Anonymous

The chronicles of Jerahmeel

Anonymous

The chronicles of Jerahmeel

ISBN/EAN: 9783337730925

Printed in Europe, USA, Canada, Australia, Japan

Cover: Foto ©ninafisch / pixelio.de

More available books at **www.hansebooks.com**

ORIENTAL TRANSLATION FUND.
NEW SERIES.
IV.

THE
CHRONICLES OF JERAHMEEL;

OR,

The Hebrew Bible Historiale.

BEING

A COLLECTION OF APOCRYPHAL AND PSEUDO-EPIGRAPHICAL BOOKS DEALING WITH THE HISTORY OF THE WORLD FROM THE CREATION TO THE DEATH OF JUDAS MACCABEUS.

Translated for the First Time from an unique Manuscript in the Bodleian Library,

BY

M. GASTER, Ph.D.

TOGETHER WITH

AN INTRODUCTION, CRITICAL NOTES, A FULL INDEX, AND FIVE FACSIMILES.

PRINTED AND PUBLISHED UNDER THE PATRONAGE OF THE
ROYAL ASIATIC SOCIETY;
AND SOLD AT
22, ALBEMARLE STREET, LONDON.
1899.

To

F. F. ARBUTHNOT, Esq.,

THIS BOOK

IS GRATEFULLY DEDICATED.

PREFACE.

THE present volume contains a collection of old-world legends and tales. The heroes are mostly biblical personages; hence the name given to it by me, 'Bible Historiale.' It resembles in tendency and spirit these mediæval compilations, and is their oldest representative. The Hebrew text exists only in one single manuscript. My translation is as faithful and literal a rendering as such a subject requires. Unlike others, I have followed the older example and have added a full index. It is a complete digest of the whole matter contained in the book. No incident of any importance has wilfully been omitted. For the purpose of preparing it and of facilitating critical and bibliographical investigations, I have divided the text into chapters and paragraphs. Indications in the manuscript guided me.

In a long introduction I have investigated firstly the question as to the date and authorship of the chronicle as a whole; then discussed the place of its composition; the relation in which the chronicle of Jerahmeel stands to the Book of Yashar and to Yosippon. I have laid bare the connection with the 'Genesis Rabba Major' of Moses ha Darshan; and drawn attention to the parallelism between this chronicle, the 'Historia Scholastica' of Comestor, and other similar Christian compilations.

In a second part of the introduction I have studied each chapter and each text separately, and I have minutely investigated each paragraph and smaller incident. Parallels have been adduced by me not only from the Hebrew but also from non-Hebrew literatures. An attempt has been made to ascertain the probable age of each of these legends, to show the historical background of some, and the value for textual criticism of the other texts contained in this chronicle.

Five pages of the Hebrew manuscript of decisive importance for the date and for the original character of this compilation have been added. In short, no pains have been spared to make this book a worthy contribution to the study of Biblical Apocrypha, and to place in the hand of the student the means of testing the truth and cogency of the conclusions to which I have arrived.

It remains now for me to fulfil a pleasant duty in thanking my friends Dr. W. H. Greenburg and Dr. H. Barnstein for the assistance they have rendered me, and above all Mr. F. F. Arbuthnot, to whose generosity the book owes its appearance.

M. GASTER.

LONDON,
June 16, 1899.
Tammuz 8, 5659.

TABLE OF CONTENTS.

	CHAPTER	PAGE
Author's Preface	-	-
The Creation of the World	I.-III.	1
Introduction	-	lix
The Seven Planets and their Functions	IV.	11
Introduction	-	lxi
Creation of Man	VI.-VII.	14
Introduction	-	lxii
The Formation of the Child	IX.	19
Introduction	-	lxiii
Admonition against Sin	X.	23
Introduction	-	lxiv
Punishments and Rewards	XI.-XII.	27
Introduction	-	lxv
The Beating of the Grave	XIII.	30
Introduction	-	lxvi
Descriptions of Hell and Paradise	XIV.-XXI.	32
Introduction	-	lxvii
Fall of Adam and Eve	XXII.	46
Introduction	-	lxix
History of Methushelah and Enosh	XXIII.	48
Introduction	-	lxxi
History of Cain and his Descendants	XXIV.	50
Introduction	-	lxxii
The Midrash of Shemḥazai and Azael	XXV.	52
Introduction	-	lxxiii
The Descendants of Adam till Noah	XXVI.	54
Introduction	-	xxxiv, lxxiii
The Descendants of Noah	XXVII.-XXVIII.	57
Introduction	-	xxxiv, lxxv
History of Abraham and Yoqtan	XXIX.-XXX.	60
Introduction	-	lxxv
The Generations of Noah	XXXI.	65
Introduction	-	xliii, lxxvi
History of Jonithes, Nimrod, and Bel	XXXII.	69
Introduction	-	lxxvii
Abraham Legends	XXXIII.-XXXV.	71
Introduction	-	lxxviii
The Wars of the Children of Jacob	XXXVI.-XXXVII.	80
Introduction	-	lxxxi
The Will of Naphtali	XXXVIII.	87
Introduction	-	lxxxiv
Joseph Legends	XXXIX.	94
Introduction	-	lxxxv

	CHAPTER	PAGE
History of Sefo, Kittim and Rome (from Yosippon)	XL.-XLI.	94
Introduction		lxxxvi
The Chronicle of Moses	XLII.-XLVIII.	102
Introduction		lxxxvii
Death of Aaron	XLIX.	130
Introduction		xci
Death of Moses	L.-LI.	133
Introduction		xcii
Ascension of Moses	LII.	144
Introduction		xciii
The Camping in the Wilderness and the Legends of the Twelve Stones	LIII.	149
Introduction		xciv
The Smiting of the Firstborn	LIV.	156
Introduction		xcvi
The Rebellion of Korah	LV.	160
Introduction		xcvii
History of Greece	LVI.	164
Introduction		xcvii
Legend of Kenaz	LVII.	165
Introduction		xcviii
Legend of Sisera, Gideon and Yair	LVIII.	174
Introduction		xcviii
The Lamentation of Seelah, Jephthah's Daughter	LIX.	176
Introduction		xcix
The Eight Exiles	LX.	182
Introduction		c
The Children of Moses and the Ten Tribes	LXI.-LXII.	186
Introduction		ci
The History of Elhanan the Merchant	LXIII.	192
Introduction		ciii
The Midrash of Ahab and Zedekiah	LXIV.	200
Introduction		civ
The History of Susanna	LXV.	202
Introduction		cv
The History of Nebuchadnezzar	LXVI.	205
Introduction		cvi
Daniel Legends	LXVII.-LXXIII.	207
Introduction		cvi
Zerubbabel and the Riddles	LXXIV.-LXXVI.	223
Introduction		cvii
Rebuilding of the Temple—Holy Fire	LXXVII.	231
Introduction		cviii
Mordecai's Dream and Esther's Prayer—Haman Legends	LXXIX.-LXXXIII.	236
Introduction		cviii
The Throne of Solomon	LXXXIV.	251
Introduction		cix
The Book of the Maccabee	LXXXV.-C.	254
Introduction		cx

INTRODUCTION.

THE chronicle which I publish here for the first time is not a chronicle in the strict sense of the word. It does not relate true events which have happened in the history of mankind, but it belongs more to that class of legendary history which was so much in vogue in the Middle Ages, and which owes its original conception to the attempt, from very ancient times, to embellish the biblical narrative. The history of the world began with the narrative of the Bible —first for the Jews, and then for all the nations who have derived their knowledge and their faith from the same source. The careful reader of the Bible must have been struck with what appeared to him to be incoherence of narrative, want of details, and at times great lacunæ. Hence the desire for filling them up.

An old problem has also been to establish a fixed chronology upon the basis of the biblical narrative. This last was, in fact, the oldest attempt to construct exact history out of the Bible. The computation of the era of the world, and the desire for fixing the age of every person mentioned in the Bible, and of every event contained therein, was imposed upon Jews almost as soon as they came in contact with the highly fantastical chronologies of Manetho and Berossus, who gave to the world and to the reigning dynasties of Egypt and Assyria millions of years. The Jews, especially those who lived in Alexandria, the ancient focus of civilization, where all the currents of thought, myth and learning combined, felt the necessity of comparing these fabulous histories with the true history of the world as contained in the Bible. We therefore find among the oldest Alexandrian writers like Demetrios and others the very first rudiments of biblical chronology. Egypt was also the land where myths and legends flourished in abundance, and no wonder that the lives of Biblical personages connected especially with Egypt and Egyptian history, like Joseph, Moses, Solomon and others, should have been embellished with legendary and poetic details drawn from sources hitherto not yet accounted for.

Biblical legends occur, therefore, very frequently in the works of the Alexandrian writers referred to, especially in Artapanos and Philo, and, derived from such sources, also in Josephus. This activity was, however, not limited to Egypt. The desire for rounding off the biblical narrative, for filling up the lacunæ, for answering all the questions of the enquiring mind of the ancient reader, was also carried on in Palestine and probably so in Babylon. Hence a new literature grew out of the Bible, and clustered round the Bible, which goes under the name of the Apocrypha, or pseudo-epigraphical literature.

Some of these writings are written with a special purpose, either to inculcate certain doctrines, or to show the antiquity of certain precepts in order to justify some religious ceremony. Some assume the form of historical narratives of events that happened to the Patriarchs, others appear in the form of ancient revelations also ascribed to biblical personages, and either try to lift the veil of the future or to encourage the people in time of trial and trouble. This literature has had a chequered career; very little has come down to us in its primitive form, and in the Hebrew language. Even those that were written in Greek, and have been translated from that language, had to undergo considerable changes at the hands of those who afterwards utilized the ancient records for the purpose of spreading their own religious views. Books that went under the names of Patriarchs claimed a great respect and veneration. And, therefore, if they contained announcements as to events that were to happen, Christian writers and then heads of sects would not fail to interpret or to interpolate sentences or passages by which Christian or specific doctrines would appear to have been foretold from ancient times. Such interpolations and the use made of the books sufficed to condemn them in the eyes of the Jews, and even in the eyes of the ruling Church, and to cause their disappearance at a very early period. Others that were written in Hebrew and claimed to be a kind of prophecy, having been belied by the non-fulfilment of those prophecies, fell into contempt, were disregarded, and therefore partly lost; the purely historical and legendary portions, however, seem to have fared somewhat better. They lived on because age did not affect them, and people at all times were inclined to bestow benevolent attention upon poetical descriptions or pseudo-historical narratives.

The critical spirit belongs to modern times. The discrimination between true and false history is the result of modern discipline. Much that we consider as impossible and legendary would pass, and did pass for centuries, as true history; and legendary history ranked very high in popular favour from ancient times onward. The texts suffered considerably because they were considered 'No man's property.' Every copyist, every author, handled them in the freest possible manner: adding, changing, altering, leaving out what he considered useless or superfluous, and dwelling at length upon details for which he had a special predilection. The liberty taken with that class of literature greatly increases the difficulties of the critical student, and makes the task much more onerous for those who attempt to winnow the chaff from the corn and to trace legendary history to its ultimate literary source.

With the Jews, history—that is, a description of battles or of internal political development—had ceased from the time that the political entity had come to an end. Scattered throughout the world, they dwelt much more passionately upon the records of the Bible, and favoured all those legendary embroideries more highly than probably any other nation which lived in the actuality, and had to shape its course in the various lands where they had established themselves. That accounts for the paucity of Jewish chronicles—there was practically nothing to record. From the time of the first Temple, that is, from the time at which the Bible closes down to the Dispersion under Titus and Vespasianus, there was a long period, in which the Jewish polity again flourished in Palestine, and wherein the Maccabeans fill such a prominent place. True, a brief allusion to these three hundred years and more of the existence of the second Temple is all that is to be found in Jewish literature; a stray passage among the thousands of pages of the homiletic or legal literature of those times, and no more. But, in spite of this poverty in reference, that period was one of intensive literary activity, the outlines of which have hitherto been only dimly recognised.

Of the literature that flourished during the second Temple, some of the books are known as the Apocrypha of the Bible. A few pretend to contain contemporary real history, like Judith, additions to Daniel, Susanna, Maccabees; others are books of wisdom, like Ben Sira's Ecclesiasticus; or, the Wisdom of Solomon; and I may also mention here the so-called Psalms of Solomon.

Greater activity was displayed in the production of the so-called pseudo-epigraphical books such as the Book of Enoch, the Book of the Jubilees, the Testaments of the Twelve Patriarchs, and a host of other similar productions which have the Bible as their centre, and poetical imagination as their characteristic. A true appreciation of this literature has been reserved for our times. These books were used in the composition of the mediæval Bible Historiale; but not one single text, according to the common notion, has been preserved in its original language. They have come down in Greek or in Latin, or in translations derived from these secondary sources. Old Hebrew parallels to the Apocrypha proper, not to speak of the pseudo-epigraphical, seemed completely lost. As far as the Apocrypha proper are concerned, there exists, however, a book which covers this whole period: a kind of continuation of the biblical narrative from the point at which it closes—viz.: the rebuilding under Ezra and Nehemiah, down to the destruction of the second Temple. It goes under the name of Yosippon (by the way, a Byzantine form of Josephus, in so far absolutely identical with the Hebrew form יוסיפון). This book contains a special version of all those Apocryphal tales, it goes on to describe the history of the Maccabeeans, and afterwards at great length the details of the war with the Romans up to the fatal conclusion. The authenticity of this Hebrew version has been questioned by almost everyone who has dealt with it, although, till now, no complete or perfect edition of this work has been attempted. It exists in at least two distinctly different forms, and the manuscripts, which are not very numerous, have scarcely yet been touched. A huge interpolation—namely, the legendary history of Alexander, of which I published an English translation from old manuscripts—has induced men like Zunz to consider the whole work as being of the same age as that portion which had been interpolated at a later time. Zunz came to the conclusion that it was a translation made in the South of Italy sometime in the eleventh or twelfth century, based probably upon the Latin 'Egesippus.' Copyists' errors, and especially the changes introduced by the final editor, Moscone, who owns to having compiled the book out of a number of different manuscripts, have been taken as sufficient proof for declaring the whole work to be a late fabrication. Before attempting to show the futility of the arguments hitherto adduced, suffice it to mention that this was the only post-biblical Jewish history known for a long time, the origin of which awaits still further elucidation.

The pseudo-epigraphical writings have also left more than a few traces. In connection with them I now mention another book which attempts for the Bible itself that which Yosippon attempts for the post-biblical period. I mean the book which goes under the name of 'Sefer Hayashar.' It is a consecutive narrative from the creation of the world down to the time of the Judges, following closely the description given by the Bible, omitting all the legal portions, and filling up the lacunæ with numerous legends drawn from those sources. If Yosippon has hitherto been treated with scant respect, in spite of Breithaupt's excellent work, this latter book—of which, curiously enough, no manuscripts are known to exist in any library of the world, at any rate not to my knowledge—has been treated with absolute contempt, as a tissue of ridiculous fables and of a modern make. The discovery of the whole series of pseudo-epigraphical writings, such as the Book of Jubilees and others; the close attention given in modern times to this whole branch of biblical Apocrypha; the investigations into the phases of development and into the origin of the Book of Enoch; the 'Assumption of Moses' (by Charles); the publication of the 'Apocrypha Anecdota' by James and Robinson in this country, and similar studies carried out by scholars in other countries, have contributed largely to change our opinion of the value and antiquity of such books.

In the above-mentioned books, especially in the Book of Yosippon and in that of Yashar, the various legendary elements have been deftly woven into one consecutive narrative. The editor or compiler has used his materials somewhat freely, just as an artist would use his colours, and he has succeeded in producing a most interesting book, both as far as contents and style are concerned. For, curiously enough, these two works alone (limiting myself to those presented in Hebrew), *i.e.*, the book called Yosippon and the Book of Yashar, are written in the purest Hebrew style. Unlike any other Hebrew writing of ancient or modern times, they imitate the Scriptural form of the language, and use almost exclusively the lexicon of the Bible. A very few non-biblical words are to be met with, especially in the Yosippon, but altogether the reading is as pleasant as that of a biblical book in the form of an attractive historical novel. This very peculiarity of style has been put down by Zunz and others as proof of their recent origin. For what reason a book written in a pure style should be considered as modern and not archaic, has not been made clear by anyone, and it does not seem to have struck any critics to demand a reason.

To assume the reverse, however, would be quite natural. The essential characteristic of this literature is that it pretends to be of high antiquity; it claims patriarchs and prophets as its author. Could anyone conceive, then, that such a claim would be maintained with any hope of success, or that such a poetical deception would meet with any acceptance, if the book, purporting to be written by Enoch, Moses, Daniel, etc., would not be in a language resembling very closely that of the Bible, or that it should have appealed to a Jewish public in Greek? It would have at once betrayed its spurious origin, and neither Synagogue nor Church would have taken cognizance of its existence.

It is, furthermore, incomprehensible that, for no visible reason, writers of a later period should have so successfully avoided adopting the current literary language of their time, and have purposely written in that pure, simple, biblical form. I do not suggest that this alone is a stringent proof of antiquity, but at any rate I wish to point out that at no time do we know this literary canon to have been established or to have been acted upon, that writers should imitate the diction of the Bible. The language therefore is no proof whatsoever of the recent origin of this or any such book. Internal evidence alone must finally decide the true character and date of each composition. The necessity for writing in such a pure biblical phraseology has never been felt at a later time. In fact, the whole Hebrew literature, from the second or third century onward, betrays in its grammatical forms the successive changes to which it has been subjected. Neither the poetical literature nor the Halachic or Hagadic, during the time which followed the destruction of the Temple, shows, as far as contemporary records go, this tendency of

b

adopting the pure biblical language; and when we come to the eleventh century, in which the so-called Poetanic literature flourished in Palestine and in Spain, it cannot be shown that even the remotest attempt was made by anyone to mould his language entirely upon the biblical types. True, these authors use biblical words, but in a manner so different from the Bible—playing with their meaning, changing their forms, and even adapting them to their own grammatical views in the use they make of those words—that it requires in many cases great ingenuity to detect original biblical words in these strange changelings. The reason for writing in that old biblical style becomes more incomprehensible if we compare it, for instance, with the Chronicle of Ahimaaz, composed in the beginning of the eleventh century in South Italy (Neubauer, 'Medieval Jewish Chronicles,' ii., p. 111 *et seq.*), written all in rhymed prose, and totally different in style and conception from those in biblical idiom. One main point that stands out clearly in dealing with a subject which has hitherto been treated in a rather indifferent manner, is that assertions were freely made, whilst convincing proofs are still greatly wanting to support them. We have no right to blindly accept the conclusions thus arrived at. Caution has specially to be exercised in the case of a book like Yashar, so lightly put down to be of modern make, solely on account of the language. In examining the contents, we shall find them to be full of legends which do not owe their origin to the fancy or poetical imagination of writers of a late period. We find in it a portion of the legend of Enoch; the legendary history of Moses, of his birth as well as that of his death; of Aaron's death, and many other similar elements to which we find parallel in the writings of the Fathers of the Church, in Josephus, and in that very old Apocryphal literature, the Book of Jubilees, the Testaments of the Twelve Patriarchs, and the cycle of writings to which reference will be made anon. In virtue of these new facts, we are now differently placed when dealing with Apocryphal matter, and we are in a far better position to estimate the true value of this compilation than has hitherto been the case.

The publication of the present chronicle, which I have called 'The Chronicles of Jerahmeel,' will now contribute much to the elucidation of many problems connected therewith, and with biblical Apocrypha in general. It combines the Yosippon with the Yashar—*i.e.*, it is a continuous narrative from the Creation down to the destruction of the Temple—and contains a great number of either unknown or little known Apocryphal texts in what I believe to be their original form. It must be borne in mind that the Book of Jubilees, for instance, has not yet been found in its old Hebrew form, only parallels to portions of it are known to exist in Hebrew writings. The whole book has thus far disappeared. How old, now, are these parallels, and in what relation do they stand to the lost original? The same may be said of the Testaments of the Twelve Patriarchs, and of ever so many other old Apocryphal writings to which we shall refer in the course of our investigation. Here in this Chronicle we now have a series of similar texts all in Hebrew, the value of which remains to be proved, but which I have no hesitation in declaring to be very great.

We are in the fortunate position that this Chronicle is not like the Book of Yashar—a continuous narrative by one author who has mixed up more or less skilfully various elements, and has utilized the old texts to make a single book of them, in a manner which obliterates the traces separating one from the other, and making it almost impossible for us to follow each of the component parts to their original source. Here, on the contrary, we have a compilation in its most primitive state, and therefore much more valuable from the critical point of view. The texts are placed one next to the other in their integrity without any attempt at changing their original form, or of weaving them together and combining them in any artificial manner. It is, on the whole, more a mechanical compilation than a scientific composition. The compiler of the complete work, which contains not merely the Chronicle, but a host of other texts, is not Jerahmeel himself, nor is the date of the compilation identical with that of the texts which make the volume. As will be shown later on, some of these texts go back to remote antiquity, others may be put down as of a more recent origin, but one and all of the texts in the Chronicle proper are by many centuries older than the date at which the compiler connected them into one volume. This volume—hitherto a unique manuscript—is now the property of the Bodleian Library in Oxford. It belonged originally to the late Rabbinowitz, who bought it from an unknown source in Italy, and it was purchased, whilst I was in treaty with Rabbinowitz, by the Bodleian Library in the year 1887. I had the whole manuscript copied out, with a view to its ultimate publication, in 1888. And now the first part of it, dealing with Scripture history from the Creation down to the death of Judas Maccabeus, forms the present publication. The compilation of the manuscript is due to a certain Eleasar ben Asher the Levite, who lived at the beginning of the fourteenth century somewhere in the Rhine Provinces, and whose preface I have reproduced as faithfully as possible. In it he states that he has collected the books from far and wide, and combined them into one consecutive whole, fully conscious of the fact that no such book had ever been prepared before, and charging his children with the faithful preservation of this record of his labours of many years, continued under great stress and with great difficulties. Thus, as we can see, Eleasar the Levite introduced into his work in the first place a legendary compilation, written in the style of the old legendary Chronicles, filling up from ancient records all that appeared to him wanting in the Scriptural narrative. But he continues this history down to the destruction of the Temple; and then in a very keen way he passes over centuries, filling up the gap with the legendary history of Alexander mentioned above, and other similar tales, and alights on the persecution of the Jews in the time of the Crusades. The rest of the book contains the poetical works of Gabirol, of Berachia, the Lapidarius, astronomical notes, and so on. Dr. Neubauer will probably give a detailed description of this manuscript in his forthcoming supplement to the catalogue of the Bodleian Library. Now, this compilation ought to have been called the 'Chronicle of Eleasar ben Asher the Levite,' were it not for the fact that, except one or two texts and a few lines in which he shows in what manner he has utilized the books at his disposal, nothing in the whole first part can directly be proved to be his. So I have selected to call this Chronicle by the name of the writer whose work, next to Yosippon, forms the most interesting and the most remarkable portion of this compilation.

In comparison with this source from which Eleasar the Levite has drawn his elements, the chronicle of Jerahmeel is second in size; for he has embodied in it almost the whole of the Yosippon. Jerahmeel, on his side, has utilized a great number of ancient biblical Hagadic writings, and it might be stated here at once that he has introduced into his Chronicle only and solely Hebrew writings, not translations made by him from more Hebrew texts; that there is not in the volume a single text whose Hebrew origin or character the compiler had a reason to doubt. This must be stated as emphatically as possible, in view especially of 'Jerahmeel' and of other minor legendary elements which are found in this work of Eleasar the Levite. He had, moreover, access to very good texts. A minute comparison of the contents with other sources and parallels which I shall bring forward later on will, I hope, prove the superiority and the excellence of the texts contained in this chronicle over any other similar or identical texts found in other works of Hebrew literature. These latter have all been more or less deteriorated or altered, and we shall see that portions missing everywhere else are found in our text.

Having only one manuscript at my disposal, as no other copy of this work seems to be in existence anywhere, and as the writing—the facsimiles I have added here show it—is not often easily readable, I had to contend with many a difficulty on the question of textual criticism and accuracy of reading. But in spite of these obstacles, and in spite of other difficulties inherent in a work resting upon one single manuscript, it will be seen that these contentions of mine are perfectly justified; first of all, that all the texts contained in this chronicle are Hebrew originals, or rest upon purely Hebrew originals, and, secondly, that the readings are more archaic and far superior to the parallels existing in other manuscripts or prints. As regards a few, I have even been able to find parallels among the ancient fragments which I have got from the Geniza in Fostat, near Cairo. And although some may be of greater antiquity than the actual manuscript of Eleasar the Levite, they corroborate the accuracy of the latter. One will easily understand, furthermore, the importance which this compilation has for the textual criticism of Yosippon and for the antiquity of that compilation; as we have here a complete text of Yosippon, written down not later than the twelfth century in the Rhine Provinces. The original manuscript must have had to pass many vicissitudes until it reached the hands of the last compiler or copyist; and yet it will be seen that the old edition of Conte (Mantua, *circa* 1480) does not differ very much from our manuscript, preceding the edition, as it does, by at least three hundred years.

Any new edition of the Yosippon will have to be based exclusively upon this compilation, of which I have been preparing an edition for many years. But 'Jerahmeel' has many interesting things in store for us. His work is a collection of a number of old Apocrypha, some known, some quite unknown. He begins his Chronicle with the very creation of the world, and he draws his information from the book that goes under the name of R. Eliezer the son of Hyrqanos, and is quoted as the Chapters of R. Eliezer. Jerahmeel utilizes also the calendristic work ascribed to Mar Samuel, unless it be proved that the chapter derived from it belonged to the Chapters of Eliezer

Hyrqanos, which is very probable (*vide* later on). Jeraḥmeel then gives a minute description of the Visions of heaven and hell and paradise, the Beating of the grave, in two or even three recensions; the fall of the two angels Shemḥazai and Aza'el, following upon the history of Adam and Eve, separate texts one independent of the other. He writes of the war between the children of Jacob and the Sichemites, and of the kings that had leagued themselves against them. He tells of the war between Esau and the children of Jacob. He gives us in full the Chronicle of Moses, the history of the death of Aaron, and that of Moses; a minute description of the Tabernacle, of the way in which the tribes used to encamp in the Wilderness, and many other legendary tales, but each of them forming as it were a separate chapter, not connected one with the other, but simply placed one next to the other, showing how he arranged mechanically the materials to which he had access. He further gives us one of the oldest versions of the legend of the children of Moses, of the history of the Ten Tribes after the Exile, the travels of Elḥanan, which throw light on the history of that other legendary traveller Eldad the Danite.

And then we have such other texts known as biblical Apocrypha, either in Aramaic, like the history of Daniel and the Dragon, the Song of the three Children in the Furnace, with the Dream of Mordecai, the Prayer of Esther, and the history of Susanna, and the rest of the biblical Apocrypha as given also by Yosippon, but in a slightly differing form.

If we compare the contents of this Chronicle with the Book of Yashar, we shall be struck by the remarkable coincidence in a good number of those legends which deal with biblical personages. Moreover, we shall find in the Book of Yashar traces of the author's acquaintance with a chronicle similar to 'Jeraḥmeel.' Did the author of the Book of Yashar, who owns to having compiled it in Spain, follow the example of some other chronicle hitherto not identified, but absolutely like the Chronicle of Jeraḥmeel?

Did they both work in different countries, at different times, exactly under the same influences, and almost with the same result, having the same texts at their disposal? This is one of the literary problems which suggest themselves when we peruse this Chronicle side by side with the Book of Yashar. We find, furthermore, in the Book of Yashar a trace of the first chapters of the Yosippon. The question is, did the author of the Yashar take only the beginning and leave the rest? Did he limit his book to the history of the Israelites comprised within the boundary of the Pentateuch? or is that chapter a later interpolation, remarkable enough in so far as the same chapter occurs also in the chronicle of Jeraḥmeel and in the name of Yosippon, but added by Eleasar the Levite? If we extend our inquiry a little further, and study among non-Jewish writers, in the first instance, the 'Historia Scholastica' or 'Biblia Historiale' of Petrus Comestor (Pierre le Mangeur), the famous Rector of the University of Paris in the twelfth century,* we shall also find resemblances in system and plan, and even in authorities quoted, which are fairly startling.

The difficulties connected with this chronicle thicken and grow, especially on close examination of that portion to which I have not yet alluded, and which gives to our chronicle an almost unique character. In my investigation, I shall in the first instance examine, as carefully as I can, the problem connected with Jeraḥmeel, as to date of compilation, origin, author and language. I shall later on follow the text of the book of the chronicle, chapter by chapter, indicating as far as possible the source whence each of them is derived, the parallels in Jewish and non-Jewish literature, so as to enable us not merely to judge of the work of Jeraḥmeel, but also as to the age of the various elements that go to make up his compilation. The ramifications are multifarious. There is scarcely a single legend in this compilation which does not find its counterpart in non-Jewish literature, and it might be profitable to discuss the connection between these and the

* *Vide* my Ilchester Lectures, p. 147 *et seq.*

point how far they depend one upon the other; whether the latter have borrowed from Jewish sources, or whether Jews are indebted to others for these legends, and for the information they give—questions of literary history and of the propagation of tales from country to country and from literature to literature. They can, however, merely be touched upon here lightly.

Before commencing a minute investigation, we must first ascertain whether Eleasar the Levite has incorporated the whole Chronicle of Jerahmeel in his compilation, and whether the last copyist has been as conscientious as Jerahmeel. I have some doubts on these points. For among the texts there is one of which it will be seen that only a portion has been incorporated. But that portion in itself is sufficiently bulky to assist us in unravelling partly the character, the origin, the date of that composition, and the personality of the author and of the first compiler, and the manner in which it has been preserved.

It is in this portion that there are found peculiar legends for which hitherto no parallel is known to exist in the whole literature of the Apocrypha that has thus far come to light. This portion of the Chronicle of Jerahmeel is to all appearances just such a legendary book as we are accustomed to expect from very ancient writers imbued with that spirit which has produced such works as the Book of Jubilees and similar writings.

A brief extract from the contents so far as they are preserved in our Hebrew version will show that this portion of the Chronicle follows up the purpose of explaining many things which did not seem quite clear in the biblical narrative, and of adding a number of legendary interpretations and embellishments to those parts of the Scriptures which seem scant in information and require some elucidation. Starting, therefore, with Adam and Eve—Chapter xxvi. in our text, and paragraphs, as I have divided the whole in chapters—our author is able to tell us exactly how many children each of the Patriarchs had. The Bible, after the birth of Seth, for instance, adds merely: 'And

Adam lived so-and-so many years, and he begat sons and daughters, and he died.' Jerahmeel knows exactly how many sons and daughters were born to Adam and Eve, and he gives us the names of these children. He knows, moreover, exactly the names of the wives of each of the biblical personages. He knows also the children of Cain, and he is able to tell us minutely what arts were invented by the wives of Lamech. Wherever he mentions a biblical name it is given exactly in the form in which it occurs in the Bible, with one notable exception, to which I shall refer later on. In our Hebrew text every portion that could be derived directly from the Bible, or any information that is found in the pages of the Bible, is studiously omitted. It would be very difficult to decide whether this is due to Jerahmeel or to the later compiler, Eleasar the Levite. It might be due to the latter's activity, considering that it coincides with the character of the whole work, which is to give merely such information as is not found in the Bible. Such information was assumed as known and accessible to all. It would therefore, in his opinion, be mere waste of time or space to repeat such well-known facts as are contained in the Bible itself.

Chapter xxvii. contains a minute description of the descendants of Noah, together with that of the countries occupied by some of them. It is filled with names which thus far defy every attempt at identifying them with any known ancient geographical or other proper names. At the end of paragraph 5 there is a peculiar vision placed in the mouth of Reu concerning the birth of Abraham. Then follows Chapter xxviii.: how the three sons of Noah and their descendants appointed princes over each of their descendants, and the number of their descendants is given.

Chapters xxix. and xxx., up to the end of paragraph 4 (maybe up to the end of that chapter), belong to the same author, and contain one of those legends completely unknown hitherto. It is the history of Yoqtan and of the people building the Tower of Babylon and worshipping the fire; how Abraham with some men refused to join to make bricks, and how he was to be put into the furnace together with the twelve men associated with him; how eleven of them were sent away into the mountains by Yoqtan, who wished to save them; but Abraham, who refused to be saved, relying upon God, was thrown into the furnace and was saved from it, whilst those who heated the furnace were all burned. Then there is the descent of God and the angels; the curse of the builders of the tower, and the promise of salvation preserved for Abraham, whom He brought into a land upon which the flood had not descended.

In our compilation then follows (Chapter xxxi.) a second genealogical table of the nations. Nothing justifies us as yet to ascribe this to the author of Chapter xxvii., as it would be an unnecessary duplicate, and in fact contradictory to the one given in the previous chapters. Eleasar the Levite describes this now as part of the work of Jerahmeel. In the beginning of Chapter xxxii. we find further the following sentence: 'I Jerahmeel have found in the Book of Strabo of Caphtor that Nimrod was the son of Shem.' And in Chapter xxxv., paragraph 2, we have the following sentence: 'And I Jerahmeel have discovered in the Book of Nicholas of Damascus,' etc. It must be noted at once that these two writers are quoted in the same connection by Josephus, and that, as far as Nicholas of Damascus is concerned, almost all our references to his work are derived exclusively from Josephus. These points will be utilized afterwards for elucidating the time when this chronicle may have been compiled, and the materials which were at the disposal of that compiler.

To the same book belongs Chapter xlii., telling us the history of Pharaoh's decree of killing the male children, of the people's decision to separate themselves from their wives, and of Amram's speech to the people, inducing them to trust in God for annulling Pharaoh's decrees. God afterwards in the night reveals Himself to Amram, and is gratified with the action he has taken.

It is difficult as yet to decide whether Chapter xliii. and the following belonged originally to that portion of the chronicle of Jeraḥmeel. They deal with the birth of Moses, his subsequent flight from Egypt, his being appointed king over the Kushites, the flight to Midian, the imprisonment by Jethro, the miraculous rescue through the intermediary of Zipporah, the history of the rod of Moses, and, above all, Chapter xlviii., filled with a very remarkable description of the ten plagues. All this exists as a separate book; the more important portion of it goes back to the time of Josephus, and is even older (*vide* later on).

We resume the thread of the older portion in Jeraḥmeel's 'Chronicle' probably from Chapter lvi. onward, although in paragraph 2 Joseph b. Gorion is mentioned. Chapter lvii., however, and the following belong undoubtedly to that ancient book, and contain such legends as have hitherto not been found elsewhere outside of this work.

We have here the history of the Israelites after the death of Joshua. They appoint as leader, contrary to the Bible, Kenaz, not Othniel, as the first judge, who, together with Eleazar the High-priest, finds out that a number of people from each tribe had committed grievous sins in the eyes of the Lord, and also that they had found idols among the Amorites and other nations living in Canaan and kept them. We then get a very circumstantial description of precious stones that cannot be destroyed, and of magical books that cannot be burned, and of what happened to them at the hand of God; then the fight between the Israelites and the Amorites, the marvellous deeds of Kenaz, who slew 45,000 single-handed, and whose hand had cleaved to the sword until it was freed by pouring warm blood over it. Before his death Kenaz delivers a most peculiar and obscure piece of prophecy. After Kenaz Othniel comes, and then we have a short history of Sisera, a miracle of Gideon not mentioned in the Bible; the idol-worship of Jair, the Gileadite, the worship of Baal, the history of Jephthah, the vow he made to which his daughter

Seelah fell a victim, and then the lamentation of Seelah before her death.

Interspersed between these Apocryphal legends, we find attempts at synchronistic history. The author is at pains to inform us what happened contemporaneously among other nations of the world, *e.g.*, what kings reigned in Egypt, in Greece, and afterwards in the Latin kingdom— all features peculiar to this chronicle.

The concluding portion of this part of the chronicle, as far as it has been preserved, is the fight between the Israelites and the tribe of Benjamin; the prayer of Phineas, and the remarkable end of Phineas, who is evidently identified with the future prophet Elijah, because he is not to die, but to remain in God's mountain, where the ravens and crows would feed him, and he would come down again when the end has arrived. 'Then he will close the heavens, and at his command they will be opened again, and he will be lifted up to the place where his fathers have gone before him, and there he shall remain until God shall remember the world.' A clear indication of the activity of Elijah, who was fed by the ravens, at whose word drought set in, at whose request the rain came, who was taken up in the chariot to the abode of his forefathers, and who is to remain there until God remembers the world.

All this narrative is written in a pure biblical style, easily flowing, and divided into small verses. Here and there some obscurity is to be noticed, but on the whole it is very clear; biblical terms and forms abound at every turn, and scarcely a few new Hebrew words have I been able to detect.

This portion has come down to us, unfortunately, in a fragmentary form. Its contents are so unique in character, and so different from what is known till now in Apocryphal or legendary biblical literature, that one is confronted with very great difficulties in trying to ascertain the sources from which the author drew, and the immediate surroundings in which he lived. The date is also, thus far, a matter of speculation. The only book in Hebrew literature which shows some relation in conception and in details is the Sepher Hayashar, which I have mentioned above. The similarity extends to the following points: both present us with lists of names of biblical persons before the Flood. In the Yashar we find, furthermore, a list of the names of the descendants of the sons of Noah as unintelligible and as unknown, and not met with anywhere else, as in this part of the Chronicle of Jeraḥmeel. We, further, find the same desire to give us attempts at synchronistic history; and in matters of contents there is also a very great similarity, but these very prominent legends of Yoqtan and Kenaz, so unique in the chronicle of Jeraḥmeel, are missing in the Book of Yashar. Another trace of our book, at any rate as far as the names of the wives of the patriarchs are concerned, has been preserved in 'Toledoth Adam,' by Samuel Algazi, printed in Venice, 1600. The names in this latter are, however, not identical. The oldest parallels to these names we find in the Book of Jubilees. (As for the Byzantine and other literatures, cf. H. Rönsch, 'Das Buch der Jubileen,' Leipzig, 1874, who has collected the whole material in connection with the Book of Jubilees.) A Syriac list of such names of the wives of the patriarchs has been reprinted by Charles in his Appendix III. to the Ethiopic version of the Book of Jubilees (Oxford, 1895, p. 183).

I have found, however, not merely fragments and stray parallels to this portion of our chronicle, but the whole text, and even more than our Hebrew, in a Latin translation. The Latin version of this book has been preserved in manuscript and in print. Mr. M. R. James, in his 'Apocrypha Anecdota' (Cambridge, 1893), had published four fragments from a manuscript of the eleventh century, the original of which he did not know. As he says, 'There seems to be no corner of Apocryphal literature on which you can fit this fragment.' He gives us first a prayer of Moses on the day of his death, the vision of Kenaz, the lamentation of Seelah, and the song of David. Feeling that the Latin text might be a translation from the Greek, he translated the three former into Greek, but he gives up the attempt with the fourth. (In line 11 of the latter *virginitate mea* should be read instead of *ingenuitate mea;* it was probably badly written in the manuscript.)

Mr. James, when publishing these fragments, was quite unaware that they belonged to a book which had been printed as far back as 1527, in Basle, under the title 'Philonis Judaei Alexandrini. Libri Antiquitatum. Quaestionum et Solvtionum in Genesin. de Essaeis. de Nominibus hebraicis. de Mundo.' All his speculations as to their probable origin fall to the ground in face of the fact that they belonged to the 'Antiquitates,' a larger work of a totally different character from that which he surmised. This work is that very portion in the Chronicle of Jerahmeel! There is, however, some difference between the two versions. The Latin is much fuller, and seems to be the complete text, whilst the Hebrew is merely fragmentary. In the Latin text the second genealogical table, or the distribution of the children of Noah among the various countries, and the origin of the nations traced to the three sons of Noah in the second version of Jerahmeel (Chapters xxxi., xxxii.), and the synchronistic element, are missing altogether, but, on the whole, the Latin version is much fuller. The legendary history proper is carried further down, for the book concludes with the death of Saul. It contains also some portions taken from the Bible, so as to form a consecutive narrative, more in the style of the Sepher Hayashar. On closer examination, we find in it a great number of speeches and other details with which the Biblical narrative is filled out, whilst everything found in Jerahmeel occurs in it also, and corresponds literally with it. This book is ascribed in the Latin text to Philo, and seems to have been entirely forgotten and neglected. Mangey excluded it altogether in his edition of Philo, and up to quite recently it had escaped the notice of all scholars, until Dr. Cohn published in the *Jewish Quarterly Review* of 1898 an abstract of the book under the title, 'An

Apocryphal Work ascribed to Philo of Alexandria' (vol. x., pp. 227-332).

In this study Dr. Cohn is quite unaware of the existence of the Hebrew manuscript. The discovery of the Hebrew original may stimulate someone to undertake anew a critical edition of the Latin text, with the aid of the other manuscripts to which Dr. Cohn refers in his note (p. 279, note 2). He is also not aware how widely it was read in ancient times, and how deeply it has influenced medieval literature, as will be shown later on. The famous 'Bible Historiale' of Comestor, the 'Fasciculus Temporum,' and Forresti's (Jacob de Bergamo) 'Supplementum Chronicarum,' derive their information from this source. The quotations from 'Philo' are, as it appears now, taken from this very book.

Now, curiously enough, the very same name of 'Philo' occurs also in the Hebrew text. The history of the legends of the Judges (Chapters lvii. *et seq.* of my edition here) is ascribed to Philo, the friend of Joseph ben Gorion, and we must ascribe to the same author the first part containing the legends of Abraham and the first genealogical table. Evidently the book bore from the beginning the name of Philo as author. Now, comparing in this Philo-Jerahmeel the dates given to the patriarchs, the number of years they lived before and after the birth of their children, Dr. Cohn shows that these chronological data agree more with the Septuagint than with the Massoretic text. In the Hebrew text these dates are unfortunately omitted, with the exception of those given for the lives of Adam, Seth and Enosh, where the dates agree with those of the Latin text. It can be shown, however, that almost every one of the Apocryphal writings, the Samaritan tradition, and Josephus differ from the dates given in the Bible. This point alone would not justify us in drawing conclusions as to the source of, or the influence of the Septuagint upon this text. And even as far as the relation to the Septuagint is concerned, Philo is in many places at variance with it, and in closer agreement with the Hebrew text. The work contains merely the evidence of the use of a Greek version of the Bible, which, moreover, was not identical with the Septuagint, but standing in much closer relation to the Hebrew text than the Septuagint itself. From the vast number of Greek words in the Latin text of Philo-Jerahmeel, it is furthermore clear that the Latin, at any rate, is not the original language in which this work was composed, but that it is a translation made from a Greek text. Moreover, from the very archaic form of the language, and from the words that are used in it, which agree with the language of the Latin translation of the Bible of the period before Jerome, and the identity of language with the Latin translations known as the 'Itala,' Dr. Cohn concludes with irresistible force that the Latin translation dates back not later than from the *third* or *fourth* century. Neither was then Greek the primitive language. Even through the Latin one can recognise so many Hebrew forms that we are forced to conclude that the book must originally have been written in Hebrew. The Greek is merely the intermediary between the old original and the later Latin. The original must have been moulded entirely upon the character and style of the Hebrew Bible. As Cohn rightly says: 'The author himself used as his model and sole authority the Hebrew text of the Old Testament, and imitated its style and method of narration even in the smallest details. Had the author written in Greek, he could not possibly have reproduced so faithfully the style and accent of the Bible. Among all the Apocryphal books which were written in Greek, there is none in which the biblical style is so faithfully reproduced as in Philo' (p. 312).

He next brings some arguments for his contention, showing, in the first instance, that the sentences are almost universally connected with 'and,' like in the Bible, that paragraphs are unknown, for there is no break in the narrative from beginning to end, which is exactly the style of Hebrew narration. Also peculiar forms and turns of phrases and other peculiarities of language derived from Hebrew have been retained in the Latin, which is thus a faithful reproduction of the Greek, and this of the Hebrew original. The original, surmised by Dr. Cohn, now lies before us in the text which I am publishing, and bears out all the characteristics that might be expected from this old Hebrew legendary chronicle.

The question may well be asked whether the Hebrew text which we have before us is the very original, or a later retranslation, and whether it is dependent, supposing it be a translation, upon the Greek or upon the Latin. In order to satisfy us as to the relation existing between the Latin, the only one thus far accessible, and the Hebrew text, I will limit myself to the investigation of the genealogical tables that are to be found in both texts. Decisive to my mind is this comparison between the two lists of proper names. As those names are probably of Semitic origin, they must have been written in the original, with the full use of the whole Hebrew alphabet. If, now, they were transliterated from Hebrew into Greek, and from Greek into Latin, the differences between ה and ח, א and ע, ט and ת, כ and ק, ס, שׁ and צ, would have disappeared, as those sounds have no corresponding letters in Greek or in Latin. Assuming now that the Hebrew text is a re-translation from the Latin, none of these double letters, or letters representing peculiar Semitic sounds, that had disappeared in the Latin or Greek, could reappear in the Hebrew text. It would tax the ingenuity of any man to be able to distinguish between the ח and the ה when they are both written with the Latin 'H'; or between the א, צ, and ע as 'A,' when both are written by 'S'; in the same way כ and ק being reproduced by one letter, 'K,' there will be no hint or indication for the re-translator to substitute the one for the other. If we apply this test to the names contained in Chapter xxvi., we shall find a very careful distinction made between all these letters. Take, for instance, the very first names, the eleven sons and eight daughters of Adam, which are, by the way, fearfully corrupted, like all the other names in the Basle edition (words are often combined, names run into one another, lacunæ are artificially created, all due to misreading of the original). These very first names show already marked differences in the Hebrew spelling; for we find various specific sounds being carefully separated, whilst the Latin shows one and the same letter for all: ש and צ are represented by 'S', ח and ה, א and ע are represented by 'A'. In the middle of a word ה is entirely omitted, as they could not distinguish between this letter and א or ח—in names like Naat and Maathal, which in Hebrew are written מחתל נחת. We find also that ב and כ are sometimes confused with one another because of the similarity of the form, *e.g.*, the third name in the Latin, which is a combination of two names in the Hebrew text. It is written 'Barabal' in Latin, whilst in Hebrew it is ברוך כעל, 'Berok Ke'al,' where it is to be noted that in Latin the ע is also omitted in the second word. Then the proper names in Chapter xxix., paragraph 3, which are fearfully corrupted in Latin, appear much clearer in Hebrew; by which we recognise that they are the names of the children of Yoqtan, as given in Genesis (x. 26). This identification helps us, by the way, to see by what means they invented those names; they simply took them from other biblical passages. Now, the Latin form is so corrupt that no man would be able to re-translate them into their biblical prototype. One single exception I have to point out, which is certainly very surprising, and that is the same names of the children of Yoqtan occurring once more in Chapter xxvii., § 5, are written in the same corrupt form as in the Latin.

In the corresponding portion in the Sepher Hayashar, chapter vii., vers. 1-21, we find exactly similar lists, also extremely curious readings; but in the last the names of the children of Yoqtan are given exactly in the same form as they are in our Hebrew text of the Bible. The copyist in Jerahmeel has probably run them together, thinking he had to deal with similar fanciful names as those which fill the whole preceding portion of the chapter.

In order to facilitate the comparison between these genealogical tables in Hebrew with the corresponding

Latin text, I have added them to this book in photographic reproduction; I have also given the Latin text in an Appendix at the end of the volume. We find, also, mistranslations which can only be explained by reading Hebrew words differently. So we have in Chapter xxvii., paragraph 4, the name וּבְנֵי corresponding in Latin to *et filii*, because he must have read it for the Hebrew בְּנִי׳ In Chapter xxviii., paragraph 3, instead of 640 the Latin has 340; he must have read probably שלש for שש. And in Chapter xxix., paragraph 13, where the Hebrew text has 'appeased the wrath of the people,' the Latin has *liquefactus*. He read the Hebrew וישפך instead of וישכך. All these examples, which can easily be multiplied, prove at any rate that the Hebrew text cannot be a translation from any non-Semitic original, and that the Latin itself, though it adheres verbatim to the Hebrew text, can only be considered as a faithful though secondary translation from the intermediary Greek now lost. This Latin translation, as I have already observed, has become in its turn the primary source of much of the legendary lore which has got into the writings of the early Fathers of the Church, and of medieval compilations, coming as far down as Foresti's 'Supplementum Chronicarum.'

The next point for investigation will be to ascertain the *date* of these 'Antiquities' and the probable author. Having established the fact that the book was originally composed in Hebrew, and that the language was one of biblical purity, *i.e.*, in imitation of the style of the Bible, which is entirely borne out by the character of the texts recovered—as in it scarcely a word occurs that is not biblical in origin or of a biblical turn—and the fact that the book had early been translated into Greek, and before the end of the third century into Latin, it will not be difficult to determine the date of the original composition. It must be noted that not a trace or allusion to Christianity is to be found in the whole book. In the vision of 'Cenes,' in the Latin form (folio 32) the words 'Nomen hominis illius' is a wrong translation of the Hebrew text; the Latin read שמו as

= םָקֻיַו, instead of םָקָיַו corresponding to Hebrew, Chapter lvii., paragraph 41, and is not to be taken as referring to Christ, for not a single trace of Christianity is to be found in it. Furthermore, the destruction of the second Temple is only indirectly touched upon. The twelve stones which Kenaz recovers will be utilized, we are told in Chapter lvii., paragraphs 23 and 25, at the time of the building of the Temple. When it again will be destroyed, they will be kept for a future revelation, but nowhere is there a direct indication to the second Temple.

The question, however, which Moses puts to God (fol. 20d), and which has been reprinted by James ('Apocrypha Anecdota,' i., p. 172) offers a date which, if sufficiently clear, might assist us in fixing the probable time of the composition. Moses asks how much of the world's time has already passed and how much is still to come. And the answer is, $4\frac{1}{2}$ times have past, and $2\frac{1}{2}$ times have still to come, that means altogether that out of 7,000 years probably 4,500 had passed. The only question is, according to which computation these 4,500 are to be taken. If they are according to the Jewish reckoning, of which, however, not a trace is to be found anywhere in the rest of the book —except the dates mentioned above concerning the lives of the patriarchs, where the sum total agrees with the Massoretic text—that would bring us down somewhere to the middle of the eighth century, a date that is utterly out of question, considering that the Latin translation belongs to the third or fourth century. If the date could have been reversed, viz., $2\frac{1}{2}$ passed, that would agree with the calculation of the Book of Jubilees, according to which 2,410 had passed from the Creation to the exodus from Egypt. Adding 40 years of wandering in the wilderness, it would bring us to 2,450 as the year of Moses' death, and as near as possible to 2,500. But there is another date mentioned in connection with the death of Moses (folio 19b), immediately preceding in the original the portion printed by James, in which it is said that God commands Moses to ascend the Mount Nebo, and says to him, ' I will shew thee the place in which they will serve Me 740 years, and after that it will be given into the hands of their enemies, and they will destroy it. Strangers will surround it, and that day will be in accordance with the same day in which I have obliterated the Tables of the Covenant, which I had given to them on Oreb. And when they sinned, that which was written upon them flew away, and that day was the 17th of the fourth month.'

The allusion to the 17th day of the fourth month, the day on which Moses came down from the mountain, as a day of bad omen for the future, agrees with the date of the destruction of the second Temple, the 17th of Tamuz. We would then have clear indication that the book belonged to a period after the destruction of the Temple.

Referring again in other places to worship in congregations, the author shows himself to be a Jew who lived immediately after the destruction of the Temple, and, as Dr. Cohn rightly remarks, a book that has been adopted by the Church must belong to an early period, as otherwise such a book would never have been adopted by, or translated for it. The place where such a book could have been written can obviously only be Palestine, as only in that country, and at that period, Hebrew literature still flourished, and there alone attempts at chronology were made concurrently with embellishments of the Bible, as is attested by those Apocryphal books like the Book of Jubilees and Henoch, with which our author seems to have been acquainted, and also with that old attempt at chronology which goes under the name of Seder 'Olām. Without entering into an examination of the exact date of its composition, I consider the origin of the last-mentioned work, and the reason for it, to have been the establishment of a true chronology in contradiction to those apocryphal and incorrect chronologies—a new one that should clearly represent Rabbinical tradition and be in accordance with the then recognised interpretation of the Bible. The Seder 'Olām in its original form belongs probably to the same period. It is more than mere chance to find there a remarkable coincidence in the circumstance (chap. xi. Editio Ratner, page 48), that from the entrance of the Israelites into Palestine until the Exile 850 years are reckoned to have passed. If we alter (and I see Dr. Cohn suggests the same alteration) the figures DCCXL, as given above, into DCCCL, we have exactly the same date, 850. We may safely assume the date of the original composition to be somewhere in the first centuries of the common era; and this work to be thus far the oldest example of a Bible Historiale—*i.e.*, a description of events contemporary with those narrated in the Bible, adding new elements, supplementing and amplifying the latter. The period covered in this narrative agrees exactly with the most famous of mediæval compositions of a similar character, in which the whole of the legal and prophetic portion of the Bible is omitted, stress being laid exclusively on the historical part contained in the Bible. All these historiated Bibles proceed on the same lines. They start with the Creation, and close, at any rate, as far as legends are concerned, with David or the building of the Temple by Solomon. I have dealt fully with the history of this amplified Bible in my Ilchester Lectures on Græco-Slavonic literature (London, 1887, pp. 147-208). Such is also the character of the oldest representative in Europe, the Greek Palaia of the eighth century, upon which the Slavonic Palæa rests, published since by A. Vassiliev in his 'Anecdota Græco-Byzantina' (Moscow, 1893, pp. 188-292; *vide* also Introduction, pp. xlii-lvi).

Shorter and more in agreement with the Hebrew text as far as the period described, is that other chronicle the Yashar, to which I have alluded above. Therein the historical narrative comes virtually to a close with the death of Moses. Three or four pages out of 150 are devoted to a sketch of the period of the judges. In the Hebrew text of Philo this is exactly the terminus to which the narrative reaches. But, however much alike in general contents all the other historiated Bibles are among themselves, the Philo chronicle is distinguished from them by those very legends that are nowhere else found, by the rhetorical character of the description, by the speeches placed in the mouths of the principal persons, and especially by the fulness of details regarding the period of the Judges. All these details are missing in the whole known cycle of the Bible Historiale, and prove the greater antiquity and independence of Philo. Whilst preserving the frame, later compilers made additions and introduced better known and generally adopted legends. Thus we can understand the total disappearance of the primitive form of the Bible Historiale. The same thing has happened even to the latter, being superseded by Comestor.

Turning now to the Hebrew text, it is a remarkable coincidence that this legendary chronicle should in this text tally absolutely with the Samaritan chronicle. In both the ancient Jewish history comes abruptly to a close with the establishment of the Tabernacle in Shiloh under the High Priest Eli. The Samaritans consider this period to be the beginning of the secession from the true ancient Israelitish worship, which they claim to have carried on uninterruptedly in its primitive purity.

Their biblical history, and especially their famous Book of Joshua, treats only of the same space of time and of the same events as contained in our chronicle. All the rest is ignored by them completely. It is an extraordinary coincidence, and may almost assist us in the elucidation of the origin of this old Philo-Jerahmeel, pointing as it does to a possible Samaritan origin. This origin would explain the peculiar chronology at the beginning, and the reason why our Chronicle should dilate on the events that happened in the time of the Judges. It is only remarkable that Joshua himself, who plays such a prominent rôle in the Samaritan chronicle, should be missing here altogether, and that the Latin should continue the history down to the time of David and Solomon, the two kings most hated by the Samaritans. The name of the mountain, Tlag (lix. 5), would also point to some such Aramaic-Samaritan tradition, as this is the name for

Hermon in the Palestinian-Aramaic Targum. The Samaritan chronicle of Joshua was not unknown to the Jews, as the correspondence between Joshua and King Shobakh of Armenia carried on by means of a dove is given by Samuel Shalom in his edition of the 'Juḥasin' (Constantinople, fol. 117a).

In what relation stands this book—which in Latin is ascribed to Philo, and in one portion of the Hebrew manuscript also—to Jeraḥmeel's compilation? Who is Jeraḥmeel? This difficulty is somewhat increased by the fact that we have in that which appears now in Eleasar the Levite's compilation under the name of Jeraḥmeel portions, as it were, added to the ancient work of Philo which are missing in the Latin, unless they can be found in other manuscripts, and have been omitted by the editor of the hitherto single edition of Basle. Principally we must note in this connection the *second* genealogical table, to which I have already drawn attention once or twice, forming Chapters xxxi. and xxxii., and the synchronistic element which pervades the whole compilation. Is this an addition made by Jeraḥmeel, or is it the work of another and more ancient compiler, whom Jeraḥmeel utilized for his own work?

How great is his share in the work before us, at what time and where did he live and write? I assume him to have been a person other than the author of the legendary part, and not identical with 'Philo,' although the names seem identical; the Hebrew is the counterpart and perfect translation of the Greek word 'Philo,' both meaning 'the beloved of God.' I ascribe to him most of the chapters that precede and follow that portion of the book which is found in 'Philo.' Eleasar, the last compiler, moreover, states distinctly that he intercalates portions from other books, notably from the Yosippon, or whole texts, breaking up the narrative of Jeraḥmeel. Dr. Perles, who was the first to have the manuscript of Jeraḥmeel in his hands (and whilst dilating on Eleasar, the author of the actual full compilation, fixing his date correctly and connecting him with a family of great scholars), draws attention to Jerahmeel, and comes to the following conclusion: That all the statements of Jerahmeel wherein he refers to Nicolaos of Damascus and to Strabo are not to be taken literally; that he must have used the Yosippon; and, because a German word occurs in one of these chapters, Jerahmeel must have lived somewhere in Germany in the thirteenth century. The truth, however, is that the German word does not belong to Jerahmeel, but is undoubtedly a gloss added by Eleasar, the compiler, who was a German. This is not the only instance in the present work. In the first chapters, which owe their place in this book also probably to Eleasar, we have a list of the names of the week given in that very old German dialect which belonged to the Rhine Province of the twelfth century. In another place, Chapter lviii. 8, we have the explanation of the Sirenes as Niks (Nix in German), and in the genealogical table Eleasar the Levite gives an explanation, in his own name, of one of the names of the nations; the Flamingos he considers to be identical with the Lehabim of the Bible. A curious popular etymology, by which the Flamingos, the Flemish people, would be derived from the 'flame,' the burning ones. We may dismiss, therefore, this conjecture of Dr. Perles altogether, as being contrary to the internal evidence furnished by the text.

The next one who deals with Jerahmeel is Dr. Neubauer (*vide* later on), and he declares him to have been a writer of the eleventh century, living in Magna Græcia or in South Italy, the proof for it being that he knew Greek, and also that he made use of the Yosippon, which goes back to Greek sources. The supposed knowledge of Greek is evidenced, according to Dr. Neubauer, by the names of the genealogical table; but, if anything, just the reverse is the fact. Forms like 'Isides' for 'Isis,' 'Palante' for 'Palas,' and any number of them, show distinctly that the author knew anything but Greek. More proofs to the contrary will be brought forward in the course of this investigation. And the reason for declaring that he lived in the South of Italy xliii

is of so flimsy a nature that it can also not be considered seriously, for it rests mostly upon Jerahmeel's acquaintance with the Yosippon. The South-Italian origin of this book is one of those assumptions in Hebrew literature for which the proof is still wanting. This very acquaintance with Yosippon will lead exactly to different conclusions. Before approaching this more problematical part of our investigation, we take first into consideration those portions which may yield a more positive result. I start with the synchronistic element, that is, with those portions which deal with non-Jewish history, and especially with the second genealogical table (Chapter xxxi., et seq.). Examining it, we find that it rests primarily upon Josephus. In this second version we have a totally different tradition from that in the preceding chapters, and, moreover, this new genealogical table is entirely missing in the Latin Philo. The basis of it seems to be identical with the geographical table given by Josephus in his 'Antiquities' (book i., chapter vi., paragraph 1, et seq.). If we turn, then, to the Book of Jubilees (chapter viii., verse 12 onward) we find an absolute identity in the general outline of the geographical divisions of the world among the three sons of Noah. And if we look at the other Jewish traditions connected with that division of the world, and contained, for instance, in the Jerusalemitan Targum to Genesis (chapter x.), and in other parallel passages in Midrash and Talmud, we shall find that they all seem to go back to one and the same ancient tradition, represented in its fullest form by Josephus. This has been adopted afterwards by all the Fathers of the Church.

It recurs, then, almost in the same form, with slight alterations in, or additions to, the names of the descendants of Noah, in the writings of ancient Christian authors who lived or wrote in Palestine and Asia Minor, such as Epiphanius, of the fourth century, in his 'Ancoratus,' c. 114, 115, and 'Heresies,' c. 46, et seq., in the fifth century. The text of Epiphanius had been copied verbatim in the 'Chronicon Paschale' of the seventh (ed. Bonn, i., pp. 45-64). (Full notes and parallels from the whole cycle of the ancient Greek chronicles, *ibid.*, ii., pp. 235-249.) Hippolytus, third century, Eusebius, fourth century, Jerome of the fifth, and then Malalas of the sixth. It entered also the Latin writers through the intermediary of Jerome, notably into the 'Origines' of Isidorus of Spain, of the seventh, and in Beda's writings of the eighth century; it found a place in the later Byzantine and Slavonic Chronographs, as well as in the writings of Eutychius and Bar-Hebræus Abulpharadj.

They all seem to have repeated one another, and have all one and the same old tradition. In the course of time they substituted new names for the old ones. The same has happened also in Hebrew literature. So, in the Targum, in the introductory chapters to the Hebrew Yosippon, where we find also such a division, together with a list of names reproduced in our chronicle side by side with the old and also in the Sepher Hayashar (chapter x., verse 7, *et seq.*). These names assist us now to show, at any rate, to what late period we may bring down the date of the composition. If any nation is mentioned which appears at a certain date on the stage of history, we are able then to assign the book that mentions it to the period after the appearance of that nation. In this manner we are able to establish that the introductory chapter to the Yosippon is probably a later substitution for an older one, and belongs to the eighth or ninth century. On the other hand, the names mentioned in 'Jerahmeel,' if that chapter really belongs to the original 'Jerahmeel,' cannot be earlier than the fifth or sixth century; that chapter might belong to even a later period, but we cannot consider it to be earlier than the fifth or sixth century, as among others the Nordmani, Bayuvori, and Langobardi are already mentioned—all nations which appear in the fifth or sixth century.

If we examine, then, the form of these names, we shall be able to decide whether the author had access to Greek or to Latin sources of information, and, by the pronunciation or transliteration of certain names, even to what period they belong. The oldest source of information was undoubtedly Josephus, or a similar source identical with that from which Josephus drew his information — the old imperial road lists, the 'Itineraria.' The form of these names proves clearly that the immediate source for Jeraḥmeel was certainly not a Greek text. Dr. Neubauer in his study on Jeraḥmeel (in the *Jewish Quarterly Review* of April, 1899, page 367) suggests such a source. The very examples brought forward by him prove the reverse, as the transliteration of the names and the oblique form of the tenses show them to have been dependent, not on Greek, but on Latin sources. Forms like Gresi, Fransi, Kapadoses are certainly a transliteration of the corresponding Latin forms written with *C*, and not of the Greek that are written with *K*. A form like Frozes undoubtedly corresponds much more with the Latin Phryges, already with that palatal pronunciation of the Latin *g*, in its change to the Romance forms, than with Greek. The same is to be said of Silicia, which in Greek would be Kilikia. (I must mention that Cyprus is still written Kipros.) We have further Phenise, which is certainly the representative of Phoenicae, Luṣifer, corresponding to Lucifer — the Greek word would be Eōsphoros — which all prove that the immediate source must have been written in Latin and not in Greek. None of the peculiar Hebrew letters such as ח and ע are found here!

The old Latin translation of Josephus's 'Antiquities' made in the sixth century cannot have served as basis for our genealogical table, for the latter contains many additions and changes that are not to be found in Josephus's work itself; they agree, however, partly with Jerome's version in his 'Quaestiones in Genesin.' Much more close is the identity between 'Jeraḥmeel' and Isidor of Spain (Origines, xx., 2, in Opera, Paris, 1601, f. 116 *et seq.*). We shall find later on, especially concerning the synchronistic portion, a remarkable closeness between Isidor's 'Chronicon' (*ibid.*, f. 374 *et seq.*) and 'Jeraḥmeel,' and also between the latter and the 'Historia Scholastica' of Comestor, who probably had access to the same Latin source for his information as Jeraḥmeel. This points to a Latin-speaking or Latin-writing country in the South of Europe as the home of the author of these additional elements in 'Jeraḥmeel's Chronicle.' I believe this to have been neither Germany nor Greece, but Spain. Spain is the only country where this kind of early Latin chronograph was written. But besides this possible acquaintance with Isidor's works, there are a number of other cogent reasons for looking to Spain as the home of this chronicle.

We must remember in the first instance the close similarity in contents and sources so often pointed out between the Book of Yashar and this Chronicle even as far as genealogical tables are concerned. In one instance the Book of Yashar contains even more than that which is preserved in our Jeraḥmeel. I am alluding to Yashar, chapter xxii., verses 20-39, containing an apocryphal list of the children of Teraḥ, which is not to be found anywhere else. This Book of Yashar has been compiled, as it is stated in the introduction, in Spain, and there is no reason to doubt the accuracy of this statement. In Spain we find, further, the Book of Yosippon having been used on an extensive scale by a man of the standing of Rabbi Abraham b. David, who lived in the twelfth century (1161). He, curiously enough, writes also an abstract of Roman history, which in many details is absolutely identical with the narrative of Jeraḥmeel, especially in that concerning the establishment of the Republic. The senators are ruled by a man whom he, just as Jeraḥmeel, calls 'Yashish,' or 'Zaqoen,' 'the old man,' a curious literal translation of the word 'Senatus.' If the use of the Yosippon would prove the author to have lived in the South of Italy, then Abraham b. David, the first one who quotes from it extensively, in fact, who makes an abstract of the history of the second Temple agreeing almost verbatim with our text, should also have lived in the South of Italy. It is established, however, and is beyond doubt, that he lived and died in Spain. Saadyah knows Yosippon in the ninth century in Egypt, and Qalir in Palestine, probably in the seventh ; from the argument adduced by others, these authors ought to have lived in South Italy in the twelfth. The use of a book can prove merely the age of the author, but not in any way the country in which he lived.

We thus find two works in Spain agreeing in the main with the bulk of Jerahmeel's work—the Yashar, an apocryphal history from the Creation, together with peculiar genealogical tables, with the introduction of legendary elements drawn from ancient sources, and portions of the history of the Romans; and Abraham b. David's work containing a long abstract from Yosippon, these two being the characteristic elements of the Chronicle of Jerahmeel.

We may go now one step further. One portion of his book consists of a translation of the Aramaic portions of Daniel into Hebrew. It is now a recognised fact that among all the countries where Jews lived in ancient times, those of Spain were the only ones that either neglected Aramaic, or did not possess any knowledge of it. So late as the tenth century Dunash b. Tamim, the great grammarian, had to write an epistle recommending strongly the study of Aramaic for the purpose of elucidating and understanding the Hebrew. Missives and information that came from Babylon are known to exist in an Aramaic and in a Hebrew form, like the famous letters of Sherira and Haya Gaon, and it is now an admitted fact that the Hebrew was intended for the Jews in Spain, whilst the Aramaic went to those in Italy, France, and Germany. As regards the liturgical poetry, we find Aramaic poems known only in the liturgy of the latter countries, composed by authors living there, whilst almost everything in Aramaic was discarded in Spain. This was probably due to the connection between Spain and Palestine. The translation, therefore, of Aramaic portions of the Bible into Hebrew could only have been of value and appreciated as such in a country like Spain—an additional argument, therefore, for my contention that we have to seek in Spain, and nowhere else, for the origin of the Chronicle of Jerahmeel.

xlviii

Everything points to that conclusion : Jerahmeel's acquaintance with the books that are known to have existed there, viz., Biblical Apocrypha and the Book of Yosippon; the identity also in style between his writing and these two other writings. Now, as to the other activity of Jerahmeel, we find in the same manuscript some poetical compositions which show him to have been a man versed in mathematical disciplines, especially addicted to chronological calculations and in preference to mathematical puzzles. In one of these poems a peculiar era is mentioned by him which agrees with the Era Seleucidarum, but in Chapter lix., paragraph 10, of the Chronicle itself he distinctly states that the *era* which 'we use is that from the destruction of the Temple.' This era is known to have existed solely in Spain.

A more decisive proof for the Spanish origin of this compilation is furnished to us by another legendary collection, which in itself is a problem hitherto not sufficiently elucidated. It was known from the quotations made by Reymundus Martini, in his 'Pugio Fidei,' that, besides the so-called 'Genesis Rabba,' another similar compilation of a homiletical character also existed, which went under the name of 'Genesis Rabba Major,' or 'Rabbati,' and in many cases it is ascribed to a certain Moses the Darshan. This 'Genesis Rabba Major' has disappeared, however, save a few fragments preserved in a manuscript of late date now in the Bodleian Library, and in some quotations which Gedaliah made in his edition of the 'Genesis Rabba' in ed. Salonik. Many were the speculations connected with the origin and character of this last compilation, which was characterized by the fact that it contained many curious Apocryphal legends and tales almost of a unique character. It so happened that a manuscript was found in Prague, which seemed to be a kind of reflex or an imperfect copy of that old compilation of the 'Rabbati' ascribed to Rabbi Moses Hadarschan. Zunz, Rappaport, and Jellinek drew attention to it, and also conclusions from it. Mr. Epstein has recently examined this manuscript, and published a study, the result of which is that the authenticity and correctness of the quotations of Martini are now placed beyond doubt; and this manuscript represents, to a certain extent, that old and more perfect compilation which was known and utilized in the thirteenth century.

In comparing the most important legends in 'Rabbati' with Jerahmeel we are forced to conclude that Moses the Darshan, who lived in the twelfth century in Narbonne, must have had access to our Chronicle. From it he has drawn most of those peculiar elements so characteristic of his compilation; for we find the Aramaic fragments in 'Pugio Fidei' of Daniel in the lions' den are also in Aramaic, and absolutely identical with Jerahmeel's version. This, by the way, is one proof more of the extreme antiquity of this Aramaic text, and of the authenticity of Jerahmeel's information, that he has copied it from the old version, which served as basis to Thedotion ('Pugio Fidei,' ed. Paris, p. 742). The same text is found in the fragment of the 'Rabbati,' published by Dr. Neubauer ('Book of Tobit,' pp. 41, 42), and in the manuscript examined by Epstein ('Bereschit Rabbati,' 1888, p. 14, No. 1), which agrees still more closely with the text of Jerahmeel. The following comparison will prove that we have now found the hitherto unknown and unsuspected source for the 'Rabbati.' For the identity of the legends in 'Rabbati' with those in our collection goes much further. The legend of the bird Milham, which is a variation of the phœnix legend given by Martini in the 'Pugio,' 543, in the name of Moses the Darshan, is found also in the manuscript 'Rabbati' (*vide* Jellinek, 'Bet. Ham.,' vol. vi., p. xii, note), and is identical with the legend in Jerahmeel, Chapter xxii., verse 6, for which hitherto the only known parallel was in the 'Alphabetum Sirac.' (*cf.* later on). This last identification between Martini and the 'Rabbati' has been overlooked by Epstein.

We find in it, further, the legend of the fallen angels, for which we have known hitherto only the parallel in the 'Mid. Abkir.' It is found in the 'Pugio' and in the

'Rabbati' manuscript of Prague (Epstein, p. 21, No. 17), and in Jerahmeel, Chapter xxv. It also contains a description of Paradise ('Pugio Fidei,' p. 335; and in the manuscript 'Rabbati,' Epstein, p. 16, No. 9), which agrees with Jerahmeel, Chapter xx., paragraph 7 following, being absolutely identical. A short description of hell is given in 'Pugio,' pp. 482, 483, which agrees in the main with Jerahmeel, Chapter xxi., paragraphs 2, 3; and still more convincing, if necessary, is the absolute identity of the history of the Children of Moses, as mentioned by Epstein (p. 19), agreeing entirely with Jerahmeel, Chapter lxii. This legend is the only one fully reprinted by Epstein, from manuscript Prague (in his 'Eldad,' pp. 42-45), and we can see the absolute identity between the two texts. Epstein mentions further (p. 30) that in the 'Rabbati' are to be found similar legends about Eliphaz, the son of Esau, and the war between Esau and the children of Jacob, which he believes to have been taken from the Book of Yashar. As this very same legend is given in full in Jerahmeel, we need not go to the Sepher Hayashar for the solitary instance of a possible borrowing. The coincidence between the two compilations having exactly the same legends not known elsewhere, and the fact that these legends agree literally with one another, prove absolutely that one must have been borrowed from the other. The priority will easily be conceded to Jerahmeel, whose work consists exclusively of such legends placed one next to the other and collected into one volume, and not to the author of a homiletical commentary to the Bible, where he would introduce, by way of illustration, legends culled from different sources. I consider all the texts that occur in homiletical collections as of but secondary value, altered and utilized for a special purpose. In many cases the whole text has been reproduced; in other cases that text has been curtailed, and only the principal incidents which were of interest in connection with the homily were retained. In that compilation known as 'Rabbati,' in the form quoted by Reymundus, we see the very same thing.

Some legends are retained in full, others have been shortened and adapted to the homiletic purpose.

This evidence overwhelmingly proves that our compilation must have been known and extensively used by writers who lived in Spain, and who had direct literary connections with Spain; and our 'Jeraḥmeel' assists us, by the way, to solve an important problem in the history of Jewish literature. This alone would have sufficed to justify the publication of his Chronicle.

The date of this part of the Chronicle is fixed, to a certain extent, by the names of the nations which are mentioned, and by the dependence upon the 'Chronicon' and 'Origenes' of Isidor. They carry us down to the middle of the sixth century. It is noteworthy that in the whole book not a single allusion to Christianity is made. In the legends of the Ten Tribes Mohammed is mentioned, but this would also not carry us further down than to the seventh century, as no Chaliphate is alluded to, and the Jews are fighting apparently small Ishmaelite kingdoms. On the contrary, in one instance (Chapter xxxii., paragraph 6) our author states distinctly that the Kings of Rome are *still in existence*, and are called Cæsar, after the name of Julius Cæsar, unless this note be taken to refer to the Emperor of the Holy Roman Empire from the ninth century onward. But there is not the slightest allusion to *German* Emperors in our text, or even to a German kingdom. The author of this compilation evidently limited himself to the biblical period, with this solitary exceptional reference to the *Cæsars* that *are* still ruling in Rome.

As a result of this investigation I ascribe the synchronistic element, as well as the second genealogical table, to the same author. Both are derived from one and the same source; and as they occur mostly in conjunction with the 'Philo' portion, I am inclined to believe that they have been incorporated with that chronicle not later than the sixth or seventh century, when, in every probability, all the other biblical Apocrypha were added, which would contribute to amplify that legendary chronicle. The histories of Abraham, Moses, Haman and Mordecai, of the Ten Tribes, and the children of Moses, living beyond the borders of the mythical Sambatyon, would thus have amplified and enriched the older Chronicle of Jeraḥmeel, form the basis for the Yashar, with which it would agree in most elements, and would thus be the nucleus for the larger work, unless it could be proved that Yashar is dependent on another similar compilation, and not directly on the present work.

The question of the relation between the Yashar and Jeraḥmeel still requires further elucidation before I can venture upon a definite reply, and very much depends upon the fact whether another manuscript of Jeraḥmeel will ever be available. But there can be no doubt as to the intimate relation between these two books, and as to the independence and priority of Jeraḥmeel.

Throughout this introduction I have called the whole compilation by the name of Jeraḥmeel. Of the part which he has taken in it nothing definite can be said, the date when he lived and wrote being still a matter of conjecture. If the poems found at the beginning of this manuscript with the acrostic Jeraḥmeel belong to the same man, and his references are to the well-known Rashi and probably to his grandson, he must have lived in the twelfth century. His activity would then have consisted merely in enriching the already existing older compilation of at latest the seventh century by the addition of new and similar material and possibly the omission of some of the older materials, without changing however in the least the wording of the texts which he retained. The 'Duplicates,' if I may call them so, would be due to him; then, the portion from Daniel translated from Aramaic into Hebrew; but, on the other hand, he took great care *not* to incorporate larger portions of Yosippon in the middle of the actual chronicle. The genealogical table from Yosippon was interpolated (Chapter xxxi.) by the last compiler, Eleazar, who mentions this fact expressly, stating that he was, by so doing, interrupting the narrative of Jeraḥmeel.

The literary tradition of Spain also favours this theory. In that country alone writers of chronicles, following the old example, strive after a simple, pure Hebrew style. Curiously enough, all of them, like the later writers: Ibn Verga, the author of the Shebet Yehudah; Ibn Yahya, the author of the Shalshelet Haqqabbalah; Joseph Ha-Cohen, the author of the Emeq Habakhah, and others, follow the same old example of imitating the biblical style, exactly in the same manner, but with less originality and less freedom as was done by the author of the old Chronicle Philo-Jerahmeel, by the Yosippon, and by the compiler of the Sepher Hayashar.

His reference to the writings of Nic. of Damascus and Strabo of Caftor as books consulted by him could not be taken literally, as he quotes them probably from the Yosippon, in which they, in fact, are found in identical terms. Like all mediæval chroniclers, he both copied the ancient chronicle, and embellished it with legends and information of his own. The texts are not altered in the wording; whole portions are omitted or added. The same operation was afterwards repeated by Eleazar the Levite, who utilized it in the fourteenth century for the compilation of his own great chronicle.

It is noteworthy that the name Jerahmeel is as perfect a translation as one could wish for the Greek name Philo. To assume two Jerahmeels, one of a very early date, the author of that portion of our Chronicle which in the Latin goes under the name of Philo, and another of a comparatively very recent date, the compiler of the larger work, would be somewhat hazardous. But the name of Philo in itself requires to be explained, unless it can be shown that that legendary work could not be the work of Philo the Alexandrian, or some other Philo. The fact is that these Apocryphal 'Antiquities' are found together in that translation with other genuine works of Philo. They all have the same character as far as the language is concerned, and belong to the same early period before Jerome, and are probably all the work of one and the same translator. He therefore knew them as the work of the same author, Philo, as the rest. However that may be, until the question of Jerahmeel and his part in our Chronicle has been further elucidated, I call this Chronicle by the name of Jerahmeel or Philo-Jerahmeel, for if it is not the name of the real author, it is undoubtedly due to him that this most precious and unique monument of ancient Hebrew legendary literature has been preserved. It is one of the few old Apocryphal books which have come down in their original form and in the Hebrew language, whilst most other books of the same period and of the same character have either perished entirely or have been preserved in a mutilated and incomplete translation, like the Book of Enoch, in Ethiopian; the Assumption of Moses, in Latin; or the Testaments of the Twelve Patriarchs, in Greek, and so on. The close similarity between the Latin of Philo and the Hebrew preserved to us by Jerahmeel, at any rate, shows that it is a very ancient original Hebrew text. The possibility of its being a translation from the Latin being absolutely excluded, Jerahmeel proves thus to be, if not the author, at any rate a faithful transcriber of very ancient documents.

The language of this Philo-Jerahmeel portion is exactly the same as in the Yashar and in the Book of Yosippon, with which Jerahmeel is evidently well acquainted. The argument, therefore, that a book written in imitation of the biblical style must be of recent origin, is thus disproved at the hand of authentic documents. I need not point out the extreme importance which this fact has for the other Apocryphal texts in our compilation of uncertain date, those considered to be of comparatively recent origin, only and solely because of the fluency of the style, of the purity of the language, and of the imitation of the biblical diction. The fact once established that the older a book the purer its Hebrew style (unless it is shown to be a late artificial production purposely written in that style), will throw some side-light on recently recovered fragments of the ancient Apocrypha, which differ very considerably, by reason of the artificial character of their style, and the numerous new forms and words they contain, from the simple and natural sentences and words of the Bible, and from such historical or legendary books as the Chronicle of Philo-Jerahmeel, and as the legends that go towards making up the Yashar, such as the history of Abraham, Chronicle of Moses, etc.

A comparison between Jerahmeel's texts and their ancient parallels, prove him to have been a faithful copyist of the documents which he wrote down exactly in the form in which he found them; otherwise such names as occur in the genealogical lists and in the historical notices interspersed throughout the book, would not have been allowed by him to retain their original form in the Hebrew transliteration, but would have been recast by him into a form more akin to the Hebrew language. In the one instance where he acts as a translator he mentions the fact expressly, and states that he had translated the Aramaic portions in Daniel into Hebrew. Comparing that language of his own translation with the language of the legends, say, of Abraham or Kenaz, we find them differing so much from one another that both cannot be the work of one and the same author. This is another proof for the authenticity and the accuracy of his transcript of the ancient Chronicle; always assuming this Jerahmeel not to be identical with Philo, but to be the name of a later compiler, who incorporated into his work the old composition that went under the name of Philo. We thus set at rest the gratuitous assumption of Neubauer and others, who have completely misunderstood Jerahmeel's introductory sentences to the Aramaic version of the Song of the Three Children in the furnace and the Daniel-legends, published by me, viz., that they had been translated by Jerahmeel from a Greek or another source. They are old and genuine original texts, as already remarked above.

It is not at all unlikely that the original Jerahmeel or the original chronicle which Jerahmeel copied out was as full as the Latin text, and may have gone further than the

Latin, including also a short reference to the destruction of the Temple, so as to cover the whole ground of the Bible, to which Yosippon would then be the natural continuation. Has Jerahmeel curtailed it, or is it due to the editorial activity of Eleazar the Levite, who seems to have taken some liberties with his text? This must remain an open question until a new manuscript is discovered. Eleazar, at any rate, is under the impression that the older portion coincides with the biblical period, and connects the text of Yosippon almost immediately with the account of the Exiles to which the Jews had been subjected. The version of the Yosippon in our manuscript agrees on the whole with the old text printed by Conte* (*ante* 1480); and the Apocrypha which it contains, and with which I intend dealing later on when studying each chapter by itself, prove them not to be translated from the Latin or from the Greek, as some have rather hastily assumed, but to be independent versions of ancient origin, maybe reflecting the originals. For one or two at least, like the dream of Mordecai, it will be shown that they are extant in manuscripts much older than the date which Neubauer, and Perles before him, agreed to assign to Jerahmeel. He, therefore, could not have been the translator of texts that exist in Hebrew or in Aramaic before his time. And as it can be proved regarding some of the texts contained in our compilation that they are much older than the time of the compiler, we are justified to claim great age for the rest of the biblical Apocrypha in this Chronicle, which also go back to a far greater antiquity than scholars have hitherto assumed. It is for this reason that I have brought this Chronicle to a close with the Book of the Maccabee, the last Biblical Apocryphum in the volume. It must be left to special studies to ascertain the exact date of each of them, and the relation in which these Apocrypha of the Bible stand to the known Syriac, Greek, and Latin versions.

I shall now proceed to discuss each chapter separately;

* Guided by the spelling of this name in the colophon to some of his editions, I have been the first to substitute this reading of 'Conte' for the hitherto current form 'Cunath.'

to show, if possible, the immediate source whence each has been drawn ; to trace its parallels in the Hebrew literature, and whenever possible in cognate literatures. In order to facilitate references, I have divided the text into chapters and paragraphs, following in the main the indications in the manuscript. This investigation will form at the same time a commentary to the various texts, and will show in many instances the value that is to be attached to each text from a critical point of view. In a few instances, we shall find two versions of one and the same legend, which proves the faithfulness of the compiler. When he found two texts dealing with the same subject, but somewhat different in form, he did not hesitate to copy both and to place them one next to the other. Each of them will be treated by itself.

The works to which reference is chiefly made, in so far as Hebrew parallels and bibliography are concerned, are : Zunz, 'Die Gottesdienstlichen Vorträge der Juden,' second edition, Frankfurt-a-M., 1892 (Zunz, G. V.²) ; A. Jellinek, ' Bet ha-Midrasch,' vols. i.-vi. (Jellinek, ' B. H.') ; and the ' Sepher Hayashar,' ed Princeps, Venice, 1625 (Yashar). I have subdivided this last work into chapters and verses, following the English translation, ' The Book of Jasher,' New York, 1840. As all the Hebrew editions are divided in accordance with the biblical large divisions of the Pentateuch, I add a comparative table : Chapters i.-ii., Bereshit ; iii.-xiii., 21, Noah ; xiii. 22-xvii., Lekhlekha ; xviii-xxiii., Vayera ; xxiv.-xxv., Ḥayyei Sarah ; xxvi.-xxix., Tóledóth ; xxx.-xxxi, Vayeṣe ; xxxii.-xl., Vayishlaḥ ; xli.-xlvii., Vayesheb ; xlviii.-liii., Miqēṣ ; liv.-lv., Vayigash ; lvi.-lviii., Vayeḥi ; lix.-lxxix., Shemóth ; lxxx.-lxxvii., Bó ; lxxxiii., Vayiqra ; lxxxiv.-lxxxvi., Bemidbar ; lxxxvii., Eleh ha-debarim ; lxxxviii.-xc., Yehóshua ; xci., Shófeṭim.

In the notes that I give I do not aim at reproducing the whole bibliography, when it is already given by Zunz, or by Buber, or in any of the books referred to. It is a useless show of erudition, and does not further our investigation. My principal aim is to mention, in the first instance, those texts which show the closest similarity with our compilation, and which are either direct sources, or, at any rate, stand nearest in age and in form to the immediate source from which the compiler drew his text. Reference is necessarily made to non-Jewish parallels, in the first place to Syriac and Arabic. I refer, in the first instance, to M. Gruenbaum, 'Neue Beiträge für Semitischen Sagenkunde, Leiden, 1893.' Many scholars have assumed that legends and parallels found, for instance, in the Book of Yashar, or in the chapters of Rabbi Eliezer, son of Hyrqanos, parallel to Mahomedan legends, must have been borrowed from the latter source. But conclusive evidence is still missing, and I do not think that the time has yet come to draw final conclusions. Many more legendary texts may surge up from the depth of antiquity hitherto unknown, which will throw a new light upon the materials existing in Hebrew literature. The recent discovery of the Yemenite homiletical literature, such as the Midrash Haggadol, for instance; then my find of the old collection of 'Rabbinical Exempla' (legends), dating probably from the fifth or sixth century, fragments found by me among the pieces from the Geniza in Cairo, may modify, and have to a certain extent modified, such views. But as these literatures have undoubtedly borrowed one from the other, I thought it right to refer to them whenever I considered necessary. The Slavonic Palæa, being a reflex of the Greek compilation, which, in the light of this discovery of Philo-Jerahmeel, I believe to have stood in close relation to the Greek text, as well as to some old translation of the Book of Yashar, or with the elements contained therein, has also been referred to by me, when the similarity proved striking. Special attention have I given, then, to Petrus Comestor's 'Historia Scholastica' (ed. Migne, Patrologia, vol. cxciii., Paris, 1855), in which he has utilized, as he states distinctly (in Genesis, chapter xxxvii.) the work of 'Philo,' and who has also all those synchronistic elements so prominent a feature of Jerahmeel. Comestor says: 'Narrat autem Philo Judaeus vel ut alii volunt Gentiliis philosophus in libro *Quaestionum* super Genesim,' and finally Fabricius's invaluable 'Codex Pseudo-Epigraphus Veteris Testamenti.' All the other authorities will be quoted in full when referred to singly.

Chapter I.—Starting from the history of the Creation, our compiler takes as basis for this description a fragmentary collection of legends known as the chapters of Rabbi Eliezer. It is not my intention here to enter into a detailed examination of each of these sources. I am referring to the principal ones, especially to those which, by being utilized to a larger extent by the compiler, claim our special consideration. In that book of 'Eliezer,' for instance, we find for the first time a description of the fall of Satan, and many details which, by a long process of transmission, have had also an influence upon Milton's 'Paradise Lost.' The last word has not yet been spoken about this book, whose reputed author is Eliezer, the son of Hyrqanos, of the first century of the Common Era. Some scholars have ascribed that book to the seventh or eighth century, because a few allusions to Mahomedanism are found in it; but the book belongs unquestionably to a much higher antiquity, and many incidents point to more ancient sources, akin with those utilized by the author of the Book of Jubilees and the Book of Enoch. My references are to the edition made by David Lurya (Warsaw, 1852), whose commentary contains to each detail in the book the whole parallel literature; when I add numbers to the chapters quoted, I refer to the numbers of the notes.

Chapter I. of Jerahmeel corresponds, then, with Chapter iii. of Eliezer Hyrqanos. In a few instances biblical references are omitted in our text; such is the case at the end of paragraph 2 and the end of paragraph 7. Chapter II. Jerahmeel corresponds to Eliezer, Chapter v.; Chapter III., paragraph 1, is taken from Eliezer, Chapter vi. In the latter book there follows a minute description of the rules of the Jewish Calendar, of the movement of the planets, in which point that book resembles other ancient Apocryphal books. The calculation of the calendar is one of the chief items of interest with almost every one of those ancient writers; it fills many chapters in the Book of Enoch, and the whole of the Book of Jubilees is unquestionably an attempt to establish such a calendar. The Rabbinical dissentient calendar finds, then, its expression in these chapters of Eliezer, and in a book, lost up to quite recent time, attributed to Mar Samuel. A small portion of this 'Barayta,' as it is called, has been recovered and published in Salonic, 1861. Zunz describes (in 'Hamazkir,' vol. v., p. 15, 1862) the history of this astronomical work. There seems to have existed an intimate connection, hitherto not sufficiently explained, between this work, ascribed to Samuel, and the astronomical portions in the Book of Eliezer Hyrqanos, as ancient quotations from the latter, now missing in our text, are found in that Barayta of Samuel. I mention these points here because similar portions are found in the following chapters of Jerahmeel, which at first sight appear intercalated from Samuel's Barayta, between the continuous quotations from the Chapters of Rabbi Eliezer. Their appearance here proves the text preserved in Jerahmeel's compilation, which agrees with the old quotations, to be the fullest and more correct than that found in the edition of the Chapters of Rabbi Eliezer. The order in which the things are quoted by Jerahmeel is slightly different from that of the published text; for Chapter III., paragraphs 2, 3, are taken literally from the beginning of Chapter vii. of Rabbi Eliezer; whilst Chapter IV., paragraph 4, is identical with a portion from Chapter vi. of Rabbi Eliezer. Instead of continuing the text as in Rabbi Eliezer, Chapter vii., with that calendaristic calculation (which is probably a later interpolation from a different source or an abstract from a larger work), we have, in our text of Jerahmeel, paragraph 6 *et seq.*, totally different elements, now missing in Eliezer, but preserved in that very book which is ascribed to Samuel. But of this only a fragment has hitherto been recovered, and that explains why paragraph 6 is missing in this text; we find it, however, in the 'Barayta of Creation,' published by Buber and Chones ('Yerioth Shelomo,' Warsaw, 1896, p. 50). A similar text is to be found in the 'Pardes' ascribed to Rashi (*vide* Lurya to end of Chapter vii. of Rabbi Eliezer, No. 68, *et seq.*), then in 'Sode Razaya,' and in the Yalqut Makhiri to Ps. lxxxi. (my codex, No. 100, fol. 191*a*).

Jerahmeel, Chapter IV., agrees remotely with the actual text of Rabbi Eliezer, Chapter vii. Concerning the planets, we find their names, etc., mentioned in the book 'Yeṣira,' chap. iv., then Rashi to the following treatises of the Talmud: Berakoth, 59*b*, Sabbath, 129*b*, Erubin, 56*a*; in the Zohar to Haazinu, fol. 287*a*, also in the Midrash Haggadol to Genesis (my manuscript, No. 1, fol. 15*c*). In paragraph 2, which is undoubtedly an interpolation of Eleazar the Levite, the last compiler of the book, we have the oldest list of German names of the days of the week and their primitive form as known in the Rhine Province about the end of the twelfth century. The same list is repeated once more at the end of the whole manuscript, proving this interpolation to be due to Eleazar the Levite. Paragraphs 3 and 4 agree with chap. vii. of the Barayta of Samuel. But our text is much shorter than the parallels, which we find also in the 'Sode Razaya' quoted in 'Yalqut Reubeni' (fol. 7*a*), and in that book which goes under the name of the Angel 'Raziel' (ed. Amsterdam, fol. 17*b*). The two books 'Sode Razaya' and 'Raziel' owe their present form to Rabbi Eleazar of Worms, who lived in the thirteenth century, and made use of extremely ancient Midrashim. Paragraphs 5-9 are identical with chap. ix. of the Barayta of Samuel. Here the reverse has taken place, for the fuller form seems to have been preserved in Jerahmeel, as many details, such as the form of each of the seven planets, and the description of the things over which they are appointed, are missing in the Barayta of Samuel. We are dealing in this chapter with some of the old astrological data current in ancient times (*cf.* Boucher Leclerque, ' L'astrologie Grecque,' Paris, 1899).

Chapter V.—The thread of the narrative according to the

chapters of Eliezer Hyrqanos is resumed with Chapter V., which corresponds with part of Chapter ix.

Chapter VI., paragraph 1, is taken from Chapter xi. of Eliezer. Chapter VI., paragraph 2, and part of paragraph 3, cf. Treat. Sanhedrin, fol. 38a, b, where the text is much shorter. Paragraphs 3-5, the consultation of God with the angels about the creation of man, are identical in form with the book that goes under the title 'Midrash Kônên' (ed. Jellinek, 'B. H.,' ii., pp. 26-27), also dealing with the Creation. It is very much like the first chapters of our book, and it is attributed to the compiler of the book 'Raziel.' Everything, however, seems to point to the conclusion that the text in Jerahmeel has retained the very original form, and that all the quotations in other writings are merely portions from what originally has been a continuous narrative in the chapters of Eliezer, though it is now missing in the printed text of that book. The abstract from this work of Eliezer is, in fact, continued here as if no break had occurred between. The very beginning and end of Jerahmeel, Chapter VI., are identical with Eliezer, Chapter xi., though the intermediate portions are now missing there, and are found scattered through the pages of the Talmud, in the 'Midrash Kônên,' and other books. I have not been able hitherto to find a single parallel to paragraph 6 in the Hebrew literature; only Arabic writers like Tabari, Iben El Atîr, and Masudi have it (cf. Greenbaum, 'Beiträge,' p. 62); cf. also (ibid., p. 55) all the Hebrew, Arabic, and Syriac parallels to paragraph 7, concerning the elements out of which the human body was created.

Chapter VI., paragraph 7, to the end of Chapter VII., is taken continuously from Eliezer, Chapter xi., No. 28, to Chapter xii., No. 60. The first seven chapters dealing with the Creation are thus undoubtedly all taken from one and the same book—the Chapters of Eliezer—and not pieced together from quotations and minor fragments collected from various writings. We have thus a different recension, more complete and better rounded off, of that book of Eliezer, which in itself is also a problem in Hebrew literary history. Concerning various details in these last two chapters, especially those that have been admitted into many other literatures, I would give a few more parallels from the Hebrew. So we find to Chapter VI., paragraphs 8, 9 identical wording in the Tanḥuma, Parasha Pequdei, paragraph 3 to the end (ed. Venice, folio 51b). To paragraphs 7 to 10 also 'Midrash Haggadol,' loc. cit. (folio 20c). To paragraph 10, about the hours in which Adam and Eve were created, sinned, etc., cf. Tanḥuma, (ed. Buber, vol. i., p. 18, No. 195), where the whole parallel literature is given. How long Adam and Eve lived in Paradise is a question that agitated ancient writers, and we find an echo in the old Slavonic Lucidarius, in the so-called Questions of St. Athanasius, etc. To paragraph 11 cf. Targum Jerushalmi to Genesis, chapter ii., ver. 7; and, moreover, Greenbaum, loc. cit., p. 60, who refers to the Book of Adam, to the Korân, and other Oriental writings. To Chapter VII., paragraph 1, et seq., cf. Tanḥuma, ed. Buber, i., folio 58b, and Pesiqta of Rabbi Kahana, ed. Buber, folio 37b.

Chapter IX.—Following upon the creation of the world comes now the treatise of the formation of the human being. Between these two I have omitted a chapter (VIII.) of the Hebrew text, giving anatomical details, and quoting, among others, as an authority Ibn Ezra. Independent of that is Chapter IX., probably a very ancient legend. Fragments of it occur in various old writings. Paragraphs 4, 5 are found in the Talmud, Tr. Niddah, folio 30b. Paragraph 9, vide 'Midrash Ecclesiastes,' chapter i., ver. 1; cf. 'Yalqut,' vol. ii., folio 182b, paragraph 966. We find it, moreover, in an anonymous compilation, which goes under the name of 'Abqath Rokhel,' folio 23a (ed. Amsterdam), from which it has been reprinted by Jellinek, 'B. H.,' vol. i., p. 153 et seq. But our text is much more like the one incorporated into the Tanḥuma, loc. cit., paragraph 3, (folio 51b), where it follows immediately upon the same tales as that at the end of Jeraḥmeel, Chapter VI., paragraph 9, being thus a direct continuation of the description how God created man. Paragraphs 1 to 4 are also found in the Midrash to the Ten Commandments (Precept 6). Güdemann has treated these legends in the 'Monatschrift f. d. Gesch. d. Judent,' and tried to identify them with the legends of Horus—the child God with a finger at His mouth. We may have here some reminiscences of the old Platonic ideas of man's soul knowing everything before birth, and that our learning in this world is merely a recollection of things known before.

In Chapter X. we have one of those old books which have been preserved in an incomplete form in various compilations, of which I have, moreover, found fragments among the texts recovered from the Geniza in Cairo. Eliah de Vidas, in his work 'Reshit Hokhmah,' has incorporated many such old Apocryphal legends which he found in the sixteenth century in Palestine. He has reprinted there also this very text, though not in the same order, it forming in his book chapter xii. of the division 'Sha'ar hayirah' (ed. Amsterdam, folio 40a; ed. Constantinople, folio 37b). The order in Vidas as compared to the paragraphs in Jerahmeel is as follows: Vidas begins with what is in Jerahmeel paragraph 9, then follows first part of paragraph 12, a little of paragraph 10, then the second half of paragraph 7, and finally the whole of the paragraphs 8, 2, 3, 5, 6, 7, to end. It is evident that paragraphs 2-7 formed probably the kernel of this 'Admonition to the sinner.' This text is called the 'Pearl of Rabbi Meir' by Vidas, whilst it figures as the 'Pearl of Rab' in an abstract made of this chapter in the 'Shebet Musar,' p. 7, of Eliah Hacohen, of Smyrna (*vide* also Jellinek, 'B. H.,' ii., pp. 120-122). My fragment from the Geniza (codex No. 289), from which the beginning is missing, is absolutely identical with our text from paragraph 3 on to the middle of paragraph 7. Some of it is found also in my codex, No. 220, a manuscript probably of the eighteenth century, coming from Yemen. The second half of the text, from paragraph 10 onwards, is only found in Jerahmeel. The knowledge of this 'Admonition' seems to have been limited to writers who have lived, and to compilations that have been made, in the East. This points to the East as the source whence also the other element contained in our present compilation may have been drawn. To the same source belongs also Chapter XI. Only to paragraphs 1-4 have I been able to find a parallel legend, viz., with Vision V., paragraphs 13, 14, of the 'Visions of Heaven and Hell,' published by me (*Journal of the Royal Asiatic Society*, 1893, p. 603). The source for it I found in a manuscript of the Orḥot Ḥayim, vol. ii. It is also in Jellinek, 'B. H.' v., p. 50. To paragraph 4 compare T. Berakhoth, folio 17a, and in Vidas, 'Resh. Ḥokhma,' Chapter xii., paragraph 4; whilst paragraph 5 is also found in the work 'Ḥibbuṭ Haqeber,' that is 'The Beating of the Grave' (Jellinek, 'B. H.,' ii., pp. 151, 152). No parallel have I been able to find to our text from paragraph 6 to the end of the chapter.

Chapter XII., as well as the following chapters, deals with the eschatological questions of life after death, of punishment and reward. They belong to that large circle of Apocalyptic visions of Heaven, Hell and Paradise, to which attention has recently been drawn again in a prominent form by the discovery of the Apocalypse of Peter. The time has not yet arrived to decide as to whence all these notions have come, whether they are of Jewish origin or of Egyptian origin, and in how far the Orphic mysteries have anything to do with them. All these teachings seem to have had a share in these Apocalypses, but it is impossible to believe that such notions should have been admitted into Jewish and Christian circles, and still less in the latter, unless they were already current in the minds of the people, and were considered as genuine religious representations of life after death. In spite of Dietriech's strictures in his 'Nekyia' (Leipzig, 1893), especially p. 223, and his attempt to find their origin exclusively in Greek classical antiquity, he must look to the East as the true source of these mystical inspirations and mystical teachings. New-Pythagorean and New-Platonic views are not an original growth upon the soil of Hellas. And the whole magical literature that is so closely connected with the cult of the dead, and with these eschatological views of life after death, was evolved by the Greeks only after they had imbibed those teachings in the East.

The pure Hebrew language of these texts, especially those dealing with visions of heaven and hell, proves their extreme antiquity. Although for various statements reference is made to the Bible, the Rabbinical literature is entirely ignored in them, save a few later interpolations. Dietriech has entirely misunderstood the drift of my arguments and the value of the texts of those Hebrew visions published by me. A fragment, moreover, which I consider to be the oldest in existence, which has come to light also from the 'Geniza' and is now my property, carries us far back, maybe to the eighth or ninth century. No text as yet shown to exist can be proved to be a translation from a non-Jewish source. Not that I claim special priority for them. The views expressed therein are not countenanced by the representative teachers of Judaism, and their existence is in fact surprising in Jewish literature; but I consider them to stand on a par, as to age and importance, with the whole cycle of Apocryphal and Apocalyptic literature, to which I reckon also the books of magic; and much may be due to the hitherto not yet sufficiently recognised literary activity of some such Jewish sect as the Essenes or other unknown authorities, who are known to have been addicted to this kind of mystic speculation. Just as much as the Essenes can be credited with the description of the heavenly halls in the Hekhalôth and the place of Paradise, so also may we credit them with a description of the tortures of hell. Fragments of, and parallels to, such descriptions are found already in the Book of Enoch in abundance, and not a few are mentioned in the Testaments of the Twelve Patriarchs, not to speak of the New Testament and other Apocalyptic writings.

Chapter XII. is probably the beginning of that Apocryphal tale which is continued in Chapter XIII. under the title of 'The Beating of the Grave.' Eliah de Vidas has the whole of it, beginning from Chapter XII., paragraph 3, up to Chapter XIII., end of paragraph 6, forming paragraphs 1-3 in his Chapter xii. He evidently has left out the beginning, which was known to Eliah Levita in his 'Tishbi,' and which is also found in a very mutilated form in a late manuscript; reprinted hence by Jellinek ('B. H.,' vol. v., p. 48).

Our text again appears to be the fullest and the most coherent. From paragraph 7 on we have here a kind of short abstract from what is given afterwards in a very complete form in Chapters XIV.-XVII., containing a minute description of hell. In the parallels of this description I limit myself almost exclusively to the reference to my edition of those Apocalyptic Visions where I have indicated the whole Jewish and non-Jewish literature, including references to the Apocalypses of Peter, Paul, Virgin Mary, etc. I add here the reference to the 'Reshith Hokhmah,' Chapter xiii., which agrees with our Chapters XIV. and XV., and to the extremely ancient manuscript from the Geniza, mentioned above, with which this portion agrees absolutely.

Passing on to the detailed parallelism, we find Chapter XIV., paragraph 2, up to Chapter XV., paragraph 6, identical with Vision No. V., paragraphs 1-9 (p. 599 *et seq*.). Chapter XV., paragraphs 7-9, is identical with Vision No. V., paragraphs 20-22 (pp. 604, 605).

Chapter XVI., paragraphs 1-5, is identical with the text of Orḥot Hayim, to which I have referred already above, being a continuation of Chapter XI., paragraph 4, and is to be found in that same Vision V., paragraphs 15-19 (pp. 603-605). The continuation to Chapter XV., paragraph 9, reappears here in Chapter XVI., paragraph 6, corresponding with paragraph 23 of Vision V. Paragraph 7 of Chapter XVI. is identical with paragraph 24 of Vision V., whilst paragraph 8 differs here from the version published in the 'Visions.'

Chapter XVII.—Portions of this chapter are found in

Vision VII., paragraph 4, but in a different order and altered form. There are also parallels to it in Vision I., paragraph 42, and Vision V., paragraph 24; to paragraph 1 here *cf.* also 'Yalqut Reubeni,' fol. 3*b*. 'Midrash Konèn,' 5*b* and 6*a* (Jellinek, 'B. H.,' vol. ii., pp. 35, 36), has a parallel legend to end of paragraph 1 and of paragraph 4. Concerning the names of Hell, *cf.* also the Talmudic treatise Erubin, fol. 19*a*. Paragraph 6 leads from hell to Paradise.

Chapters XVIII., XIX.—The chief personage in these two Visions, the man to whom these revelations are made and who is the hero in the oldest documents, is Rabbi *Joshua*, son of Levi. We have here probably an unintentional alteration from *Isaiah*, as in one place Isaiah is suddenly mentioned, and we know of the existence of such an Apocalypse of Isaiah, the 'Ascensio Isaiae.' Maybe it is a later ascription to the man of whom legend told that he was in friendly relations with the Angel of Death. Whether it is due to popular etymology and analogy of name, or to a definite intentional alteration, it is difficult to determine. The oldest texts all agree, at any rate, in ascribing these revelations to Rabbi Joshua, the son of Levi. The text published in Chapter XVIII. is probably the oldest of all known, and agrees in the main with the version contained in 'Mahazor Vitry' (pp. 735-736). It is found further in 'Yalqut,' i., fol. 7*a*, par. 20; 'Shebet Musar,' ch. xxv.; and Jellinek, 'B. H.,' vol. 2, pp. 52, 53; also 'Midrash Talpiyoth' (ed. Lemberg, 1875), p. 59*b*; and in 'Visions,' No. IV., p. 596 *et seq.*

Chapter XIX., paragraph 1, recurs thus far in its complete form once more in the manuscript reprinted by Jellinek, vol. v., p. 48. Its contents occur also in the Midrash to Psalm xi., ver. 6 (ed. Buber, pp. 101, 102; *cf.* note No. 48). The whole is also mentioned by Eleazar of Worms in his work 'Hokhmath Hanephesh,' and is partly alluded to in the 'Pesiqta Rabbati' (ed. Friedman), fol. 198*a*. To paragraph 4 *cf.* 'Visions,' No. I., paragraph 48 (p. 584); the 'Apocalypse of Paul,' ch. xliv.; and 'Pesiqta

Rabbati,' fol. 112a ; vide also the study of Israel Levi in the *Revue des Études Juives.*

Chapters XX., XXI.—The first two paragraphs of Chapter XX. are missing in every other parallel text, but from paragraph 3 on our text is identical with Vision III., paragraphs 10-17. A short version of the journey of Joshua, the son of Levi, accompanied by the Angel of Death, is to be found in my 'Exempla of the Rabbis,' No. 138, where also a short description of what he sees in Paradise is given. The description is continued, as here, in Chapter XIII., paragraphs 1-3, in 'Visions,' No. III., paragraphs 20-21. From paragraph 4 to the end a new description of hell is ascribed to Joshua, the son of Levi. It agrees with the version preserved by Nachmanides, reprinted in the 'B. H.' by Jellinek, vol. v., p. 43 *et seq.*, as well as with that contained in 'Orḥot Ḥayim,' and in 'Midrash Konên,' 4a, published by me, 'Visions,' No. VI., pp. 605-607. Our text agrees best with that of Nachmanides, reprinted by Eisenmenger, 'Entdecktes Judenthum,' vol. ii., pp. 340, 341.

Chapter XXII.—After this long interpolation, dealing with eschatological subjects, our author returns to the history of Adam and Eve and their progeny on earth. Chapter XXII., paragraphs 1-4, is an abstract from the Book of Eliezer, chap. xiii. The cause of the fall of the Angel Samael is here given in a totally different form, and agrees in the main with the first chapter of the Latin version of the 'Historia Adæ.' A close parallel to this version we find in the manuscript 'Genesis Rabbati,' from which Epstein has published a similar legend in his 'Eldad ha Dani' (Presburg, 1891, pp. 66-68, and notes, p. 75 *et seq.*). The reprint by Epstein, who has not noticed that the text is found also in Martini's 'Pugio' (p. 425, ed. Paris), does not, however, go far enough, for we find in the 'Genesis Rabbati,' according to the quotation in the 'Pugio' (*vide* above, p. xlix), also the phœnix legend, agreeing with the latter part of this legend in Jeraḥmeel.

It is evident, as already noted above, that the author, Moses Hadarshan, must have had our collection of legendary tales at his disposal. The form of the legends in the 'Ber. Rabbati' proves it to be a later development, especially as the name of *Samael* is changed into *Satan* (*cf.* also the Syriac Legends in 'Schatzhoele,' ed. Betzold, pp. 4, 8; *vide* Weil, 'Biblische Legenden,' p. 15). There is no necessity now to assume with Epstein that this is one of the legends invented by, or derived from, Eldad; still less can we consider it as being of a Christian Abyssinian origin, and borrowed hence; it is much more likely that the reverse has happened. The Hebrew represents an older tradition, retained in a most complete form in this chapter of Jerahmeel's compilation. There are other details also in it (from paragraph 4 onwards), which are found nowhere else together except in the 'Rabbati,' whilst only to a few details parallels can be found scattered through various works of the Hebrew literature. Quotations of such a kind are not, as some have hitherto believed, proofs that a later author has taken pains to collect scattered allusions and legends from numberless books and treatises, and has welded them together so as to form one single small tale. The reverse has undoubtedly taken place. A complete legend has been composed at a given time, and portions of it are then quoted and utilized by writers of various ages, everyone selecting from it that portion which suited his fancy or his subject best.

The occurrence, therefore, of details or elements of a long and complete text in other compositions is, to my mind, rather a proof that the complete tale is the older, which has been laid under contribution by later writers, and not that the reverse has taken place, so that the complete legend has been compiled in a mosaic-artic fashion from most heterogeneous books and writings. In this case, we have thus in Jerahmeel the primitive and complete legend. We find an allusion to the second half of paragraph 5 in 'Genesis Rabba' (section 19, paragraph 9, and section 20, paragraph 19). Paragraphs 6 and 7 as well as 8 contain two versions of the old famous legend of the phœnix, which forms part of the old Physiologus. In the Hebrew literature we find both: the one corresponding to the first tradition (paragraphs 6, 7) occurring in the 'Alphabetum Siracidis' (ed. Steinschneider, Berlin, 1858, fol. 29a, b) in a somewhat shorter form, and the other in 'Genesis Rabba' (loc. cit.; further, Midrash Samuel, chapter xii., paragraph 81), also a little different, then in the Genesis Rabbati, MS. Prague, and in Martini's quotation 'Pugio,' p. 453.

Chapter XXIII., a similar legendary composition, from which fragments only can be traced in various writings, but nowhere is the whole text found, as here, in a continuous narrative. To paragraph 1, the history of Lilith and the origin of the Demons, there is a parallel in the same 'Alphabetum Siracidis,' fol. 23a, b, which shows that the author of that work, which I place latest in the seventh century, knew already those legends and tales (cf. Treatise of Erubin, fol. 18; Genesis Rabba, chap. xx., xxiv.). In our version the chief hero is Methusela, not Adam, as in Sira, who must have been one of the old heroes of Apocalyptic literature. Enoch reveals visions to Methusela (Book of Enoch, chap. lxxxii., et seq.), and many ancient interpretations of his name are to be found in the old 'Onomastica' (ed. Lagarde, p. 8, line 10, and p. 65, line 10). Fabricius, pp. 224-226, refers to the Midrash Abkir, which must have been a similar collection of biblical Apocrypha very much alike in character to Philo-Jerahmeel and to the Yashar; only fragments have been preserved. A manuscript of it still known to de Rossi, in the sixteenth century has since disappeared; only stray fragments are to be found. In one of these (Yalqut, i., fol. 42, and No. 4 in the separate edition of Buber, pp. 2-3) we find a literal parallel to paragraph 5, and also an indication of Methusela's knowledge of magic. A preceding and now lost portion of the Abkir may have contained these paragraphs which precede it here. To paragraphs 1-4, cf. also Book of Jubilees, chap. viii., ver. 5, and a similar fragment from Abkir is quoted by Buber in 'Yerioth Shelomo' (Warsaw, 1896, p. 47).

Concerning the images made by Enosh, paragraphs 6, 7, we find only a remote parallel, probably only an abbreviated quotation from here, in Genesis Rabba, chap. xxiii., section 9, and an allusion to it in Ibn Yahya's 'Shalsheleth Haqqab-bala' (ed. Venice, fol. 92*b*). But this is derived probably from the 'Supplementum Chronicarum' of Foresti. I am inclined to believe that the ancient chronicle of Philo-Jerahmeel must have commenced with this Chapter XXIII., although the Latin text begins much later.

Chapter XXIV. is of a similar character, with very few parallels in Hebrew literature. The name of Cain's wife, Qalmana, is mentioned by Ibn Yahya, *loc. cit.*, fol. 92*b*, and long before him in Pseudo-Methodius. The oldest source thus far is the Book of Jubilees (*vide* Rönsch, p. 373, where the names of the two daughters of Adam according to all the ancient traditions are given). Our text, especially paragraphs 1-4 and paragraphs 7, 8, corresponds in many details with Josephus, 'Antiquities,' book i., chap. ii., sections 2, 3; *vide* also Fabricius, p. 119. In many details we find from here onwards a close resemblance with Comestor's 'Historia Scholastica,' *cf.* 'Genesis,' chap. xxv., and for paragraphs 5-8 of our text, *vide* Comestor, *ibid.*, chap. xxviii. Comestor assigns the erection of the two pillars to Tubal Cain, like our Hebrew text, whilst other authorities ascribe these to Adam, Seth, or to others (*vide* Fabricius, p. 148).

From paragraph 8 to end of chapter *cf.* Comestor, 'Genesis,' chap. xxxi. In the Hebrew literature we find merely a reference to Tubal's activity in the Jerusal. Targum to Genesis, chap. iv., vers. 21, 22, and in Rashi, *ibid*.

The origin of the Elohim and their identification with the seed of Seth and not with fallen angels, as set forth here in paragraph 10, *et seq.*, differs completely from the tradition in the chapters of Rabbi Eliezer (Chapter xxii.), where the giants are considered to be the children of angels that had intermarried with human beings. According to the tradition in our text, they are the offspring from the mixture between the seed of Seth and the seed of Cain. The same tradition is found especially in Christian pseudo-epigraphic literature like the Christian Book of Adam (pp. 82-93); the 'Cave of Treasures' (p. 10), in Cedrenus, ed. Bonn, vol. i., p. 19, and Eutychius's 'Annals,' vol. i., pp. 21-26; further, in Arabic authors like Tabari, Jaḳubi, Ibn el Atîr (vide Gruenbaum, loc. cit., pp. 73, 74, and 76, 77). Ibn Ezra to Genesis, chap. vi., ver. 2, has a similar tradition.

Chapter XXV., the legend of the fallen angels, brings us back to the Midrash Abkir, because there alone we find an absolutely identical legend. It seems also to have entered into the Midrash Rabbati in a somewhat shorter form. In the name of Moses the Darshan it is quoted by Reymundus in his 'Pugio Fidei' (Paris, 1651), pp. 7-9. In his version paragraphs 7-11 of our text are omitted.

The longer version, identical with ours, has been preserved by the 'Yalqut' (paragraph 44, fol. 12b-12c) from the Midrash Abkir. The antiquity of this legend is shown by the fact that the central portion of it is found in the Book of Enoch, chap. vi.-x. (ed. Charles, pp. 62-77). The tendency is here somewhat different, as the angels are lustful after women and therefore descend from heaven, whilst in the Hebrew version it is a more ethical principle which induces them to descend from heaven, viz., to show that they are above human vices, but they, like human beings, fall also a victim to their presumption. The name of the virtuous girl who ascends to heaven and is placed among the Pleiades is Estira (=star). The whole of the first part is entirely omitted in the Book of Enoch, which is, however, no proof that this version is not at least as old as the Book of Enoch. Concerning the activity of the two fallen angels, especially of Azael, vide Lagarde, 'Materialien,' etc., vol. ii., p. 57, and Gruenbaum, p. 74.

Chapters XXVI.-XXX. inclusive are absolutely identical with the Latin 'Philo,' which commences here. In the first part of this introduction I have dealt largely with the proof that the Latin text cannot be considered as the original, and that the Hebrew proves to be the older of the two versions. The spirit that breathes through the pages of this book is the same which animated the author of the Book of Jubilees and other similar attempts of a genealogical character; it is the same which pervades the Hellenistic literature and the Hagadic literature of later times. We find traces of it in the fragment of Malchus Kleodemas and other writers, who lived two or three centuries before the Common Era. Concerning them, I refer to the admirable work of Professor Freudenthal ('Hellenistiche Studien,' i., ii., Breslau, 1874, 1875).

The source for the peculiar names that occur in these chapters has not been laid bare, nor do we know the system which the ancients followed in the invention of such mythical names. Here and there one can discover biblical names in a somewhat changed form. But until all these names will have been collected and the manuscripts carefully collated, taking as basis our Jeraḥmeel, and comparing these names with those contained in the Sepher Hayashar and those scattered through the pages of the rabbinical literature, such an attempt will be fruitless. My transliteration of these names is merely tentative, as the original manuscript in many cases has no vowel signs, so as to indicate the correct pronunciation of the names, and the similarity of letters in the Hebrew script may account for changes or differences between the Hebrew and the Latin version. In order to assist further investigation, I have added in the Appendix the corresponding pages from the Latin edition, and a reproduction in facsimile of those chapters of the Hebrew manuscript which contain the genealogical tables and geographical names, viz., Chapter XXVI., paragraphs 1-13; XXVI. 27 to XXVIII. 3; XXXI. 1-20. I have already drawn attention (p. xxx) to the similarity in various details between these chapters and some portions in the Book of Jubilees.

In Chapter XXVI. our compiler seems to have intercalated from the middle of paragraph 15 on to the end of 20 a tradition that occurs already once before in Chapter XXIV., paragraphs 6-9, and which is missing in the Latin. It is not at all improbable that this portion belongs to the old original. Some apocryphal names occur also in it, but are omitted in the Latin. A parallel to paragraph 20 is found in Eutychius, i., p. 60. In paragraph 13 we could read *Sheth* with the Latin instead of *Shem*.

Chapter XXVII.—The Yashar has in chap. vii., vers. 1-22, a list of the sons of Noah of a similar apocryphal and unintelligible character as the one contained here in Chapter XXVII. Both must have borrowed from the same apocryphal source, represented more correctly by Jerahmeel, who agrees entirely with the Latin, unless the change in the Yashar is due to careless copyists. It is curious that the names of the children of Yoqtan (Jeptan in the Latin) at the end of paragraph 5, which are given correctly by Josephus ('Antiquities,' book i., chap. vi., par. 4) and in Yashar, are so fearfully mutilated in Jerahmeel as well as in the Latin; for, if read carefully, they reveal themselves to be the very names given in Genesis, chap. x., vers. 26-28. The preceding lists may have misled the copyist, who did not recognise the true form of those names. To paragraph 9, *cf.* Eutychius, i., pp. 56, 57. In paragraph 7 we find an old tradition that Terah took to wife Amtalai, the daughter of Barnabo, or Karnabo (*cf.* Beer, 'Leben Abrahams,' pp. 1, 96, 97).

Chapter XXVIII. contains the number of the children of the generations of Noah. The numbering is mentioned also in the Book of Yashar, chap. vii., vers. 9, 14, 18; but the numbers are very much smaller; the thousands seem to have dropped out. But absolutely identical numbers are given by Comestor at the end of Genesis, chap. xxxvii., whose authority is, as he states, our very Philo.

Chapter XXIX. corresponds to 'Philo,' fol. 6*d*, *et seq.* The name of the place (paragraph 13) is called 'Linguæ Chaldæorum Deli.' (The Hebrew has, 'Elohe'—אלהי.)

Chapter XXX.—Of this chapter only paragraphs 1-4 are found in the Latin, which has some very curious expressions not represented in the Hebrew. In paragraph 3, 'Et tanquam stillicidium arbitrator eos, et in scuto approximabo eos,' the first part is missing altogether in the Hebrew. I am at a loss to suggest the word for 'drops' ('stillicidium') in the original, which the translator has evidently misunderstood. For 'approximabo' we have in the Hebrew ואקרבם, which I take to be from קְרָב = fight, battle—and I have translated accordingly, 'I will fight them.' The parallelism with Philo finishes with paragraph 4. Paragraph 5, et seq., is found again in Hebrew writings. The transformation of the builders of the Tower of Babel into monkeys and the confusion of tongues, paragraph 5, finds its counterpart in the Yashar, chap. ix., vers. 33-54; cf. also vers. 24-33, Jerusalemitan Targum, in Genesis, ad loc.; further, 'Gen. Rabba,' sect. 38, paragraph 15; and at the end of the version of the Abraham legends (ed. Horowitz), p. 46; whilst the whole of the chapter, beginning from the middle of paragraph 5, is taken verbatim from Chap. xxiv. of Eliezer.

Chapter XXXI. is a duplicate to the genealogies hitherto treated. In the beginning of this introduction I have drawn special attention to it (p. xlii et seq.), showing how old these geographical explanations of the tenth chapter of Genesis are; which all rest upon one and the same old tradition, found in general outline in the Book of Jubilees, and in a much more elaborate form in Josephus's 'Antiquities,' book i., chap. vi., paragraph 1, et seq. This chapter represents in our text, in every probability, the second layer of geographical tradition, superposed over the other represented by Philo-Jerahmeel, which has an air of greater antiquity. In this text, which, as shown, rests upon a Latin original, we do not find any of the specifically Semitic letters ע and ח so often met with in the older portion. A third layer covering these two is that one which is represented by Yosippon, and introduced here by Eleazar the Levite as the first chapter from the work of Yosippon the Great; this interpolation forms here paragraphs 6-15. The same genealogies, without the mention of Yosippon, as the sources are never mentioned, is to be found in Yashar, chap. x., ver. 7, et seq. The question whether this chapter has been added later on from the Yashar to Yosippon, or whether the compiler of the Yashar borrowed it from the Yosippon, can be decided only after a careful investigation and an exhaustive study of the history and origin of each of these books. I am inclined to give to Yosippon the priority, and to consider the Yashar as being a later compilation. As one of the sources of information for such genealogical terms, I refer here especially to the letter of the King of the Kozars to Ḥasdai Ibn Shaprut in Spain in the tenth century. The information which he gives about the origin of his own people agrees in many details almost absolutely with the details contained here as to the descendants of Togarma. In paragraph 15, which is so very corrupt in the Yosippon, I should like to interpret the names in the following manner: Sorbin would be Servians; Lousisii would be Lausatians; Liech'an would be Poles; Chrabat would be Croatians; Bosniin would be Bosnians. Then, for Asidinia, in paragraph 14, I would read 'Ascania.' The last name almost that occurs in the whole list, that of Qualiron, may assist us in fixing the origin of the most famous Hebrew liturgical poet, Qalir. The identification of his place of birth, after which he got the name, has hitherto baffled every investigation. It would thus turn out to be 'Lesha' in Palestine—the 'Callirhoë' of later times. The end of the chapter (paragraph 20) agrees with chap. xxiv. of Eliezer. As we see, Jeraḥmeel utilizes the Book of Eliezer Hyrqanos as the frame into which he fixes all the other texts gathered from various quarters. This paragraph agrees also with the beginning of No. IIa of my 'Exempla of the Rabbis' (p. 2).

Chapter XXXII. begins with the history of the third son of Noah, Ionithem or Ionithes. We find this legend in Comestor, 'Genes.,' chap. xxxvii., who refers to Pseudo-Methodius as his source. Fabricius knows the Greek form 'Monethon,' from which undoubtedly is derived the Slavonic version 'Muntu' (Palæa, ed. Popoff, Moscow, 1881; appendix, p. 15, from a manuscript of the fourteenth century). Ibn Jaḥya, in 'Shalsheleth,' fol. 92b, has 'Ioniko'; and the same short note reappears in Zakuto's 'Juḥasin,' ed. Philipowski, p. 232; *cf.* also I. Perles, Graetz, Jubelschrift, Breslau, 1887, pp. 22, 23. The same legend also occurs in the Arabic work of Jakubi (Gruenbaum, p. 94). But the diacritical points are wrongly placed on the name, which reads now Bentek (بطك), but which, if differently placed, would read Ionites or Ionitem (بطس or يطم).

Paragraphs 2-5 we find in Comestor, chapters xxxix., xl.; paragraph 4, in Isidor, 'Chronicon,' p. 378*h*, *vide* note to it. In Eutychius (i., pp. 58, 59) occurs a somewhat similar legend about the origin of the God Bel (here paragraph 5). The historical note in paragraphs 6, 7 occurs also in Comestor, 'Genesis,' chap. lxiii., but in a somewhat different form. Both go back undoubtedly to an older source, which I have not yet been able to identify. Eusebius, in his Canon (third book of his 'Chronicles'), has similar but not identical information, which is to be found also in Syncellus. But none of these are the direct source for Comestor or Jeraḥmeel. The one which approaches them nearest is only the 'Chronicon' of Isidor of Spain.

Chapters XXXIII.-XXXV.—In the history of the world, we have reached now the period of Abraham. The following chapters contain Abraham legends, for which we find already indications in Josephus and in other Hellenistic writers. We have at least two distinct legends already in that old collection of Rabbinical 'Exempla' published by me (Nos. II*a*, II*b*, p. 2, *et seq.*), and in a similar manner we have here in Chapter XXXIII. one version, the other in Chapter XXXIV. Of the first version, I have found parallels only to paragraph 1, viz., my Exampla, No. II*a*, p. 3, lines 11-24; *cf.* 'Gen. Rabba,' sec. 38, paragraph 19; Jalqut, i., paragraph 62. For the Arabic parallels *vide* Gruenbaum, *loc. cit.*, p. 129 *et seq.* The whole literature concerning the legends clustering round Abraham has been collected by Beer in his 'Leben Abrahams' (Leipzig, 1859), but gathering it from various sources, almost indiscriminately, he has not separated the material sufficiently, and has combined old and new into one consecutive narrative. In spite of the riches of his materials, there is no parallel to the details contained in paragraphs 2, 3, 4, exactly in the form as we have them here. To paragraph 5 we find, curiously enough, a parallel in the 'Zohar' (vol. i., fol. 77b; *vide* Beer, p. 16, note 125).

Chapter XXXIV. is the most complete and perfect, as well as the oldest and best known Abraham legend. It is identical with the version in the Midrash to the Ten Commandments (Precept 2); *cf.* also my Exempla, IIa and b. Of this version of the Midrash 'Ten Com.,' Bahya has incorporated an abstract in his commentary to the Bible (ed. Venice, folio 25c), which has been reprinted by Jellinek, 'B. H.,' ii., pp. 118-119. It is absolutely identical also with codex Oxford, No. 1,466 (Ctlg. Neubauer), folio 303b-305b, a copy of which is in my codex, No. 185, pp. 8-11. The same legend is also found in the Book of Yashar, from chap. xi., ver. 15, to the end of chap xii. It is in the main identical, but very much more expanded, and also differing in a few details, especially concerning the death of Haran, which in our text (Chapter XXXV., paragraph 1) is mentioned to have occurred in a totally different manner. The only parallel to the version in Jerahmeel I have been able to find is in Comestor, 'Genesis,' chap. xli. Jerahmeel refers in paragraph 2 to Nicolaos of Damascus. The very same passage is to be found in Josephus, 'Antiquities,' book i., chap. vii., sec. 2, in the name of the same authority; and we meet the same quotation also, in the name of Nicolaos of Damascus, in Comestor, 'Genesis,' chap. xliii. paragraph 3. Abraham in the fiery furnace forms the end of the Abraham legend in the version contained in the Midrash to the Ten Commandments.

More elaborate than this is the version which appeared for the first time in Constantinople, 1519, reprinted by Jellinek, 'B. H.,' i., pp. 25-35; *vide ibid.*, pp. xv-xvi, and a similar text has been published by Horowitz, 'Eqed Agadoth,' i., pp. 43-46, who gives the literature, *ibid.*, p. 40. In this form the legend has been adapted to homiletic purposes. I consider all the texts which have been thus utilized as of secondary value, representing no longer the simple old original tale, but one recast, altered, and either enlarged or shortened—at any rate, subjected to a remodelling process. Almost every one of these old biblical legends has undergone such a change. The essential difference between these two forms has not been sufficiently appreciated by those who have studied this branch of Hebrew literature; conclusions to which they have arrived are vitiated in consequence thereof. Guided by the modernized form of the legends in homilies, they have been declared to be of a similar modern origin. I am now the first to point out the difference between the two, and to insist that only the primitive simple legend is to guide us in our conclusions. Our chronicle has preserved most of these in their primitive form.

Arabic parallels to the Abraham legend, *vide* Gruenbaum, pp. 91-93; that of d'Herbelot more closely resembles our version (Fabricius, i., p. 345 *et seq.*). Abraham burning the idols, *vide* Book of Jubilees, chap. xii.; Rönsch (Jubiläen, pp. 224, 267, 308, etc.); also in the Slavonic 'Palæa' (*loc. cit.*, p. 21 *et seq.*). Paragraph 4 treats of Abraham's knowledge of magic. This belongs to those old Greek legends circulating in Egypt, and connected with the name of Artapanos. Josephus knows it ('Antiq.,' i., chap. viii., section 2). The whole literature has been collected by Fabricius (i., pp. 336 *et seq.*, 345 *et seq.*, and 359 *et seq.*) and Beer (p. 207, No. 978); *vide* also Migne, 'Dict. des Apocryphes,' ii., col. 31 *et seq.* In all other versions Abraham is the teacher of astrology, whilst in our Hebrew text he is the one who acquired it in Egypt. A close parallel we find to this paragraph in Comestor, 'Genesis,' chap. xlvii., who also brings Abraham in connection with Zoroaster. The reference to Rabbi Eleazar of Modiin (paragraph 4) is found in the Talmudic treatise, 'Baba Bathra,' fol. 16*b*. In paragraph 5 Jerahmeel refers to Yosippon concerning the oak under which Abraham used to sit, which lasted until the reign of Theodosius in Rome. The same is found also in Comestor, chap. xlv., and Add. II., where reference is made to Jerome. Again reference is made to Yosippon in paragraph 6; this seems to refer to Josephus ('Wars,' book iv., chap. viii., sec. 4), as in the Hebrew text of the Yosippon it is not to be found; also mentioned in Comestor, 'Genesis,' chap. liii., and Add. I.

The rest of the chapter is devoted to the synchronistic history of the Kings in Argos and in Egypt. We find the same information in P. Orosius, ed. Zangemeister, i., 4, 7, in the same order first in Eusebius, Canon, ed. Migne, col. 357; then Isidorus, 'Chronic.,' 378g and note 3; Syncellus, 126a. Comestor (chaps. lxvii., lxx., lxxvi.) evidently has drawn from the same sources, but Comestor separated these items, and placed them differently, whilst Jerahmeel kept probably to the old original without separating them. Jerahmeel has also a peculiar description of the origin of the Apis—the magic calf—made by the King Apis, who was afterwards called 'Sarapis,' which description he repeats in Chapter XLII., paragraph 2. It is found also in Comestor's narrative, but much later, in 'Exodus,' chap. iv., absolutely identical with Jerahmeel, and he refers to Plinius as his source. The same legend of Apis—Sarapis, son of Jupiter, etc.—is mentioned already by Clemens of Alexandria in his 'Stromata,' i.; Eusebius, *loc. cit.* (Cols. 360, 362); Isidorus, 378h, 379a; *vide* especially note 5, where the whole literature is given. I have drawn attention to the difference between Jerahmeel and Comestor in the arrangement of these synchronistic notes, in order to avoid the impression which one might have, that Jerahmeel had borrowed directly from Comestor. The latter indicates our Philo as one of the sources from which he has drawn his materials, and it is more and more clearly established by this minute comparison.

Chapters XXXVI. and XXXVII. contain an extremely ancient biblical legend, of which, happily, not merely fragments, but almost the whole is found in some of those well-known old Apocryphal books which I have had occasion to mention hitherto more than once. These two chapters form a separate legend, known under the title of

f

'Midrash Vayisau,' a continuation of the narrative in Gen. xxxv. 5, beginning with this word, וַיִּסָּעוּ, to which the legend is added. It is also known as the 'Book of the Wars of the Children of Jacob.' Chapter XXXVI. contains a detailed description of the war between the children of Jacob after the incident of Shechem with the allied kings of Palestine, and upon it follows (Chapter XXXVII.) the fight between them and Esau's army. Down to the minutest details, which extend also to the identity in the names of these kings, we find this legend in the Apocryphal Testament of Judah, the son of Jacob, chaps. iii.-vii.; and a short abstract of it with the same names occurs in the Book of Jubilees, chap. xxxiv., vers. 1-9. The legend, limited only to the description of the wars between the children of Jacob and the combined forces of the Kings of Palestine, occurs in a very expanded form and is very elaborately worked out in Yashar (chaps. xxxvii.-xl.). A version identical with ours has been preserved in the 'Yalqut' (i., fol. 40d and 41b, reprinted hence by Jellinek, 'B. H.,' vol. iii., pp. 1-5). I have found, moreover, a manuscript agreeing absolutely with it in the British Museum (Add. 27,089, fol. 165-169b), which I have collated with my text, and the few additions (in brackets) are taken from this text (*vide* also Zunz, G. V.,[2] p. 153, and Rab Pealim, pp. 54, 55).

Concerning the fight between Esau and Jacob, the Book of Yashar differs considerably from our version. According to it, this fight takes place on the occasion of Jacob's burial, whilst in our version it follows upon the first battle, and Esau is killed whilst fighting before Shechem. Our version is undoubtedly the original form of the legend, as we find it already in the same connection in the Testament of Judah (chap. ix.), following upon the other fight, like in our text and in the 'Yalqut' (also 'B. H.,' *loc. cit.*, pp. 3-5). R. H. Charles, in his edition of the Ethiopic version of the Book of Jubilees (Oxford, 1895), has reprinted (pp. 180-182) this chapter, and has in the margins indicated the parallels to it in the Book of

Jubilees, showing how it often agrees to the letter with the text of the Book of Jubilees. By means of our text we are able to explain the name of the place where Esau was buried. Given in the Greek text of the Testament of Judah in a corrupted form as Iramna, it stands for Irodia, corresponding in one of the Hebrew texts with Erodin, ארודין, Herodion, in another MS., Merodin, מרודין, this last due to a wrong reading of the first letter, מ for א. If this place where Esau was said to have been buried is Herodion, as I believe it to be, we have under this legendary form a piece of contemporary history, and this legend offers us a key to the understanding of the origin and composition of these legendary tales. Herodion is the name of the place which Herod the Great built, and in which he was afterwards buried. Herod was, as is well known, an Edomite by origin, a descendant of Esau. Those fights, placed far back into antiquity, are now a reflex of the wars of the Jews against Herod, described by Josephus ('Antiquities,' book xiv., chap. xvi., and book xv., chap. xiv.), clothed under that form. The other legends as to the fight between Esau and the children of Jacob at the latter's burial we find alluded to in the Acts of the Apostles (chap. vii., ver. 16) and in Josephus ('Antiquities,' book ii., chap. viii., sec. 2). If this conjecture of mine be right, that we have under the form of legend contemporary history—and, as a matter of fact, apocalyptic visions also reflect contemporary history; it is delineated clearly in the similitudes of the Book of Enoch, in the fourth Book of Ezra, in the Assumption of Moses, and in other apocalyptic writings of that period—it will help us to determine the accurate date of the composition of such legends by their historical background. Purporting to give us history of the past, they in fact describe contemporary events. If now this legend refers to the period of Herod the Great, this legend would therefore belong latest to the beginning of the first century of the Common Era. That it is so old is proved by the undoubted fact of its inclusion in the Testaments of the Twelve Patriarchs and in the Book of Jubilees, both of the same

period, thus mutually corroborating the high antiquity
assigned to each of them. Being utilized by the authors
of the last two books, the legend of the children of Jacob
is prior to them in composition. I now go one step
further, and affirm that also our Hebrew text is the old
original text, preserved with much fidelity and accuracy,
and on the whole retaining the original form very little
impaired.

Chapter XXXVIII. contains the Testament of Naphtali.
In publishing the Hebrew text (Proceedings of the Society
of Biblical Archæology), I have dealt at length with the
relation that exists between this text and the Greek version
of the Testaments of the Twelve Patriarchs, and I have
endeavoured to show not only that the original language
in which that book had been written was Hebrew, and that
the Greek was merely a translation made at a somewhat
later period, but also that the original form had been better
preserved in the Hebrew version. This view is now fully
corroborated by C. Resch, who has reprinted my text
('Theolog. Studien u. Kritiken,' 1899, pp. 206-33) and has
retranslated it into Greek. Schürer's objections ('Gesch.
d. Jued. Volkes,' III.,[3] p. 259) rest upon an insufficient
knowledge of Jerahmeel's Chronicle and of his literary
activity. The contents of it bear out my contention fully
that *all the texts* contained therein without exception *are
originals*, and not translations. Only the synchronistic notes
and the second genealogical table, dealing as they are with
non-Jewish history, are derived from a non-Jewish source,
and are therefore no real exceptions; they are mere notes,
not long legend, and not having biblical personages as their
heroes. Jerahmeel, or whoever goes under that name, has
simply collected into one volume separate Hebrew Midrashim or Aggadoth, the majority of which are either known
also from other collections, or are referred to and used in
homilies. Immediate sources or direct parallels in any other
language are not known to exist. Even of the Philo portions,
though we have a perfect Latin counterpart, the Hebrew
text is the ancient original; the style of the diction and the

form of the language preclude the gratuitous assumption of their being translations. Stronger arguments than used hitherto will have to be adduced to shake the belief in the original character of the Hebrew versions of these legends. The historical background of this 'Testament' is, however, not so clear as in the legend of the warlike exploits of Judah and his brethren. One point, however, is to be remarked. The strong antagonism against Joseph, who separates himself from the rest of his brethren, might be a direct allusion to the Samaritans, with whom the tribes of Judah and Levi, so prominently singled out in this Testament of Naphtali, lived in strong feud. Against them Hyrqanos had led a successful war, destroying the temple on Gerizim and the town of Samaria; but the same Herodes rebuilt them, and favoured thus the very tribe so strongly denounced in this Testament by Naphtali and Jacob.

Chapter XXXIX.—The history of Joseph seems also to be an echo from the Testament of Joseph, at least as far as paragraph 1 is concerned. Paragraph 2, about the beauty of Joseph, occurs also in the Aramaic Targum to the seventh of the Ten Commandments. The Book of Yashar has a much more elaborate romance of Joseph from chap. xl. onwards. In chap. xliv. of Yashar we find the old legend of Joseph and Zelikah (Arabic, Suleikah), which has been considered to be of Arabic origin. The fact that almost everything mentioned therein, with the exception of the name, is found already in the Testament of Joseph (one of the 'Twelve Patriarchs') and a small portion of it preserved here in our chronicle prove that the narrative in Yashar may also be independent of any Arabic sources. No Arabic etymology has as yet been found for Suleikah, which, moreover, would be the only one borrowed from strange sources, whilst we find in Yashar, Philo-Jerahmeel, Kleodemus, and others many extraordinary names that are not vouched for by the biblical narrative. An old romance of Joseph's life in Egypt of a pre-Arabic period exists in a full form, at least in Greek, under the title of 'Joseph and Asenath,' published by P. Batiffol (Studia Patristica, Paris,

1889). Fragments and even the most important incidents are found in the old Hebrew legendary works, in the Midrash and Hagadah.

It is here again a case of mutual borrowing, and the priority is by no means yet decisively proved, even for the incident describing Joseph's beauty and the women cutting their hands whilst looking at him, as it occurs in our text, paragraph 2, and in the Book of Yashar, chap. xliv., ver. 27 *et seq.* Gruenbaum has studied exhaustively all the legends connected with Joseph in the Jewish and Arabic literature in 'Zeitschrift d. Deutsch Morgenländ. Gesellschaft,' lxiii., p. 1 *et seq.*

Chapter XL.—With this chapter begin the voluminous abstracts taken verbatim from Yosippon, and intercalated here by Eleazar the Levite. Concerning the literature about Yosippon, *vide* Zunz, G. V.,[2] p. 154 *et seq.* Chapter XL. corresponds in Breithaupt's edition to Book I., chap. i., p. 9, to end of chap. iv., p. 22. As I am preparing a critical edition of the Yosippon based upon this manuscript of Jeraḥmeel and upon the collations I have made with other editions and manuscripts, I limit myself here, as in the future, wherever Yosippon has been copied directly by our compiler, to refer to the corresponding chapters in that edition. Breithaupt has already referred in his footnotes to the Conte-Münster edition, to Josephus, Titus Livius, and other authorities which contribute to elucidate the true meaning of the text of Yosippon published by him, and indirectly of our text translated here.

The very same chapters from Yosippon, forming here Chapter XL., in the same full form are reproduced in Yashar from chap. lx. to chap. lxvi., with slight intercalations from other sources that are not named; Yosippon is also not mentioned. Baḥya (commentary to Genesis portion Vayeḥi) knows the legend of Ṣefo migrating to Italy and establishing himself there, which is contained in this portion (*cf.* Zunz, G. V.[2], p. 161, note *a*). We find in this chapter also a reference to the Midrash to Psalms, under the name of Shoḥer Tob.

lxxxvii

Chapter XLI.—In Chapter XLI. we find, as it were, a second edition of the history of the building of Rome, mentioned once in the preceding chapter. It agrees partly with the treatise of Abraham ben David under the heading 'Short Memorabilia of Rome.'

Chapters XLII.-XLVIII.—From Chapter XLII. on to Chapter XLVIII. inclusive we have two or three different versions of the Chronicle of Moses. Of these various versions, the longest and most coherent, which also has a separate title beginning from Chapter XLIII. on, is the oldest. The first version in Chapter XLII. belongs probably to the Latin Chronicle of Philo-Jerahmeel, with the usual additions and intercalations. The first paragraphs have similar synchronistic elements as all the other additions of Jerahmeel. The description of the bull Apis as given here in paragraph 2 is identical with that given above (Chapter XXXV., paragraph 8). The king is called throughout 'Amenophis' in the Hebrew text. To paragraphs 2 and 3 cf. Comestor, Exodus, chap. ii., giving the same reference to Psalm lxxx. in describing the forms of slavery to which the Children of Israel were subjected, as we find them in paragraph 3.

The fact that these elements are to be found in Comestor preceding the abstract from Philo seems to indicate again that in the Latin text of Philo used by Comestor this portion may have been in it, just as we find it in the Hebrew text. Paragraph 5 onwards is identical with Philo (fol. 9b to 11a). In the Latin text we have the peculiar form *Anra* for *Amram*, and instead of *Jochebed*, which, according to tradition, was the name of Moses' mother (correctly given so in paragraph 9), we find in the Latin *Jacob!*

Chapter XLIII.—Of far greater antiquity is a subsequent legend known in the Hebrew literature as the Chronicle of Moses (*vide* Zunz, G. V.², p. 153). It is found in a very elaborate form in the Yashar (from chap. lxvii. to chap. lxxxii.); but one can see that the Yashar already takes liberties with the text. Further, in the Yalqut (i., fol. 52 *et seq.*). Jellinek, in reprinting ('B. H.,' ii., pp. 1-11; *vide* pp. vii-xi) the editio princeps, Constantinople, 1516, with which our text completely agrees, believes the latter as well as the text in the Yalqut to be an abstract from the Book of Yashar, and refers, as a significant indication of this dependence on the Book of Yashar, to the reference which is made in one place to 'the Book of Yashar.' But Jellinek (p. viii, note 5) mistook the true meaning of this word. Its occurrence here, by the way, proves the extreme antiquity of the text; for in the very old Massoretic treatise published by Baer and Strack under the title of 'Diqduqei Hateamim' (Leipzig, 1879, p. 57, *vide* note *b*, where reference is made to the Talmud and Midrash), the Book of Genesis especially, and then the Pentateuch as a whole, are called by this very name, either 'Yashar' or 'Sepher Yesharim,' the 'Book of the Pious Ones,' the Patriarchs. If this reference would mean that the author of the Yalqut has copied the text from our Book of Yashar, this reference would certainly be missing in the supposed original. In referring now to the editio princeps of the Yashar, we find the very same passage verbatim identical with the quotation in the Yalqut, but with the one significant difference that instead of 'Sepher ha-Yashar,' we read there, and properly so, 'Sepher ha-Torah'; as the author, who calls his compilation 'Yashar,' could not refer to himself, and he, therefore, in copying the old text and embodying it into his compilation, was bound to change the word 'Yashar,' as it stood in the old original, into 'Sepher Torah.' But that old word was retained in the editio princeps, in the text from which the Yalqut made his abstract, and in our text.

Another evident proof that in the old original preserved by Jerahmeel and by the Yalqut the name of 'Yashar' meant 'the Bible' is furnished by the very last sentence in this Chronicle of Moses (chap. xlviii., paragraph 18),[where we read, 'is written in the S. ha-yashar,' with the explanatory addition, 'which is the law of God.' I have translated it accordingly in chap. xlv., paragraph 8, 'the

Bible.' The same legends are also met with in the Midrash which goes under the title 'Midrash Vayosha,' which deals with the Exodus proper, and is a kind of homiletic commentary to the Song of Moses. A complete recension has been printed by Moses Ashkenazi in 'Dibre Ḥakhamim' (Metz, 1849, pp. 1-16), reprinted Jellinek, 'B. H.,' vol. i., p. 35 *et seq*.

This Moses legend can now be proved, even in its Hebrew form, to go back to one of those ancient Hellenistic writings which existed undoubtedly in the second century before the Common Era. Artapanos, whoever he may have been, is the author of what we may call a Græco-Jewish romance with Moses as central figure. Ezekiel, the Greek Jewish poet in Egypt, has already derived information from it, and utilized in his poem details borrowed from Artapanos' novel. Josephus has reproduced the main part. Of this Greek composition Eusebius has preserved in the name of Alexander Polyhistor a very large portion, and through his intermediary it has become the common property of all the ancient and mediæval Chronographs. Comestor makes long quotations (Exodus, chaps. v.-vii.). He mentions the prophetic dream of Pharaoh. He knows that Moses flees from Egypt, is made King in Ethiopia, marries the Ethiopian Queen, and accounts for the forty years of his absence from Egypt, until he reappears in Midian, in the house of Jethro. Freudenthal, in his work already mentioned, has subjected this work of Artapanos to a searching investigation, and he has proved, among others, not only the extreme antiquity of the novel of Artapanos, but also—and this is a point on which I lay the greatest stress—that the Hebrew version stands in immediate close connection with this old text, having many more details than any of the Greek fragments that have come down to us ('Hellenistische Studien,' pp. 169-174).

But such a version could only have been made at a time when the Hebrew writer had access to the more complete text of Alexander Polyhistor, or of Artapanos himself, that is, at a time near that in which Josephus flourished ; as

from that time on these books have disappeared, and we
cannot trace all these details to any other source or any
later compilation. The apparent anachronism in Chapter
XLVI., paragraphs 1-6, is easily explained when compared
with the version in the Yalqut, where the sequence of events
is reversed, the legend commencing with this very chapter,
and XLVI., paragraph 6, following upon Chapter XLV.
In our text the incidents connected with Balaam are added
later, as an explanation to the reference that Balaam was
one of the wizards that had counselled Pharaoh to wipe
out the name of Jacob from off the face of the earth. It is
merely a question of the order in which the chapters follow
upon one another. The antiquity of this version is also
shown in a few of the names mentioned. Mobras (Yashar,
chap. xlvi. 8, Menkeros) is the name of the son of the
Queen of Kush. If we change 'Mobras' into 'Monbras,'
then we have the very name 'Menophras' of Artapanos;
so is also 'Kikanos' identical with 'Kikinos' of older
versions. Janis and Jambres, the two wizard sons of
Balaam (XLVII. 6), are well-known figures of ancient tradition, and are also, as Freudenthal proves, Egyptian names
that have been adapted to Greek forms. The references to
classical literature are given by Freudenthal, *loc. cit.*, who
also refers to Fabricius (pp. 813-825); for further information, *vide* now also Schürer, *loc. cit.*, II^2., p. 689. Of all
the versions of this Chronicle of Moses, the one preserved in
our manuscript seems to be the most complete. It begins
with the birth of Moses, and contains in full all the subsequent events that happened to him, until the time when
he leads the people out of Egypt. In it are embodied
also some of the legends concerning the death of
Balaam, the death of Aaron, treated here very briefly,
similarly the death of Moses; and it finishes with a reference to Joshua leading the people across the Jordan. This
Chronicle of Moses has evidently supplanted the portion
dealing with Moses in Philo-Jerahmeel, with the speeches
therein, and the last oration of Moses, in which those dates
occur to which I have referred above (Philo, fol. 13-20).

Here we have instead (Chap. XLVI., paragraphs 2, 3), the speech of Reuel. Further parallels to some of the legends contained in this apocryphal chronicle, *vide* Gaster, ' Literatura Populara Romana,' Bucuresci, 1883, p. 318 *et seq.*; Gaster (Ilchester Lectures), ' Greco-Slavonic Literature,' London, 1887, p. 156 *et seq*.

Concerning the Rod of Moses (Chap. XLVI., paragraph 11, *et seq.*), *vide* Chapters of R. Eliezer, chap. xl. and notes; Arabic Parallels, *vide* Gruenbaum, p. 161. The Syriac version in 'Book of the Bee,' chap. xxx.; Is. Abraham, 'The Rod of Moses,' London, etc. Chapter XLVI., paragraph 13, occurs already in the Mekhilta to Exodus, chap. xviii. 3. The legend that Pharaoh alone was saved from drowning and became King of Nineveh (XLVIII. 12) is found also in the Koran, Sure x., vers. 90-92, but before it in R. Eliezer, chap. xliii.

Chapter XLIX.—The death of Aaron has been added here, preceding as it does also in the Bible that of Moses. It appeared in an expanded form, turned into a Homily, Constantinople, 1516, reprinted by Jellinek, ' B. Ham.,' ii., pp. 91-95. The text in our version is much shorter, differing from that printed hitherto in so far as it neither contains any reference to the rock which was smitten by Aaron, nor the concluding portion of the version published hitherto, referring to Miriam, which is evidently a later addition. Our text is a much more harmonious and complete, though short, description of the last days of Aaron, finishing exactly with the same quotation with which it begins. We have thus in our text evidently the oldest and most perfect version, which has been later on elaborated and altered, being used as a Homily, as it is also called in the old edition, viz., ' Derash Lepetirat Aharon.' Parallels to parts of it are found scattered throughout the Midrashic literature. Sharastani mentions an Arabic legend identical with that here in paragraph 6. *Cf.* also Treatise Erubin, fol. 54*b*. For paragraphs 6 and 7, *vide* Numbers Rabba, section 19, paragraph 11, and Yalqut, i., fol. 238*d*, paragraph 763, which quotation is taken from the lost

Midrash 'Espha.' Yalqut, fol. 240a, paragraph 755, has a somewhat different version from the Jelamdenu running parallel with our text, from paragraph 3 on to the end.

Chapter L.—The tale of the Death of Moses is also represented by two versions, Chapters L. and LI. The first concludes with a reference to the Midrash Deuteronomy Rabba, as if taken from there. The date of the composition of this work falls between the tenth and eleventh century; it may be older; but this reference has evidently been inserted by Eleazar the Levite. The text is absolutely identical with the version contained in Deuteronomy Rabba, chap. xi., paragraph 6. But an 'Assumptio Mosis' is mentioned already in the first centuries of the Common Era (*vide* Schürer II.^{2}, pp. 630 and 635-636, the whole literature; *vide* also R. H. Charles, 'The Assumption of Moses,' London, 1897), and in the letter of Judah the Apostle allusion is made to the dispute between Samael the wicked, or Satan, and the Archangel, concerning the death of Moses. We are therefore justified in considering the Hebrew text as being of ancient origin, and afterwards added to that collection known as Deuteronomy Rabba, borrowed from an independent and much older source. It forms now the concluding chapter of Deuteronomy Rabba (Hebrew literature, *cf.* Zunz, G. V.^{2}, p. 154). It may be noted that those very passages from which Zunz wished to deduct the recent origin of the composition are missing in our text. They are evidently due to a later interpolation.

The substance of this very legend of the last hours of Moses has been much elaborated and expanded in the text which appeared in Constantinople for the first time in 1516, and since reprinted by Jellinek in 'B. Ham.,' i., p. 115 *et seq.* I call this version the 'Homily,' although it has not the title 'Derash,' as that of Aaron, for the Death of Moses has been worked up in it in the same manner as other biblical legends, such as the Abraham legend, the 'Death of Aaron' (above, pp. lxxix ,xci), have been worked up in homilies.

The Christian homiletic literature furnishes us with very

numerous examples of a similar process; the life of a saint is here embodied wholly into a sermon or into a homily delivered on the day of the saint. I refer to Ephraim Syrus, Chrysostomos, St. Gregorius, and innumerable others. The same thing happened there as in the Hebrew literature. The Church followed the example of the Synagogue also in this homiletic literature. The Homily of the Death of Moses was delivered probably on the last day of Tabernacles, when the last chapter of the Bible was read, in which the Blessing and the Death of Moses is described. We find thus in this Homily ('B. Ham.,' vol. i., p. 120), a parallel to Chapter L., paragraph 2 of our text. Paragraph 10 to the end of the legend are faithfully and literally reproduced in the Homily (p. 127 *et seq.*).

Chapter LI.—The second version contained in Chapter LI. has not fared so well. It is not found in its entirety anywhere else; only parallels to portions of it, and probably quotations from it, are found. The author of the 'Homily' has used some of it as material for the completion of his text, and the same has been done by the compilers of Deuteronomy Rabba, Tanhuma, etc. Paragraphs 1-3 and 6 have been utilized for the first part of the 'Homily' (p. 115 *et seq.*, p. 122); paragraphs 1-4 occur also in Deuteronomy Rabba, chap. xi., from the middle of paragraph 5 on, and Exodus Rabba, chap. xx., paragraph 17; paragraphs 5 and 6 are found in Deuteronomy Rabba, chap. ix.; paragraphs 4-5 being a kind of duplicate from Chapter L., paragraph 1, whilst our paragraphs 7, 8 of Chapter LI. correspond to Deuteronomy Rabba, chap. xi., paragraph 4. Paragraph 6 is found: Sifrei, i., section 135, and Mid. Tanhuma, Numbers, portion Vaethanan; and paragraph 7 is like Tanhuma Vezôth Haberakha, section 3. As one can see, portions of this legend recur in various ancient writings. Arabic parallels to paragraphs 1, 2 in Tabari and others, *vide* Gruenbaum, p. 150 *et seq.*

In Chapter LII. we have a complete 'Apocalypse of Moses,' his assumption to heaven in order to obtain the law, and a minute description of all that he sees in the heavenly abodes. I have reproduced this text in my 'Visions' as No. II., p. 588 et seq., where I have also mentioned the comparative literature. Jellinek considers it to be a portion of the Hekhaloth, viz., a mystical description of the heavenly halls; but I consider it to be 'A Revelation of Moses,' independent of the latter, and running on parallel lines to it. Of this Revelation we have two versions: a very elaborate one, and a shorter one. Our text represents the shorter one. The more elaborate has also been published by me (ibid., No. I., p. 172 et seq. A further Hebrew text of this version has since been published by Wertheimer in his 'Bate Midrashoth,' Jerusalem, 1897, vol. iv., pp. 22-30).

Our text is again the more complete and the more perfect of all hitherto known. They agree with this only as far as paragraph 9. The following paragraphs (10-13) are entirely new, and merely fragments or quotations from them are found in the Hebrew literature. Paragraph 11, cf. Exod. Rabba, chap. xxix., vide Gruenbaum, loc. cit., p. 169. For paragraph 12 I must refer to my Codex (No. 83, fol. 70a), which contains a Commentary to the Bible, probably of the twelfth century. This Apocalypse has also been utilized in a homily for the day of the Giving of the Law, as it reads like an introduction to it; and we are, therefore, not surprised to find a somewhat similar description of the Heavenly Halls as an introduction to the 'Midrash of the Ten Commandments,' and in it a direct parallel to paragraphs 12 and 13.

In Chapter LIII. we have recovered one of those very old legendary compilations of which only portions were known, and these under different names. The description of the Tabernacle erected in the wilderness had been the subject of an old legendary treatise known under the name of 'Barayta di Malekhet Hamishkan,' the text of which has been printed by Jellinek, and has since been reprinted by H. Flesch from the MS. copy of the Talmud in Munich. This text appears to be incomplete, as it contains merely a detailed description of the vessels of the Temple, whilst everything else concerning the camp and the order in which the tribes were settled in the camp seems to have dropped out completely.

The last two chapters of that Barayta are then a fragment of, what in the light of our text must have been, a full description of the incidents connected with the camping in the desert, and the manner in which the tribes started on their journeys. Traces of this and of other portions are found elsewhere too, as will be seen anon, but unconnected one with the other. Jellinek and Flesch, not being aware of the intimate relation that exists between the portion dealing with the travelling in the wilderness with that dealing with the camping, have not been able to treat them as parts of one and the same legend. Our text is now undoubtedly the complete form of the missing old legend, being, as all the other texts in the Jerahmeel compilation, in a perfect state of preservation. I recognise in this chapter the 'Barayta' which had been utilized by the author of the 'Jerusalemitan Targum,' by Maimonides, Barzeloni, and all those authorities who are mentioned by Epstein in his book 'Mi-Kadmonioth,' or 'Beiträge zur Jüdischen Alterthumskunde,' Vienna, 1887 (pp. 83-90), where he deals merely with what is here paragraph 13. I have discovered in the 'Sepher ha Qana,' that old mystical book published in Kores (fol. 32*b* and 32*c*), an absolutely identical parallel to the whole of the first portion from paragraph 1 to paragraph 13 of our text. Judah Barcelloni, or Jehudah Barzillai, who lived at the beginning of the twelfth century, in his Commentary to the Book Yeṣira (ed. Halberstam, p. 8), has also a fragment of our text which he mentions under the name of 'Midrash.' We see already how old this text must be. Epstein, studying the parallels to our paragraphs 11, 12, 13 and 14 (*loc. cit.*, p. 83, quotes this portion from the work called 'Arugath ha-Bósem.' As the author of this work is one of the few who mention our Jerahmeel (*vide* Perles, *loc. cit.*), there cannot be any doubt that the immediate source from which he derived his information was evidently our text, unknown to Epstein.

For some portions we can go even much further back, for we find parallels already in Josephus ('Antiquities,' iii., 12, vi.); the description of the trumpets and the manner in which they were used correspond with paragraphs 8, 9, and the symbolical interpretation of the twelve stones of the Ephod and of the four banners of the Jewish camp, the latter representing the four elements of the world and the former the twelve signs of the Zodiac, is almost identical with that of Josephus ('Antiquities,' Book iii., 7, vii.).

A detailed description of the stone of each tribe we find further in our Philo-Jerahmeel (fol. 28*d*) corresponding almost verbatim with paragraph 13, with the only exception that in Philo-Jerahmeel the signs of the Zodiac are omitted. I do not wish to dwell here on the connection between this portion and the Lapidaria, of which the oldest is ascribed to Epiphanius, who lived in Palestine; concerning Hebrew Lapidaria *vide* Steinschneider, 'Uebersetzungen,' pp. 236 *et seq.*, 963 *et seq.* The Latin text is very obscure, and shows that the original from which it was translated must have been a very difficult one. Somewhat similar to paragraph 13 is the Jerusalem. Targum to Num., chap. ii., ver. 2 *et seq.* All this denotes extreme antiquity, and as it was evidently known to Josephus, it is not at all improbable that it belongs to an extremely ancient period.

In our Hebrew text paragraph 14 has a marginal note indicating that it had been borrowed from, or probably found in, the Glosses of Ephraim Alibha, but as this text is quoted already by older authorities, the marginal note can only refer to the copy that existed also among the manuscripts of this unknown Ephraim of Bonn (eleventh century?) or Ephraim of Regensbourg, the teacher of Rabbi Jehudah ha-Ḥasid. No parallels have I been able to find for paragraphs 15-17, whilst paragraph 18 corresponds to a certain extent with the 'Barayta of the making of the Tabernacle,' ed. Flesch, chap. xii., ed. Jellinek, chap. xiii., but these two are incomplete and faulty.

In Chapter LIV. we return to the history of the Exodus, and have a minute description of the smiting of the firstborn, also a continued narrative which must have been known in ancient times, as portions of it are found elsewhere. To paragraph 1, cf. Chapter xlviii. of Rabbi Eliezer, and to paragraph 2 Pesiqta di R. Kahana (ed. Buber, fol. 65a) (vide note 56), cf. Mekhilta, paragraph 13 (ed. Friedman, fol. 13b), Tanḥuma, Parashat Bó, sec. 7, and in Midrash 'Vayosha' to Exodus, chap. xv., ver. 6, in a somewhat different order. Nowhere are all these combined together into one legend as in our text. Parallels to paragraphs 8 and 9, where the two wizards Johanai and Mamre (who were mentioned in the Chronicle of Moses) appear in a totally different form, being able to ascend to the heavenly throne, have I found only in 'Vayosha' (to chap. xv., vers. 9, 10). But our version is much more complete than the fragmentary, in the Midrash 'Vayosha.'

Chapter LV.—The history of Korah and his rebellion forms the contents of this Chapter. To the various incidents and parables mentioned therein we find here and there a parallel in other books, evidently borrowed from this more complete legend. So do we find a parallel to paragraph 1 in the Midrash to Psalm i. (edit. Buber, p. 14); in a better form in Yalquṭ (I., fol. 229d, paragraph 750); in fol. 229c there are parallels to paragraphs 5, 6, and 7, which are also found in the Tanḥuma (ad loc.). The manner in which On was saved by the wisdom of his wife, described here in paragraph 9 et seq., is found in the Talmudic treatise 'Sanhedrin,' fol. 109b. The deep counsel which Balaam is said by tradition to have given to the King of Moab in order to entice the Israelites to sin, is set forth in paragraphs 10 and 11. We find the parallel to it in the same treatise 'Sanhedrin,' fol. 106a; a very elaborate description of it in the Book of Yashar, chap. lxxxv., ver. 53 et seq.; then in Sifrei (i., paragraph 131 (ed. Friedman, p. 47b); chapters of Rabbi Eliezer (xlvii.); Comestor (Num., chap. xxxiv.); and in the Slavonic 'Palæa' (first version, p. 106).

Chapter LVI. is full of non-Jewish history. All the historical details given therein, except paragraph 2, are found in Eusebius, Isidorus, and in Comestor. Paragraph 1, Commestor, Exodus, chap. xxiv.; paragraphs 3 and 4, Eusebius, column 383 and 384; Isidorus, p. 380e and note; Comestor, Joshua, chap. xvii.; paragraph 5, Isidorus, *ibid.*; Comestor, Judges, chap. v. In paragraph 2 reference is made to Joseph ben Gorion, but nothing like it is found in our text of Yosippon.

Chapter LVII. contains that apocryphal history of Kenaz to which I have referred above, which is here quoted as the work of 'Philo, the friend of Joseph, the son of Gorion.' It is literally identical with our 'Philo,' fol. 25b onwards. Paragraph 39 here is the vision of Kenaz published by M. R. James in Latin ('Apocrypha Anecdota,' Cambridge, 1893, p. 178).

Chapter LVIII. is a peculiar mixture of legends, partly consisting of abstracts from Philo-Jerahmeel, and partly intercalations of incidents from non-Jewish history. In no chapter throughout this book can we see so clearly as in this chapter the interweaving of these two elements, and this strengthens me in the belief that the last copyist must have found these two texts already intimately blended in his original. Comestor, as I have already remarked, follows exactly the same system ; but it is the system of all ancient chroniclers, and in a remoter degree we find an attempt at synchronistic history even in Josephus himself. Of Chapter LVIII., the paragraphs 4 and 5, and 7-10 correspond entirely with Philo, fol. 34d, 38c, 39b; whilst to paragraph 2 we find parallels in Comestor, Judges, chap. vi.; paragraph 6, *ibid.*, chap. vii.; to paragraph 8, *ibid.*, chap. viii. The difference, however, between these versions is very considerable. Here we can at once recognise that the interpolation is derived from a Latin source. Mistakes in spelling, misunderstandings of the original, abound. What Jerahmeel calls 'Syrenis' appears there as 'Syringas.' All that which follows is either missing or is in a different order. Paragraph 9 (where the word 'chorus' is left untranslated, and merely transliterated כור, so that I translated wrongly 'measure') is equal to Isidor, p. 380a and note 18, and Comestor, Judges ix. and x.; and paragraph 11 to Comestor, Judges xi. What we read in the Hebrew as 'Nizpah' (my copy may, perhaps, not have been quite clear) is read correctly by Isidor (p. 380*h*) and by Comestor 'Nympha,' the name 'Carmenta' has entirely dropped out in the Hebrew. 'Dialus' in paragraph 8 is probably 'Dædalus' (so Isidor, but somewhat different legend).

Chapter LIX. is also partly literally identical with Philo; so paragraphs 1-8 equal to Philo, fol. 40*d*. Then follow paragraphs 8-12, taken from non-Jewish history. From paragraph 12 on up to the Assumption of Phineas, who is clearly identified here with the prophet Elijah, we have in two pages an abstract from a narrative which is very much spread-out in Philo and filled up with prayers and exhortations (fol. 44*d*-46*d*). Passing to details, we have in paragraph 4 the Lamentation of Seelah, published also by Mr. James in the 'Anecdota' (p. 182). The name of the mountain which appears here in the Hebrew as 'Telag' reads in the Latin 'Telach,' and in James's copy 'Stellac.' Here we have an evident proof for the Semitic origin. This name is none other but the local Aramaic name for Mount 'Ḥermon.' The Targum to Deuteronomy, chap. iii., ver. 9, has for the Hebrew Ḥermon 'Tur Talga'—the mountain of Telag; that is, the snow-capped mountain.

To paragraph 8 *et seq.*, containing non-Jewish history, I refer as parallel Comestor, Judges, chap. xii.; paragraph 9, *ibid.*, chap. xiii.; paragraph 14, *ibid.*, chap. xiv.; but still more identical with Isidorus, 'Chronicon,' p. 381, where all these incidents, together with many more missing in Jeraḥmeel, follow upon one another as one consecutive text, just as we have it here, and not broken up over the whole period from the time of the Judges to that of the last kings, as is the case in Comestor's work. In this paragraph 14 we find the very remarkable and thus far the only reference, by the author, to the era which he used. He says distinctly, 'We calculate the date from the destruction of the Temple.' The dating of the era from the destruction of the Temple lasted for a short time only, and was almost exclusively limited to Spain.

To the second half of paragraph 10, *cf.* Comestor, Kings IV., chap. xxv.; and to section 11, *ibid.*, chap. xxxi.-xxxiii. With this chapter finishes the parallelism between Philo's Latin and Jeraḥmeel's Hebrew chronicle, which apparently stopped at the period of Samuel. Paragraphs 8 to 11 are apparently intercalated. In them history is carried down to the time of Hezekiah; but the writer takes up the thread of his, thus interrupted, narrative with the beginning of paragraph 11, saying, 'We now return to the Judges.' Everything from the time of Samuel to the destruction of the first Temple is omitted. There are no Hebrew legends known elsewhere that treat of this period; hence, also, none in our 'Jeraḥmeel.'

The following chapters deal with the fate that befell the Ten Tribes in the Exile, and included therein are also versions of the ancient legends concerning the history of the Children of Moses, who were taken up immediately after they had left Palestine, were carried far away miraculously, and settled behind the river Sambatyon, to lead an idyllic life in absolute peace.

Chapter LX. contains a description of the 'eight times' the Jews were exiled from Palestine by Sancherib and Nebuchadnezzar. The description of these Exiles differs entirely from all the other versions that are known to exist. All these speak of *ten*, and carry history down till after the destruction of the second Temple, under Titus and Vespasianus, whilst our text stops short at the destruction of the first Temple by the Chaldeans. Those other texts have been published first in a Mantua edition (1514), as an addition to Abraham ibn Daud's abstract from Yosippon, who probably had found this legend in the same MS. as the Yosippon, of which he made an abstract exactly as it is here in our text of 'Jeraḥmeel,' where we have also this legend side by side with 'Yosippon.' Sebastianus Münster has reprinted the abstract and this addition in Basle, 1527; and another reprint has appeared in Basle in 1599, pp. 276-287, which seems to have escaped the notice of our bibliographers. Jellinek has reprinted what pretends to be an exact copy of this Basle edition, but not correctly ('Bet. Ham.,' vol. iv., pp. 133-136), and a still more different version (*ibid.*, vol. v., p. 113 *et seq.*). Comparing now his text with ours, we find in the first instance that all the others number ten Exiles, while this limits the number to eight; furthermore, that all those printed editions are much shorter, leaving out sometimes half and more of our text. Our version is evidently the more primitive, as it counts only eight, up to the destruction of the first Temple, and at the same time the most complete, for this text alone has preserved also that Jeremiah legend for which I know no other parallel, save those in the 'Baruch' cycle. The substance agrees, furthermore, with the tradition as given in the 'Seder 'Olām Rabba,' chap. xxv. *et seq.* (edit. Ratner, p. 110). *Cf.* notes thereto by the editor, note 9 *et seq.*

Chapters LXI. to LXIII.—The fate of the Ten Tribes and, connected with them, that of the Levites, or Children of Moses going into exile, has exercised the mind of the people from very ancient times. The question is already discussed in the fourth Book of Ezra, in the apocryphal letter of Baruch. It was, moreover, mixed up from very early times with the history of the Rechabites, and later on with that of the Gymnosophistes and the Brachmans; it entered into the Alexander legend, *vide* the Romance published by me (*Journ. Royal Asiatic Soc.*, 1897, chaps. lii.-liii.), and into Christian apocryphal literature, such as the narrative of Zosimus, concerning the life of the blessed, alluded to already in the third century, and in the various versions of the Macarius legend. We know of its existence in Hebrew literature in the seventh century, and later on it got into the narrative of that mysterious traveller Eldad ha-Dani, who pretends to have visited those various tribes, and to have learned of the existence of the Children of Moses beyond the river Sambatyon. As he flourished in the ninth century, our legend must perforce be much older, and it is as yet not known distinctly how much of his narrative is due to his own experience, and how much he has borrowed from older legends already in circulation and has incorporated into his sailor's yarn.

A contribution to the solution of the problem connected with that name is furnished by our book, with no less than three different versions of the cycle of these legends. The most amplified is here ascribed not to Eldad, but to a certain Elḥanan, and this version again seems to be the most primitive of that legend which has been connected with the name of Eldad. Various texts have been published which contain either the legends of the tribes, or of the Children of Moses, either singly, or mixed up with those of Eldad (Jellinek, 'Bet. Ham.,' vol. ii., pp. 102-13; vol. iii., pp. 6-11; vol. v., pp. 17-21; and vol. vi., pp. 15-18). The whole cycle of the Eldad legends has been subjected to a critical investigation by Mr. Epstein, in his work called 'Eldad ha-Dani' (Pressburg, 1891). I do not agree with the results at which he arrives. He connects the narrative of Eldad with Abyssinian legends, forgetting that the information obtained from Abyssinia is of recent origin, and can in no way prove anything for facts at least a thousand years older, recorded among Jews living in the Arabian Peninsula or around the Persian Gulf. It is not at all improbable, in fact it is very likely, that some of the customs and ceremonies noted now among the Jewish Fallashas in Abyssinia have been introduced from those parts, either from Egypt or from the Persian Gulf, which latter I consider to be the starting-point of Elḥanan's travels. Of the texts published by Epstein, we find the one incorporated into the first version of Eldad's narrative to be identical with the greater part of our Chapter LXI. The beginning has evidently been omitted when this legend was tacked on to the cycle of Eldad. It follows, therefrom, that our text, being more complete, is the more primitive. Paragraphs 2-4 correspond with Eldad, i., paragraphs 7-9 (pp. 5-6; *cf.* p. 13, also note 10 *et seq.*). Concerning paragraph 1, which gives us the exact date of the banishment, *cf.* ' Seder Olām Rabba,' chap. xxx., ed. Ratner, pp. 147-149, *vide* note 93 *et seq.*

Chapter LXII.—The second version has the peculiar superscription, 'The ten banishments of the Sanhedrin,' although not a word of the Sanhedrin is mentioned in the text. It may mean the banishment of the ten communities or tribes. This is absolutely identical with the version contained in the 'Midrash Rabba Rabbati,' and it is, if anything, more perfect than the copy preserved in the manuscript of Prague, from which Epstein has reprinted it (*loc. cit.*, pp. 42-45). This again proves the author of the 'Midrash Rabba Rabbati' to have borrowed his legendary material from our compilation.

Chapter LXIII. is an amplified recapitulation of the last legend. This time it is presented under the form of a recital of the adventures of Elḥanan the sailor, who happened to come to the country occupied by the descendants of Dan. From them he learned all about their past, and he went from them to visit the other tribes. In his narrative he has incorporated (paragraphs 11-14) the legendary history of the Children of Moses and of the happy land in which they are living, surrounded by the river Sambatyon, that flows for six days of the week, but rests on the Sabbath day, when a flame descends and covers the river, protecting them from any possible contact with the outer world. From them he goes on to visit other tribes, until he comes to the sons of Judah and Simeon, which means to the Jews scattered in this part of the world, and when Danite merchants come he returns with them to their country. We see here distinctly how the older material has been bodily incorporated into this tale, which forms a kind of traveller's romance—the oldest version of the Sinbad cycle —in the same manner in which biblical legends have been used for liturgical purposes, and have been incorporated into homilies. Elḥanan's tale agrees in the main with the fourth version of Eldad (Epstein, *loc. cit.*, p. 47 *et seq.*), having many points in common with it; among other things, the names of the various kings with whom they are fighting (paragraph 6) corresponding in our edition to paragraph 8. Professor David Heinrich Müller has attempted to examine the names of these nations, which occur also in the second version published by Epstein (p. 22 *et seq.*, and grouped together by him on p. 38). In our text we have a list of eighteen names, which in the other versions have been reduced to *seven*. A few of these names agree with those in our text, but on the whole they are different and difficult to identify.

Having as it were finished with the history of the Ten Tribes, Jerahmeel very skilfully returns to the history of the Jews in the Exile, and translates into Hebrew the Aramaic portions of Daniel, who lived there. He retains, however, those portions of Daniel which are not forming part of the Hebrew Bible, viz., the old Apocrypha, in their original Aramaic language, in the very form in which they served as basis to Theodotion for his Greek translation, as I have set forth in my edition of those two chapters containing the history of Daniel and the Dragon, and the history of Daniel and Bel, as well as the Song of the Three Children in the Fiery Furnace. These apocryphal portions have been declared by some scholars not to be the original texts, but probably late translations from the Latin or Greek. It now so happens, as stated above (p. xlix), that Reymundus Martini, in his 'Pugio Fidei,' has preserved to us a portion of this very Aramaic text of Daniel in the lion's den, which he had taken from the 'Midrash Rabbati' of Moses Hadarschan. It is a literal quotation from our book, being absolutely identical also with the manuscript of the 'Rabbati' published by Neubauer. Every doubt as to its antiquity and authenticity is undoubtedly hypercritical. I have omitted the texts here, as they have already been published elsewhere by me.

Chapter LXIV.—From this incident Jerahmeel proceeds to the description of the evil deeds of two false prophets in the Exile, who are mentioned in the Bible, together with the peculiar punishment inflicted upon them by Nebuchadnezzar. This old legend explains the reason for their being roasted alive as a consequence of the attempt to commit adultery with the daughter of Nebuchadnezzar. It is identical in every detail with the same tale contained in Talmud treatise ' Sanhedrin,' fol. 93a, my ' Exempla of the Rabbis,' No. 28, and both identical with the Jerusalem treatise ' Sanhedrin,' fol. 93a. An abstract of it, *vide* Tanhuma, ed. Buber, Levit. Rabba, section 10, paragraph 7 ; Yalqut to Jeremiah, paragraph 309, and in the Midrash Haggadol, Exodus, portion Jethro.

Chapter LXV.—Jerahmeel now leads on to the History of Susanna, where the two elders and judges attempt the very same sin for which those false prophets had been punished. An old tradition identifies these elders with those false prophets. Here we are entering already into the domain of the known biblical apocryphal literature, and I cannot do better than refer to Schürer's ' Geschichte d. Jüd. Volkes,' II.², p. 716 *et seq*. I refer also specially to Bruell's study in his ' Jahrbuch ' (vol. iii., pp. 1-69). The crucial point in this history is the Greek names of the trees under which Susanna is said to have been seen by the two elders committing adultery, which names, being a play upon the words, seemed to indicate Greek origin. We find here totally different names. The Hebrew version in our text is thus far the only ancient Hebrew text of this History of Susanna known to exist, and it is noteworthy that it is not to be found even in Yosippon, which contains all the other apocryphal additions to the Book of Daniel in full. A modern Hebrew text, which may rest upon some older translation, is printed in ' Otzar Hakodesh,' Lemberg, 1851 (probably a reprint from an older edition which I have not yet been able to trace); but it is undoubtedly derived from a Latin original. Jellinek has not reprinted this version in his ' B. Ham.,' nor has any scholar found hitherto another ancient Hebrew text of the History of Susanna. Jerahmeel alone has preserved such a Hebrew version of the Susanna legend. In some details this text agrees more with the Syriac than with the Latino-Greek version. Especially noteworthy is the difference in the names. In our text the father of Susanna is called 'Shealtiel,' whilst in all the other versions he is called 'Chelkia.' In connection with this it might be pointed out that Shealtiel was the father of Zerubbabel; Susanna is probably taken to be his sister, and her husband King Jehoiachin. Hippolytus, Syncellus, and others identify him indeed with the King of Judah, who was carried away into the captivity at Babylon (2 Kings, chap. xxiv., ver. 15; and chap. xxv., ver. 27). This name seems to be more appropriate, and to represent the older tradition, which would centre round the prominent figure of the former King of Judah in preference to any obscure personage. The parallel history in Comestor, Daniel, chap. xiii., differs completely from the Hebrew.

Chapter LXVI.—In this chapter follows a short history of Nebuchadnezzar's apparent but not real change into an animal, who behaves like a wild beast for seven months. No other trace of this version have I found in the Hebrew literature. Parallels we find to it, however, in Epiphanius, 'Vita Danielis'; 'Chronicon Paschale,' ed. Bonn, i., pp. 299, 300; Fabricius, p. 1124 *et seq.*; and also Comestor, Daniel, chap. iv., who quotes Epiphanius. Paragraphs 3-6, *vide* Comestor, Daniel, chap. v., but already so in Josephus, 'Antiquities,' x., 11, i.-ii. The names of the sons of Evil Merodach (here paragraph 6) are given by Josephus as Niglissar, Labsardacus, and Naboandelus (who is the well-known Naboned). Comestor has Egessar, Labosardoch, and Nabar. Paragraph 6, less fully in Second Targum to Esther, chap. i., *vide* Levit. Rabba, section 18, p. 2; Tanḥuma Tazri'a, section 10; 'Seder Olām Rabba,' chap. xxviii., ed. Ratner, p. 125, and note 7.

Chapter LXVII.—From paragraph 67 on, the bulk of the rest of the Chronicle—with few exceptions, which will be treated separately—is taken bodily from the Yosippon, or, as the compiler says, from the 'Book of Joseph ben Gorion.'

A short reference, which shows the relation in which our

text stands to the edition of Breithaupt, will suffice, always remembering that the text of Jerahmeel is simpler, the names much more correct and clear, and in the main agreeing with the old edition of Conte (Mantua, *circa* 1480). According to his custom, Jerahmeel copies here once more the history of Daniel in the lion's den, because he finds it also in Yosippon, although he had already included it previously in his collection from an independent, older source.

Chapter LXVII. corresponds with Breithaupt, Book I., chap. v.

Chapter LXVIII. corresponds with Breithaupt, Book I., chaps. vi., vii.

Chapter LXIX. corresponds with Breithaupt, Book I., chap. viii.

Chapter LXX. corresponds with Breithaupt, Book I., chaps. ix., x., xi. (The history of Daniel in the lion's den.)

Chapter LXXI. corresponds with Breithaupt, Book I., chap. xii.

Chapter LXXII. corresponds with Breithaupt, Book I., chap. xiii. (The history of Daniel and the Temple of Bel.)

Chapter LXXIII. corresponds with Breithaupt, Book I., chap. xiv. (The history of Daniel and the dragon.)

In Chapter LXXIV. *et seq.*, which corresponds with Breithaupt, I., chaps. xv., xvi., we have the Hebrew parallel (in Yosippon and in Jerahmeel) to the so-called Apocryphal Third Ezra (chap. iii. *et seq.*). The order in the Hebrew text is different, and the interpretation of the riddles much more correct and much clearer than in the Greek text. The marked divergence from any other text proves that there cannot be a question of our text being a translation from the Greek or from the Latin texts known. In spite of the opinion expressed by Zunz (G. V.^{2}, p. 154 *et seq.*; and p. 160, note *d*), not a single trace of Latin influence can be detected thus far in the Hebrew text of Yosippon, and in the corresponding portion in Jerahmeel.

Chapter LXXV. corresponds with Breithaupt, I., xvii., xviii., and the beginning of xix.

Chapter LXXVI. corresponds with middle of xix. (Breithaupt, p. 56).

Chapter LXXVII. corresponds with chaps. xx., xxi.

Chapter LXXVIII. is a continuation of chap. xxi. (Breithaupt, only as far as p. 65). It is to be remarked that the personal note in p. 65 (ed. Breithaupt), where Joseph ben Gorion identifies himself with Josephus, is entirely missing in our text, and in the ed. Conte (folio 13, column *b*). The text continues in our copy exactly in the same manner as in the ed. Conte, corresponding with beginning of chap. xxii. of ed. Breithaupt. The whole portion from pp. 65-68 being entirely omitted.

With Chapter LXXIX.-LXXXIV. begins the cycle of Apocryphal legends round the Book of Esther. Of these only the first two chapters containing the dream and prayer of Mordecai and Esther's prayer form part of the known biblical Apocrypha, and are taken here from Yosippon. This chapter corresponds with Book II., chaps. i.-iv., ed. Breithaupt. I have found the whole text of this dream of Mordecai in a fragment from the Geniza, which seems to be a portion of an old chronicle (Yosippon? — or a similar), and is characterized by the fact that the Hebrew words have the vowel signs. Two old Aramaic texts have been published by de Rossi, and then reprinted by Jellinek ('B. Ham.,' i., pp. 1-8). Merx in his 'Chrestomathia Targumica' (pp. 164-174) has reprinted a text from a manuscript written in the year 1189. I necessarily ignore the translation made from the Latin by Jacob ben Machir, and printed by Jellinek (*ibid.*, p. 9 *et seq.*). For the further history of these texts in the Apocrypha, *cf.* Schürer, *loc. cit.*, II.^{2}, p. 715. Josephus has also introduced the same legends into his text ('Antiquities,' xi. 6), as he has done with the other Apocrypha of Daniel in x. 11, and the Solutions of the Problems by Zerubbabel, xi. 3.

Chapter LXXXI.—To these biblical Apocrypha Jeraḥmeel had added a series of similar legends. First we have the letter which Haman sent to the princes and rulers of the Persian kingdom to destroy the Jews. It is absolutely identical with the text found in the Midrash Aba Gorion (ed. Buber, p. 42), and I am inclined to believe that this Aba Gorion is none other than our Joseph ben Gorion, and that the text of the letter has been borrowed from a more complete recension of the Yosippon than that which we have before us. From a Codex de Rossi a similar letter has been published by Perreau in the 'Hamazkir' (1864, v.-vii., pp. 46, 47). To paragraph 3, *cf.* Haggadoth Esther (ed. Buber, p. 37), *vide* especially Aba Gorion, folio 16*a*, and Esther Rabba, chap. vii., paragraph 13; Midrash Esther (ed. Horowitz, p. 68), and Jellinek, 'Bet. Ham.,' vi. (p. 54).

The whole text contained in Chapter LXXXI., paragraph 7, up to Chapter LXXXII., paragraph 6, is found in Aba Gorion (p. 32 *et seq*.). Our text is again fuller and more harmonious in its details than the parallel passage, showing it to have retained the primitive form, which has been curtailed when utilized for homiletic purposes in that Hagadic collection. The same has happened to this text as to the other biblical legends mentioned above, for the beginning of Chapter LXXXIII. has been omitted, whilst from the middle of paragraph 1 to the middle of paragraph 7 is found verbatim in the Haggadoth Esther (ed. Buber, pp. 60-61, and note 8 *et seq*., where the whole parallel literature is referred to).

Chapter LXXXIV.—A description of the wonderful throne of King Solomon. Its place in our collection is easily explained by the fact that from very ancient times the throne upon which Ahasuerus was sitting (in Esther, chap. i. 5) is said to have been the throne of Solomon carried away by Nebuchadnezzar. A description of it occurs, therefore, at the very beginning of the so-called second Targum to the Book of Esther. (The English translation of it, by P. Cassel, appeared together with his commentary to the Book of Esther, as Appendix I., p. 207 *et seq*.). The literature that has gathered round this throne is very vast. This description is also found in the Midrash Aba Gorion (pp. 52-58), in my 'Exempla of the

Rabbis,' No. 115. Another text has been printed by Perles, reprinted by Jellinek, 'B. Ham.,' vol. v., p. 89 (see pp. vi-viii.) An elaborate monograph on it by P. Cassel, cf. also Massmann, 'Kaiser Chronik,' vol. iii., p. 889, a description of a similar throne made by Kosroe, King of Persia.

Chapter LXXXV.-C.—The concluding chapters bear the title the Book of the Maccabee, being limited to the history of Judah 'the' Maccabee. They are identical with the corresponding portion of Yosippon, with the exception of the history of Alexander the Great, interpolated into the ed. Breithaupt, and missing in Jerahmeel and ed. Conte.

The close parallelism begins with LXXXV., paragraph 2 = ed. Breithaupt II., chapter vi. and vii.; LXXXVI. = III., chapter i.; Chapter LXXXVII. = Book III., chapters ii. and iii.; LXXXVIII. = III., chapters iii. and iv. In Chapter LXXXIX. we have the history of the Mother and the Seven Sons, the martyrs = Book III., chapters v. and vi. This is one of the well-known Apocrypha, and stands at the head of a very large cycle of legends. In most of the Hebrew parallels she is called Hannah, or Miriam, *vide* my 'Exempla' of the Rabbis. No. 57; 'Echa Rabb,' chap. i., paras. 47-50; 'Pesiqta Rabbati,' chap. xxix.; 'Yalqut,' i., paragraph 93; Talmud treatise 'Kethuboth,' fol. 64, etc.; Zunz, G. V.², pp. 131, 152, 190. Chapter XC. = III., chapters vii., viii.; XCI. = III., chapter ix.; XCII. = III., chapters x., xi.; XCIII. = III., chapter xii. The general is called *Bakires*, as in the Scroll of the Hasmoneans, and not Bacchides, as the Greek texts have it.

Chapter XCIV. = III., chap. xiii.; Chapter XCV. = III., chap. xiv.; the place of the fight mentioned here in paragraphs 2 and 3 is written in the Hebrew 'Bethtur'; in the Greek texts, 2 Maccab. (chap. xi., ver. 5), it is called Bethzura; so also Josephus. In Yosippon (ed. Breithaupt, p. 216) Beter (*vide* note 6). By the orthography in Jerahmeel, and by this identity of names, it is becoming clear which place is meant by the town of the same name, famous in the war of Barcochba. It is evidently none else than this Bethtur, the fortress near Jerusalem. The old geographical puzzle is now solved with the assistance of our 'Jerahmeel.'

Chapter XCVI. = III., chaps. xv. and part of xvii.; Chapter XCVII. corresponds to the continuation of chap. xvii. and xviii.; Chapter XCVIII. = chaps. xix. and xx.; Chapter XCIX. = chaps. xxi. and xxii.; and finally Chapter C. = chap. xxiii., end of Book III. (ed. Breithaupt).

We have thus rounded off the history of the world as told by Jerahmeel with the aid of old Apocrypha, beginning with the Creation and finishing with the death of Judas Maccabeus. We have in our book the oldest example of the Bible Historiale, an amplification of the Bible narrative by means of legendary tales, many of which, in fact most of which, have their roots in extreme antiquity, written down, with perhaps a few exceptions, in the first centuries before or after the Common Era, handed on in a surprisingly perfect form, preserved through the love, the industry, and conscientiousness of one compiler who could not have lived later than the sixth or seventh century, copied a second time with the same conscientious care and enlarged by a man who may have lived in the tenth or eleventh century, and forming, then, the starting-point for a third equally conscientious continuator in the thirteenth or fourteenth century. It is at once the oldest and best corpus of Apocryphal and Pseudo-epigraphical books of which any literature can boast.

We are now in a better position to review the whole field of that ancient literary activity, and to prepare a critical edition of the texts contained in this compilation. Through the comparison with the existing parallels, I have endeavoured to show that these represent the oldest and most complete recensions. I have laid bare unsuspected connections between the literatures of many tongues and many lands. I have followed up not merely the main stream of literary tradition to its remotest course, but also some lateral channels. I have endeavoured to trace the oldest available sources of all the stores of legends which have enriched the literatures of the world, Jewish, Christian, and Mahomedan alike, which have so deeply influenced poetry and art in the middle ages, and which have kept human fancy playing for two thousand years round the stern figures of the Old Testament.

CHRONICLES OF JERAHMEEL.

COMPILER'S PREFACE.

Behold I have sworn not to lend anybody this book to take away, with the exception of three, whom I shall mention by name, but whoever desires to read it at my house is at liberty to do so.

Behold I am the youngest of all my family. I, Elazar, son of R. Asher, the Levite, have set my mind upon writing from precious and valuable secular books, for my spirit bore me aloft and filled me with enthusiasm in the days of my youth, when I was easygoing and keen-witted. For I saw many books scattered and dispersed here and there. I then resolved to collect them, and unite them in one book. I then made a collection of the words of the wise and their aphorisms, and wrote them down in a book for the use of those who love parable and history, and for wise men generally who are not otherwise occupied, in order that they may reflect upon these things, so that they may see, understand, and know the truth concerning a few of the events which have taken place under the sun, and of a few of the troubles and afflictions which our ancestors endured in their exile, and what vicissitudes they underwent when the tempest swept over them, so that they may not be forgotten by their seed. Therefore I called this book the 'Book of Chronicles,' wherein may be recorded many varied events. For I have collected in this book records of all events and incidents which have happened from the creation of the world until the present day as it is written in this book, and as I found, so I copied, and I have deftly woven the materials to form one book.

Nor did I write them to make myself a great name, but to the glory of my Creator, who truly knows, and so that this book should be a memorial for future generations; and whoever chooses to add to this book may add, and may blessing fall upon him. Behold I hope that God may make my son worthy of inheriting this Book of Chronicles, which I have collected from many books. I wrote it, and laid aside many affairs for its sake, so as to be able to complete it. The bulk of it I wrote in the autumn and winter, for I only had leisure at that time. 'In the day the drought consumed me, and the cold at night, and drove my sleep from my eyes.' And many events have happened, and what I was not able to do in the daytime, I did at night, for I neither rested nor reposed until I had completed its composition. For I gave a long time to it, and I was constantly occupied upon its composition, and I was continually busy with it, and I worked and laboured vigorously until I had selected each subject and placed it in its proper position, like a pearl in its setting and like a hook in its eye, and had I done it for payment no sum would have satisfied me, for I dwelt upon it days and years until I had completed its composition, for I had not always the books to copy it from, nor had I often the leisure, whilst occasionally I was not in the humour, on account of many misfortunes which befell me in my captivity. Therefore I conjure and command my son—since I bequeath him this Book of Chronicles—that I hand it to him on his undertaking to fulfil the solemn conditions which I impose upon him, a father to his son. He may not sell it, nor may he give it away nor pledge it, neither he nor his posterity, neither may he exchange it nor substitute anything else for it. For what will a small amount of money avail him, since he could not succeed in purchasing its equal or its like in the whole world, either for a large or small sum of money? For I have searched in many places before I composed it; for this reason rather let a man pledge or sell the cloak from his back before he disposes of this. For I know that nobody can obtain half its worth or value, for no scribe could be found to write it for less than six small pieces of gold, to say nothing of the parchment. And who sells it will soon squander the money on frivolity; then he will immediately repent his transaction, but in vain. Moreover, I can assure him that he will never obtain its like, inasmuch as I know full well that no man would compose another such work, on account of the magnitude of the task; further, I know that nobody is broad-minded enough to resolve to compose and publish such a book as this, for it appears at first sight a collection of tales. Nevertheless, if he wishes to dispose of it to one of his sons or to one of his brothers, he may do so, but the one who acquires it may not override my conditions, but must observe everything as set down here. And he may only bequeath this book to one of his sons, or, failing male issue, he should bequeath it to one of his brothers, but not to one of his daughters, who have no portion or inheritance in it, that this book may not pass from one tribe to another. And do not, my sons, resolve to divide the work into two or three portions, so that each one of you may have a share in it, but let the one who inherits it receive it in one volume. May the one who ignores my writing, transgresses my command, or does not fulfil my words, be cursed; but blessed be my descendants, and may they be established if they fulfil my wishes. Neither scoff at me when you notice in what detail I have communicated my wishes concerning this book to my sons, for do ye not know that whatever man completes by the labour and toil of his hands he values highly? And I knew that unless I did it myself, unassisted, I should never have completed it. For who can depend upon scribes in the case of a book of this kind? Besides, even if I had the will, could I order scribes to be present just as books came to my hand; and where could I get the books from? Therefore I said, 'If I do not do it for myself, who, then, will do it for me?' And God enlightened me, and I girded my loins like a mighty man, and composed this Book of Chronicles. May God remember it for me for good!

(1) WITH the help of God I commence to write this my book without interruption. These are the generations of the heavens and the earth when they were created on the day when the Lord God made heaven and earth. R. Eliezer, son of Hyrqanos, began his homily thus : ' Who can express all the mighty acts of God ?' Is there anybody who can possibly give utterance to the mighty deeds of God and proclaim all His praise ? Not even the ministering angels can do this. It is only possible to recount part of His mighty deeds, to explain what He has done and what He in future will do, so that His great name may be exalted among the creatures whom He has created from one end of the world to the other, as it is said, 'Every generation shall praise Thy works.' Before the world was created God and His name alone existed. When it entered His mind to create the world, He drew the plan of a world, but it would not stand. This may be compared to the action of a man who wishes to build a palace: unless he plans out its foundations, its exits and its entrances, he cannot commence to build. Thus God planned the world before Him, but it would not stand until He created repentance. (2) Seven things were created prior to the creation of the world, viz. : the Law, repentance, the throne of glory, the Garden of Eden, Gehinnom, the site of the temple, and the name of the Messiah, and for all these things proof is to be found in the Scriptures.

(3) Eight things were created on the first day, viz., heaven and earth, light and darkness, that which was without form and void (Tohu va-Bohu), air and water ; and the Spirit of God hovered over the surface of the waters. Some say day

and night were also included in the first day of the creation, as it is said: 'And it was evening, and it was morning, one day.' Eight things were also created on the second day: The well (of Miriam), manna, the rod (of Moses), the rainbow, the letters and the writing, the clothes (of Adam and Eve), and demons (Maziqim).

(4) Ten things were paramount in the thought of God at the creation, viz.: Jerusalem, the spirits of the patriarchs, the ways of the righteous, Gehinnom, the flood, the double tables of stone, the Sabbath, the temple, the ark, and the light of the future world. (5) Wherefrom were the heavens created? From the brilliancy of God's covering which He took up and spread as a garment, and the heavens went on extending until He said unto them, 'Be stayed,' and they stopped. (6) Whence was the earth created? From the snow beneath the throne of glory. God took it up and scattered it upon the waters, then the waters were congealed and became the dust of the earth, as it is said, 'For He says unto the snow, Become earth.' The boundaries of the heavens touch the waters of the ocean, for the waters of the ocean (Oqeanos) flow round the extremities of the heavens and the earth, and the extremities of the heavens are spread upon the waters of the ocean, as it is said, 'Who layeth the foundation of His upper chambers in the waters.' The heavens rise to an immense height in the form of a tent that is spread out, and mortals stand beneath it; its extremity is below, and its centre is above. This is the form of the heavens, their extremity is below and their centre above, so that all (God's) creatures, as it were, sit beneath it as in a tent, as it is said, 'He spread them out as a tent for dwelling therein.' (7) Four winds were created in the world, viz., the winds coming from the east, south, north, and west. From the eastern corner the light of the world goeth forth; from the south, the dews of blessing descend upon the world; from the west emanate the stores of snow, hail, cold and heat, and rains for the benefit of the world; the north corner of the world He created, but did not complete, for He said: Whoever declares himself

to be God, let him come and finish this corner which I have left, and then shall all know that he is a God. There the demons, earthquakes, evil spirits, and Shiddim dwell, and from there they come forth to the world, as it is said, 'Out of the north evil shall break forth' (Jer. i. 14).

(8) On the second day He created the firmament, the angels, the heat of the living bodies, and the heat of Gehinnom. But were not the heavens created on the first day? as it is said, 'In the beginning God created the heavens.' What, then, is this heaven which was created on the second day? R. Eliezer says: That firmament which is above the heads of the four holy creatures, as it is said, 'In the likeness of a firmament above the holy creatures.' It appears like unto hoar-frost, consisting of precious stones and pearls; it lights up the whole heavens as the light which lights up the house, and as the sun which lights up the world at noon, as it is said, 'And light dwells with Him.' Similarly the righteous are destined in the future to enlighten the world, as it is said, 'And the wise will shine as the brightness of the firmament.' And if the firmament had not been created on the second day, the whole world would have been drowned by the waters from above, but the firmament now separates the upper from the lower waters. These angels, which were created on the second day, when sent by God, become winds, as it is said: 'He made His angels winds.' When they minister before Him, they become like fire, as it is said, 'His ministering angels are a flaming fire.' (9) Four bands of angels minister unto God, the first band, under Michael, on His right, the second, under Gabriel, in front of Him, the third, under Uriel, on His left, and the fourth, under Raphael, behind Him. The Divine presence of God sits in the centre on a high and exalted throne, which is exceedingly majestic, and is suspended above in the air, and the appearance of its glory is like unto a carbuncle, one half is as fire, and the other half is as snow; a resplendent crown of glory rests upon His head, and upon His forehead is written the ineffable name of 'God.' His eyes overlook the whole earth; on

His right is life, on His left death; a sceptre of fire is in His hand; a curtain is spread out before Him, (10) and the seven angels which were created first minister before Him within the curtain. His footstool is like fire and hail, and beneath the throne of glory, it has the appearance of sapphires; fire plays round about it; righteousness and justice are the supports of His throne; clouds of glory surround it, and the wheel, the ophan, the cherub, and the holy creatures sing praises unto Him. The throne is like sapphire; it stands upon four legs, and four holy creatures are attached to it; on each side are four faces and four wings, as it is said: 'There were four faces, which were four angels.' (11) When He speaks from the east, from between the two cherubim, He speaks in the direction of the face of man; when He speaks from the south, He speaks in the direction of the face of the lion; when from the west, He speaks in the direction of the oxen; when from the north, in the direction of the eagle; and opposite Him are the ophanim and the wheels of the chariot. When He sits upon the throne, high and exalted, and looks round the earth, His chariot being upon wheels, through the noise caused by the wheels of the chariot, lightnings and earthquakes are caused in the world. But when He traverses the heavens, He rides upon a swift cherub, as it is said, 'And He rode upon a swift cherub.' When He hastens to do a thing, He flies upon the wings of the wind, as it is said, 'And He flew upon the wings of the wind." (12) Two seraphim stand near Him, one on His right side and another on His left, each of which has six wings; with two each of them covers his face to prevent them gazing upon the Shekinah, and with two they each hide their legs so as not to remember the sin of the golden calf, and with two they fly, exulting in, and sanctifying, His great name. One answers while another proclaims, and one proclaims while the other answers, and they say, 'Holy, holy, holy, is the Lord of Hosts.' (13) The holy creatures stand with reverence and awe, with trembling and quaking, lest they be consumed by the fire of the angels; and from their faces streams down a fiery river, as it is said, 'And a river of fire flows before Him;' and the holy creatures do not know the place of His glory, but answer and exclaim wherever His glory be, 'Blessed is the glory of the Lord in His place.'

II. (1) On the third day the earth was like a plain, and the waters covered the face of the whole earth. When the word of God went forth, saying, 'Let the waters be gathered together,' the mountains were lifted up and scattered over the earth, and deep valleys were dug down in the bowels of the earth, into which the waters rolled and were gathered, as it is said, 'The gathering of waters He called seas.' The waters then immediately rose tumultuously to a great height and covered the face of the earth as at first, until God rebuked them and subdued them, and placed them under the hollow of His feet, and measured them in His palm, so that they could neither diminish nor increase. He surrounded the sea with sand as a fence, just as a man makes a fence for his vineyard. So that when the waters approach and see the fence before them they recede, as it is said, 'Will they not fear My signs, says the Lord.' (2) Before the waters were finally gathered together, the rivers and the fountains of the deep were created, for the earth was stretched over the waters just as a ship floating in the midst of the sea, as it is said, 'To spread out the earth over the waters.' (3) And God opened a gate in the Garden of Eden and brought forth all kinds of plants, every kind of tree yielding fruit after its kind, and every kind of grass. He took their seeds and planted them upon the earth, as it is said, 'Whose seed is within itself upon the earth.' He prepared food for His creatures before they were created, as it is said, 'Thou preparest a table before me.' (4) All the fountains of waters rise from the depths. R. Joshua said that the depth of the earth would take sixty years to walk through. There is one fountain close to Gehinnom which receives and gives out hot waters that delight man. (5) R. Jehudah says: Once every month rivulets ascend from the depths and water the face of the whole earth, as it is said, 'And a spray went up from the earth to water the garden.' The thick clouds pass on the sound of the water-courses to the seas, and the seas to the depths, and the depths to each other, and finally rise and give moisture to the clouds, as it is said, 'Who causes the vapours to ascend at the end of the earth.'

(6) The rains descend upon every place bidden them by the King, so that the earth immediately flourishes and becomes fertile. But when God wishes to bless the land and make it fertile and prosperous, so as to feed His creatures, He then opens His storehouse of good contained in the heavens and rains upon the earth, so that it immediately becomes fertile and produces the seed of blessing, as it is said, 'The Lord will open for thee His treasure of good.'

III. (1) On the fourth day he formed two lights, one not larger than the other; they were identical both in their form and in their light, as it is said, 'And God made the two lights.' A quarrel ensued between them; one said to the other, 'I am greater than thou.' Therefore God, in order to make peace between them, enlarged the one and diminished the other, as it is said, 'And the greater to rule by day.' (2) R. Eliezer said that God uttered one word and the heavens were created to become the dwelling-place of the throne of the glory of His kingdom, as it is said, 'By the word of the Lord the heavens were made,' but for the numerous host of heaven God exerted Himself more; He blew with the breath of His mouth, and all the host of the heavens were created, as it is said, 'And with the breath of His mouth all their host.' (3) All the stars and planets and the two lights were created at the beginning of the fourth night. One did not precede the other except by one minute particle of time; therefore, all the work of the sun is done slowly, while that of the moon is done quickly; what the sun takes twelve days to do the moon can do in one day; what the sun does during the whole year the moon does in thirty days, as it is explained in the chapters of R. Eliezer. (4) Three letters of the ineffable name of God are written upon the heart of the sun, and angels lead it. Those that lead it in the day do not lead it in the night, and those that lead it in the night do not lead it in the day. The sun rises in a chariot, and rides forth crowned as a bridegroom, as it is said, 'And he goeth forth from his canopy as a bridegroom.' The horns (the rays) and the fiery face of the sun look upon the earth in the summer, they would consume it with fire if the ice above would not temper the heat, as it is said, 'Nothing is hidden from his heat.' In the winter-time the sun turns his icy face to the earth, and were it not for the fire which warms the cold, the world would not be able to endure it, as it is said, 'Who can stand before his cold?' (5) The sun rises in the east and sets opposite in the west. The Shekinah always resides in the west, and the sun enters in its presence, and, bowing down before the King of kings, says: 'O Lord of the universe, I have fulfilled all Thy commands.' These are some of the ways of the sun. (6) The habitation of the moon is placed between the clouds and the thick darkness, which are like two dishes one above the other; within them the moon travels. These two clouds turn themselves towards the west, and the moon peeps out from between the two in the form of a little horn. On the first night of the new month one part is visible, on the second night a second portion, and so on until the middle of the month, when it is full moon. From the middle of the month onwards these two clouds turn themselves eastwards, and that part of the moon which appeared first is the first to be covered by the two clouds—on the first night one part, on the second night a second part, until the end of the month, when it is entirely covered. Whence do we know that the moon is between two clouds? Because it is said, 'The cloud is its clothing, and clouds of darkness its covering.'

IV. (1) The following seven planets God created and placed in order in the firmament for the benefit of the world; for by means of them people calculate the signs, seasons, and astronomical computations; the time of summer, the number of the hours, days and months, periods and festivals (appointed times), as it is said, 'They shall be for signs, for seasons, for days and for years.' (2) The seven days of the week are called after the seven planets, the Sun, Venus, Mercury, the Moon, Saturn, Jupiter, and Mars. On the first day Sol, *i.e.* the sun, rules, and this day is called Zondakh. On the second day the moon serves; it is called Luna, therefore the second day is called Lunedi, *i.e.*, Mondakh. On the third day Mars serves; it is called Mars, hence Marsdi, *i.e.*, Diensdakh. On the fourth day Mercury, or Marcurios, serves, therefore it is called Markusdi, *i.e.*, Godansdakh. On the fifth day Jupiter serves; it is called Iovis, hence Iovisdi, *i.e.*, Donnersdakh. On the sixth day Venus, *i.e.*, Veneri, serves, therefore the day is called Vindredi, that is Vredakh. On the seventh day Saturnus serves, therefore the day is called Sabbatdi, *i.e.*, Satuldakh. (3) In what order are they placed in heaven? They are distributed there as sun and moon and the five planets. The firmament is divided into seven degrees, one above the other. There are seven distinct places for these seven planets; and this is their order: (4) The first degree is near the earth, and this lowest degree is the habitation of the moon, in which the moon makes a circuit round the firmament. The second degree is the habitation of Mercury, in which it describes its circuit in the firmament. The third degree is the habitation of Venus, in which it also describes its circuit in the firmament. The fourth degree is the middle of them, viz., the habitation of the sun, which completes its circuit of the heaven in twelve months. The fifth degree is the habitation of Mars, which makes its circuit in the firmament.[1] The seventh degree is the highest of all, viz., the habitation of Saturn, which completes its circuit in three years. (5) This is the order of their work: Saturn is appointed over the poor and needy women, over faintness and sickness, diseases of the body, and over death. His appearance is like that of an

[1] The sixth degree is missing in the MS.

old man with a sickle in his hand. (6) Mars is appointed over war (bloodshed) and the sword, over the wicked, over slander, over strife, battle, hatred, jealousy, quarrels, over warriors, wounds, injuries, bruises, over fire, water, and destruction. His appearance is like that of an armed warrior with a sword in his right hand, and he appears like a man of wrath and a stirrer up of strife. Wherever he turns wickedness ensues; he looks terrible in his coat of mail, and with the spear which he bears in his left hand. (7) Jupiter is appointed over life, peace and good, over prosperity, tranquillity, joy, pleasant conversation, rejoicings, riches, greatness, sovereignty and majesty. His appearance is like that of a valiant and noble-looking man, and his head is that of a ram. (8) Venus is appointed over kindness, favour, love, lust, passion, desire, marriage, the birth of man and animals, the fruits of the earth and the fruits of the tree. Its form is that of a young girl beautifully adorned, and swaying a branch of a tree in her hand. Mercury is appointed over wisdom, discretion, understanding, knowledge, and the active intellect enabling one to unravel mysteries, to devise plans in every branch of work, and in the writings of any language. Its form is that of an old man with thin lips; he possesses wings, and the lower part of the body is like a dragon. (9) The sun is appointed over light, to separate light from darkness, and through it to enable us to calculate the days, months and years, and to do every kind of work, to make any cunning work, to walk any distance, and to migrate from city to city and from town to town. The moon holds the key of heaven and earth, and is appointed over morning and evening. She is set over all creatures, to lead them in the right or wrong way, although she has no power in herself either to do good or evil. But everything is done by order and command. Everything was created by means of the word of God. (10) Hence the Rabbis have said that the orbit of the sun and the circuit of the moon, the order of the stars, the arrangement of the planets, the calculation of the circuits, the lengths of the days and the division of the hours, which are at first long and then become gradually shorter, are all the work of God.

V. On the fifth day He brought forth from the waters all manner of winged birds, male and female, all manner of locusts, and also the Leviathan, a serpent which holds all the dwellers of the lower waters between his two fins. The centre of the earth rests upon the huge serpents, which form food for the Leviathan. Every day he opens his mouth, and a huge serpent comes every day to feed him. It flies and flutters and enters the mouth of Leviathan, while God sports with it, as it is said, 'Thou hast created this Leviathan to sport with it.'

VI. (1) On the sixth day He brought forth from the earth all kinds of animals, male and female, and the Behemoth that lies on a thousand hills, from which it obtains its food every day. In the night-time the food grows again as if the hills had not been touched, as it is said, 'Its food is from the produce of the mountains, and it drinks from the waters of the Jordan;' for the waters of the Jordan encompass all the land of Israel, one half of which is above, and the other of which is below the earth, as it is said, 'For He can draw up the Jordan in his mouth.' The Behemoth is preserved for the day on which it is to be brought as a sacrifice on the occasion of the great banquet of the righteous, as it is said, 'Its Maker will approach it with His sword.' (2) Everything in the world was originally created before Adam, who was created last, on the sixth day, on the eve of Sabbath, lest people might say that God had a helper in the work of the creation.

(3) When God wished to create the world He called the company of angels commanded by the archangel Michael, and said unto them: 'Let us make man in our image, according to our likeness.' Whereupon they replied: 'What is man, that Thou shouldst remember him; and the son of man, that Thou shouldst think of him?' At this God immediately stretched forth His little finger among them and destroyed them, so that Michael alone was left.

He then called the company of angels commanded by Gabriel, and said: 'Let us make man in our image.' They also replied: 'What is man, that Thou shouldst remember him?' God again stretched forth His finger and destroyed them. (4) He then called Boël and his company, and said to them: 'Let us make man in our own image.' At which Boël said to his associates: 'See what has happened to those who said, What is man that Thou shouldst remember him? they were all destroyed. If we repeat what they have said, He will do the same to us, and in the end He will perform His will. It is therefore better that we comply with His wish.' They therefore immediately answered, and said: 'Lord of the world, it is well that Thou hast thought to create man; do Thou create him according to Thy will, and we shall act as attendants and servants upon him, and reveal unto him all our secrets.' (5) God then said to Boël: 'From this day henceforth thy name shall not be called Boël, but Raphael, because, through thy counsel, thou hast saved all thy host, so that they were not consumed like the other companies.' (6) God then called Gabriel, and said unto him: 'Go and bring Me dust from the four corners of the earth, and I will create man out of it.' Gabriel then went to gather dust from the earth, but the earth drove him away and would not allow him to take dust from it. Gabriel thereupon said: 'Why, O earth, dost thou not hearken to the voice of thy Lord, who founded thee upon the waters without props and without pillars?' The earth replied, and said: 'I am destined to become a curse, and to be cursed through man, and if God Himself does not take the dust from me, no one else shall ever do so.' (7) When God saw this He stretched forth His hand, took of the dust, and created therewith the first man on the sixth day. God created the matter of man in four colours, white, black, red and green. The bones and the sinews are white, the intestines black, the blood red, and the skin of the body green (livid). When the soul departs from the body, the body immediately becomes livid. (8) The Torah (Law) then said to God, 'O Lord of the universe, this man whom Thou hast created will be short-lived, and he will sin before Thee; what will become of him?' God replied: 'Is it to no purpose that I am called slow to anger, of abundant mercy and truth? He who returns to Me in repentance, I will pardon.' The Torah said, 'If so, do Thy will. (9) But why did God create man from the four corners of the earth, and not from the dust of one single spot?' 'Because man goeth to the four corners of the earth, and when he dies, the earth shall not be able to say, Thou wast not created from me, therefore thou shalt not be buried in me; go to the place whence thou wast created, and there be buried. Thus, wherever a man ends his days, there shall he rest. God created man poor and from dust, and to dust shall he return; therefore has the dust been taken from the four corners of the earth.'

(10) There are twelve hours in the day; in the first hour He gathered the dust for man, in the second He hardened it, in the third He shaped it in the form of man, in the fourth the soul was thrust into it, in the fifth man stood on his legs, in the sixth he gave names to all the birds and animals, in the seventh Eve was joined to him, in the eighth they produced two children, in the ninth they were commanded concerning the fruits of the trees, in the tenth he transgressed the command, in the eleventh he was judged, in the twelfth hour he was driven out, as it is said, 'And He drove Adam out of the Garden of Eden.' (11) God kneaded and moulded the dust for the first man in a pure place, He covered him with skin and sinews, and gave to it a human shape, but there was not yet any breath or soul in it. What did God do? He breathed with the breath of His mouth, and thrust the soul into him, as it is said, 'And He breathed in his nostrils the breath of life' Adam then stood up and gazed above and below, saw all the creatures which God had created, and was amazed with wonderment, and he began to extol and praise his Creator, and said: 'How great are Thy works, O Lord!' (12) He stood upon his feet, and was in the likeness of

God; his height extended from the east to the west, as it is said, 'Behind and in front Thou hast formed me.' Behind, that is the west, and in front, that is the east. All the creatures saw him and were afraid of him; they thought he was their creator, and prostrated themselves before him. Adam then said to the animals: 'Why do you come and prostrate yourselves before me? Come, let us all go and invest Him who created us with majesty and strength, and crown Him King over us. If the people do not show allegiance to the King, the King claims it by Himself, and if the people do not praise the King, the King causes Himself to be praised.' As soon as Adam had spoken, all the creatures assented and invested their Creator with majesty and strength, and proclaimed Him King over them, and said: 'The Lord the King is clothed with majesty.'

(13) Now, Adam walked about the Garden of Eden like one of the ministering angels. God said: 'Just as I am alone in My world, so is Adam; just as I have no companion, neither has Adam. To-morrow the creatures will say, "He does not propagate, he is surely our creator." It is not good for man to be alone, I will make a helpmeet for him.' (14) When the earth heard the word 'helpmeet' it shook and trembled, and said to its Creator: 'O Lord of the world, I am not able to provide for the whole of mankind.' To which God replied: 'I will feed the whole of mankind.' And God made a compact with the earth, and God created the sleep of life, so that when man lies down and goes to sleep, he is fed, strengthened and refreshed, and this is the healing and the feeding which God provides, as it is said, 'Then I slept, then I felt refreshed.' God moreover assists the earth and waters it, so that it yields its fruits as food for all the creatures; but, in spite of all this, man obtains his food in toil and trouble.

(15) God had pity upon Adam; in order not to give him pain He caused a deep sleep to fall upon him, during which time He took the bone of one of his ribs and flesh from his heart and made of it a helpmeet for him, and placed her before him. When he awoke from his sleep and saw

her standing before him, he said: 'This is woman; bone of my bone, and flesh of my flesh.' (16) While he was yet alone, he was called Adam. R. Joshua b. Qorḥa said that his name was Adam on account of the flesh and blood (of which he was composed). God said to him, 'Thou art Adam.' But when a helpmeet was made for him he was called Living Being—*i.e.*, Fiery Being (Heb. איש). God then added two letters of His name to it and made the name of man to be איש, and the name of woman אשה, saying, 'If they walk in My ways and observe My Commandments, behold My name will abide with them and deliver them from all trouble; but if not, behold I will take away My name from them, so that their names will become again אש, אש'—*i.e.*, fire consuming fire.

VII. (1) God created ten canopies for Adam in the Garden of Eden, and all of them were made of precious stones, of pearls and of gold. Each bridegroom has as a rule but one canopy, a king has three, but in order to show great honour to the first man He made ten canopies for him in the Garden of Eden, as it is said, 'Thou hast been in Eden, the garden of God; every precious stone was thy covering, the sardius, the topaz, and the diamond, the beryl, the onyx, and the jasper, the sapphire, the emerald, and the carbuncle, and gold; the workmanship of thy tabrets and of thy pipes (was prepared) for thee on the day when thou wast created.' These represent the ten canopies. The angels were beating their timbrels and dancing to the pipes, as it is said, 'The workmanship of thy tabrets and of thy pipes.'

(2) On the day when the first man was created God said to the ministering angels, 'Come, let us descend and show kindness to man and his helper, for upon kindness the world rests.' He further said, 'Kindness is much more acceptable to Me than the sacrifices of burnt-offerings which the Israelites are destined in the future to offer to Me upon the altar,' as it is said, 'For kindness do I desire and not sacrifices.' The ministering angels walked before Adam like shepherds who watch the flocks of birds, as it

is said, 'For He commanded His angels to watch over thee in all thy ways.' They were like unto a bridal pair, and God may be compared to a precentor, for just as the precentor in the midst of the congregation blesses the bridal pair under the canopy, so did God bless man and his helpmeet, as it is said, 'And God blessed them, and said unto them, Be fruitful and multiply.' And they did so, as it is said, 'And Adam knew Eve his wife; and she conceived and bore him Cain, and said, I have begotten a man of the Lord.' Why was Cain thus called? Because he was formed from Adam and his wife and from God.

I will now add here the description of the formation of a child by these three agencies, as it is contained in the book called יצירת הוולד (Yeṣirath ha-velad), which is as follows:

The Formation of the Child.

IX. (1) I will now proceed to explain the formation of the fœtus which God created when man approaches his wife. God indicates it to the angel appointed over conception, whose name is Lailah. God says, 'Know that this night a woman will conceive. Take this sperm, place it in thy hand, and break it on the threshing-floor into three hundred and sixty-five particles.' He does so. He then takes the sperm in his hand, brings it to God, and says, 'O Lord of the world, I have done as Thou hast commanded me, and now decree what is to become of it.' God then decrees that it will be either strong or weak, male or female, rich or poor, beautiful or ugly, long or short, wicked or righteous. (2) God then makes a sign to the angel appointed over spirits, and says, 'Bring me a certain spirit which is hidden in the Garden of Eden, whose name is So-and-so, and whose form is So-and-so.' This applies to all the spirits which are destined to be created, for from the very moment when the world was created all (these spirits) were prepared for men, as it is said, 'What has

already been has been called by name.' The angel brings
the (said) spirit, which, when it comes before God, bows
down and prostrates itself before Him. (3) At that
moment God says to the spirit, 'Enter thou this sperm.'
The spirit then opens its mouth, and says, 'O Lord of the
universe, I am satisfied with the world in which I have
lived from the day on which Thou didst create me; if it
please Thee, do not suffer me to enter this impure being, for
I am holy and pure.' God replies, 'The world which I will
cause thee to enter is better than the world in which thou
hast lived; and when I created thee, I created thee only for
this purpose.' (4) God then causes it to enter this new
being against its will. The angel then returns and causes
it to enter the womb of its mother. Two angels are prepared
to watch the embryo (during pregnancy). A light shines
upon the head of the child, by which it sees from one end of
the world to the other. (5) In the morning the angel takes
it, carries it into the Garden of Eden and shows it the
righteous men who sit there in glory with crowns on their
heads. The angel then says to the soul, 'My child, dost
thou know who these are?' 'No,' it replies. The angel then
says, 'These people whom thou seest here were formed like
thee in the womb of their mother. They went forth into
the world and observed God's statutes, therefore they
became worthy of this bliss. Know also that thou wilt at
the end of thy days depart from the world, and if thou
wilt be thought worthy to hearken unto the Law and the
Commandments then thou wilt be likewise worthy of sitting
with these in the place where I showed thee.'

(6) In the evening he carries it into Gehinnom, and shows
it the sinners, whom the wicked angels beat with fiery
staves. They cry 'Woe, woe!' but no mercy is shown them.
The angel then says to the soul, 'Dost thou know, my child,
who these are that burn?' 'No,' it replies. The angel
answers, 'These were of the same mean origin as thou art.
They went forth to the world and did not observe the
commandments and judgments of God. Therefore they
have come to this place of punishment. Know also, child,

that thou must ultimately quit this world.' (7) The angel walks about with it from morning until evening, and shows it every place which it is destined to tread, and the place where it will be buried. After this he shows it the world of the good and the world of the wicked, and in the evening he places it back again in the womb of its mother. God then encloses it within folded doors, as it is said, 'And He shut in the sea with doors, until it burst forth from the womb and became free.' It is further said, 'I will lay My words in thy mouth, and I will protect thee in the shadow of My hand.' God then said, 'Thus far shalt thou go, and no further;' and He sustains the child in the womb of its mother for nine months.

(8) At the end of that time the same angel comes and says to it, 'Come forth, for the time has come for thee to go forth into the world.' It replies, 'Have I not already told God that I am satisfied to remain in the place where I was accustomed to dwell? And He replied, "The place I will cause thee to enter is better than that world from which thou hast come." Now that it pleases me to remain here, why dost thou wish to remove me hence?' The angel replies, 'Thou must know that thou wast formed in the womb of thy mother against thy will, and now know that against thy will thou wilt be born, and wilt come forth into the world.' He then immediately strikes it, extinguishes the light, and brings it forth against its will. It then forgets whatever it had seen. As soon as it comes forth unto the world, it cries.

(9) And why does it cry? Because of the world it has left behind. For at that moment seven new worlds are awaiting it. In the first world it is like unto a king after whose welfare all people ask; all desire to see it and embrace it, and kiss it, because it is in the first year. In the second world it is like unto a swine which wallows in mire; a child does the same until it reaches two years. In the third world it is like unto a kid that skips and gambols about on the meadows. Thus, a child skips about here and there until it is five years of age. In the fourth world it is like unto a horse which strides along haughtily.

In the same way does a child walk along proud of his youth until he is eighteen years old. In the fifth world he is like unto an ass upon whose shoulders burdens are placed. In the same manner burdens are heaped upon man's shoulders; he is given a wife by whom he begets children. He must wander to and fro in order to obtain food for them until he is about forty years old. In the sixth stage he is like unto a dog, insolent and wandering about in all places for food: stealing and robbing in one place and enjoying it in another. In the seventh stage he is like unto an ape, whose appearance is changed in every respect. All the household curse him and desire his death. Even the young children make fun of him, and even the smallest bird wakes him from his sleep. (10) Finally, the time arrives for him to quit this world. When that time arrives the same angel comes beside him and says to him, What is thy name?' To which he replies 'So-and-so, and Why dost thou come to me to-day?' 'To take thee away from this world.' When he hears this he weeps, and his voice reaches from one end of the world to the other, but no creature hears his voice except the cock. 'Have I not already told thee,' he says, 'not to bring me forth from the world in which I have lived?' But the angel replies, 'Have I not already told thee that against thy will thou wast created, against thy will thou wast born, against thy will thou livest, and against thy will thou shalt die, also against thy will thou art bound to render account and reckoning before Him who said, and the world was made?'

(11) Behold, these are the four Divine hosts which God showed to Elijah the prophet, as it is said, 'And He said, Go out and stand upon the mountain before God.' God then said to Elijah, 'Behold, these are the four worlds through which man must pass. The great and strong wind is this world. After the wind comes the earthquake, *i.e.*, after this world comes death, which causes the whole body of man to quake. After the earthquake comes the fire, *i.e.*, after death there follows the judgment of Gehinnom,

which is fire, and after the judgment of Gehinnom there follows a voice, as it is said, 'A still, soft voice,' which is the voice of the last judgment. After this follows the judgment of the spirits that flit about in the air, and no one is left except God, as it is said, 'God alone shall be exalted on that day.' All this is included in the words of holy tradition spoken by David, King of Israel, who said, 'I was made in secret, I was formed in the nethermost parts of the earth.'

X. (1) The fear of God is the beginning of wisdom. Happy is the man in whom there is wisdom combined with fear; one may be doing more, another less, provided that his heart is turned to heaven. (2) Woe to him whom this world leads astray; woe unto him who does not walk in the ways of God; woe unto him who hearkens to his evil inclination, or who does not listen to his Creator; woe to him whose pleader becomes his accuser; woe unto him who does not devote his heart to his Father in heaven; woe to him whose wheel of life has turned; woe unto the man who has been righteous and has turned wicked; woe to him who loses his life's work in a rash moment, or causes the profanation of God's name.

(3) Certain punishments follow immediately upon the committal of sin, others come after a time. There are punishments which come one after the other, others simultaneously. Some punishments come upon man while he is asleep, others while he is awake; some come upon him heavily, others lightly; some affect part of the body, others the whole body; some, again, come upon one in his youth, while others come in his old age; some which he anticipates, others which he does not anticipate; some are open and some are hidden, others, again, are revealed to the whole world. And all the trouble, misery, and shame come upon man in consequence of sin and transgression. (4) Some bear their punishments with love; some worship God for fear of suffering in their sustenance or in their livelihood, or through the ill-health of their children, or through the punishment of Gehinnom. Some worship Him

in simplicity, in purity, in joy, and some in the hope that they may make others worthy of reward. Some, again, worship Him to guard themselves against punishments, as it is said, 'When they are in trouble, they seek Me early.' Everyone is judged while he is in full consciousness, and this applies to the living and the dead alike.

(5) When man is about to quit this world the angel appointed over him says, 'Pity this body that goes out of this world without having performed any good actions.' He looks at his two legs, and says, 'Woe unto those legs which have not walked in the ways of the Lord. Woe unto those thighs which have not been eager to run after God's Commandments. Woe unto the bowels which have enjoyed stolen property. Woe unto those hands which have occupied themselves with sin. Woe unto the mouth which has consumed the property of others. Woe unto the eyes which have desired the property of strangers. Woe unto those ears which have not hearkened to reproof. Woe to that proud stature that has not bent in repentance. Woe unto the spirit that has not humbled itself before its Creator.' (6) The angel in anger bids him stand up for judgment to relate his deeds. He says, 'Know whence thou hast come, and whither thou art going — to a place of dust and worms. Who is the Judge, and before whom art thou to give account and reckoning? If thou art able to answer, then answer, for no one else can answer for thee; there is no remedy except good deeds, as it is written, " Thy righteousness shall go before thee."' (7) What enjoyment can it be for man to look upon sin, since it is like fire to stubble, and like a sword to the neck, as an arrow to the liver, as chains to the feet, as darkness to the eyes, as gall to the mouth, and as chastisement to the body? Whoever induces another to swerve from the good path is cut off in the midst of his days, and whoever flatters a sinner, his days shall be shortened in this world. Whoever scoffs at the Commandments will have no mercy shown to him from heaven. (8) Whoever causes another to blush in

public will cause the book in which the sins of man are inscribed to be opened. Whoever scoffs at the poverty of the poor, behold he shall be brought low, he will be ahungered while others shall eat before him. Whoever commits fraudulent transactions shall have no rest on the eve of *the* Sabbath ; behold, all the joys which gladden his heart will be turned into mourning. He will be visited on the day of reckoning with terrible judgment and with much shame by relentless angels in the world to come. Therefore it is said, 'And what wilt thou do on the day of visitation ?' (9) He who sins with his eyes, those eyes shall become dim ; he who sins with his mouth, behold his words shall not be heard ; he who sins by giving false advice, behold his own prosperity shall vanish ; he who sins in his thoughts, his days shall be a constant vexation ; he who sins with his tongue, behold chastisement will overtake him ; he who sins with his hand shall lose his honour ; he who sins with his legs, the years of his life shall be shortened ; whoever sins in his heart shall die of grief ; whoever sins with his inclination, this very inclination shall turn his accuser ; he who sins and causes others to sin shall bury his wife and his children during his lifetime ; he who sins purposely, the decree of Divine judgment will be sealed against him ; he who sins unwittingly is not in a good moral condition.

(10) What benefit has a man by sinning? his ultimate end is to quit this world for another, to go from light to darkness, from life to death, from sleep which is sweet to a sleep that is troubled ; he is a prey for the worms ; he passes from sweet dainties to the taste of dust; from beautiful garments to the shroud in the grave. But this is not all : he moreover loses his soul. Many rich men have lost their souls through their riches, such as Dathan and Abiram; and the wisdom of many a wise man has caused him to come to grief, as, for instance, Ahitophel, Doeg the Edomite, and Balaam, the wicked one. Likewise many mighty men have existed whose power has been the cause of their fall, as Samson, Abner, Asael, and Joab. Many also have reared

sons, but have had no joy from them, as Aaron, the High Priest, who had no joy from Nadab and Abihu. All this applies equally to the righteous as well as the wicked; death overtakes them all. There were also many beautiful ones, whose beauty was the cause of their downfall, such as Absalom and Adonijah ben Ḥagith. There have been many elders of the community who have departed this life without honour, such as the great Sanhedrin in the time of Zedekiah, who were slain by Nebuchadnezzar. And again, how many young people have been snatched away from their bridal canopy! (11) Thus, what advantage can possibly accrue to man by robbing and stealing? for, although he may thereby derive some temporal comfort, he must nevertheless render account and reckoning before God. What benefit can man's joy be to him when it brings sorrow and grief upon him? What benefit is it for a man to inspire fear, since punishment will overtake him? What benefit his proud strut if it brings pains upon him? What benefit his evil meditation, which brings in its train many kinds of death? What benefit his deception, which dashes his prosperity to the ground? On account of this the righteous and the pious have no desire whatever for this world which is fleeting. But how do we know that this world is fleeting? Because it is said, 'For a wind has passed over it, and it is no more.'

(12) On the other hand, he is heir to the future world who keeps aloof from strife, from evil talk, from causeless hatred, from inciting quarrels, who is truly modest, who is devout in his prayer, and confesses his sins before God. He it is who is loved by God. Therefore the righteous have resolved to claim no honours, and to refrain from pleasure. They have therefore placed a check upon their eyes, their mouths, their hands, and their feet, to prevent them from doing evil. The eye which does not sin is worthy to behold the face of the Divine glory, as it is said, 'Thine eyes shall behold the King in his beauty.' The heart that does not sin shall be worthy to see the Divine glory with abundant joy. The hand that does not

sin will be worthy of receiving every reward, as it is said, 'Behold the Lord God shall come with strength, and give him mastery in his arm.' The mouth that does not sin will be worthy of singing praises before God, as it is written, 'And thou shalt say, On that day I will praise Thee, O God.'

XI. (1) R. Abahu told the parable of three different men. One tills the ground, another works in silver and gold, and the third studies the law. When the time approaches for him who tills the ground to die, he says to his household, 'Give me some of my work, so that I do not go to the next world empty-handed.' To which they reply, 'Thou art foolish. Hast thou not worked the field? and Scripture has already said, "The earth and its fulness belong to God," therefore thou hast nothing of thine own to bring.'

(2) When the end of him who works in silver and gold arrives, he says to his household, 'Give me some of my labour (work), that I may not go to the next world empty-handed.' But they reply, 'Thou art foolish. Thou hast worked in this world in silver and gold. Scripture has already said, "Mine is the silver, and Mine is the gold, saith the Lord;" therefore thou hast nothing of thine own to bring.'

(3) When the time arrives for him who studies the law (Torah) to quit this world, he says to his household, 'Give me of my labour, that I may not go to the next world empty-handed.' To him they say, 'O thou pious and righteous man, how can *we* give thee (the fruits) of thy labour? Hast thou not constantly occupied thyself with the law? But God will grant thee the reward of thy work, and shall receive thee with good grace. The ministering angels shall go forth to meet thee and exclaim, "Come thou in peace;" and concerning thee Scripture says, "Then shall thy light break forth as the morning."'

(4) Rabbi Jose says, 'If thou desirest to know the reward of the righteous in the world to come, come hither and learn it from what has befallen Adam. He was commanded to perform an easy precept, and because he transgressed it,

God punished him and all subsequent generations with many kinds of death. Therefore the sages have said that, on the contrary, whoever studies and observes the law and performs good deeds shall be delivered from the punishment of Gehinnom and the sorrows of the grave.' R. Abahu mentions one of the proverbial sayings of Rabbi Isaac that the end of man is death, the end of animals is slaughter, and all are destined to die. (5) R. Jose says, 'Come hither and see the difference existing between man and animals; the latter are slain and flayed, and are not subjected to any judgment: whilst with reference to man, how many chastisements and troubles does he bear in this world; and after his death, if he is a righteous man, his judgment is delayed; but if he is wicked, he is brought before the tribunal every year between Passover and Pentecost, as it is said, "And they shall go forth and look upon the carcases of the men, and it shall be at every new moon." (6) After man's death he is seen by all the other dead, and he appears to each just as they last saw him alive: some see him as a youth, others as an old man, just as each saw him before his own death, so that they should not think that any man lives for ever, and say when we were among the living we saw this or that man, and now how many hundreds of years have passed since we have seen them alive? (7) Therefore, when one dies the angel who guards the dead makes his soul assume various forms, so that all shall recognise him by seeing him just as they saw him in life. Then, in the event of one being condemned afterwards to Gehinnom, he is enveloped with smoke and brimstone, so that one should not see the punishment of the other; and none should be put to shame before the other, except those who have publicly put others to shame.'

(8) Every man after death is brought to judgment, even if he should belong to the section of the righteous, still, after a time his sins are visited. Thus Samuel said to Saul, 'To-morrow thou shalt be in my division.' Was not Samuel in Ramah, and Saul in another place? The

explanation is that he (Samuel) referred to the soul when he said, 'Thou wilt be with me in my division.' And we see that after a long lapse of time the house of Saul was judged on account of Saul and on account of the house of blood. Thus, the house of Saul was visited. Although he was called 'the chosen of the Lord,' yet His seed was judged.

XII. (1) R. Isaac ben Parnach has said that all man's iniquities are engraved upon his bones, as it is said, 'Their iniquities shall be upon their bones,' and all his merits shall be engraved upon his right hand, as it is said, 'The Lord is thy guard and thy protection on thy right hand.' (2) R. Joshua ben Levi says that man's merits and sins are not testified to until the day of his death. Even frivolous conversation, which is not accounted as a sin, is mentioned only at the time of his death, as it is said, 'For behold He who has formed the mountains and created the wind will tell man what his conversation hath been.' (3) Thus at his death three ministering angels come to him, one the angel of death, one a scribe, and a third who is appointed to accompany them. They say to him, 'Arise, for thy end has come.' To which he replies, 'I shall not rise, for my end has not yet arrived.' (4) Then the scribe proceeds to number his days and years. At that moment the man opens his eyes and sees the angel of death, whose length extends from one end of the world to the other; he quakes exceedingly and falls upon his face. (5) From the sole of his (the angel's) foot to the crown of his head he is full of eyes, his clothing is of fire, his covering of fire, he is surrounded by fire, he is all fire. In his hand he carries a fiery blade, from which hangs a bitter drop. This drop causes first death, then decomposition and the lividness of appearance, but man does not die until he has seen God, as it is said, 'For no man shall see Me and live;' but when he dies he shall see Him, as it is said, 'Before Him there shall bend all those who go down to the dust when he ceases to live.' (6) Then the man confesses everything he has done in the world. His mouth bears witness, and the Lord writes it down. 'By Myself have I sworn, saith the Lord, that from My mouth shall go forth righteousness.' (7) If he is a man of perfect righteousness his soul is handed over to its owner. But if a man of consummate wickedness, he stiffens his neck and allows his evil inclination to prevail over him; hence the sages have said that a wicked man's evil inclination prevails over him even at his death. (8) R. Eliezer has said that just as he is stiffnecked in this world so is he at the Day of Judgment, as it is said, 'The wicked shall see and be angry.' (9) At the death of the righteous man three companies of ministering angels come to him. The first company says, 'A righteous man has perished from the earth.' The second company says, 'Let him in peace come and rest upon their couches.' The third company says, 'He goeth the straight path.' (10) But at the death of the wicked five angels of destruction come to him and say, 'The wicked shall return to Sheol.'

The Beating of the Grave.

XIII. (1) R. Eliezer's pupils asked him, 'What judgment is there in the grave?' He replied, 'When a man quits this world, the angel of death comes to him and sits by his grave, and beating it with his hands, says, "Tell me thy name." "Flesh and blood is my name. It is revealed and known to Him who said, and the world was. But I do not know what my name is." Then immediately the soul re-enters his body. He stands up and is brought to judgment.' (2) R. Joshua ben Levi says, 'They bring a chain of iron, half of it burning like fire, half as cold as ice, and they beat him with it. At the first stroke his limbs get separated; at the second, his bones are scattered. Then the ministering angels gather them together, and restoring him, beat him a third time, and demand of him an account and reckoning, and judge him measure for measure. (3) On the second day they judge him in the same manner. (4) On the third day they judge him further, and they punish his two eyes, his two hands, his two feet and his two ears, his mouth and his tongue. Why are his eyes punished? Because he looked with them upon transgression. Why his ears? Because he heard sinful utterances with them. Why his lips? Because he uttered with them words of foolishness. And why his tongue? Because he has testified falsely with it. Why his two hands? He committed violence and robbery with them. Why his two legs? Because he hastened with them to transgression.' R. Jehudah says, 'Whoever has gone to a married woman shall hang ignominiously in Gehinnom; and whoever slanders his neighbour shall be suspended by his tongue. (5) R. Meir, in the name of R. Joshua, says, 'The judgment in the grave is more severe than that in Gehinnom, for in Gehinnom only they are judged who are thirteen years old and upwards; but in the grave, stillborn children and perfectly righteous men, and even sucklings, are brought to judgment.' Hence the sages have said, 'He who dwells in the land of Israel and dies on Sabbath eve at the time of the blowing of the Shofar, as long as the sun shines he shall not see the judgment in the grave; whilst he who loves righteousness and chastisement, charitable deeds and hospitality to strangers, although not living in the land of Israel, shall see neither the judgment of the grave nor that in Gehinnom, as it is said, "From the midst of trouble I called to God, and He answered me." "From my trouble" refers to the beating in the grave. "From the depth of Sheol I cried." This refers to the punishment in Gehinnom.' (6) Ben Azay says, 'There are three kinds of punishments, one more severe than the other; moreover, they are all inflicted in the presence of God.' 'But,' asks R. Aqiba, 'are they *all* in God's presence?' 'Verily the angels inflict the punishment in the grave and also that in Gehinnom, but only the punishment of heaven alone is inflicted in the presence of God!' Three days are given over to the punishment in the grave, three days to that in Gehinnom, and three days to the punishment in heaven. If there is no charge against a man, he is not brought up for judgment; but if there are charges against him, the judgment may last long. (7) The punishment of transgressing Israelites is twelve months in Gehinnom, as it is said, 'And it shall come to pass at the renewal of the new moon and at the renewal of the Sabbath.' Just as the weeks form a cycle, so the months form an annual cycle, and then shall all flesh prostrate themselves before God. R. Johanan ben Nuri says, 'The time extends from Passover until Pentecost, as it is said, "And from one festival to the other," during which the sabbaths are counted.' Some sinners are judged in Gehinnom from Passover until Pentecost, after which time they are acquitted; others, again, such as the consummately wicked of Israel, obtain no rest for the whole twelve months; (8) while others who have violated the whole of the law and the precepts and have sinned against the law of God, going the idolatrous way of the nations, shall have their bodies and souls burnt. Gehinnom vomits them out, and the north wind scatters them, so that they become ashes under the soles of the feet of the righteous, as it is said, 'And on account of the doings of the wicked, behold they shall become ashes beneath your feet on the day when I execute judgment.' (9) Further, those who leave the community, the apostates, traitors, renegades, scoffers, those who despise the festivals, deny the resurrection of the dead and the divinity of the law, are swallowed up by Gehinnom; the doors are locked upon them, and there they are left a prey to eternal punishment, as it is said, 'And they go forth and look upon the carcasses of those that have transgressed against Me, for their worm shall not die, neither shall their fire be quenched.'

THIS IS THE DESCRIPTION OF GEHINNOM (HELL).

XIV. (1) Who can stand before its might, who can withstand the fury of its wrath? R. Abahu opened his homily with the verse: 'Aluqah has two daughters called Hab, Hab.' R. Eliezer says that these are the two bands of angels that stand at the gates of Gehinnom and say, 'Come! come!' Why is it called Gehinnom (Valley of Wailing)? Because the voice of its wailing traverses the world from one end to the other. And why is it called 'Tofteh' (Enticer)? Because all enter therein enticed by their evil inclination.

(2) R. Joḥanan began his homily with the verse, 'Passing through the valley of weeping, they make it a valley of springs.' This means to say that the sinner confesses, just as the leper confesses; and he says: 'I have committed such and such a transgression in that place, on that day, in the presence of So-and-so, in that society.'

(3) Hell has three gates: one at the sea, the other in the wilderness, and the third in the inhabited part of the world. That at the sea is alluded to in Jonah: 'Out of the belly of Sheol cried I, and thou heardest my voice.' That of the wilderness is alluded to in Numbers: 'So they and all that appertained to them went down alive unto Sheol.' And that in the inhabited portion of the world in Isaiah: 'Saith the Lord, whose fire is in Zion and His furnace in Jerusalem.'

(4) Five different kinds of fires are in hell: one devours and absorbs, another absorbs and does not devour, while another, again, neither devours nor absorbs. There is further fire devouring fire. (5) There are coals big as mountains, and coals big as hills, and coals huge like unto the Dead Sea, and coals like huge stones. There are rivers of pitch and sulphur flowing and fuming and seething.

(6) The punishment of the sinner is thus: The angels of destruction throw him to the flame of hell; this opens its mouth wide and swallows him, as it is said, 'Therefore Sheol hath enlarged her desire and opened her mouth without measure, and their glory and their multitude and their pomp, and he that rejoices among them, descends into it.' This all happens to him who has not done one single pious act which would incline the balance towards mercy; (7) whilst that man who possesses many virtues and good actions and learning, and who has suffered much, he is

saved from hell, as it is said, 'Yea, though I walk through the valley of the shadow of death, I will fear no evil, for Thou art with me; Thy rod and Thy staff shall comfort me.' 'Thy rod' means the suffering, and 'Thy staff' signifies the law.

(8) R. Johanan began : 'The eyes of the wicked shall fail, and refuge is perished from them, and their hope shall be the giving up of the ghost.' That means, a body which is never destroyed, and whose soul enters a fire which is never extinguished; of these speaks also the verse, 'For their worm shall not die, neither shall their fire be quenched.'

XV. (1) R. Joshua, son of Levi, said, ' Once upon a time I was walking on my way, when I met the prophet Elijah. He said to me, "Would you like to be brought to the gate of hell?" I answered, "Yes!" So he showed me men hanging by their hair; and he said to me, "These were the men that let their hair grow to adorn themselves for sin." Others were hanging by their eyes; these were they that followed their eyes to sin, and did not set God before them. Others were hanging by their noses; these were they that perfumed themselves to sin. Others were hanging by their tongues; these were they that had slandered. Others were hanging by their hands; these were they that had stolen and robbed. Others were hanging ignominiously; these were they that had committed adultery. Others were hanging by their feet; these were they that had run to sin. He showed me women hanging by their breasts; these were they that uncovered their breasts before men, to make them sin. (2) He showed me further men that were fed on fiery coals; these were they who had blasphemed. Others were forced to eat bitter gall; these were they that ate on fast-days. (3) He showed me further men eating fine sand; they are forced to eat it, and their teeth are broken; and the Almighty says to them, "O ye sinners! when you used to eat that which you stole and robbed it was sweet in your mouth; now you are not able to eat even this," as it is said, "Thou hast broken the teeth of the wicked" (4) He showed me further men who are thrown from fire to snow, and from snow to fire; these were they that abused the poor who came to them for assistance; therefore are they thus punished, as it is said, "Thou hast caused men to ride over our heads; we went through fire and through water." He showed me others who were driven from mountain to mountain, as a shepherd leads the flock from one mountain to another. Of these speaks the verse: "They are appointed as a flock for Sheol. Death shall be their shepherd, and the upright shall have the dominion over them in the morning, and their form shall be for Sheol to consume, that there be no habitation for it."'

(5) R. Joḥanan said, For every sin there is an angel appointed to obtain the expiation thereof; one comes first and obtains his expiation, then follows another, and so on until all the sins are expiated. As with a debtor who has many creditors, and who come before the king to claim their debts, and the king delivers him to them, and says, 'Take him and divide him between yourselves,' so also is the soul delivered in hell to cruel angels, and they divide it among themselves.

(6) Three descend to hell for ever, and do not ascend any more—the man who commits adultery, who blames his neighbour in public, and who is guilty of perjury. Others say, Those who seek honour for themselves by slandering their neighbours, and those who make intrigues between man and wife in order to create strife among them.

(7) On the eve of the Sabbath the sinners are led to two mountains of snow, where they are left until the end of the Sabbath, when they are taken back from there and brought again to their former places. An angel comes and thrusts them back to their former place in hell. Some of them take, however, snow and hide it in their armpits to cool them during the six days of the week, but the Almighty says unto them, 'Woe unto you who steal even in hell,' as it is said, 'Draught and heat consume the snow waters, in Sheol they sin.' That means to say, 'They sin even in Sheol.'

(8) Every twelvemonth the sinners are burned to ashes,

and the wind disperses them and carries those ashes under the feet of the just, as it is said, 'And ye shall tread down the wicked, for they shall be ashes under the sole of your feet.' Afterwards, the soul is returned to them, and they come out black as the blackness of a pot, and they acknowledge the justice of their punishment, and say, 'Thou hast rightly sentenced us and rightly judged us. With Thee is righteousness and with us shame, as it is with us to-day.'

XVI. (1) There are five kinds of punishment in hell, and Isaiah, the son of Amos, saw them all. He entered the first compartment and saw there two men carrying pails full of water on their shoulders, and they pour that water into a pit, which, however, never fills. Isaiah said to God, 'O Thou who unveilest all that is hidden, unveil to me the secret of this.' And the Spirit of the Lord answered, 'These are the men who coveted the property of their neighbours, and this is their punishment.'

(2) He entered the second compartment, and he saw two men hanging by their tongues; and he said, 'O Thou who unveilest the hidden, reveal to me the secret of this.' He answered, 'These are the men who slandered, therefore they are thus punished.'

(3) He entered the third compartment, and he saw there men hanging by their organs. He said, 'O Thou who unveilest the hidden, reveal to me the secret of this.' And He answered, 'These are the men who neglected their own wives, and committed adultery with the daughters of Israel.'

(4) He entered the fourth compartment and saw there women hanging by their breasts, and he said, 'O Thou who unveilest the hidden, reveal to me the secret of this.' And He answered, 'These are the women who uncovered their hair and rent their veil, and sat in the open market-place to suckle their children, in order to attract the gaze of men and to make them sin; therefore they are punished thus.'

(5) He entered the fifth compartment, and found it full of smoke. There were all the princes, chiefs, and great

men, and Pharaoh, the wicked, presides over them and watches at the gate of hell, and he saith unto them, 'Why did you not learn from me when I was in Egypt?' Thus he sits there and watches at the gates of hell.

(6) There are seven compartments in hell, and in each of them are 7,000 rooms, in each room 7,000 windows, in each window (recess) there are 7,000 vessels filled with venom, all destined for slanderous writers and iniquitous judges. It is to that that Solomon alludes when he says, 'And thou mournest at thy latter end when thy flesh and thy body are consumed.'

(7) The other nations, however, and the idolators are punished in the seven compartments of hell, in each compartment for a twelvemonth. And the river 'Dinur' floweth from beneath the throne of glory and falleth over the heads of the sinners, and the sound travels from one end of the world to the other.'

(8) All these punishments are prepared for the apostates, for those who deny the resurrection of the dead, for the renegades, slanderers, and traitors. Of these King Solomon said, 'Their end shall be as bitter as wormwood.' None of these are saved unless they repent, acquire learning, and perform pious deeds. But at the end the Almighty will have pity on *all* His creatures, as it is said, 'For I will not contend for ever, neither will I be always wroth, for the spirit shall pass before Me and the souls which I have made.'

XVII. (1) There are besides in every compartment 7,000 holes (crevices), and in every hole there are 7,000 scorpions. Every scorpion has 300 slits (cavities); in every slit are 7,000 pouches of venom, and from each of these flow six rivers of deadly poison. When a man touches it, he immediately bursts, every limb is torn from him, his body is cleft asunder, and he falls dead upon his face. The angels of destruction collect his limbs, set them aright, and revive the man and place him upon his feet, and take their revenge upon him anew. This takes place in the uppermost compartment, which is called Sheol. The height thereof is 300 years' journey, the width 300 years' journey, and its length the same.

(2) The second compartment is Beer Shahat, of the same height, width, and length. The third is Tit-Hayaven, of equal size. The fourth is Sha'are Mavet, of the same size. The fifth, Abadon, of the same size. The sixth, Sha'are Salmavet, of the same size. The seventh, Gehinnom, of the same size. Thus the length of hell is altogether 6,300 years' journey. [We read further that the fire of Gehinnom is one-sixtieth of the fire of Sha'are Salmavet, and so of every consecutive compartment till the fire of Sheol.] Sheol consists half of fire and half of hail (ice), and when the sinners contained therein emerge from the fire they are tortured by the hail (ice), and when they emerge from the hail (ice) the fire burns them, and the angels who preside over them keep their souls within their bodies. As it is said, 'For their worm shall not die, neither shall their fire be quenched.'

(3) Every day the angel of death comes and drives them on like cattle from mountain to valley and from valley to mountain, as it is said, 'They are sent down to Sheol like sheep; death acts like a shepherd unto them.' The angels of destruction punish the sinners for twelve months in Gehinnom. After twelve months they revive their bodies and lower them to Sha'are Mavet, where they are again punished for twelve months. Thence they are lowered into Sha'are Salmavet, and after twelve months' punishment they are lowered into Tit-Hayaven, and again after twelve months' punishment they are lowered into Beer Shahat. Thence, after the same lapse of time, to Abadon, and finally, after twelve months' punishment, they are lowered thence into Sheol, where they are seen by the righteous, who say, 'O Lord, who art merciful to all Thy creatures, let it be enough for them!' But God answers, 'It is not yet enough, for they have destroyed My temple, and have sold My children as slaves among the nations.' Thence they are lowered to Arqa, and placed beneath the river of fire that flows from beneath the heavenly throne, and he who is lowered into Arqa ascends no more.

(4) Above Arqa is Tehom, and above Tehom is Tohu.

Above this is Bohu, and above Bohu is the sea, and above the bottom of the sea are the waters. Above the waters is the inhabited world, on the surface of which rise the mountains and dales. This earth is inhabited by man and beasts, by the birds of the air and the fish of the sea. Therein is law, charity, and piety, and the fear of the Lord.

(5) At the time of judgment 6,000 angels of trembling surround man and lead him to the place of judgment, where they weigh his merit and his guilt in the balance. Then if his guilt turns the scale they lead him to Gehinnom and hand him over to the angels of terror, and these again to the angels of anguish, and these to the angels of trembling; the angels of trembling then to the angels of destruction, who hand him over to the angel of death. He throws him into the depth of Gehinnom, as it is said, 'And the angel of the Lord pushes him.'

(6) If, however, his merits turn the scale, they lead him to the gates of Paradise and hand him over to the ministering angels, who hand him over to the angels of peace, and these to the angels of mercy, who bestow great honour upon him in the Garden of Eden.

PARADISE.

XVIII. (1) R. Joshua, son of Levi, tells, 'Paradise has two gates of carbuncle, and sixty myriads of ministering angels keep watch over them. Each of these angels shines with the lustre of the heavens. When the just man approaches them they divest him of the clothes in which he had been buried, and clothe him with eight cloths, woven out of clouds of glory, and place upon his head two crowns, one of precious stones and pearls, and the other of gold, and they place eight myrtles in his hand and praise him, and say to him, " Go and eat thy bread with joy." And they lead him to a place full of rivers (waters) surrounded by 800 species of roses and myrtles. Each one has a canopy according to his merits, as it is said, " For over all the glory shall be spread a canopy."

(2) ' And through it flow four rivers, one of oil, the other of

balsam, the third of wine, and the fourth of honey. Every canopy is overgrown by a vine of gold, and thirty pearls hang down from it, each of them shining like the morning star. (3) In every canopy there is a table of precious stones and pearls, and sixty angels stand at the head of every just man, saying unto him, " Go and eat with joy of the honey, for thou hast worked assiduously in the law," of which it is said, " And it is sweeter than honey," " and drink of the wine preserved from the six days of Creation, for thou hast worked in the law which is compared with the wine," as it is said, "I would cause thee to drink of spiced wine." The least fair of them is as beautiful as Joseph and Johanan, and as the grains of the pomegranate lit up by the rays of the sun. There is no night, as it is said, " And the light of the righteous is as the shining light."

(4) 'And they undergo four transformations according to the four watches of the day. In the first watch the just is changed into a child, and he enters the compartment of children and tastes the joys of childhood. In the second watch he is changed into a youth, and there he enjoys the delights of youth. In the third watch he becomes a middle-aged man and rejoices accordingly. In the fourth watch he is changed into an old man: he enters the compartment of the old and enjoys the pleasures of mature age.

(5) ' In Paradise there are eighty myriads of trees in every corner; the meanest among them choicer than a garden of spices. In every corner there are sixty myriads of angels singing with sweet voices, and the tree of life stands in the middle and overshadoweth the whole of Paradise; and it has 500 tastes, each different from the others, and the perfumes thereof vary likewise. (6) Over it hang seven clouds of glory, and the winds blow from all the four corners and waft its many odours from one end of the world to the other. Underneath sit the scholars and explain the law. These have each two canopies, one of stars and the other of sun and moon, and clouds of glory separate one from the other. Within this is the Eden containing 310 worlds,

as it is said, "That I may cause those that love Me to inherit Substance" (Prov. viii. 21) [the numerical value of the Hebrew word (שׁ) *Substance* is equivalent to 310].

(7) 'Here are the seven compartments of the just. In the first are the martyrs, as, for instance, R. 'Aqiba and his companions. In the second, those who were drowned. In the third, R. Joḥanan ben Zakkai and his disciples. The fourth group consists of those who were covered by the cloud of glory. The fifth group is that of the penitents, for the place occupied by a penitent not even a perfectly just man can occupy. The sixth group is that of children who have not yet tasted sin in their lives. The seventh group is that of the poor, who, notwithstanding their poverty, studied the law and the Talmud, and had followed a moral life. Of these speaks the verse, "For all that put their trust in Thee rejoice, and they shout for ever for joy.'

(8) 'And God Almighty sitteth in their midst, and expounds to them the law, as it is said, "Mine eyes shall be upon the faithful of the land, that they may dwell with Me." And God hath not yet fully unveiled the glory which awaiteth the pious in the world to come, as it is said, "The eye hath not seen, O God, beside Thee, that which Thou workest for him that waiteth for Him."'

XIX. (1) The sages tell that the dead have a large habitation, in front of which there flows a brook from the Garden of Eden, and by the side of this brook is a field. On every Sabbath eve between the afternoon and evening services the souls of the dead go forth from their secret abode and eat on this field and drink from this brook, (2) and every Israelite who drinks water between the afternoon and evening services of the Sabbath robs the dead. When the congregation on Sabbath eve exclaim, 'Bless the Lord, who is blessed,' they return to their graves, and God revives them, and causes them to stand upon their feet alive; (3) and all the dead of Israel rest on the Sabbath, and all stand up alive from their graves, and great multitudes come before God and sing praises unto Him upon their graves, and going to the synagogues, prostrate themselves before Him, as it is said, 'The pious exult in honour, and they sing upon their resting-places.'

(4) Every Sabbath and every new moon they rise from their graves, and coming before the Divine Presence, prostrate themselves before Him, as it is said, 'And the people of the earth shall worship Me, on Sabbaths and on the new moons.' What is meant by the people of the earth? Those who are hidden in the earth, as it is written, 'And it shall come to pass that on each new moon and upon each Sabbath all flesh shall come to worship Me.'

XX. (1) There are nine palaces in the Garden of Eden, and all of them consist of well-built houses with upper chambers, and the length of the houses is sixty myriads of miles. Each one of them is presided over by sixty myriads of ministering angels, and in each of these houses there are well-arranged canopies made of species of rose and myrtle trees. Every pious man has his place allotted to him according to his deeds, and to their appointed places the ministering angels lead them. There the angels of mercy dance and sing praises before him, as it is mentioned above. (2) In the midst of the Garden of Eden there are sixty myriads of species of trees, the fruit of which the pupils of the sages eat. There the light of the righteous is as the light of the sun, and sixty myriads of ministering angels attend them and feed them, while sixty myriads of angels of mercy sing and dance before them, and they bring spiced wine and the juice of the pomegranates, which they drink with delight. (3) R. Joshua ben Levi said, 'I saw in the Garden of Eden ten companies and (well) built houses, each one of which was twelve myriads of miles in length, one hundred and ten myriads of miles in breadth, and one hundred myriads of miles in height. (4) The first house was opposite the first entrance of the Garden of Eden, wherein there dwelt those proselytes who had converted themselves (to the Jewish religion) from love. The beams thereof were of white glass, and the walls thereof of cedar-wood. When I went to measure it, all the proselytes stood up and tried to prevent me, when Obadiah immediately rose and said to them, "Happy would ye be if you should be deemed worthy to dwell with such a righteous man." They thereupon allowed me to measure it. (5) The second house, corresponding with the second gate, is built of silver and its walls of cedar; therein do the penitent dwell, presided over by Manasseh. (6) The third house is built of gold and silver, wherein are to be found all the good things of heaven and earth, and wherein every kind of food and drink is arranged. In this house Abraham, Isaac, and Jacob dwell, as well as those who died in the wilderness— the generation of the wilderness, all the sons of Jacob, and the twelve tribes, with Moses and Aaron presiding over all of them. There also are David and Solomon and Caleb, who is alive, and every generation except those of Absalom and Korah. (7) I saw there precious stones, beds of gold and of precious stones, and couches and prepared lights. David exclaimed, "These are prepared for my children, who dwell in the world from which I have come." I then said to him, "Are not all the Israelites here?" At this our ancestor Jacob interposed and said, "All Israel are my children, and they are not like the other nations of the world, nor are they like the children of Abraham, my (grand)father, nor like the children of Esau, my brother; for whosoever of these performs good deeds in the world from which thou comest is rewarded there, and afterwards descends to Gehinnom; but my children, even the wicked among them, though they are punished, it is only during their lifetime, but after death they inherit the Garden of Eden." (8) The fourth house is built corresponding to the first man (Adam): its walls are of olive-wood, and those who dwell there are those who, though they have been punished in this world, have not rebelled against Providence. Why is this house built of olive-wood? Because their life had been bitter to them as olive-wood. (9) The fifth house is built of onyx stones and of precious stones. Its walls are of gold, and of fine gold, and it is perfumed with balsam. Thence the river Gihon flows forth and illumines the upper world; a fragrance breathes through it, which is more exquisite than the perfume of Lebanon. There are couches of gold and silver, covered with blue, purple, and vermilion covers woven together. In this place dwells the Messiah, the son of David and Elijah the Tishbite, and there is a palanquin of the wood of Lebanon, which Moses made in the wilderness [*i.e.*, the Tabernacle], covered (overlaid) with silver. Its floor is of gold and its seat of purple, and in the midst of this palanquin sits the Messiah, the son of David, the beloved one of the daughters of Jerusalem. Elijah takes him by his head, and placing him in his bosom, holds him and says, "Bear the judgment, O my master, for the end is near." (10) And every Monday and Thursday and every Sabbath and holy-day the patriarchs and the pious and the tribes, Moses and Aaron, David and Solomon, and all the kings of the house of David, come to him, and, weeping, take hold of him and say, " Oh, bear thou the judgment of thy Master, for the end is near." Korah and his company and Absalom come also to him every Thursday, and ask, "When is the end to come? When wilt thou return and bring us to life?" To which he replies, " Go ye to your ancestors and ask them." They are then abashed, and do not go to ask them. When I came before the Messiah, the son of David, he asked and said, "What are my children doing in the captivity?" And I answered, "Every day they await thee in their captivity among the nations of the world, which oppress them." He then lifted up his voice and wept.

XXI. (1) 'After this I implored him and said, "Do thou show me Gehinnom, which I desire to behold." But he would not allow me. And I said unto him, "Why wilt thou not let me see it?" To which the Messiah answered and said, "It is not meet for the righteous to see it, for there are no righteous people in hell." (2) I then forthwith sent to the angel Qipōd that he might measure hell from beginning to end; but he was not able to do so, because at that time R. Ishmael, R. Shim'on, son of Gamliel, and ten other pious men were put to death. I tried, but could not succeed. (3) After this, I went to the angel Qipōd, who went with me until I came before the fire at the gates of hell. The Messiah (also) went with me, and when the wicked in hell saw the light of the Messiah, they rejoiced and said, "This one will bring us forth from this fire." They showed me then a compartment in hell, which I entered, and, going round it, I measured it.' (4) R. Joshua said, ' When I measured the first compartment of hell, I found it to be one mile in length and breadth, and behold, there were many open pits in which were lions, and the lions were of fire. There were also two brooks, and when the wicked people fall therein, they are swallowed up, and lions of fire standing above cast them into the fire. (5) When I measured the second, I found it as the first, and I asked the same questions as I asked about the first, and they made the same reply. There were in it some of the nations of the world, presided over by Absalom, and one nation says to the other, " If we have sinned, it is because we did not wish to accept the law; but you, what sin have you committed?" And they reply, "We have committed the same sin as you." And they say to Absalom, "If thou hast not listened, thy ancestors have done so. And why hast thou then been punished in such a manner?" "Because," he replied, "I did not listen to the exhortations of my father." (6) An angel stands with a rod of fire, and this angel that smites them is named Qushiel. He orders the other angels to throw them down and to burn them, and one by one they are brought in, and after smiting them, they are cast upon the fire and burned until all the people have been consumed. After this, Absalom is brought in to be smitten, when a voice is heard to say, "Do not smite him nor burn him because he is one of the sons of those whom I love, who said on Mount Sinai, 'We shall do, and we shall hear.'" After they have finished smiting and burning the wicked these emerge from the fire just as if they had not been burnt; they are then smitten again, and again thrust into the fire, and this is repeated seven times every day and three times every night. But Absalom is saved from all this because he is one of the sons of David. (7) The third compartment contains seven nations of the world, who are judged in the same manner, and Korah and his company are with them. The name of him who smites them is Shabṭil (שבטיל). But Korah and his company are saved from all this, because they exclaimed on Mount Sinai, "We shall do, and we shall hear." (8) The fourth compartment contains four nations of the world, with Jeroboam to preside over them, and the one who smites them is named Maktiel. But Jeroboam is delivered from all these punishments, because he descended from those who exclaimed, "We shall do, and we shall hearken." (9) In the fifth house they are judged likewise. It contains seven nations, with Ahab among them, and he who smites them is named Ḥushiel. But Ahab is delivered from all this, because his ancestors said on Mount Sinai, " We shall do, and we shall hearken." (10) The sixth house, containing ten nations of the world, is judged likewise, and Micah is among them, and the angel who smites them is named Parhiel (פרחאל). But Micah is rescued from all this, because his ancestors also exclaimed on Mount Sinai, " We shall do, and we shall hear." (11) The seventh compartment contains six nations of the world, which are judged in the same manner, and among them is Elisha ben Abuya ; and so in all the compartments. But one cannot see the other on account of the darkness, for the darkness that existed before the creation of the world is now there.'

XXII. (1) Before Adam gave the animals their names God brought them before the angels, and said to them, ' Give names to everyone ;' but they could not. God thereupon brought them before Adam, and he gave them the names by which they were ever afterwards known. Then God said to the angels, ' Were you not saying, "What is man, that Thou shouldst remember him "? Now his wisdom is greater than yours !' The angels then began to envy him, saying, ' Indeed, God will now love him more than He does us ; if we can entice him to sin he will be destroyed from the earth. (2) Forthwith Samael, the angel of death, descended and looked at every creature, but he could find none as cunning and malignant as the serpent. The serpent then went to Eve, and began to speak of various things, until he broached the tree. 'Is it true,' he said, 'that God commanded you not to eat of any tree in the garden?' 'No; He only forbade us the one tree, which stands in the midst of the garden; we are not allowed to eat of its fruit, nor touch it, for on the day that we touch it we shall die.' (3) The serpent laughed at her, saying, 'It is only out of jealousy that God has said this, for He well knows that if you eat thereof your eyes will be opened, and you will know how to create the world just as He. Indeed, who can believe that for that thou shouldst die? Forsooth, I shall go and pluck (gather) some fruit.' The serpent accordingly stood on his feet and shook the tree, so that some of the fruit fell upon the ground; and the tree cried, 'O wicked one, do not touch me!' (4) When Eve saw the serpent touch the tree and not die, she said to herself, that the words of her husband were false. Therefore, on seeing that the fruit was beautiful, she desired it and ate of it. As soon as she had eaten thereof her teeth were set on edge, and she saw the angel of death with drawn sword standing before her. She then said in her heart, 'Woe unto me that I have eaten of this death, for now I will die; and Adam, my husband, who has not eaten of it will live for ever, and God will couple him with another woman. It is better that we die together, for God has created us together even unto death.' So when her husband came she gave him some of the fruit to taste. (5) As soon as he had eaten thereof his teeth were set on edge, and he saw the angel of death standing before him with drawn sword. 'What is this evil food,' he said to Eve, 'which thou hast given me to eat? perchance thou hast given me to eat of the tree of which I was forbidden to eat.' He was then exceedingly grieved. 'Why art thou so troubled?' she said, 'since what has happened was destined to happen.' She then thought, 'I and my husband are to die for having eaten of the fruit, whilst all the other creatures which have not eaten thereof will live on for ever in joy. It is better that we either die together or live together, since our Creator formed us together.' She therefore forthwith fed all the creatures of the world with the fruit—beasts, animals, and birds alike—until she came to a certain bird named Ḥōl (חול) or, as some say, Milḥam (so called because it had pity upon itself, and refused, in spite of her exceedingly strong persuasions, to eat of the fruit or to listen to her voice). Eve said, 'Eat of this fruit, just as thy fellows have done.' But it replied, 'Woe unto thee, thou afflicted one, who hast brought death upon thyself, upon thy husband, and upon all the creatures of the world. I alone remained to be killed by thee, but I swear that I shall never eat of that fruit.'

(6) According to another tradition, the bird Milḥam said to Adam and his wife, 'You have sinned, and have caused many others to sin; you are not satisfied with having brought death upon all the creatures of the world, but you wish me also to sin against God. Indeed, I shall not listen to you.' (7) At that moment a voice was heard saying to Adam, 'Thee I have commanded not to eat of the fruit, and thou hast not obeyed My commands, but Milḥam the bird I did not command to keep My ordinances and My decrees, yet he has fulfilled what I commanded thee; behold, I will establish him and his descendants for all generations to be an everlasting witness for Israel.' And therefore they live for ever, and exist in that city which the angel of death built, and they increase and multiply as all other creatures.

(8) The sages say that these birds live for ever, and that during the space of a thousand years they become smaller and smaller until they are like very young chickens, so that their feathers fall off, and their limbs are divided. Then God sends two angels, who restore them to their eggs as at first, and they feed them until they are grown up again. This is their natural change from one thousand years to another, so that they become revivified like the eagle.

XXIII. (1) Know and understand that, when Adam was separated for 130 years from Eve, he slept alone, and the first Eve—that is, Lilith—found him, and being charmed with his beauty, went and lay by his side, and there were begotten from her demons, spirits, and imps in thousands and myriads, and whomever they lighted upon they injured and killed outright, until Methushelah appeared and besought the mercy of God. (2) After fasting for three days, God gave him permission to write the ineffable name of God upon (his sword ?), through which he slew ninety-four myriads of them in a minute, (3) until Agrimus, the firstborn of Adam, came to him and entreated him (to stop); he then handed over to him the names of the demons and imps. And so he placed their kings in iron fetters, while the remainder fled away and hid themselves in the innermost chambers and recesses of the ocean. (4) Ḥanoch called his son Methushelaḥ, and said to him, 'All the men died (מתו), and they came into the power (שלט) of the angel of death.' When Methuselah died (מת), his missile (weapon, שלח) died with him, and they buried his sword with him. (5) It is said of Methushelaḥ that out of every word uttered by the mouth of God he used to make 230 parables in praise of God, and he studied 900 sections of the Mishna (Traditional Law). When he died, a voice of thunder was heard in the heavens, where the angels made a funeral oration, and they took him up, and the people saw 900 rows of mourners corresponding with the 900 sections of the Mishna, and the tears flowed from the eyes of the holy creatures on to the place where he died. (6) Enosh, the son of Seth, was asked, 'Who was thy father?' 'Seth,' he replied. 'Who was the father of Seth?' 'Adam.' 'And who was Adam's father?' 'He had neither father nor mother, but God formed him (shaped him) from the dust of the earth.' 'But man has not the appearance of dust.' 'After death man returns to dust, as it is said, "He will return to his dust"; but on the day of his creation man was made in the image of God.' 'How was the woman created?' He said, 'Male and female He created them.' 'But how?' asked they (his questioners). He answered, 'God took water and earth and moulded it together in the form of man.' They asked, 'But how?

(7) Enosh then took six clods of earth, mixed them, and moulded them and formed an image of dust and clay. 'But,' said they, 'this image does not walk, nor does it possess any breath of life.' He then showed them how God breathed into his nostrils the breath of life. But when He began to breathe into it, Satan entered the image so that it walked, and they went astray after it, saying, 'What is the difference between the bowing down before this image and before man?' That is what is meant when it is said, 'Then they began to apply the name of the Lord'; that is, they gave this name to other gods. On this account Enosh is mentioned in Scripture immediately before the word 'his image.'

XXIV. (1) And Cain knew Qalmana, his wife, and Enoch was born; and he built a city and called it Enoch, after the name of his son, and he used to entice the people, and to rob and plunder them. He built that city, and surrounded it with a wall and dug trenches. (2) He was the first to surround a city (with a wall), for he was afraid of his enemies. And this city, called by the name Enoch, is the first of all cities. He was, moreover, the counterpart of Enoch the righteous whom God took to Himself and trained for the day which is entirely Sabbath. (3) Cain dedicated the city to his son's name. When the city called Enoch was finished, it was inhabited by his children, who were about double the number of those who went forth from Egypt. Now the city became very corrupt until the other Enoch will arise, the seventh from Adam, and dedicate it anew with a holy dedication, together with the sons of Lemech, who slew Cain in the seventh generation, after Cain had confessed his sin, repented, and his punishment had been suspended until the seventh generation. (4) And Enoch begat Irad, and Irad Mehuyael, and Mehuyael Metushael, and Metushael Lemech, the seventh from Adam. They were all wicked, for all the descendants of Cain were called the seed of evil-doers, and all his descendants were swallowed up by the flood. (5) The wicked Lemech had two wives, 'Adah and Ṣillah, and 'Adah bare

Jabal; he was the father of such as live in tents and feed the cattle. He discovered the work appertaining to shepherds, and made tents and pens for the cattle, one for the sheep, and another for the oxen, distinct from each other. He also invented the locks which are made to prevent thieves entering the house, which are like unto this, χ. And the name of his brother was Jubal, the father of all who play on the harp and the reed-pipe. (6) At this time the inhabitants of the earth began to commit violence, to defile each other, and kindle the anger of the Lord. They began to sing with the harp and the reed-pipe, and to sport with all kinds of song corrupting the earth. This Jubal discovered the science of music, whence arose all the tunes for the above two instruments. This art is very great. (7) And it came to pass, when he heard of the judgments which Adam prophesied concerning the two trials to come upon his descendants by the flood, the dispersion and fire, he wrote down the science of music upon two pillars, one of white marble, and the other of brick, so that if one would melt and crumble away on account of the water, the other would be saved. (8) And Sillah bare Tubal Cain, who forged all the iron implements of war, and was an artificer in all kinds of ironwork. He also discovered the art of joining lead and iron together, in order to temper the iron and to make the blade sharper. He also invented the pincers, the hammer, and the axe, and other instruments of iron. Tubal was a worker in all kinds of tin and lead, iron and copper, silver and gold. Then men began to make graven images for worship. The sister of Tubal Cain was called Naamah. It was she who invented all kinds of instruments used for weaving and sewing silk, wool and flax, and the entire art of the fancy-worker and the weaver. (9) In the days of Enosh men began to be designated by the names of princes and judges, to be made gods, applying to them the name of the Lord. They also erected temples for them, but in the time of Re'u they were all overthrown. (10) It came to pass when man began to multiply upon the face of the earth, that the children of Elohim—that is, the seed of Seth—looked upon the daughters of man—that is, the seed of Cain—and they took them wives of all which they chose, and begat those giants that peopled the earth in the days of Noah. (11) During the whole lifetime of Adam the sons of Seth had not intermarried with the seed of Cain, but when Adam died they intermarried. The sons of Seth dwelt in the mountains by the Garden of Eden, while Cain dwelt in the fields of Damascus, where Abel was killed. For seven generations the descendants of Seth kept righteous, but thenceforward they became wicked. It was for this reason that God repented that He had made man. (12) From the seed of Seth and Cain there came forth the giants, who, from their haughtiness of spirit, fell and became corrupt, and were therefore swept away by the waters of the flood, and therefore they were called 'Nefilim' (the fallen). They claimed the same pedigree as the descendants of Seth, and compared themselves to princes and to men of noble descent—sons of Elohim, lords and judges. Concerning them it is said, 'Therefore like unto man ye shall die, and as like unto princes ye shall fall.'

THE MIDRASH OF SHEMḤAZAI AND 'AZAEL.

XXV. (1) R. Joseph was once asked what was the story of Shemḥazai and Azael, and he replied, 'When the generation of Enosh arose and worshipped idols, and when the generation of the flood arose and went astray, God was grieved that He had created man, as it is said, "And the Lord repented that He had made man, and He was grieved at heart." (2) Then two angels, whose names were Shemḥazai and 'Azael, appeared before God, and said, "O Lord of the universe, did we not say unto Thee when Thou didst create Thy world, 'Do not create man'?" as it is said, "What is man, that Thou shouldst remember him?" "Then what shall become of the world?" said God. They replied, "We will occupy ourselves with it." (3) God said, "It is revealed and well known to Me that if peradventure you had lived in that earthly world, the evil inclination would have swayed you just as much as it rules over the sons of man, but you would be more stubborn than they." "Give us Thy sanction, then, and let us descend among the creatures, and then Thou shalt see how we shall sanctify Thy name." "Descend," spake the Lord, "and dwell ye among them." Forthwith He allowed the evil inclination to sway them. (4) As soon as they descended and beheld the daughters of man that they were beautiful, they began to disport themselves with them, as it is said, "When the sons of Elohim saw the daughters of man," they could not restrain their inclination. (5) Shemḥazai beheld a girl whose name was Esṭirah (איסטירה). When he beheld her, he said, "Listen to my request." But she replied, "I will not listen to thee until thou teachest me the name by the mention of which thou art enabled to ascend to heaven." He forthwith taught her the Ineffable Name. (6) She then uttered the Ineffable Name and thereby ascended to heaven. God said, "Since she has departed from sin, go and set her among the stars"—it is she who shines brightly in the midst of the seven stars of Pleiades; for that she may always be remembered God fixed her among the Pleiades. (7) When Shemḥazai and 'Azael saw this they took to them wives, and begat children. The former begat two children, whose names were Heyya (הִיָּא), and Aheyya (אַהְיָא). And 'Azael was appointed chief over all the dyes, and over all kinds of ornaments by which women entice men to thoughts of sin.

(8) 'God then sent Meṭaṭron a messenger to Shemḥazai, and said to him, "God will destroy His world, and bring upon it a flood." Shemḥazai then raised his voice and wept aloud, for he was sorely troubled about his sons and his own iniquity. "How shall my children live, and what shall they eat, and if the world is destroyed what shall become of my children, for each one of them eats 1,000 camels, 1,000 horses, and 1,000 oxen daily?" (9) One night the sons of Shemḥazai—Heyya and Aheyyah—dreamt dreams. One

dreamt that he saw a great stone spread over the earth like a table, the whole of which was covered with writing. An angel descended from heaven with a knife in his hand and obliterated all the lines, save one line only with four words upon it. (10) The other dreamt that he saw a lovely garden, planted with all kinds of trees and beautiful things. An angel descended from heaven with an axe in his hand, and cut down all the trees, so that there remained only one tree containing three branches. (11) When they awoke from their sleep they were much confused, and, going to their father, they related their dreams. He said to them, " God is about to bring a flood upon the world, to destroy it, so that there will remain but one man and his three sons." They thereupon cried in anguish, and wept, saying, " What shall become of us, and how shall our names be perpetuated?" " Do not trouble yourselves about your names. Heyya and Aheyya will never cease from the mouths of creatures, because every time that men raise heavy stones, or ships, or any heavy load or burden, they will sigh and call your names." With this his sons were satisfied (quieted).

(12) 'Shemḥazai repented and suspended himself between heaven and earth, head downwards, because he durst not appear before God, and he still hangs between heaven and earth. (13) 'Azael, however, did not repent. He is appointed over all kinds of dyes which entice man to commit sin, and he still continues to sin. Therefore, when the Israelites used to bring sacrifices on the day of atonement, they cast one lot for the Lord that it might atone for the iniquities of the Israelites, and one lot for Azael that he might bear the burden of Israel's iniquity. This is the 'Azazel that is mentioned in the Scripture.'

XXVI. (1) Adam begat three sons and three daughters, Cain and his twin wife Qalmana, Abel and his twin wife Deborah, and Seth and his twin wife Nōba. (2) And Adam, after he had begotten Seth, lived 700 years, and there were eleven sons and eight daughters born to him. These are the names of his sons : 'Eli, Shēēl, Ṣurēi, 'Almiel,

Berokh, Ke'al, Nahath, Zarhamah, Sisha, Māhtel, and 'Anat
(אֱלִי שֵׁאָל עוּרִי עֲלֻמִיאֵל בְּרוֹךְ כְּאָל נַחַת זַרְחֲמָה צִישָׁא מַחְתֵּל עֲנָת);
and the names of his daughters are: Havah, Gitsh,
Harē, Bikha, Zifath, Hēkhiah, Shaba, and 'Azin. (3) And
Seth lived 105 years and begat Enosh. After he begat
Enosh, Seth lived 707 years and begat three sons and
two daughters. The names of his sons were: Elide'ah,
Funa, and Matath, and the names of his daughters were
Melila and Tēla. (4) And Enosh lived 180 years and begat
Qeinan; and after Enosh had begotten Qeinan he lived
715 years, and begat two sons, Ehor and Aal, and one
daughter, Qatēnath. (5) And Qeinan begat, after Mahalalel,
three sons, Hatak, Mōkro, and Lupa, and two daughters,
Hannah and Liba. (6) And after Yered, Mahalalel begat
seven sons, viz., Ṭeqa, Māya, Nēkhar, Mēli, Aesh, Uriel,
Luriūṭin, and five daughters, 'Adah, Nō'ah, Yebal, Ma'adah,
and Sillah. (7) After Enoch, Yered begat four sons, viz.,
L'ei'ad, 'Anaq, Sabkhē, Yeter, and two daughters, Zēzēkho
and Lēzēkh. (8) After Methuselah, Enoch begat five sons,
viz., 'Anaz, Lū'on, 'Akhaon, Pĕlēdi, and Elēd, and three
daughters, viz., Tūid, Lēfīd, Laēad. Then God desired
Enoch and took him away. (9) After Lemech, Methuselah
begat two sons and two daughters, viz., 'Enab, Rapo,
'Alumah and 'Amugah. And Lemech begat Noah, and said,
'This one will comfort us and give rest to the earth and
all its inhabitants when God will visit the earth with evil
on account of the wickedness of the evildoers.' (10) And
Noah begat three sons, Shem, Ham, and Japheth.
(11) Cain and his wife Temed dwelt in the land of Nod.
And Cain knew his wife Tūmēd when he was fifteen years
old, and she bore him Enoch, and he built seven cities and
called the first Enoch, after the name of his son. (The
names of the remaining six were): Maōlē, Lūed, Gōzeh,
Yeshbah, Qeled, and Yūbab. (12) And after Enoch, Cain
begat three sons, Ulaf, Lēzef, and Fuzal, and two
daughters, Sēṭa and Mahat. (13) And Enoch took Nība,
the daughter of Shem, to wife, and she bore him Zēra,
Qu'ith, and Maddaf. And Zera begat Methushael, and

Methushael, Lemech. (14) And Lemech took two wives. Ada bore Jabal, the father of all those who dwell in tents, and Jubal, the father of all who play upon the harp and the reed-pipe. (15) Then the inhabitants of the land began to commit violence and to defile the wives of their neighbours, thus kindling the anger of the Lord. And they then began to play upon the harp and the reed-pipe, and to sport with every kind of song, corrupting the earth. This same Jubal discovered the science of music, whence arose all the melodies for the two above-named instruments. This is a great science, as I have explained in its proper place (above). (16) And it came to pass, when Jubal heard the prophecy of Adam concerning the two judgments about to come upon the world by means of the flood, the dispersion and fire, that he wrote down the science of music upon two pillars, one of fine white marble and the other of brick, so that in the event of the one melting and being destroyed by the waters, the other would be saved. (17) And Ṣillah bore Tubal Cain, who used to sharpen all instruments of iron for war, and worked in all manner of iron. He also invented the art of alloying lead and iron together, so as to temper the iron and to make the blade sharper. He also invented the pincers, the hammer, and the axe, and all instruments of iron. (18) The sister of Tubal Cain was Na'amah. It was she who invented the art of weaving and sewing silk, wool, and flax, and the whole art of the fancy-worker and the weaver. Ṣillah also bore Miza and Tipa. Tubal was a worker in tin, lead, iron, copper, silver, and gold. Then men began to make graven images for their worship. (19) 'Adah also bore Jabal, who was the father of those who dwell in tents and attend to the flock. He discovered the work appertaining to shepherds, and made tents and pens for the cattle, one for the sheep and another for the oxen, distinct from each other. He also invented the locks, as a safeguard to prevent robbers entering the house, like this, χ. (20) In the time of Enosh men were called princes, judges, and made gods, applying to them the name of God; and temples were made for them, but they were overthrown in the time of Re'u. And Enoch—who was the author of many writings—walked with God, and was no more, for God had taken him away and placed him in the Garden of Eden, where he will remain until Elijah shall appear and restore the hearts of the fathers to the children. (21) And the flood took place, and Noah went forth from the ark and offered sacrifices, and the Lord, smelling the sweet savour, said, 'I shall no more curse the earth and smite every living being, but if they sin against Me, I shall judge them by famine, sword, fire, pestilence, and earthquake, and I shall scatter them hither and thither. And I shall remember this for the inhabitants of the earth until the end. And it shall come to pass, when the end of the world shall have arrived, that the light shall cease and the darkness shall weep, and I shall revive the dead and awaken those who slumber in the dust, and Sheol will repay its debt, and Abadon return its portion, and I shall requite the wicked according to their deeds and judge between the flesh and the soul. And the world shall rest in quietness (peace), and I shall destroy death for ever. The grave shall close its mouth and the earth shall no longer be without produce, nor shall its inhabitants be rooted out nor be defiled by iniquitous judgments, for there shall be a new earth and new heavens for an everlasting habitation.'

XXVII. (1) The sons of Jepheth were Gomer, Magog, Madai, Yavan, Tubal, Meshekh, and Tiras; and the sons of Gomar were Ashkenaz, Riphath, and Togarmah; and the sons of Yavan, Elishah, Tarshish, Kittim, and Dodanim. (2) The sons of Gomer were Ṭeled, Lud, Deber, and Led; the sons of Magog, Qashē, Ṭipa, Paruṭa, 'Amiel, Pinḥas, Golaza, and Samanâkh; the sons of Dedan, Shalom, Filog, and Ṭufliṭa; the children of Tubal, Fantônya and Aṭipa; the children of Tiras, Maakh, Ṭabel, Bal'anah, Shampla, Mēah, and Elash; the children of Melech, Aburdad, Horad, and Boṣrah. The children of Ashkenaz were Vekhal, Sardana, and Anakh; the children of Hēri, Eṣudad, Do'ath, Dēpasēat, and Ḥanokh; the children of Togarmah, Abihud, Shāfaṭ, and Yaftir; the children of Elishah, Zaaq, Qenath, and Mastizrida; the children of Zipthai, Mafshiel, Ṭina, Avla, and Jinòn. The children of Tisai were, Maqôl, Luon, Ṣilagtaba; the children of Dodanim, Iteb, Bēath, and Faneg. And of these the inhabitants of the land of Persia, Media, and those of the isles of the sea were divided. (3) And Faneg, son of Dodanim, was the first to ride the ships of the sea. At that time a third part of the land of Romidath was flooded. And his sons subdued Yedid; and the sons of Magog subdued Dēgel, and the sons of Madai subdued Biṭṭo; the sons of Yavan, Ṣēel; the sons of Tubal, Paḥath; the sons of Meshek, Nephṭī; the sons of Tiras, Roó; the sons of Dinim, Gudah. And Riphath without his sons conquered Gódò; and the sons of Riphath, Boṣrah; and the sons of Targômah, Phut; the sons of Elishah, Ṭablo; the sons of Tarshish, Meriba; and the sons of Kittim . . .; and the sons of Dodanim, Qaduba. Then did men begin to till the ground, and when the land was parched, they cried to God, and He caused a fructifying rain to descend. And it came to pass, when the rain descended, the bow was seen in the clouds. When the inhabitants perceived the sign of the covenant, they blessed the Lord. (4) The children of Ham were Cush, Misraim, Put, and Canaan; and these are the children of Cush, Sheba, Tudan, Vabni (?), Māipòn, Tinòs, Siliò, Ṭiluf, Gilug, Lipukh. The children of Canaan were Ṣidon, Andaïm, Reṣin, Simim, Óròin, Nimigim, Ḥamatim, Nipim, Ṭilas, Ilag, and Cushim. Cush begat Nimrod, who was the first giant in pride before God. Misraim begat Ludim, 'Anamim, Lehabim, Naftuḥim, Pathrosim, Kasluḥim, and Kaftorim. These began to build the following cities: Ṣidon and its villages, Risôn, Kiūza, Mazāger, Ashqalon, Debir, Qamo, Tilón, Lakhish, Sodom, Gomorrah, Admah, and Ṣebòim. (5) The children of Shem were Elam, Ashur, Arpakhshad, Lud, and Aran. The sons of Ashur were Gezròn, Ishai; and Arpakhshad begat Shelaḥ, and Shelaḥ begat 'Eber. Two sons were born to Eber: the name of the one was Peleg, for in his days the earth was divided, and the name of his brother, Yoqtan, who begat Almodad, Shalaphtra, Muzam, Riadura, 'Uzim, Diqalbel, Mimöel, Shabethfin, Havilah, Yobab. And the children of Peleg were Re'u, Rifud, Shafra, Aqòlôn, Zakar, Zifd, Gebi, Shuri, Shzēūr, Palabus, Rafa, Palṭia, Shafdifal, Shayish, Harṭman, Elifaz. These are the children of Peleg, and these are their names. They took to them wives of the daughters of Yoqtan, by whom were born sons and daughters, so that the whole earth was filled with them. (6) And Re'u took to him Malkah, the daughter of Ruth, to wife, and begat Serug. When the days of her pregnancy were drawing to an end, Re'u said, 'From this one will issue a child, in the fourth generation, whose throne will be established on high; he will be called a perfect righteous man, the father of a multitude of nations. His testimonies will not be forsaken, and his seed shall fill the world.' And Re'u begat after Serug seven sons, Abiel, Obed, Shalma, Dedazal, Qīniza, 'Akur, Nefesh, and five daughters, Qadima, Derifa, Sheifa, Firiṭa, and Tehilah. (7) After Naḥor, Serug begat four sons, Ṣillah, Diga, Sòba, and Pòra, and three daughters, Gizla, Hôglah, and Shelifa. And after Teraḥ, Naḥor begat six sons, viz., Rekab, Deriab, Berikhab, Shibalshaf, Nidab, and Qemuel, and eight (?) daughters, Yiskah, Tipa, Berona, Qaniṭa. He took to wife Amtalai, the daughter of Karnabo. (8) And Terah lived seventy years, and begat Abram, Naḥor, and Haran, and Haran begat Loṭ. (9) Then the inhabitants of the land began to prognosticate by the planets and to become astrologers and to practise divination. They also passed their sons and daughters through fire, but Serug and his sons did not walk in their ways.

XXVIII. (1) These are the generations of Noah in their lands, according to their families, and according to their tongues. After the flood they were spread over the earth according to their nations. The children of Ham then went and appointed Nimrod to be a prince and a chief over them; while the children of Japheth appointed Pinḥas to be a prince and a chief over them. And the children of Ham appointed for themselves Yoqtan as their prince and chief. (2) These three chiefs came and took counsel together to assemble all their people while Noah their father was yet alive. And all the people accordingly drew near to them, and were as one body, and peace reigned in the land. (3) It came to pass, 640 years after Noah went out of the ark, that each chief numbered his people. Pinḥas numbered the children of Japheth and the children of Gomar, and the total number of those which Pinḥas numbered was 5,800 ; that of the children of Magog under him, 6,200 ; that of Madai under him, 5,700 ; that of the children of Tubal, 9,400 ; and the children of Meshech, 7,200 ; the children of Riphath numbered 11,500 ; those of Togarmah, 14,400 ; those of Elishah, 14,900 ; of Tarshish, 12,100 ; of Kittim, 18,800 ; of Dodanim, 17,700. The number of the children of Japheth, the men of war and the armour-bearers, as Pinḥas their prince had numbered them was 142,000, besides women and children. (4) Nimrod the chief numbered the children of Ham under his sway, and found them to be 12,600 ; the children of Misraim under him were, 24,900 ; the children of Phut, 27,700; of Canaan, 82,900; of Sheba, 4,300 (?); of Ḥavilah, 24,800; of Sabta, 25,300; of Ra'amah, 30,600; of Sabtecha, 46,400. And the number of the children of Ham, according to the numbering of Nimrod the prince, was 492,000 valiant men who went out to war, besides the women and children.[1] (5) And the number of the children of Noah was 714,100. All these were numbered during the lifetime of Noah, and Noah lived after the flood 350 years. And all the days of Noah were 950 years, and he died.

XXIX. (1) Now, it came to pass, when the inhabitants of the land were already spread abroad, that they gathered together and journeyed from the East, and arrived at a valley in the land of Babylon, where they stayed. Then each man said to his neighbour, 'Behold the time is coming when at the end of days man will be separated from his neighbour, and brother from brother, and there will be war

---

[1] N.B.—Shem has evidently dropped out in the MS.

between us. Come, therefore, and let us build a city and a tower, the top of which is to reach heaven, and let us make for us a great name upon the earth.' (2) And each one said to his neighbour, ' Come, and let us make bricks, and let each one write his name upon his brick, and let us burn them, and each brick will be to us as a stone and the pitch for mortar.' Each one made his brick and wrote his name upon it, with the exception of twelve men, who did not wish to be with them. (3) These are the names of the men who were not in their counsel: Abram, Naḥor, Lot, Re'u, Tinuto, Ṣeba, Almodad, Jobab, Eṣer, Abïmael, Sheba, and Ofir. The people of the land seized these, and, bringing them to their princes, said, ' These are the men who have transgressed the counsel we have advised, and they do not wish to tread in our paths.' (4) The princes then said to them, ' Why did you refuse to make bricks, the same as the other people of the land?' And they answered, ' We shall not make bricks nor remain with you, for we know but one God, and Him we serve; even if you burn us in the fire together with the bricks, we shall not walk in your ways.' (5) The princes were very wroth thereat, and said, ' As they have spoken, so shall we do; for unless they act as we do, you shall cast them in the fire together with the bricks.' (6) And Yoqtan, the head of the princes, answered and said, ' We shall not do this, but we will grant them seven days, and then, if they desire to make the bricks with us, they shall live; but if they refuse, they shall die by the fire.' For he sought to save them from their hands, as he was the head of the house of their fathers, notwithstanding that they served the Lord. So the people did, and placed the transgressors in the prison, in the house of Yoqtan. (7) And it came to pass in the evening that Yoqtan the prince called fifty men of valour, and commanded them, saying, 'Gird yourselves, and this very night take these men that are imprisoned in my house, place them upon ten (twelve) mules, and, providing both the men and the animals with food, bring them to the mountains, and there remain with them ; but if you betray this thing to anyone, you shall die by fire.' (8) The men accordingly went forth to do as they were commanded. In the night they took them and brought them before Yoqtan the prince. He said to them, 'Ye who remain steadfast in God, trust in Him for ever, for He shall deliver you and save you. Therefore behold I have commanded these fifty men to take you to the mountains with provender and food, and there do you conceal yourselves in the valleys, for in the valleys there is sufficient water, and stay there for thirty days, for by that time either the thoughts of the people will have passed from you, or the anger of the Lord will be kindled against them so that He shall destroy them, for I know that they will not abide by their wicked counsel which they devised, for their plan will be frustrated. (9) And at the end of the seven days, when they seek you, I will say to them, "They have broken the door of the prison and fled during the night, and I sent a hundred men to pursue and seek them: I shall do all this to appease their wrath."' And eleven men answered him, saying, 'Behold we have found favour in thine eyes, for thou hast delivered our lives from the hands of our enemies.' (10) Abram alone was silent, and Yoqtan the prince said to him, 'Why dost thou not answer together with thy friends?' And Abram replied, 'Behold to-day we flee to the mountains to escape from the fire; but if wild beasts rush out of the mountains and devour us, or if food is lacking so that we die by famine, we shall be found fleeing before the people of the land and dying by our sins. Now, as the Lord in whom I trust liveth, I shall not depart from this place, wherein they have imprisoned me, and if I am to die through any iniquity, then I shall die by the will of God according to His desire.' (11) 'Thy blood be upon thine own head,' said the prince, 'if thou wilt not flee with these men; for if thou wilt flee thou art sure to be saved.' Abram replied, 'I shall not flee, but remain.' He was accordingly put into prison again, and the prince sent the eleven men away in charge of fifty others, whom he commanded to remain with them for fifteen days, and to return and say, 'We have not been able to find them.' 'If you do not do this I shall have you burnt to death.' (12) At the end of seven days all the people assembled and said to their princes, 'Give us the men who refused to abide by our counsel, and let us burn them in the fire.' They thereupon sent for them, but found only Abram. 'Where are those men who were bound in the prison of thy house?' asked the chiefs, Pinhas and Nimrod. Yoqtan replied: 'They broke away in the middle of the night and escaped, and I have sent a hundred men after them to discover and to slay them.' And the people exclaimed, 'Since we have only found Abram, let us burn him in the fire.' (13) And they took Abram and brought him before the princes, who asked him, saying, 'Where are the men whom we imprisoned with thee?' 'I do not know, for I slept all the night, and when I awoke I did not find them.' So they made a brick-kiln, and heated it until the bricks in it glowed fiercely; they then placed Abram in the furnace of fire, and Yoqtan appeased the wrath of the people by the burning of Abram. (14) The Lord at that moment caused a great earthquake throughout the land, so that the fire leaped from the furnace and became a huge blaze, which devoured all the men that surrounded it, and the number of men burnt on that day was 84,500. But Abram was not burnt, and he came forth from the furnace of the Chaldees (*i.e.*, the fire of the Chaldees), and, having escaped, he went to his friends upon the mountains and related all that had befallen him. They thereupon returned with him from the mountains, happy and rejoicing in the name of the Lord, nor did the people speak against them any longer. They thenceforward called the name of that place 'The God of Abraham.'

XXX. (1) It came to pass, after these things, that the people did not turn from their evil counsels, but coming to their princes, they said, 'Behold, will not man be able to conquer the world? Come and let us build for ourselves a city and tower, the top of which shall reach heaven, so that it shall stand for ever.' (2) And it happened, when they began to build, that God saw the city and the tower, and said, 'Behold this people is of one speech; now the earth will not bear them, neither will the heaven support them. (3) Therefore I shall scatter them over the whole earth, and shall confuse their tongue, so that one shall neither be able to recognise his brother nor understand the speech of his neighbour. (8) And I will order them to the clefts, and they shall prepare for themselves dwellings made of reeds and straw, and they shall dig for themselves caves and holes in the dust, and the beasts of the field shall dwell among them. There they shall remain all their days, and shall not again counsel such a deed. And I will fight (or: I will draw near unto) them with shields (or: thorns, בצנינות), and I shall destroy one portion by water and another by fire, and I shall destroy them with thirst, but Abram, My servant, I shall select; I shall bring him out of their land to the land upon which my eyes have long dwelt. (4) And when the people sinned and I brought a flood upon them, this land was not destroyed, for I did not cause the flood to descend upon it in My wrath, and I shall bring thither Abram, My servant, and shall make a covenant with him and his seed for ever, and I shall bless him and be to him a God for ever.'

(5) And it came to pass, when they commenced to build the tower, that God confused their tongue and changed their form into that of monkeys, so that one could not recognise his own brother nor could one man understand the language of his neighbour, so that when the builders ordered the people to bring stones they brought water, and when they told them to bring water they brought stubble. In this way their evil intentions were frustrated, and they ceased building the tower, and the Lord scattered them over the face of the whole earth. (6) For they had said, 'Come and let us build for ourselves a city, and let us take axes and break open the firmament so that the water flow from there and descend below, that He may not do unto us as He did to the generation of the flood. And let us wage war with those in heaven and establish ourselves there as Gods.' (7) But how could they build the city, since they

had no stones? They made bricks from clay and pitch, and burnt them as a potter burns his pots in the oven and hardens them. In this way they made the bricks, and built the city and the tower exceedingly high, with seventy steps. The ascent was made from the east and the descent was from the west. If a man fell therefrom they did not heed it much, whereas if a brick fell, they wept bitterly and said, ' When, oh, when, will another be brought up?' (8) When Abram saw their wicked ways he cursed them in the name of the Lord, but they did not pay attention to his words. The Lord then descended with the seventy (thousand) angels that surround His throne, and at that time of the dispersion He confounded their tongue into seventy different languages.

XXXI. (1) These are the generations of the sons of Noah: Shem, Ham, and Japheth. Children were born to them after the flood, for from Noah there came forth 72 families—from Japheth, 15; from Ham, 30; and from Shem, 27. And these 72 families were separated each according to his lineage in his own land, with their several nations, into 72 languages, the Hebrew language in Eber, the Egyptian in Egypt, the Greek in Greece, Latin in Rome, the Aramean in Syria, the Chaldean in Chaldea, etc. The nations which descended from Shem were 406, Briṭania, Qalabra, Tosqana, Luqa, Piqenṣa, etc. The whole earth was divided into three parts. (2) Shem, the eldest, chose his portion in the land of 'Asya (עֲסָיא), that is, the land of Persia, from Baqṭris to Endiana, from the Persian River until the Ocean in the west and the whole Rīnós. They numbered 27 languages, and 406 peoples. Ham took his portion in the land of Afriqia, which comprises Aram, Hamath, and the mountain of Lebanon, in a well-watered land, until the Red Sea and the Sea of Philistia, from Rīnós as far as Gadaira. The number of their languages was 22, and that of the peoples 394. (3) Japheth chose his portion in the land of Eoropa (אֱיאוֹרוֹפָּא), that is, in the south from Media to Bodeá (בּוּדְיָאה), and their boundaries extended from the mountains of Ṭaòrò (טאורו) and Manò (מָאנוֹ), in Syria and Sisilia, until the river Ṭanais (טָנָאס), until Gadaira, that is, the land of Eoropa (אִיאורוּפָּא, Europe). The number of their languages was 23, and that of their peoples 300. The land of Shem contained the river Euphrates; Ham, G(iḥón) which is called the Nile; Japheth, Hiddeqel (Tigris), in Media and Babylon. (4) The children of Japheth are Gomer, i.e., Gavathi (or Gãlãthi, נָאלָאתִי) and Regini; Magog, i.e., Sqitē (שְׂקְטִי) (Scythes), from whom arose Gog and Magog. These were the peoples which Alexander of Macedon enclosed in the Caspian Mountains; and from them arose the Guti (Goths), Pirāṭi (פִּירָאטִי), Nordmani (נוֹרְדְמָנִי), Bauvēri (בַּאוּבֵּירִי), Langobardi, Saqsonēi, Gasqonēi. Madai are: Mēdi, Yavan-Greṣi (גְרֵיצִי), Armenēi (אַרְמֵנְיָאִי), and Franṣi (פְרַנְצִי). The river of the Greṣi (גְרֵיצִי) is called Yoniñ. Tubal are Ibēri and Ispamia; Mēsech are the Qapadòṣes (קְפָאדוֹצֵש). The name of the city was formerly Mesekhah (מֵשְׂכָה), and the royal city was Qapadoqia (קפודקיא), now called Cæsarea (Kesari, קסרי), in the land of Kaftor; Tiras are Tráṣes (תְרָאצֵיש). The children of Gomer were Ashkenaz, in the land of the Greeks, or Greṣi (גריצי), Rifath (ריפת) is Paflagronas (Paphlagonians) (פָּאפְלַאגְרוֹנַש). Togarmah are the Frēzes (Phryges, פְרֵיזֵיש). The children of Yavan were Elisa' (אלישע), i.e., Eòlides (אִיאולִידֵש), and they are one-fifth of the Greek tongue. Tarshish is Sīlīṣīa (סִילִיצְאָה)—this is the Tarshish in the Book of Jonah—Kittim are Qipres (קִיפְרֵס), Dodanim are Rodiē (רוֹדִיאִי). All these live from the mountain Amone (אמוֹנִי) and Ṭaòrò (טאוֹרוּ), in Brittania, as far as the sea Oqeanòs. [Eliezer the Levite thought fit to add here the chapter, from the beginning of Jossipon the Great's work, because it is similar to the above; and this is the very beginning of the Book of Jossipon.]

(6) And the children of Japheth were Gomer, Magog, Madai, Yavan, Tubal, Mesekh, and Tiras; and these are the names of the countries of the children of Yapheth who were scattered at the time of the dispersion. The children of Gomer were the Frankos (פרנקוס), who inhabited the

country of the Frankos (פרנקוס), in the land of Franṣelni (פרנצלני), on the river Segna (שיגנא). Riphath are the Britanos (בריטנוס), who inhabit the land of Riphtania (ריפתניא), on the river Lira (לירא). The Segna and Lira both flow into the Ocean. Togarmah branched into ten families, who are the Cuzar (כּוּזָר), Paṣinaq (פּצינק), Alan (אלן), Bulgar (בולגר), Kanbina (כנבינא), Turq (טוּרְקְ), Buz (בוז), Zakhukh (זכוך), Ugar (אוגר), and Tulmeṣ (תולמין). All of these dwell in the North, and the names of their lands are taken from their own names, and they live by the river Hetel (התל); but Ugar, Bulgar, and Paṣinaq live by the great river called Danube (רָגוּבִּי), *i.e.*, the Dunai (דוּנַיִ). (8) The children of Javan are the Greeks, who dwell in the land of Nsa (נשא)[1] and Macedonia. (9) Madai, that is, Edalus (אִידלוּס), dwell in the land of Turkhan (טָרְבָּן or Kurasan (כּוּרָסָן).[2] (10) Tubal are the Tuscans (תּיּשְׁקַנֵי), who dwell in the land of Tuscania, by the river Pisa (פּיסָא); Mesech, *i.e.*, the Saqsoni (סקסני). (11) Tirus, *i.e.*, the Rossi (רוסי); the Saqsni (שקיסני) and the Iglesusi (אִינְגְלֶקְסִי) dwell by the river of the great sea. The Rossi dwell by the river Kiô (or Kiva, כיוא), which flows into the Gergan (גירגאן) Sea. (12) Elisa, *i.e.*, Alamania (אלמניא), inhabit the mountains of Iov and Sebtimo (יוב וישבתימו); and from them arose the Lungobardi (לְנגוֹבַּרְדִי), who came from the other side of the mountains of Iov and Septimo (יוב וישבתימו), and having conquered Italia, dwelt in it until this very day on the river Pao (פּאו), and Tiṣio (תצִיאוּ); and from them again arose the Borgonia (ברגוניא), who dwell by the river Rodano (רודנו), and the Bidria (בידריא), dwelling by the river Rinos (רינוס), which flows into the Great Sea. And the rivers Tiṣio and Pio (תציאו ופיאו) flow into the sea Venitiqia (בניטיקיא). (13) Tarshish, *i.e.*, the Trkisiani (תרקיסיאני), who accepted the law of the Macedonians; and from them come Trasos (תרשום). And it came to pass, when the Ishmaelites captured the land of Trasos, that its inhabitants fled to the land of Greece, and fought hence with the Ishmaelites in Trasos. (14) Kittim, *i.e.*, the

[1] [2] N.B.—These words scarcely legible in the MS.

Romans, who dwell in the valley Kapania (כפניא), by the river Tiberio. Dodanim (רודנים), these are the Danisqi (דנײשקי), who dwell in the midst of the tongues of the sea, in the land of Danemarka (דנמרכא) and Aṣidania (אצידניא ?), in the Great Sea, who swore not to serve the Romans, and they hid themselves in the midst of the waves of the sea; but they could not (withstand) them, for the power of Rome extended as far as the end of the isles of the sea. (15) And thus the Moraia (מוראיה), Bruti (ברוטאי), Sorbin (סורבין), Lusinin (לוצניו), Liumin (ליומן), Krākar (כראכר), and Bazimin (בזימין) are reckoned among the descendants of the Dodanim. They dwell by the seashore, from the border of Bulgar (בופנר) until Venitiqia (ביניטיקיא) on the sea, and from there they spread as far as the border of Saqsni (שקשני) to the Great Sea; they are called Isqlabi (איסקלבי). Some say they are descendants of Canaan, but they trace their descent to the Dodanim (רודנים). [Thus far the Hebrew of Josippon; from the next sentence beginning, 'And it came to pass when the Lord scattered,' etc., I shall copy in connection with Esau and the kings of Edom later on. Let us now return to the narrative of Jeraḥmeel.]

(16) The children of Shem were Elam 'Elamitēi (עילמיטט), Ashur, i.e., Assyria (אשׁירִיא); Arpachshad, i.e., Qaldea (קלדײאה); Lud, i.e., Lydia (לידיאה); and Aram, i.e., Syria (שׁירי). The children of Aram were 'Uṣ, where Job was born, Geter (נתר), Qarnani (קרנאני), Menes (מיגש). These dwell from the Persian Gulf until the Ocean. (17) The children of Ḥam were Cush, Miṣraim, Phut, and Canaan. Cush is called Ethiopia (אתיופיאה); Miṣraim, Egypt (איניפטא), Phut, Libia (ליביאה); and Canaan the Land of Israel. The children of Cush were Saba, Havilah, Sabta, Ra'amah, and Sabtecha. The children of Ra'amah were Sheba and Dedan. Sheba comprises the Sabeans, Arabians, and Indians (אינדיא); Havilah, i.e., Getili (גיתילי); Sabta, i.e., Asṭabari (אשטברי); Sabtecha and Ra'amah I have not been able to find. From the children of Ra'amah (came) the Queen of Sheba, and Dedan is a nation to the east of Cush. (18) And Cush begat Nimrod. The begin-

ning of his kingdom was Babylon and Erekh, *i.e.*, Edessa (אֶרֶךְ ,אִידֵיְשָׂא); Accad, *i.e.*, the city of Nisibis (נִיבִּיש). Kalnah, Selevqos gave to the city of Kalna the name of Selevqia (סליוקיא); from this land came Ashur, *i.e.*, Bel, the son of Nimrod. And Bel begat Ninus, who built the great city of Nineveh; and Rehoboth, *i.e.*, the wide city; and Miṣraim begat Ludim, and 'Anamim, and Lehabim, and the rest I do not know, for a war broke out between Ethiopia and Egypt, and all these nations were ultimately merged into one, so that they could no longer be distinguished. [And I, Eliezer, the scribe, have heard that the Lehabim are the Flaminga (וּלְמִיְנְגָא), and their appearance is like blazing fire, as it is said, 'And their faces are the faces of torches.'] And Canaan begat Sidon, his firstborn, by whose name the city of Sidon is called; it is in the land of Phēniṣe (פֵינִיצְ). The Hittites, Jebusites, Amorites, and Girgashites and Hivites were destroyed by the Israelites. 'Arqi, the city of 'Arqes (אָרְקִיָ), near Tripolis; Arvadi is the name of an island, Arvodios (אַרוֹדִיאוֹס); Ṣemari, *i.e.*, Edessa, in the land of Syria; Ḥamathi built Ḥamath, *i.e.*, Antochia. And the Canaanite boundary extended from Ṣidon, reaching as far as 'Azzah, and as far as Lesha, *i.e.*, Qaliron (קלירון). Its waters are warm, and flow into the Salt Sea. These are the sons of Ham, according to their families, their tongues, in their countries and provinces. (20) And Cush, the son of Ham, begat Nimrod, who was a mighty hunter in the land before the Lord. He caught men through his strength, and forced them to bow down to him, to make him a god, and to worship him. He therefore counselled the people to erect the city and the tower of Babel, where he established his kingdom, in order to rebel against God; and therefore, according to an ancient proverb, whosoever rebelled against the Lord was compared to Nimrod, the mighty hunter before God.

XXXII. (1) I, Jeraḥmeel, have found in the book of Strabon of Caphtor that Nimrod was the son of Shem; and when Noah was one hundred years old a son was born to him in his form and in his image, and he called his name

Jonithes (יוֹנִיתֻם). His father, Noah, gave him gifts, and sent him to the land of Itan (אִיתָן), of which he took possession as far as the sea of Eliochora (אִילִיאוֹבוֹרָא). And Nimrod the wicked went to Jonithes to learn of his wisdom, for the spirit of the Lord was with him. But Jonithes foresaw by means of astrology that the wicked Nimrod would come to him to take counsel with him how he could obtain sovereignty; he gave him the explanation of the four kings whom Daniel saw. And Jonithes said to Nimrod that the descendants of Ashur would reign first, *i.e.*, the children of Shem, as it is said: 'And the sons of Shem were Elam and Ashur.' (2) The beginning of Nimrod's reign was in Babylon, and there Nimrod begat Bel. At the time of the dispersion Nimrod departed thence, and allied himself with the children of Ham; therefore it is said, 'And Cush begat Nimrod.' (3) After Nimrod, Bel, his son, succeeded to the kingdom in Babylon, in the days of Serug. And Bel went to the land of Ashur, but did not capture it. When Bel died, Ninus, his son, succeeded him, and, capturing the land of Assur, reigned over it, and built Nineveh and Rehoboth; and the length of the city was a distance of thirty days' walk; it became the royal residence of Assur. From this land Assur, that is, Ninus, the son of Bel, the son of Nimrod, went forth. (4) Ninus vanquished Zoroastres the Wise, who discovered the art of Nigromancia, *i.e.*, Nagirā (נָגִירָא). He reigned in Bractia (Bactria), and had written down the seven sciences (or arts) on fourteen pillars, seven of brass and seven of brick, so that they should be proof against the water—of the flood—and against the fire—of the day of judgment. But Ninus vanquished him, and burnt the books of wisdom. (5) And Ninus wrote (?) another book of wisdom. When Bel, his father, died, he (Ninus) made an image in the likeness and form of his father, and called it Bel, after the name of his father; and he was always grieving at the loss of his father. He called all the gods Bel, after his name, as it is said, 'Nebo bowed Bel bent down.' Whosoever Ninus hated was pardoned when he came in the name of Bel and supplicated him for mercy. Thus, all the world honoured and worshipped the god Bel, and made obeisance to him. Some gods were called Baʻal, and there is a Baʻal Peʻor and a Baʻal Zebub. (6) In the forty-third year of the reign of Ninus Abraham was born, and on that very day the first King Pharaoh began to reign in Egypt, who was called Tibei (תִּיבִיאִי); and after him all the kings of Egypt were called Pharaoh until the reign of Ptolemy, the son of Lagos, in Egypt, after whom all the kings of Egypt were called Ptolemy (תלמי). All the kings of Assyria were called Antiochus; and all the kings of Rome were called Cæsar, after the name of Julius Cæsar, *until this very day*. (7) When Abraham was ten years of age, Ninus, the son of Bel, died, and his wife, Semēramit, reigned after him in Assyria forty-two years. After her there reigned Shimʻi (שִׁמְעִי), the son of Ninus, who built the city of Babylon. At that time all the kings were under the king of Assyria, *i.e.*, under Shimʻi, the son of Ninus, and whoever had greater power than his fellow-man forced the other to serve him (Shimʻi).

XXXIII. (1) As this is simply to be taken as a legend, we do not care to reconcile it with the other, which makes Abraham live in the time of Nimrod the Wicked. According to the latter we find that Nimrod acted as judge over him, since it is related that the whole household of Abraham's father were idol-worshippers, moreover they made idols and sold them in the streets. But when a man approached Abraham to sell him an idol, he would ask him, 'How much is this image?' 'Three manas,' he would reply. 'How old art thou?' Abraham would add. 'Thirty years.' 'Thou art thirty years of age, and yet worshippest this idol which we made but to-day!' The man would depart and go his way. Again, another would come to Abraham, and ask, 'How much is this idol?' 'Five manas,' he would say. 'How old art thou?' would Abraham continue. 'Fifty years.' 'And dost thou, who art fifty years of age, bow down to this idol which we made but to-day?' With this the man would depart and go his way.

(2) When Nimrod heard of Abraham's utterances, he ordered him to be brought before him, and said, 'Thou son of Terah, make me a beautiful god.' Abraham then entered his father's house, and said, 'Make a beautiful image for me.' They accordingly made it, finished it, and painted it with many colours. He went and brought it to Nimrod. [Here probably a lacuna in MS.] (3) And on that day Abraham's righteousness shone forth. It was a cloudy day, and rain fell. Therefore, when they were about to thrust him into the burning furnace, Nimrod sat down, and all the people of the dispersion did likewise. Abraham then entered, and standing in the centre, he pleaded his cause. After which Nimrod asked, 'If not the gods, whom shall I serve?' Abraham replied, 'The God of gods and Lord of lords, whose kingdom is everlasting in heaven and on earth, and in the heavens of the high heavens.' 'I shall worship,' said Nimrod, 'the god of fire; and, behold, I shall cast thee therein. Let, then, the God to whom thou testifiest deliver thee from the burning furnace.' (4) They then immediately bound him strongly and tightly, and placed him on the ground. They then surrounded him with wood on the four sides, 500 cubits thickness to the north, 500 cubits to the south, 500 to the west, and 500 to the east. They then set the pile on fire. (5) The whole house of Terah were worshippers of idols, and until that moment had not recognised their Creator. Their neighbours and fellow-citizens assembled, and, beating their heads, said to Terah, 'O shame—great shame! thy son, of whom thou didst say that he will inherit this world and the world to come has Nimrod burnt in the fire.' (6) Immediately then God's mercy was moved, so that He descended from the habitation of His glory, His greatness, His majesty, and the holiness of His great name, and delivered Abraham, our ancestor, from that shame, from that reproach, and from the burning furnace, as it is said, 'I am the Lord who brought thee out of the fire of the Chaldeans'; and since a miracle was wrought for our forefather Abraham, he and Terah were able to refute the generation of the

Dispersion, as it is said, 'Be wise, O my son, and let my heart rejoice, and then I shall be able to answer those who reproach me.'

XXXIV. (1) The sages tell that when our forefather Abraham was born a star appeared, which swallowed up four other stars from the four sides of the heavens. When the astrologers of Nimrod saw this they forthwith went to Nimrod and said, 'Nimrod, of a certainty there is born to-day a lad who is destined to inherit both this world and the world to come. Now, if it is thy wish, let us give his father and mother a large sum of money, and then kill him. Whatever his father and mother wish shall be given to them.' 'What kind of child is he whom ye seek to kill?' asked Nimrod. 'A boy,' said they, 'was born to-day, and a star appeared which swallowed up four stars of the heavens, and he is destined to inherit this world and the world to come.'

(2) Then said Terah, for Terah, the father of Abraham, was present there, 'This thing which you suggest is to be compared to a mule, to which man says, "I will give thee a quantity of barley, as much as a houseful, on condition that I cut off thy head." The mule replies, "Fool that thou art; if thou cuttest off my head, of what use will the barley be to me, and who will eat it when thou givest it to me?" Thus I say unto you, if ye slay the son, who will inherit the goods and the money which ye give to his parents?' To this they answered, 'From thy words we perceive that a son has been born to thee.' 'A son has been born to me, but he is now dead.' 'But we speak of a living son, and not of one dead,' added they.

(3) When Terah heard their words he immediately went home, and hid his son Abraham in a cave for three years. After that time he brought him forth. As soon as Abraham saw the rising sun in the east he said to himself, 'Of a certainty this is the lord of the whole world, and to him I pray; he created me and the whole world.' When he saw the moon he said, 'This is the lord of the whole world, and to him I shall supplicate; he created me and

the whole world.' Thus when evening came, and the sun had set and the moon had risen, he prayed to the moon the whole night. When, however, the morning came, the moon set and the sun rose. As soon as he saw the sun on the morrow Abraham said, 'Now do I know that neither the one nor the other is lord of the world, but that both of them are servants of another Master, and that is Lord who created the heavens and the earth and the whole world.'

(4) Then Abraham forthwith asked his father, 'Who created this world, the heavens, and the earth?' And Terah, his father, replied, 'This great image is our god.' 'If this is true,' said Abraham, 'I shall bring a sacrifice to him, and he will be pleased with me, as he is with other people.' He thereupon went to his father, and said, 'Make for me a cake of fine flour that I may offer it to him.' His father, complying with his request, made him a cake of fine flour, which Abraham took and offered before the great idol, saying, 'Accept this offering from me;' but he neither took it nor ate it nor drank it. (6) When Abraham saw this he went to his mother, and said, 'Make me a meal offering better than this, that I may offer it to the god of my father.' When she made it Abraham took the meal offering to the little image, saying, 'Accept thou this meal offering from my hand, and be pleased with me as thou art with other men.' Seeing that he did not reply, Abraham said, 'This offering has not been made to his liking.' (7) Then going once more to his mother, he said, 'Prepare a meal offering better still than this.' She did so, and Abraham presented the offering to the image. When he perceived that it neither ate nor drank nor answered him a word he went once more to the large image, and said, 'I entreat thee to receive this offering from me; do thou eat and drink and be pleased with me as thou art with other men.' But as neither of them replied to him, Abraham waxed very angry, and the spirit of prophecy rested upon him, and he said, 'They have eyes, but see not; ears, but hear not; they have hands, but do not move them; and feet, but do not walk; nor do their throats

give utterance. Like them are their makers and all those who trust in them.' He then kindled a fire and burned them.

(9) When Terah arrived home and found his idols burnt, he went to Abraham, and said, 'Who has burnt my gods?' And Abraham replied, 'The large one picked a quarrel with the little ones, and burnt them because he was angry with them.' 'Fool that thou art,' said his father, 'how canst thou say that he who cannot see nor hear nor walk, that he who has no power could burn them?' Then said Abraham to his father, 'O my father, hear what thy mouth utters; why dost thou forsake the living God who created the heavens and the earth, and servest gods that neither see nor hear?' (10) Thereupon Terah took Abraham, our ancestor, and went with him to Nimrod. And Terah said to Nimrod, 'O my lord the king, judge this my son who has burned my gods, and find out who is the God which he makes for himself.' 'Who is this man?' said Nimrod. 'My son.' Then added Nimrod, 'Why hast thou acted thus and burned the idols?' 'I did not do this, nor did I burn them,' said Abraham. 'Who, then, did act thus and burn them?' 'The great idol burnt them,' said he. 'Fool that thou art,' replied Nimrod. 'how canst thou say that that which cannot stand by itself, cannot hear nor see, nor hath any power could burn them?' 'Hear thou, my lord, what thy mouth utters. Why dost thou forsake the living God, who created the heavens and the earth and who created thee, and in whose hand is the Spirit of all living, and worshippest other gods of wood and stone, which do not hear nor see nor speak?' (11) 'Who, then,' said Nimrod, 'created the heavens and the earth, if not I?' 'Art thou he?' queried Abraham. 'I am,' replied he. 'Then by this I shall know that thou art the creator of everything. Behold, the sun rises in the east and sets in the west: if thou canst by thy command cause the sun to rise in the west and to set in the east, I shall then know and believe that thou didst create all.' When Nimrod heard Abraham's words he was

dumbfounded; he put his hand to his beard and was wonderstruck at his words.

(12) As soon as the astrologers saw Abraham they recognised him at once, and said to Nimrod, 'O lord the king, this is the child of whom we spoke on the day of his birth, and whom thou didst desire to slay. If it be thy will, we shall bring thee wood and burn him to death, and then compensate his parents with a large sum of money. Now, O lord, since he has come into our hands, let us burn him in the fire.' 'Do then your will,' said Nimrod. They forthwith went away, and having heated the furnace for seven (whole) days, cast him into it.

(13) Then spake the angels to God, saying, 'O Lord of the universe, let us go and deliver this man from the fiery furnace.' At that moment a dispute arose among the angels who said, 'Let us descend and deliver this man from the furnace.' One said, 'I shall go down to deliver him,' and another said, 'I shall go down to deliver him.' Michael said, 'I shall go down,' and Gabriel said, 'I shall go down.' Then spake God himself to Gabriel, and said, 'I am One in My world, and so is this man, who was the first to declare the unity of My name in the world. It is, therefore, meet that I the One should go down and rescue him who is also one in his generation. It is pleasing to Me to descend and rescue him from the fiery furnace.' At that moment God descended in His glory and in His strength, and delivered him from the furnace of fire. He brought him forth without a blemish. When all the nations saw that Abraham was thus delivered from the burning furnace, they forthwith sanctified the name of God, and some of them were made proselytes through the means of Abraham our ancestor.

XXXV. (1) These are the generations of Terah, etc.: Haran, the firstborn, begat Lot and Yiskah, *i.e.*, Sarai, and Milkah. And Haran died in the presence of his father Terah in Ur of the Chaldees. On account of the idols of Terah he died in the fire of the Chaldeans, for the Chaldeans worshipped the fire. Terah used to make the idols of their gods, and Haran, his eldest son, used to sell them. But Abram did not worship them. The Chaldeans came to dip both Haran and Abram in the fire, for they were accustomed to dip them in the fire, just as some nations dip their sons in the water. Abram, who did not worship, and who did not bow down to the idol, was saved from the fire of the Chaldeans and was not burnt; but Haran, who feared the idols, who honoured them and sold them for worship, was burnt in the fire of the Chaldeans and died. When Terah saw that God delivered Abram, he deserted his former faith, and went forth with him (Abram) to dwell in a foreign country; and he gave Milkah, the daughter of Haran, to Nahor, his son, to wife, and Yiskah, that is Sarai, he gave to Abram, his youngest son, after he had weaned her and brought her up in his own house on the death of her father Haran. And he gave Lot, the son of Haran, to Abram as an adopted son, for Sarai was barren. And they went forth towards the land of Canaan. (2) Now, it came to pass, when Abram came from Babylon—*i.e.*, Ur of the Chaldees—he betook himself to Damascus, he and his household, and was made king over that city; for Eliezer was then the ruler of Damascus; but when he saw that the Lord was with Abram he presented him with the kingdom and surrendered himself to his service. And I, Jerahmeel, have discovered in the Book of Nicolaos of Damascus that there existed a certain neighbourhood in Damascus called the dwelling-place of Abram. This they honoured exceedingly.

(3) And the Lord said to him (Abram), 'I am the Lord, who brought thee forth from the fire of the Chaldeans.' The sages say that when Nimrod the Wicked cast Abram into the fiery furnace, Gabriel said to God, 'I shall go down and cool the furnace, and deliver this righteous man.' But God replied, 'I am One in My world, and he is one in this world; it is therefore proper for the One to deliver the other one.' But since God does not withhold reward from any creature, He added to Gabriel, 'Thou shalt deliver three of his posterity.' For when Nebuchadnezzar cast Hananya,

Mishael, and 'Azaria, into the burning furnace Laqmi (לאקמי), the angel who rules over hail, spake to God, and said, 'I shall go down and cool the furnace, and thus deliver the righteous men.' But Gabriel interposed, and said, 'The greatness of God would not be shown in this manner, for thou art the ruler over hail, and all people know that water quenches fire; but I who am the ruler over fire shall go down and cool the inside while I am at the same time heating the outside of the furnace. Thus I shall perform a double miracle.' Then spake God to Gabriel, 'Descend.' And Gabriel at once exclaimed, 'The truth of God is everlasting.' (4) And Abram was rich in cattle, silver, gold, and in all the wisdom of 'hermetica' and astrology which he had acquired in Egypt from Pharaoh's magicians, so that there was none so wise as he. From Egypt these sciences spread over Greece. And Abram was able to foretell the future by the observance of the stars, and was very wise in astrology. He taught his magic science to Zoroastres, the philosopher, and he saw from the planets that the order of the world was not as before, for the order of creation was changed on account of the flood and the dispersion. Rabbi El'azar, of Modiin, asserted that Abraham was exceedingly great in magic, so much so that all the kings of the East and West waited upon him.

(5) And the Lord appeared unto him in the plains of Mamre. Josippon relates that Abram used to sit in an oak-tree, and that that oak lasted until the reign of Theodosius in Rome, when it withered, and despite the fact that it had dried up, yet its wood was excellent for medicinal purposes, for whoever took of its wood, whether animal or man, did not experience any illness to the day of his death.

(6) Then supervened the destruction of the cities of the plain. And Lot said, 'I am not able to flee to the mountain, for I am an old man, and the cold will kill me, and my soul is also weary. Behold there is a little city near to flee to; I pray thee let me escape thither, for the way is short, and my soul shall live.' And the name of the city had formerly been 'Bela'.' Now, there was a great earth-

quake; and Lot went and dwelt in a cave, for he feared the earthquake. And the Lord rained brimstone and fire from heaven upon Sodom, so that on the third day all the plain was filled with water. This they now call the Salt Sea, or 'Leber Meer' (לִיבֶּר מֵיר). Neither fish nor fowl are found there. It separates the land of Israel from Arabia. During the whole of the forty years the Israelites were in the wilderness they travelled round this sea. No ships are able to travel thereon, because the sea is like pitch, so that nothing can sink in it, but remains on the surface on account of the pitch; and if one places a burning torch upon the pitch, all the while it floats it burns, but as soon as it is extinguished it sinks to the bottom. And the sea vomits a kind of black pitch with which the things are joined together, for it is good for sticking. Josippon relates that he saw Vespasian cast a man into that sea, and that he hurled him with great force into it so that he should sink, but the sea brought him up again. The sand on the shores of the sea is salty, and one finds there the 'salty stones of Sodom' looking like pieces of marble.

(7) When Jacob was born Inachus was then the first King of Argos, and reigned for fifty years, and in the third year of his reign a daughter was born to Inachus whose name was Io, and the Egyptians gave her a surname and called her Izides (אִיזִידֶשׁ), and worshipped her as a God. (8) And in the nineteenth year of Jacob's life the Egyptians made Apis King of Egypt; they made him a god and called his name Sarapis. And Apis made for himself a calf by means of the magic of his magicians. On the right eye of the calf there was a white mark in the likeness of the moon, and once every day at the fourth hour it used to rise up from the river and fly in the air. And the Egyptians used to worship and pray and sing praises to it with all kinds of instruments, and prostrate themselves before it. And in a moment the calf vanished and was no more, and it was hidden and concealed as before in the river, so that the Egyptians could not see it until the morrow at the fourth hour. This the calf repeated every day. The Egyptians

called it Sarapis, and for this idol-worship the Egyptians were punished by water when they perished in the Red Sea. (9) In the ninety-second year of Jacob's life Joseph was born, and at that time there was a flood in the land of Achayā (אַכַיָא), which was a very large kingdom. There reigned in it a king whose name was Ogiges (אוֹגִיגִיס). This king built anew the city Akta (אַקְטָא), and called its name Eliozin (אִילִיאוֹזִין, Eleusis). At that time there arose a virgin, whose name was Titonide (טִיטוֹנִידֵי). She was versed in all the seven sciences. They called her Pallas, because she killed a giant called Palante (פלנטי). At that place the city of Palini (פְּלִינִי) was built.

XXXVI. (1) And a great terror was upon the cities that were round about them, and they did not pursue after the sons of Jacob; for they said, 'If two sons of Jacob were able to do this thing' (namely, to exterminate a whole town), 'how much more would they exterminate the whole world if all the sons of Jacob gathered together?' This terror of them fell upon the cities, for the Lord let the terror fall upon all the nations, and they did not pursue the sons of Jacob. The sages say, 'They did not pursue them during that same year, but after (seven) years they pursued them, for they came back and settled there again.' The kings of the Amorites assembled themselves, when they heard that Jacob and his sons had again settled in Shekhem. They came to slay them, saying, 'It is not enough for them to have killed all the men of Shekhem, now they come also to take possession of their land.'

(2) When Judah beheld them coming, he was the first to spring in the midst of their ranks, and was soon engaged in fight with Ishub, King of Tapuaḥ, who was covered with iron and brass from head to foot, standing in the middle of his lines (of soldiers). He rode a powerful steed, and he could throw his javelins with both hands from horseback, in front and behind, and never missed his aim even to a hair's breadth, for he was a mighty and powerful man, and could manage his spear with either hand. Judah was not at all frightened when he saw him, despite his strength,

but he picked up a heavy stone from the ground, weighing about sixty shekels, and threw it at him at a distance of two parts of a furlong; *i.e.*, 170 cubits and one-third of a cubit. Whilst the king was advancing against Judah, dressed in iron armour and throwing his spears, Judah struck him with the stone upon his shield and rolled him off his horse. (3) Judah hastened to approach him, in order to kill him before he could get up again from the ground, but the king rallied quickly and sprang upon his feet. Now he began to fight with Judah, shield against shield. He drew his sword and tried to smite the head of Judah, but Judah lifted up his shield and received the blow aimed at him; the shield broke into two pieces. Judah thereupon ducked and slashed with his sword at the feet of the king and cut them off from the ankles. The king fell to the ground and his sword slipped out of his hands. Judah sprang upon him and cut off his head.

(4) Whilst he was busy stripping him of his armour, nine comrades of the dead man attacked him. Judah broke the head of the first who approached him with a stone, and killed him on the spot. He let his shield drop out of his hand, which Judah seized, and defended himself with it against the other eight. His brother Levi came to his rescue and shot the King of Ga'ash with an arrow. Judah succeeded then in killing the eight. Jacob then killed (Zehori), King of Shiloh, with an arrow, and they could not stand against the children of Jacob, but all turned and fled, and the sons of Jacob pursued them. And Judah killed on that day a thousand men before sunset.

(5) The remaining sons of Jacob came out from Shekhem, from the side where they had been standing, and pursued them among the mountains, until they came to Ḥaṣor. There, before the town of Ḥaṣor, they had to fight more than they had fought in the vale of Shekhem. (6) Jacob shot with his arrows and killed Pir'athaho, King of Ḥaṣor, and Susi, King of Sartan, and Laban, King of Horan (or Ḥeldon, חלדון), and Shakir (or Shikkor), King of Mahna(im). Judah was the first to climb up the wall of Ḥaṣor. Four

warriors attacked Judah and fought with him, till Naphtali came to his rescue, for he followed Judah upon the wall; but before he came up, Judah had killed the four warriors. Judah stood now on the right side of the wall, and Naphtali on the left, and they killed all the people that were there. The other sons of Jacob jumped upon the wall after them, and destroyed it, and on that same day they took the town of Haṣor, and killed all the warriors, and they did not leave one single man. After that they carried away the booty.

(7) The following day they went to Sartan. There was a great multitude of people, and the fight was a very heavy one, for it was a town built upon a height, with high walls, and it was difficult to approach in consequence of these walls; yet they subdued it on that same day, and got upon the walls. The first to climb them was Judah, on the east, after him came Gad on the west, Simeon and Levi climbed up on the north, and Reuben and Dan on the south, whilst Naphtali and Issachar put fire to the gates of the town. The fight was very fierce upon the walls, and their remaining comrades went up to their assistance. They all stood now against a huge tower (wherein the inhabitants had fled, defying from there the assailants). That was before Judah had taken the tower. But he soon went up to the top of the tower and killed two hundred men on the roof, and the other sons of Israel killed the rest, not leaving one single man, for these were all powerful and valiant warriors. They carried away the whole booty and returned to their places.

(8) Now they went against Tapuah, for its inhabitants had tried to rob them of their spoil. First they killed all the men who had come out for the purpose of robbing them of the booty. Afterwards they rested on the waters of Jishub (ישוב), north of Tapuah. Early in the morning of the third day they marched towards Tapuah. Whilst they were gathering their booty, the inhabitants of Shilo came out and attacked them. But they were all beaten and killed before noon, and they entered with the fugitives

into Shilo, and did not allow them to stand up against the sons of Jacob. On that same day they occupied the town and carried away the spoil thereof. The troop of their company which they had left against Tapuaḥ came now to meet them with the booty from Tapuaḥ.

(9) On the fourth day they marched against the camp of Shakir (שביר). Some of the camp came out to rob them of the booty. They (the sons of Jacob) had gone down into the valley, and the (men from Shakir) ran after them, but when they tried to ascend again they were killed. After that the men from the camp of Shakir threw stones upon them; but the sons of Jacob occupied the town, and killed all the warriors, and added the booty from this town to the booty they had formerly collected.

(10) On the fifth day they went to Mount Ga'ash. There lived a great multitude of the Amorites. Ga'ash was a fortified town of the Amorites. They fought against it, but could not well subdue it because it had three walls, one wall inside the other. And the inhabitants began to defy and to reproach the sons of Jacob. (11) Judah waxed wroth, and he was the first to jump upon the wall. He would have met his death there had not his father Jacob come to his rescue. He first bent his bow and shot his arrows with his right hand, then he drew his sword and killed right and left, until Dan sprang upon the wall and assisted Judah. (From the right-hand side the inhabitants threw stones at him, and from inside they fought him, and they all tried to push him down the wall.) Dan drove them away from the wall. After Dan, Simeon, Levi and Naphtali came up, and they killed so many of the inhabitants that the blood flowed like a river. (And when the sun was near its setting they had taken the town and killed all the warriors) and they carried away the booty.

(12) On the sixth day all the Amorites came without arms and promised to keep peace (and friendship, and they gave unto Jacob Timna' and the whole land of Hararyah). Then made Jacob peace with them, and the sons of Jacob restored them all the sheep they had

captured from them, and in returning them gave double, two for one. And Jacob built Timnah (תימנה), and Judah built Zabel (זבאל). And from that time on they lived in peace with the Amorites. This it was that Jacob said to Joseph, "I have given thee a portion above thy brethren, which I took out of the hand of the Amorite with my sword and with my bow."

XXXVII. (1) And Esau went into a land away from his brother Jacob. He made a contract with him. Some say he went out of shame. The sages say: Esau went away because he had moved his property away, and not because his hatred had subsided, for "his anger did he bear perpetually and he kept his wrath for ever." Although he went away at that time, he came again to fight Jacob afterwards. Leah had just died, and Jacob and his sons were sitting in mourning, and some of his children had come to comfort him. At that time Esau came against him with a mighty host, all clad in iron and brass coats of mail, all armed with shields, and bows, and lances. They were altogether four thousand men, and they surrounded the fortress. Jacob, his sons, his servants, and his cattle, and all that belonged to them, were gathered, for they had all congregated to comfort Jacob during his mourning. (2) So they were all sitting peacefully, and never thought of any attack from any side whatsoever until that host approached the place where Jacob and his sons were dwelling. There were with them in all two hundred servants.

(3) When Jacob saw that Esau dared to war with him, and that he had come to take the fortress and to slay them, and that he shot arrows against them, Jacob stood upon the wall of the tower and spoke to Esau words of peace, friendship and brotherhood. But Esau did not heed them.

(4) After that, Judah spoke to his father Jacob, and said to him: "How long wilt thou speak unto him words of friendship and love, whilst he comes against us like an armed enemy, with coats of mail and with bows to slay us?" And immediately Jacob bent the bow, and killed Adoram

the Edomite. (5) And again he drew his bow, sent forth his arrow, and hit Esau on the right shoulder. Esau became weak from the wound, and so his sons took him up and placed him upon a white mule, and they carried him to Adoram, where he died. [Others say he did not die there.]

(6) And then came Judah, and Gad and Naphtali with him, out of the south side of the fortress, and fifty young men-servants of their father. And Levi, and Dan, and Asher came out from the east side of the fortress, and fifty servants with them. And Reuben, Issachar and Zebulun came out from the north of the fortress, and with them fifty servants. And Simeon, and Benjamin, and Enoch, the son of Reuben, came out from the west side of the fortress, and fifty servants with them. Joseph was not with them at that time, for he had already been sold.

(7) Judah strengthened himself for the battle, and he, Naphtali and Gad first rushed against the host. And they captured the iron tower (?), and caught on their shields the stones which were hurled at them. The sun was darkened through the stones, and through the arrows which were shot at them, and through the missiles which the catapults hurled at them. And Judah rushed first against the enemy, and killed sixty men. Naphtali and Gad went with him, one kept watch over him to the right, and the other to the left, guarding him lest he should be slain by the enemy. They also slew two men each, and the fifty servants who were with them helped them, and each of them slew his man, fifty in all. (8) And yet Judah, Naphtali and Gad could not drive away the host from the north side of the fortress, nor even move them from their position. Again they strengthened themselves for the battle, and each of them slew two of his adversaries. (9) And when Judah saw that they still kept their ground and that they could not move them from their place, his wrath was kindled, and he clothed himself with strength, and he slew twenty men, whilst Naphtali and Gad slew ten men. And when the servants saw that Judah, Naphtali and Gad were standing in the midst of the battle, they came to their assistance, and

fought together with them. Judah was slaying to the right and left, and Naphtali and Gad slew behind him. (10) At that time they drove the army away from the city, a distance of a furlong (Ris רים). And they wanted to bury (their dead), but could not do it. When the enemy saw that those who had fought against Judah had been dispersed by Judah and his brothers, they gathered together and strengthened themselves to fight with Judah and his brothers, and they arrayed their ranks to fight with strength and might. In the same manner Levi and those with him, and Simeon and those with him, prepared themselves for battle with those arrayed against them, and they were ready to fight for life or death.

(11) When Judah beheld that the whole army of the enemy had gathered against him, and that all would fight at one time, and that they stood in battle-array, he lifted up his eyes to God (imploringly) that He might help them, for they were very fatigued from the heavy fight, and they could not by any means fight any longer.

(12) At that moment God accepted Judah's prayer. He saw their trouble, and He helped them, for He sent forth a storm from His treasuries, which blew in the faces of the army and filled their eyes with darkness and obscurity, so that they could not see how to fight, whilst the eyes of Judah and his brothers were clear, as the wind came from behind them. So Judah, Naphtali and Gad began to slay them, and they felled them to the ground, like the harvest cut by the reaper, who binds it into sheaves and heaps them up into stacks. So did they do until they had destroyed the whole army which stood against them on the north side of the fortress.

(13) Reuben, Simeon and Levi fought on their side with another portion of the army. And after Judah, Naphtali and Gad had slain those who fought with them, they went to the assistance of their brothers. The storm was still blowing, filling the eyes of the enemies with darkness and obscurity. Thereupon Reuben, Simeon and Levi, and those with them, fell upon the enemies, and felled them

to the ground in heaps, whilst Judah, Naphtali and Gad were driving them before them, until all those were destroyed who fought against Levi and Reuben; and out of those who fought against Simeon four hundred were slain. The remaining six hundred ran away; with them were the four sons of Esau: Reuel, Yeush, Ya'alam and Korah. Eliphaz did not accompany them in the war, for Jacob had been his teacher.

(14) The sons of Jacob pursued them up to the city Merodio (Herodia). There in the citadel of Merodio they left the body of Esau lying on the ground, and they ran away to Mount Se'ïr, to the place leading up to 'Aqrabim. The sons of Jacob entered Merodio and encamped there over night. Finding there the body of Esau, they buried him out of respect for their father, Jacob. (Some say he did not die there, but left Merodio, though ill, and went with his children to Mount Se'ïr.)

The sons of Jacob armed themselves and pursued them the way leading to 'Aqrabim, where they found the children of Esau, and all those that had fled with them. They all came out, prostrated themselves before the sons of Jacob, and sued for peace. The children of Jacob made peace with them, and made them tributary for ever.

THIS IS THE WILL (TESTAMENT) OF NAPHTALI, SON OF JACOB.

XXXVIII. (1) When Naphtali grew old and came to an old age, and had completed his years of strength, and fulfilled the duty of the earth-born man, he began to command his children, and he said unto them, 'My children, come and draw near and receive the command of your father.' They answered, and said, 'Lo, we hearken to fulfil all that thou wilt command us.' And he said unto them, 'I do not command you concerning my silver, nor concerning my gold, nor concerning all my substance that I leave unto you here under the sun, nor do I command you any difficult thing which you may not be able to accomplish; but I speak to you about a very easy matter, which you can easily fulfil.'

(2) His sons answered, and said a second time, 'Speak, O father, for we listen. Then he said unto them, 'I leave you no command save concerning the fear of God; Him ye shall serve, to Him ye shall cling.' They said unto him, 'What need hath He of our service?' And he answered, 'It is not that God hath need of any creature, but that all the creatures need Him. Neither hath He created the world for naught, but that His creatures should fear Him, and that none should do to his neighbour what he would not have done to himself.' They then said, 'Our father, hast thou, forsooth, seen us departing from thy ways, or from the ways of our fathers, either to the right or to the left?' And he answered, 'God and I are witnesses that it is even as ye say; but I dread only the future, that ye may not err after the gods of strange nations; that ye should not go in the ways of the peoples of the lands, and that you should not join the children of Joseph; only the children of Levi and the children of Judah shall you join.'

(3) They said to him, 'What dost thou see that thou commandest us concerning it?' He answered, 'Because I see that in the future the children of Joseph will depart from the Lord, the God of their fathers, and induce the children of Israel to sin, and will cause them to be banished from the good land into another that is not ours, as we have been exiled through him to the bondage of Egypt. I will also tell you the vision I have seen. When I was pasturing the flock I saw my twelve (?) brothers feeding with me in the field; and lo, our father came, and said to us, "My children, go (run) and let everyone lay hold here before me on anything that he can get." And we answered, and said, "What shall we take possession of, as we do not see anything else but the sun, the moon, and the stars?" And he said, "Take hold of them." When Levi heard it, he took a staff (rod) in his hands, and jumped upon the sun and rode on it. When Judah saw it, he did in like wise; he also took a rod and jumped upon the moon, and rode on it. So also every one

of the nine tribes rode upon his star and his planet in the heavens; Joseph alone remained upon the earth.

(4) 'Jacob, our father, said to him, "My son, why hast thou not done as thy brothers?" He answered, "What availeth the woman-born in heaven, as in the end he must needs stand upon the earth?" Whilst Joseph was speaking, behold there stood near by him a mighty bull with wings like the wings of a stork, and his horns were like unto the horns of the Reëm. And Jacob said to him, "Get up, my son Joseph, and ride upon him." And Joseph got up and mounted upon the bull. And Jacob left us. For about four hours Joseph gloried in the bull; now he walked and ran, anon he flew up with him, till he came near to Judah, and with the staff he had in his hands he began to beat his brother Judah. Judah said to him, "My brother, why dost thou beat me?" He answered, "Because thou holdest in thy hands twelve rods, and I have only one; give them unto me, and then there will be peace."

(5) 'But Judah refused to give them to him, and Joseph beat him till he had taken from him ten against his will, and had left only two with him. Joseph then said to his ten brothers, "Wherefore run ye after Judah and Levi? Depart from them at once!" When the brothers of Joseph heard his words, they departed from Judah and Levi like one man, and followed Joseph, and there remained with Judah only Benjamin and Levi. When Levi beheld this, he descended from the sun full of anger (sadness). And Joseph said unto Benjamin, "Benjamin, my brother, art thou not my brother? Come thou also with me." But Benjamin refused to go with Joseph. When the day drew to an end, there arose a mighty storm, which separated Joseph from his brothers, so that no two were left together. When I beheld this vision, I related it unto my father Jacob, and he said unto me, "My son, it is only a dream, which will not come to pass (will neither ascend nor descend), for it hath not been repeated."

(6) 'Not a long period, however, elapsed after that before I saw another vision. We were standing all together

with our father Jacob, at the shore of the Great Sea. And, behold, there was a ship sailing in the middle of the sea without a sailor and a man (pilot). Our father said to us, "Do ye see what I am seeing?" We answered, "We see it." He then said to us, "Look what I am doing, and do the same." He took off his clothes, threw himself into the sea, and we all followed him. The first were Levi and Judah and they jumped in (to the ship), and Jacob with them. In that ship there was all the goodness of the world. Jacob said, "Look at the mast and see what is written on it; for there is no ship on which the name of the master should not be written on the mast."

(7) 'Levi and Judah looked up, and they saw there was written, "This ship and all the good therein belongs to the son of Berakhel (the one whom God had blessed)." When Jacob heard that, he rejoiced very much, bowed down and thanked God, and said, "Not only hast Thou blessed me on earth, but Thou hast blessed me on the sea too!" He then said, "My children, be men, and whatever each one of you will seize, that shall be his share." Thereupon Levi ascended the big mast and sat upon it; the second after him to ascend the other mast was Judah, and he sat upon it. My other brothers then took each his oar, and Jacob our father grasped the two rudders to steer the ship by them. Joseph alone was left, and Jacob said unto him, "My son Joseph, take thou also thine oar." But Joseph refused. When my father saw that Joseph refused to take his oar, he said unto him, "Come here, my son, and grasp one of the rudders which I hold in my hands, and steer the ship, whilst thy brothers row with the oars until you reach land." And he taught each one of us, and he said to us, "Thus ye shall steer the ship, and ye will not be afraid of the waves of the sea, nor of the blast of the wind when it shall rise against you."

(8) 'When he had made an end of speaking, he disappeared from us. Joseph grasped both the rudders, one with the right hand and one with the left, and my other brothers were rowing, and the ship sailed on and floated

over the waters. Levi and Judah sat upon the mast to look out for the way (course) the ship was to take. As long as Joseph and Judah were of one mind, so that when Judah showed to Joseph which was the right way, Joseph accordingly directed thither the ship, the ship sailed on peaceably without hindrance. After a while, however, a quarrel arose between Joseph and Judah, and Joseph did not steer any longer the ship according to the words of his father, and to the teaching of Judah; and the ship went wrong, and the waves of the sea dashed it on a rock, so that the ship foundered.

(9) 'Levi and Judah then descended from the mast to save their lives, and every one of the brothers went to the shore to save himself. Behold, there came our father, Jacob, and found us cast about, one here and the other there. He said to us, "What is the matter with you, my sons? Have you not steered the ship as it ought to be steered, and as I had taught you?" We answered, "By the life of thy servants, we did not depart from anything that thou hast commanded us, but Joseph transgressed the word (sinned in the affair), for he did not keep the ship right according to thy command, and as he was told (taught) by Judah and Levi, for he was jealous of them." And he (Jacob) said unto us, " Show me the place (of the ship)." And he saw, and only the tops of the masts were visible. But lo, the ship floated on the surface of the water. My father whistled, and we gathered round him. He again threw himself into the sea as before, and he healed (repaired) the ship, and entered it; and he reproved Joseph, and said, "My son, thou shalt no more deceive and be jealous of thy brothers, for they were nearly lost through thee."

(10) 'When I had told this vision to my father he clapped his hands and he sighed, and his eyes shed tears. I waited for awhile, but he did not answer. So I took the hand of my father to embrace it, and to kiss it, and I said to him, "O servant of the Lord, why do thine eyes shed tears?" He answered, "My son, the repetition of thy vision hath made my heart sink within me, and my body

is shaken with tremor by reason of my son Joseph, for I loved him above you all; and for the wickedness of my son Joseph you will be sent into captivity, and you will be scattered among the nations. For thy first and second visions are both but one." I therefore command you not to unite (combine) with the sons of Joseph, but only with Levi and Judah. I further tell you that my lot will be in the best of the middle of the land, and ye shall eat and be satisfied with the choice of its products. But I warn you not to kick in your fatness and not to rebel and not to oppose the will of God, who satisfies you with the best of His earth; and not to forget the Lord your God, the God of your fathers, who was chosen by our father Abraham when the nations of the earth were divided in the time of Phaleg.

(11) 'At that time the Lord—blessed be He!—came down from His high heavens, and brought down with Him seventy ministering angels, Michael being the first among them. He commanded them to teach the seventy descendants of Noah seventy languages. The angels descended immediately and fulfilled the command of their Creator. The holy language, the Hebrew, remained only in the house of Sem and Eber, and in the house of our father Abraham, who is one of their descendants.

(12) 'On that day the angel Michael took a message from the Lord, and said to each of the seventy nations separately, "You know the rebellion you undertook and the treacherous confederacy into which you entered against the Lord of heaven and earth, now choose to-day whom you will worship and who shall be your Protector in heaven." Nimrod, the wicked, answered, "I do not know anyone greater than those who taught me and my nation the languages of Kush." In like manner answered also Put, and Mizraim, and Tubal, and Javan, and Meseh, and Tiras; and every nation chose its own angel, and none of them mentioned the name of the Lord, blessed be He!

(13) 'But when Michael said unto our father Abraham, "Abram, whom dost thou choose, and whom wilt thou

worship?" Abram answered, "I choose and I will worship only Him who said and the world was created, Him who has created me in the womb of my mother, body within body, Him who has given unto me spirit and soul—Him I choose and to Him will I cling, I and my seed after me, all the days of the world." Then He divided the nations and apportioned to every nation its lot and share; and from that time all the nations separated themselves from the Lord, blessed be He! Only Abraham and his house remained with his Creator to worship Him, and after him Isaac and Jacob and myself. I therefore conjure you not to err and not to worship any other god than that one chosen by your fathers.

(14) 'For ye shall know there is no other god like unto Him, and no other who can do like His works in heaven and on earth, and there is none to do such wondrous and mighty deeds like unto Him. A portion only of His power you can see in the creation of man; how many remarkable wonders are there not in him! He created him perfect from head to foot; to listen with the ears, to see with the eyes, to understand with his brains, to smell with his nose, to bring forth the voice with his windpipe, to eat and drink with his gullet, to speak with his tongue, to pronounce with his mouth, to do work with his hands, to think with his heart, to laugh with his spleen, to be angry with his liver, to digest with his belly (stomach), to walk with his feet, to breathe with his lungs, to be counselled by his kidneys, and none of his members changes its function, but every one remains at its own.

(15) 'It is therefore proper for man to bear in mind all these things—to remember who hath created him, and who it is that hath wrought him out of a drop in the womb of the woman, and who it is that bringeth him out into the light of the world, and who hath given him the sight of the eyes and the walking of the feet, and who standeth him upright and hath given him intelligence for doing good deeds, and hath breathed into him a living soul and the spirit of purity. Blessed is the man who does not defile the Divine spirit which hath been put and breathed into him, and blessed is

he who returns it as pure as it was on the day when it was entrusted to (him by his) Creator.'

These are the words of Naphtali, the son of Israel, which he (commended) to his sons; they are sweeter than honey to the palate.

XXXIX. (1) After these things the wife of his master raised her eyes unto Joseph. Potiphar's wife, his mistress, used to entice him every day by her conversation, and used to bedeck herself with all kinds of ornaments and array herself in many dresses in order to find favour in his eyes. But he prevailed over his inclination. It was for this strength of mind that he became worthy of being made king and ruler over Egypt.

(2) One day all the Egyptian women assembled together to see Joseph's beauty. When Joseph was brought before them to wait upon them, his mistress offered each of them an apple and knife to peel it; but when they started peeling their apples they all cut their hands, since they were so much captivated with Joseph's beauty that they could not take their eyes from him. She (Potiphar's wife) then said, 'If you do this after seeing him but for one hour, how much more should I be captivated who see him continually?'

[Here I think it right to return to the book of Josippon at the place where we left, viz., the generations of Noah's sons. Josippon commenced to enumerate the generations of Adam, Seth, and Anosh, and gave a list of the names of the families of the children of Japheth, and the boundaries of their lands until Kittim and Dudanim, as I have written above, among the generations of Noah's sons. Afterwards he wrote the following, which I write down here, as it seems to belong to this portion.]

XL. (1) It came to pass when the Lord scattered the sons of man all over the surface of the earth that they became separated into different companies. The Kittim formed one company, and encamping in the plain of Kapanya (Campania כפניא), they dwelt there by the river Tiberio (תבריאו), while the children of Tubal encamped in

Toscana (תוישכנא), and their frontier was the river Tiberio. They built a city and called it Sabino (סבינו), after the name of its builders. And the Kittim also built a city for themselves, and called its name Poṣomanga (פוצומננא). Now, the children of Tubal were overbearing to the Kittim, and said, 'They shall not intermarry among us.' But it happened at the harvest time, when the children of Tubal had gone to their fields, that the young men of the Kittim gathered together, and, going to Sabino, they took their daughters captives, and then climbed the mountain of Kaporiṣio (כפוריציאו). As soon as the children of Tubal heard of this they arrayed themselves in battle against them, but could not prevail over them on account of the height of the mountain, so they gathered all the young warriors to the mountain.

(2) In the next year the children of Tubal went out again to battle, but the Kittim brought up all the children that were born of their (Tubal's) daughters upon the wall which they had built, and said, 'You have come to fight against your own sons and daughters; are we not now your own bone and flesh?' At this they ceased fighting, and the Kittim gathered together and built a city by the sea which they called Porto (פורתו), and another which they called Albano (אלבאנו), and yet another which they named Arēṣah (אריצה).

(3) In those days Ṣefo (צפו), the son of Eliphaz, fled from Egypt. Joseph had captured him when he went up to Hebron to bury his father. It was then that the children of Esau tried to entice him to evil, but Joseph prevailed over him and (capturing) Ṣefo from them, brought him to Egypt. After the death of Joseph, Ṣefo fled from Egypt, to Africa, to Agnias (אנניאס), King of Carthage, where he was received with great honour and appointed captain of the host.

(4) At the same time there lived a man in the land of the Kittim, in the city of Poṣomanga (פוצומננא), named 'Uṣi (עוצי). He was to the Kittim as a vain god. He died and left no son, but only one daughter, named Iania (יניאה).

She was beautiful and very wise, nor was the like of her beauty to be found in all the land. Agnias sought her for his wife, as did Turnus, King of Benevento (בנבנטו); but they (the Kittim) said to the latter, 'We cannot give her to thee, because Agnias, King of Afriqia, seeks her; we fear lest he wage war against us, and in that case thou couldst not deliver us from his power.'

(5) The inhabitants of Poṣomanga (פוצומנגא) then sent a letter to that effect to Agnias. Thereupon he mustered all his host and came to the island of Sardinia (איסרדניא). Palos, his nephew, went out to meet him, and said, 'When thou askest my father to come to thy assistance, ask him to appoint me the head of the army.' Agnias did so, and came into the province of Astiras (אישתיראיש) in ships. Turnus went out to meet him, and a very severe battle ensued in the valley Kapanya (Campania), in which Palos, his nephew, fell by the sword. Agnias then embalmed him, and having made a golden human image (mask ?), placed him therein. After that he once more set his men in battle array and captured Turnus (טורנוס), King of Benevento, and having slain him, made a mask (image) of brass, and placed him therein. He then built a tower in the highway in his honour, and another for Palos, his nephew, and called the one 'The tower of Palos,' and the other 'The tower of Turnus,' and the latter were separated by a marble pavement, which remains unto this day. They were built between Albano (אלבנו) and Rome. Agnias then took Iania to wife and returned to his own country. From that day henceforth Gondalas (גונדלוס) and the armies of the kings of Afriqia used to ravage the land of the Kittim for spoil and plunder, Ṣefo (צפו) always accompanying them.

(6) When this Ṣefo, the son of Eliphaz, travelled from Afriqia (אפריקיא) to the Kittim, the inhabitants received him with great honour, and presented him with many gifts so that he became very rich. And the troops of Afriqia (אפריקיא) spread themselves over all the land of the Kittim, and they having assembled, ascended the mountain of Kaporiṣio (Campo-Marzio ?) (כפוריציאו) on account of the

troops of Gondalos. (7) One day one of the herd of Ṣefo was missing, and after starting in search of it he heard the lowing of a bull in the neighbourhood of the mountain. On going to the bottom of the mountain, he discovered a cave with a great stone placed at its mouth. When he removed the stone he beheld to his surprise a huge animal devouring the bullock. From the middle downwards it presented the likeness of man, while from the middle upwards that of a goat. Ṣefo instantly sprang upon it, and split its head open. The inhabitants of Kittim then said, 'What shall be done for the man who has slain the beast that continually devoured our cattle?' On a festival day they assembled together and called his name Janus, after the name of the beast. They offered him drink offerings on that day and brought him meal offerings, and from that time they named the day 'The festival of Janus.'

(8) When the troops of Gondalos once more invaded the land of the Kittim for plunder, as heretofore, Janus went out against them, and having smitten them and put them to flight, he delivered the land from their raids. The Kittim then assembled and appointed Ṣefo to the throne of the kingdom. The Kittim then went forth to subdue the children of Tubal and the nations round about. And Janus their king went before them and subdued them. After this Ṣefo was called Saturnus, in addition to Janus: Janus after the name of the beast, and Saturnus after the name of the star which they worshipped in those days, *i.e.*, the planet 'Shabtai' (Saturnus). (9) He reigned at first in the valley of Kapanya, in the land of the Kittim, and built an exceedingly large temple there. He then extended his kingdom over the whole of the Kittim, and over all Italy. Janus Saturnus, after a reign of fifty-five years, died and was buried.

(10) His successor was Piqos Faunos (פיקוס פאונוס), who reigned fifty years. He also erected a huge temple in the valley of Kapanya, and soon after died. His successor was named Latinus; it was he who explained the language and its letters. He likewise built a temple for his dwelling, and

many ships. He went to battle with Astrubel (אסתרובל), the son of Agnias, whom Iania bore him, in order to take his daughter Yaspiṣi (יספיצי) to wife, as Agnias had done to the Kittim when he took Iania from them in battle. And this woman was very beautiful, so much so that the men of her generation weaved her image upon their clothes in honour of her beauty. A fierce battle ensued between Astrubel, King of the Carthaginians, and Latinus, King of Kittim, and Latinus captured the fountain of water which Agnias, when he took Iania, had brought with her to Carthage.

(11) For Iania the queen, when arriving there, was taken ill, and Agnias and his servants were sorely grieved. Agnias said to his wise men, 'How can I cure Iania's illness?' His servants replied, 'The air of our land is not like unto that of Kittim, nor our waters like theirs. Therefore the queen is ill through the change of air and water, for in her own land she only drank the water drawn from Forma (פורמה), which her ancestors drew upon bridges (aqueducts).' Agnias then ordered his ministers (princes) to bring water from Forma in Kittim in a vessel. They weighed these waters against all the waters of Africa, and found that only those of Goqar (גוקר) corresponded with them. Agnias then ordered his princes to gather together stonemasons by thousands and myriads. So they hewed a vast number of stones for building; and, being in great numbers, they built a bridge (an aqueduct) from the fountain of the water as far as Carthage. All these waters were for the sole use of Iania, who used them for drinking, baking, washing clothes, ordinary washing, and for watering all the seeds which provided her food. They also brought earth from Kittim in many ships, as well as stones and bricks, and they built therewith temples. All this they did for the great love they bore her, for through her wiles she charmed the people, and through her they called themselves blessed, and she was to them as a goddess.

(12) Now, it happened when Latinus waged war with Astrubel that he overthrew part of the bridge, so that the

troops of Gondalos were exceedingly furious, and fought desperately. Astrubel being mortally wounded, Latinus by main force captured Yaspiṣi (יספיצי), his daughter, for his wife. He brought her to Kittim and made her queen. And Latinus reigned forty-five years.

(13) When Latinus died, Anias reigned in his stead for three years, and, after his death, Asqinus (Ascanias, אסקינוס) reigned thirty-eight years. He also built a large temple. After him Seliaqos (סליאקוס) reigned twenty-nine years, and he built a large temple. After his death Latinus, who reigned for fifty years, succeeded him. This was the king who fought with Almania (אלמניא) and Burgunia (בורגניא), the sons of Elisa (אלישה), whom he took as tribute. He built a temple to 'Luṣifer' (לוצפרי), *i.e.*, Nogah, and closed that of Saturnus, which was 'the Temple of Shabbetai.' He passed his priests through the fire on the altar of his temple, dedicated to 'Luṣifer.'

(14) After the death of Latinus, Anias Trognos (Tarquinius) reigned in his stead thirty-three years. He also erected a temple to Saturn. After him Alba reigned thirty-nine years. When he died, Aviṣianos (אביציאנוס) reigned for twenty-four years, and built a large temple. After him Qapis (קאפיס) reigned twenty-eight years, and built a temple. After him Karpitos (קרפיטוס) reigned for twenty-three years, and built a temple. After him Tiberios reigned for eight years. Agrippa reigned after him for forty years. Romulus succeeded him, and reigned nine years, during which time he built several temples. After him Abṭinos reigned for thirty-seven years. This is the king who waged war with the children of Rifath, who dwelt by the Lira (לירא), and with the sons of Turnus, who dwelt in Toronia (טורוניא) by the river Lira. It was they who fled from Agnias, King of Afriqi (אפריקי), and who built Purnus (פורניס) and Anba (אנבא). These Abṭinos brought to submission. After him Procas (פרוקאיס) reigned twenty-three years; and after him Æmilius reigned for forty-three years.

(15) After his death Romulus reigned for thirty-eight

years. In his days David smote the land of Syria, so that Hadarezer and his sons fled into the land of the Kittim. He there obtained a place on the seashore and a place on the mountain. He there built a city, and called its name Sorento (סורנטו). (16) At that place there dwelt a young man of a descendant of the family of Hadarezer, who had fled from David. He built the old city Albano (אלבנו), where his posterity dwell unto this day. But within the city of Sorento (סורנטו) a well of oil sprung up, and after some years the city subsided, and the sea swept over it, *i.e.*, between Napoli (נאפולי) and New Sorento; yet the well did not cease from flowing, for until this very day the oil bubbles and rises upon the waters of the sea, while the inhabitants are continually collecting it.

(17) Romulus was greatly afraid of David. He therefore built a wall higher than any other wall hitherto erected by any king that preceded him, and he surrounded all the mountains and hills round about with this wall. Its length was forty-five miles, and he called the name of the city Roma, after the name of Romulus. And they yet continued to be greatly afraid of David. He made the name of the Kittim great, and they called the place Romania (רומניאה), as it is called unto this very day. He built a temple in honour of Jovis, *i.e.*, 'Ṣedek,' and removed that dedicated to 'Luṣifer.' And Romulus waged great wars. He also made a covenant with David. (18) After the death of Romulus, Numa Popilios reigned in his stead forty-one years. After him Polios (פוליאום) reigned for thirty-two years. After him Tarkinos (תרכינום) reigned for thirty-seven years. After his death Servios (שריאום) reigned thirty-four years. After him Tarkinos reigned. This Tarkinos was he who fell in love with a Roman woman. But as she was already married, he took her by force. The woman was thereat grieved, and she stabbed herself with a dagger and met her death. Her brothers rose up, and, going to the temple of Jovis, they lay in wait for Tarkinos. When he came to pray they fell upon him with drawn swords and killed him.

(19) On that day the Romans took an oath that no king should henceforth reign in Rome. They then selected seventy Roman counsellors and appointed them to rule and to guide the kingdom. 'The Old Man' and his seven counsellors then ruled over them and subdued all the West.

(20) After the lapse of 205 years battles were fought by sea and land between Babylon and Rome, because the Romans assisted Greece when the Greeks fought with Babylon. At that time, when they rebelled, they caused the Tiber to flow into other channels, and made a bottom to the river from one gate (of Rome) to the other, from its entrance to its exit, a distance of eighteen miles, all of which covered with brass, from the gate of Rome where it flows into the sea until the gate where it takes its source, a distance of eighteen miles, for three-fourths of the people were on one side of the river and one-fourth on the other side. The river flowed in the midst of the city, and the inhabitants of Rome paved its bed. No ships or boats of the King of Babylon could henceforth enter. The Romans feared and trembled, as they had heard that the King of Babylon had captured Jerusalem. They sent him presents by messengers, and made a treaty after that war so that wars ceased between them until the reign of Darius the Mede.

[Thus far the narrative of Josippon. After this Josippon wrote of the kingdom of Darius and Cyrus, and the book of the Maccabees, and of the kings who lived during the time of the second temple until its destruction. I shall, with the help of God, write it all in its proper place just as it is written in the book of Josippon until the end.]

XLI. (1) I also find that during the first temple, in the time of Jotham, King of Judah, two brothers, Remus and Romilus, arose who were the first kings of Rome. They reigned thirty-eight years. (2) I also find in 'Ṣoher Ṭob' that their mother from the pains of travail died at their birth, and that God appointed a she-wolf to suckle them until they were grown up. Romulus built the city of Roma. He, the first king, then appointed 100 elders as counsellers. He also built a temple in Rome, and erected the walls of Rome. (3) After him, Huma (Numa) Pompilios (הוּמָא פּוֹמְפִּילִיאוּשׁ) reigned for forty-one years. This Huma Pompilios added two months to the year, viz., Januarius and Febrius (פֶבְּרִיאוּשׁ), for the Romans had originally but ten months to the year. After him Tullus Ostilius (אוּיְשְׁטִילִיאוֹם) reigned for thirty-two years. This Tullus, King of Rome, was the first to clothe himself in purple robes. (4) These are the seven kings that reigned in Rome: 1. Romulus; 2. Numa Pompilius; 3. Tullus Ostilius; 4. Ancus Marcus; 5. Tarquinius Priscus; 6. Servius (שֶׂרְבִיאוּשׁ); 7. Tarquinus (טַרְקוּינוּשׁ). Their rule over Rome lasted altogether 240 years. After them Rome remained without a king for 464 years until the reign of Julius Cæsar.

[Here finishes the 'Book of Genealogies.' I now commence the 'Chronicles of Moses, our Teacher.']

XLII. (1) From the time that Jacob and his sons came to the land of Goshen, there reigned in it certain shepherds, for the land of Egypt was divided into three kingdoms, viz., the land of Ramses, where the Tibei (טִיבִיאִי) reigned. This was situated at the extreme end of Egypt. The Israelites built this town, which was afterwards called Ramses on account of the evil (רַע, Rá) and the tribute (מַס, Mas) which were imposed upon the Israelites. The former name of the city was Heroës (הֵירוֹעֵשׁ). Another capital was Mof, that is Menfis (מִינְפִּישׁ), for Apis, King of Egypt, built it, and was made a god because Jovis, the god of Egypt, revealed himself to them in the form of a calf and a ram, and therefore they called him Sarapis. On this account shepherds were the abomination of Egypt in the land of Menfis, Nof, Pathros, and Tahpanhes, for the Egyptians did not eat sheep or rams because they worshipped them as gods. But the land of Goshen was the kingdom of the shepherds in honour of Joseph and Jacob and his sons, all of whom were shepherds.

(2) Now, a new king arose in Egypt who did not know

Joseph and his good deeds. This was Pharaoh Amenofis
(אֲמֶנוֹפִיס). In his days there arose in the air the likeness
of an ox. On its right side it had a mark resembling
the moon, from which there issued sparks. When it arose
in the morning with the sun, it used to fly in the air of
the heaven. All the Egyptians worshipped it, and praised
it with every kind of song. When it moved they also
moved, and when it stood they also stood. The ox used
also to sing hymns. This it did once in each year. It
became a festival day in Egypt, and they called it the day
of Sarapis. On account of this, the Israelites afterwards
made the calf in the wilderness, as it is said, 'And he
passed through the sea of affliction.'

(3) Then he (Pharaoh) said to his people, 'Behold the
people of Israel are becoming mightier and stronger than
we; and the Egyptians envy and hate them on account of
the multitude of their families, the greatness of their riches,
and their mighty strength. Come, let us take counsel
lest they multiply, and let us appoint rulers over Israel,
and taskmasters over these rulers from among our own
people, for the purpose of subjecting them to rigorous
servitude, and let us further appoint tax-gatherers over
them that they may be reduced to poverty.' And they
built store-cities for Pharaoh, Pithom and Ramses, great
cities which stood on the border of Pithom at the extremity
of the land of Egypt, and Ramses at the other extremity.
In these two cities were the stores of the king and his
implements of war. They were built in such a manner
that no one could possibly enter or go out of the land of
Egypt without the king's knowledge. And the Egyptians
enslaved the Israelites with rigour; they appointed taskmasters, who beat them to obtain the taxes. They
embittered their lives with hard bondage, in that they had
to dig all the channels in the land of Egypt, and to carry
the manure upon their shoulders in pots and in baskets to
manure the fields, as it is said, 'I shall remove the burden
of manure from his shoulder, and his hands shall be
removed from the pots.' They had to cleanse all the

channels of the land on account of the Nile, which filled them once in forty years.

(4) The Egyptians decreed three kinds of punishment against Israel. One was to embitter their lives; the second to impose upon them the slavery in the field; and the third to cast all their males into the river, for they said to King Pharaoh Amenofis, 'We shall slay the males that they may not increase, and allow the females to live to be our servants and our wives, and the males that we beget from them shall be our slaves.' On this account their misery went up before the Lord. And it came to pass when the time of the pregnancy of the women had almost come to an end, they went out in the field and there gave birth to their children, and they left them in the field. The Lord then sent an angel, who washed the children and placed in their hand two stones, from one of which they sucked milk, and from the other honey. When the children were weaned they returned to their father's house. When the Egyptians saw the children in the field, they tried to take them away, but the earth opened its mouth and swallowed them up. The Egyptians brought their ploughshares and ploughed the field over them, but could not harm them, for the Lord had saved them.

(5) The elders and all the people then gathered together, wept and wailed, saying, 'It would have been better had our wives been barren, for the fruit of the womb has now been annihilated. Now let no man approach his wife for some time; for it is preferable to die childless than to see our children defiled by the Gentile, until we know what the Lord will do.' Now Amram answered and said, 'Are you willing to destroy by obstinacy or with premeditation the world? But even when misery has reached the bottom of the abyss the seed of Israel will not be destroyed; for the Lord has sworn to Abraham to afflict his seed for 400 years, and behold from the time of the covenant between the pieces which God made with Abraham, 350 years have already passed, and 130 years of these we have been slaves in Egypt. Now I shall not abide by your counsel, to fix a time

for God's intercession, and to restrain my wife from helping to people the world, for the anger of the Lord will not last for ever, nor will He forsake His people for ever, nor has He made the covenant with our ancestors in vain, neither has He increased the seed of Israel to no purpose.

(6) 'Now I shall therefore go to my wife according to the commandment of God, and, if it is pleasing to you, do you act likewise, and it shall come to pass when our wives shall conceive, that they shall conceal the fruit of their conception for three months, just as Tamar, our mother, did. She did not designedly go astray, for she said, "It is better for me to die than to mix with the heathen." She therefore concealed the fruit of her womb for three months and then confessed. Now let us do likewise, even we. And when the time of bearing comes to an end, we shall not withhold the fruit of our womb, for perchance the Lord will be zealous, and save us from our affliction.'

(7) The advice of Amram seemed good in the eyes of God, and He said to him, 'Thy words are pleasing in My sight. Therefore there shall be born to thee a son who shall be My servant for ever, who shall perform wonders in the house of Jacob, and signs and miracles among the people. And I shall show him My glory, and make My ways known to him. In him I shall cause My light to burn, and shall teach him My statutes and laws. I shall lead him on the high places of My righteousness and My judgments, and through him shall the light of the world be kindled. Of him have I thought from the beginning when I said, "My spirit shall not strive any longer with man, since he is to be in the flesh. His days shall be 120 years."'

(8) Amram, of the tribe of Levi, went forth and took Jochebed, the daughter of Levi, to wife. All the people likewise took to them wives. And Amram begat a son and daughter, Aaron and Miriam. And the spirit of the Lord came upon Miriam so that she had a dream in the night. She told her father, saying, 'In the night I saw a man clothed in fine linen. "Tell thy father and mother," he said, "that whatever is born to thee in the night will be

cast upon the waters, and by him the waters shall become dry. And through him shall wonders and miracles be performed, and he shall save My people Israel, and he shall be their leader for ever."' This dream Miriam told her father and mother. But they did not believe it.

(9) Now, Jochebed had conceived for six months, and in the seventh month she bore a son. They could no longer conceal him, for the Egyptians had made houses by which they knew of the birth of a child. They therefore made a little ark, and placed the child among the bulrushes. The elders then said to Amram, 'Did we not say to thee "It is better for us to die childless than to see the fruit of our womb cast into the sea"?' Then said Amram to his daughter Miriam, 'Where is thy prophecy?' So his sister stood a little distance off to know what would become of the child. And Pharaoh's daughter went down to wash. And she took the child and adopted him as a son.

The Chronicles of Moses.

XLIII. (1) In the 130th year after the Israelites had gone down to Egypt, Pharaoh dreamt a dream. While he was sitting on the throne of his kingdom he lifted up his eyes, and beheld an old man standing before him. In his hand he held a pair of scales as used by merchants. The old man then took the scales and, holding them up before Pharaoh, he laid hold of all the elders of Egypt and its princes, together with all its great men, and, having bound them together, placed them in one pan of the scales. After that he took a milch goat, and, placing it in the other pan, it outweighed all the others. Pharaoh then awoke, and it was a dream.

(2) Rising early next morning, he called all his servants, and told them the dream. They were sorely frightened by it, and one of the king's eunuchs said, 'This is nothing else than the foreboding of a great evil about to fall upon Egypt.' On hearing this the king said to the eunuch, 'What will it be?' And the eunuch replied, 'A child will be born in Israel, who will destroy all the land of Egypt.

If it is pleasing to the king, let the royal command go forth in all the land of Egypt that every male born among the Hebrews should be slain, so that this evil be averted from the land of Egypt.

(3) The king did so, and accordingly sent for the Hebrew midwives, one of whom was named Shifrah, and another Puah, and said to them, 'When the Hebrew women give birth, and ye see upon the stools that it is a son, ye slay it; but if a daughter, then let it live.' But the midwives feared God, and did not act according to the king's word, but let the males live. The king, therefore, summoned the midwives, and said to them, 'Why have ye done this thing, and kept the males alive?' And the midwives answered Pharaoh, saying, 'The Hebrew women are not like the Egyptian women, for they are like the free animals of the field which do not require midwives; before the midwives come to them the children are born.'

(4) When Pharaoh saw that he could not do anything with them, he commanded all his people, saying, 'Every male that is born ye shall cast into the river; but all the females ye shall keep alive.' When the Israelites heard this command of Pharaoh to cast their males into the river, some of the people separated from their wives, while others remained with them. It came to pass, about the time of childbirth, that the women went out into the field, and the Lord, who swore to their ancestors that He would multiply them, sent them an angel, one of his ministers, who was appointed over childbirth, to wash it, and rub it with salt; and the angel bound it in swaddling clothes, and placed in the child's hand two smooth stones, from the one of which it sucked milk, and from the other honey. God also caused its hair to grow down to its knees, so as to be well covered by it; and the angel rocked it caressingly.

(5) And when God had compassion upon them and sought to increase them upon the face of the whole land, He commanded the earth to swallow the children up, and protect them until they grew up, after which time it should open its mouth and let them go forth so that they should

sprout as the grass of the field, and as the young trees of the forest. Then they would return to their families, and to the house of their fathers, where they would remain. (6) Accordingly, it happened that after the earth had swallowed up, through the mercy of God, the males born of the house of Jacob, that the Egyptians went out into the field to plough with teams of oxen and with the ploughshare. They worked (ploughed) upon them as the spoiler in time of the harvest. But although they ploughed never so hard they were unable to injure them, and thus they increased abundantly.

[ANOTHER VERSION.—It came to pass at the time of birth that they left their children in the field, and the Lord, who swore to their ancestors that He would cause them to inherit the land, tamed for them the beasts of the field, and sustained and reared them, as it is said, 'And the beasts of the field were at peace with thee.' When the Egyptians saw that they (the Israelites) left their sons in the field, and that the wild beasts helped them, and led them in the forests until they had grown to manhood, they said, 'These have surely reared them in the caverns and vaults of the earth,' and each of them brought their ploughshare and their plough, and ploughed above them, etc.]

XLIV. (1) There was a Levite in the land of Egypt whose name was Amram, the son of Qehath, the son of Levi, the son of Jacob. This man betrothed Jochebed, the daughter of Levi, the sister of his father, and she conceived and bare a daughter, and called her name Miriam (the bitter), because in those days people began to embitter the lives of the Israelites. She conceived again and bare a son, whose name she called Aaron (pregnancy), because during the time of her pregnancy Pharaoh began to shed the blood of their males upon the ground, and to cast them into the river of Egypt. When, however, the word of the king and his decree became known respecting the casting of their males into the river, many of God's people separated from their wives, as did Amram from his wife.

(2) After the lapse of three years the Spirit of God came

upon Miriam, so that she went forth and prophesied in the house, saying, 'Behold, a son shall be born to my mother and father, and he shall rescue the Israelites from the hands of the Egyptians.' When Amram heard his young daughter's prophecy he took back his wife, from whom he had separated in consequence of Pharaoh's decree to destroy all the male line of the house of Jacob. After three years of separation he went to her and she conceived. And it came to pass at the end of six months from the time of her conception that she bare a son. The whole house was at that moment filled with a great light, as the light of the sun and the moon in their splendour. The woman saw that the child was good and beautiful to behold, so she hid him in an inner room for three months.

(3) At that time the Egyptian women took secret counsel together to destroy the Hebrew women; they, therefore, went to the land of Goshen, where the Israelites were carrying their little children who could not speak upon their shoulders. The Hebrew women then hid their children from the Egyptians, so that their existence might not become known to them, in order to preserve them from destruction and annihilation. The Egyptian women came thus to Goshen with their children who could not speak, and when one of them came into the house of the Hebrew she made her own child chatter in the child's language, and the hidden child, hearing it, replied in the same manner. The Egyptian women thereupon went to Pharaoh's house to tell him of it, and Pharaoh sent his officers to slay those children.

(4) After that child (Moses) had been hidden now for three months and it thus became known to Pharaoh, the mother took the child and placed it in a little ark of bulrushes, which she daubed with slime and with pitch. She then hurriedly placed the child among the flags by the river's brink, while his sister stood at a distance to wit what would be done to him.

(5) God then sent drought and great heat in the land of Egypt, so that it burnt one's very flesh upon him just

as when the sun is in its strength. The Egyptians were therefore sorely troubled. Pharaoh's daughter went down by the river-side to bathe, as did all the Egyptian women, on account of the heat and the drought. Her handmaids and all Pharaoh's concubines went with her. While thus occupied, she beheld the ark floating on the water, and sent her handmaid to fetch it. On opening the box, she discovered the child. It began to cry, and she had pity upon it, and said, 'This is one of the Hebrew children.' (6) At this the Egyptian women by the river came up for the purpose of suckling it, but it refused to take them. God wished to return it to the breast of its mother. The child's sister Miriam then said to Pharaoh's daughter, 'Shall I go and call a Hebrew nurse to suckle the child?' 'Yes,' said she. And she forthwith called the child's own mother. Then said Pharaoh's daughter, 'Take this child and suckle it for me, and I will give thee as a reward a monthly wage of two pieces of silver;' so the woman took the child and nursed it. (7) After two years she brought it to Pharaoh's daughter, who adopted it, and she called its name Moses, 'for from the waters I drew him.' But his father called him 'Heber,' because for his sake he joined his wife again from whom he had separated himself; while his mother called him 'Yequtiel,' because 'I placed my hope in God the Almighty,' and He returned him to her. His sister called him 'Yered,' because she went down to the river after him to know what his end would be; while his brother called him 'Abi Zanoah,' saying, 'My father separated from my mother, but returned to her on account of this child.' Kehath, his grandfather, named him 'Abigedor,' because for his sake God closed up the breach of the house of Jacob, so that they no more cast the children into the water. His nurse called him 'Abi Sokho,' saying that he was hidden in a tent (or box) for three months out of fear of the descendants of Ham; and all Israel called him 'Ben Nethanel,' because in his days God heard their groaning.

(8) In the third year of Moses' birth, when Pharaoh was sitting at his meal, with his mistress on his right hand, his

daughter on his left, and the child in her lap, and all the princes of the kingdom sitting round the table, it happened that the child stretched out his hand, and, taking the crown from the king's head, placed it upon his own. The king and the princes, on seeing this, were confused and exceedingly astonished. (9) Then Balaam, the enchanter, one of the king's eunûchs, said,'' Rememberest thou, my lord the king, the dream which thou didst dream and the interpretation thy servant gave it? Now, is this not one of the children of the Hebrews in whom the spirit of God is? By his wisdom he has done this and has chosen for himself the kingdom of Egypt. Thus did Abraham, who weakened the power of Nimrod, the King of the Chaldeans, and Abimelech, King of Gerar, and inherited the land of the children of Ḥeth and all the kingdoms of Canaan. He also went down to Egypt, and said of his wife, "She is my sister," for the purpose of placing a stumbling-block in the way of the Egyptians and their king. Isaac did the same in Philistia when he sojourned in Gerar. He grew stronger than all the Philistines. Their king he also wished to lead astray when he said of his wife, "She is my sister." Jacob also went stealthily and took away his only brother's birthright and his blessing withal. He then went to Padan Aram, to the house of Laban, his maternal uncle, and by his cunning obtained his daughters, his cattle, and all that he had. He then fled to the land of Canaan. (10) His sons again sold Joseph into Egypt, where he was put in prison for two years, until the Pharaoh before thee dreamt dreams. He was then taken from prison and appointed over the princes of Egypt, on account of the interpretation of these dreams. When God brought a famine upon the land he brought his father and his brothers to Egypt. He maintained them without paying for it, and us he bought for slaves. If, now, it seems good to the king, let us shed the blood of this child, lest, when he grows up, he take the kingdom from thy hands, and Egypt perish.'

(11) God at that moment sent one of his angels, named

Gabriel, who assumed the form of one of them. 'If it pleaseth the king,' said the angel, 'let onyx stones and live-coals be brought and placed before the child, and it shall come to pass, if he stretches forth his hand to the coals, then know that he has not done this by his wisdom, and let him live.' This thing being good in the eyes of the king and the princes, they acted according to the word of the angel, and they brought him the onyx and the coals. The angel then placed the child's hand near the coal so that his fingers touched it. He lifted it to his mouth and burnt his lips and his tongue, so that he became heavy of speech. The king and the princes then desisted from killing the child. (12) He lived for fifteen years afterwards in the king's palace, clothed in garments of purple, for he was reared together with the king's sons. When he was in his eighteenth year the lad longed for his parents, and consequently went to them. He went out to his brethren in the field and looked upon their burdens. He there saw an Egyptian smite one of his Hebrew brethren. When the man that was beaten saw Moses he ran to him for help, for Moses was a greatly-honoured man in Pharaoh's house. He said to him, 'O my Lord, this Egyptian came into my house in the night and, binding me with cords, went to my wife in my very presence, and he now seeks my life.' When Moses heard this evil deed he was exceedingly angry, and, turning this way and that to see that nobody was looking, he smote the Egyptian and hid him in the sand. He thus saved the Hebrew from the hand of the Egyptian. (13) Moses then returned to the palace, and the Hebrew to his house. When the man returned to his house he told his wife that he wished to divorce her, because it was not right for one of the house of Jacob to lie with his wife after she had been defiled. So the woman went out and told her brothers, who thereupon sought to kill him, but he fled into his house, and thus escaped.

(14) On the next day Moses went out to his brethren, and, seeing that some were quarrelling, he said to the wicked

one, 'Why dost thou beat thy neighbour?' But one of them retorted, 'Who made thee to be a prince and judge over us? Wilt thou slay us as thou didst slay the Egyptian?' Moses by this perceived that the thing was already known. (15) Pharaoh immediately got to hear of it, and ordered Moses to be slain. But God sent Michael, the captain of His heavenly host, in the likeness of the chief butcher (slayer). He then took his sword and severed the head of the chief butcher, for his face was changed to the exact likeness of Moses. The angel then took hold of Moses' hand, and, bringing him forth from Egypt, placed him outside its border, a distance of forty days' journey. But Aaron yet remained in Egypt, who prophesied to the Israelites in the midst of the Egyptians, saying, 'Cast away from you the abominations of the Egyptians, and do not defile yourselves with their idols.' But the Israelites rebelled and would not listen. The Lord then said that He would have destroyed them, were it not that He remembered the covenant He had made with Abraham, Isaac, and Jacob. But the hand of Pharaoh was constantly becoming heavier upon the Israelites, so that he persecuted and oppressed them until God sent forth His word and redeemed them.

XLV. (1) At that time a war broke out between Cush on the one side and the people of Qedem (East) and Syria on the other; for these rebelled against the King of Cush. Qinqanos, King of Cush, then went out to war against the other two nations, and smote Syria and the East. He took many captives and made them submit to Cush. (2) When Qinqanos went out to war against Syria and the people of the East he left behind Bala'am the enchanter, i.e., Laban the Aramean, who came from Caphtor, together with his two sons, Janis and Jambris, to guard the city and the poor people. But Bala'am counselled the people to rebel against Qinqanos, so that he should not be able to come into the city. The people, listening to him, swore to act accordingly. Him they made king over them, and his two sons they appointed as captains of the host of the people. On two sides of the city they raised very high walls, while on the third side they dug an innumerable number of pits between the city and the river that surrounds the whole land of Cush, and from there the people drew into them the waters of the river. On the fourth side they collected by their wiles and witchcraft an immense number of serpents, so that no one could approach them.

(3) When the king and all the captains of the army returned from the war and saw the very high walls of the city they were greatly astonished, and said, 'Behold, while we have been detained at war, they have built walls to the city and strengthened themselves to prevent the Canaanitish kings from waging war against them.' But when they came near the city and discovered that the gates were closed, they shouted to the keepers, 'Open the gates for us, that we may enter the city.' But they refused to open them, just as Bala'am the enchanter had ordered them, and would not allow them to enter the city. They therefore drew up their line of battle opposite the gate, and fought so that on that day there fell 130 men of Qinqanos's army. On the second day they fought on the side of the river. But when thirty cavalrymen tried to cross they sank into the pits and were drowned. The king then commanded them to hew some wood, which they were to use as rafts upon which to cross, and they did so. When, however, they came to the walls, the rafts rolled from under them like a mill, and on that day 200 men that had gone upon ten rafts were sunk in the wells. On the third day they went on that side of the city where the serpents lay, but they dared not approach. After 170 men had been killed by these serpents they ceased fighting against Cush. They besieged it for nine years, so that no one went out or entered the city.

(4) During this siege Moses, having fled from Egypt, came to the camp of Qinqanos, the King of Cush. He was then but eighteen years old. This young man entered their ranks, and was much beloved by the king, the princes, and all the army, because he was mighty and beautiful.

His height was like the cedar and his face like the rising
sun, and his strength like that of a lion. He was therefore
made the king's counsellor. It came to pass after nine
years that the Cushite king was seized with an illness by
which he died, so that after seven days Qinqanos departed
this life. His servants embalmed him, and buried him
opposite the gate of the city looking towards Egypt. There
they erected a beautiful building and a very high temple,
and engraved upon the stones his arms and the record of
his mighty deeds.

(5) When they had completed the building, they said to
each other, 'What shall we now do? If we try to get into
the city and fight there will be many more of us slain than
before. If we give up the siege, then all the Syrian kings
and those of the East, having heard of the death of our
king, will come upon us suddenly, and none of us will be
left. Now, let us appoint a king over us, and we shall then
continue the siege until the city falls into our hands.'
They then hastily stripped themselves of their garments,
and, casting them upon the ground, they made a large
platform, upon which they placed Moses. They then blew
the trumpets, and exclaimed, 'Long live the king!' And
all the princes and all the people took the oath of obedience
to him, and gave him a Cushite wife, the widow of Qinqanos.
They then crowned him King of Cush. He was twenty-
seven years old when he was made king.

(6) On the second day of his reign they all assembled
before the king, and said, 'If it is pleasing to the king, give
us advice what to do. For these last nine years we have
not seen our wives nor our sons, but have remained in the
siege.' The king then answered the people, saying, 'Be
certain that the city will be delivered into our hands if you
hearken to my advice. Now, if we fight with them, many
of us will fall as at first, and if we determine to cross the
water we shall fare similarly. Now, go to the forest, and
let each one bring a young stork, which he shall keep until
it has grown up and be taught to hunt just as the hawk.'
The people immediately hastened to the forest, and, climb-

ing the fir-trees, they each brought the young (of the stork) in their hands according to the king's word.

(7) When the young storks had grown up, the king commanded them to starve them for two days, and on the third day he said to them, 'Let each man put on his armour and harness the horses and mules to the chariots; and when each man has taken his stork in his hand, let us rise and war against the city on the side where the serpents are lying.' This they did. When they approached the place, the king said, 'Let each send forth his young stork.' As soon as they did so the storks flew upon the serpents and devoured them, thus ridding the place of them.

(8) When the king and the people saw that the serpents had disappeared they raised a great shout, fought against the city, and captured it, so that each man went to his own house, to his own wife, and to his goods. On that day 1,100 inhabitants were killed, but of the besiegers not one. When Bala'am the enchanter saw that the city was taken, opening the gate, he and his two sons fled away upon their horses to Egypt, to Pharaoh, King of Egypt. These were the magicians and the wizards, as it is written in the 'Sefer Hayashar' (Book of the Just = Bible), that counselled Pharaoh to wipe out the name of Jacob from off the face of the earth.

XLVI. (1) And it came to pass when Pharaoh reigned over Egypt that he changed the statutes of the first kings and their laws, and made the yoke heavy upon all the inhabitants of his land, and also upon the house of Jacob he had no pity, through the counsel of Bala'am the enchanter and his two sons, for they were then the king's counsellors. The king then took counsel with his three advisers—one of whom was named Reuel the Midianite, the second Job, and the third Bala'am of Petor—and said, 'Behold, the Israelites are becoming more numerous, and mightier than we. Come, let us be wise, lest they grow too numerous, and in the event of a war breaking out they will assemble against us and fight us, and go up from the land.'

(2) Then Reuel the Midianite exclaimed, 'Long live the king! If it pleases the king, do not stretch forth thy hand against them, because God has selected them of old and taken them from all nations of the earth to be His inheritance. For whoever of all the kings of the earth stretches forth his hand against them their God will take vengeance upon him. When Abraham went down to Egypt, and Pharaoh ordered his wife Sarah to be brought to him, did not the Lord their God send great plagues upon him and upon his house until he restored Abraham's wife, and only through Abraham's prayer was he healed? Also in the case of Abimelech in Gerar. As a punishment all his house was struck with barrenness, even unto the animals. In a vision Abimelech learned the cause, and that he must restore Abraham's wife whom he had taken. After Isaac prayed for him and his household, and entreated God on their behalf, they were healed. (3) When Isaac was separated from his wife all their fountains were dried up, and their fruit-bearing trees did not yield their produce, and the breasts of their wives and cows were dried up. Then Abimelech went to him from Gerar, his pasturage, and Phichol, the captain of his host. They prostrated themselves, and asked him to entreat God for them and pray to Him. When he besought God they were healed. Jacob was a simple man dwelling in tents; by his integrity he was delivered from Esau, and Laban the Aramean, and from all the kings of Canaan. Who can stretch forth his hand against them without being punished? Was it not thy father that promoted Joseph over all the princes of Egypt, for through his wisdom he rescued all the inhabitants from famine, and commanded Jacob and his sons to go down to Egypt that the land of Egypt be saved from further evil through their piety? Now, if it seems good to thee, cease destroying them, and if thou dost not wish to allow them to dwell in Egypt, send them hence, and they will go to the land of Canaan.'

(4) Pharaoh was exceedingly angry with Reuel, so he left the kingdom and went to Midian. He took Jacob's staff with him. The king then said to Job, 'Give thy

counsel. What shall be done with these people?' But Job briefly replied, 'Are not all the inhabitants of thy country in thy hand? Do thou what is pleasing in thine eyes.' Then spake Bala'am of Petor to the king, 'If thou thinkest to diminish them by fire, has not their God delivered Abraham from the furnace of the Chaldeans? And if thou thinkest to destroy them by the sword, has not Isaac been tested thereby, and a ram been given in his stead? Now, my lord the king, if thou seekest to blot out their name, order their babes to be thrown into the sea, because not one of them has yet been put to this test.'

(5) This advice pleasing the king, he issued a decree all over Egypt, saying that every male born to the Hebrews should be cast into the water. And it came to pass when the males of the house of Jacob were cast into the river that Moses was one of them. The Lord thereupon sent an angel to deliver them, and thus he also was saved through the daughter of Pharaoh. When Moses grew up in the king's palace Pharaoh's daughter adopted him as her son, and the whole of Pharaoh's household was afraid of him.

(6) One day it was reported to Bala'am that the son of Bityah (Pharaoh's daughter) wished to take his life. Bala'am the enchanter and his two sons therefore fled for their lives and escaped to the land of Cush. And when Qinqanos waged war with the peoples of the East and Syria, Bala'am revolted against him and did not allow him to enter the city. Cush was therefore besieged for nine years, and during the siege Qinqanos died. The people then crowned Moses the Levite as their king. (7) By his wisdom Moses captured the city, and was placed upon the throne of the kingdom with the crown upon his head. They also gave him to wife the Cushite wife of the late monarch. But Moses, fearing the God of his fathers, did not approach her, for he remembered the oath which Abraham made Eleazar his servant swear, saying, 'Thou shalt not take a wife of the daughters of Canaan for my sons.' Isaac said likewise to Jacob when he fled on account of Esau. 'Thou shalt not intermarry,' said he, 'with the

children of Ham, for remember that Noah said, "The children of Ham should be servants to the children of Shem and Jafeth."' Therefore Moses feared the Lord, and walked before Him in truth with all his heart. Nor did he deviate from the path wherein his ancestors Abraham, Isaac, and Jacob walked. The kingdom of Cush was firmly established through him, and, going to war with Edom, the East of Palestine, and Syria, he conquered them, and made them submit to Cush. The number of years during which he sat upon the throne was forty, and in all his battles he was successful, because the Lord God of his fathers was with him.

(8) In the fortieth year of his reign, when he was sitting upon the throne with his queen by his side, the queen said to the princes in the presence of the people, 'Behold now, during the whole of the forty years that this king has reigned he has not once approached me, nor has he worshipped the gods of Cush. Now, hearken ye unto me, O sons of Cush, do not allow this man to reign over you any longer, but let my son Mobros (מוברים) reign over you, for it is better that you serve the son of your master than a stranger, a servant of the King of Egypt.' The people discussed the matter until the evening. They then rose up early next morning and crowned Mobros (מוברים), the son of Qinqanos, king over them. But the Cushites feared to lay hands on Moses, for they remembered the oath they took to him. So they gave him valuable gifts and sent him away with great honour. Moses accordingly went forth thence, and his reign over Cush thus came to an end.

(9) Moses was sixty-seven years of age when he went out of Cush; for the thing came from God, as the time had arrived which had been fixed from olden times when the Israelites were to be freed from the children of Ham. Moses then went to Midian, for he feared to return to Egypt through fear of Pharaoh, and stayed by a well of water. When the seven daughters of Reuel the Midianite came out to feed the sheep of their father, they came to the well to draw the water for the sheep. But the Midianite

shepherds drove them away, and Moses rose up and assisted them in watering the sheep. Returning to their father, they told him what the man had done for them. Reuel (*i.e.*, Jethro the Kenite) then invited him into the house to take a meal with him. Moses then related to him that he hailed from Egypt, and that he had reigned over Cush; that they had wrested the kingdom from him and had sent him away. When Reuel heard this, he said to himself, 'I shall put this man in prison, by which I shall please the Cushites from whom he fled.' Accordingly he put him in prison, where he remained for ten years. But Zipporah, the daughter of Reuel, had pity upon him, and fed him with bread and water.

(10) At the end of the ten years she said to her father, 'Nobody seeks or inquires after this Hebrew whom thou hast imprisoned these ten years. Now, if it seemeth good to thee, my father, let us send and see whether he is dead or alive.' Her father did not know that she had supplied him with food. Reuel then answered and said, 'Is it possible for a man to be imprisoned twelve (?) years without food and yet live?' But Zipporah replied, 'Hast thou not heard, O my lord, that the God of the Hebrews is great and powerful, and that He works wonders at all times? That he delivered Abraham from the furnace of the Chaldeans, Isaac from the sword, and Jacob from the angel with whom he wrestled by the brook of Jabbok? That even for this man He has done many wonders; that He delivered him from the river of Egypt and from the sword of Pharaoh? He will also be able to deliver him from this place.' (11) This word pleased Reuel, and he acted as she had asked. He therefore sent to the pit to see what had become of him, and found him alive, standing erect, and praying to the God of his ancestors. Having brought him forth from the pit, he shaved him, changed his prison garments, and gave him to eat. The man then went to the garden of Reuel at the back of the palace, and prayed to his God, who had done so many wonders for him. While he was praying, he suddenly beheld a staff made of

sapphire fixed in the ground in the midst of the garden. When he approached it, he found engraved thereon the name of the Lord of Hosts, the ineffable name. He read that name, and pulled up the staff as lightly as a branch is lifted up in a thickly-wooded forest, and it was a rod in his hand.

(12) This was the same staff that was created in the world among the works of God after He created the heavens and the earth and all their hosts, the seas, rivers, and all the fishes thereof. When Adam was driven from the garden of Eden he took the staff with him and tilled the ground from which he was taken. It then came into the hands of Noah (son of Lamek), who handed it down to Shem and his descendants until it reached Abraham the Hebrew. He then handed over all his possessions to Isaac, including the staff of wonders, which Isaac also inherited. When Jacob fled to Padan Aram he took it with him, and when he came to his father in Beersheba he did not leave it behind. When he went down to Egypt he handed it over to Joseph as a separate gift above that which he gave to his other sons. After Joseph's death the princes of Egypt dwelt in his house, and the staff came into the hand of Reuel the Midianite, who, when he left Egypt, took it away with him and planted it in his own garden. All the mighty men of King Qinqanos (קינקנוס) who wished to wed his daughter Zipporah tried to uproot it, but without avail, so that it remained there in the garden until Moses, to whom it rightly belonged, came and took it away. When Reuel saw the staff in Moses' hand he was astonished (and knew that he was the redeemer of Israel). Reuel then gave Zipporah his daughter to Moses.

(13) Moses was seventy-seven years old when he came out of prison, and took Zipporah the Midianite to wife. And Zipporah went the ways of the women of Israel; she did not even in the smallest thing fall short of the righteousness of Sarah, Rebecca, Rachel, and Leah, the pinnacles of the world. She conceived and bare a son, whom she called Gershon, for he (Moses) said: 'I was a

wanderer in a strange land'; but by the order of Reuel his father-in-law the child was not circumcised. After the lapse of three years she conceived again and bare another son. After his circumcision Moses called his name Eleazar, because (he said) 'The God of my father is my help, and He delivered me from the sword of Pharaoh.'

XLVII. (1) At that time Moses used to tend the flocks of Reuel the Midianite behind the wilderness of Sin, with his staff in his hand. But the Lord was zealous for His people and His inheritance, and, hearing their cry, said He would rescue them from the descendants of Ham, and give them the land of Canaan. He appeared to Moses, His servant, in Horeb, in a burning bush; but the fire did not consume the bush. Then God called him from the midst of the bush, and commanded him to go down to Egypt to Pharaoh, King of Egypt, and to ask him to send away His chosen people as free men. He showed him signs and wonders to perform in Egypt that they might believe that the Lord had sent him. God gave him confidence by saying, 'Go, and return to Egypt, for those that sought thy life are now dead, and they have no power to do thee harm.' (2) Moses then returned to Midian, and related to his father-in-law all that had happened. 'Go in peace,' said he. So Moses arose and went away with his wife and sons. They lodged at a certain place, and an angel came down and attacked him for his transgression of the covenant which God made with Abraham His servant, in that he did not circumcise his eldest son, and he wanted to slay him. Zipporah then immediately took one of the sharp flint stones which she found there and circumcised her son, and she rescued her husband from the power of the angel.

(3) As Aaron the Levite was walking in Egypt by the river God appeared to him, and said, 'Go now, and meet thy brother Moses in the wilderness.' He accordingly went and met him on the mountain of God, and kissed him. On beholding the woman and her children, he said to Moses, 'Who are these?' 'These are,' said he, 'my wife

and sons whom God gave me in Midian.' But Aaron was displeased, and he told him to send the woman and her sons back to her father's house. This Moses did. And Zipporah and her sons remained in the house of Reuel, her father, until the Lord visited His people, and delivered them from Egypt from the hand of Pharaoh. (4) Moses and Aaron then went alone to Egypt to the Israelites, whom they told all that the Lord had spoken. Thereat the people exceedingly rejoiced. The next morning they rose up early and went to Pharaoh's house, taking the staff of God with them.

(5) When they came to the gate of the king's palace they saw there two young lions bound in iron chains. No one could enter or pass out from within unless the king commanded it. The keepers on seeing them loosened the chains, and by charms set the lions free to pounce upon them; but Moses hastily waved his wand upon them, and Moses and Aaron entered the king's palace, followed by the young lions playing round them as a dog plays on seeing its master coming home from the field. When Pharaoh saw this he was greatly astonished, and still more confused on account of these men, whose appearance was like that of the children of God. The king then said to them, 'What do you wish?' And Moses said, 'The Lord God of the Hebrews has sent us to thee, saying, " Send out My people, that they may serve Me." ' Pharaoh was greatly afraid of them, and told them to go away and come again to-morrow, which they did.

(6) When they were gone Pharaoh ordered Bala'am the enchanter, and Janis (ינים) and Jambris (ימברים), his sons, the wizards, and all the magicians of Egypt to be summoned before him. He then related to them what these men had spoken. The magicians then asked, 'How did these men pass the lions that were chained at the gate of the palace?' 'They waved their staves upon the lions,' said the king, ' and they let them loose, and they followed them just as dogs who were pleased to meet them.' 'They are nothing else than wizards like ourselves,' said Bala'am. ' Send now

after them and let them come, and we shall try them.' The king acted accordingly.

(7) Taking the staff, they came before the king, and repeated the words which they had spoken at first. 'But how can one believe,' said Pharaoh, 'that you are messengers of God, and that by His word you have come here? Give us a sign and we shall believe you.' Aaron then threw his staff upon the ground, and it was immediately changed into a serpent. The magicians, seeing this, did the same by their incantations, and the staff of each one of them became a serpent; but Aaron's serpent at that moment lifted its head, and, opening its mouth, swallowed up the serpents of Pharaoh's magicians. Bala'am the wizard, seeing this, said, 'This has been done from time immemorial, that one serpent should swallow up his neighbour just as the fish swallow each other. But change it back to a staff as we shall do, and then if thy staff is able to swallow ours we shall thereby know that the Spirit of the Lord is with thee; but if it cannot swallow them, then thou art a wizard as we are.' Aaron then hastily took hold of the serpent by its tail, and it became a stick again. This the magicians likewise did. Then Aaron, as previously, cast his staff upon the ground, and it swallowed up those of the magicians.

(8) Pharaoh then ordered the Book of Chronicles of the Kings of Egypt to be brought to him; therein were contained the names of all the gods of Egypt. When the list was read over to Pharaoh, he said, 'I do not find your God written in this book, nor do I know Him.' 'The Lord God of gods is His name,' replied they (Moses and Aaron). 'But who is the Lord,' added Pharaoh, 'that I should listen to His voice and send Israel forth? I do not know Him, and shall not allow the Israelites to go.' 'From the days of our forefathers He has been called "The God of the Hebrews." Now give us permission to go a journey of three days in the wilderness to sacrifice unto the Lord, for ever since we came down to Egypt He has not received from our hands a burnt offering, meal offering, or sacrifice.

If, however, thou wilt not let us go forth, the Lord will assuredly wax angry and smite the land of Egypt with pestilence or with the sword.'

(9) 'Tell us something of His might and power,' said Pharaoh. 'He created the heavens and all their host; the earth and all it contains; the seas with all their fishes. He it was who formed the light and who created the darkness; who caused the rain to fall upon the earth to irrigate it. He caused the young plants and the grass to spring forth. He created man, animals, the beasts in the forest, the birds in the heavens, and the fish in the seas. Through Him they live, through Him they die. Did He not create thee in the womb of thy mother, and give thee the spirit of life? did He not make thee grow up, and place thee on the royal throne of Egypt? He shall also take away thy spirit and thy soul, and return thee to the dust from which thou wast taken.' The anger of Pharaoh was kindled, and he said, 'Who is there among all the gods of the people that can do this? Behold, I it was who created the river, and who created myself.' He then drove them out of his presence, and from that day he made the slavery more oppressive than heretofore.

XLVIII. (1) The Lord rose in His strength and smote Pharaoh and his people with many great and terrible plagues, and turned all their rivers to blood, so that whenever an Egyptian came to the river to draw water, as soon as he looked into his pitcher, he found it turned to blood. Whether for drinking or for kneading the dough, or for boiling, it always looked like blood.

(2) After this all their waters brought forth frogs, so that whenever an Egyptian drank of them, his stomach became full of frogs, which croaked about in his entrails just as they did in the river. Whether they kneaded or whether they boiled, the water was filled with frogs. Even when they lay down upon their beds, their very perspiration was turned into frogs. (3) He then smote their dust so that it became lice two cubits high; on their very bodies they lay a handbreadth, as well on the king and queen as on the

people. Following this, the Lord sent against them the wild beasts of the field to destroy them; serpents, vipers and scorpions to injure them; mice, weasels, lizards, and noxious reptiles; flies, hornets, and other insects to fly into their eyes and ears; fleas, ants, and every species of winged insect to torture them; they filled the innermost recesses of their houses. When the Egyptians tried to hide themselves in order to shut out and to escape the wild beasts, the Lord ordered the sea-monster (octopus? סילונית) to ascend to Egypt. It has arms ten cubits in length, according to the cubit of man. Rising to the roof, it uncovered the roof and exposed the rafters; and it then slid its arm inside the house; it wrenched off the bolt and lock, and thus forced open the houses of the Egyptians. In this manner the hordes of wild beasts got into the palace of Pharaoh and his servants, and they worried them greatly.

(4) And God sent a pestilence among the horses, asses, camels, cattle and sheep. When the Egyptian rose early in the morning and went out to his pasture, he found his animals lying about dead, there remaining alive but one in ten. (5) The Lord next sent a plague of fever among the Egyptians, which afterwards broke out into severe boils, which covered them from the sole of the foot to the crown of the head. They broke, and their flesh was running with streams of matter, until they wasted away and rotted, and (6) the hail devastated all their vines and trees so that not even the bark or the leaves were left: all their produce was dried up, and a burning fiery flame played in the midst of it. Even the men and animals found abroad were slain by the flame, and all the libraries (houses of books) were overthrown. (7) Various kinds of locust devoured everything left by the hail; what one species left, the other destroyed. The Egyptians, however, were glad to hunt them and salt them for food. The Lord then raised a very strong wind, which carried them all, including the salted ones, into the Red Sea, so that not a solitary one remained in the whole of Egypt. (8) Darkness then covered the

earth for three days, so that one could not see his own hand before his eyes. During this period of darkness many Hebrews who had rebelled against their Creator, rebelled also against Moses and Aaron, saying: 'We shall not go forth lest we die in the desolate wilderness by famine.' God smote them by a plague, and they were buried during these three days, lest the Egyptians should see them and rejoice at their downfall. (9) All the firstborn of the Egyptians were then slain from man to animal, even the likeness of their firstborn engraved on the walls of their houses was effaced and thrown to the ground. The bones of their firstborn that were buried in their houses the dogs of Egypt dragged away, and, breaking them to pieces, devoured them before the very eyes of the people, so that their descendants cried out in anguish. The people of Egypt then hastened to accompany the servants of God, whom they sent away with much riches and many gifts, according to the oath which God sware at the Covenant between the pieces.

(10) Moses went to Shiḥor (the Nile), and drawing up the coffin of Joseph, took it away with him. The heads of the tribes of Israel also assisted in bringing up each one the coffins of his forefathers. Many of the heathen joined them in their departure from Egypt and in their journey of three days in the wilderness. (11) On the third day, however, they said to one another, 'Did not Moses and Aaron tell Pharaoh that they wished to go a journey of three days in the wilderness in order to sacrifice to the Lord their God? now let us rise early to-morrow morning and see if they return to Egypt to our lord; we shall thereby know that they are to be believed, but if not, we shall go to war against them and bring them back by main force.' On the fourth day they accordingly rose early, and found Moses and Aaron eating and drinking, and celebrating a festival to their God. The rabble said to them, 'Why do you not return to your master?' Moses replied: 'Because the Lord has warned us, saying, "Ye shall no more return to Egypt, but ye shall go to a

land flowing with milk and honey, as I have sworn to your fathers." '

(12) As soon as the rabble saw that they refused to return, they went to war against the Israelites; but the Israelites prevailed against them, causing great slaughter. The remainder fled to Egypt to inform Pharaoh that the people had fled. And the heart of Pharaoh and of his servants was forthwith turned against them, so that they pursued after them to bring them back to their burdens; for the Egyptians repented after they had sent them away. Pursuing them hastily, they at length overtook them while they were encamping by the Red Sea. There the Lord wrought many miracles for the Hebrews through Moses, His chosen servant, who stretched his staff upon the sea, when the waters were immediately divided into twelve rents (for the twelve tribes), through which they all passed over dryshod, just as one passes along the highway. After them came all the Egyptians. But they were all drowned except Pharaoh, King of Egypt, who thereupon offered a thanksgiving offering to the living God, and believed that He was the living God. God then commanded Michael, Gabriel, and Uriel, the heavenly princes, to bring him up from the sea. So they brought him to the land of Nineveh, where he remained for 500 years.

(13) The Israelites then journeyed into the wilderness, and Amaleq, the son of Eliphaz, the son of Esau, went to war against them. With him there came an innumerable army of wizards and enchanters. But the Lord delivered them into the hand of Moses His servant and Joshua the son of Nun, the Ephrathite, who put them to the edge of the sword. Reuel the Midianite, Moses' father-in-law, then came out into the wilderness to Moses, where he was encamping by the mountain of God with Zipporah and his sons, and dwelt with them among the Israelites. Moses next fought against Sihon and Og, and captured their land. He then fought against Midian and slew Evi, Reqem, Ṣur, Ḥur and Reb'a, the five kings of Midian. (14) He put Bala'am the enchanter and his two sons to the edge of the sword.

When Bala'am the enchanter saw Eleazar, the son of Aaron the priest, and Pineḥas his son, captains of the host of Israel, following him for the purpose of slaying him, by means of witchcraft he flew in the air, just as an eagle is seen to fly heavenward. But, uttering the ineffable, revered name of God, they brought him down to the earth, and, capturing him, slew him with the rest of the princes of Midian. The Canaanites who dwelt in the mountains also descended with the Amaleqites to fight against Israel, but the Lord delivered them into the hand of Moses and the Israelites, who smote them utterly. (15) Moses was eighty years old when he stood before Pharaoh, King of Egypt. Through him the Lord redeemed Israel from Egypt. He reigned over them in the wilderness forty years, during which time the Lord maintained them by His mercy with the bread of the mighty and the fowl of the heaven, and from the flinty rock He brought forth fountains of water for them. The cloud of the Lord gently guided them by day like children, and a pillar of fire by night, and during the whole time of their travels in the wilderness neither their garments nor their shoes wore out, and no goodness lacked them there. (16) After travelling through the wilderness of Sin, they arrived at Mount Sinai on the third day of the third month after their departure from Egypt. The word of the Lord then came to Moses the Levite, saying, 'Come up to the mountain, and I will give thee the tablets of stone, the Law and the Commandments which I have written to teach the Israelites.' Moses accordingly told the people to sanctify themselves for three days, and on the third day, that is, on the sixth day of the third month, he ascended the mount. The Lord then gave the Israelites through Moses the 613 precepts refined as silver and tried as gold, accompanied by the sound of the trumpet, by thunders and lightnings. They next erected a tabernacle, with its vessels, for ministering to God, and the ark for the two tablets and for the scroll of the Law. They also prepared burnt-offerings, sacrifices, incense, frankincense, oil for the consecration and for anointing therewith the tabernacle with its vessels and the priests of God, viz., Aaron and his sons, who ministered before God and offered sacrifices and incense for the congregation. They also made for them garments of honour, and appointed the sons of Levi to guard the tabernacle of the Lord, to minister to their fellow-priests, and to sing hymns during the sacrifice. They also offered frankincense within to avert the anger and punishment of the Lord.

(17) In the fortieth year of their wanderings, Miriam the prophetess died, on the tenth day of the first month, and was buried in the wilderness of Sin, which is Qadesh. In the same year, on the first day of the fifth month, Aaron the priest died, and was buried on Mount Hor, and Eleazar and Ithamar were appointed to minister in the place of their father. The priesthood has remained in that family as an inheritance throughout all generations. (18) In that same year on the seventh day of the twelfth month—*i.e.*, Adar—Moses, the servant of the Lord, died, 120 years old, and was buried in the valley at the nethermost part of the Mount of Ebarim, and Joshua the son of Nun, the Ephrathite, was appointed leader of the people. The rest of the words of Moses relating to his power, his military deeds, his entreaties and prayers on behalf of his people, are they not written in the 'Sefer Hayashar,' which is the Law of our God? Joshua the son of Nun rose up after him. He led the Israelites across the Jordan and divided the land by lots according to the word of God.

THE DEATH OF AARON, OF BLESSED MEMORY.

XLIX. (1) 'Better is a good name than precious oil.' Thus it was with Aaron. God said to Moses, our teacher, 'The time has arrived for Aaron to quit this world. Do thou go and tell him that his life is nearing the end.' Moses then rose and prayed the whole night. He said, 'Lord of the world, how can I say to Aaron, "Thy time has arrived to quit this world"? And God said to Moses, 'Give him the message of a great thing and of good tidings, that I will not deliver his soul into the hand of the angel of death.'

(2) Moses then determined to change the order of things for that day. It was customary for some of the princes to rise early and wait at the door of Eleazar and Ithamar, and for all the elders to wait on Moses; but on that day the order was reversed, for Moses, Eleazar, and all the princes rose early to wait on Aaron. When Aaron came to the door and saw them all standing, with Moses among them, he asked, 'O my brother, why hast thou changed thy custom to-day?' 'Because God has bidden me to tell thee something to-day,' said Moses. 'But canst thou not tell me privately?' 'No.' 'Speak, I entreat thee!' 'I cannot,' replied Moses, 'until we depart hence.' They then immediately went away. On other occasions Moses, Aaron, and Eleazar used to walk together—Moses in the middle Aaron at his right, Eleazar at his left, and all the Israelites behind them; but on this day Aaron walked in the middle. When the Israelites perceived this they said to each other, 'The Holy Spirit has been removed from Moses, and has been given to Aaron.' They all rejoiced, because they loved Aaron with a greater love than they did Moses, because he loved peace and pursued it.

(3) 'Why,' asked Aaron, 'dost thou confer this great honour upon me to-day?' 'Because God has commanded me to tell thee something.' 'And what is that which thou hast been commanded to tell me?' 'Do thou wait until we are seated.' When they were seated Aaron repeated his question, 'Now tell me, my brother.' 'Wait until we mount the hill.' And he did all this in order not to frighten him too much. The three of them, Moses, Aaron, and Eleazar, then ascended the hill, when Moses said, 'O my brother Aaron, return unto me what God has entrusted thee with.' 'Is it the tent of the congregation with all its vessels which is entrusted to me?' 'Has he handed over a light to thee?' 'Yes,' said Aaron; 'the lamp with its seven lights has been entrusted to my care.' He did not yet understand that Moses referred to his soul, which is com-

pared to a light, as the verse says, 'The light of God is the soul of man, penetrating the inmost chambers of the heart.' 'Aaron, my brother, why did Abraham, our forefather, die? Was it not because the time had arrived for Isaac's rule? And Isaac, why did he die?—why, do you think? Because of the time having arrived for Jacob's rule, which was then to be transferred to him.' Even yet Aaron did not understand the drift of Moses' conversation. 'O Aaron, my brother, if one were to ask thee to give twenty years, or ten years, or one year, or even one day of thy life to that person, when that day should arrive wouldst thou deny his claim?'

(4) Aaron then at last understood that the time had come for him to die, and he said to Moses, 'Moses, the time of my death has arrived.' Moses remained silent and did not reply, for he was inwardly weeping. Aaron then, placing his hands upon his head, wept bitterly, saying, 'What avails me the good name, when I am about to quit this world, in which I have always loved peace and pursued it, and made peace between man and his neighbour, between man and wife?' While they were sitting in that place, the ground suddenly opened, showing them the cave of Machpelah. After entering it, Moses said, 'Aaron, my brother, perhaps this is the cave of Machpelah—that is, the vault of Abraham, Isaac, and Jacob; thou art clothed in thy priestly garments, and they will become defiled. If now thou art willing, clothe thy son Eleazar with thine own garments, and array thyself in his, then thou and I will enter this vault.' Aaron forthwith stripped himself of his garments and put them upon Eleazar, his son, while he clothed himself in those of Eleazar. When they entered the cave they looked and beheld a burning lamp, a prepared bed, and a table spread. 'Go up, my brother,' said Moses, 'and lie upon this bed. Stretch out thy legs and close thine eyes and mouth.' He did so, and his soul departed.

(5) When Moses saw this he coveted such a death, saying, 'Happy the man that is born to such a death.' And God replied, 'By thy life thou shalt end thy days by

such a death.' At once Moses went out from the cave, and the mouth of it closed up by itself.

(6) Moses and Eleazar then descended the hill. When the Israelites saw Moses and Eleazar without Aaron they said to Moses, 'Where is thy brother Aaron?' 'His time had arrived to die, and he is no more,' answered Moses. Thereupon they sought to stone him, saying, 'Thou hast slain him, because we loved him more than thee.' At this Moses raised his eyes on high and stood in prayer.

(7) At that moment God said to the ministering angels, 'Lift up Aaron's coffin, and suspend it in the air that the Israelites may see it and believe Moses.' Thus they did, and the Israelites believed. They mourned for him thirty days. The ministering angels also lamented his death, saying, 'Wail, ye cypresses, for the cedar has fallen.' Even God himself uttered this verse over him, 'The law of truth was in his mouth, iniquity was never found on his lips; he walked with Me in peace and righteousness, and gave many a place of refuge.' Concerning his death, it is said, 'A good name is better than precious oil, and the day of death better than the day of one's birth.'

[End of the death of Aaron. May the Lord deliver us on the last day. With the help of God, I, Eleazar the Levite, add here the account of the death of Moses, our teacher.]

L. (1) The Lord said to Moses, '*Behold*, the time draws near when thou shalt die.' R. Aybo related that Moses addressed God in the following manner, 'Through the very word with which I praised Thee in the law in the presence of sixty myriads of those who sanctify Thy name Thou hast sentenced me to death,' as it is said, '*Behold*, thy days draw near for thee to die; all thy gifts and punishments are meted out measure for measure, each one meted out in full, how now evil for good.' And God replied, 'Even this word which I told thee is a mark of goodness, as, *e.g.*, "*Behold*, I send before thee an angel. *Behold*, the righteous man will be rewarded in the land."

"*Behold*, I shall send to you Elijah, the prophet," and just as thou hast proclaimed Me before sixty myriads, so shall I, in the future, exalt thee in the midst of fifty-five myriads of perfectly righteous people.' Therefore He used the word 'behold' (הן), the numerical value of הן is 50 and 5, viz., ה = 5, and נ = 50.

(2) Rabbi said that the death of Moses is referred to ten times, viz.: 'Behold, the time draws near for thee to die.' 'He died upon the mount.' 'For I am about to die.' 'Thou knowest that after my death.' 'After my death.' 'And before his death.' 'He was one hundred and twenty years old when he died.' 'And Moses, the servant of God, died there.' 'And it came to pass after the death of Moses, the servant of God.' 'Moses My servant is dead.' From all these instances we learn that it was ten times decreed that Moses was not to enter the land of Israel; but this harsh decree was, nevertheless, not sealed until the decision of the Great Tribunal was revealed to him. (3) For God said to him, 'A decree has been passed that thou shalt not pass (into the land of Israel), as it is said, Thou shalt not pass this Jordan.' This decree was, however, lightly felt by Moses, for he said, 'The Israelites have committed many grievous sins; and whenever I interceded for mercy on their behalf my prayer was accepted, as it is said, "Let me alone, that I may destroy them"; yet at the same place it is written, "And the Lord repented of the evil." At the same place it is further written: '"And the Lord said, I have pardoned according to thy word." I, Moses, therefore, who have not sinned from my youth, if I entreat God on my own behalf, how much more will God hear my words?' When God saw that the decree was lightly felt by Moses, and that he did not turn his mind to prayer, He immediately swore by His great name that he would not enter the land, as it is said, 'Therefore thou shalt not bring this congregation.' 'Therefore' means nothing else than an oath, as it is similarly said, 'Therefore, I sware to the house of Eli.' (4) As soon as Moses became aware that the judgment concerning him was finally decreed, he fasted, and drawing

a circle he stood within it and said, 'I shall not move from this place until that decree has been annulled.' Having then clothed himself in sackcloth and scattered ashes upon his head, he prayed and supplicated before God until heaven and earth and the very creation were moved, and said, 'Perhaps the will of God to renew the world is being accomplished.' A Divine voice then went forth, and said, 'It is not God's will to renew the world; in His hand is the soul of every Man, and the spirit of all flesh.' 'Man' is applied to Moses, as it is said, 'And the Man Moses was exceedingly meek.' (5) At that moment God made a proclamation at every gate, and in every firmament, and at every door of the Great Tribunal that they should not accept Moses' prayer. They, therefore, did not allow his prayer to reach God as the decree had already been sealed. The angel appointed to carry out this decree was named Akhzariel. God forthwith cried out to his ministering angels, 'Hasten to go down and close all those gates of heaven so long as his prayer continues.' For his prayer strove to penetrate the heavens, for like unto a sword it rent and cut, and was not impeded. It drew its strength from the 'Ineffable Name,' which Moses learnt from Zagzagel, his teacher, who is the scribe of all the heavenly host. To this event refers the verse: 'Behind me I heard the sound of a great noise, saying: "Blessed be the Lord from His abode."' The voice was the cry of one supplicating, and the word 'great' can only be applied to Moses, as it is said, 'The man Moses was very great.'

(6) What is the true meaning of the expression, 'Blessed be the glory of the Lord from His abode'? The reply is that when the wheels of the chariot and the seraphim of fire perceived that God said, 'Ye shall not receive Moses' prayer, nor show him favour, nor grant him life, nor allow him to enter the land of Israel,' they exclaimed, 'Blessed be the glory of the Lord from His abode, who is no respecter of persons either small or great.'

(7) At that time Moses said to God, 'O Lord of the universe, it is well known to Thee what cares and troubles

I have undergone for Israel until they became " The chosen ones " to observe Thy Law, and how much anxiety I have suffered for them until I established for them the Law and the Commandments. I said, " As I saw their evil, may I also look upon their good ;" and now that they have reached that state Thou sayest to me, " Thou shalt not pass over this Jordan," behold Thou makest Thy law a falsity; for it is said, " Thou shalt give him his reward on the day due." Is this the payment for the forty years' service during which I have toiled, until they (the Israelites) became holy and faithful ?' as it is said, ' While Judah was yet rebelling against God, they became a holy and faithful people.'

(8) The angel Samael, the wicked, was the chief of the Satans. Every hour he used to dilate upon the coming death of Moses, saying, ' When will the moment arrive at which Moses is to die, so that I may go and take away his soul?' Concerning this David said, ' The wicked are always watching the righteous, seeking to take their life.' But of all the Satans Samael was the most wicked, while, on the contrary, there was no man so righteous among the prophets as Moses, as it is said, ' There has not yet arisen in Israel a prophet like Moses.' This may be compared to a man who is preparing for a wedding-feast, and who anxiously inquires, ' When will thy festivity begin, that I may participate in the joy?' Thus did the wicked Samael remain on the watch for the soul of Moses, and say, ' When will Michael commence to weep, and when shall I obtain the consummation of my joy?' Michael replied, ' I shall weep when (or while) thou rejoicest.' Some are of opinion that he said, ' Do not rejoice, mine enemy; although I fall, yet I rise again, for I fall at the death of Moses, but I shall rise again at the prosperity of Joshua, when he conquers thirty-one kings. I sit in darkness at the destruction of the first temple, but afterwards the Lord shall be my light, the light of the Messiah.' In the meantime one hour had passed.

(9) Moses then said to God, ' Lord of the universe, if

Thou wilt not permit me to enter the land of Israel, allow me to live in this world, and not die.' But the Lord replied, 'If I do not kill thee in this world, how can I bring thee to life in the world to come? And, further, thou wouldst by this falsify My law, for it is written in My law, "None shall deliver (him) from My hand."' Thus far God forbore. Moses added, 'Lord of the universe, if I am not allowed to enter the land of Israel, allow me to remain as one of the beasts of the field, which eat the grass and drink the water, but live and see the world. Let my soul be as one of them.' God replied, 'You ask too much.' Moses continued, ' If not, allow me to remain in this world as a bird that flieth every day to the four corners of the earth, and in the evening returns to its nest. Let me be as one of them.' God still said, 'You ask too much.' 'O Lord of the universe, then place one of my eyes behind the door, and let them shut the door upon it three times in each year, that I may live and not die.' 'It is too much.' 'What dost thou mean, O Lord, when thou sayest, "It is too much"?' And God replied, 'Thou hast spoken too much.' (10) When, at length, Moses perceived that there was no creature that could deliver him from death, he immediately exclaimed, ' The Rock, whose work is perfect.' Then, taking a scroll, he wrote upon it the Ineffable Name, and recited his last ' Song' until the moment arrived for him to die. Then spake the Lord to Gabriel, ' Go thou and bring to Me the soul of Moses.' But he replied, ' How can I look upon the death of him who is worth sixty myriads of creatures? and how can I make him angry who uttereth such words as he?' Then spake God to Michael, ' Go and bring me the soul of Moses.' And he replied, ' Lord of the universe, how can I, who was his instructor, look upon the death of him who was my pupil?'

(11) At length God addressed Samael, the wicked, saying, ' Go thou and bring to Me the soul of Moses.' Then, clothing himself with anger, girding himself with his sword, and enveloping himself with eagerness, he set out to find Moses. When he saw Moses writing the Ineffable Name,

that his brilliancy was like that of the sun, and that he looked like an angel of the Lord of hosts, Samael was seized with a great fear for Moses, and said, 'The angels cannot of a surety take away the soul of Moses.' But before Samael appeared Moses knew that he was coming.

(12) When he (again) looked on Moses he was exceedingly terrified, and trembled as a woman in travail, so that he could find no courage to speak to Moses, until Moses himself said, 'Samael, "There is no peace for the wicked," saith the Lord. What dost thou here?' 'I have come here to take away thy life.' 'But who sent thee?' 'He who formed all creatures,' replied Samael. 'Thou shalt not take my life,' added Moses. 'But the souls of all living beings are entrusted to me.' 'And I am,' said Moses, 'the son of Amram, who was born circumcised. On the day of my birth I found speech; I walked on my feet, and spoke to my parents; even the milk I did not suck. When I was three months old, I prophesied that I would in the future receive the Law on this day, from the midst of the flames of fire. When I went abroad I entered the king's palace and took the crown from off the king's head. When I was eighty years old, I performed signs and wonders in Egypt, and brought out thence sixty myriads under the very eyes of the Egyptians. I also rent the sea into twelve parts; I made the bitter waters sweet; I went up to heaven and trod its path; in the wars of the kings I conquered them; I received the law of fire from the fiery throne, and I was hidden behind a cloud; and I spake face to face to God, and I conquered the host of heaven, and I revealed hidden mysteries to mankind; I received the law from the right hand of God, and taught it to the Israelites; I went to war with Siḥon and 'Og, the two mightiest warriors of the world, for even at the time of the flood the waters would not reach their knees on account of their enormous height; I caused the sun and the moon to stand still in the horizon, while I smote those two kings with the staff that is in my hand and killed them. Who is there in the world that can do like this? Away hence,

thou wicked one. Thou hast not the permission to stay here. Depart from me, for I shall not give thee my soul.'

(13) Samael accordingly returned and brought back word to God, who again said, 'Go forth and bring to Me the soul of Moses.' Samael immediately drew his sword from its sheath and thus stood over Moses. But Moses' anger was kindled against him, and he took the staff of God in his hand, on which the Ineffable Name was engraved, and beat Samael with all his might until he fled before him. Moses ran after him, took away the horn of his glory from him, and deprived him of his sight. Thus far did Moses' power prevail. The last moment of Moses' life had then drawn near, when a voice (Bath Kol) was heard to say: 'Thy last moment, the time of thy death, has arrived.' But Moses entreated thus, 'O Lord God of the world, remember the day on which thou didst reveal Thyself to me in the bush, when Thou didst say, "Go forth and I will send thee to Pharaoh." Remember (O Lord) the day when I stood upon Mount Sinai, where I remained forty days and forty nights. I entreat Thee not to deliver me into the hand of the angel of death.' A voice (Bath Kol) then went forth and said, 'Do not be afraid, for I myself will attend to thy burial.'

(14) At that moment Moses stood up, and having sanctified himself just as one of the Seraphim, the Holy One, blessed be He, descended from the highest heavens together with Michael, Gabriel, and Zagzael. Michael arranged Moses' bed, Gabriel spread a garment of fine linen at his head and Zagzael a rug at his feet; Michael stood on one side and Gabriel on the other. Then spake the Lord to Moses, 'Close thy eyes one after the other, and gather up thy feet.' Then, addressing the soul of Moses from the midst of his body, He said to it, 'My daughter, after I have placed thee in Moses' body for 120 successive years, the time has now arrived for thee to go forth from it; therefore depart and do not delay.' The soul of Moses said: 'O Lord of the universe, I know that Thou art the

Lord God of the spirits of all flesh, and that all souls, both of life and death, are delivered into Thy hand. Thou it was who createdst me; Thou it was who formedst me and didst place me in the body of Moses for 120 years; and no human body has ever been purer than the body of Moses, in which no evil germ was seen, no worm or insect, wherein there never was any over-estimation. On account of all this I love him, and do not wish to depart from him.' 'O soul,' added God, 'depart and do not delay. I shall then carry thee up into the highest heavens, and place thee beneath the throne of My glory, with the Cherubim, Seraphim and Gedudim' (troops of angels).

(15) Once more entreating the Lord, it said: 'Lord of the universe, from Thy Divine Presence on high there once descended two angels, 'Azah and 'Azazel, who in their desire for the daughters of the earth, corrupted their way upon the earth, until Thou didst suspend them between heaven and earth. But from the very day on which Thou didst reveal Thyself in the bush, the son of Amram did not approach his wife, as it is said, "And Miriam and Aaron spoke against Moses on account of his wife." I entreat Thee, O Lord, allow me to remain in the body of Moses.' At that moment, by a kiss of God, the soul of Moses was taken from him, and, as if weeping, God exclaimed, 'Who will now rise up to correct the evil-doers? who will now stand up for the workers of iniquity?' The Spirit of God then wept and said, 'There has never yet arisen in Israel a prophet like Moses.' The heavens wept and said, 'A pious man has perished from the earth.' The earth wept, saying, 'There is no upright man left on the earth.' When Joshua had sought for his master and could not find him, he also wept, saying, 'Save me, O Lord, for the pious one is no more, and the faithful have ceased from among men.' The Israelites then wept, saying, 'He performed the righteousness of God.' And the angels of every heaven exclaimed, 'His judgments are with Israel: the remembrance of the righteous is for a blessing, and his soul returns to everlasting life.'

LI. (1) Now, what was the special merit of Moses, that God Himself should attend on his burial? It was for the following reason. When he went down to Egypt and the time for the redemption of Israel had arrived, all the Israelites busied themselves with the silver and gold, while Moses, for three days and three nights, wearied himself by walking round the city silently searching for Joseph's coffin, since they could not depart from Egypt without Joseph, for he had made them promise him before his death and swear that they would do it, as it is said, 'And Joseph made the children of Israel swear.'

(2) When Moses was already exceedingly tired, a woman, Serah, the daughter of Asher, met him, and, seeing him very faint and weary, she said to him, 'My lord Moses, why art thou faint?' 'Because,' said he, 'I have been wandering round the city for three days and three nights in search of Joseph's coffin, but have not yet been able to find it.' 'Come with me, and I will show thee where it is.' Leading him to a brook in that place, she then related to him that the magicians and wizards of Pharaoh had made a coffin of lead for Joseph, weighing 500 talents, and cast it into the brook. They thus spoke to Pharaoh, 'If it please the king, this nation will now not be able to go forth from this place as it cannot discover Joseph's coffin.'

(3) Standing by the edge of the brook, Moses exclaimed, 'Joseph, Joseph, thou knowest how thou didst cause Israel to swear, saying, "The Lord will surely visit you," Now bestow glory upon the God of Israel, and do not prevent their redemption. Beseech, I pray thee, thy Creator that thou mayest rise from these depths.' Immediately after this the coffin ascended from the depths, preceded by a bubbling of the waters, floating as lightly as a reed. Lifting it upon his shoulders, he carried it along, followed by all the Israelites. They carried the silver and the gold which they took from Egypt, whilst Moses carried the coffin. Then said the Lord to Moses, 'Thou sayest that thou hast in this done a small thing; by thy life, the

mercy which thou hast shown is great, since thou didst not think of the silver and the gold. I shall, therefore, show thee the same mercy when thou departest this life. I shall with My glory bestow kindness on thee.'

(4) Thus, when the time had arrived for Moses to quit this world, and God said to him, 'Behold, the time approaches for thee to die,' he exclaimed, 'O Lord of the universe, after having received the law, and having suffered such weariness, dost Thou tell me, "The day of thy death draws near"? I shall not die, but will live.' 'Thou canst not, for this is the way of man.' 'Lord of the universe,' entreated Moses, 'I beseech thee before my death to allow me to enter and search all the gates of the heavens and the depths of the earth, that they may see there is none besides Thee, as it is said, "And thou shalt know this day, and lay it up in thy heart that the Lord is God and no one else."' God said, 'Thou hast written of Me: "and no one else." I say of thee there has not yet arisen in Israel any one like Moses, who knew the Lord face to face.' What is the meaning of the words, 'Behold, thy day draws near to its end'? R. Simon said, 'The very day appeared before God, and said, "Lord of the universe, I shall not move nor end, so that Moses may continue to live."'

(5) The sages asked, 'What did Moses do as soon as he knew the day on which he was to die? R. Janai said, that on that day he wrote thirteen scrolls, twelve for the tribes, and one he placed in the Ark. In the event of their seeking to falsify a word, they might refer to the one in the Ark. Then said Moses, 'While I have been occupying myself with the Torah which is living, the day has set and the decree is thus annulled.' God then forthwith made a sign to the heavens, and the day remained at a standstill, saying, 'I will not set, so that Moses shall live.' Therefore Job uttered, 'Did not I weep for him that was in trouble (whose day was fixed), that is, the day was hardened (fixed) for him?' What is the meaning of the words, 'Behold, thy day draws near'? Just as one man

says to his neighbour, 'Behold, someone has sued thee before the King.'

(6) He called Joshua, and addressed God thus, 'Lord of the universe, let Joshua, my servant, be the ruler, and I shall live.' God replied, 'Serve thou him as he did serve thee.' Moses then rose up and hastened to the house of Joshua, who was greatly afraid, and said, 'Moses, my teacher, has come to me.' When he went out Moses walked on Joshua's left side. When they entered the tent of the congregation, the pillar of cloud descended and separated them; as soon as it departed Moses went up to Joshua, and asked, 'What did the Word say to thee?' And Joshua replied, 'When the Word was revealed to thee, I knew what was said to thee.' Moses then wept, saying, 'Better one hundred deaths, than one jealousy.' Solomon explains it thus, that love was as strong as death, and jealousy as Sheol, *i.e.*, the love which Moses bare Joshua, and the jealousy which he showed towards him. When Moses was about to die, God tried to appease him, saying, 'By thy life, as thou hast guarded My children in this world, so will I in the future world make thee the leader of My children,' as it is said, 'And He will remember the days of old.'

(7) This is the blessing with which Moses blessed the children of Israel before his death. What is the meaning of the expression, 'Before his death'? The sages say that Moses took hold of the angel of death, and compelled him to go before him while he blessed each one of the twelve tribes. R. Meir says that the angel of death approached Moses, and said to him, 'The Lord has sent me to thee, because thou must depart on this day.' Moses said, 'I seek to praise God, as it is said, "I shall not die, but live to tell of the works of God."' 'But why,' said the angel, 'art thou so boastful? for there are others who praise Him; the heavens and the earth glorify Him every hour, as it is said, "The heavens declare the glory of God." But I will silence them,' continued Moses, 'as it is said, "Listen, O heavens, while I speak."' For the second time the angel

of death approached him, but as soon as Moses uttered the 'Shem Hammeforash' (Ineffable Name), he fled, as it is said, 'When I call upon the name of the Lord, bring ye greatness to our God.' When the angel of death approached him the third time, Moses said, ' It is now necessary for me to justify the Divine judgment upon me,' for it is said, ' The Rock, whose work is perfect.'

(8) R. Isaac said that the soul of Moses refused to depart from him, so that Moses communed with it, saying, 'Dost thou aver that the angel of death tried to overcome thee?' 'God will not do this,' it replied, ' for " thou hast delivered my soul from death."' 'Has he caused thee to see them crying, and made thee weep with them?' 'No, for "(thou hast delivered) my eye from tears."' ' But did he try to make me fall among them (the people)?' ' "Thou hast prevented my foot,"' said it, ' " from slipping."' 'And where wilt thou in the future walk?' The soul replied, ' I shall walk before the Lord in the lands of the living.' As soon as Moses heard this, he exclaimed, 'Return, O my soul, to thy rest.' R. Abin said that as soon as they departed the mortals glorified God, saying, ' Moses has commanded us a law, an everlasting inheritance to the congregation of Jacob.'

LII. (1) R. Joshua ben Levi said that when Moses ascended on high to receive the Law, a cloud appeared before him in a crouching position, so that he did not know whether to ride upon it or to take hold of it. However, it soon opened, and having entered it, the cloud carried him aloft. Moses then walked along the firmament, just as one walks along the earth, as it is said, 'And Moses went in the midst of the cloud.' Qemuel, the angel appointed over 12,000 other angels of destruction, keeping guard at the gates of heaven, met him. When he saw Moses he rebuked him, saying: ' Thou comest from a place of defilement, and darest walk in this place of purity. What dost thou, who wert born of woman, in this place of fire?' ' I am Moses, the son of Amram, and have come here to receive the law for Israel.'

(2) Moses walked along the firmament just as a man walks

along a pathway, until he came to Hadarniel. The sages say of Hadarniel that he stands 60,000 parasangs above his fellow-angels, and that every word he utters is accompanied by 12,000 sparks of fire. On seeing Moses, he in his turn rebuked him, saying, 'What doest thou in this sublime and holy place?' But as soon as Moses heard the voice of Hadarniel, he became frightened, confused, and trembled exceedingly in his presence, and the tears flowed from his eyes. He therefore entreated the cloud to cast him forth; (3) but God's mercy was moved for Moses, and He thus addressed Hadarniel: 'From the very day that I created you, you have striven before Me; when I wished to create man, all of you became his accusers before Me, saying: "What is man, that Thou shouldst remember him, and the son of man, that Thou shouldst visit him?" You gave Me no rest until I consumed many of your companies; and now, seeing that My desire is to give My law to My children, you stand in the way and will not allow My law to descend to My chosen people Israel. Indeed, were it not for Israel, who are to receive My law, there would be no dwelling in the firmament, either for Me or for you,' as it is said, 'If I had not created the day and the night, I would never have decreed the statutes of heaven and earth.'

(4) When Hadarniel heard this he rose and prayed and made supplication before God, saying, 'O Lord of the universe, it is revealed and known before Thee that I did not know that Moses came here with Thy permission. Now that I know it I shall act as a messenger to him, I shall go before him as a pupil before his teacher.' Thus humbling himself, he went before Moses as a pupil before his instructor, until he came to the fire of Saldalphon; (5) and then Hadarniel said: 'Moses, do thou proceed, for I am not able to stand before the fire of Saldalphon. I fear lest he consume me with the breath of his mouth.' When Moses perceived Saldalphon, he was confused and trembled, and the tears flowed from his eyes. He then desired to be thrown from the cloud, and besought the

mercy of God. His prayer was answered, for at that moment the Holy One, blessed be He, Himself descended and stood before Moses until he passed the fire of Saldalphon. Concerning this it is said, 'And the Lord passed before him and he exclaimed, "The Lord, the Lord, the God of mercy and kindness."'

(6) Of Saldalphon the sages say that he towers above his fellow-angels a distance that would take 500 years to walk, and that he stands in front of the curtain weaving crowns for his Maker. The ministering angels do not know where God dwells, for it is said, 'Blessed be the Lord *from* His abode,' and it is not said *in*, but *from*, His abode. He (Saldalphon) therefore conjures with the Ineffable Name, and the crown departs to rest by itself on the head of the Almighty. As soon as the crown leaves the hand of Saldalphon, all the heavenly hosts are moved, and the holy creatures, till now silent, roar like lions, and they exclaim with one voice, 'Holy, Holy, Holy is the Lord of Hosts, the whole earth is filled with His glory.' When the crown reaches the throne of God, all the wheels of His chariot and throne commence rolling; the sockets of fire blaze forth, and all the heavens are seized with terror. When it passes on to the throne all the heavenly hosts with their own crowns on break forth into glorification of God, saying, 'Blessed be the glory of the Lord from His abode.' Come and see the glory and greatness of God. As soon as the crown reaches His head, He strengthens Himself to receive the prayers of His servants. Then all the Hayoth, Ophanim, Seraphim, the wheels of His chariot, the throne of His glory, and the hosts above and below exalt, glorify, and break forth in words of praise, honour and glory, and all as with one mouth proclaim His Sovereignty, saying, 'The Lord will reign for ever and ever.'

(7) As soon as Moses passed away from Saldalphon, he came to Rigion, a river of fire, whose flames burn the angels of fire just as the fire which consumes man. Moses, however, was taken across by God. (8) He then met Galisur, an angel to whom is attributed the saying that

out of the mouth of the Most High proceedeth evil and good. Why was his name called Galiṣur? Because he reveals the secrets of God. His wings are spread out to receive the fiery breath of the holy creatures, for, were he not to do so, no creature would be able to endure it. Galiṣur is appointed for another kind of work: he prophesies that this year shall be a good wheat crop; the barley shall ripen, and the wine shall be cheap. And yet another kind of work: taking a thick covering of iron and spreading it on the river Rigion, he places certain people upon it opposite the angels and princes, so that they may prosper, and that their fear shall fall upon the creatures. God took Moses up and brought him across the river.

(9) After this, Moses met a troop of angels of terror that surround the Throne of Glory, and that are mightier and stronger than all the ministering angels. As soon as they espied Moses, they tried to consume him with the breath of their mouths, saying, 'What doest thou in this place of glory?' But God immediately spread the glory of His throne round about him, as it is said, 'He closeth in the face of His throne and spreadeth His cloud upon it.' Moses, thereby strengthened, returned the following answer: 'What avails the Torah to you? The Exodus from Egypt does not apply to you, nor the worshipping of strange gods, nor the taking of oaths.' At this they immediately rendered their thanksgiving to God, as it is said, 'Our Lord, how mighty is Thy name in all the earth! Thou whose majesty extends over the heavens.' From that moment every one became Moses' friend; every one handed over to him a secret cure, and even the angel of death revealed to him his secret, as it is said, 'And he gave the frankincense and atoned for the people.' (10) Then, opening the seven firmaments, God showed him the heavenly temple and the four different hues in which the tabernacle was made, as it is said, 'And thou shalt erect the tabernacle according to the plan which thou sawest on the mount.' 'O Lord of the universe,' said

Moses, 'I do not know its form.' Then spake God to him, 'Turn to the right.' He did so, and seeing angels clothed in a colour like that of the sea, God said, 'This is blue.' 'Now turn to the left,' said God. He did so, and seeing angels clothed in white, God said, 'This is the fine linen.' Then turning in front of him and seeing angels clothed in red, God said, 'This is scarlet.' 'Now turn behind thee.' Turning behind, he saw angels clothed neither in red nor green, and God said, 'This is purple.'

(11) The Lord then opened the seven doors of the seven heavens, and revealed Himself to Israel face to face in His glory and with His crown. As soon as the Israelites heard the words, 'I am the Lord thy God' from God's own mouth, their souls departed forthwith, as it is said, 'The souls of the Israelites departed when He spoke.' The Law went forth to Israel and found them all dead. Returning to God, it said, 'Lord of the universe, to whom hast Thou given me, to the living or to the dead?' 'To the living,' said He. 'Hast thou not applied to me the verse, "It shall be thy life and the length of thy days"? and yet here are they all dead.' 'Then for thy sake I shall restore their souls;' and causing that dew to descend which is destined to revive the dead, He thus brought them to life, as it is said, 'Thou, O God, didst send a plentiful rain; Thou didst confirm Thine inheritance when it was weary.' He then restored their souls, as it is said, 'The law of God is perfect, refreshing the soul.'

(12) There then descended, at the command of God, 120 myriads of ministering angels, of whom a pair went to each of the Israelites, one to place his hand upon his heart to prevent his soul from departing, and the other to straighten his neck that he might behold God. But why did God reveal Himself to them face to face? Because He said to them, 'Know that I reveal Myself to you in My glory and in My majesty, so that in the event of one of you leading others astray and saying to them, "Forsake your God and let us go and serve other gods," you may then say to him, "Is there anyone who, after beholding his

Creator in His glory and in His majesty and upon the throne of His glory, would go and serve other gods?"' (13) Then said the Lord to Moses, 'My angels are afraid of thee because the fire of thy lightnings is stronger than theirs. Let Michael My archangel go before thee, for My great name is engraved upon his heart, as it is said, "For My name is within him." The glory of the heights is on thy right hand, and the image of Jacob thy forefather on thy left.' Moses was inwardly pleased when he saw the Most High condescending to argue with him. All the inhabitants of the world were confused; the inhabitants of every country were astonished when they saw Moses the son of Amram, who had captured the King's daughter (the Law), descending in great exultation, as it is written, 'Thou didst ascend on high; thou didst take captive and receive presents for man.' It is further written, 'A wise man scaleth the city of the mighty, and bringeth down the strength of the confidence thereof.' The mountains and hills skipped like rams when they saw the canopy erected, and the daughter of God as a bride decked with precious stones. The daughter of God is the Torah (Law), and the precious stones represent the twelve tribes, who said, 'All that the Lord has spoken we shall do and hearken thereunto.' As soon as they exclaimed, 'We shall do and we shall obey,' there descended 120 myriads of ministering angels, who placed two crowns upon every one of the Israelites: one because they said, 'We shall do,' and the other because they exclaimed, 'We shall obey.' And the glory of the Lord was revealed from heaven, from the habitation of His holiness. He gave the Torah to the children of Jacob, His chosen one, and gave them righteous judgments, a true law, statutes and commandments for their good, by which to prolong the life, to obliterate the sins, and to sow the seeds of righteousness.

LIII. (1) The sages say that while the Israelites were travelling in the wilderness they were surrounded by seven clouds of glory, one in front of them, one behind them, two on each side, and one above them to protect them from the sun and the cold. Another cloud went before them, which levelled the high places and raised the lower places that they might not stumble, as it is said, 'And Thy cloud stood above them, and in a pillar of cloud Thou wentest before them.' This was the one in front of them, and the seventh was that which was placed at the head of the standards, and the light of the Divine Presence was refulgent in it. But how did it shine there? (2) The Rabbis say that there were four standards, of which the standard of Judah was in the east, and similar in shape to a lion, as it is said, 'Judah is a lion's whelp.' On the top of the banner was the form of a lion, out of which hooks of gold protruded, which ended in a sword-like pike, and on this there rested one arm of the seventh cloud, on which the three letters representing the three forefathers were engraved, viz., Alef, Yod, Yod. 'Alef' for Abraham, 'Yod' for Isaac, and 'Yod' for Jacob (אי״י being the mnemonic sign). These letters were illuminated by the Shechinah. (3) In the south the banner of Reuben was placed. It had the appearance of a man similar to mandrakes, on account of the passage, 'And he found mandrakes.' On the top of the banner hooks of gold, which ended in a sword-like pike, and upon them rested one arm of the cloud, on which the three letters representing the three ancestors were engraved—'Beth' for Abraham, 'Ṣade' for Isaac, and ''Ayin' for Jacob (בצע being the mnemonic sign). These letters also shone from the splendour of the Shechinah.

(4) In the west the banner of Ephraim was encamped, being in appearance like a fish, on account of the expression, 'And they shall increase like the fish abundantly.' On the top of the banner were placed hooks of gold ending in a sword-like pike, on which rested one arm of the cloud, with the three letters representing the three forefathers engraved upon it, viz., 'Resh' for Abraham, 'Ḥeth' for Isaac, and 'Qof' for Jacob (the mnemonic sign being רחק). Likewise these letters shone through the splendour of the Shechinah. (5) Lastly, in the north was encamped the banner of Dan, in the form of a serpent, on account of the

expression, 'Dan shall be like a serpent by the way.' On the top of the banner were placed hooks of gold ending in a sword-like pike, above which one arm of the cloud rested, with three letters representing the three ancestors engraved thereon, viz., 'Mem' for Abraham, 'Qof' for Isaac, and 'Beth' for Jacob (the mnemonic letters being מקב), which shone through the splendour of the Shechinah.

(6) Now, there was one letter remaining, viz., the Hē of Abraham, which God added to Abram from His own name, which is spelt Yod Hē (יה). With this God created the world, as it is said, ' For with " Yah " the Lord created the worlds.' God placed the pillar of cloud above the ark, which was surrounded by all the banners, as it is said, 'They encamped round about the tent of the congregation.' On this cloud now those sacred letters Yad, Hē, were fixed, and during the seven days of each week it went the round of all the camps of Israel, giving light as the sun by day and as the moon by night. They were thus able to distinguish between day and night. (7) When God wished them to remove their camps, the cloud on which the letters Yod, Hē were engraved moved upwards from the ark of the covenant. The four clouds on which were respectively engraved the letters אייצ, עצב, רחק and מקב followed after them, and as soon as the priests noticed these clouds following in the wake of the pillar of cloud, with the letters יה on it, they blew their trumpets, and the four winds of the earth blew myrrh and frankincense, as it is said, ' Who is this coming up from the wilderness like pillars of smoke, perfumed with myrrh and frankincense?'

(8) These trumpets were used first for assembling the people together, then as the signal to continue their journeying for war, and also for the Sabbaths and festivals. Every trumpet was hollow and emitted a loud sound. It was one cubit in length and broad at the mouth, and a thin reed was placed in its mouth to receive the breath, and thus to discourse music in the hearing of the people. When they were used to assemble the people, and to bring the princes together, the sons of Aaron blew on one trumpet one long

even sound (teqi'ah תקיעה), and not a tremolo (תרועה). A Teqi'ah, or one long even sound, on two trumpets meant the assembling of the whole congregation, but the same on only one trumpet was the signal for the assembling of the princes. If a tribe required its prince, they blew a Teqi'ah on one trumpet, but not a Teru'ah or tremolo. In the same manner the assembling of all the congregation was sounded.

(9) As a signal for continuing their journey they used two trumpets and sounded the Teru'ah. At the first sound the three camps eastward, under the banner of Judah, moved onwards; at the second the three camps in the south, under the banner of Reuben; at the third, the three camps in the west, under the banner of Ephraim; and at the fourth sound of the Teru'ah, the three camps in the north, under the banner of Dan, started on their journey. For all these the Teru'ah sound was blown. In war, however, and on a day of rejoicing, or a festival, or a new moon, the sons of Aaron blew the two sounds Teqi'ah and Teru'ah. (10) These four banners correspond with the four elements of which the world is composed, and the twelve tribes correspond with the twelve stones of the ephod, as it is said, 'And the stones shall be called after the names of the children of Israel.' The banner of Judah in the east corresponds to one of the four elements, viz., fire, and of the constellations, to Aries, Leo and Sagittarius, which consist of fire, and to the first row of the stones of the ephod, viz., the sardius, topaz and carbuncle.

(11) The standard of Reuben in the south corresponded to earth, the second of the four elements; to Taurus, Virgo and Capricornus of the constellations which are of the dust; and to the second row of the stones of the ephod, viz., the emerald, sapphire, and diamond. The banner of Ephraim in the west corresponded to water, the third of the four elements; to Gemini, Libra, and Aquarius of the constellations, which consist of water; and to the third row of the stones of the ephod, viz., the jacinth, agate, and amethyst.

(12) The standard of Dan in the north corresponded to air, the fourth of the four elements; to Cancer, Scorpio, and Pisces of the constellations, which were created of air; and to the fourth row of the stones of the ephod, viz., the beryl, onyx, and the jasper. (13) Judah's constellation is Leo and his stone the sardius; Isaachar's is Aries and his stone the topaz; Zebulun's Sagittarius and his stone the carbuncle, *i.e.*, altogether nine corresponding to fire.* Reuben's constellation is Taurus, and his stone the emerald; Simeon's Virgo and his stone the sapphire; Gad's Capricornus and his stone the diamond, *i.e.*, altogether nine* corresponding to dust. Ephraim's constellation is Gemini and his stone the jacinth; Menasseh's Libra and his stone the agate; Benjamin's Aquarius and his stone the amethyst, which are together nine corresponding to air.* Dan's constellation is Cancer and his stone the beryl; Asher's Scorpio and his stone the onyx; Naphtali's Pisces and his stone the jasper, which are altogether nine corresponding to water.*

(14) Each man stood by his standard, together with the ensign of his father's house, thus: Reuben, mandrakes; Simeon, the city of Shechem; Judah, the lion's whelp; Issachar, a strong ass; Zebulun, a ship; Ephraim, an ox; Menasseh, a buffalo (or Rëem); Benjamin, a wolf; Dan, a serpent; Naphtali, a hind; Gad, a troop (according to the passage, 'a troop will overtake him'); Asher, an olive, on account of the passage, 'He dipped his foot in oil.' Thus, a sign was given to every banner, according to the deeds and according to the name of the tribe.

(15) And these are the four camps of the standards. 'Every man by his standard, according to the house of their fathers, shall encamp round about the tent of the congregation.' Between the tabernacle and the camps of the standards there was a very wide space. Three tribes formed under one banner, that is, in three separate camps according to their order, and each camp was like a large city. The camps of Judah, Issachar, and Zebulun, were

* *I. e.*, if we include the names of the tribes.

placed in the east; Reuben, Simeon and Gad in the south; Ephraim, Benjamin and Menasseh in the west; and Dan, Asher and Naphtali in the north. The Levites encamped between the tabernacle and the camps, on the four sides of the tabernacle, at a distance from the camps, but near the tabernacle, and kept guard in the tabernacle of the Lord. Moses and Aaron and his sons encamped in the east of the tabernacle, opposite Judah's standard. The sons of Kehath encamped in the south, opposite Reuben's banner; the children of Gershon in the west, opposite Ephraim's banner, and the children of Merari in the north, opposite Dan's banner. The tent of the congregation stood in the centre, surrounded on all sides by the Levites, while the four standards of the Israelites surrounded the Levites, and the clouds of glory surrounded the Israelites. That is the meaning of the verse, 'The angel of the Lord encamps round about those who fear Him.' The four standards, Moses, Aaron and the tabernacle, which are altogether seven, correspond to the seven planets, viz., Sun, Venus, Mercury, Moon, Saturn, Jupiter and Mars, and the twelve tribes to the twelve constellations.

(16) R. Ele'azar asked R. Simeon, 'When the Israelites went out of Egypt, did they take weavers with them?' 'No,' replied R. Simeon. 'How, then, did they clothe themselves during the whole of the forty years?' 'The ministering angels clothed them, as it is said, "And I shall clothe thee in fine network." 'But did not the children grow to men?' said he. 'Learn the reply from the purple snail whose shell grows simultaneously with it.' Thus the Israelites fared, nor did they become dirty, for the clouds were cleansing them. Further, they did not emit a malodorous smell from the perspiration of their bodies, although they did not change their clothes.

(17) The well caused to grow various kinds of spices and sweet-smelling herbs, upon which they lay, as it is said, 'He will cause me to lie down in the well-watered pastures,' the perfume of which travelled from one end of the world to the other. The well of Miriam was placed at the entrance of

the court near Moses' tent, and indicated to all (the camps) where they were to encamp. It indicated it in this manner: When the curtains of the court were set up, the twelve pillars by the well sang the 'Shirah,' as it is said, 'They dug the well with songs.' And the waters of the well swelled into rivers, one of which surrounded the camp of the Shechinah. From that river there issued four other rivers into the four corners of the court, each one of which flowed through the four corners, such as south-east, etc., to the camp of the Israelites. After passing the camp of the Levites, these rivers flowed together into one channel, encompassing first the whole camp of the Levites; and flowing between each family, and surrounding the camp of the Shechinah, there were seen many small channels. Then this great river encompassed the whole camp of the Israelites from without, forming into smaller rivers running between each tribe. These rivers marked the boundary of each camp, so that one did not encroach upon his neighbour. But do not think that they obtained nothing from the waters, because they produced all kinds of dainties similar to those of the world to come, as it is written, 'Thou art a fountain of gardens.' And all kinds of spices grew for them, as it is said, 'Thy shoots are a garden of pomegranates . . . . with spikenard and saffron,' etc.

(18) At the end of each camp on the east, west, north and south, there stretched an area of 4,000 cubits. Moses and Aaron and his sons were encamped in the east; the children of Kehath in the south; the children of Gershon in the west; and the children of Merari in the north. Each one of them occupied 100 cubits within the 4,000. In addition to this there were those 4,000 cubits on each side. Thus the Levites occupied one-eighth of the whole area of the tribes. But where did the animals pasture? The whole encampment extended over an area of 12 square miles, comprising the camp of the Shechinah, that of the Levites, and that of the camp of the Israelites. In the corners on each side their cattle pastured, *i.e.*, opposite (or facing) their own encampment. The rivers

surrounded them from within and without, forming channels for them all round, so that the people had permission to walk on the Sabbath from one camp to the other. The cloud being spread over them, divided them from their cattle, as it is said, 'And the cloud of the Lord rested over them by day.' From the splendour of the blue used in the tabernacle the rivers appeared blue as the blue of the morning and the light of the moon and the sun was reflected in them. When the nations beheld them from afar praising God, they said, 'Who are these people looking at us from the wilderness?' and fear and dread fell upon them all, as it is said, 'Fear and dread shall fall upon them.'

The Smiting of the Firstborn.

LIV. (1) The sages say that when God brought the plague of the firstborn upon the Egyptians, He started first upon their gods, as it is said, 'I shall execute judgment on all the gods of Egypt; I am the Lord.' And what was this smiting of their gods, since they were but images of stone? They were broken up into small pieces; every idol of wood rotted and became a heap of dust, and all idols of silver, brass, iron and lead were melted to metal sheets on the ground; and when the Egyptians were drowned in the Red Sea fire descended upon their gods and consumed them, as it is said, 'And in the abundance of Thy majesty, Thou wilt overthrow all those who rise up against Thee.'

(2) The sages further say that before the plague of the firstborn descended upon them Moses went among the firstborn in Egypt and said to them, 'Thus saith the Lord, About the time of midnight I shall go forth in the midst of the Egyptians, and all their firstborn shall die.' Thereupon all the firstborn went to their fathers and said, 'All the plagues which Moses foretold have come to pass; he now says that all the firstborn are to die.' 'Go to Pharaoh,' replied their fathers, 'for he is a firstborn.'

Going to him, they said, 'Send this people away, for if you do not, all the firstborn will perish.' Pharaoh immediately ordered his servants to go and smite them, and he said, 'I have once declared either my soul shall be taken or those of the Israelites, and now you wish them to be sent away.' Each one of them took his sword and slew his father, as it is said, 'The smiting of the Egyptians by their firstborn.' Nevertheless, at midnight, all the firstborn were slain, as it is said, 'And the Lord smote all the firstborn of the land of Egypt, from the firstborn of Pharaoh, *i.e.*, his son, who also died. And Pharaoh and his servants arose in the night on that account. (3) If an Egyptian married five wives, having had five sons, the next day these sons were found dead, because they were all firstborn to their mothers. In the same manner, if a woman had married five times and had obtained a son of each husband, all these sons died, because they were all firstborn to their fathers. Thus was fulfilled the statement that 'All the firstborn of the land of Egypt should die.' In the event of a house containing no firstborn, the eldest in the house died. The house wherein the firstborn had died long before, the dead came out again from the grave and died anew within the house, causing great wailing. Therefore it is written, 'There was no house into which death did not enter.'

(4) As soon as Pharaoh saw that his son, the son of his wife, and the sons of his servants were dead, he meditated within him that Moses had never once yet lied to him, and said to his servants, 'All the time that he was near me he used to appease; and he prayed before his Creator, and we were then healed of all our plagues. But, a little while ago, I was incensed against Moses, and said to him, "Thou shalt not any longer look upon my face." Therefore it is incumbent upon myself to go to seek him.' Pharaoh and all his servants accordingly rose from their beds with great weeping, and Pharaoh, going the round of all the streets, inquired, 'Where is Moses? Where is Moses? Where does he dwell?' When the Israelites saw

him they laughed, saying to him, 'Pharaoh, where art thou going, and whom dost thou seek?' 'It is Moses your master that I am searching for.' 'Here he lives, here he lives,' said the children, all the while laughing at him, until he at last said, 'Arise, go forth from among my people.' But the Israelites took no notice of him until he went to Moses' house and said, 'I entreat thee, O my lord, pray to God for us.' But Moses and Aaron and all the Israelites were at that moment in their several houses, eating their paschal lambs and singing praises to the King of kings, the Holy One, blessed be He, and sitting at home, and no one went out of his house, because God said to the Israelites, 'And no man of you shall go out of his house until the morning.' (5) So that when Pharaoh came to Moses' door, Moses said to him from within his house, 'Who art thou calling?' 'I am Pharaoh,' said he. 'Why dost thou thyself come to me? Surely it is not customary for kings to come to men's houses, and, moreover, at night-time.' 'I entreat thee, go forth and pray for us, for there is no man left in Egypt that is not dead.' 'But I cannot go forth, for I have heard it from the mouth of God, saying, "You shall not go forth."' 'I beseech thee,' said Pharaoh, 'stand at the window and let me behold thy pleasant face.' 'But,' added Moses, 'didst thou not say to me, "Thou shalt no more see my face"?' 'I said this to thee before the firstborn died, but now they are already dead. Thou hast indeed never lied before me: now, why are they all dead?' And Moses said, 'Dost thou wish them to be brought to life again?' 'Yes,' said he. (6) 'If so, then raise thy voice and say, "O children of Israel, behold ye are free men, behold ye are your own masters. Now arise and go forth from the midst of my people. But now ye were the servants of Pharaoh, henceforward ye are the servants of God."' These words Pharaoh repeated. 'Say them again.' And Pharaoh did so. 'Say them a third time.' And Pharaoh said them a third time. When Pharaoh raised his voice, it was heard in all the land of Egypt, a distance of forty days or 400 parasangs.

(7) And in that night he called Moses and Aaron and said to them, 'Arise, go forth from among my people.' 'But why dost thou trouble me the whole night?' said Moses. 'Because,' answered Pharaoh, 'I am a firstborn, and I fear lest I die.' 'Do not fear this, because thou art destined for greatness.' And the Egyptians forced Pharaoh, and persuaded him to send the Israelites from among them, as it is said, 'And the Egyptians strengthened themselves to hasten the people out of their land, for they said, "Behold we shall all of us die."' But God answered them, saying, 'By your life you shall not all of you die here, but I shall destroy you in the sea.' When the Egyptians were drowned in the sea, fire descended upon their gods so that they were consumed.

(8) Among these Egyptians there were two wizards whose names were Johanai and Mamre. As soon as they entered the sea and saw that the waters encompassed them, by means of their wiles they flew into the air as high as the firmament. There was not another nation in the world so much addicted to witchcraft as the Egyptians. Thus our sages have said, 'Ten measures of witchcraft descended into the world: nine parts the Egyptians took, and one remained for the rest of the world.' Johanai and Mamre were the princes of witchcraft, and, from their great knowledge of it, they ascended to the firmament; nor were Michael and Gabriel able to do anything against them. They therefore cried to God in supplication, saying, 'O Lord of the universe, these wicked men who oppressed Thy children with hard bondage dare to stand here without fear, and not only this, but they dare to defy even Thee.' (Whence do we know that God Himself descended in Egypt? Because it is said, 'I shall go down with thee to Egypt.') 'Now, if it is Thy will, O Lord of the universe, execute punishment for Thy children.' At this God immediately ordered Metatron, saying, 'Throw them down and cast them to the ground, but be careful that they only fall into the sea.' Metatron accordingly cast them forcibly into the midst of the sea. It was then that the Israelites broke forth with the 'Shirah' (the

song), 'And in the abundance of Thy majesty Thou hast overthrown those who rise up against Thee.'

(9) 'The nations heard it and trembled,' The sages say that when the Egyptians pursued the Israelites and beheld them, they were seized with great fear and dread, and did not wish to enter into the sea after them. God therefore sent Gabriel to them, and he appeared like a mare entering the sea. Pharaoh's horse immediately followed into the sea after it, and he was followed by all the Egyptians. Then spake God to Moses, saying, ' Stretch forth thy hand over the sea, and the waters shall return upon the heads of Pharaoh and his chariot and his riders.' Moses thus stretched forth his hand upon the sea, which was cleft asunder and rent. When the nations of the world heard the report of the exodus from Egypt, and the rending of the Red Sea, they trembled, and in terror fled from their habitations.

THE REBELLION OF KORAH.

LV. (1) And the children of Israel went up from the sea, and they came to the wilderness. While they were journeying in the wilderness a quarrel broke out between Korah and Moses. A certain woman had a ewe-lamb which she fed from her bread and gave to drink from her own cup, so that it was as a daughter to her. When she one day sheared the wool of her lamb, Aaron the priest came and took the wool away. Going immediately to Korah, she said to him, ' O my lord, I am exceedingly poor, my whole possession being but one ewe-lamb. When I sheared its wool for the purpose of clothing myself, for I am naked, Aaron the priest came up and took it away by force.' (2) Korah then went up to Aaron and said to him, 'Hast thou not sufficient with the tithes and heave-offerings of the Israelites, that thou must needs take away the wool of this poor woman, who is esteemed as a dead person ?' But Aaron retorted, ' Thou shalt not die in the natural way. I shall not annul, for thy sake, one letter of the law. It is written therein, "The first of the shearing of thy flock shall be given to me."' In three months' time the ewe bore a lamb, and Aaron came and took it away. The woman immediately went again to Korah and complained, 'O my lord, behold Aaron has no compassion on me, for but yesterday he took away the wool, and to-day he has taken the firstborn.' And he replied, 'The law says that every male firstborn of thy cattle and of thy sheep shall be dedicated to the Lord thy God.' (3) The woman then went forth and slew the ewe, and Aaron immediately came and took the shoulder, the jaws and the maw. Seeing this, the woman, sorely troubled, cried, saying, 'Thou hast all the flesh.' 'I take all the flesh,' added Aaron, it has now become our portion, as it is said, "The flesh of everything that is dedicated belongs to thee."'

(4) The woman, going to Korah, related all that had happened, and Korah, exceedingly enraged, said to Aaron, 'What claim hast thou upon this poor woman? Thou didst first take the wool, then the firstborn, and now the whole ewe itself.' 'I shall not transgress one letter of the law on account of thy anger, for it is said, "All the flesh shall be the priest's."' (5) Korah was then filled with wrath, and when God commanded Moses to tell the children of Israel to make for themselves fringes, Korah arose in the night, and weaving 400 garments of blue, put them on 400 men. Then, standing before Moses, he said to him, 'Do these garments require fringes, as they are now made wholly of the תכלת' (blue)? Moses replied, 'Korah, does a house full of holy books require a Mezuzah.' 'Yes,' said Korah. 'So also do these garments require fringes.'

(6) Thus the jealousy (envy) between them grew to such an extent that God said to Moses, 'Take the Levites, and thus thou shalt do to purify them.' He then made four decrees concerning the Levites, two of which they accepted and two of which they did not accept. They then said to Moses, 'Sprinkle upon us the water of the sin-offering, and we shall also wash our clothes, but to the heaving and the razor we shall not submit.' (7) Moses then forcibly lifted

them up from the ground against their will. When it came to the decree of the shaving their bodies, Moses was not able to attend to them alone, so he said to the Israelites, 'A decree has been issued concerning the Levites to pass the razor over their flesh, and they have refused to submit.' Thereupon, all the Israelites stood up, laid hold of the Levites by force, and made them submit.

(8) At that time the wife of Korah said to her husband, 'The King of Life makes both you and Moses subservient to Him, but now, having passed the razor over your own flesh and over your beards, you will be a reproach and a shame to all. It is surely preferable to die than to live.' Concerning this Scripture says, 'The wisdom of woman buildeth her house, but the hands of the foolish one overthrow it.' (9) 'The wisdom of woman buildeth her house.' This refers to the wife of On, the son of Peleth, who, when she saw that the quarrel was coming to a head, said to her husband, 'My lord, hearken to my counsel: whether Korah is the prince and thou art the pupil, or Moses is the prince and thou art the pupil, what avails thee this quarrel? It is surely better to free thy soul from the punishment.' 'But what shall I do now,' he answered, 'since I have already sworn to Korah that I shall abide by his counsel?' 'Thy oath will be fulfilled,' she replied, 'if thou sidest with Moses, since all the Israelites are holy.' 'May I trust thee?' said he. She answered: 'Yes.' Thereupon, on the day of visitation, she killed a lamb, and gave him to eat and to drink until he was drunk. She then put him to bed, and while he slept she sat at the street-door and uncovered her head, and combed her hair; and whoever came to call for On, the son of Peleth, saw his wife with uncovered head, and being shamed, turned away until the time passed, and On was thus saved. With reference to this the text says, 'Hide thyself for a moment until the anger has passed away.'

'But the foolish woman overthroweth it (her house) with her hands.' This alludes to the wife of Korah, who wickedly counselled her husband to quarrel with Moses, and thus he perished from this world and from the next also, as it is said, 'And they perished from the midst of the congregation.'

(10) The sages say that through the deep counsel of Balaam the Israelites were diminished, for the sons of Moab and Midian took counsel together, and, gathering all the beautiful women of their land, they made tents for them and placed them therein close by the camp of the Israelites. And the women dwelling within the tents were decked with all conceivable kinds of ornaments and had every kind of saleable garment. At the door of the tent stood an old woman holding a garment for sale. Whenever any Israelite passed by and asked the old woman the price, she placed a very high value upon it, but said, 'Step inside the tent, and there you can choose what you desire at a low price.' As soon as he entered a beautiful maiden would stand up, beautifully decked and sprayed with scent, and, looking at him, say, 'I will sell thee these ornaments at a very low price; and if thou desirest, I will give thee these others for nothing.' Before her was placed excellent strong wine. She would then say to him, 'Drink this cup of wine for my love, and I will present thee with any precious ornament thou mayest wish.' At this time the wine of the heathen was not yet a prohibited thing. He therefore would accept the offer and drink the wine, and as soon as he had finished it he would be very drunk. She then would take hold of him and begin kissing him, so that the evil inclination should burn within him, and he would lie with her. For the great love that sprang up between them, she would not leave him until at length she would say to him, 'Worship this idol for the love you bare me;' and he would worship it.

(11) Thus the Israelites sinned through fornication as it is said, 'And the people began to commit fornication with the daughters of Moab, who enticed the people to sacrifice to their god; and the people ate of their sacrifices and bowed down to their gods.' The Lord was therefore angry with Israel, so that there died by a plague 24,000 men. (12) And all the Israelites, and all the princes, and Eleazar, and Pinehas, seeing the angel of destruction among

the people, sat down and wept, and did not know how to act. Pineḥas saw Zimri publicly going with a Midianite woman, and, burning with zeal, he snatched the spear from Moses. Some say that, raising his spear, he ran after him from behind, and pierced them both, so that it entered the stomach of the woman. On account of this God gave him and his sons the maw of the animals as his reward, and strengthened his arm. He fixed the spear in the ground, and both were found on the top of it, one above the other. Then Pineḥas smote the young men of Israel without remorse, and dragged them, scourging them all the while, through the whole camp of Israel, that all should see and fear. R. Eleazar of Modâi relates that Pineḥas cast the ban of excommunication upon all Israel by means of the secret of the Ineffable Name as written upon the tables of the law—the terrestrial and celestial Tribunal sanctioned an excommunication prohibiting every man of Israel to drink of the wine of the heathen.

LVI. (1) When the ten plagues with which the Egyptians were smitten commenced, Ṣiqrops fled from Egypt to the city of Aqtēs, in Greece, which he built as the Metropolis. There he established the throne of the kingdom of the So'anites, and became the first king of the Atinisim (Athenians)—*i.e.*, the Ṣo'anites. After him there reigned seventeen kings and nineteen princes, until the reign of Cambyses, the son of Cyrus, King of Persia. (2) At the end of the Book of Joshua it is written, ' So Joshua made a covenant with the people that day, and set them a statute and an ordinance in Shechem.' Joseph ben Gorion asserts in his book that when the heathen made a covenant, after shedding the blood of the calf and sprinkling it upon the ground, they used to say, ' Thus shall the blood of him who breaks this covenant which we have made be shed.' Joshua then issued a decree to the Israelites that they should pour water upon the ground instead of blood, to fulfil the command, ' Thou shalt not do according to their deeds.'

(3) In those days, in the time of Joshua, there lived a certain man Eriqtonios, who was the first to construct

a chariot in Greece. And Cadmus, King of Egypt, went from Thebes (תִּיבְּיאִי) and came to Tyre and Sidon, and there reigned. In the land of Greece there also reigned Cadmus Europes Tahpanhes, and he called the name of the royal city Tahpanhes.

(4) Now, Danaus had fifty sons, and they took to them the fifty daughters of Egisates, their brother. But one day one of the brothers arose, and, killing all the others, reigned in their stead. (5) At that time, in the days of Othniel, Cadmus reigned in Thebes, and the city of Biṭanya (בְּטַנְיָא) was built by Tahpanhes. He first introduced the letters of the Greek writing. The city of Epira (אֲפִירָה), now called Corinthus, was also then built by Sisipo. Minos, the son of Eoripi (אִיאוֹרִיפִּי), reigned then in Crete (קְרִיטָא).

LVII. (1) Philo, the friend of Joseph, the son of Gorion, has narrated in his book that after the death of Joshua the Israelites did not possess a friend to lead them. So that the Israelites asked the Lord, 'Who shall go up before us to fight against the Canaanites as in the olden times?' And the Lord replied, 'If the heart of this people is perfect with the Lord, let Judah go up, but if not, nobody shall go up.' 'But whereby shall we know the heart of the people?' they asked further. And the Lord said, 'Draw lots according to your tribes, and the tribe which the Lord shall take shall assemble according to their families, and ye shall thus know the heart of the people.' (2) The people then addressed God, saying, 'O Lord, appoint over us a head and a chief to assemble us for casting the lots, that he may take us out and bring us in.' And the angel of God replied, 'Cast lots in the tribe of Caleb, and the person selected by lot shall be to you the head and the chief.' They did so, and the lot fell upon Kenaz. They therefore made him a prince over Israel. Kenaz then said to the people, 'Bring me your tribes and hearken to the voice of the Lord.' And they came to him.

(3) 'You know,' said he, 'that Moses, the servant of the Lord, commanded you, saying, "Ye shall not depart from

the way which I commanded you in the Torah, neither to the right nor to the left;" this Joshua has also exhorted you to do. (4) Now, hear and mark my words, for the heart of the people is not with Him, and He has commanded us each tribe to approach for the lot to be cast. Let not the anger of the Lord be kindled against us. If I and my house be caught, then burn us with fire.' 'Thou hast spoken well,' answered the people. (5) Accordingly, the tribes assembled before him by lot, and of the tribe of Judah 345 men were taken, of Reuben 540, of Simeon 385, of Levi 350, of Isaachar 665, of Zebulun 545, of Gad, 380, of Asher 665, of Menasseh 480, and of Ephraim 468. (6) Thus, the total number of those that were caught by lot was 6,110, all of whom Kenaz placed in a ward to inquire the word of the Lord concerning them, and said, 'Of such did Moses, the servant of the Lord, speak when he said, "Lest there be among you a root, a poisonous plant or wormwood," blessed be the Lord, who reveals our sins to us that we may not stumble through them.' (7) And Kenaz, and Eleazar the priest, and all the elders of the assembly, prayed to the Lord, saying, 'Thou, O Lord, hast made known unto us the men who did not believe in Thy wonders what Thou didst for our forefathers from the time when Thou didst bring them forth from the land of Egypt until this very day.' (8) And the Lord replied, 'Ask these people now to confess their iniquity, and they shall be burnt with fire.' And Kenaz addressed them thus, 'You know that Achan ben Zabdi sinned by appropriating the devoted spoil, was taken by lot and confessed his sin: do you also make a confession unto the Lord, that ye may live with those whom the Lord will revive at the resurrection of the dead.'

(9) And one of them, whose name was Elah (אלה), answered, 'We shall only die once by this fire. Now ask each tribe separately.' Kenaz thereupon commenced with his own tribe, the tribe of Judah. And they said, 'Behold, we have chosen to make a calf for ourselves, just as our forefathers did in the wilderness.'

(10) Coming next to the tribe of Reuben, they said, 'We have chosen to sacrifice to the gods of the nations.' The children of Levi said, 'We desired to try and test if the tabernacle is holy.' The children of Isaachar replied, 'We desired to ask the idols what will become of us.' (11) And the children of Zebulun, 'We wished to eat the flesh of our sons and our daughters, to know whether the Lord loved them.' The children of Dan replied, 'We desired to teach our sons what we learned from the Amorites; behold, their books are hidden and concealed under the Mount Ebarim, where thou wilt find them.' And Kenaz sent for them and found them.

(12) Coming next to Naphtali, they answered, 'We have done all that the Amorites have done, and hidden them (?) in the tent of Elah, who requested thee to ask each tribe separately.' And Kenaz sent for them and found them there. (13) Then the sons of Gad said, 'We have lain with the wives of our neighbours.' And the sons of Asher said, 'We found seven golden idols, which the Amorites called "The holy ones of Ninfe," (יְנִפֵּה); and upon them were many precious stones. We hid them beneath Mount Shechem. Send thither now and thou wilt find them.' He acted accordingly and found them. These were the idols which informed the Amorites at certain periods the deeds they should perform.

(14) Now, these are the names of the seven sinners that made them after the Flood: Canaan, Phut, Shelah, Nimrod, Elah, Diul, and Shuah. Nor was their work like that of ordinary artificers. The precious stones they brought from Havilah, where the bdellium and the onyx are found. These were the stones used by the Amorites for their idols. In the night they shone as the light of day, and when the blind Amorites kissed the idols and touched their eyes they could see. Kenaz then placed them in a ward until he knew what was to become of them. (15) Continuing his questions, Kenaz came to Menasseh, who said, 'We have not observed the Sabbath to sanctify it.' Ephraim answered, 'We have been pleased to pass our sons and our daughters

through the fire, according to the custom of the Amorites.' And Benjamin said, 'We desired to test whether the law of God emanated from God or from Moses.' Kenaz thereupon entered all their replies in a book and recited them before the Lord.

(16) And the Lord said, 'Take these men, and everything that belongs to them, and bring them down to the river Pishon. There shalt thou burn them with fire.' 'Shall we also burn,' asked Kenaz, 'the precious stones which are priceless or shall we dedicate them to Thee?' And the Lord answered, 'If God would take of the accursed, why then not also man? (17) Take the books and the precious stones and keep them until I make known to thee what thou shalt do with them and how thou shalt destroy them, because fire will not consume them; but the men shall be consumed with fire. And they shall say to all the people, "Thus shall be done to the man who turneth his heart away from the Lord." (18) When they are consumed by the fire, then take the precious stones which fire will not injure, and which iron will not break, and place them on the top of the mountain by the side of the new altar, and there I shall command the thick clouds to cause their dew to fall upon them and thus destroy them; and I shall command My angels to take these stones and cast them into the depths of the sea, so that they shall no more be seen, and to bring up to Me instead of them twelve stones more precious than those. These thou shalt place in the ephod and in the breast-plate, and sanctify them to Me.'

(19) Accordingly Kenaz, fetching everything found upon these sinners, said to the people, 'Ye have seen the miracles and the wonders which the Lord has shown us until this very day, and how He has made known unto us these sinning men so that they have been requited according to their deeds. (20) Now, cursed be the man who acts in the same manner in Israel.' And the people answered, 'Amen.' Thus those men perished in the flames. After this, Kenaz wished to test the stones in the fire, but the fire was extin-

guished. He then took the iron and tried to crush them in pieces, but the iron slipped away from them. (21) Even the books he placed in water, in order to destroy them, but the water became dry upon them. Kenaz then burst forth in praise of God, saying, 'Blessed be the Lord, for this day He has wrought miracles and wonders with the sons of man, when they sinned and did not deny their guilt.' He then took the stones and the books of the law, and placed them on the mount by the new altar, just as God had commanded him; and upon the altar he offered sacrifices of peace-offerings, and all the people ate there together.

(22) On that night the Lord did with those stones and books just as He had spoken, and in the morning Kenaz found twelve precious stones, upon which were engraved the names of the sons of Israel. And the Lord said, ' Take these stones and place them in the ark together with the tables of the law, until Solomon shall have built a temple dedicated to My name, and shall place them on two cherubim, and it shall be to Me as a memorial of the children of Israel. (23) And it shall come to pass, when the sin of the children of man shall have been completed by defiling My temple, which they will have made, that I shall take these stones, together with the tables of the law, and shall put them in the place whence they were taken of old, and there shall they remain until the end of the world, when I shall visit the inhabitants of the earth; and then I shall take them up, and they shall be as an everlasting light to those who love Me and keep My commandments. The moon shall be confounded and the sun ashamed before that light, for it shall be seven times more powerful than either of them.' (24) Then Kenaz said, 'Behold the innumerable good actions which God has done for man, and of which they have been deprived through their sins; now I know that man's work is nothing and his life vanity.'

(25) When he took the stones from the place where they were put, they illumined the whole earth just as the sun at noonday. He put them in the ark of the testimony, together with the tables of the Covenant, just as the

Lord had commanded, and there they remain until this very day.

(26) Having chosen 300,000 armed men of war, on the second day he waged war with their enemies and slew of them 5,000. On the third day the people spoke against Kenaz, saying, 'Behold Kenaz stays in his house with his wives and his concubines; whilst we arm ourselves for battle and destroy our enemies.' (27) The servants of Kenaz, hearing of this, told their master. And he commanded them to summon before him the captains of fifties, and ordered them to place those thirty-seven men in prison who had spoken evilly against him; and they acted accordingly.

(28) He then said, 'When the Lord shall work salvation for His people, will I order the death of these men.' He commanded the captains of the fifties, saying, 'Go and choose 300 of my servants and 300 horses. Let it not become known that we are going to battle, and let them be ready to march with me to-night.'

(29) Sending spies to view the position of the Amorites' encampment, they saw at once that the Amorites were too mighty for the Israelites to fight against. The spies, therefore, returned and reported to Kenaz. (30) He rose up in the middle of the night, holding a shofar in his hand, and taking with him 300 men. When he approached the camp he said to his servants, 'Stay here while I alone go and look at the camp of the Amorites; but as soon as you hear the sound of the shofar, come to me, but if you do not hear it, then return home.' (31) Kenaz thus went down to the camp alone, and he prayed to God, saying, 'O Lord God of our fathers, Thou hast shown Thy servants all the great wonders which Thou hast performed: do Thou now likewise work Thy miracles with Thy servant, and I will go to battle against Thine enemy, that all the nations may know that Thy hand is not too short to send salvation either by means of a multitude or by a few, for Thou O Lord art mighty in war.' (32) And Kenaz continued, 'Let this be the sign of the salvation which Thou wilt show me this day. If when

I draw my sword from its sheath and brandish it so that it glitters in the camp of the Amorites, the latter know that I am Kenaz, I shall then know that Thou wilt deliver them into my hand; and if not, then I shall know that Thou hast not heard my prayer, but hast delivered me into the hand of the enemy for my sins.' (33) After this Kenaz overheard the Amorites say, 'Let us arise and fight against the Israelites, for our holy gods Ninfe (נִינְפֵּי) are in their possession, and they will deliver them into our hands.' At that moment the Spirit of God rested upon Kenaz, so that he rose up, and brandished his sword against the Amorites; and when they saw it they exclaimed, 'Behold, this is the sword of Kenaz, to afflict us with wounds and gashes; but we know that our gods which are with them will deliver them into our hands. Now arise and give them battle.'

(34) When Kenaz heard their words, he went down to the camp of the Amorites and smote them, and the Lord sent the angel Gabriel to afflict the Amorites with blindness, so that they killed each other. And Kenaz slew of them 45,000. (35) Now, when Kenaz had finished the slaughter, it happened that his sword clave to his hand, and, noticing an Amorite fleeing from the camp, he said to him, 'Behold, thou knowest what I have done to the Amorites; now tell me, pray, by what means I can separate my sword from my hand.' And the Amorite answered, 'Slay a Hebrew and pour his warm blood over thy hand, and it will be separated.' Kenaz then slew that Amorite, and pouring his blood upon his hand, separated it from his sword. Then returning to his army, he found them all asleep, for a deep sleep had fallen upon them, so that they did not know what Kenaz had done in the night. When they awoke from their sleep and saw the whole plain full of dead men they expressed great astonishment; at which Kenaz said, 'Are the ways of God like the ways of man? The Lord hath sent salvation through me to His people; now arise and return to your tents.'

(36) As soon as all the Israelites heard of the salvation which the Lord had wrought through the hand of Kenaz,

they went forth to meet him, saying, 'Blessed be the Lord, who appointed thee to be the captain of His people, for now we know that the Lord has chosen His people.' And Kenaz replied, 'Ask the men who were with me of the work I have done.' On asking them, they replied, 'As the Lord liveth, we do not know, for we found the plain full of dead bodies.' (37) After this Kenaz ordered the captains of the fifties to bring forth the prisoners, that they might obtain a hearing. When they were brought before him he said to them, 'Now, what is the complaint you have against me?' And they replied, 'Why dost thou ask us, seeing that the Lord has delivered us into thy hands, and commanded that we should be burnt, not for our complaint, but in connection with those former men who confessed their iniquity. We were not found out among the people when we had joined the sinners. It was for this that the Lord has delivered us into your hands.' Kenaz then said, 'Since you thus testify against yourselves, why should I withhold you from your punishment?' They were, therefore, ordered to be burnt to death in the flames. (38) Now, the days of the life of Kenaz were drawing to a close, and he called the two prophets Pineḥas and Jabin, and also Pineḥas, the son of Eleazar the priest, and said to them, 'I know the heart of this people, for they will turn from following the Lord. I therefore testify against them.' And Pineḥas said, 'Just as Moses and Joshua testified, so do I testify against them; for they prophesied concerning the vineyard, the beautiful plantation of God which did not know its planter, and did not recognise its worker, so that the vineyard was destroyed and did not give forth its fruit. These are the words which my father commanded me to tell this people.' Kenaz then lifted up his voice and wept aloud, as did all the elders and the people until the evening, when they said, 'Is it for the iniquity of the sheep that the shepherd must perish? May the Lord have compassion upon His inheritance that they may not work in vain.'

(39) And the Spirit of the Lord came upon Kenaz, so that he prophesied, saying, 'I have seen what I had not hoped for, and have looked upon what I had not imagined.

(40) Behold, I saw a flame which did not burn, and I heard in my dream the noise of the rushing of waters which had no source and no way upon the mountains, and no base in the air, but they appeared according to their form. They had no fixed place, and since the eye does not know what to see, how can the heart understand it? (41) From this flame which was not burning I saw a spark fly out and remain in the air as a shield, as a spider's web in a beam. Then I saw that this was the base and its source vomited hot foam, and became changed to the foundation of the deep, and ways (paths) were between the upper and lower bases; there shone the hidden light, and beings, in the form of men, were walking about. And then I heard a voice saying, " Between these foundations (bases) shall the sons of man dwell 7,000 years, when the lower foundation shall be destroyed, and the upper one which is like hot foam shall be the foundation, and the light which is between them and illumines the path of man is Jerusalem, and there the men will dwell. But when the sons of man shall sin against Me, and the time of their sinning shall have been completed, then shall the spark be extinguished, and the fountain dry up, and everything pass away."'

(42) When Kenaz had thus finished prophesying, the spirit of his soul returned to him, and he no longer knew what he had uttered in his prophecy. He then said to the people, ' If such be the rest which the righteous obtain after their death, it would be preferable for them to die at their birth in this world and not sin.' And Kenaz died, and Othniel his son arose in his stead.

LVIII. (1) Josippon says that the incident of Micah and the concubine of Gibeah occurred between the time of the death of Joshua and Othniel, between the times to which the following verses refer, viz.: ' And Judah captured Azah and its boundary, and Ekron and Askalon'; and the other, ' And the children of Israel did evil in the sight of the Lord, and He delivered them into the hands of the Canaanites. Then the children of Dan built Laish and the mountain.' For the purpose of enabling us to calculate the days of the judges, this portion was placed at the end of the Book of Judges.

(2) After Othniel came Ehud. At that time, in the days of Ehud, the city Cinnereth in Lybia (ליביא) was built, and many ships were built by Tritolymus (טְרִיטוֹלִימוּשׁ), for carrying wheat, for merchandise. Dionysius built the city of Niza, in Media; Troy (טרויא) was built about the same time in Dardania. There a dog killed Piritius (פיריטיאש), and attempted to slay Tisius, and Heraclones (הֲרַקְלוֹנִישׁ) saved him. In the sixty-ninth year of Ehud the city Sirine (צִירִיגִי) in Libia was built. (3) Shamgar succeeded him, and was followed by Deborah and Barak, who fought with Sisera. And the Lord confounded Sisera and all his charioteers and his whole camp with a fierce tempest; and He overwhelmed them all with hail, and blinding rain and lightnings and thunders, so that they could no longer stand, but fell by the sword.

(4) Sisera then fled on foot to the tent of Jael, who went out to meet him and embraced him. Then, covering him well, he fell into a deep sleep. And Jael prayed to God, saying, 'I pray Thee, O Lord, strengthen Thy handmaid against Thy enemy, and by this I shall know that Thou wilt deliver him into my hand, viz., if I bring him down from his bed on to the ground, and he does not awake.' She did accordingly. Then, taking a nail of the tent and a hammer, she knocked the nail into his temple, according to Deborah's prophecy. And Barak captured Ḥaṣor and slew its king, and all its inhabitants.

(5) Now, when Sisera went out to fight against Israel his mother, Tamar, with her maidens and princesses, by means of their enchantments prophesied, saying that Sisera would bring as spoil one or more of the women of Israel with their coloured garments, for she saw in her charms that he would lie upon the bed of Jael, the wife of Heber, and be covered with a coloured garment of needlework. Therefore she said, 'A damsel, two damsels to every man.'

(6) At that time the kings of Argos, who had reigned for

544 years, were destroyed and exterminated, and their kingdom passed into the hands of Mesenes (מֵישַׁאגָשׁ). In the thirty-ninth year of Deborah's reign the city of Meletus was built. Gideon succeeded Barak and Deborah. He asked a sign of the Lord from the fleece of wool. (7) I find that Gideon asked for yet another sign, for he said, 'Give me a sign that God has chosen me to deliver Israel just as He gave to Moses, who delivered the Israelites from Egypt.' And the angel replied, 'Run and fetch me some water from that pool and pour it upon this rock. I shall then give thee a sign.' Having done as he was requested, the angel said, 'Tell me, shall this water be turned into blood or fire?' And Gideon answered, 'Let part of it be turned into fire and part into blood.' And thus it was, the blood neither quenching the fire, nor the fire drying up the blood.

(8) At that time, during the reign of Gideon, Mercorius (מֵרְקוֹרִיאוּשׁ) discovered certain islands called Sirenes (שִׁירֵינֵי); in Ashkenaz they are called Nikes (Nix) (נִיקֵשׁ). The inhabitants were like beautiful women, their lower parts resembling fishes; and the inhabitants of the forests of the islands were half men and the other half wild animals and horses. The wise man Dialus, by means of his cunning (אַרְטִיפִיסִיאוֹ), made images and idols and birds of gold and brass, and having breathed into them, the idols spoke and the images prophesied while the birds flew about, for he was exceedingly clever in this art. The city of Tyre was built 240 years before the Temple at Jerusalem. (9) After Gideon Abimelech, the son of his concubine, succeeded him, and at that time the measure of the Kor (כּוֹר) and the art of playing upon the timbrel were discovered in Greece. Tola, the son of Phua, succeeded Abimelech. During his reign Erkules (אַרְקוּלִישׁ) conquered Anteos (אַנְתֵּיאוּם), in Lybia, in the water, and destroyed the city of Elios (אִילִיאוּם) when Priamus reigned in Troy.

(10) Yair the Gileadite rose up after him. He made an altar unto Baal, and all the Israelites turned after it and worshipped Baal, except seven righteous men, who did not worship it. These were their names, Da'al, Abi Yezre'el,

Gutiel, Shalom, Ashchor, Jonadab, and Shim'i. These said to Yair, 'We remember what Moses commanded Israel, saying, "Take care lest ye turn aside from following the Lord to worship Baal."' Yair then commanded his servants to burn those men with fire, because they spoke against Baal. Then, taking the men they cast them into the fire, but the fire swerved from them and burned instead the servants of Yair who cast them therein, together with all his household. And these seven men escaped from the fire and went on their way, for the men round about them were struck with blindness so that they could not see them, and the fire reached the house of Yair, who heard the voice of the Lord, saying, 'I have promoted thee to be a judge over Israel; but thou hast corrupted the people and caused them to turn aside from following the Lord and to worship Baal, and those who remain steadfast to Me thou hast burned with fire. But they shall live, and thou shalt die by being consumed in the flames which shall never be extinguished.' Thus the Lord consumed Yair and all his house, and Baal with 10,000 of his followers; and Yair was buried in Qamon.

(11) At that time Theseus captured Helena, but Castor and Pollux, the brothers of Theseus, and his mother, were captured. The city of Carthage (Qar Laini, קרסאיני) was then built. Nizpa (נִצְפָּא) invented the Latin alphabet.

LIX. (1) Yair was succeeded by Jephthah the Gileadite, who delivered the Israelites from the hands of the Ammonites. And Jephthah and all Israel prayed to God in Mizpah, saying, 'We pray Thee, O Lord, save us, and do not deliver Thy inheritance to the slaughter and Thy vineyard to be a spoil. Remember, we beseech Thee, the vine which Thou hast planted and which Thou hast brought up from Egypt.' Jephthah then sent messengers to Giteal (גתאל), King of the Ammonites, saying, 'What dost thou want, since thou hast come to me?' etc.

(2) And the Spirit of the Lord came upon Jephthah, and he went out to wage war against the Ammonites; and he made a vow unto the Lord, saying, 'If Thou wilt deliver

the Ammonites into my hand, then that which cometh forth from my house to meet me on my peaceful return from the Ammonites shall be the Lord's, and I shall offer it to God as a burnt-offering.' And Jephthah smote the Ammonites so that they were humbled before the Israelites. When Jephthah returned to Mizpah, behold, all the virgins and women came forth with timbrels and dances to meet him, and his daughter, the only child he had, went in front of the others and was the first to greet him.

(3) When, however, he saw her, he rent his garments, saying, 'Alas! my daughter, thou hast sorely grieved and troubled me. Who will put my heart and my flesh in one pan of the scale to see it go down? for thou hast grieved me sorely at the feast in honour of my victories in battle, for I have opened my mouth unto the Lord, and now I am not able to retract.'

(4) Then said his daughter Seelah (שְׁאֵילָה), 'Why dost thou grieve for my death, since the Lord hath wrought vengeance for thee upon thine enemies? Remember our forefathers, one of whom offered up his son as a burnt-offering, and the offerer and the offered were both accepted by God. Therefore, my father, do unto me as thou hast spoken. But before I die I will ask thee a favour. Grant me two months' liberty, that I may during that time pray unto Him to whom I return my soul. I shall go upon the mountains and sojourn among the hills; I shall tread the clefts of the rock and lament my virginity, I and my companions; there I shall shed my tears and thus soften the grief of my youth. The trees of the field shall weep for me, and the wild beasts of the fields shall mourn for me; but I do not grieve for my death, nor do I grieve that I must give up my soul on account of the vow which my father made to sacrifice me as a holocaust to God. The one thing I fear, however, is that the offering of my soul may not be accepted, that my death shall have been for nothing.'

(5) Her father having granted her request, she went forth

with her maidens and told the sages of her people, but they answered not a word. She then went up to the mount Tlag (תְּלַג), and the Lord remembered her in the night, saying, 'Behold, I have closed the mouth of the sages of My people, so that they answered not the daughter of Jephthah; now her soul shall be accepted at her request, and her death shall be very precious in My sight, for the wisdom of the sage belongs to her.'

(6) Seelah, the daughter of Jephthah, then fell upon her mother's bosom, and went on the mountain of Tlag weeping, and bewailed her fate in these words, 'Hearken, O ye mountains, to the lamentation of my grief; mark, O ye hills, the tears of mine eyes; and ye clefts of the rocks, testify to the weeping of my soul. Alas! how has my soul been delivered to death! but not in vain; my words will be atoned for in heaven, and my tears shall be written on the firmament, for the father who has vowed to sacrifice his daughter did not have compassion on her. He did not listen to his princes, but said that he would confirm his vow by offering his only daughter. I have not beheld my bridal canopy, nor has the crown of my betrothal been completed. I have not been decked with the lovely ornaments of the bride who sits in her virginity, nor have I been perfumed with the myrrh and the sweet-smelling (odoriferous) aloe. (7) I have not been anointed with the oil of anointment that was prepared for me. Alas! O my mother, it was in vain that thou didst give me birth. Behold, thine only one is destined for the bridal chamber of the grave. Thou hast wearied thyself for me to no purpose. The oil with which I was anointed will be wasted, and the white garments with which I was clothed the moths will eat; the garlands of my crown with which thou hast exalted me will wither and dry up, and my garments of fine needlework in blue and purple the worm shall destroy. And now my friends will lament all the days of my mourning; the trees shall incline their branches and their shoots and weep for my youth. The beasts of the forest shall come together and trample upon my virginity,

for my years are cut off and the days of my life grow old in darkness.'

(8) It came to pass, at the end of two months, that she returned to her father. He then fulfilled the vow he had made, and the virgins of Israel buried her, and mourned for her, and from time immemorial the daughters of Israel have adhered to the custom of devoting four days in the year to Jephthah's daughter. At the time of the death of Jephthah's daughter Ercules committed suicide by throwing himself in the fire, and was consumed by the flames. (9) Ibṣan, of Bethlehem, succeeded Jephthah, and was followed by Elon the Zebulonite. About this time Alexander captured Helena (for his wife). (10) After Elon came Abdon, the son of Hillel the Pirathonite. During his reign the royal city of Troy was captured, and 406 years after its capture began the Olympiad, for after the victory of the Greeks they began to calculate their Olympiad, which consisted of four years, just as we calculate the date from the destruction of the temple. Then Menelaus and Helena came to Egypt, and in the third year after the capture of Troy Agnios reigned over Italy, where Janus, Saturnus, Ficus, and Faunus reigned. Three years after the capture of Troy—some say eight years—Aeneas ruled the empire, and during his reign there arose the city of Rome—*i.e.*, the Latini, so called because the inhabitants spoke the Latin language. In the reign of Ahaz, King of Judah, two twin brothers were born, Remus and Romulus, who founded the great city. They were the first kings of Rome, and reigned in Rome thirty-eight years. (11) In the 'Shocher Tob' I have found it narrated that at the birth of these twins their mother died from the pangs of travail, and that God prepared a young she-wolf to suckle them until they were grown up. Romulus it was who built the city of Rome. At the end of the reign of Hezekiah, King of Judah, Huma Pompilius (הוּמָא פּוֹמְפִּילִיאוּשׂ) succeeded Romulus and reigned forty-one years. He added two months to the calendar year, viz., Januarius and Februarius (פֶּבְרָאיִישׂ), which were not included in the

Roman year, which originally consisted of ten months. At the end of the reign of Menasseh, King of Judah, Tullus Ostilius succeeded Numa, and reigned for thirty-two years. This Tullus, King of Rome, was the first person to clothe himself in purple robes.

(12) We now return to the judges. Many people say that in the days of Abdon, the son of Hillel the Pirathonite, occurred the incidents of Gibeah and Micah. Micah acted just as his mother bade him. He made for himself three images of man, and three of calves, and the likeness of an eagle, lion, and serpent. Whoever desired to obtain sons had to pray to the images of man; whoever desired riches had to entreat the eagle; whoever wished for strength had to entreat the lion; whoever desired sons and daughters had to beseech the calves; whoever desired long life had to entreat the serpent; and whoever desired something of everything had to entreat the dove. Thus all the Israelites went astray, forsook the Lord, and worshipped these idols, so that the Lord sold them to the nations of the earth; but when they at intervals repented the Lord visited them.

(13) It came to pass, when the Israelites, on account of the concubine who was found dead in Gibeah, waged war against the tribe of Dan (!) that they were smitten by the Danites (!), so that on that day 22,000 men of them were destroyed. The Israelites, then going up, wept before the Lord until the evening, and said, 'Let us ask of the Lord, saying, "What is this iniquity through which we have stumbled?"' Thus they asked the Lord, saying, 'Shall we still continue to wage war against Benjamin our brother?' And the Lord replied, 'Go up, and I shall afterwards make known to you whereby ye have stumbled.' On the second day they accordingly went forth again to battle with Benjamin, and there fell of the Israelites 18,000 more men. The Israelites then went up to Bethel, for there the ark of the Lord was placed, and on that day they wept and fasted until the evening, and they offered burnt-offerings and peace-offerings unto the Lord.

(14) Then Pineḥas, the son of Eleazar the priest, prayed unto God, saying, ' O Lord God, if what we have done was considered right in Thine eyes, why hast Thou caused us to fall into the hands of our brother? And if it was evil in Thy sight what these have done, why have we fallen before them? I pray Thee, tell Thy servant in whom this iniquity rests and we shall set it right, for, behold, I remember what I have done. In my jealousy I pierced Zimri with the sword, and Thou didst deliver me from his people, and didst slay of them 24,000 men. Now Thou didst say to the tribes of Israel, "Go up and fight with Benjamin." '

(15) The Lord heard the entreaty of Pineḥas, and said, ' The Israelites showed their zeal for Me in this wickedness which was committed (in Gibeah), but they do not show it against Micah and his idols, who caused all the Israelites to go astray after them. Therefore, I was jealous, and wreaked my vengeance on them, for they were astounded at the one sin of the concubine and wanted to root it out, but they did not root out the worshippers of Micah's idols. Now, let the Israelites go up once more against Benjamin, and to-morrow I shall deliver him into their hands.' (16) Thus the Lord smote Benjamin before the Israelites, so that there fell 18,000 men. The total number of the Benjaminites that were slain was 25,000 ; 600 of them fled to the cleft of Rimmon and escaped. The Israelites then had pity upon their brother Benjamin, and made peace with those that remained, restoring them to their inheritance, where they built cities and dwelt therein; and the Israelites went each one to his tribe and his inheritance.

(17) Now, the days of Pineḥas drew nigh to die, and the Lord said to him, ' To-day thou art 120 years old, which are the years of a man's life; now arise and get thee to My mountain, where thou shalt remain many days. I shall command the ravens and the eagles to feed thee, but do not go down until the end has arrived. Then thou shalt close the heavens, and at thy command they shall again be opened. And then thou shalt be lifted up to the (Divine) place, where thy fathers have been before

thee, and there thou shalt remain until I remember the world.' And Pinehas, the son of Eleazar the priest, did as God had commanded him.

The Eight Exiles.

LX. (1) From the time our ancestors were brought out of Egypt until the destruction of the first temple they were exiled eight times. This happened on the following occasions: Four times Sennacherib banished them, and four times Nebuchadnezzar. The first time Sennacherib, King of Assyria, going up to Jerusalem, sent the tribes of Reuben, Gad, and the half-tribe of Menasseh into exile, and captured the golden calf which Jeroboam had placed in Dan; and the children of Gad and Reuben had brought it up from Dan, and made a holy temple (sanctuary) for it. For this they were exiled from the land of their possession to another land until this very day. When Sennacherib banished them he made them dwell in Lahlah, Habor, the river Gozan, and the cities of Media. At that time Pekah, the son of Remalyahu, reigned over Israel. When Hosea, the son of Elah, perceived that the armies of Pekah were considerably diminished, he went out to war against him and killed him. He reigned over Israel, in Samaria, five years. This was the first exile.

(2) When Sennacherib heard of this he went up against Hosea, the son of Elah, and fought against him, and Hosea, the son of Elah, going to Sennacherib, gave him a present of silver and gold and brought him the golden calf, which Jeroboam had placed in Bethel. After this he (Sennacherib) exiled the tribes of Asher, Zebulun, Naphtali, and Isaachar, because they refused to allow Hosea, the son of Elah, to reign over them. He then appointed Hosea, the son of Elah, over Samaria, and thus fulfilled the scriptural passage, 'Thus saith the Lord, Just as the shepherd delivers two legs, or the tip of the ear, from the clutches of the lion, so shall the Israelites be rescued (that sit in Samaria) in the corner of a couch, and in Damascus on a bed.'

And Hosea, the son of Elah, reigned over Israel, and Ahaz over Judah. This was the second exile.

(3) When this king died Hezekiah reigned over the whole of Judah, and at the beginning of the fourth year of Hezekiah's reign Sennacherib went up against Samaria and besieged it for three years, in the third (!) year of Hezekiah's reign, and he exiled the tribes of Ephraim and Menasseh from Samaria. This was the third exile.

(4) After an interval of five years he mustered together the Babylonians, Kuthim, Avim, the B'ne Hamath, and the Sapharvaim, and then going against Judah, besieged all the fortified cities in Judah, among the 150 places in which were the tribes of Judah and Simeon. He besieged them and took them captive, and sought to bring them to Lahlah and Habor, to the other tribes. Hearing that Tirhakah, King of Ethiopia, whose land was near Egypt, had rebelled against him, he took with him the tribes of Judah and Simeon, and ascended the mountains of Ethiopia to wage war with the Ethiopian king, and to test the strength of the tribes of Judah and Simeon. He then took these tribes and concealed them behind the mountains of darkness on the other side of the rivers of Ethiopia. Concerning them the prophetess 'Athrai (עתרי), the daughter of Pusai (פוסי), prophesied, ' They shall bring my offering.' This was the fourth captivity brought about by Sennacherib, King of Assyria.

(5) There remained in Jerusalem of the tribes of Judah and Benjamin 130,000, over whom the righteous Hezekiah reigned. Sennacherib, King of Assyria, now once more became proud, and setting his face towards the holy city of Jerusalem, he assembled all his host, to the number of 40,000 and 2,590,000 warriors, and went up to besiege Jerusalem. When Hezekiah saw the great multitude he was greatly afraid, and, praying to the Lord, he called upon the people of Judah and Benjamin to proclaim a fast. Then, covering themselves with sackcloth, they went into the house of the Lord, and, repenting with all their heart, they cried unto the Lord, and He heard the prayer of the

righteous Hezekiah, and sent His angel who smote the Assyrian camp, slaying 185,000 men, together with the kings and princes. Not one of the kings and princes of his army remained except Sennacherib and Nebuchadnezzar. Thus Isaiah's prophecy was fulfilled, who said, 'On that day the Lord shall shave with a razor that is hired, the parts beyond the river of Ethiopia, even the King of Assyria, the head, and the hair of the feet; and it shall also consume the beard.' The head represents the kings, the hair of the feet represents the armies, and the beard the wicked Sannacherib, whose two sons slew him. From the fall of Sennacherib to the time of Nebuchadnezzar passed 107 years.

(6) In the fourth year of the reign of Jehoiakim the decree was sealed on account of the sins of the Israelites, and the remnant of those who were delivered from the mouth of the lion and the mouth of the bear, the remnant of Judah and Benjamin, and the rest of the people that remained of the tribes were banished by Nebuchadnezzar during his first captivity. Of the tribes of Judah and Benjamin 3,023, and of the remaining tribes 7,000. All these were warriors skilled in the art of battle, but their sin lay heavy upon them, and he exiled them to Babylon. This was the first captivity brought about by Nebuchadnezzar.

(7) After an interval of seven years he went up to Jerusalem for the second time, and besieging it, he captured it, and exiled of the tribes of Judah and Benjamin 4,600 men, and of the remaining tribes 10,000, together with the free and the imprisoned, i.e., the kings and queens. Others explain the words חרש and מסגר to refer to the pupils of the sages who study the Torah, and thus open and shut the books. In the time of David these people were called Kerethi and Pelethi. Yet another explanation makes the words refer to the mighty men of Judah and their children. All these were banished through Jechoniah and his sons. This constituted the second captivity of Nebuchadnezzar.

(8) He made Zedekiah King of Judah, over which and Jerusalem he reigned eleven years. In the nineteenth year

of the reign of Nebuchadnezzar, while he was yet seated on the throne of his kingdom, he sent Nebuzaraddan, his captain of the guard, against Jerusalem. Having besieged it, he caught Zedekiah, and bringing him to Riblah, to the King of Babylon, he executed his judgment upon him. He then took the pillars, the sea of brass, and all the vessels of the house of the Lord, and the bases which Solomon had made, and the treasures found in Jerusalem, and carried them to Babylon. In Jerusalem he slew 940,000 (?) men, besides those he slew in avenging the blood of Zechariah.

(9) He also besieged sixty cities of the Levites, the sons of Moses, in which there were 600,000 men, as we know from the verses, 'And the sons of Moses were Gershom and Eliezer; and of the sons of Eliezer the eldest was Rehabya,' and it is said, 'And the children of Rehabya continually increased, *i.e.*, increased beyond the number of 600,000 men.' The total number of those exiled from Jerusalem was 802,000, all of whom consisted of the youths of Judah and Benjamin. Concerning them the prophet says, 'And he exiled the flower of Judah,' so that there only remained in Jerusalem the poverty of the people, as it is said, 'The people of the land which Nebuzaraddan left were vile,' etc. He made the son of Ahikam king over them, and giving the land over to him, the exiles were carried to Babylon, which constituted the third exile.

(10) When Ishmael, the son of Netaniah, of the royal seed, heard that Gedaliah, the son of Ahikam, was appointed over the remnant of the people, he came in stealth and slew him and all his men. The Israelites were exceedingly afraid of this and fled to Egypt, in the twenty-seventh year of Nebuchadnezzar's reign, when he besieged Tyre, and capturing it, killed all its inhabitants and sent its king into captivity. On his return he went to Egypt, captured it, and reduced it to desolation, thus fulfilling the prophecy of Scripture, 'Egypt shall be a desolation.' He then slew all the Jews found in Ammon and Moab, and in the surrounding parts of Egypt. There, in Egypt, he discovered the

prophet Jeremiah and Baruch, the son of Neriya, and carried them to Babylon. When the Israelites dwelling in Egypt heard that Nebuchadnezzar had announced his intention to come there, in fear and trembling they fled to Amon, a little fortified city in Egypt, near the Salt Sea. This was the fourth captivity through Nebuchadnezzar.

(11) When Jeremiah saw that scarcely any of the Israelites were left, he lifted up his heart in prayer to God, saying, 'Why dost Thou cause me to see grief and iniquity? Why hast Thou caused the flock of Thy chosen people to fall into the hands of their enemy? I am sorely grieved and my soul is crushed within me, and mine eye sheddeth tears, and ceaseth not, for the destruction of the daughter of my people am I hurt. Mine eye weepeth with my soul, and for this do I weep day and night. Therefore do I pour forth my supplication before Thee that Thou wilt take my soul from me, for it is better for me to die than to live.' A voice was forthwith heard to say, 'By thy life wait, and behold the downfall of Babylon. Afterwards I shall preserve thee until I build the everlasting building.' Immediately upon these words, God hid him.

The Children of Moses.

LXI. (1) The banishment brought about by Titus, Vespasianus, and Hadrian, occurred on the eve of the ninth of Ab, on the outgoing of the Sabbath and the Sabbatical year. The Levites were then occupied with their ministrations, and, with their harps in their hands, were singing their hymns. But Scripture saith, 'He hath brought upon them their own iniquity, and shall cut them off in their own evil.' The words 'He shall cut them off' were not yet fully uttered ere their enemies came upon them, slaughtered many of them, and sent the rest into exile. Thus, also, when Nebuchadnezzar the wicked sent them into exile it fell upon the eve of the ninth of Ab, the outgoing of the Sabbatical year and the Sabbath, when the Levites were standing on their 'Duchan,' being sixty myriads in number, who were, moreover, of the seed of Moses our instructor. While the harps were in their hands, the verse 'He hath brought upon them their own iniquity, and shall cut them off in their own evil,' was not yet fully uttered, ere the enemy came and exiled them to Babylon. When they arrived in Babylon, their enemies and captors said to them, 'Sing us a song of Zion.' And they replied, 'How can we sing a song of Zion upon strange ground?'

(2) 'Now,' retorted their captors, 'ye shall sing by force.' But they at once cut off their fingers with their teeth, and cast them before them. And they replied, 'How can those fingers which struck the strings of the harps in the temple strike them here in a strange land?' And God exclaimed, 'If I forget Jerusalem, My right hand shall be forgotten.'

(3) A cloud then descended, and lifting all the children of Moses, with their sheep and cattle, brought them to the east of Havila. In the night they were let down, and on that same night they heard a great noise surrounding them, like that of a river, without seeing a drop of water descending, but heard only the rolling of stones and sand, where there had never been a river. This river then rolled great stones, and the sand, without any water, made a noise as of a great earthquake, so that if anyone came near that river, he was dashed to pieces. This continued until the Sabbath. The river they called Sabbatyon or Sabbatianus. In some part the river is less than sixty cubits in width; there the people stand and speak with those of the other side. On the Sabbath it ceases to flow, and on the eve of Sabbath a cloud descends full of smoke. No one is able to approach them, neither do they approach us. There are no wild beasts, no unclean animals, nor any reptiles or creeping things; nothing except their flocks and herds.

(4) They reap and sow, and they ask the others, and thus they learned of the destruction of the second temple. Behind the sons of Moses we do not know who may be dwelling; but Naphtali, Gad, and Asher came to Dan after the destruction of the second temple; for Isaachar, who lived at the mountains of the deep, quarrelled with them and

called them 'the sons of the handmaids.' At length, being afraid lest they be coming to battle, those three tribes went away until they came to Dan, and these four tribes were thus living in one place.

THE TEN BANISHMENTS OF THE SANHEDRIM.

LXII. (1) The Levites, the sons of Moses, made ten journeys and encamped on the other side of the river Sabbatyon. Our sages say that when the Israelites were exiled to Babylon, and came to the Euphrates, as it is said, 'We sat by the waters of Babylon,' etc., they said to them, 'O Levites, stand up before our gods, and sing a song just as you sang in the temple.' But they replied, 'O ye fools, if we had sung a song of thanksgiving for every miracle which God wrought for us, we should not have been exiled from our land, but would, on the contrary, have added honour upon honour; and shall we now sing a song to your idols?' Being angered at this reply, they immediately rose up and slew the Jews in heaps, and although the slaughter was so great, yet their joy had ceased, because the Jews did not worship idols. Therefore it is said, 'Their joy was turned into wailing.' The remaining Levites then cut off their fingers that they might avoid playing on their harps; so that when they were told to play and sing on their harps, just as they had done in the temple, they showed them their mutilated fingers.

(2) When night came on a cloud covered them, together with their wives, and sons, and daughters, and the Lord gave them light by a pillar of fire, which showed them the way the whole night until the dawn of day, and brought them to the seashore. When the sun rose the cloud departed as well as the pillar of fire. And the Lord extended the length of the river Sabbatianus, so that it surrounded them completely. It hems them in so that no one can cross over to them, and He extended it all round to a distance of nine months' journey. The river surrounds them from three sides, and on the fourth is the sea. The

depth of the river is 200 cubits, and it is full of sand and stones. The noise is that of an earthquake, and reaches the distance of half a day's journey, and causes the sand and stones to roll all the six days of the week.

(3) But on the Sabbath it rests, and immediately a fire bursts forth from the western side, which lasts from the eve of Sabbath until the end. Its flames shoot out in every direction, so that one can not approach nearer the river than a distance of thirty-four miles, and this fire burns all round and consumes everything. There is not seen among them any unclean animal or bird, and no creeping thing, but only their flocks and herds. There are six fountains, which gather together and form one pool. From these they water the land and obtain in abundance all kinds of clean fishes, and all kinds of birds and fruits. They sow one seed and reap a hundredfold. They are men of faith, students of the Law, the Scripture, Mishna and Agadah. They are pious and pure and never swear falsely. They attain the ripe old age of 120 years, nor does a son or daughter die in the lifetime of their father. (4) They see three successive generations and build for themselves houses; they sow and plough themselves, because they have no manservants or maidservants. They do not close their houses in the night-time, and a young child walks fearlessly with the cattle for many a day, without having any fear either of robbers or of any possible injury, because they are holy and remained in the holiness of Moses our teacher. Therefore God gave them all this and chose them. They do not see any man, nor does any of the sons of men see them, except the four tribes, Dan, Naphtali, Gad, and Asher, all of whom dwell on the other side of the rivers of Kush, with the Sabbatyon between them, and there they will remain until the end of the world. Concerning them it is said, 'To say to the captives " Go out," ' viz., referring to those behind the river Sabbatyon.

(5) There the tribes of Dan, Naphtali, Gad, and Asher, were enclosed. The question as to how they arrived at that

place our sages have thus answered: When Jeroboam, the son of Nebat, sinned, and caused Israel to sin, and the house of David became separated from the ten tribes of Israel, he said to the people, 'Go ye forth and fight with Rehoboam and the inhabitants of Jerusalem.' But they said, 'Wherefore should we go to war against our brethren, against the house of our master, David, King of Israel and Judah?' And the elders of Israel said to him, 'In all the land of Israel there do not exist such mighty warriors and men so trained to battle as those of the tribe of Dan.' Then, commanding them forthwith to wage war with Judah, they said, 'By the life of Dan, our forefather, we shall never go to battle with our brethren, and we shall not shed their blood without any cause.' And immediately afterwards the sons of Dan, taking up their swords and spears and bows, determined to fight unto death with Jeroboam, but God saved them from the crime of shedding the blood of their brethren. (6) They spread the news then throughout the whole tribe of Dan, and the sons of Dan took counsel together to depart from Canaan and to go down to Egypt to destroy it and kill all its inhabitants. But their princes asked, 'Why will you go to Egypt? Is it not written in the Torah, "Ye shall never again behold them"?' At this they gave way, but again took counsel concerning Edom, Moab, and the Ammonites. When, however, they heard that God had withheld Israel from fighting them they again gave up their intentions, until the Lord advised them better what to do. So they went to the brook of Pishon, and journeyed on their camels until they arrived at the other side of the river Pishon. There they discovered that the country was fruitful and extensive, containing fruitful fields and gardens. The sons of Dan therefore determined to dwell there, and made a covenant with the inhabitants, the sons of Kush, who paid them tribute, and also dwelt among them until they increased and multiplied exceedingly.

(7) On the death of Sennacherib the three tribes of Gad, Asher, and Naphtali left the country, and travelled until

they arrived near the border of that tribe, when they slaughtered the Kushites, a distance of four days' journey. They war with six Kushite kings, which every tribe continues to do for three months in the year until this very day, each tribe separately, but the descendants of Simeon go with those of Dan. (8) The Levites journeyed and encamped in Havila, which abounds in gold, that is as common as stones, also in sheep, cattle, camels, asses, and horses. There they sow and reap, and dwell in tents made of skin. They journey from one border to another, a distance of four days each way; and where they encamp there no man dares enter, and they only stay in the fields and vineyards, and punish in accordance with the different kinds of capital punishments meted out by the Jewish Law. Concerning them it is said, 'Those on the other side of the mountains of Kush,' etc.

(9) The tribe of Isaachar dwell on the mountains of the great deep in the nethermost parts of Media and Persia, and there they fulfil the commandment, 'the book of the Torah shall not depart from their mouth;' nor do they take upon themselves the yoke of any earthly kingdom, but only the yoke of Heaven and the yoke of the Law. They have many captains of the army, but never fight with man, but discuss the Torah. They dwell in peace and tranquillity, and no rebellious thought or evil of any kind enters their minds. They possess a country whose area covers land of ten days' journey, and they have an abundance of cattle, camels, and servants, but do not breed horses, nor do they possess any warlike instruments, except knives for preparing food, and to kill the animals for that purpose. They are men of great faith, hating oppression or robbery. If even their servant finds money by the way they will not stretch forth their hand to take it. (10) But their wicked neighbours worship fire, and take their mothers and their sisters to wives. They neither till the ground, nor reap, nor gather in the harvest, but they purchase it for money. They have a judge and a chief who metes out the four capital punish-

ments. They speak the Hebrew and Persian languages, and that of Kedar.

(11) The children of Zebulun encamp on the mountains of Paran, and pitch tents made of the hair of Armania (ארמניא) and stretch as far as the Euphrates. The tribe of Reuben dwells opposite them behind the mountains of Paran, and between them there is love, unity, and peace. They infest the roads leading to Mecoth (מכו) and the way to Babylon. All their spoil they divide equally between them, and food is so cheap that two camel-loads can be bought for two drachmas. They speak among themselves the language of Kedar, and possess the Bible, Mishna, Talmud, and Agadoth. But every Sabbath a lecture is given in Hebrew, and interpreted in the language of Kedar. (12) The tribe of Ephraim and half the tribe of Menasseh dwells opposite the city of Meyuqa (מיוקא). They have to toil for their living by the sweat of their brow, and are hard-hearted. They are riders of horses, infesting the roads, and having pity on no man. They possess no money, but only the spoil they acquire from their enemies. They are a distance of six months' march from the temple, and their numbers are incalculable and without number. They exact tribute from twenty-five kingdoms, as well as from a portion of Ishmael, but the tribes of Judah and Benjamin are scattered over the whole world. 'May the Rock of Israel gather together our dispersed brethren. Amen.'

ELCHANAN THE MERCHANT.

LXIII. (1) The story of Elchanan. Elchanan, the son of Joseph, was a large export merchant, and owned many vessels. He hailed from the province of the tribe of Dan, and was exceedingly wise and pious. He passed the day in praying, maintaining the poor, and giving a helping hand to orphan boys and girls. By means of his great skill he made a ship containing sixty chambers, of which each one of his servants made one for himself and his goods. In the centre of the vessel he constructed a tower which enabled him to see all his servants and their chambers. All the rooms were placed far away from his, and his servants could also not easily enter their neighbour's compartment, nor make any designs upon his property.

(2) Elchanan himself was a mighty man of valour, as were also his sons, being altogether four in the tower. The ship was loaded with 10,000 talents' worth of pepper, 10,000 talents' worth of frankincense, 10,000 of calamus and cinnamon, 1,000 litres of machik (מכיק), which they call saffron (ש׳ רון), and every other kind of spice, filling the whole vessel from top to bottom. Some of the servants appointed to guard the merchandise were Jews and others Ishmaelites. Besides these, there were, of course, the sailors. He had with him also 10,000 talents of silver to buy beautiful garments in various parts of the world.

(3) He acted as captain himself. His intention was to travel to a large kingdom, but was overtaken by a severe storm, which resulted in his ship drifting on to the sand in the Sea of Havila. (4) There R. Elchanan came across a certain people who spoke Hebrew. 'Who are ye?' said he. 'We are descendants of Dan,' answered they. And they forthwith invited him among them, and did very great honour to him, for R. Elchanan was beautiful and majestic in appearance. He then told them all his trouble and everything that befell him, and asked them many questions how they came to that place. Thereupon they related to him all their adventures. At the time when Jeroboam resigned, he said to the Israelites, 'Go ye and wage war with Rehoboam, the son of David.' And then the elders told him, Among all the tribes of Israel there is not one containing such mighty men of war and men so trained to battle as the tribe of Dan, and that they should therefore go to battle with Rehoboam and the inhabitants of Jerusalem. Thereupon he (Jeroboam) said to them, 'Arise, ye sons of Dan, and fight the men of Judah.' But they replied, 'By the life of our father, Dan, we shall never go against our brothers the house of David and against the King of Judah, and

why should we shed innocent blood?' 'If that is so,' said he, 'then depart from this land of Canaan.' For Jeroboam had made two calves of gold, by which he caused Israel to sin, so that the kingdom of the house of David was divided from that time. (5) They then took counsel against the Egyptians to destroy their land and kill its inhabitants. But their chiefs said to them, 'Is it not written in the Torah, "Ye shall no more see them?" How can we therefore go down to Egypt?' They then had designs (counselled) against Edom, Ammon and Moab, but found it stated in the Torah that God had forbidden Israel to inherit their borderland. But God gave them good advice, and they left the land and marched until they reached the brook of Pishon, a journey of seven years from Canaan. Then, journeying upon camels, they came to Kush, *i.e.*, Havila, a land both rich and fertile, abounding in fields, vineyards, gardens and palaces. There they dwelt by the sea, where there were Ethiopians without number. (6) The news of their advent having reached the ears of the king, they gathered themselves together as one man, and said, 'It is better for us to die all on one day than little by little by the hand of this strange nation.' The Kushite kings, numbering sixty-five, encamped on the one side of the brook of Pishon, facing the others, the town being between the two hosts. The descendants of Dan, consisting of 200,000 foot, took their bows in their hands and crossed the brook, and a battle took place by the water, in which twenty-five Ethiopian kings were slain. Each one of these kings possessed 1,000 horsemen and 80,000 infantry.

(7) Soon after this, the descendants of Dan, while they were in their camp, heard a great shouting and a loud noise of trumpets. Almost immediately they set up a great shouting themselves, for about 300,000 men of the tribes of Naphtali, as well as of Gad and Asher, had come to their assistance on their horses, and said, 'Brethren, ye must be weary now; rest until the morrow, and we shall join you.' Accordingly, on the morrow they slew all the

kings of Kush, and, taking all the spoil, divided it by lot, the silver and gold being as plentiful as stones. The land of Havila measured a distance of a square, one side of which would take four months to travel, each of the four tribes occupying one side. There they dwell now securely. Concerning them it is written, 'How good and how pleasant it is for brothers to dwell together.' A king is appointed over them, and they have an abundance of sheep and oxen, silver and gold, horses, camels and asses; and they sow and gather in the harvest. The king and the judges appointed by themselves give battle every day to the kings of Kush and to strange kingdoms.

(8) These are the names of the kingdoms: Zaqlah the first (or the Eastern), Batuaḥ, Qelalah, Arirah, 'Adirah, Zeridah, Zaryonah, Latusqah (לתוסקה), Tiráh, Tiqunah, Qomah, Qalmah, Ahalah, Aholibah, Riphtah, Saqvah, Qadvah (Qadovah), and Horiyah. They converse with each of these peoples in their own language, and, having made a covenant with them, they dwell by the rivers of Kush called 'Zahab Tob,' which is on the border of the land of Ḥavila.

(9) These four tribes having given battle to these strange kings, they (the kings) brought them presents. Concerning this it is written, "Othri, the daughter of Puṣi (פוצי), shall bring them gifts. . . .' They possess vineyards and large fields, and dwell in tents made of hair, and no stranger can enter the land of Havila. Therein also dwells their king, Abiel, the son of Shaphat, and also the captain of the host, Abihail, the son of Shaphat, both of them of the tribe of Dan. When the trumpeter sounds the trumpet, the captain of the host comes forth with the armies, consisting of 173 banners, under each one serving 1,500 men of each tribe, and just as they go out, so they return.

(10) Then the second tribe comes forth, each of the four tribes serving three months. Each tribe keeps its own spoil, and they converse with each other in Hebrew, and in the language of Kedar, and they are all of them pious men. I dwelt among them for twelve months.

(11) They inflict the four capital punishments in accordance with the decisions of the Beth Din. The tribe of Moses is also among them, as it is said, 'And all the children of Levi gathered unto him.' They encamp by the brook of Kedron, together with scattered remnants of the exiles. The brook is called Sambatyon (שאמבטיון), which encompasses them with a radius of two months' walk. They sleep in houses built like towers, nor is any unclean bird or animal found among them, not even flies, or gnats, or vermin, but only their flocks and herds, which breed twice every year. Nor is there any scorpion or serpent. They reap a hundredfold for every measure of corn they sow, and they possess all kinds of fruits, herbs, spelt, leeks, melons, onions and garlic. They are living together as one nation, and possess many wells, from the waters of which all the lands are irrigated. They also possess all kinds of spices, and round about them there fly about all manner of clean birds. The river, the sand and stones continue in a whirl during the six days of the week, but on the Sabbath they rest. On the eve of every Sabbath a flaming fire ascends from one side of the river, so that no one can approach it until the Sabbath has come to an end. No man has ever seen these flames of the river Sambatyon except the descendants of Dan, Asher, Gad and Naphtali. They alone commune with them, and with reference to them it is said, 'To say to those that are bound, Go forth,' etc.

(12) They have an abundance of silver and gold; they sow and reap, and grow the worms that make the crimson colour, and they make unto themselves beautiful garments and robes, and they are more numerous than they were when they left Egypt. Concerning these four tribes it is written, 'Ah! the land of the rustling of wings which is beyond the rivers of Kush.' The river Sambatyon is four cubits wide, as far as a bowshot reaches. The noise it makes is exceedingly loud, like the billows of the sea and like a mighty tempest, and in the night-time the sound is heard at a distance of half a day's journey. If sand from

that river is placed in a flask, it whirls about during the six days of the week, but on the Sabbath it rests.

(13) The four tribes, together with their cattle, go near the river Sambatyon to shear their flock, for the land is plain and smooth, where neither thorns nor herbs grow. When the descendants of Moses see them, they assemble at the side of the brook, and, raising their voices, say, 'O children of Dan, show us a camel, or ass, or dog.' And they exclaim, 'How long is this camel! and see the length of its neck! How short its ear is! It is very ugly!' These men are pious and charitable, besides being well versed in the Torah, Mishna, and Talmud. When they study they use to say, 'We have received this by tradition from Joshua and Moses, our teachers, and from God.' They do not know the other sages and their traditions are written down in the language in which our teacher Moses delivered them to them. The laws of the killing of animals are according to the words of the sages. They never swore by the name of God.

(14) But the children of Dan did so, and the children of Levi said to them, 'Why do ye take the name of God (in vain)? for has He not given thee bread to eat and water to drink? Why do ye therefore do this thing? Know now that your sons and your daughters shall die in their youth on account of your iniquities, but as for us, no son or daughter shall die in the lifetime of their father, but shall live to the ripe age of 120.' These people do not possess any manservants or maidservants, since they are themselves skilled workmen and merchants. They have shutters with which to close their shops, but never do so because there are no thieves. It is usual for a child to go a distance of several days with the cattle, without any fear of wild beasts, evil spirits, demons or injurious beings, since they are pure and still sanctified with the holiness of Moses our teacher, as it is said, 'For they shall eat the fruit of their actions.'

(15) The children of Isaachar are as numerous as the sand of the sea, without number. They dwell on the

mountains of the deep, behind the land of the Medes and Persians, and a distance of four months' journey from those who dwell by the brook of Pishon. The law does not depart from their mouth, thus fulfilling the command, 'The Torah shall not depart from thy mouth; thou shalt meditate upon it day and night.' They accepted no earthly yoke, but only the yoke of the kingdom of heaven, and do not fight with their fellow-men, but discuss the Talmud and the Torah. They live in peace and tranquillity, with no injurious thought or evil of any kind to tempt them, and dwell on an area of thirteen days' journey in each direction. Silver and gold, servants, camels, flocks and herds, they have in plenty, but they breed none. The only warlike instruments they use are knives for killing the sheep, oxen and birds. They receive a tribute from the heathen kingdoms, of all produce, a fourth, and of the oxen and sheep a fifth every year. From this tribute they accumulate immense riches. They have judges and they inflict the four capital punishments according to the decisions of the Beth Din. They converse in the Hebrew language and in that of Kedar.

(16) I dwelt among them for a period of two months, and then, taking my departure on board ship, I fell in among the tribe of Zebulun, who dwell on the mountains of Paran, in tents of hair, in the land of Lud and Pul. Entering their land, I found them to be farmers, tilling the ground and reaping the harvest. They possess all kinds of dainties and are men of valour. For four months they go out to plunder, fighting and robbing people of their riches. They possess the Torah, the Talmud and Mishna, and are men of great faith, who observe all the Commandments. They are also good riders, having innumerable servants, horses, sheep and oxen, as well as camels and asses. They dwell in peace and tranquillity, where no man can intrude.

(17) Thence, after six days' journey, I came to the tribe of Reuben, opposite them, between Paran and Bethel, where they dwell without war. Concerning them it is written,

'And I shall cause the wild beast to cease from the land, and no sword shall pass over their land.' In the midst of the mountains of darkness they possess a fertile and fruitful land, the stones of which are iron, and from the mountains of which brass is hewn. It is a land in which one could eat his bread without any danger, for no man passes among them. They watch the roads and capture spoil without end. They dwell safely in tents of hair, and speak the Hebrew language and another strange one (לשון).

(18) Thence I came to an extensive land by way of Shin'ar, through Elam; it was the kingdom of Mehumat (מהומט) on the border of Madia, a distance of four months' journey from the city of (Medinat). I saw the river Gozan (גוזן), and a part of the tribes of Ephraim and Menasseh, who were harsh and hard-hearted. They also are good riders, watching the roads, and having pity on no man. All their possessions were plunder. They are men of valour and skilled in war; one of them alone could smite a thousand men. Among themselves a large amount of food could be obtained for two pieces of silver, and grapes could be obtained in the same way. Concerning them it is said, 'Five of you shall pursue 100, and 100 of you 10,000.'

(19) A half of the tribe of Simeon lives together with the tribe of Judah in the land of the Chasdim, near Jerusalem, a distance of four months' journey. They are countless and innumerable, and their faces are like lions' faces. They are all of them proficient riders, archers, spearsmen, and swordsmen, and dwell in tents made of hair, in a wilderness the extent of which is a journey of two months each way. They receive tribute from twenty-five kings, all of whom are white, some belonging to the Ishmaelites and others to the descendants of Keturah. They wage war with heathen kingdoms, always seeking battle. They journey the way of Mathol (מטחול), and the way of Babylon, until the city of the madman (מישוגע); in all directions they

journey with their cattle from border to border, and nobody ever dares speak to them. Among themselves they speak Hebrew and Greek, and are men of faith, skilled in the Torah, Talmud, Mishna, and Agada, and also spoke the language of Togarma.

(20) I dwelt among the sons of Judah and Simeon for three years, until merchants from the land of the Danites came to buy the spoil of which they had great quantities, and also spices captured from merchants on the way, and which they had acquired for nothing. I travelled with them on board ship until we came to Elam, after a journey of four months. After the lapse of ten years from the day I departed from the Danites I returned. Those heathen whose land I passed through, and among whom the tribes dwell, were some of them worshippers of the earth, while some worshipped fire, and others worshipped a white horse and were cannibals. [End of the words of R. Elchanan the Danite. I have heard that this R. Elchanan was simple and upright, eschewing evil, and fearing God. He came from the land of India.[1]]

THE MIDRASH OF AHAB BEN QOLAYA AND ZEDEKIAH BEN MA'ASEYAH.

LXIV. (1) 'Thus saith the Lord of Ahab ben Qolaya and of Zedekiah ben Ma'aseyah, which prophesy falsely in My name, behold I will deliver them into the hand of Nebuchadnezzar, King of Babylon, and he shall slay them before your very eyes. From them a curse shall be taken up by all the captivity of Judah and Israel in Babylon, saying, "May the Lord make thee like Zedekiah and Ahab, whom the King of Babylon 'roasted' in the fire."' It is not said, 'They were burnt,' but 'roasted.' R. Johanan, in the name of R. Simeon ben Johai, said, 'We learn from

[1] Here follows in the MS. the Hebrew translation of Daniel, which is therefore omitted in the English translation; and then the history of Bel and the Dragon, and the 'Song of Three Children,' translated and published by me in the Proceedings of the Society of *Biblical Archæology*, 1894-95.

the above that He made them like parched ears of corn.' 'Because they committed abomination in Israel, they committed adultery with the wives of their neighbours, and spoke falsely in My name that which I had not commanded them, even I who know and testify against them, saith the Lord.' (2) Ahab went to the daughter of Nebuchadnezzar, and said to her, 'The Lord said, "Hearken to Zedekiah, and there shall come forth from thee kings and prophets who will prophesy against Israel."' Hearing this, Zedekiah also went to her, and said, 'In the same manner as Ahab has said about me, so also listen to him, and there shall come forth from thee kings and prophets who will prophesy against Israel.' When she heard this, she immediately went to her father and told him all that had happened, saying, 'Thus and thus did Ahab and Zedekiah say unto me.' And her father replied, 'The God of these men hateth lewdness. As soon as they come to thee a second time again send them to me.' When they came, she accordingly said to them, 'I cannot do anything without my father's knowledge; therefore, go ye to my father, and, placing your request before him, listen to his reply.'

(3) Going to Nebuchadnezzar, they repeated what they had told his daughter. And he replied, 'What is the cause of it that your God did not tell this prophecy to Hananya, Mishael, and Azariah? Are they not prophets?' And they said, 'He did not command Hananya, Mishael, and Azariah to do anything, but it was us He commanded to do this thing.' At this Nebuchadnezzar retorted, 'I asked Hananya, Mishael, and Azariah, saying, "Is this thing which you ask my daughter prohibited or permitted?" "It is prohibited," said they.' 'But we are prophets,' answered Zedekiah and Ahab, 'as they. He did not command them but us to do this thing.' (4) 'I desire, then, to test you as I tested Hananya, Mishael, and Azariah, viz., in the fiery furnace.' 'But they were three, and we are only two,' added they. 'Then choose ye one whomsoever ye wish to be tried with you.' And they said, 'We desire Joshua the

son of Jehozadak, the high priest.' They knew that his merit was so great that he would protect them also. Accordingly the three of them were brought and cast into the fiery furnace. Ahab and Zedekiah were consumed by the fire, but Joshua, the high priest, was not touched by it; his garments merely smelt of fire, as it is said, 'He showed me Joshua, the high priest, standing before the angel of the Lord, and Satan standing at his right hand to tempt him.' It is further written, 'And the Lord said unto Satan, "The Lord rebuke thee, O Satan ; the Lord who chose Jerusalem shall rebuke thee. Is this not a brand plucked out of the fire?'

(5) 'I know now,' said Nebuchadnezzar, 'that thou art very righteous, but how is it that thy garments were touched a little by the fire, while in the case of Hananya, Mishael, and Azariah the fire did not touch them at all?' 'Because,' said Joshua, 'they were three and I was alone.' 'But,' said he, 'Abraham was also alone.' 'True, but there were no wicked people in his company, and the Lord therefore did not allow the fire to touch him ; but with me there were two wicked men, and on this account the Lord allowed the fire to touch me a little.' This is the parable of the two dry torches and the one moist, where the two dry ones burn the moist.

The History of Susanna.

LXV. (1) There dwelt a man in Babylon named Jehoiachin, and he took a wife whose name was Susanna, one that feared the Lord. She was the daughter of righteous and good parents, who brought her up in the ways of the Lord, according to the precepts of the law of Moses. Now, this man Jehoiachin was greater and more respected than any of his generation. To him all the Jews resorted daily, for no one like him was found among God's people. He had a beautiful garden adjoining his house, where his wife Susanna used to retire for bathing. (2) At this time two judges were appointed over the people, who came in the early morning and evening to Jehoiachin's house to deliver judgment to the people. But when they beheld the beautiful Susanna their lust was inflamed towards her. They renounced their hope in heavenly reward, and, whilst separating themselves from the righteous, yet neither one revealed to the other the evil thought of his heart. But when the crowd had dispersed to their homes, they spoke to each other, and then, confessing their lust to each other, they took counsel together in which way they might lead her astray, and, watching diligently every day to defile her, they neither stopped nor rested from their sin.

(3) One day when all the people had departed to their homes they remained behind according to custom, nor did they remove the evil of their heart, but lay in wait to commit the evil. When Susanna entered the garden accompanied by her maids to wash herself on account of the heat, she sent them to bring her some oil wherewith to anoint herself, at the same time telling them to close the door behind them. When they went out they accordingly bolted the doors after them, but the old men were concealed in the beautiful garden, and when she stripped to wash they ran out of their hiding-place, and, taking hold of her, said, 'Lie with us, for if thou wilt not consent we shall bear witness against thee that a young man has lain with thee.' In fear and trembling she then said, 'What am I to do? I cannot escape these men. It is better for me to resign myself to the Lord, the righteous, the good, the great, the mighty, and the awe-inspiring God, the Deliverer, Saviour, and mighty Redeemer, whose name is the Lord of Hosts.' (4) Then, raising her voice on high, she cried, 'Save me, O Lord my God, from the hands of the wicked who rebel against Thee.' But they also cried aloud, and bore false witness against her. At their cry the men of her house came forth, and, entering the garden, beheld the elders bearing this testimony against her, and they and all their kindred were astonished, since they knew that the like of this was not seen or heard of her.

(5) On the morrow all the people gathered together to the house of Jehoiachin according to their custom, and

with them the elders who rose up and testified that they had seen this woman enter the garden with her two maids, and that a young man came and lay with her. 'We then took hold of the young man, but he slipped from our hands.' The people believed their words, for the elders were held to be good and God-fearing men.

(6) Then, sending for the woman, they brought her, and there came with her her relatives, friends, and acquaintances; but she was very feeble, and came there with her face covered. But the elders cried angrily from their evil desires, 'Remove the veil from her face!' that they might satisfy the wickedness of their eyes, and, condemning her to death, they led her forth. Then, raising her eyes on high, she said, 'O truthful and righteous Judge, O faithful Witness, behold me and save me from a death through false witnesses; let me not be found a sinner in the sight of all these people; and let not the words of these wicked men be fulfilled against me.'

(7) And the Lord heard her cry and sent a helper, for the Lord aroused the spirit of Daniel, who raised his voice, and said, 'Lord God, clear us of the death of this righteous woman.' Hearing this, the people asked, 'Who art thou that speaketh?' And they replied, 'The voice is that of Daniel;' he was then a young man in the king's household and a chamberlain in his palace. 'But why dost thou speak in this manner?' And he said, 'Will ye condemn to death one in Israel without investigation? Will ye slay the innocent and the righteous in a manner contrary to the law? Return to me, that I may investigate the matter.'

(8) The woman and all the people then returned, and the elders who bore witness against her said to him, 'Why does my Lord say, she is not to die, since she has done such and such a thing?' And Daniel said to the people, 'Be ye seated;' and they sat down. 'Now separate these elders one from the other.' Then, interrogating one of them, he said, 'O sinful old man, thou art surely condemned to death, and the angel stands over thee to cut thee in two.

Under what tree didst thou find her?' 'Under the terebinth' (אלין). And Daniel said to the people, 'Behold, this man shall die, for there is no such tree in the garden.'

(9) He was accordingly taken away, and the second one brought. And he said to him, 'O thou of the seed of Kainan, who art not of Judah. Thus did ye act in our land. Ye enticed beautiful maidens by your false testimony, so that we became a curse and a reproach, we were led captive and became a spoil; behold, thou art destined to be slain, and no soul is to be left within thee. Tell me, before the people, under what tree didst thou find her?' 'Under a trellis of the vine' (דלית). Then said Daniel, 'Behold, the angel stands over thee with a drawn sword in his hand to saw thy loins asunder, for there is no such tree in the garden.'

(10) They went and found that it was the truth. Then Daniel appeared to the people in all his wisdom, and it was done to those judges just as they devised against their sister. From that day Daniel was exalted in the sight of the people of Judah, and they gave thanks and praises to the Lord God of their fathers, as did Shealtiel, the father of Susanna, and her mother, as well as all her relatives and acquaintances, and her husband Jehoiachin.

LXVI. (1) Nebuchadnezzar was not very much changed in his being from other men; but only in his appearance, in his mind, and in his language. He appeared to men like an ox as far as his navel (or stomach), and from his navel to his feet like a lion. He ate the herbs at first which other men eat, to show that he chewed his food like an ox, and became at last like a lion, in that he killed all the wicked. Many people went out to see him, but Daniel did not, because, during the time of his change, he was praying for him, so that the seven years became seven months. For forty days he roamed about among the wild beasts, and for the next forty days his heart became like that of any other man, and he wept on account of his sins. Again, for forty days he wandered about in caves, and for yet another forty days he roamed among the wild beasts until the seven months were completed.

(2) When, however, the Lord restored him to his former position he no longer reigned alone, but appointed seven judges, one for each year until the expiration of the seven years. And during this time, while he was repenting for his sins, he neither ate meat nor bread, nor drank any wine, but his food consisted of herbs and seed, according to Daniel's counsel. When, after the seven years of his punishment, he sat once more on the throne of his kingdom, he wished to make Daniel an heir among his sons, but Daniel said, 'Far be it from me to leave the inheritance of my fathers for that of the uncircumcised.'

(3) On the death of Nebuchadnezzar the Great, his son of the same name succeeded him. He built a temple to Bel in Babylon, and completed the city of Babylon. He surrounded it with the river, so that the enemy could not prevail against it. He increased the city and the temple of Bel tenfold, and added glory and honour, and in fifteen days (?) the building was complete.

(4) The king then, having placed a huge stone upon a mountain, planted a garden upon it, which was raised to a great height so as to enable his wife to gaze upon Media, the land of her birth, for she longed to behold it. This was the king who besieged Tyre for three years and ten months. When Nebuchadnezzar, the son of Nebuchadnezzar the Great, died, Evil Merodach reigned in his stead.

(5) Now, in the thirty-seventh year of the captivity of Jehoiachin, King of Judah, on the twenty-seventh day of the twelfth month, Evil Merodach, King of Babylon, in the first year of his reign, rescued Jehoiachin, King of Judah, from prison, and raised his throne above that of any other king in Babylon, and, changing his prison garments, he maintained him as long as he lived. He did this because Nebuchadnezzar the Great did not keep his faith with him, for Evil Merodach was really his eldest son; but he made Nebuchadnezzar the Younger king, because he had humbled the wicked. They slandered him to his father, who

placed him (Evil Merodach) in prison together with Jehoiachin, where they remained together until the death of Nebuchadnezzar, his brother, after whom he reigned.

(6) 'I fear my father Nebuchadnezzar,' he said, 'lest he rise from his grave, for just as he was changed back from an animal to a man, so in the same manner he may rise up from death to life.' But Jehoiachin advised him to take the corpse out of the grave, and, cutting it into 300 pieces, to give it to 300 vultures, and he said to him, 'Thy father will not rise up until these vultures have brought back the flesh of thy father, which they have eaten.' Evil Merodach had three sons, whose names were Regosar (רִיגוֹסַר), Lebuzer-Dukh (לְבוּזֶר דוּךְ), and Nabar (נְבָאר), who was Belshazzar, with whom the Chaldean kingdom came to an end.

[Here commences the book of Joseph ben Gorion, with the exception of the first two pages, which contain an enumeration of the families and ancient kings, which I have written above in its proper place in the Book of the Generations.]

LXVII. (1) When God had visited upon Babylon all that He spake to His servants Isaiah and Jeremiah, the prophets, on behalf of Jerusalem, He raised up against them two mighty kings: Darius, King of Media, and Cyrus, King of Persia. And Cyrus entered into close friendship with Darius by taking his daughter to wife, so that they jointly rebelled against Belshazzar, King of the Chaldeans. This was the commencement of many fierce battles. At the outset the Chaldeans were victorious; but many fell on either side, and the Chaldeans fleeing, Cyrus and Darius pursued them until a distance of one day's journey from Babylon, and smote them and cut them to pieces. There Cyrus and Darius encamped with all their armies, and when the king Belshazzar saw them he sent out all the host of his mighty men—a thousand princes and the troops that were in the temple, a numerous and powerful band. At twilight all these marched out of Babylon, continuing their march during the whole night. But at the break of morn they began to attack the camp of Darius and Cyrus, which at the onset became bewildered, and the camp of Media fled in confusion; but Cyrus and his men braced themselves up to fight against the Chaldeans, and prevented them from following the Median camp. In the night, when the battle had ceased, the slain of the Medes and Persians were found to be very numerous.

(2) On that same day, as the princes of Belshazzar saw that they had gained a victory, they came before King Belshazzar full of victory and strength. The king made a great feast for them, and many presents of silver and gold were given to them; and the king rejoiced with his 1,000 princes, and sat down to eat and drink with them. They prolonged the banquet until night. Now, Belshazzar had drunk too much, and while he was in a state of intoxication he ordered the golden vessels which had been in the temple of our God at Jerusalem to be brought to him—viz., those holy vessels which Nebuchadnezzar had seized when he exiled the Jews from Jerusalem to Babylon. He then defiled the holy vessels by drinking wine out of them, together with his 1,000 princes, his wives, and his concubines.

(3) But when our God beheld this profanation, He was angry and jealous (zealous) for His vessels, so He sent from His throne a scribe to write a severe rebuke for the king, and to acquaint him with the judgment which our God had decreed concerning his life and his kingdom. The scribe accordingly wrote upon the wall in red ink by the lamp of the king the following: 'He thought, He weighed, He separated.' The letters were written in Hebrew characters, but the writing was Aramaic. When the king saw the fingers writing—the other parts of the body he did not see, for the fingers were terrible and beautiful—he became bewildered and very much afraid, so that every limb of his body, his heart, and his very bones trembled.

LXVIII. (1) Daniel was then brought before the king to read and interpret the writing, and he said to the king:

'Thou hast acted very foolishly, in that thou hast defiled the vessels of the temple of our God. Therefore our God, being zealous for His children and for His sanctuary, sent an angel to write these words. And these are the words which he has written, 'Shekel,' *i.e.*, the enemy of the Lord, 'has been weighed in the balance and been found wanting. He will therefore rend the kingdom from His enemy, and will give it to Darius and Cyrus, who have given thee battle. Between them the kingdom shall be divided.'

(2) And the princes of the king heard this explanation from Daniel and that he reproved the king, saying, 'Hearken to me, I pray thee, King Belshazzar, and mark and understand my words. Didst thou not know that the Lord God of the heavens made thy father great, and raised him over all the kingdoms of the earth; that He caused him to rule, in His greatness, over the holy Land, over the kingdom of priests and the holy nation; and that he (Nebuchadnezzar) treated them with great cruelty; that he shed their blood as water, burnt the holy temple with fire, and sent the whole of God's inheritance into captivity to Babylon? That then his heart waxed mighty and his spirit proud, so that he said, "My hand is exalted, and my power has stood by me"; that he did not remember that the God of the world, who exalteth and maketh humble, had delivered all these things into his hands; nor did he think of this until the Lord humbled him by making him wander among the wild beasts of the field and the birds of the heavens; and not until he believed that the Lord God of heaven is He who slayeth and bringeth to life was he restored again to his palace? And thou, Belshazzar, hast received thy father's kingdom by the will of the God of heaven, and reignest over all the land in the same manner as thy father.

(3) 'When thy two vassals, Darius and Cyrus, rebelled and made a conspiracy against thee, and went to battle against thy mighty army, thou didst send forth thy warriors to subdue them, and they returned to thee exceedingly elated with strength and glory; but thou

didst not give thanks to thy Creator, who gave thee the very breath of thy life, but to thy idols of silver and gold, of iron and brass, of clay and earthenware, which cannot rescue nor save, which can do neither evil nor good. And thou didst burn bright the lamp for thy 1,000 warriors and princes. Then didst thou send for the holy vessels, which were sanctified to the God of heaven, who breathed into thee the breath of life, and in whose hand is thy spirit, to slay or to keep alive. And thou didst defile His vessels by drinking out of them, together with all thy servants, princes, wives, and concubines, and didst sing praises to thy idols. For this the Lord's anger was kindled against thee and thy people, since thou hast foolishly done this. He therefore sent His scribe to write down upon the wall of thy house thy end, and the end of thy kingdom. Behold the writing is written in Hebrew characters, but the language is Aramaic. The words are "Mene, Mene, Tekel, Upharsin," which means that God has "numbered" the years of thy kingdom, which have been found completed; the seventy years (of the captivity) having come to an end. Thou hast been "weighed," and been found wanting. Therefore thy kingdom shall be "taken away" from thee, and given to the Medes and Persians.'

(4) When the king, the princes and the dignitaries of the kingdom heard this interpretation from Daniel, they were all greatly afraid, every one of them, their heart beat violently, and they were alarmed and trembled, and the king, being seized with dreadful pains through Daniel's words, fell upon his bed, sad and troubled, and mourning bitterly, while the rest of the princes returned to their houses in fear. When they went out through the gate they were in their excitement crushed and trampled on, and the king remained alone with his messengers and his household, and, being in great excitement and bewildered, he fell into a deep sleep, and slumbered like one of the dead through his fright and trembling. (5) Now, there was in the bedroom of the king a doorkeeper, one of the old servants of Nebuchadnezzar, who was much honoured and

respected. Meditating in his heart, he said, 'Did not Daniel interpret all Nebuchadnezzar's dreams? and did not all his words come true, so that nothing he prophesied failed to be realized? Now he has told the king what is decreed concerning him, for the spirit of God is with him, and he does not lie. Why, therefore, should I not go, and, severing Belshazzar's head, run with it to Cyrus and Darius, the Kings of Media and Persia, and thereby find favour in their eyes?' And as he thought, so he did. Rising hastily in the twilight, he drew the sword from beneath the king's pillows, and with it smote Belshazzar, severing his head. He wandered all through the night until daybreak, and then went to the two kings with the head of Belshazzar in his hand.

(6) But when they saw it, both they and all the men trembled and gazed in fear at each other, as well as all the army. On asking the man for an explanation, he related all that Daniel had told Belshazzar, how he had defiled the holy vessels of the temple, and thus kindled the anger of the God of the heavens, who sent a messenger to write upon the wall in red ink opposite the candlestick. 'When I heard Daniel tell these things, I knew that it was all true and that nothing would fail to come to pass. On account of this I planned and hastened to perform this deed which now your eyes behold.'

(7) When the two kings heard the words of the servant they feared the wrath of the God of heaven, and consequently humbled, prostrated and bowed themselves before the Lord of all things, saying, 'We know that Thou alone art God over all the hosts of heaven and over all the kingdoms of the earth, who removest and establishest kings, and who doest whatever Thou desirest. Thou knowest that this Belshazzar, the wicked grandson of the wicked Nebuchadnezzar, acted wickedly, and Thou hast therefore visited him to destroy him in the wrath of Thy anger in that he defiled the vessels of Thy holy sanctuary. Thou didst hand him over to be slaughtered by this chamberlain that his head may be brought before

us. We now give thanks unto Thee, O God of the heavens, for the wonders which Thou hast wrought. If Thou wilt deliver his land into our possession and the valiant, mighty men thereof, we shall wreak vengeance upon them to satisfy the wrath of Thine anger. Then Thou wilt help us to free Thy servants from their captivity, to build Thy holy temple in Jerusalem, and to gather together the outcasts of Thy people, that they may once again worship Thee alone.' Having said this, they made a feast and rejoiced for three days.

(8) Then, marching into Babylon, they captured it, and, overthrowing the fortresses, slew the warriors at the edge of the sword, ripped up their women with child, slaughtered their old men in the streets, strangled their young men with ropes and dragged them with their horses along the streets, their virgins they trampled to death, and their young children they dashed against the rocks. (9) Thus God avenged the blood of His servants that was shed by the Babylonians and Chaldeans, and took vengeance for His city and His temple. These two kings overran all the streets with their mighty army, and, overthrowing all their palaces, burnt their most precious things, and, blowing upon their trumpets, raised a loud cry so that the earth was cleft asunder at their noise, and they said: 'Where are ye, ye mighty men of Babylon and ye valiant men, ye sinners of the whole earth. The battle is no longer yours.' They then set fire to everything that came before them until they rendered the whole of Babylon a waste land, like Sodom and Gomorrah, according to the word which God spake to His servants the prophets. (10) After this the two kings divided the whole kingdom of the Chaldeans by lot, so that Darius took for his portion Babylon, with all its inhabitants, and the great temple of the palace which Nebuchadnezzar had built; and Darius sat upon the throne of Belshazzar. Thus, while the great Babylon, with all its inhabitants, together with the land of Media, fell to the lot of Darius, the land of the Chaldeans, Assyria and Persia fell to the lot of Cyrus.

LXIX. (1) Now it came to pass, when Darius was firmly seated upon the throne of his kingdom in Babylon, that he ordered Daniel to be brought before him, and, placing for him a throne, he sat before Darius. Then said the king, 'Art thou Daniel?' 'I am,' said he. 'Then give me counsel what to do, for the spirit of the God of heaven is with thee; do not withhold it from me, for I am old now and wanting in strength. My active life wearies me, and continual wars make me faint; and now that my old age has begun, I am no longer able to bear the burden of my people, to judge between man and man, to reward the righteous and punish the wicked, for the thing is too heavy for me.'

(2) And Daniel replied: 'Let my lord the king appoint three officers, men of valour and truth, to take upon themselves part of the responsibility, and let them judge between man and man in order to relieve thee of the heaviness of the burden, and let the king rest in his palace. Then every matter that is too weighty for the judges shall be brought before the king, who shall decide. Thus the king and his throne shall be pure.' He did as he was advised, for he appointed two princes of his host, with Daniel in authority over them, to judge the people, while he himself remained peaceably in his palace.

(3) Darius issued a decree throughout all his kingdom, saying, 'The God of the heavens hath given me all these kingdoms of the earth, and the burden is too great for me to bear, for my soul is weary through old age. I have therefore taken advice of Daniel, who has given me true counsel, and I have hearkened unto him. I shall now rest in my palace so that the heaviness of the burden will be taken off my shoulders. Now give honour to the God of Daniel and believe in Him. Rise up early and seek Him, for He is the great God over all other gods. Let it be known to you that by the advice of Daniel have I done this. I have appointed over all my kingdom two princes of the host, to whose decisions all the people shall listen in all cases of trouble, so that the burden is made

lighter for me; and Daniel have I appointed as overseer to these two princes, who are to obey him and to listen to all that he teaches them, and not to change his words, but to perform everything he commands them, for I have appointed him as a vicegerent, with the two princes of the army under him, and whoever violates this decree of the king shall forfeit his life.' All the people obeyed this decree, and the princes, governors, commanders and rulers of the provinces bestowed honour upon Daniel, for the holy Spirit was with him.

LXX. (1) Soon after this, however, the princes of the army, as well as the other chiefs, governors and dignitaries of the kingdom envied Daniel, and, meeting in counsel, they sought for some pretext by which they might overthrow Daniel. So they resolved to make a decree and a covenant that every man, old or young, belonging to the rulers or the princes, who shall during the next thirty days entreat any god, or ask a request from any being, except from the king alone, shall be given as food to lions, nor shall he be rescued by the hand of the king, or redeemed by his great wealth to annul the decree. Daniel was ignorant of their machinations, for they cunningly kept their secret from him, saying, 'If we do not trap him in a religious matter we shall not be able to overthrow him.' But they did not know that, as Daniel was faithful to his God, so would his God prove faithful to him.

(2) The men, having then written down what they had resolved to do, they each one of them signed it and sealed it with his seal, in order to give it greater authority. They then waited upon the king with their writing, who took it and read it innocently without suspecting that it was a secret plot cunningly devised against Daniel. Therefore he confirmed the decree by sealing it with the king's seal, and giving it to his scribes to guard for the appointed time. (3) One day the men went to Daniel's house to spy, and, finding a girl playing about opposite the entrance of his house, they asked, 'Where is Daniel, and what is he doing?' And she replied, 'Behold, he is in

the upper chamber of his house, praying near the window which looks towards the holy temple at Jerusalem, and uttering praises and words of thanksgiving to his God.' Believing her, they went to the upper chamber, and found him on his knees with his hands spread towards heaven, for Daniel supplicated to God three times during the day.

(4) When these men came into Daniel's chamber he was not frightened, nor did he tremble at the noise of their voice, and he finished his prayer, when they all immediately seized him and brought him to the king. But when the king saw Daniel in the hands of the princes he trembled very greatly, and was astounded, for he then knew that it was against Daniel they had made and established such a decree. Then said the king to the princes, 'What have ye done to Daniel, and what have ye to do with him?' (5) And they replied, 'Have we not written down and sealed the decree in accordance with the law of Media and Persia, which cannot be changed or frustrated, that whoever prostrates himself to any being for the whole of this month other than to the king shall be consigned as food for the lions? Behold, Daniel was found in his house praying to his God, and thus this decree of the King of Media and Persia was violated, which cannot be. Now, since Daniel has mocked us in trying to set our laws at naught, give him into our hands, and we shall cast him into the den of lions, that no other person may attempt such a thing again in opposition to the laws of Media and Persia.' And the king answered the princes, saying, 'Ye have devised this plan against Daniel to attack him for your envy. Now, cease pursuing him, for he is a Jew, and his God is revered, glorious and mighty, who may visit you with His anger, and destroy you.' But the princes seized Daniel with their hands, ready to destroy him by casting him into the den of lions. The king, therefore, exerted all his strength to rescue him, but not one of them helped the king to save Daniel, for they were all eager for his downfall, and refused, therefore, to release him. But the king would not listen to the princes,

and they strove with each other, the princes and the king, until sunset.

(6) When, however, they saw that the king was with him, they said with one accord, 'O king, know and mark well, if thou wilt not deliver him into our hands, we shall know that thou annullest the laws of Media and Persia.' As soon as the king saw that they were all of them bent on conspiring against him on account of Daniel, he let him go, delivering him into their power, and saying to them, 'Tell me, if God delivers him from the mouth of the lions, how will you hide your reproach and your shame, for ye shall surely be cast to the lions as food.' And they all replied, 'So it shall be.' The king, having striven with the princes until it was late, said to Daniel, 'Behold, the princes have determined to cast thee into the den of lions, but the Lord God of the heavens, who hath given thee His holy Spirit, shall close their mouths and prevent them injuring thee; but I am innocent before thy God, for I sought to rescue thee, but could not.' Then, drawing Daniel forth, they cast him into the den in which ten lions were enclosed. Their daily fare consisted of ten sheep and ten human bodies. But they starved them, depriving them of their food, giving them nothing to eat, so that they should hasten to devour Daniel. When Daniel had, however, descended to the den of lions they showed him a kind face, licked him, wagged their tails, and were as rejoiced to meet him as dogs are to see their master arrive home from the field. The princes rolled a great stone over the mouth of the pit, which the king sealed with his ring as well as with that of the princes, and they each went their way.

(7) Daniel, in the meantime, praised the name of his God all the night until the next morning with the voice of song and thanksgiving, while the lions crouched round about him, eager to hearken unto his song. But the king went to his house grieved and bitterly sad, eating no food, and drinking neither wine nor water. He forbad the musical instruments to be played before him, and did not

remove his garments, for he was grieved at heart for Daniel; his sleep also left him, for he was saddened at the princes' plot against Daniel. Then, turning over on his side and sighing, he said, ' Would that it were morning, to see what has become of Daniel.'

(8) On that same day, and at the same time as Daniel was cast into the den, behold the prophet Habakkuk, in the land of Judah, returned that evening from harvesting, and prepared a large dish to feed the reapers. While he was carrying his burden in his hand to supply the reapers with food, the word of the Lord came to him, saying, ' Go thou with this food to My servant Daniel, in the land of the Chaldeans, to the den of lions, where he is cast.' ' But, O Lord God, who will lead me there,' said he, ' at this time, since the distance is so great for me?' And forthwith an angel of God lifted him by the lock of his hair, together with his food, and placed him in the midst of Daniel's den, where he put down the food. The angel then brought him forth thence, and restored him to his native place, whence he was taken before the reapers had had their meal. And Daniel uttered thanksgiving and praises to his God, in whose salvation he trusted, for whoever supplicates to his God communes with Him as well as one who studies His law, and he need not despair of His kindness.

(9) On the following morning at daybreak the king arose and hastily went to the den, and when he heard Daniel's voice singing and the beauty of his praises, he was not able to speak to him, for his voice was stifled through his sobbing. But, strengthening himself, he called out, ' Daniel, Daniel, has God withheld thee from the mouth of the lions, and art thou not torn to pieces?' And Daniel replied, ' Indeed, God hath withheld me from the mouth of the lions, and hath closed their mouths, and prevented them from injuring me. They, on the contrary, rejoiced to meet me, just as my own household would rejoice, for thus my God, in whom I trust, has commanded, and yesterday food was even given to me through Habakkuk, through the spirit of my God ; but, my lord the king, I have

not sinned against thee, nor will any iniquity be found in me.'

(10) The king then sending for the princes, Daniel's enemies, they came to him as he was standing by the den. 'Know,' said he, 'and behold the seals of your rings; are they as ye sealed them, and has there been any mischief?' And examining the seals, they said, 'They are untouched and just as we have sealed them.' Then, commanding the stone to be rolled away from the mouth of the pit, Daniel they brought forth, sound and perfect, without any blemish or hurt. The bystanders, being struck with wonder at the miracles of the God of Daniel, with a loud voice shouted, 'The God of Daniel is greater than all other gods.' The king then ordered his servants to lay hold of those princes, Daniel's enemies, together with their wives and children, and to cast them into the den of lions, and before they reached the floor of the den, the lions, who had not eaten any food since yesterday, roared at them, and, tearing them, crushed their bones and ground them to dust. They then continued roaring from their den so that the noise could be heard far off, and all the people trembled, and said, 'The lions have escaped from their den.'

LXXI. (1) The king then returned to his palace with Daniel, and the Lord showered upon Daniel honour and greatness, and he found favour and kindness in the eyes of the king. A command was then issued in the kingdom, saying: 'In all the land there is no god like the God of Daniel who performs miracles and wonders. May his God be with all the people of His inheritance, and cause them to prosper; and let the great temple of God be built in Judah, and I shall give silver and gold of my treasures for the building until it is completed.'

(2) He then issued orders to all the cities in the land of his rule, by means of runners and horsemen, to permit the Jews to go up to Jerusalem to build the temple of God. This happened in the first year of Cyrus's reign over the Chaldeans. Letters of the king were also sent to all the

princes on the other side of the river and to the governors, to be in readiness to assist the Jews by attending to all their wants in the matter of the building, such as the supply of wood, stones, wheat, oil, and wine, until the building was completed, and rams and lambs for their sacrifices.

(3) The Jews then rose, all whose hearts were willing, to go up to the house of God. They numbered about four myriads, with Ezra the priest and scribe at their head, as well as Eliakim the priest, Jeshu'a, Mordecai, and the rest of the chiefs of the fathers belonging to Judah and Benjamin; and, journeying, they came to the other side of the river, and arrived at Jerusalem, where they commenced to lay the foundation of the house of God. When this was finished, the work prospered. There then arose certain wicked men, enemies of the Jews, from the remnant of the nations, *e.g.*, Sanballat the Horonite, Tobiya the Ammonite, and Geshem the Arabian, all of whom wrote evil against the Jews. They sent a letter to the Kings of Media and Persia, saying, 'Be it known to you that if ye build the city of Jerusalem it will be to you a snare, a great evil, and there will arise a great conspiracy against you; for in days of yore the Jews who dealt therein were strong and very hard, and destroyed the whole country. It was for this reason that Nebuchadnezzar, their enemy, exiled them to Babylon. Then the kings had rest, and each dwelt peacefully in his own place. Therefore we send to inform you of it, as we are faithful, for we have eaten at the table of the king, and far be it from us to allow the downfall of the kingdom.' As soon as the letter reached the King of Persia, the work was discontinued until the second year of the reign of Darius.

LXXII. (1) Now, when Darius was seated on the throne of his kingdom, he sent for Daniel, the servant of God, to test his wisdom and to obtain his counsel. Having come before him, he tried him and proved him, and found him sevenfold wiser than report had told of him. He was therefore very pleased with him, and loved him, and appointed him to be his counsellor, as Darius had done before him.

(2) One day Darius held a feast in honour of Bel, the god of Babylon, and the king accordingly prepared an offering to be brought before Bel, the god of Babylon. The daily order of the offering consisted of 1 bullock, 10 rams, 10 sheep, 100 doves, 70 loaves of bread, and 10 barrels of wine, for the table of the god. On the day in question they arranged the table before Bel, and the king said to Daniel, ' Would that thou didst believe in the glory of our god Bel, who consumes what is laid upon this table.'

(3) And Daniel replied, ' Let not the heart of the king be deceived and be led astray, for it is vanity. There is no breath in it, but it is simply the work of the craftsman. How can it therefore eat or drink anything? It is the priests of Bel who eat the contents of this table, as well as the meal-offering and burnt-offering. Now, if thou wilt hearken unto me, and deliver these priests into my hand, I will show thee the deceit they practise upon thee and thy people, which causes you to prostrate yourselves to vanity and emptiness.' ' Let it be as thou hast spoken,' said the king. Daniel then commanded the porters of Bel to lock the temple and all its gates, except the one which the king and Daniel entered.

(4) Then said the king, ' Bring me some ashes.' When they were brought he scattered them upon the floor of the house, and the priests were kept in ignorance of Daniel's advice. As soon as they had done this, the king and Daniel went out with their young men by the same gate, and, locking the door, the king sealed it with his own seal and with that of Daniel, and then both of them went back to the palace, and retired for the night.

(5) On the following morning the king sent for Daniel, to let him see and know what Bel had done. Coming to the gate of the temple, they found the seals just as they had been left; and the king said, ' Has there been any tampering with these seals ?' And Daniel said ' No,' and

commanded the seals to be removed. They then opened the gate, and saw that the contents of the table which they had arranged, from the bread even to the meat and wine, had all been consumed.

(6) As soon as the king saw this, he fell prostrate before Bel, and exclaimed, 'O Bel, great is thy name in the world, and who is like unto thee in might among all the other gods?' But Daniel answered, 'Let not the king say that, for Bel is but clay, earthenware, and brass, and cannot eat or drink. Look but upon the ashes which we have spread on the floor, and round about the temple and the table, and see whose footprints are these, for they are the traces of the consumers of Bel's table.' The king looked, and beheld the footprints of men, women, and children; (7) and sending forthwith for these seventy priests and ministers of Bel, he swore to them, saying, 'If ye will not tell me the truth, ye shall surely die.' They then showed him the secret entrances through which they came in and went out in the night, to eat the contents of the table. [Here one leaf of the MS. is missing.]

LXXIII. (1) The dragon felt the smell of the ashes and of the sacrifice, and he rejoiced to go out and see the offering, and it opened its mouth, according to custom, and they cast it therein. After swallowing it, it raised itself on high, and turned to enter the cave again, when the princes said to the king, 'Is Daniel also able to destroy this god, which is a living god, just as he destroyed Bel and his priests and his altar, thus putting an end to his worship? Why does he not strive with this god, for, if he does, then we shall be avenged for the destruction of Bel and his temple.

(2) Then said the king to Daniel, 'Hearken to me, pray, and give ear to what I say. Canst thou lift up thy thoughts also against this great and mighty serpent god, and subdue him as thou didst Bel, in which there was no life? This, however, is mighty and strong, and who would dare rise up against it to do it evil? But Daniel replied, 'Let not the king err also in this, for it is but a beast, and can be subdued by the hand of man. It hath no spirit, and now,

if my lord the king will permit me to go against this dragon, I shall slay it without either sword or stick or any warlike instrument, for it is but a reptile that crawls upon the earth, and the Lord set the fear of man in every beast, insect, and reptile, for in the image of God did He make man. I shall therefore destroy it just as I destroyed one of the graven images, but do not give power unto thy princes to do me evil.' 'Go thou and do what thou canst,' replied the king. The princes were, however, greatly rejoiced when the king told Daniel to strive with the dragon, for they said, 'Now will Daniel surely perish, for it is impossible for him to make a stand against the dragon.'

(3) Daniel then went from the king, and making iron instruments like wool combs, he joined them together back to back, with the points outward, forming a circle of hard and sharp points. This he rolled in all manner of poisonous fat and grease and other fatty substances, and beneath it he placed pitch and brimstone, until the points of the brass and the other piercing metals were concealed. Then, making it in the shape of an oblation, Daniel cast it into the dragon's mouth. The dragon hastily and greedily swallowed it, and seemed to enjoy it. But when it entered its mouth, and passed on to the entrails of its belly, the fat melted from off the iron prongs, so the sharp spikes pierced its entrails, and gave it such agony that it died on the morrow.

(4) It came to pass, three days after its death, that the Chaldeans and Babylonians came, as was their daily custom, to propitiate the dragon with an oblation, but it was not visible; only a horrible stench issued from the cave. When they searched the cave they found that their god was slain, swollen up, and decaying. They became very grieved and full of wrath against Daniel, and they said, 'Behold what is this Daniel has done to the two gods! for he has destroyed Bel and smitten the dragon. Now if the king deliver him into our hands, he shall surely be slain; and if not, it must be made known to the king that he also shall surely not live.' When it reached the ears

of the king that the people had made a conspiracy against him, a command was issued to smite the leaders and princes, as well as those that rose up against Daniel, with the edge of the sword.

LXXIV. (1) Daniel having now grown old in years, came one day to the king, and prostrating himself before him, said, 'O my lord the king, behold old age has crept upon me, and I have now no more strength to stand and go to and fro. Behold, the lawless men of thy people have humbled me through their enmity, and have cast me twice into the den of lions, but God, in whom I put my trust, has delivered me. They meditated to take my soul, to deprive me of my life, through their zeal on behalf of their gods, but my God withheld me from their destruction. My three friends also they cast into the fiery furnace to be burnt, and yet after all this we have not forsaken our God. Now, my lord the king, I pray thee allow me to go back to my native city and to my house, to worship the God of my fathers for the remainder of my days, for I am old and have no longer the power to restrain (check) the multitude of thy host.' And the king answered Daniel, saying, 'How can I listen to thy request to send thee away, seeing thou art a man of the God of heaven? If thou leavest me and departest from my side, how can my kingdom remain in its integrity? I am indeed aware that thou art an old man, and that thou hast no longer that strength for active life which the rulers of the kingdom ought to have; therefore, if thou wilt give me from among thy people a man of wisdom and understanding, and withal filled with the spirit of thy God as thou art, to remain with me in thy stead, then will I send thee away in peace to rest in thine own house, although my soul knoweth there is none esteemed thy equal among the sons of thy people.'

(2) Daniel then went forth from the presence of the king to the assembly of the exiles, and, finding there Zerubbabel, the son of Shealtiel, the son of Jechoniah, King of Judah, he selected him from among the people, and taking him by the hand, led him to the king, and said, 'Behold before

thee the man who is to take my place. He is esteemed my equal, and is descended from Judah and from the chiefs of the royal seed. He is withal a man of valour, filled with the spirit of God, with knowledge and wisdom as myself, falling short of nothing that is in me, and he will be, as I have been, a faithful counsellor to thee. And now, do thou give me permission to depart for my native place for the short time I have to live.' The king, being confident of the truth of everything Daniel told him, gave him permission to depart. Daniel then made his obeisance, and the king embraced and kissed him, and having ordered many gifts to be presented to him, he sent him away.

(3) Thus did Zerubbabel take the place of Daniel, who gave all that the king presented him with to the suffering exiles, and then left for Shushan, his native place, in the land of Elam. There he worshipped the Lord among his brother exiles until the day of his death.

(4) Now, Zerubbabel was a man of valour, young and prosperous, understanding and wise, filled with the spirit of wisdom, for Daniel had put his hand upon him. He found favour in the eyes of the king, who loved him and appointed him chief of all the princes, and overseer of the two captains of the host and guardians of the king.

(5) One day, according to custom, all the princes assembled before the king, and the king said to them, 'Have ye seen in the whole of this land a man as wise and as full of understanding, in whom is the spirit of Daniel, as this man Zerubbabel?' And they answered, 'The king hath spoken the truth.'

(6) Now, about the time of noon, after they had all eaten, the king, as usual, lay upon his bed and slept. The two princes and guardians of the king then arose, as was customary, and Zerubbabel with them, and stood round the king's bedside until he awoke. On this occasion the king slept heavily, for he was drunk with wine; and the three young men, being weary of standing, proposed to test each other's wisdom by means of riddles, each one according to his wit, and they said, 'Let us write them down in a

book, and place the book under the head of the king until he awake from his sleep,' when he would see the book, and understand its meaning.

(7) 'Then it shall be that the man whose words appear wiser than his two colleagues,' and whose riddles are superior to those of his brethren, should be made vicegerent, and should also sit on the royal throne and in the royal chariot; that he should have free access to the presence of the king; that the vessels of his table should be of silver, and the reins of his horse of gold. That the crown of the vicegerent be placed upon his head; that he receive the portion of the vicegerent from the hand of the king; that every request be granted him, and that he be a friend of the king.' To this they all agreed, and, making a covenant in accordance therewith, they established it according to the laws of Media and Persia, which can never be altered.

(8) Then, bringing the pen and the scroll, they cast lots as to who should be the first to inscribe. The first wrote, 'On the earth there is no one so powerful as a king.' The second wrote, 'Wine is the strongest thing on earth.' And Zerubbabel, who was the third, wrote, 'There is nothing on the earth so powerful as woman.' When they had finished writing their words of wisdom, they placed the scroll under the king's pillow, but the king was awake, for though his eyes were closed yet he heard their whisperings; and when they placed the scroll under his pillow the king arose as if he had just woke from his sleep, and, rubbing his eyes with his two hands, he looked under his pillow, and saw the scroll which the three young men had written. Then opening it, he read it, and was perplexed about it, until all the princes, pashas, chiefs, governors, and heads of the provinces came to him. Then calling the three young men, he said, 'Bring me each one of you his writing, and let me listen to the interpretation of your riddles; then will I fulfil for the wisest of you three everything that is stated in the scroll to honour and exalt him.'

(9) The first one then approached to read what he had written, and said, 'Hearken, O king and princes, to my words. There is nobody on earth so powerful as a king.' The second, drawing near (the king), said, 'There is nothing on earth so powerful as wine.' And the third, viz., Zerubbabel, exclaimed, 'There is nothing on earth so powerful as woman.' At this the king and the princes said, 'We have hearkened to your hidden sayings; now tell us the explanation, and we shall listen.'

LXXV. (1) And the first answered and said, 'O my lord the king, princes and mighty men, do ye not know the power of the king and the strength of his dominion over all the earth, over the sea, the isles, and over all languages? to slay or to keep alive? If he commands an army to march forth, they march forth armed; they turn not their heads, though they may stand face to face with death. If he command them to overthrow cities, they overthrow them; if to hew down mountains, or to pull down walls, they obey. If he command them to plough for him, they plough; they sow and reap his produce, for they fear the wrath of the king, who is mighty and lord over all, and no one dares frustrate his word; therefore believe ye my words that there is no one on earth so powerful as a king.' All the bystanders were astonished at his speech.

(2) The second now replied, saying, 'Though ye know the power of a king and the strength of his might, for he has dominion and rules over the land; yet wine is stronger than a king. It is true he has great power, but as soon as he drinks freely of wine, it overpowers him and inclines his heart to other things, he sings, plays and dances, for his heart is turned by the wine, so that he repulses his kin, approaches strangers, slays his friends, and confers honour upon strangers, and respects neither his father nor mother. (3) Do ye not know that such is the power of wine, when a man is drunk he cannot learn, but is rather prone to singing; he whispers to his neighbour and reveals secrets, and hidden things drop out of his mouth. Men full of sorrow the wine makes glad,

and even if mourners and those whose hearts are grieved drink thereof, they rejoice and are merry. The drunken one draws his sword against his neighbour, and he gets fierce, and bashful men it makes bold. But when the wine has disappeared from them, they have forgotten all, and say, "We have not done this thing." Is thus wine not stronger than a king, as it rules over him; it makes man walk crookedly, he cannot see straight, and he continues babbling things which he has not learned. Do ye not think that wine is therefore more powerful than a king, for such it does?' Thereat the men were greatly surprised.

(4) After that the king summoned Zerubbabel, and said, 'Tell me, I pray thee, thy riddle and its interpretation, as thy friends have done.' And he answered and said, 'Give ear and hearken unto me, O king and princes, governors and rulers, and all ye who stand here. Indeed, the king is stronger and greater than all; it is true that wine weakens the king through its strength, as my friends have said. Thus the power of both the king and wine cannot be denied; but woman is yet more powerful than either king or wine or any other strong drink. For why should she not be more powerful than the king? Did she not give birth to him, suckle him, sustain him, rear him, clothe him, wash him, and sometimes chastise him? Did she not rule over him as a mother does the child of her womb? When she was angry with him, did he not fear her rebuke? Did she not sometimes beat him and at other times censure him? If she lifted the rod to him, did he not run away from her in fear of her? Moreover, when he grows up to be a young man, he cannot forget his instructress, nor will rebel against her call. He always respects her as a son honours her who conceived him.

(5) 'Then looking about him, he beholds a woman fair to look upon, and desires her beauty to sport with. His heart inclines towards her, and he will not change his love for her for all the riches. It is then that he leaves his father and mother, forsaking them for her love and her beauty, and many are they that have been led astray

through the love of woman; many are they that have acted foolishly, and become mad for her sake; and many that have met their death for the sake of woman, and have fallen for her pride down into hell. Wise men also have been caught in her net, and much hatred has the frivolous one caused among brothers. Do ye not know and understand that if a man sees a comely woman, and he carries in his hands goodly things, will not his eyes gaze upon her, for his heart inclines towards her? If she answers him when he speaks to her on account of her beauty, will he not leave everything that he keeps in his hands to speak to her? for his heart is drawn near to her.

(6) 'Who is there that will not believe this, and confess the truth of this power of woman? Tell me, for whom do ye steal, for whom do ye rob, and for whom do ye gird yourselves—is it not for woman? Is it not for her that ye buy all the precious ornaments? is not the myrrh and the aloe for her? are not all the spices, perfumed oils, and frankincense for her? If a man break into a house, if he keeps the high roads, goes on the sea, on dry land, on the mountains; if he fight, commit murder, rob, plunder, and shed blood, to whom will he bring his spoil, if not to woman? Have I not seen the concubine of the King Apumaṣia (אפומצ״יא), the daughter of Abyaush (אביאוש) of Makeden, take the crown of honour from off the king's head and place it on her own head, while he was seated on the throne beside her, and the king was pleased with her? But when she became angry, did not the king then hasten to appease her, and to reconcile her, and remove her anger?

(7) 'Who, then, is there that will not believe that woman's power is stronger than everything? She subdued Samson, enticed David, and inclined the heart of Solomon towards her. Many are her captives, and innumerable are those that are slain through her, and their number increases. And even if there be one man who rules the whole world, and before whose wrath all people tremble and shake, since he would be supreme, and although man is appointed

to be the prince, ruler, and king over her, and to her is given the desire of him, yet not even he would be able to conquer her and to rule over her. Even Adam, the father of all mankind, was induced by his wife to transgress the word of God, by which she destined him and his offspring to death. Also, in the days of Noah, the heavenly angels were led astray and took to them women. Who does not believe that this is known from the very beginning of the world, and will last to the end unaltered? This is the truth that I utter.

(8) 'Now, finally, let it be known to the king and to all my hearers that all is vanity here—the king who rules the earth, the wine that rules the king, and woman with her iniquity, who rules the three; but truth reigns supreme in heaven and on earth; in the seas and in the depths truth prevails before God and man; for where truth dwells there wickedness cannot abide, for the heavens and the earth are founded upon truth, and the Lord our God is true for ever.'

(9) After this all the people assembled there before the king exclaimed, 'It is true.' Then said the king to Zerubbabel, 'Come near to me.' When he approached, the king kissed him and embraced him in the presence of all the people, and said, 'Blessed be the Lord God of Zerubbabel, who hath given him the spirit of truth, for there is nothing like God's truth; everything else is vanity.' And the princes also exclaimed, 'Indeed, truth is greater than all things; nor can one stand up against it since it dwells in the heaven and in the earth, and upon it is everything based. True is the God of Zerubbabel, who hath given him the spirit of truth to praise and to glorify truth before God and man.'

LXXVI. (1) The king then commanded all the honours written in the scroll to be carried out for Zerubbabel, for he had found great favour in the eyes of the king and the two princes, his colleagues. And the king further said to Zerubbabel, 'Ask, in addition to what is written in the scroll, whatever thy soul desires and I will grant it, even to half the kingdom.' And Zerubbabel answered and said, 'Remember, my lord the king, the vow which thou and King Cyrus made to the God of heaven, viz., to build His house, and to restore His holy vessels, and to allow His captive people to worship Him in the temple that is called by His name, that they may pray to the great God of heaven for the welfare of thy reign, for thou must not delay the vow which thou madest to the heavenly God.'

(2) The king thereupon commanded the scribes to hasten and write down Zerubbabel's request, to rebuild the ruins of Jerusalem. He then sent a message to Cyrus, King of Persia, to join hands with him in this work, and thus to fulfil their vow by establishing the house of God in Jerusalem. And Cyrus issued a proclamation throughout his kingdom, saying, 'Every one of God's people whose heart prompts him to go up to Jerusalem to lay the foundation of the temple and to build it, let him go, and I shall give everyone the pay of his labour from my treasures until the building is completed.'

(3) The king's scribes thereupon wrote down this proclamation on behalf of Darius, King of Media, and Cyrus, King of Persia, to the princes, governors, and rulers on the other side of the river, and to the Arameans, Tyrians, Samaritans, and to Asaph, governor of the garden of Lebanon, 'Be it known to you that it is our pleasure to send back to God's holy city the captives of His people, whom Nebuchadnezzar, King of Babylon, sent into exile; to restore the vessels of the great and holy temple which is called by the name of the God of heaven; to build His altar, and to sacrifice thereon every day; to build the temple, and the Holy of Holies; to establish the palace according to its old form; and to restore the walls of Jerusalem. (4) When this edict reaches you, exert yourselves to assist them by supplying all their wants in silver and gold, brass, wood, and stones for the builders and hewers until the building is finished, and to give them whatever they ask for, wheat, barley, oil, or wine, and whatever they want for the buildings. For re-establishing

the sacrifices upon the altar ye shall give them oxen, calves, rams, sheep, he-goats, doves, flour, oil, salt, to enable them to re-establish the altar, and to finish the whole work.'

(5) The Edomites were also commanded by these two kings to contribute their share in the service of the house of the Lord, because they had helped the Chaldeans to overthrow it; they were to give a yearly tribute of five talents of gold for strengthening the breach of the house, to rebuild the temple and the holy city. The Sidonians, Tyrians, and Edomites, as well as the servants of the king in the Lebanon, under the command of Asaph, keeper of the garden, were ordered to hew the wood from the Lebanon, and to drag it to the sea from the Lebanon and thence to the Sea of Joppa, to complete the work of the house of God. No man was to hinder them until everything was completed. Having written down all these details as the two kings commanded, the scribes sealed it, and handed it over to Zerubbabel, the son of Shealtiel, and to Nehemiah, the son of Hachaliah.

LXXVII. (1) About this time Darius, King of Media, was taken very ill, and, being about to die, he called Cyrus, King of Persia, his son-in-law, his daughter's husband, and made him king in his stead, so that the kingdoms of Media and Persia were united into one; and when Darius the Mede was gathered to his people, Cyrus reigned over Media and Persia and the remainder of the country. He then issued a proclamation in all his kingdom, saying, 'Whoever of you among the people of the Lord God of heaven is willing to go up to Jerusalem to the footstool of the great and mighty God, to build His house and His temple which the wicked Nebuchadnezzar, who was more wicked than all his predecessors, overthrew, let him go up and assist in the building, and may His God be with everyone whose heart prompts him to do so. And I, Cyrus, servant of the living God, who set me upon this throne, shall provide from my riches and my treasury all the wants of the house of this mighty God who made me King of Media and Persia, and who assisted me to destroy the kingdom of the Chaldeans.'

(2) Thus all the elders of the captivity, Ezra the scribe, Nehemiah, the son of Hachaliah, with the other chiefs of the captivity and the priests, went up to Jerusalem and built the temple of God and His altar, and arranged the wood and placed the flesh of sacrifice upon the altar. (3) Then they lifted up their voices and wept, while Ezra and Nehemiah, with the other chiefs of the captivity, prayed to God, and said: ' O Lord of the whole universe, Thou hast put it into the heart of the King of Persia to do honour to Thy house, and to send Thy servants and priests to make sacrifices to Thee and to offer Thy burnt-offerings as Thy servants, our pious forefathers, did before Thee. Behold we, also Thy servants, have come to this place, and have rebuilt Thy altar after the same pattern, and we offer sacrifices to Thee, and arrange the wood beneath the burnt-offering. But how can it be pleasing to Thee, O God, seeing that we offer strange fire, for the holy fire is no more, since it has been hidden by Jeremiah the prophet, Thy servant, and the other chiefs of the captivity whom Nebuchadnezzar sent into exile. What shall we do, O God of heaven? Give us counsel and help, for to Thee belongs dominion, to help us and to strengthen our hands.'

(4) Now, it happened while they were praying to the Lord in this wise, a very old man about 100 years of age, belonging to those priests who were exiled in the days of Nebuchadnezzar, was heard calling. Being rather deaf through old age, he summoned his six sons before him, and said, ' O my sons, if I have found favour in your eyes, carry me near the altar and place me opposite it that I may inhale the sweet-smelling frankincense of the altar, for I have not been deemed worthy of that pleasure for many years now. Let your kindness be extended to me that ye may hearken to me this once, that I may be enabled to smell it once more before I die. Ye shall be rewarded by the holy God, for I have been a great burden to you.'

(5) His sons forthwith carried him into the midst of the assembled priests opposite the altar. When he heard the

noise of the multitude and the priests crying to God for the holy fire, the old man said to his sons, 'What ails the people that they cry?' And they replied, 'The priests are seeking the holy fire which is no longer to be found, as it has been hidden from them.' 'Carry me, then, near the priests and the heads of the fathers, and I shall tell them where it is, and where Jeremiah the prophet and the other priests who went into exile had concealed it.' (6) His sons carried him in the midst of the chiefs of the fathers, who asked him about it, and he told them where it was. Then, carrying the old man, and crossing the Brook of Kedron and the Valley of Hinnom, they ascended Mount Olives; and during their descent, when they faced the valley in the plain, the old man showed them a large stone sunk in the earth. Digging up the dust round about the stone, they rolled the stone away, and removing the lime beneath it, they opened the pit.

(7) Then said he to the young priests, 'Descend thither and take the fire, for there it was placed.' He repeated his command, whereupon they descended, and found there at the bottom of the pit something like the lees of oil, and like mud and honey. When they related this to Ezra and the priests, they replied, 'Bring up whatever ye find, and no stranger touch you until ye come to the altar. Then place what ye have carried away upon the altar, upon the burnt-offering, and upon the wood.' They went down and did as they were commanded; (8) and as soon as they did this a great fire suddenly burnt upon the altar, and grew into such huge flames that the priests and the people fled from before it, for they could not endure it. It licked the burnt-offering, and, travelling round the temple, cleansed it, after which it got considerably smaller, so that it remained only on the altar, as usual. From that day thenceforward a continual fire burnt upon the altar, as they placed the wood regularly upon it until the second captivity.

(9) But the ark was not there, because Jeremiah took the ark with all the curtains which Moses, the servant of God,

made in the wilderness, and he carried them up to Mount Nebo and placed them in a cave. The priests of that time pursued him to find out the place of the ark, and of the tablets, of the curtains of the tabernacle, and of the tent of the congregation. When Jeremiah looked behind him and saw the priests, he became angry with them, and swore to them 'you shall never discover the place you desired to know until I and Elijah appear. Then we shall restore the tabernacle and the tent of the congregation to its original place, as well as the ark of the testimony and the two tables of stone which it contains. Then we shall enter the Holy of Holies.'

(10) From that day our ancestors offered their sacrifices and burnt-offerings and continual offerings every day, for the kings of Persia had assisted them with gold and silver, with wheat, oil and wine, with oxen, sheep and rams, everything that they desired, year after year, for the kings of Persia loved the temple of our God, and its sanctuary they greatly honoured.

LXXVIII. (1) And Cyrus reigned over all the kingdoms of the earth, for our God strengthened his right hand so that he subdued many nations. He (God) opened before him the gates of iron and broke the doors of brass, and revealed to him hidden treasures, just as He had told through Isaiah the prophet to his people, the servants of Jacob and Israel whom He had chosen. And the hand of Cyrus was strengthened, and, going to battle, he captured all the land, all the fords of India, as well as those in the south, the whole land of Ethiopia, all the nations dwelling in the lands of the south (Arabia), and in the west as far as Sefarad, and in the north, the land of Moqedon, and all the land of Kaftor and Ararat, the whole of Alan (אלן), Alasar (אלסר), and the mountains of Alaf (אלף), *i.e.*, the mountains of darkness, as far as the Snow Mountains, which are impassable. The rest of his mighty deeds and his battles, are they not written in the Book of Chronicles of the kings of Media and Persia, and in the book of Joseph ben Gorion, the anointed priest of battle, who was exiled from Jerusalem in the reign of Vespasianus, and in the Book of Chronicles of the kings of Rome?

(2) Cyrus the king ended his days in battle, and died in the land of the Shittim; but this need not cause surprise, for we know that Saul, the anointed of the Lord, also died in battle, as well as King Josiah, the beloved of God. (3) When Cyrus went to the land of Shittim, he smote their king at the edge of the sword, together with his warriors, because they raised their hands against the king (*i.e.*, himself). And when they fell, the Shittites fled with their queen, Tamirah (תמירה), and her son until they came to their fortresses, and there they shut themselves in. As soon as Cyrus saw that they had shut themselves in their castles and that no one went out or in, he enticed them out by a ruse, for he departed with all his camp as if seeking to find an escape, whereupon the Shittites, with Tamirah's son, came out of their castles to pursue them. When they had come out into the plain, Cyrus suddenly turned upon them, and smote 300,000 of their warriors, and among the slain was found the son of their queen Tamirah. Cyrus then took all the Shittites prisoners, except those who had escaped to the mountains with the warriors. When Tamyris saw that her son had been slain with the other soldiers, she was exceedingly grieved, and went wandering about the mountains and valleys of the Shittites, lying in ambush. When Cyrus left the land of the Shittites, he being confident of his victory, never thought of any possible ambush; therefore his army passed on before him, and, being left behind with a few followers, he encamped between two mountains and lay there down to sleep.

(4) On the same night he was attacked by the woman, who was like a wild beast, like a lioness bereaved of her cubs, and like a bereaved bear. She smote the whole camp of Cyrus, numbering 200,000 mighty men of Persia, together with their king. Then, strengthening herself, she went to the dead body of Cyrus, and, cutting off his head and placing it in a leather bottle, which she filled with the blood of the slain,

she said, 'Drink and satisfy thyself with the blood which thou hast been so fond of shedding these thirty years without tiring.'

(5) Cyrus being thus gathered to his people, Cambisa, his son, reigned in his stead. As soon as he was enthroned he went to Shittim and destroyed the remainder of its inhabitants, together with their queen, Tamirah, and all her offspring. After him, Ahasuerus arose and abolished all the work of the temple, for the enemies of the Jews had increased, and had written accusations at the beginning of Ahasuerus' reign. Thus the service of the temple was stopped until the second year of the reign of Darius, King of Persia.

LXXIX. (1) But our ancestors served the kings of Media and Persia with great loyalty, for they neither did them harm nor oppressed them. It was only in the time of Ahasuerus that the memory of Judah was nearly destroyed through the enmity of Haman the Amalekite, because Mordecai, a descendant of Saul, who smote the Amalekites from Havilah to Shur, a distance of several days, would not rise before him. He slew more than 500,000 Amalekites, and put to the sword their men, women, and children, to the number of thousands of thousands. It was for this reason that Haman, who was descended from them, cherished that hatred against the people of Judah, and especially against the tribe of Benjamin.

(2) Now, in the days of Ahasuerus, when Mordecai was sitting at the gate of the king he discovered a secret plot of two Persian princes, Bigthan and Teresh, whom he heard whispering and plotting to sever the head of the king while he lay in his bed, in order to carry it to the Macedonian king, for at that time the Macedonian empire was warring against the Persian kingdom. This plot Mordecai revealed to Esther, and she in her turn to the king, who commanded this act of loyalty on the part of Mordecai to be noted down in the Book of Chronicles, as well as the reward due to him. When, however, these two chamberlains were hanged it incurred the wrath of Haman,

for they were his counsellors, and he, therefore, sought to blot out the name of Judah from under the heavens. But Mordecai discovered this plan of his and remembered the dream he had in the second year of the reign of Ahasuerus. (3) It was the following: There was a great earthquake, accompanied by a noise and the sound of wailing in the land, so that fear and terror fell upon all the inhabitants, and two immense dragons with terrible noise went against each other in battle, whereupon all the inhabitants ran towards the spot. Living among them was a small nation, and all the nations round about it rose up to destroy their memory from the face of the earth. On that day everywhere it was thick darkness, and the small nation, being much oppressed, cried unto the Lord. The dragons continued to fight furiously and nobody could separate them; when lo! Mordecai saw a small brook of water passing between the two dragons, which separated them, for the brook soon grew into an overflowing river, like the overflowing of the Great Sea, so that it flooded the whole earth. The sun then shone upon the earth, and the small nation was raised to exaltation, while the proud ones were humbled, and peace and truth were restored in the world.

(4) Mordecai from that day always nursed that dream in his heart, and when Haman oppressed him, he said to Esther, 'Remember the dream I narrated to thee in the days of thy youth. Now arise, and, beseeching the Lord for mercy, go into the presence of Ahasuerus; stand before him in all thy beauty, and plead the cause of thy people and thy kindred.' And Mordecai supplicated to God, saying, 'It is well known and revealed to the throne of Thy glory, O Lord of the universe, that it was not from pride or haughtiness I refused to bow down to this Amalekite, but on account of the reverence I have for Thee I opposed him, refusing to bow down, for I fear Thee alone, O Lord of the universe, and would not, therefore, give Thine honour to flesh and blood; therefore, I would prostrate myself to no being except Thy holy presence. And who am I that would not bow down to

Haman? Yet for Israel's salvation I would lick the shoe upon his foot, and the dust upon which he walks. (5) O Lord, deliver them from his hand, that he may fall into the pit which he has dug for us, and be caught in the net which he has spread (hidden) under the feet of Thy pious men, that they may thereby know that Thou hast not forgotten the oath Thou didst swear; for Thou didst not deliver us into captivity because Thou wert not able to save us, but because of our sins and our iniquities, for we have sinned against Thee. But Thou, our God, art mighty in salvation; therefore save us, O Lord, from his hand; in our distress we call upon Thee to protect us, and to stand up in our midst to fight those who rise up against us. Remember, we beseech Thee, that we are Thy portion; for of old, when Thou didst give the nations their inheritance, and when Thou didst separate the sons of men, we were Thy portion; the lot which Thou didst cast fell upon us to be chosen for Thy name. (6) Why, O God, should our enemies say we have no God? why should they open wide their mouth to swallow up Thy portion and praise their idols and vanities? We beseech Thee, O Lord, send salvation unto us; let them be ashamed of their idols and vanities, and let them place their hand upon their mouth and see Thy salvation, O Lord. Have mercy upon Thy people, and upon Thine inheritance. Do not close the mouths of those who praise Thee and proclaim Thy unity evening and morning continually. Turn our sorrow to joy and gladness, that we may live and give Thee thanks for the blessed salvation by which Thou wilt save us.' And all Israel cried unto the Lord for the trouble and sorrow which had come upon them.

Esther's Prayer.

LXXX. (1) And Esther fled to the Lord, for she feared the evil which was growing; and, stripping herself of her royal garments and the ornaments of her majesty, she clothed herself in sackcloth, and dishevelling the hair of her head, she put dust and ashes upon it. Then, afflicting her soul with fasting, she fell upon her face in prayer, saying, 'O Lord God of Israel, who art the King of kings, who art to be feared, who createdst the world, and who rulest over us, help Thine handmaid in her desolation, for she has no saviour except Thee. Behold, I dwell in the king's palace alone, without father or mother. Like an afflicted orphan begging charity from house to house, so do I beg for Thy mercy, from one window to the other in the palace of King Ahasuerus, and have done so from the time I was brought here until this present day. (2) O Lord, if it is pleasing to Thee, take my soul from my own hand; and if not, then deliver, I beseech Thee, the flock of Thy pasture from those lions who have risen up against them; for my father taught me that Thou didst redeem our forefathers from Egypt, and didst slay all the firstborn of the Egyptians. Thou didst bring Thy people forth thence with a strong hand and an outstretched arm, and didst cause them to pass over the sea like a horse on dry land. Thou didst give them food from heaven, water from the cleft of the rock, and meat in plenty. Thou didst smite great and mighty kings before them, and caused them to inherit the goodly land. But when our ancestors sinned against Thy great name, then didst Thou deliver them into captivity; and here we are in exile to this day. My father further told me that, through Moses Thy servant, Thou didst say, "When also they shall be in the land of their enemies, I will never forsake them."

(3) 'Now, O Lord, Father of the fatherless, stand at the right hand of this orphan, who trusts in Thee, and grant me mercy when I am in the presence of King Ahasuerus, for I fear him as a kid fears the lion. Make lowly all his counsellors, that he may be humbled and subdued before the grace and beauty Thou hast given me. O my God, cause his heart to hate our enemies and to love Thy servants, for the heart of kings is in Thy hand. O Thou mighty, revered, and exalted God, deliver me from the fear and trembling which have taken hold of me, that I may go into his presence in Thy name, and come out in peace.'

(4) On the third day Esther accordingly clothed herself in royal garments, and came before the king, who was sitting upon the throne, accompanied by her two handmaidens. Upon one of them she placed her right hand, and leaned upon her, according to the royal custom, while the other maiden followed behind her to hold up her train, that the gold and precious stones should not touch the ground. Before him were seated all the potentates of the kingdom, who said one to the other, 'This woman is sure to be killed, since she has entered here without an appointed time.' One said, 'I will then take her royal garments'; another, 'I shall take the ornaments on her feet'; and another, 'I will take the ornaments on her hands.' When Esther heard these remarks, she kept her face serene, and concealed the grief of her soul.

(5) The king, then raising his eyes to her, was much enraged that she had transgressed the law by coming into his presence without being called. When Esther noticed the king's anger and fury, she trembled, and, feeling faint, placed her head upon the maid at her right; but our Lord saw the oppression of His people, and had pity upon Israel and upon the trouble of the orphan who trusted in Him, and He made her find favour in the eyes of the king, for the Lord added beauty to her beauty and majesty to her majesty, and the king, rising in haste from his throne, ran towards Esther, and embraced and kissed her, and, taking her in his arms, said to her, 'What is this fear, O Queen Esther? for this decree of ours does not apply to thee, since thou art the queen, my friend and companion;' and, taking up the golden sceptre, he placed it into her hand, and added, 'Why dost thou not speak to me?' And Esther replied, 'When I saw thee, O lord, my soul trembled before thine honour, and on account of the greatness of thy glory.'

(6) She then leaned her head once more upon her handmaid, for she was faint from fasting and from trouble. The king, however, was now very much alarmed at this, and wept before his wife, while all his ministers entreated her to speak to the king, in order to appease

his soul. And the Lord brought about that great salvation through Queen Esther and Mordecai. Haman and his sons were hanged upon the gallows, and all those who devised evil against Israel were slain at the edge of the sword, and Mordecai from that day forth was honoured in the king's palace.

[This is the letter which Haman sent (to the nations), for the purpose of causing the house of Jacob to perish.]

LXXXI. (1) 'I, Haman, who am great before the king, and second to him, who am the chief of the potentates, and seventh among the princes, and who am the most favoured in the kingdom—I, Haman, do write with the consent of all the prefects (eparchs), governors, rulers, and of all the kings of the East who lend their aid, and with the consent of all the royal princes. We all with one consent, with one mouth, with one speech, and in one language, write down, with the permission of King Ahasuerus, and seal it with his ring, so that it cannot be retracted, concerning the great eagle, whose wings were spread over the whole world, so that no bird, beast, or animal was able to stand before it, until the great Mede arose and smote it with one great blow, by which its wings were broken, its feathers plucked out, and its legs cut off, thereby giving the whole world rest, peace, and tranquillity, from the time it wandered from its nest until this very day. We now see that it wishes to grow and to increase its feathers and to spread out its wings again to cover us and the whole world, and to rend us in pieces in the same manner as it rent our forefathers who preceded us.

(2) 'On this account all the great men of Media and Persia have here assembled, and with the permission of the king we all of us with one counsel write to you to spread out nets to catch this eagle, whose strength again increases, and bring her back to her nest, to pluck out her feathers and to break her wings, to give her flesh to the birds of the heaven, to destroy her seed, to crush her young, and to root out her memory from the world. Our

counsel is not like Pharaoh's, who decreed only concerning the males, leaving the females; nor as Esau's, who said, "Now that the days of my father's mourning draw nigh, I will kill my brother Jacob, and make his sons my servants"; nor like Amalek's, who pursued Israel, and slew the weak, but let the strong remain; nor like Nebuchadnezzar's, who exiled them, and, giving them rest, promoted some to the throne of the kingdom; nor like Sennacherib's, who brought them to a land like their own; (3) but with a united wish, we have decided to destroy and to blot out all the Jews, young and old, women and children, and all on one day, so that there be no seed left in the world, that their children act not as they did to our ancestors, to our fathers, and our great men, for those who did good to them they rewarded with evil. We would be justified even if we took only revenge for Pharaoh, who did many good deeds for them, for he made Joseph, a servant, king over them and over all Egypt, and when his father and brothers came to him, he gave them the very best part of the land to dwell in, and maintained them during the years of famine, so that his people increased and multiplied in the land, and a prophet arose among them, Moses by name, the son of Amram. He was a wizard, and brought upon Pharaoh, upon his household, and upon his land, great plagues, awful and extraordinary. The people then rose up in the middle of the night like thieves, and, after robbing their neighbours, went out of the land. But Pharaoh, with his army, pursued them for their property, and they entered the sea through the enchantments of the Israelites; but they did not know by what means they had entered, and they were all drowned in the sea, thus returning evil for good.

(4) 'When they arrived in the wilderness, a certain old man, a descendant of Esau, offered them a feast in honour of their ancestor Jacob, and after they had eaten and drunk and enjoyed his feast—Joshua their wizard did not cease with his enchantments—but they spread their hands and whispered with their lips, until our ancestors

became weak through him, as it is said, "And Joshua weakened them"; nor was this alone sufficient for them, but they made a decree that our name should be blotted out, as it is said, "Thou shalt destroy the memory of Amalek." They did likewise to the kings of Midian who dwelt there, for they spoiled and slew the Midianite kings, their prophets and their priest they slew at the edge of the sword, and had no mercy upon them, as it is said, "And Balaam, the son of Beor, they slew with the sword, also Sihon and Og, the two Amorite kings." Also the thirty-one kings and seventy elders. Then arose their king, Saul, who destroyed all the seed of Amalek, and had not our ancestor Agag been preserved, there would not have been one single survivor. They strengthened themselves against our kingdom, and destroyed us, not by means of the spear or the sword, but, having built a large house, they entered therein, and when they came out, they caused the nations to fall down before their words by means of their wiles.'

(5) When the nations of the world read this writing, they sent back word to Haman, saying, 'Whatever thou hast written we know, but we fear lest they do the same to us as they did to our forefathers and our ancestors, for we shall perish at their hands. Cease, therefore, from them, for whoever touches them touches the apple of God's eye, for they are called "The people near to Him," as it is said, "And the children of Israel are the people near to Him; they are His beloved, His treasure, and His inheritance." Now, Haman, what wilt thou do? for see what happens to those who pursue them, see how the mighty men of the world have fallen beneath them. We therefore do not wish to lay hand upon them, for their God has called them the stone of foundation, and whenever it is moved He shall replace it.'

(6) Haman once more wrote to them, saying that 'their God, whom you fear so much, does not fight their battles, nor does He avenge their wrongs; He only did so in His youth, but now He has become weak, and has no more

power to wreak vengeance; for if He had, why did He not deliver them from Nebuchadnezzar, who destroyed His house, burnt His temple, and slew His young men, and before whom He had no power, for the remnant was then exiled to his land (Babylon). And now though they are prisoners in our hands, we wish to intermarry with them, but they do not wish it. They, on the contrary, despise us, and account us as reptiles and creeping things; if a fly happens to fall into one of their cups, he throws it out and drinks the wine, and if one of us happens to touch the cup of one of them, he throws it on the ground and breaks it. If we ask them for anything, although we desire to return them double, in order to unite them to us, they do not wish it, but despise us and our kingdom. It is therefore our desire, with the king's consent, as well as the consent of the princes, rulers, governors, and pashas, to destroy them utterly from the world, both young and old, women and children, in one day, as it is said, "Come, and let us destroy them."'

(7) As soon as the surrounding nations heard this, with one accord they consented to destroy the Israelites, as it is said, 'Those kings counselled together,' etc. One day when Haman was walking along, with the princes of the kingdom following him, Mordecai, while walking in front of them, met three children just coming from school, and said to them, 'Tell me each of you what lesson you have learnt to-day.' The first one replied, 'Do not be hastily terrified.' The second replied, 'Take counsel together, and it shall be brought to nought;' and the third said, 'Until old age I am He.' On hearing these replies Mordecai rejoiced, and gave thanks to God. When Haman met him, he said, 'What did these children tell thee?' And he replied, 'They told me good tidings.' At this Haman's anger was kindled, and he commanded the children to be captured, saying, 'I will stretch forth my hand first against these children.' [End of the letter.]

LXXXII. (1) R. Isaak Napha said Haman worked cunningly against Israel, for it is written, 'And when these days were fulfilled, the king made a feast unto all the people.' 'The people' here referred to is Israel. Haman said to Ahasuerus, 'The God of these people hates lewdness, for it is written in the Torah, "Thou shalt not commit adultery."' He, therefore, brought together lewd women, and making the banquet for them, decreed that they should comply with any man's wish, so as not to give the accused the excuse of saying that they had been forced to do such a thing by a decree of the king. As soon, however, as Mordecai perceived this, he said to the people, 'Do not go to this banquet, that you may not be led into temptation.' But the Jews disregarded Mordecai's advice, and went.

(2) R. Levi said that 18,560 men went to this banquet, and ate and drank until they were intoxicated with the wine. Our sages say that while they were at the table of this wicked man, Satan appeared before God, and accused Israel in these words, 'O Lord of the universe, how long wilt Thou cleave to this nation, who turn their hearts from Thee, who forsake Thee, and separate themselves from Thee? Moreover, they do not turn to Thee in repentance, although the verse has been fulfilled in which it is written, "I shall scatter you among the heathen." Therefore, if it is Thy will, let them perish from the world.' But God asked, 'What will become of My law?' And he replied, 'Let it remain for the higher beings.' Then said the Holy One, blessed be He, 'My mind is satisfied to destroy Israel.' (3) At that moment He wished to blot Israel out of the world, as it is said, 'I shall cease to remember man.' 'What is this nation to Me,' said the Lord, 'for whom My sorrow increases every day?' And God said to Satan, 'Go, and bring Me a scroll, that I may write thereon their destruction.' When Satan went out to fetch the scroll, he came face to face with the Law, which came forth to meet him in widow's garments groaning and weeping, and at the voice of her weeping the ministering angels cried, saying, 'If the Israelites are to be destroyed, what is the use of us?' And they wept aloud, as it is said, 'The Arēlīm cried abroad, and

the angels of peace wept bitterly.' As soon as the sun, moon, stars, and planets heard it they clothed themselves with sackcloth, and lifted up their voice in lamentation, as it is said, 'The heavens and the earth clothed themselves in blackness, and girded themselves with sackcloth;' as it is said, 'I will clothe the heavens with blackness, and make sackcloth their garment.' Then they all exclaimed, 'O Lord of the universe, shall Israel be destroyed, who go from door to door wishing to study the law, observe the Sabbath, circumcision, and the commandments, and for whose sakes we were created? as it is said, "If not for My covenant, the day and the night and the ordinances of heaven and earth would not have been founded," and now shall they perish from the world?'

(4) At that moment Elijah went to beseech the righteous men of yore, the patriarchs, Abraham, Isaac, and Jacob, and said to them, 'O patriarchs, do ye not know that the heavens and the earth and all the heavenly host weep in the day, and cry in the night, and that the whole world is now like a travailing woman, while ye remain silent?' 'But why is this?' said they. 'Because Israel has been handed over to the slaughterer like sheep, to be blotted out from the face of the earth, and their name is to perish, as it is said, "Come, and let us destroy them."' Then said Moses to Elijah, 'Is there a righteous man in this generation?' And he replied, 'Yes, there is one, and his name is Mordecai, the son of Jair.' 'Then go, and tell him to supplicate continually for mercy, and I shall do likewise.' 'But,' said Elijah, 'Moses, O faithful shepherd, against thy flock the decree has already been written down, and now they desire to put the seal on it.'

(5) 'Notice,' then said Moses to Elijah, 'whether it has been sealed with clay, for then our prayers may still be heard; but if it is sealed with blood, then what has been decreed will happen.' After this conversation Elijah, of blessed memory, forthwith went to Mordecai, as it is said, 'And Mordecai knew all that had happened,' and when he heard this, he rent his clothes, as it is said, 'And

Mordecai rent his clothes.' Then said Mordecai before God, 'O Lord of the universe, Thou hast sworn to our forefathers to make their seed as numerous as the stars of the heavens, and now we are accounted for as sheep to be slaughtered. Remember Abraham, Isaac, and Israel, thy servants.'

(6) Then, gathering all the children of the school together, he afflicted them by depriving them of bread and water, and, clothing them in sackcloth, he placed them on ashes, so that they cried day and night, while the wicked Haman went to his house rejoicing, as it is written, 'And on that day Haman went home rejoicing, and with a merry heart, and calling his friends, said, "Thus and thus has Queen Esther done." And he told them of his greatness, adding, "But all this is not enough for me." And Zeresh, his wife, said to him to erect gallows for Mordecai, and it pleased him, and he erected a gallows. Cutting down a cedar from his garden, 50 cubits high and 15 cubits wide, he brought it out, and fixed it near his door, all the while singing praises and songs, and thinking in his heart that at the time of the reading of the 'Shema'' he would hang Mordecai thereon. On the same day that he fixed it, it fell upon him; but Gabriel replaced it in its position, saying to him, 'To thee belongs this beautiful tree, and for thee was it established from the creation.'

(7) Haman then went out to seek Mordecai, and found him sitting at the head of the children, while they sat upon ashes girded with sackcloth, lamenting and crying. Having beaten them with chains of iron, he appointed keepers over them, saying, 'First shall these be slain, and afterwards I will hang Mordecai the Jew.' Their mothers then brought them bread and water, saying to them, 'Eat and drink, my children, before you die'; but they refused, and, swearing by the life of Mordecai, they placed their hands upon their books, and said, 'We shall not eat anything at all, but shall die in our fast.' (8) After rolling up his scroll, each one of them placed it at his heart, and when the hours of the night passed by their lamentation was heard on high,

and the supplications of the patriarchs. The Holy One said, 'I hear the voices of kids and goats;' at which Moses replied, 'O Lord God of the universe, Father of the fatherless, and Judge of the widows, these are not kids and goats, but the young of Thy people of the house of Israel, who sit fasting now for three days and three nights, bound in chains of iron; but to-morrow they are to be slaughtered like kids and goats, while the heart of the enemy rejoiceth.' The mercy of God was then moved for them, so that He broke the seals, rent the decree, and frustrated the counsel of Haman and his plans, causing the salvation of Israel and Mordecai to spring forth, thus fulfilling what is written, 'I shall cut off the horns of the wicked; but the horns of the righteous shall be raised on high.'

LXXXIII. (1) It is written, On that same night the sleep of the king was disturbed. God at that time said to the patriarchs, 'They have been condemned to destruction:' they replied, 'O Lord of the universe, for what reason?' 'Because in the time of Nebuchadnezzar they did not sanctify My name, and made Me to be one who hath no power to deliver.' Whereupon they replied, 'Now, O Lord, do unto them what seems good to Thee.' But as soon as God saw that they bowed to justice, He arose from His throne of justice, and sat upon the throne of mercy. Then did the heavenly host address God, saying, 'Didst Thou not create the whole world for the sake of the Torah, which Thou gavest to Israel? do not all things exist for their sake? as it is said, "If not for My covenant I would not have created day and night." Therefore, if Thou destroyest this nation, what shall become of us?' But God replied, 'My children have not done well.' 'O Lord of the world,' added they, 'it is revealed and known to Thee that they did this from fear.'

(2) The Lord was then filled with mercy for Israel, and, calling to the trees of the creation, He said, 'Who of you will be willing to serve as gallows for the wicked?' And the fig-tree replied, 'I am ready to be the gallows to hang that wicked man; for from me the Israelites brought the

first ripe fruits into the temple, and not only this, but they were compared to me,' as it is said, 'I saw your fathers as the first ripe fruit on the fig-tree in its bud.' The vine also said, 'I will offer myself, for from me they obtained the drink-offering for the temple; and, moreover, to me they were compared,' as it is said, 'Israel is a budding vine.'

(3) Then said the pomegranate, 'I will offer myself, for the Israelites were compared to me,' as it is said, 'Like the heart of a pomegranate is thy temple.' And the walnut said, 'I will offer myself, for the Israelites were compared to me,' as it is said, 'I descended to the garden of nuts.' The citron also exclaimed, 'I will offer myself, for the Israelites praised God through me,' as it is said, 'And ye shall take you the fruit of goodly trees.' The willows of the brook said, 'They were compared to me,' as it is said, 'And they shall spring up among the grass, as willows by the water-courses.' The olive said, 'I will offer myself, for from me they kindled the lights in the temple,' as it is said, 'And they shall take unto me pure olive-oil'; 'they were, moreover, compared to me,' as it is said, 'His majesty is like the olive, and, further, the green olive whose fruit is beautiful to look at.'

(4) The apple also said, 'I will offer myself, for the Israelites were compared to me,' as it is said, 'And the sweet smell of thy breath is like apples.' The cedar said, 'I will offer myself, for from me the holy temple was built, besides which the Israelites were compared to me,' as it is said, 'He shall grow like the cedar in Lebanon.' The thorn next said, 'I will serve as gallows, for the wicked were compared to me,' as it is said, 'But the ungodly shall be all as thorns to be thrust away.'

(5) As soon as the thorn had offered itself, the Lord silenced all the trees of the creation, saying, 'Since thou offerest thyself, this wicked man, who desires to destroy My children, shall be hanged upon thee.' And at that moment that wicked man, summoning his wise men, said unto them, 'I will erect a tree, to hang Mordecai thereon,

50 cubits high, that all the surrounding countries may see him hanging.' 'But there is no tree as high as that, except in thine own house.' This wicked man then destroyed the hall of his own house in order to obtain the materials required for the gallows, and taking the beam of thorn from his house, he fixed it; but it fell upon him, and thereby took his measurement. Then exclaimed Gabriel, 'This tree has been prepared for thee from the creation.'

(6) The sages say that Michael came to the bedside of Ahasuerus in the night, and disturbed his sleep, for he knocked him on the ground 366 times. When he arose, in great anger, he saw three companies before him, one of butchers, one of bakers, and the third of butlers, and said to them, 'Ye have given me poison, and you seek to kill me and to blot me out from the world.' But they answered, 'The same bread that Queen Esther and Haman ate thou atest, and the wine they drank thou also drankest. Let us see Esther and Haman, and if they are as thou art, then thou doest rightly; but if not, then why should we be killed?'

(7) When they found that Esther and Haman had suffered no harm, the king ordered the Book of Chronicles to be brought before him. On that same night Gabriel appeared in his dream before Ahasuerus, in the likeness of Haman, with a drawn sword in his hand, seeking to kill him. Rising confusedly from his sleep he exclaimed, 'Who is in the court?' And the young chamberlains of the king replied, 'Haman is in the court.' Then he thought, and said, 'The dream I have dreamt is true, and he has come here for no other reason than to sláy me.' Then, commanding Haman to come into his presence, he said, 'I know that thou art a man of thought, and whoever follows thy counsel never fails. What shall be done to the man whom the king delights to honour?' Revolving this in his mind, Haman thought, 'Whom can the king desire to honour more than me?'

(8) He therefore said to the king: 'Let the man whom the king desires to honour be clothed in the royal garments,

and let one of the greatest men of the kingdom walk in front of him and proclaim aloud these words, "Whoever will not bend himself or bow down before him shall be slain," and in addition, let the king's daughter be given him.' Then said the king to Haman, 'Go and do likewise to Mordecai the Jew who sits in the gate of the king.' 'But there are many Mordecais who sit in the king's gate, and is not a small province sufficient for him?' asked Haman. The king said, 'Let no word fail from all that thou hast said.'

[End of the letter of Haman. This is a Midrash, and is not to be found in the Book of Josippon.]

THE THRONE OF SOLOMON, KING OF ISRAEL.

LXXXIV. (1) 'In those days, when Ahasuerus sat (upon the throne).' The word כשבת can only be understood as meaning 'sitting on a throne,' as it is said, 'When Ahasuerus sat upon the throne of his kingdom;' but with reference to Solomon, it is said, 'And Solomon sat upon the throne of the Lord as king over Israel.' It is related that the assembly of Israel said unto God, 'O Lord of the universe, this wicked man sits in the same place where Solomon has been sitting; do not make abominable the throne of Thy glory.' In the third year of his reign—for he busied himself with this throne for three years—he sent for workmen to make a throne like unto that of Solomon, but they were unable to do so.

(2) And what was the throne of Solomon? The sages say that Solomon mounted his throne by six different ways, each way having steps. On each step there were two lions, one on the right and the other on the left, who did not remain quiet, but were active. And what did they do? When Solomon went up on the first step, the lions on the right stretched out their paws upon which a writing was engraved. He could not place his foot on the second step until he had read what was written on the lions' paws. It was, 'Ye shall not respect persons in judgment.'

Turning now to the left, he read what the other lions had written on their paws, 'Thou shalt not accept any bribe.' (3) Thus at every step he had to read some portion of the law of judgment. All the steps were set with precious stones and pearls, red, white and green. Kinds of trees and species of the palm-trees were fixed on both sides of each step, and upon their branches there nestled all kinds of eagles, peacocks and birds. On the highest step were two huge pillars of ivory on the heads of the lions, and two golden hollow vines fragrant with every kind of perfume, which they exhaled whenever Solomon ascended the throne. The throne itself was made of ivory, overlaid with the gold of Ophir, and surrounded with precious stones and pearls. On either side of the throne a golden seat of honour was placed, one for Gad the seer, and the other for Nathan the prophet. (4) And seventy other seats of gold for the seventy judges of the Sanhedrim formed a circle round the central throne. In front of it was a lamp of gold, with its snuffers and censers and other appurtenances; and on one side of this lamp were seen in sculptured work the seven patriarchs of the world, viz., Adam, Noah, Shem, Abraham, Isaac, Jacob and Job, while on the other side were the seven pious men of the world, viz., Kehath, Amran, Moses, Aaron, Eldad, Medad and Hur, and on the top the form of a priest was seen kindling the light.

(5) On the steps approaching the throne were placed as many unclean animals as clean, all facing each other, on the first step the ox was placed opposite the lion; on the second, the goat opposite the wolf; on the third (third missing); on the fourth, the bear opposite the hart; on the fifth, the eagle opposite the dove; and on the sixth, the hawk opposite the turtledove. The ascent to the throne was made between these animals. As soon as Solomon placed his foot on the first step he turned round, and the lion immediately stretched out its paw on the right and the eagle its talon on the left. Upon these he leaned, and was spared the trouble of ascending himself because the same thing was done by the different animals and

birds on each until he arrived at the top. (6) Then all the birds of every species began to chirp and sing, and the peacocks to shriek, and all the trees emitted their fragrant perfumes. A serpent of gold then encircled him, and, having seated him upon his throne, crept down beneath his feet. The eagles, nestling on the vines after wafting breezes of perfume with their wings, placed the crown upon his head, and, this done, all the beasts and birds with one accord exclaimed, 'Long may the kingdom of the house of David be established.' (7) After this a dove of gold opposite the throne brought a scroll of the law and placed it upon his knees. Then, laying it upon a golden reading-desk just by the throne, he read it to fulfil what is written, 'And it shall remain with him, and he shall read therein all the days of his life.' Every step on the throne contained some verse in praise of the law. On the first was written, 'The law of the Lord is perfect, refreshing the soul.' On the second, 'The testimony of the Lord is faithful, making the foolish (simple) wise.' On the third, 'The precepts of the Lord are just, rejoicing the heart.' On the fourth, 'The commandment of the Lord He created as an enlightenment to the eyes.' On the fifth, 'The fear of the Lord is pure, lasting for ever.' On the sixth, 'The judgments of the Lord are true, and are righteous, all of them.'

(8) When the people approached Solomon for judgment, the wheels of his throne turned, the oxen lowed, the lions roared, the bears howled, the lambs bleated, the eagles cried, the peacocks shrieked, the cocks crowed, the hawks screamed, and all the birds chirped, to terrify the plaintiffs and the witnesses, so that they did not plead wrong cases, and the witnesses were not testifying falsely. On account of all this, it is said, 'The like of it will never be made in any kingdom.' When Ahasuerus was king, he tried for three years to have a throne made like that of Solomon, but in vain. [End of the throne of Solomon.]

LXXXV. (1) In the first year of his reign, Cyrus tried to build the temple, but when Ahasuerus arose he prohibited it, and attempted to uproot the vineyard (of the Lord), but God exterminated him and the wicked Haman from the world, and he died. His son succeeded him. These are the kings mentioned, 'Darius,' 'Cyrus,' and 'Artaxerxes.' Then the people believed the prophets and were prosperous. In the second year of his reign he allowed the Jews to return to Jerusalem to erect the holy temple and repair Jerusalem without let or hindrance. This was, indeed, a complete redemption. Then did Ezra, Zerubbabel, and his company for the second time go up to Jerusalem with another generation of the captivity, and they rebuilt Jerusalem and its walls. The towers they erected were very high and strong, and the temple contained more than did the first one, so that the first temple was deemed insignificant in comparison to it. The people on this account served Cyrus loyally for thirty-four years.

(2) After the rebuilding of the temple, Zerubbabel returned to Babylon and there died. His son, Meshullam, succeeded him, and in his days, in the fifty-second year of the kingdom of the Medes and Persians, the kingdom was formed. The last prophets, Haggai, Zechariah, and Malachi, died at that time, and from that day prophecy ceased to exist in Israel, and the Echo of the Heavenly Voice (Bath Kol) took its place, and after that they had to consult the sages, until the Messiah will come and show us the right way.

(3) Thirty-four years after the rebuilding of the temple, Darius, the son of Ahasuerus, reigned, until Alexander the Macedonian, and first King of Greece, rose up against him in battle, and having killed him, took his kingdom. He reigned over Israel two years and captured every kingdom; he made the whole world subservient to him, for at that time, thirty-four years after the rebuilding of the temple, Alexander the Great was crowned, the son of Philippus,

King of Macedon, for he made the name of the Macedonian nation great, and smote the whole country. When he waged war against Darius he smote the land of Egypt, and slew in Alexandria double as many Jews as went out of Egypt. After conquering Edom, he marched along the sea-shore until he came to Acco, which he conquered, as well as Ashkalon and 'Aza. He then turned to go up to Jerusalem to smite it, because the Jews had made a covenant with Darius. After journeying with all his camp some distance, he arrived at a lodge, where he and his army encamped.

(4) On the same night, while he was lying in his bed in his tent, he opened his eyes and beheld a man standing over him, clothed in white linen, and with a drawn sword in his hand. The appearance of the sword was like lightning on a rainy day. When he lifted the sword over the head of the king, he was greatly afraid, and said, 'Why will my lord smite his servant?' And the man replied, 'God hath sent me to conquer kings and many nations before thee, and I will go before thee to render thee assistance, but know now that thou shalt surely be slain, because thy heart is bent upon going to Jerusalem in order to injure God's priests and God's people.' 'I beseech thee, O lord,' replied the king, 'pardon the sin of thy servant, and if it is evil in thine eyes, I will return to my home.' 'Do not be afraid,' said the man; 'go thy way to Jerusalem, and when thou comest before the gate of the city and seest a man clothed in white like me, having an appearance and form like mine, do thou immediately make thy obeisance to him and bow thyself to the ground before him; do whatever he bids thee and do not transgress his word, for the very day that thou rebellest against his word thou shalt be slain.'

(5) The king accordingly arose and went on his way to Jerusalem. When the High Priest heard that the king was coming against Jerusalem in great anger, he was exceedingly afraid, as were all the people, and he with the people went out at the gate of the city, and he stood

before them clothed in white linen. As soon as Alexander beheld the priest, quickly dismounting from his chariot, he fell upon his face and bowed down to him. But the generals of Alexander became very angry at this, and said, 'Why dost thou bow down to a man who has no strength for battle?' And the king replied, 'Because the man that goeth in front of me to subdue all the nations before me is in appearance and form like this man. I therefore bow down to him.'

(6) Then, going into our holy temple, he said to the priest, 'I will have my statue erected here, and will give much gold to the workmen, that it may be a remembrance of me. And they shall erect it between the Holy of Holies and the temple, so that my image be a remembrance in this great house of God.' But the priest replied, 'Present the gold for the maintenance of God's priests and the poor of His people, and I shall cause thee to be remembered for good, as thou wishest. All the children of the priests that are born this year shall be called by thy name, Alexander, and thou shalt be remembered when they worship in this house; but it is not permitted to place a graven image or any likeness in the house of our God.' The king then gave the gold according to the priest's request.

(7) He asked him to inquire of God on his behalf whether he should go to war with Darius, or abandon the plan. And the priest replied, 'He will surely be delivered into thy hand.' Then, bringing the Book of Daniel, he showed him the passage concerning the ram that gores on all sides, and the young of the goats which runs up to him and tramples upon him. 'Thou,' added he, 'art the young of the goats and Darius is the ram. Thou shalt therefore trample upon him and seize his kingdom.' Thereupon Alexander went to battle, and having slain Darius, captured all his kingdom, so that the Persian kingdom ceased to exist. Alexandria in Egypt was made the royal city.

(8) He ruled over all the nations just as a shepherd rules over his flock. He soon went over to India, travelling right across the country to its extremity, and extended his

dominion, as we learn from the Talmud. R. Jose said, 'For six years he reigned in Elam, and afterwards spread his kingdom over the whole world.' He reigned altogether twelve years, and when he was on his way home to his house he died. Before his death, he divided his kingdom among his four chieftains. He made Ptolemy, the son of Lagi (לאני), King of Egypt; Phillipos his brother King of Macedon, and Seleucus and Nicanor Kings of Syria and Babylon respectively; lastly, he made Antiochus, the great enemy of the Jews, King of Asia (עמיא).' Daniel prophesied this event when he said that the goat would gore the ram and break down his kingdom, which would be given to the four winds of the heaven.

LXXXVI. (1) When Seleucus reigned over Macedonia, a very wicked, rebellious man of our own people, Simeon of the tribe of Benjamin, went to Seleucus, and, slandering the Jews, informed him of the riches contained in the temple at Jerusalem, saying that the treasures were heaped up in the treasury in endless quantities, and an abundance of gold and precious stones, and that it would be preferable to have it all placed in the treasury of Seleucus. The king thereupon sent for Eliodorus, the captain of his host, and bade him go to Jerusalem with his armies. On his arrival, Honiah the priest said to him, 'Why has my lord come to his servants?' 'Because of the vast amount of gold and precious stones which, the king has been informed, is contained in the treasury of your temple.' 'The only gold in the treasury,' said the priest, 'is that which King Seleucus and other kings presented to us, for the maintenance of orphans, widows and the poor. For this, we pray to God to grant long life to the king and his sons.'

(2) Eliodorus, however, would not listen to the priest, but placed guards round the temple until the following day, when the city was in great uproar through the lamentation and cries of the people. The priests also called upon their God, and the old men and women and princes covered themselves with ashes and afflicted their souls with fasting.

They withheld food from even the young, and milk from the sucklings. They cried to God to guard the treasury and the riches deposited therein. Even the young virgins spread out their hands through the windows of their houses, and besought the Lord for protection. And as to Honiah the priest, he afflicted his soul (by fasting), and having stripped himself of his garments of honour, clothed himself in sackcloth and ashes, for he was grief-stricken, and, from his appearance, one could imagine the sorrow that was in his heart.

(3) On the next day the enemy came with all his hosts and went into the temple shouting, but the Lord caused a strong and mighty sound of thunder to be heard, together with an earthquake, and a tempest that overthrew mountains and shattered rocks. On hearing this, all his troops took to flight, and hid themselves wherever they could, so that he (Eliodorus) remained alone, and, lifting up his eyes, he saw an awe-inspiring man clothed in gold, decked with precious stones, and girt with implements of war. He was riding a splendid horse, that was plunging and rearing, trotting and galloping in the temple. Heliodorus immediately ran away, but the horse felled him to the ground, standing over him. The man then commanded his two young servants, clothed in white linen, with staves in their hands, to smite Eliodorus very severely; and the two young men at his bidding stood one on each side of him, and beat him mercilessly until he became insensible and hovered between life and death.

(4) Young priests came then, and lifting him on their shoulders, carried him into his tent and placed him in his bed, where he lay motionless and dumb. He could neither speak nor partake of any food. When the elders of Macedon saw him in this state, they came to Honiah the priest, and, crying, entreated him in the following manner, 'O my lord, we beseech thee, pray for thy servant Eliodorus and all his servants who have come with him, that we may live and not die, for we know that there is no other God except yours, since all the gods of the nations are vanity and

emptiness, whilst yours is the God that created the world, and in whose hand is the soul of every living being.'

(5) The priest, then praying to God, offered up burnt-offerings and sacrifices, and the two young men that smote Eliodorus by the temple appeared to him and said, 'Arise, go to Honiah the priest, and bow down to his feet, since for his sake the Lord has had mercy upon thee.' Eliodorus accordingly arose, and, going to the priest, prostrated himself, and blessing the Lord and the priest, gave much gold and silver to the treasury of the house of the Lord. Then hastening to Macedonia, he went to Seleucus the king, who asked, 'What of Jerusalem?' And Eliodorus replied, 'If thou hast any enemies that seek thy life, send them at once to Jerusalem, and let them go into the temple, where they will surely be killed, for the great God reigns in that place, and destroys all the enemies of Jerusalem and Judah.' He then told the king all that he had witnessed. And Seleucus no more sent his army to Jerusalem to do evil, but, on the contrary, every year until his death he sent a present to the temple, and the kings of the land loved to send their offerings to honour the temple at Jerusalem.

LXXXVII. (1) Now, Ptolemy the Macedonian, who was made King of Egypt, was a wise and clever king, who delighted much in books. He, therefore, commanded his two officers to collect very many of them. The names of these princes were Aristios and Andrios. Having collected together many Median and Persian books, besides others in all kinds of languages, the king said to them, 'How many books have you obtained?' 'Nine hundred and fifty,' they replied. Ptolemy laughed at this, and said, 'Go and add another fifty to make a thousand.'

(2) But Aristios and Andrios replied, 'O my lord, it is in vain that we weary ourselves to obtain these books, since they are useless. Now, if it please the king, let him write to the priest at Jerusalem, and he will send thee some wise men of that place, conversant with the Greek language, who will explain to thee their law, which is the holy writing, but the books we have copied are of no use.'

(3) Acting upon their advice, the king made such a request of the priest who was in those days, and the high priest sent him seventy priests with Eleazar as their chief, the same Eleazar who was afterwards tried during the reign of Antiochus, and who died a martyr's death for his God.

(4) When Eleazar and these seventy priestly interpreters came to Egypt, Ptolemy, having put them in seventy different houses, one distinct from the other, provided each one with a scribe, and the priests interpreted the whole twenty-four books of the law, which these seventy elders then translated from Hebrew into Greek. As soon as it was finished, Eleazar brought the various copies to the king, who, after reading each one of them, found that they were all of one mind, and that the interpretations of all were identical. (5) The king was much rejoiced at this, and, presenting Eleazar and the seventy elders with much money, sent them back to Jerusalem. He further gave 150,000 men of Judah their freedom, besides presenting them each with fifty drachmas of gold, and a table of pure gold weighing 1,000 talents for the temple. Upon it he engraved the land of Egypt, and the course of the river Nile in Egypt, by which the country is watered, and inlaid it with precious stones, so that the like of it had never been seen in all the land. This the King Ptolemy sent as a present to the temple of the great and awe-inspiring God of the whole world.

(6) A long time after this, Antiochus was made King of Macedonia, while Ptolemy, King of Egypt, was gathered to his people, and another Ptolemy succeeded him. But Antiochus rose up against him, and having slain him, captured the whole land of Egypt, over which he reigned. (7) In those days fierce battles began to be fought against the people of Judah, for after Antiochus had smitten Egypt he became very proud, and issued a proclamation to every people, commanding them to bow down to the image of the king. And all the nations obeyed. But the godless men of our people, Menelaos, Simeon, Alkimos, and others,

incited Antiochus to do evil to the Israelites. At this time a great miracle was seen in Jerusalem. There were seen forty men riding between heaven and earth on what seemed like horses of fire. The riders carried in their hands partly golden implements of war, with which they fought one against the other for forty days. At this the wicked men of our people went to King Antiochus, and said, 'Behold, we have seen a miracle in Jerusalem, and the people say that Antiochus the king is dead, and are rejoicing at the downfall of our lord.' (8) The king was greatly angered at this, and immediately went to Jerusalem and smote them with the edge of the sword, so that there was a great slaughter in the city. A great multitude were sent into exile, and the assembly of the Ḥassidim scattered. They fled to the forest, and fed upon the grass as animals, and hid themselves in the forest like wild beasts, for Antiochus was not satisfied with slaying many, but he sent many more into captivity, and when he left the land of Judah, he left his officers to afflict the people, and he left Phillipos the Pelusian. They are Phrygians (מפקיסי פריני), and so are also the Trojans (תרייני), of whom the Romans are descended. Phillipos belonged to that race. The king left him there to oppress the Israelites, commanding him thus, 'Whoever is willing to bow down to the image I set up, and to eat of the flesh of the swine, shall live, but all who refuse shall be slain without mercy. Prohibit also this people from observing the Sabbath, and from circumcising their children.'

LXXXVIII. (1) The king then returned to Macedonia, and, having left Phillipos in the land of Judah, he (Phillip) acted according to the word of the king, and prohibited the people of Judah from studying the Torah and from performing the service of their God. He supported the wicked and the rebellious of our people, and slew many of the congregation of the Ḥassidim.

(2) At that time two women were discovered who had circumcised their children. They hanged them by their breasts, and hurled them with their children from the top

of a tower; they burst open and died. (3) After this Eleazar, the chief of the priests, of whom we have spoken as having gone to Egypt in the days of Ptolemy, was captured and brought to Phillip. And Phillip said to him, 'Eleazar, thou art a wise man and a man of understanding, now, do not transgress the command of the king, but eat of the flesh of his sacrifice.' But Eleazar replied, 'Far be it from me to set aside the command of my God for the performance of the command of the king.' Then did Phillip call him aside and say, 'Thou knowest that I have loved thee now for many years, therefore I have pity for thy soul and for thy old age. Now let a portion of the flesh of your own sacrifices which you are allowed to eat be brought to thee, and eat it before the people so that they will say thou eatest of the flesh of the king's sacrifice. By this means thou canst save thy life and not die.'

(4) When Eleazar heard this he thought of the greatness of his honour and of the sanctity of his glory, and said to Phillip, 'I am now ninety years old, and have never yet served my God with deceit, nor is it meet for me now to do so and to deceive man, for then the young men will say, "Since Eleazar, although ninety years of age, has frustrated the law of his God, we can also do so," and they will thus bring destruction upon themselves. Now, far be it from me to defile my holiness, to taint the purity of my old age, and to cause these young men with me to waver, and give them the pretext for saying, "Eleazar, although ninety years of age, has sinned against his God, and has chosen to serve the vanities of the nations; let us do likewise." For even if I escape from your hands to-day, I cannot escape God, for no man can, either living or dead, since His dominion extends over the living to bring death upon them, and over the dead to quicken them to life. I shall therefore die true to my faith, and shall leave my power behind to my people and my young men, so that when they see me give up my life so readily, they will desire to follow my example, and thus keep their Torah precious, and will choose a worthy death.'

(5) As soon, however, as Phillipos heard these words, he turned exceedingly cruel, and commanded his men to bind the pious old man and to beat him. They thereupon smote him with all manner of weapons without pity, and he groaned, saying, 'O Lord my God, who hast caused me to reach this old age, Thou knowest that I was able to deliver my soul from such a death, but did not wish to do so on account of my love for Thee. Now they smite so cruelly and fiercely that I would not be able to bear it were it not for my fear of Thee, which renders them as nothing in my eyes, and I suffer them willingly.' While he was still speaking these words his life closed, and he left might to his people and power to his young men.

LXXXIX. (1) Seven brothers with their mother were then seized and sent to the king, for the king had not yet departed from Jerusalem, and because the swine's flesh was abhorred by the Jews and stank and was despised by them, therefore the cruelties against them were increased, and he tore their flesh as that of an ox.

(2) When the first son was brought before the king, he said, 'Why waste words to teach us, for we have already been taught by our forefathers? We are prepared to suffer death for the Lord and His law.' The king was furious at this, and, ordering a pan of brass to be brought, placed it on the fire. Then, ordering his tongue to be cut out, his hands and legs and the skin of his head to be cut off, he placed them all in the frying-pan in the sight of his brothers; the rest of his body they cast in a large brass pot placed upon the hot coals. When he was near death the king commanded the fire to be removed from under the pot so that he should not die too quickly, so as to terrify his brothers and his mother. But they, on the contrary, encouraged each other and fortified each other when they saw that their brother gave up his life for the Lord and His Torah, and said to each other, 'See what Moses, the servant of the Lord, said in his song, "He shall be comforted in His servants." Even now the Lord is comforted in us for all the evil which He has purposed to do to His people, and He will have compassion upon them.'

(3) As soon as the first died, the second brother was brought. They said to him, 'Listen to the command of the king. Why die in great torture as thy brother?' And he replied, 'Make haste with the sword and with the fire, and do not do one whit less to me than ye did to my brother, for I do not fall short of my brother in piety and the fear of God.' Every limb was then commanded to be cut off and placed in the frying-pan on the fire. He then said, 'Hear me, thou cruel king: art thou able to bind up these our souls which thou robbest us of? Behold, they shall walk to God, who has given them to us—to the light that is with the Lord. We shall yet live a life that has no limit or end when He awakeneth the dead of His people and the slain of His servants.'

(4) Thus died the second brother. When the third was brought, he looked at the king, and, stretching out his right hand towards the king, said, 'What business of thine is it to destroy us, O thou enemy and foe? All this comes from Heaven, and we receive it with love, but thy tortures are despicable in our eyes, as nothing before us, since we expect honour and favour from Heaven. He will grant us the reward of our actions.' The king and all his princes were astonished at the bravery of the youth.

(5) After his death the fourth brother was brought. 'What,' said he, 'have I to do with thee, O thou wicked man? We die for the Lord, and He will again bring us back to life, but thou shalt never rise again.'

(6) When the fifth was brought, he said, 'Do not imagine that God has forsaken us, for on account of His great love has He brought us to this honour. Thou reviler and blasphemer, the Lord hates thee and stirs thee up to do unto us whatever thou wilt, but a great vengeance will be taken upon thee and thy seed, and His anger will be kindled against thee and all thy household.'

(7) After his death the sixth brother was brought before the king, and he said, 'We know our wickedness, for we have sinned against the Lord, and now our souls are given over to death as an atonement for our people; but now be-

cause thy heart prompts thee to do this thing to the servants of our God and to fight against God; behold, He shall fight against thee and uproot thee from the face of the earth.'

(8) The seventh and last brother was but a young lad, yet the mother, who had seen her seven sons slain on one day, neither feared nor trembled, but, standing upright by the corpses of her sons, she lifted up her voice and cried, saying, 'O my son! O my son! I do not know how you were formed in my womb, nor did I give you the breath and soul which you had, nor bring you out of my womb, nor raise you, nor make you grow, or your flesh which is now offered as a sacrifice; God formed it. He wove the sinews and covered it with skin, and caused hair to grow upon it. He then breathed in your nostrils the breath of life. And since you give up all this for His sake, He will restore them to you, and will renew your body. He will give you the reward of your actions, and happy are ye, my sons, for all this.'

(9) At this the king was very much taken aback, in that the woman had subdued him. 'Bring me the seventh one,' said he, 'and perhaps, as he is but a young lad, I may be able to entice him with soft words to do our will, but do not let this woman boast of me, saying, 'I have conquered King Antiochus in exhorting my sons to die for our God.'

(10) According to the king's command, the seventh lad was brought, and the king implored him, and took an oath to enrich him with silver and gold, with cattle and many servants, to make him viceregent, and to let him rule over the whole kingdom. But when the lad despised the words of the king, the king summoned the mother to him, and said, 'O good woman, have pity upon this child, and be merciful to the fruit of thy womb; induce him to perform my will and to escape.' And the woman answered, 'Give him to me, and I shall entice him with kind words.' This being done, she led him aside, and having kissed kim, and rejoiced at the king's shame and confusion, said, 'O my son, thou whom I carried in my womb for nine months,

and whom I suckled for three years, after which I sustained thee with food until this very day, give up all this proffered honour, and fear the God of whom I taught thee. (11) Now, O my son, look toward the heaven, and behold the land, the sea, the waters, and the fire, which by the word of the Lord were created. But man is merely flesh and blood and as nothing before Him. Do not fear this cruel man, but give up thy life for the sake of the Lord. Go the same way as thy brothers. Would that I could now see where thy brothers are, and the greatness of their glory before the Lord. My son, cleave to thy brothers, and thy lot shall be cast in their glory. I shall go there with you, and rejoice with you as on the days of your marriage. I shall be with you in your righteousness.'

(12) While she was yet speaking the lad answered, and said, 'Why do you delay me, and will not leave me to go and join my holy brothers? I will not listen to the king, but to the law of our God, which He has given through the hand of Moses to the people of Israel, which this cruel enemy of God has put to shame and reviled. Woe unto thee, woe unto thee! Whither wilt thou go? whither wilt thou flee? whither wilt thou run? and where wilt thou hide thyself from our God, O enemy, foe, and wicked man, for He still keeps us alive, and has glorified and exalted us over all nations? But thou who art insolent enough to stretch forth thy hand against His servants, it were better thou hadst not been born. Thou wicked fool Antiochus, who wast begotten of tainted folly, hast committed evil against thyself, but Thou hast done good unto us, and if we endure and bear these tortures in this world, we shall be taken to the life and light of the world where there is no darkness, but eternal life without death. (13) But thou wilt be the abomination of all creatures, and wilt be abhorred of our God when He takes vengeance upon thee. Thou shalt die an unnatural death, plagued with dreadful plagues. Thou shalt descend to the bottom of hell. Thou shalt be drawn into darkness, where there is no life or light, but darkness and shades; where there

is no repose or rest, but trouble, sorrow, brimstone, and fire. This will be thy portion of the Lord and thy lot from our God, O man of blood and wicked man. But God will have mercy upon His people. Until now His wrath has rested upon us, but He will henceforth be angry no longer with His people, but will repent of what He has done to us at the beginning, although He did so in truth and in righteousness, for we acted wickedly. He will return and have mercy upon us, and will grant us eternal life.' King Antiochus now became exceedingly angry because he would not perform his will, and therefore increased the tortures, and acted much more cruelly to him than he had done to the others. Thus died the seventh.

(14) The mother then stood by the corpses of her sons, and, spreading out her hands, she said, 'O exalted and awe-inspiring God, O God of the universe, now will I come; now will I die with my sons in the place which Thou hast prepared for them.' While she was yet speaking she finished her days upon earth, falling upon the dead bodies of her sons, her spirit went forth, and she died with them.

XC. (1) The king then went on his way to Macedon, and commanded Phillip and the captains whom he had left in the land of Judah, saying, 'Blot out the very memory of Judah from the face of the earth, and let him who but mentions the name "Jew" be slain; but let all those live who are willing to be assimilated with our people, and be called "Javan."' (2) Accordingly Phillip and the captains with him destroyed all whom he discovered observing the Torah, with the exception of those who fled with Mattathiah, the son of Jochanan to Mod'aith. For Mattathiah would not bear the reproach of the uncircumcised, but was zealous for his God, and, weeping, he said, 'Woe unto me, O my mother, that thou didst give me birth to behold the breach of my people.'

(3) Then he sent his son Judah secretly to say to the Jews, 'Whoever of you are on the side of the Lord, come to me.' There gathered unto him a 'large assembly of

Hassidim, and Mattathiah addressed them in the following words, 'Why multiply words? The only thing that remains for us to do is to pray and to fight. Let us strengthen ourselves and die in battle, but not as sheep led to slaughter.' When they heard these words they all of them took courage (braced themselves up), and said each one to his neighbour, 'To thy tent, O Judah. Rule again over thine own land. It is enough, King Antiochus. Now sharpen thy sword, O people of Judah, and beware of thy life, O nation of Macedon.' From that day the Macedonian yoke was broken asunder from the shoulders of Judah.

(4) When Phillip and the chiefs of the king heard these words they went against them with a large army. When they were going against them, they found on the way men, women, and children of Judah in a cave all observing the Sabbath. Coming to the entrance of the cave, they said to them, 'Come out and profane the Sabbath, and perform the command of the king and live, and do not allow yourselves to die.' But they said, 'We shall not come out nor shall we profane the Sabbath day. Let the heavens and the earth be witness that we die in our integrity.' Phillip then commanded fire to be brought and placed at the mouth of the cave. Then, placing some wood upon it, he filled the cave with smoke, so that they were all suffocated.

(5) The chiefs of the king then marched upon Mattathiah, to the mount of Mod'aith, and found him, his sons, his brothers, and a few of his people of the assembly of the Hassidim fully armed for war, for they had brought their wives and children to that mountain. The chiefs of the king approached Mattathiah with words of peace, saying, 'O honoured among thy people, perform the command of the king and live and do not die.' (6) But Mattathiah answered very proudly, saying, 'I obey the command of my King; do you obey the command of yours.' At this the chiefs were confused, and, being silent, did not say another word; for they wondered at Mattathiah, and were thinking how they could capture and slay him as they had

slain the other pious men. (7) But suddenly one of the renegade Jews among the chiefs of the king said, 'I am astonished at the chiefs of the king and his army. How long will ye hold your peace and not perform the command of the king by rising up against Mattathiah, who was insolent enough to refuse to obey the king's command?' And after he had spoken thus he unsheathed his sword, and, cutting off the head of a swine, he took it in his hand and carried it to the altar which they had built to sacrifice to the king's vanities. Then, placing the head of the swine upon the altar, he offered it with frankincense to the idols of Antiochus. (8) When Mattathiah beheld this he was exceedingly wroth, and his fury burnt within him. Then, drawing his sword, he leaped upon the sacrificing Jew, and, severing his head from his body, he held it up on high before the chief of the king who approached Mattathiah, while the body fell down from the altar upon which he stood. He also killed the king's chief, and put the rest of them to flight, levelling to the ground a number of the crowd. Then, sounding the Shofar, he gave the signal for war. (9) He was the first one to raise his hand against the Macedonian kingdom. He also commanded us to fight on the Sabbath, and he will stand by us to defend us in this matter. It is written in the book of Joseph ben Gorion the priest. (10) Mattathiah with his sons and brothers then marched forth, and with them a large band of the Ḥassidim. They pursued those who had hidden themselves, and smote and discomfited them, until there did not remain one in the whole land of Judah. They then circumcised their sons. Thus, great salvation was brought about by the Lord through Mattathiah.

XCI. (1) Now, the days of Mattathiah were drawing to a close, so, calling his five sons to his bedside, he encouraged them and exhorted them, saying, 'I know that now fierce battles will be waged in the land of Judah, since we have been stirred up to fight for our people. Now, my sons, be zealous for your God, for His sanctuary, and for His people. Fight, and do not be afraid of death; if you die in battle, you will be received among your brethren, and their portion shall be shared with you, for to all our ancestors who have been zealous for God, God has given honour and favour. Did not our ancestor Pinehas receive the everlasting covenant, and did not our other ancestors who were zealous for the Lord receive their reward from the Lord?' (2) Then, addressing Simeon his son, he said, 'I know the wisdom that God has put in thy heart; withhold not, then, thy counsel from this people, and be to thy brethren as a father, and they shall hearken to thee and to all thy counsels, since our God has given thee might and wisdom.' (3) Next Mattathiah called his son Judah, who came and stood before him; and he said, 'O my son Judah, who art called Maccabee (מכבי) on account of thy power, I know, my son, that thou art a man of war, and that God has given thee strength and might, and a heart like a lion's that flees from nothing. Now, my son, honour the Lord with all the strength the Lord hath granted thee; fight His battles without stopping; do not be reluctant to travel the four corners of the land—east, west, south and north — to capture the country from the power of the uncircumcised; be to them the captain of their host and the anointed of battle.' Then, bringing out a horn of oil, he poured it upon his head, and thus anointed him for battle, while all the people raised a shout, and, blowing upon their trumpets, exclaimed, 'Long live the anointed!' (4) When he had finished his exhortation to his sons, he died and was gathered to his people, and Judah his son, surnamed Maccabee, arose in his place. He had the assistance of his brothers, his father's household, and all the assembly of the Hassidim. And Judah was glad to fight the battles of Israel. Having clothed himself in a coat of mail as a warrior, and equipped himself with the implements of war, he looked like one of the sons of Anak. He protected the camp of Israel with his sword, and, pursuing the enemy, he crushed out their life. He burnt the sinners with the fire of his mouth, confounded the wicked with terror, and confused all the evil-doers through fear of him, for he appeared to them just as a roaring lion seeking prey appears to cattle. Jacob rejoiced at his deeds and was glad at his actions, for he confounded great kings, so that his name rang from one end of the world to the other, and people continually spoke of the wars he waged. Blessed be his name among the people of Israel; peace and repose be upon his righteous couch, and blessing on his holy bed, for he has not withheld his soul from death to defend Israel, God's people, and has slain all the wicked of the people of Judah who led the Israelites astray.

XCII. (1) When Apolonius, the captain of the Macedonian host, heard these things, he said, 'Who is it that dared to rebel against our lord the king?' And he gathered unto him a large and strong multitude of Macedonian warriors, and marched forwards to fight against Israel. Judah went out to meet him, and a very fierce battle ensued between the Macedonians and the assembly of the Ḥassidim. During the battle Judah saw Apolonius standing in the midst of the Macedonian company, and ran towards him in the fury of his anger into the valley, and, smiting right and left and in front of him, he cut down the mighty men of Greece just as the reaper cuts down the sheaves and the corn of his harvest. Then, approaching Apolonius, he smote him with the edge of the sword and felled him to the ground. Then, putting the Greeks and Macedonians to flight, they fled in haste, and Judah and the assembly of the Ḥassidim pursued them and smote them with a very great slaughter, and, having taken their spoil, Judah seized Apolonius's sword and fought with it all his life. (2) When Seron (סֵירוֹן), the captain of the host of Syria, heard this he said, 'I will go and fight against Judah, and thus make a name for myself.' Then, summoning all his people, he went to Beth-Ḥoron. Judah, becoming aware of this, said to his men, 'There is no time for delay; let us go out to them, although our brethren the Ḥassidim have gone away from us; for if we wait until they return, our enemies will say we are afraid of them.' Therefore Judah marched all the night long; at daybreak, when the people suddenly beheld in the distance a strong and mighty army, they said to Judah, 'How can we who are so few go to war against this great multitude?' But Judah replied, 'Cry unto heaven, and ye shall be saved, for the battle is in the hands of the Lord to deliver the many into the hands of the few; it is in His power to save either with a multitude or with a few.' (3) Judah then went sideways near the enemy's camp, and suddenly leaping upon them, he struck terror into them, and thereby Seron with all his men were put in confusion. Judah pursued him, and, overtaking him, smote him. On that day as many as 800 corpses of the Syrians were found piled up in heaps on the field. Those that remained fled into the land of the Philistines, and the fear of Judah fell upon all the nations.

(4) Now, as soon as Antiochus heard these things, he was very much vexed, and gathering together all his people and all the nations under his rule, mustered a strong and mighty army, and divided it into two portions. With one half he went to (Persia), for the Persians had revolted from the Macedonian rule when they saw that the people of Judah had rebelled. The other half he handed over to Lysias (ליסיאה), of his own kin, and of royal Macedonian descent, saying to him, 'Thou knowest all that Judah, the son of Mattathiah, has done to my two chiefs, Apolonius and Seron, and to all their host. Therefore, go now and smite all the inhabitants of Judah, and my son Eopator (אֲאוֹפְטוֹר) will go with thee. I myself will go to Persia and uproot the nation that rebelled against me.'

(5) Accordingly, Antiochus the king went to Persia, and left Lysias in command to wage war against Judah and look after his son. Lysias chose for himself Tolmios (תולמאוס), who is Ptolemy, Nicanor, and Gorgias, men of valour, sending with them 40,000 young warriors on foot and 7,000 horsemen, and the entire armies of both Syria and Philistia joined them in marching against Judah to destroy it. When Judah and all the elders of Israel heard this they proclaimed a fast, and clothed themselves in sackcloth, and

placing dust upon their heads, cried unto the Lord. (6) After the fast Judah numbered his people, and appointed over them captains of thousands, captains of hundreds, captains of fifties, and captains of tens. Then marching into the field, he issued an order in the camp, saying, 'Whoever has planted a vineyard or built a house, and whoever is betrothed or faint-hearted, let him return home;' and many of them returned. There thus remained 7,000 valiant men, chosen warriors, of whom one would not have run away before a hundred enemies.

(7) Judah then marched on to meet Nicanor, who had brought many merchants with him, for he intended to sell to them the young men and the young women whom he would capture and carry into captivity from Judah. He went into the valley to meet Judah. Judah, coming out of the assembly of the Ḥassidim who were with him, called upon the Lord, saying, 'O exalted God, who hast ruled from the creation until this time, who causeth battles to cease, and in whose hands is power and might to exalt or to humble, subdue and humble this nation before the lowly of Thy people, for Thou wilt subdue nations under us and peoples under our feet.' After his prayer, the priests blew their holy trumpets, and all the people raised a shout. Then did Judah leap into battle, and smote the camp of Nicanor with heavy slaughter, so that they fled before him. Pursuing them with his army, he continued to slay them in their flight. The number of the slain was 9,000. They then returned and took their spoil, and the gold which the merchants had brought with them to purchase the Israelitish youths. This they distributed among the poor, and then rested in that place, for the battle was fought on the sixth day.

XCIII. (1) Departing thence, Judah went to Bakires (בְּכִירָס) and Timothios, and a severe battle ensued between them, in which he himself killed on that day twenty Macedonian warriors. Bakires and Timothios took to flight, and Judah pursued them, but did not overtake them, for they went to Ashtaroth Karnaim. But he captured Phillipio, the man who had done so much evil in Judah. When Judah approached him he turned from the way he was going into a house in the vicinity. Judah then ordered his men to overthrow the house upon him, and to burn him to death in that place. He thus avenged the death of Eleazar and the blood of those pious men which Phillipio had shed. They then returned to strip the slain and they sent the spoil to Jerusalem. (2) Nicanor fled thence and escaped, for he had stripped himself of his purple coat, and dressed himself in a poor man's coat, so that he could not be recognised. In this way he came to Macedon and related to Lysias all that had happened.

(3) At that time King Antiochus returned from Persia, ashamed in that the Persians had made him flee the country of Ecbatana, and when he was informed of all Judah had done to his chiefs, and how he had smitten them, he was filled with wrath and fury. He reviled and blasphemed, and said, ' I will go to Jerusalem, and make it a burial-ground, and will fill it with the carcasses of the slain.' He then summoned together all his people, his charioteers and horsemen, a large and mighty multitude. (4) But the Lord had a jealous care for His people, for His city, and His temple, and remembering all the evil Antiochus did to His people, He required the blood of those pious men from Antiochus, and therefore plagued him with boils and with an internal disease. Yet he was not humbled through this, but said, ' Press on, ye charioteers; press on, ye horsemen; press on, ye soldiers. I will go to Jerusalem, and will carry out my intention, for who can stand before me? Is not the sea and the dry land mine, to change their being according to my will? Can I not transform the earth into sea and the sea into earth?' When he had finished speaking thus he mounted his chariot, and went with his huge army in the direction of Jerusalem. With him were many elephants, and his camp was enormous.

(5) Now, while on the journey, his chariot happened to pass in front of one of the elephants, and it trumpeted.

At this the horses took fright, and slipping down, overturned the chariot, and threw Antiochus out of it. As a result of the fall, his bones were broken, for he was a stout and very heavy man. The Lord, however, heaped up plagues upon him, and his flesh stank. The stench of his body was like that of a dead man cast upon the field in the height of the summer. As soon as his servants lifted him upon their shoulders, they had to cast him back again to the ground and run away, for they could not possibly approach him or carry him on account of the dreadful stench of the flesh of that reviler, and blasphemer, and enemy of God. (6) Now, when his army became weary, and he also became sick unto death of the stench arising from his body, he knew then that the hand of the Lord had touched him, and being humbled and made lowly, he exclaimed, 'The Lord is righteous, who humbleth the proud and humiliates the wicked like me, for I have done all this wickedness to His people and to His pious men. It is for this that all these evils have overtaken me.' He then made a vow, saying, 'If the Lord will heal me from this disease, I will go to Jerusalem and fill it with silver and gold; I will spread carpets of purple in all the streets, and will give all my treasury to the temple of the great God. I will circumcise my foreskin, and will go about the whole land exclaiming in a loud voice, 'There is no God in the whole world like the God of Israel.'

(7) But the Lord did not hearken to his prayer, nor did He give ear to him, for all the way Antiochus the Cruel was travelling his flesh fell off from his bones, until finally his very bowels fell out upon the ground. Thus his life came to an end. He died in shame and disgrace and in a strange land. Eopator, his son, succeeded him.

XCIV. (1) Judah, the son of Mattathias, and with him the assembly of the Ḥassidim, now went up to Jerusalem, and overthrowing the altars which the uncircumcised had built, they cleansed the temple of the abominations of the nations, and building a new altar, they placed upon it the flesh of the sacrifice, and arranged the wood, but the holy fire they could not find. Then calling in prayer upon the Lord, fire came forth from a stone upon the altar, and they placed the wood upon it. This fire remained with them until the time of the third captivity. On the 25th of Kislev they dedicated the altar, and placing the showbread in its place and kindling the lights, they praised the name of the Lord by reading the 'Hallel Psalms' for eight days.

(2) After this dedication, Judah marched to the land of Edom, and Gorgias came to meet him with a huge multitude of men, but Judah smote Gorgias and his camp, and put them all to flight. Pursuing them, Judah's men left upon the field 20,000 of the enemy slain. Gorgias then fled to Arabia to Timotheos. And Timotheos, marching out with 120,000 men of the Macedonian and Arabian armies, went into the land of Gad and Gilead, and slew many of the Jews, so that they sent a letter to Judah, saying, 'Come up and save us, for the sword of Timotheos is consuming us.' Again another letter arrived, saying, 'The sword of Tyre and Sidon is destroying us, and the men of Macedonia who dwell there.' (3) As soon as Judah heard these words, he cried to the Lord in fasting and prayer, and selecting all the valiant men and the Ḥassidim, he made haste to pass the Jordan. Simeon also took with him 3,000 men of Judah, and hastening to Galilee, engaged in a fierce battle, in which he slew 8,000 men, and thus delivered his brethren in Galilee. Then, taking the spoil of the slain, he returned to Jerusalem.

(4) Judah the Anointed one of battle, having passed the Jordan, arrived at Gilead, where they found Timotheos attacking the city on Mount Gilead, and, having girded himself for the fray, a fierce battle ensued. The two armies stood opposite each other, that of Timotheos being mighty and strong, while Judah's army was few in number. And in the midst of the fight Judah cried unto the Lord, when he suddenly beheld five young horsemen, clothed in gold. Two of them stood in front of Judah, and then, placing themselves one on each side of him, protected him with their shields, while the other three fought against the

camp of Timotheos. As soon as Judah saw them, he at once knew that they were sent from heaven to assist the pious, and, encouraging his men, he pressed hard upon Timotheos's army and smote 20,500 of his men. Timotheos himself and his army fled thence towards the Jordan, but Judah was after him, making havoc among them all the time until they came to Aza.

(5) Here Timotheos recruited his men and prepared again for battle, for the whole army of Philistia had now joined his ranks. When Judah arrived at that place he leaped upon them as a lion upon a flock of sheep. Timotheos took to flight, and his whole army was scattered in confusion. The Hasmoneans pursued them and cut them to pieces until there were none left. Timotheos fled to Aza, and there took refuge within the closed gates of the city, from the high walls of which he still gave battle. For five days Judah and his men besieged it.

(6) On the fifth day the men of Timotheos, ascending the high tower, cursed and defied the Anointed one of battle, and taunted them all with words of insolence. At length twenty Hasmoneans, becoming heated through passion on account of the reproaches, took their shields in their left hands and their swords in their right hands, and, running towards the wall, scaled it one after another by means of a ladder. Then, smiting those upon the wall, they made room for their fellows, all of whom likewise scaled the wall. The twenty men then went into the market-place of the city, shouting and killing many of the enemy. Then, going towards the gate, they attacked it within, while the whole army of the Hasmoneans approached it from without, and set fire to it, whereupon the gate fell to the ground. In this manner was the city of Aza captured. Then, seizing the men who defied the Anointed one of battle, they burnt them to death, and put the inhabitants to the edge of the sword. For two whole days they did not cease from their deadly work of slaughter.

(7) Timotheos, fleeing, hid himself in one of the pits and could not be found. But they discovered his brothers,

Birean (בִּירִיאָן) and Apollopanis (אפולופנים), and brought them to Judah, who ordered their heads to be cut off. The spoil of the city they carried to Jerusalem with songs, praises and thanksgivings, and sang the Psalms of David, King of Israel, to the Lord, whose mercy endureth for ever.

XCV. (1) Now, when it came to the ear of Antiochus Eopator, son of Antiochus called Epiphanes, who had wrought such evil in Jerusalem, who slew the pious men, and who ultimately died from the severe plagues inflicted upon him, as we have stated above, (2) this Antiochus Eopator sent Lysias, his cousin, with an army of 80,000 horsemen and eighty elephants, a mighty army. They came to Judah and Jerusalem and gave battle at Bethter (ביתתר); building a ditch round about the city, he began to attack the city with a battering-ram and with stones, while Judah and the whole army of the Hasmoneans dwelt in the forests and on the mountains away from the Greek army. Judah said to his men, 'Come, let us approach the Lord our God in fasting and in supplication, and then let us march against the Greek army of Javan, who are attacking Bethter.'

(3) After the fast he blew the Shofar, and then gave the signal for battle, and he and all his men went to assist their brethren in Bethter. When they came to Jerusalem they entered the temple, offered peace-offerings, sacrificed burnt-offerings, and cried to the Lord. Then, departing from Jerusalem to go to Bethter to the Macedonian camp, Judah said to his men, 'Be strong and of good cheer; for the people of the Lord and for our brethren, let us rather perish together in the fight than see any evil fall upon our people.'

(4) When he had finished speaking, he lifted up his eyes and beheld between heaven and earth a man, well dressed, riding upon a horse like a flame of fire, and in his hand a spear. His back was turned towards the Hasmoneans and his face to the camp of the Greeks, with his hand stretched out ready to smite it. Judah then exclaimed, 'Blessed be He who has sent His messenger to save His people and to

smite the camp of His enemies.' Hastening thence, they went to Bethter, and, springing upon the Macedonian camp, they put them into confusion, and slaughtered 11,000 foot and 1,600 horsemen. Lysias and his men fled for their lives in shame and disorder, and Lysias then knowing that God was fighting against the enemies of Israel, made a covenant with Judah.

(5) The following is the letter which Lysias sent to the people of Judah :

'Lysias, chief of the king's army and vicegerent of Antiochus, to Judah the Anointed of battle and to all his people be there greeting ! Be it known to you that I have received letters you sent through your messengers, Johanan and Absalom, and that I have carried out whatever they told me. I read the letter with good feeling and have fulfilled everything contained therein. I have told the king the message on your behalf, and have given answer to Johanan and Absalom. I have further charged the messengers I sent to you with words of peace.'

(6) This is the contents of the letter which the king sent to Lysias, his cousin :

'King Antiochus to Lysias my brother greeting ! Be it known to thee that we have received the letter thou didst send us concerning the Jews, and that we have read it with every good feeling. My father has gone the way of all flesh, he has ceased to be with men and has been taken with angels; but I seek for the welfare of all my kingdom, to stop wars, and to establish peace. I have heard that the Jews refused to listen to my father to violate their law, and that they have therefore conquered by the sword and slain the chief men and the most honoured of my father's kingdom. Now give them thy right hand, and make a covenant with them that they may know it to be my will and my hearty desire that they live in peace and observe their law according to their own wish.'

(7) And this is the contents of the letter which the king

sent to Judah : ' King Antiochus Eopator to Judah the Anointed one of battle and to the rest of the people greeting ! Be it known to you that I have issued a decree throughout all my cities and to all the peoples subjected to my rule, that they should not oppress the Jews, but leave them to keep and to observe your law. Pardon whatever actions my father erringly did, and if we have also erred we send you Menelaos to speak to you words of peace.'

XCVI. (1) In those days the Lord began to render the fourth kingdom more powerful than the third, that is the kingdom of Rome, which was stirred up against the kingdom of Greece. The name of the Roman was exalted over all the empires of the world. That was the fourth animal which Daniel, that greatly-beloved man, saw in a vision. Just as that animal devoured, crushed and trampled upon everything, so did this nation of Romans devour and crush all the other nations. It was they who fought with Antiochus, King of Greece, his 120 elephants and a strong and powerful army of infantry and cavalry, whom they conquered in the battle, and compelled to pay the Romans tribute.

(2) They also humbled the pride of Annibal, King of Africa, who reigned over the city whose name was Carthagene. Annibal entered the field with an army as mighty and as numerous as the sand upon the seashore. With him were all the armies of Ethiopia, Phut and Lud, and other mighty nations. Having crossed the narrow sea between Africa and Sefarad, he humbled the pride of the nation of the Goths (גותים). Journeying thence, he arrived in the land of Germania by the sea Oceanus. Thence he came to Italy and engaged in battle with the Romans, who went out to meet him. It was a long and fierce contest, in which the Romans were utterly routed.

(3) The Romans, however, continued to fight, and in ten years no less than eighteen battles were fought with Annibal, but they could make no stand before him. At length, they again mustered all their warriors, at the head

of whom were two valiant men, Æmilius and Varros. Having arranged their men in line of battle by the river Eopiros (אאופירום), the battle was fought at Canusi (קנוסי), a large city. Here a fierce and desperate battle was fought, in which 90,000 Romans met their death. (4) Among them was Æmilius, one of the Roman commanders. Varros (ברום), however, managed to escape to Venosia (בנוסיאה), a city situated between the mountains and the plain. Of Annibal's men, 40,000 were killed in that battle. Having pursued the Romans up to the gates of the city, he besieged the city for eight days, and building turrets in front of the city, fought against it.

(5) Then the Roman counsellors said to each other, 'Let us open the gate and come and make a covenant with Annibal, that we may live and not be put to death.' This they determined to do, when a young man, whose name was Scipios (שיפיאום), arose, and said to the 320 counsellors of the city, 'Far be it from us to subject ourselves to Annibal.' 'But what can we do,' answered they, 'since we have not been able to make a stand before Annibal for the last eighteen years?' 'Then,' said Scipio, 'come, let us take counsel. Give me about five legions of men, and I will go to the land of Africa and attack and destroy his land. As soon as Annibal hears this, he will hasten away from Rome to deliver his own land from my hands, and thus will ye obtain rest.'

(6) Having consented to his proposal, he took with him 30,000 Romans, and marching to Africa, the country of Annibal, he engaged in battle, in which Astrubal, Annibal's brother, was slain. Scipio cut off his head and brought it to Rome, and, mounting the wall, he cried out to Annibal, 'Why art thou so eager for our land, and dost not go to deliver thy own land from my hands, which I am destroying?' He then sent Annibal his brother's head. When he recognised it he braced himself up, and hardening his heart, swore not to leave the city until he had taken it, and he besieged it for several days more.

(7) Scipio then returned to Africa and entirely destroyed

it. Thence he went to Carthagene and besieged it. And the men of Carthagene sent Annibal a letter to Rome, saying, 'Why dost thou desire a strange land, when thine own land is taken from thee? If thou wilt not hasten here and deliver us from the hand of Scipio, we shall open the gate and give the city of Carthagene with thy palace into his hands.' (8) When he read this letter he wept, and immediately raised the siege, and going to Epirus, where lay his ships, he slew there Romans without number, men, women and children who were taken prisoners. He then went to Africa with all his army. (9) But Scipio went out to meet him, and a fierce war ensued between them, in which Annibal was conquered and about 50,000 of his men slain. He was likewise conquered in three pitched battles with Scipio. After that Annibal fled to Egypt, but Scipio followed him, and Ptolemy the king delivered him into Scipio's hands. He was brought to Africa in great honour, and there he drank poison and died and was buried. Scipio then captured the whole land of Africa, and the place that abounds in gold and silver. Thus Rome was exalted above all the other nations.

XCVII. (1) The following is the contents of the letter which the Romans sent to Judah, the son of Mattathiah:

'Qinsius Minios, Scipio and Menelaos, princes of Rome, to Judah the Anointed one of battle, and to the elders of Judah greeting to you! for we have heard of your power and of your battles, and are glad, also of what Antiochus and Lysias have given you, and of what they wrote concerning the Jews. Now we also write to ask you whether you will become our associates and friends, but not the friends of the Greeks, who have afflicted you. We are now going to war against Antiochia, therefore hasten to let us know who are your enemies and who your friends.'

(2) The following is the text of the covenant made between the Romans and the Jews:

'Whether on the sea or on land, whenever war is

declared against the Romans, the Jews are to assist them with all their power. They are not to supply Rome's enemies with either implements of war, with wheat or any other food, according to the decree of the Consul and the 320 counsellors. And if, on the other hand, war be declared against the Jews, the Romans in their turn are to assist the Jews with all their power, and are not to provide the enemies of the Jews with either implements of war, or wheat or food of any kind. They should themselves not take any food from them unless in trouble. Further, neither party is to add or to diminish what had been decreed by the Consul and the 320 counsellors.'

After that the land had rest for about eight months. At that time Judah began to judge his people, and to weed out the wicked from his people.

(3) At that time the Jews lived in all the cities on the sea-coast, extending from Aza until Acco; but the Macedonian nation and the people of Joppa and Jabneh brought about great evil, for they induced the Jews living among them to board their ships, together with their wives and children, to go and have sports on the sea. The Jews, trusting them, consented to go with them, but when they arrived in mid-ocean they were thrown into the water and drowned, to the number of 200 souls.

(4) When Judah was informed of it he wept and proclaimed a fast. Then, hastening to Joppa, he besieged it, and God delivered it into his hands After separating the Jews, he smote the city with the edge of the sword, man, woman, child and suckling, and burnt the city to the ground. The same he did to Jabneh, besides burning the ships of both cities. The burning and conflagration could be seen as far as Jerusalem, a distance of 240 stadia. He thus avenged the blood of the women and children that were drowned in the sea. Journeying thence, he went to the Arabian desert, and having smitten many Arabs, imposed a tribute upon them.

(5) He then returned to the land of . . . and during

the journey had to pass a certain city by name Kaspon (כספון). It was very strongly fortified, for nations of all kinds dwelt therein. Relying upon their strongholds, they cursed Judah, and uttered countless slanders about Judah's people. At this Judah exclaimed, ' O Almighty God, at the sound of the trumpet Thou didst deliver the city of Jericho by the hands of Thy servant Joshua; now deliver this city into our hands, that I may avenge the reproach they have cast upon the people of God.' (6) Then, taking his shield in his left hand and unsheathing his sword, he marched bravely onwards, followed by the Hasmoneans, at a very quick pace until they reached the gate of the city. After besmearing it with pitch, and placing bushes and thorns of the desert upon it, they set fire to it and it fell to the ground. God delivered the city into his hands, and he effected a slaughter such as has never yet been known, for the pool of blood which flowed from the city as a pool of water was two stadia in length and two in breadth.

(7) Journeying from that place, he travelled a distance of 750 stadia. And Timotheos came out to meet him with 120,000 foot and 1,000 horse. After offering up his supplication to God, Judah marched out against Timotheos with about 10,000 chosen men. A very fierce battle ensued, in which Judah slaughtered 30,000 of Timotheos's army. Timotheos forthwith tried to escape, but Dostios (Dositheus), the captain of Judah's army, and Sosipater, a gallant warrior of Israel, pursued him and brought him back to Judah, who ordered his head to be cut off. But Timotheos wept bitterly, and implored him, saying, ' O my lord Judah, do not kill me, for there are many Jews dwelling in my land, and I swear that I will do good to them all the days of my life.' And he took an oath. Judah had pity upon him and did not kill him, but allowed him to go his way, and Timotheos did no more evil to the Jews all the days of his life, for he kept the oath he had taken.

(8) Journeying thence, Judah marched in the direction of the wilderness, and, meeting the army of the king that

had come into Arabia, he smote them, and, pursuing them further, slew 25,000 of their men. He next journeyed to Ephron, a large city, and besieged it, and the Lord delivered it into his hands. He slew 20,000 in the contest.

(9) Marching onwards a journey of 600 stadia, he came to a city the name of which was Scitopolis (שיטופולים); and the inhabitants of Scitopolis being sorely afraid of them, came out to meet them with entreaties and tears, saying, 'O lord, the Anointed one of battle, do thou, I pray thee, ask the Jews who dwell in our midst whether we have treated them kindly or not. Moreover, in the time of the cruel Antiochus many Jews made their escape to us and we maintained them.' To the truth of this the Jews among them testified. As soon as Judah heard this he blessed them, and desisted from attacking them, and he returned to Jerusalem, arriving there three days before the festival of Pentecost.

XCVIII. (1) When the festival was at an end he marched out to Gorgios, the captain of the army of Edom, with 3,000 foot and 4,000 horse. A fierce battle took place between their two armies, in which some Hasmoneans were slain, and among them was Dostios, the captain of the host, who was sorely wounded on the shoulders; some of the Hasmonean warriors were nearly thrown back. When Judah realized what had happened, he then prayed to the Lord, and, encouraging his men, leaped forward into the camp of Gorgios and slaughtered many of his men. He then shouted out, 'At thee, Gorgios!' and stretched out his right hand to smite him, but Gorgios stepped back and thus escaped the blow, and throwing down his weapons, fled and made his escape, nor has he ever since been seen or recognised alive or dead. Some hold the opinion that he fled to the desert of Maresha (מרישה), in the wilderness of Edom, and there died.

(2) Judah now returned to Edom, and, after destroying all their cities, took all the inhabitants prisoners. At this time graven images of the nations were discovered under the clothes of those Hasmoneans that were slain in battle.

Judah then knew that they had fallen through their iniquity, and said, 'Blessed be the Lord, who discovers that which is hidden, and who revealed these secrets.' He then exhorted the people to serve the Lord in holiness and purity, and returned to Jerusalem.

(3) Now, when Antiochus Eopator heard of all the battles Judah had waged and of the cities he had captured, he broke the covenant he had made with Judah, and marched out against him with an army as numerous as the sand upon the seashore, together with Lysias, his cousin, who also marched out at the head of a huge army. Having arrived in the land of Judah, he laid siege to Bethter. (4) Seeing this, Judah and all the elders of Israel called upon the Lord in fasting, tears, and in supplication. They also sacrificed burnt-offerings and offered peace-offerings. On that night Judah mustered all his chosen men of the Hasmoneans, and, dividing them round the camp of the king, he slew 4,000 men and the largest elephant. In the morning the king arranged his men in line of battle opposite Judah, and a very fierce engagement took place.

(5) Judah suddenly noticed an elephant coated with armour of gold, and as it was greater than all the other elephants, he thought the king must be riding it, and shouted out to his men, 'Who of you are with me?' And forthwith Eleazar, one of the young Hasmoneans, sprang forward and faced the elephant, felling to the ground all who came in his way, and, striking out right and left, the slain fell on either side of him; then, rushing in the thick of the fight, and placing himself between the elephant's legs, he pierced its belly with his sword, and it fell upon him, so that he died, having sacrificed his life for the Lord and for his people, and left a name after him, and courage to all who heard it. It was a day of mourning to his people. There fell in battle on that day 800 of the king's nobles, besides the other people that were slain among them.

(6) The king then ceased fighting, and returned to his tent. Soon after his return, he was informed that Phillip

had revolted against him, and that Demetrius, the son of Seleucus the king, was coming from Rome with a large army, in order to wrest the kingdom from his hands. Being sorely frightened, the king made peace, and made a covenant with Judah, embracing and kissing him, and ratified it by an oath, in which Lysias joined, saying, 'We shall never as long as we live go to war against Jerusalem.' The king then brought out much gold from his treasury, and gave it as a present to the house of God in Jerusalem.

(7) He took Menelaus, a Judæan, prisoner, who brought Antiochus to Jerusalem, and caused him to do evil, and also Eopator. The king, being very wrath with him, ordered him to be carried to a lofty tower, fifty cubits in height, and near it there was dust and ashes in immense quantities. Then, commanding him to be bound hand and foot, they cast him into the ashes, and buried him beneath them, so that he died in torment, through his iniquity, for he had committed many abominations before the altar of the Lord with the sacred dust and ashes. Thus this wicked man died, suffocated with the very ashes with which he committed abominations. Just is the Lord, who requites man according to his deeds and the fruit of his actions.

XCIX. (1) After this the king went his way to Macedon and Judah, judged his people, and did righteousness and justice. At that time Demetrius, the son of Seleucus the king, with a Roman army, engaged in battle with Antiochus Eopator, in which Antiochus and Lysias were slain, and he held the reins of government in Antiochia in Macedon.

(2) Now, Alkimos the priest, a worthless man, who ate swine's flesh during the reign of Antiochus, came to Demetrius, and said, 'Long live King Demetrius! How long wilt thou remain inactive on behalf of thy servants in the land of Judah, who have fallen by the sword of Judah, the son of Mattathias, and his people the Jews, who are called Ḥassidim? He slays us because we refuse to comply with many precepts of their law.'

(3) Demetrius, stirred to anger by this, sent Nicanor,

the captain of his army, with a strong army, and chariots, horsemen, elephants, and footmen without number. Arriving at Jerusalem, he sent word professing his friendship, and said, 'Come and let us see each other, and consult in a friendly manner.' Judah, fearing no treachery, went to meet him. When Nicanor met him, he embraced him, and asked after his welfare. Then, placing seats for both of them, they sat down and conversed. Judah, however, had commanded his young Hasmoneans to remain armed ready for battle, lest the enemy suddenly attack them. Accordingly, his men stood near him, ready at any moment for the fray, as Judah had ordered. Judah and Nicanor at length rose from their seats, and went into their respective tents, and they dwelt both in Jerusalem, there being no war between them. On the contrary, Nicanor was very fond of Judah, and said to him, 'Would it not be meet for a man like thee to take a wife and beget children?' Judah married, and begat children.

(4) When Alkimos recognised the love Judah and Nicanor bore each other, he again went to the king, and informed him what had taken place. The king thereupon sent a letter to Nicanor, saying, 'If thou wilt not send me Judah, son of Mattathiah, bound in chains, know that thou wilt surely be slain.' Judah soon became aware of this, and, leaving the city by night, he sounded the trumpet-call and gave the battle-signal, and when all the valiant Ḥassidim and Hasmoneans had mustered in full force, he went to Samaria, and remained there.

(5) In the meantime Nicanor went to the temple of the Lord, and said to the priests, 'Bring ye out the man who fled from me, that I may send him to the king bound in chains.' But the priests swore unto him, saying, 'He has not been here, nor have we seen him since the day before yesterday.' At this reply, Nicanor spoke blasphemously of the temple, and, spitting upon it, stretched out his right hand, and, baring his arm for slaughter, he said, 'I will overthrow this temple, and will not leave one single stone in its place, and I shall dig up and overturn all its founda-

tions.' With this, he departed in anger, and the priests went about crying between the porch and the altar, and said, 'O God, whose dwelling-place has of old been in this temple, now continue to rest here, for here is Thy throne, and here is Thy footstool, and all Thy service. The heart of Nicanor was filled with blasphemy towards Thy house and towards Thy habitation. He acted treacherously against the temple of Thy glory, and has committed abomination, therefore let him die as an abomination.'

(6) Nicanor searched all the houses of Jerusalem for Judah, and sent 500 troops to the house of Daqsios (דקסיאום), the Elder of Ḥassidim, who was tested in Antiochus's reign and found perfect, for he had suffered many tortures, and was called 'Father of the Jews and Judge in Jerusalem.'

(7) And as Nicanor was trying to show his bitter hatred of the Jews, he sent a messenger to fetch the old man, while his men surrounded the house to catch him; but the old man, unsheathing his sword and piercing his bowels, ran upon the wall, and threw himself upon Nicanor's troops, who made room for him, and he fell to the ground. But he soon rose up again, and went towards the troops. He stood on a large stone, and from the great loss of blood which was rapidly flowing from him, he became distracted, and took part of his entrails and threw it at the troops. Then, calling upon the Lord in prayer, he died, and was gathered to his people.

(8) When Judah heard these things, he waxed furious, and sent a message to Nicanor, saying, 'Why dost thou delay? Come into the field, and I will show thee the man thou hast been seeking in the chamber. Behold, he is here waiting for thee in the valley and in the plain.' Nicanor then gathered all his forces, and went to meet the Jews on a Sabbath. The Jews that were with him said, 'O my lord, we beseech thee, do not act presumptuously; grant Him honour who gave the Sabbath.' 'And who, indeed, gave the Sabbath?' asked Nicanor. 'The God whose dwelling is in heaven,' answered they, 'and whose

dominion extends over the whole world.' Nicanor then spoke such words of blasphemy as are not fit to be written down.

(9) Judah heard of this, and said to his men, 'How long will we be indolent, and refuse to give battle to this reviler and blasphemer? for who is this dead dog and outcast that defies the strength and glory of Israel?'

(10) He then marched in great anger and zeal to attack Nicanor, who came to meet him with a huge and powerful army. And Judah cried to the Lord, saying, 'O Lord my God, Thou didst send a messenger into the camp of Sennacherib, whose men stood up outside the city and blasphemed Thee, and Thou didst smite his multitude by slaying 175,000 men; the slain we counted, but the slayer we did not see. Now, how much more deserving of death is this man, who has stood up against Thy temple, and has blasphemed Thy might and Thy glory?'

(11) On that day a very fierce and bloody battle was fought. When Judah saw Nicanor with drawn sword, he cried out, 'At thee, Nicanor!' and then ran against him in the fury of his anger. And Nicanor turned his back to flee, but Judah laid hold of him, and, cutting him in two, cast him to the ground. There fell on that day 30,000 men of the Macedonian army. The remainder fled, but were pursued by Judah's men, who all the while were sounding the Shofar. All the cities of Judah turned out to meet the enemy, and smote them, cutting them to pieces, so that not one of them remained alive. Then, proceeding to strip the slain, they found abundance of gold, precious stones, and purple garments. They cut off the head of Nicanor and the arm that he had stretched out against God's temple, and hung them up before the gate, which has henceforth until this very day been called 'The gate of Nicanor.' The people then rejoiced exceedingly, and sang the Psalms of David, King of Israel, concluding, 'For He is good, and His mercy endureth for ever.'

(12) Ever since that time the Jews celebrate this day as a feast and a holiday, on which wine is drunk—viz., the

13th day of Adar, one day before 'Purim.' And Judah judged all his people, and did justice and righteousness in the land.

C. (1) At the end of the year, the days of Judah drew to a close, and the Lord ordained that Judah end his days, and be gathered to his people the Ḥassidim. At this time Baqidos (בקידוס) suddenly came upon Judah with 30,000 men of the Macedonian army, while he was in Laish (Leshem?). The 3,000 men that were with him fled as one man, and the only ones that remained were himself, his brothers, and 800 chosen men of Israel, who did not stir from their places. All these men were Judah's associates, tried veterans in all the wars that Judah had waged with the nations.

(2) Baqidos then brought forward 15,000 men, and arranged them in line of battle on the right of Judah, while on his left he placed another army to the number of 15,000. There was a great shouting, both on the right and left of Judah; but when he saw that the battle was very fierce, and that Baqidos stood on his right—for all the warriors of Baqidos remained on the right, and that the right wing was with him—he shouted and leaped forward followed by his brothers, and the few Hasmoneans. (3) He ran in the direction of Baqidos, and a fierce and terrible battle ensued, at the beginning of which heaps of Macedonians were slain. As soon as Judah saw Baqidos standing in the midst of the people, he ran towards him in the strength of his anger, and smote many of his warriors. He struck out right and left at all who came in his way, slaying enemies without number, until he had no place to walk except upon the slain. Upon these he made his way. (4) He then came face to face with Baqidos, with sword unsheathed and steeped in blood. As soon as Baqidos beheld Judah's face, it appeared to him like that of a lion robbed of its prey, and fear and trembling seized him. Turning his back, he attempted to flee in the direction of Ashdod, but Judah pursued him, and put all his men, 15,000, to the edge of the sword.

(5) Baqidos succeeded in effecting his escape to Ashdod, and his army, which was behind him, finding Judah faint and weary, fell upon him. Baqidos came out from the city, and war was waged on every side, and many more were slain, Judah being among the number, falling upon those he had slain. His brothers Simeon and Jonathan took him and buried him on Mount Moda'ith, and all Israel mourned for him many days. The number of years during which Judah, surnamed Maccabee, ministered unto Israel was six years, and the Lord caused him to prosper all the days of his life.

[END OF THE BOOK OF THE MACCABEE.]

APPENDIX.

PHILONIS IUDAEI ANTIQUITATUM BIBLICARUM LIBER INCERTO
INTERPRETE.

INITIO mundi Adam genuit tres filios, et unam filiam, Cain, Noaba, Abel, et Seth: Er uixit Adam, postquam genuit Seth, annos DCC. et genuit filios duodecim, et filias octo: Et haec sunt nomina uirorum, Aeliseel, Suris, Aelamiel, Brabal, Naat, Harama, Zasam, Maathal, et Anath: Et hae filiae eius, Phua, Iectas, Arebica, Siphatecia, Sabaasin. Et uixit Seth annos CV. et genuit Enos: Et uixit Seth, postquam genuit Enos annos DCCVII. et genuit filios tres, et filias tres: Et haec sunt nomina filiorum eius, Elidia, Phonna et Matha: Filiarum uero, Malida et Thila. Et uixit Enos annos CLXXX. et genuit Cainan: Et uixit Enos, postquam genuit Cainan annos DCCXV. et genuit filios duos et filiam: Et haec sunt nomina filiorum eius, Phoë, Thaal: Filiae autem, Catennath. Et uixit Cainan annos DXX. et genuit Malalech: Et uixit Cainan, postquam genuit Malalech, annos DCCXXX. et genuit tres filios et duas filias: Et haec sunt nomina uirorum, Athac, Socer, Lopha: Et nomina filiarum, Ana et Leua. Et uixit Malalech annos CLXV. et procreauit Iareth: Et uixit Malalech postquam procreauit Iareth, annos DCCXXX. et genuit filios septem, et filias quinquae: et haec sunt nomina uirorum, Leta, Mata, Cechar, Melic, Suriel, Lodootim: Et haec sunt nomina filiarum eius, Ada et Noa, Iebal, Mada, Sella. Et uixit Iareth annos CLXXII. et genuit Enoc: Et uixit Iareth postquam genuit Enoc annos DCCC., et genuit filios quatuor, et filias duas: Et haec sunt nomina uirorum, Lead, Anac, Soboac, et Ietar: Filiarum autem, Tetheco, Lesse. Et uixit Enoc annos CLX. et V. et genuit Mathusalam: Et uixit Enoc postquam genuit Mathusalam, annos CC. et genuit filios quinquae et filias tres. Placuit autem Enoc deo in tempore illo, et non inueniebatur, quoniam transtullit illum deus: Nomina autem filiorum eius, Anaz, Zeum, Achaun, Pheledi, Elid: Filiarum autem, Theth, Lephith, Leath. Et uixit Mathusalam annos CLXXXVII. et genuit Lamech: Et uixit Mathusalam, postquam genuit Lamech, annos DCCLXXXII. et genuit duos filios, et duas filias: Et haec sunt nomina uirorum, Inab et

Rapho : Filiarum autem, Aluma, et Aniuga. Et uixit Lamech annos
CLXXXII. et genuit filium et uocauit cum secundum natiuitatem suam,
Noë, dicens : Hic requiem dabit nobis, et terrae, ab his qui sunt in ea,
in quibus uisitabitur, propter iniquitatem operum malorum. Et uixit
Lamech, postquam procreauit Noë, annos DLXXX. et V. Et uixit
Noë annos CCC. et genuit filios tres, Sem, Cham, Iapheth. Cain
autem habitauit in terra tremens, secundum quod constituit ei deus,
postquam interfecit Abel, fratrem suum : Et nomen mulieris eius
Themech : Et cognouit Cain Themech mulierem suam, et concepit,
et peperit Enoc. Cain autem erat annorum quindecim, quando fecit
haec : Et ex eo (fol. 2) coepit aedificare ciuitates, quousque conderet
ciuitates septem : Et haec sunt nomina ciuitatum : Nomen primae
ciuitatis secundum nomen filij sui Enoc : Nomen autem secundae
ciuitatis Mauli, et tertiae Leed, et nomen quartae Tehe, et nomen
quintae Iesca, nomen autem sextae Celet, et nomen septimae Iebbat,
Et uixit Cain postquam genuit Enoc annos DCCXV. et genuit tres
filios et duas filias : Et haec sunt nomina filiorum eius, Olad, Lizaph,
Fosal : Et filiarum eius, Citha, et Maac. Et facti sunt omnes dies
Cain anni DCCXXX. et mortuus est. Tunc accepit Enoc mulierem
de filiabus Seth, et genuit ei Ciram, et Cuuth, et Madab : Ciram autem
genuit Matusaël, Matusaël autem genuit Lamech, Lamech autem accepit
sibi mulieres duas : nomen uni Ada : et nomen alteri Sella. Et peperit
Ada Iobab : ipse erat pater omnium habitantium in tabernaculis, et
pascentium pecora : Et iterum genuit ei Iobal, qui initiauit docere
omnem psalmum organorum. In tempore illo cum initiassent habitantes terram operari iniqua, unusquisque in uxores proximi sui, con-
taminantes eas, indignatus est deus, et coepit percutere cyneram, et
cytharam, et omne organum dulcis psalterij, et corrumpere terram.
Sella autem genuit Tobel, et Nuha, et Theffa : Et hic est Thobel, qui
ostendit hominibus artes in plumbo et stagno, et ferro, et aeramento,
et argento, et auro. Et tunc coeperunt habitantes terram facere
sculptilia et adorare ea . . . (fol. 3) . . . Et fuerunt filij, Noë qui
exierunt de arca : Sem, Cam, et Iapheth. Filij Iapheth, Magog,
Madai, Nidiazec, Tubal, Mocteras, Cenez, Riphath, et Thegorma,
Elisa, Dessin, Cethin, Tudant. Et filij Gomer, Tholez, Lud, Dober-
let. Et filij Mago, Cesse, et Thipha, Pharuta, Ammiel, Phimei,
Goloza, Samanac. Et filij Duden, Sallus, Pheluciti, Phallita. Et
filij Tubal, Phanatanoua, Eteua. Et filij Tiras, Maac, Tabel, Ballana,
Samplameae, Elaz. Et filij Mellec, Amboradat, Vrac, Bosara.
Et filij Cenez, Iubal, Zaraddana, Anac. Et filij Heri, Phuddet,
Doad, Dephad, Zeath, Enoc. Et filij Torgoma, Abiuth, Saphath,
Asapli, Zepthir. Et filij Elisa, et Zaac, Zenez, Mastisa, Rira. Et
filij Zepti, Macziel, Temna, Aela, Phinon. Et filij Tessis, Meccul,
Loon, Zelatabar. Et filij Duodennin, Itheb, Beath, Phencth. Et hi
sunt qui dispersi sunt, et habitauerunt in terra apud Persas et (fol. 4).

Monadas, in insulis, quae sunt in mari. Et ascendit Phanat, filius
Dudeni, et praecepit fieri naues maris, et tunc diuisa est pars tertia
terrae. Domereth, et filij eius acceperunt Ladech. Magoge autem,
et filij eius acceperunt Degalmadam—et filij eius acceperunt Besto.
Iuban, et filij eius acceperunt Coel. Tubal, et filij eius acceperunt
Pheod. Misech, et filij eius acceperunt Nepthi. Iras, et filij eius
acceperunt   *   Duodennut et filij eius acceperunt   *   Goda-
riphath, et filij eius acceperunt Bosarra. Tergoma, et filij eius acceperunt   *   Fudelisa et filij eius acceperunt   *   Thabolathesis,
et filij eius acceperunt Marecham. Cethim, et filij eius acceperunt
Thaan. Dudennin, et filij eius acceperunt Caruba. Et tunc coeperunt
operari terram, et seminare super eam. Et cum sitiret terra, ex-
clamauerunt habitantes eam ad dominum, et exaudiuit eos, et ampli-
auit pluuia. Et factum est cum descenderet pluuia super terram,
apparuit arcus in nube: Et uiderunt habitantes terram memoriam
testamenti, et ceciderunt in faciem suam, et immolauerunt offerentes
holocaustomata domino. Filij autem Cam, Chus, et Mestra, et Phuni,
et Chanaan. Filij Ethij, Chus, Saba, et Tudan. Et filij Effuntenus,
Zeleutelup, Geluc, Lephuc. Et filij Sidona, Endain, Racin, Simmin,
Vruin, Nenugin, Amathinnephin, Telaz, Elat, Cusin. Chus autem
genuit Nembroth, ipse initiauit esse superbus ante dominum. Mestram
uero genuit Ludin, et Iuenugin, et Labin, et Latuin, et Petrosonum,
et Ceslun: Vnde exierunt Philistini et Cappadoces. Et tunc coeperunt
etiam et ipsi aedificare ciuitates. Et hae sunt civitates, quas aedifi-
cauerunt, Sidona, et circumiacentia eius, id est, Resun, Beosamaza,
Gerras, Calon, Dabircaino, Tellunlacis, Sodoma, et Gomorra, Adama, et
Segom. Et filij Sem, Elam, Assur, Arphaxa, Luzi, Aram. Et filiarum,
Assum, Gedrummese. Arphaxas autem genuit Sala, Sala genuit Heber:
Et Heber nati sunt duo filij, nomen uni, Phalech: Quoniam in diebus
eius diuisa est terra: Et nomen fratris eius Ieptam. Ieptam autem
genuit Elimodan, et Salastra, et Mazaam, Rea, Dura, Vzia, Deglabal,
Mimoël, Sabthphin, Euilac, Iubab. Et filij Phalec, Ragau, Rephuth,
Zepheram, Aculon, Sachar, Siphaz, Nabi, Suri, Seciur, Phalacus,
Rapho, Phalthia, Zaldephal, Zaphis, et Arteman, Heliphas. Hij filij
Phalec, et haec nomina eorum. Et acceperunt sibi uxores de filiabus
Iectan, et generauerunt filios et filias, et compleuerunt terram. Ragau
autem accepit sibi mulierem, Melcham, filiam Ruth, et genuit ei Scruch.
Et quum factus fuisset dies partus eius, dixit: Ex isto nascetur in
quarta generatione, qui ponat habitationem super excelsa, et perfectus
uocabitur, et immaculatus, et pater gentium erit, et non dissoluetur
testamentum eius, et semen eius in seculum multiplicabitur. Et uixit
Ragau, postquam genuit Seruch, annos CXVIIII. Et genuit septem
filios, et quinque filias: Et haec sunt nomina filiorum eius, Abielobth,
Salma, Dedasal, Zeneza, Accur, Nephes, Et haec nomina filiarum
eius, Cedema, Derisa, Seipha, Pherita, Theila. Et uixit Scruch annos

XXIX. et genuit Nachor. Et uixit Seruch, postquam genuit Nachor, annos LXVII. et genuit quatuor filios, et tres filias. Et haec sunt nomina uirorum, Zela, Zobadica, et Phodde. Et hae filiae eius Tephila, Oda, Selipha, et uixit Nachor annos XXXIIII. et genuit Tharram. Et uixit Nachor, postquam genuit Tharram (fol. 5), annos CC. et genuit VIII. filios, et V. filias. Et haec sunt nomina uirorum, Recap, Dediap, Berechap, Iosac, Sithal, Nisab, Nadab, Camoël. Et filiae eius, Esca, Thiphabruna, Ceneta. Et uixit Tharra annos LXX. et genuit Ambram, et Nachor, et Arram. Tharram autem genuit Loth. . . .

INDEX.

AARON, the High Priest, sees no joy from his sons, x. 10; called so because in the time of his mother's pregnancy Pharaoh began to shed blood of male children, xliv. 1; prophesies to the Israelites, xliv. 15; ordered by God to meet Moses, xlvii. 8; tells Moses to send his wife and children back, xlvii. 3; staff of, swallows staves of Pharaoh's magicians, xlvii. 7; takes the ewe's wool away from the woman, lv. 1; takes the flesh of the ewe, lv. 3; death of, xlix.; waited on by Moses, Eleazar, and all the princes, xlix. 2; walks between Moses and Eleazar, contrary to the usual custom, xlix. 2; soul of, referred to by Moses as claimed by God, xlix. 3; shown the cave of Machpelah, by the ground suddenly opening, xlix. 4; sees a burning lamp, prepared bed, and a table spread on entering the cave, xlix. 4; stretches out his leg, closes his eyes and mouth, and his soul departs, xlix. 4; coffin of, suspended in mid-air by angels, to allay the suspicion against Moses, xlix. 7; loved with a greater love by Israelites than Moses, xlix. 2; death of, mourned by Israelites for thirty days, xlix. 7; dies in the same year as Miriam, on the first day of the fifth month, xlviii. 17; buried on Mount Hor, xlviii. 17

Abadon, fifth compartment of hell, xvii. 2

Abahu's, parable of three men, xi. 1; homily, xiv. 1

Abarim, mount under which books of Emorites concealed, lvii. 10

Abiel, son of Reu, xxvii. 6; son of Shaphat, king of the four tribes, lxiii. 9

Abigedor, name given Moses by his grandfather, Kehath, xliv. 7

Abihail, son of Shaphat, captain of the host of the four tribes, lxiii. 9

Abi Jezreel, did not worship Baal in the days of Yair, lviii. 10

Abiram, lost his soul through riches, x. 10

Abi Sokho, name given Moses by his nurse, xliv. 7

Abi Zanoah, name given Moses by his brother, xliv. 7

Abraham, born in forty-third year of reign of Ninus, xxxii. 6; portent appears at the birth of, xxxiv. 1; discovers that both sun and moon are subservient to a higher Master, xxxiv. 3; offers a sacrifice to image, xxxiv. 6; burns his father's idols, xxxiv. 8; difference in future reward of children of, to that of children of Jacob, xx. 7; refuses to obey Yoqtan to flee, xxix. 10; cast into the furnace, xxix. 13; selection of, xxx. 3; argument of, against idolatry, xxxiii. 1; ordered by Nimrod to make an image, xxxiii. 2; cast into furnace by Nimrod, xxxiii. 3; delivered from furnace by God Himself, xxxiv. 13; tests Nimrod, xxxiv. 11; goes from Babylon to Damascus, xxxv. 2; hidden in a cave, xxxv. 3; wise in sciences of 'hermetica' and astrology, xxxv.

4; sees the order of creation changed, xxxv. 4; teaches Zoroaster magic, xxxv. 4; the oak under which he sat still used for medicinal purposes, xxxv. 5
Absalom, downfall of, caused by beauty, x. 10; not smitten, in second compartment of hell, xx. 6; generation of, excepted from dwelling in third house in Eden, xx. 6; messenger of Lysias, xcv. 5
Abtinos, succeeds Romulus, xl. 14; wages war with the children of Rifath, who dwelt by the Lira, and with the children of Turnus, who dwell in Toronia by the Lira, xl. 14
Abyaush of Makedon, Apumasia, his daughter, concubine of Darius, lxxv. 6; daughter of, takes the crown from the head of King Darius, and places it upon her own head, lxxv. 6
Accad, i.e. Nisibis, xxxi. 18
Achan ben Zabdi, confessed, the Israelites should do likewise, lvii. 8
Achaya, flood in, xxxv. 9
Ada, wife of Lemech, xxiv. 5
Adam, creation and legends of, vi. 10 et seq.; during first twelve hours of his life, vi. 10; causes creatures to acknowledge Creator, vi. 12; helpmeet for, vi. 15; letters added to his name, vi. 16; sons and daughters of, xxvi. 1, 2; induced by his wife to transgress God's Word, lxxv. 7; lives 700 years after Seth's birth, and begets eleven sons and eight daughters, xxvi. 2
Adam and Eve, clothes of, created on second day, i. 3; like a bridal pair, vii. 2
Adirah, a kingdom in Kush, lxiii. 8; built by Misraim, xxvii. 4
Adonijah ben Hagith, downfall of, caused by beauty, x. 10
Adoram the Edomite, killed by an arrow shot from Jacob's bow, xxxvii. 4
Adulterer, descends to hell for ever, xv. 6
Adultery, punishment for, xiii. 4
Aemilius, succeeds Procas, xl. 14; at the head of the Roman army, xcvi. 3; one of the Roman commanders killed at Canusi, xcvi. 4
Aeneas rules Empire of Italy three (or eight) years after the capture of Troy, lix. 10
Afriqia in Ham's portion, xxxi. 2
Agnios, King of Carthage, to whom Sofo flies from Egypt, xl. 3; King of Afriqi, xl. 4; King of Afriqi, from whom Turnus fled, xl. 14; reigned over Italy in the third year after the capture of Troy, lix. 10
Agrimus, demon firstborn of Adam, xxiii. 3; helps Matushelah to place imps in fetters, xxiii. 3
Agrippa succeeds Tiberios, xl. 14
Ahab presides over, and not smitten, in fifth compartment of hell, xx. 9
Ahab ben Qolaya, false prophet, Midrash of, lxiv.; goes to the daughter of Nebuchadnezzar, inducing her to sin, lxiv. 2
Ahalah, a kingdom in Kush, lxiii. 8
Ahasuerus, succeeds Cambisa, lxxviii. 5; abolished all the work of the temple, lxxviii. 5; nearly destroyed the memory of Judah, lxxix. 1; orders the loyalty of Mordecai to be entered into the Book of Chronicles, lxxix. 2; embraces Esther, lxxx. 5; alarmed at the faintness of Esther, weeps, lxxx. 6; accuses the butchers, bakers, and butlers of poisoning him, lxxxii. 6; sends for workmen to make a throne like that of King Solomon, lxxxiv. 1
Aheyya, son of Shemhazai, xxv. 7; invoked by men when they bear heavy loads, xxv. 11
Ahiqam, son of, appointed king over those who remained in Jerusalem, lxi. 9
Ahitophel lost his soul through wisdom, x. 10
Aholibah, a kingdom in Kush, lxiii. 8
Air created on first day, i. 3
Akhzariel, angel appointed to carry out death of Moses, l. 5
Akta built by Ogiges, and called Eliosin (Eleusis), xxxv. 9
'Akur, son of Re'u, xxvii. 6

Alan, whole of, captured by Cyrus, lxxviii. 1
Alba succeeds Anios Trognos, xl. 14
Albano, city of, xl. 5; built by a descendant of Hadarezer, xl. 16
Alexander the Great, son of Phillippus, crowned King of Macedon, lxxxv. 3; of Macedon, enclosed peoples in Caspian Mountains, xxxi. 4; smote Egypt, and slew in Alexandria double as many Jews as went out from Egypt, lxxxv. 3; the Macedonian, King of Greece, slays Darius, lxxxv. 3; wishes to go up to smite Jerusalem, lxxxv. 3; warned against injuring Jews, lxxxv. 4; met by the High Priest in Jerusalem, lxxxv. 5; bows down before the High Priest, lxxxv. 5; informed that it was not permitted to place his image in the Temple, lxxxv. 6; informed that Darius would be delivered into his hand, lxxxv. 7; slays Darius and captures his kingdom, lxxxv. 7; subdues India, lxxxv. 8; reigns six years in Elam (according to R. Jose), lxxxv. 8; before his death divides his kingdom among his four pages, lxxxv. 8; captures Helena as wife in the time of Elon the Zebulonite, lix. 9
Alexandria, in Egypt, made the royal city by Alexander, lxxxv. 7
Alkimos, a worthless priest, incites Antiochus against the Jews, lxxxvii. 7; eats swine's flesh, stirs up Demetrius against the Jews, xcix. 2; informs Antiochus Eupator of the friendship between Judah and Nicanor, xcix. 4
Almania, son of Elisa, fought Latinus II., xl. 13
Almodad, son of Yoqtan, xxvii. 5
Alsar captured by Cyrus, lxxviii. 1
Amaleq defeated, xlviii. 13; son of Eliphaz, son of Esau, makes war upon the Israelites, xlviii. 13
Amon, a little fortified city in Egypt, near the Salt Sea, lx. 10
Amano, mountain in Brittania (?), xxxi. 4
Amorites determine to kill sons of Jacob, xxxvi. 1; come to terms with sons of Jacob, xxxvi. 12; books of, concealed under the Mount Ebarim, lvii. 10; call seven golden idols the holy Ninfe, upon which are many precious stones, lvii. 13; blind restored to sight by kissing the idols, lvii. 14; too mighty for the Israelites to fight against, lvii. 29
Amram marries Jochebed, and begets Aaron and Miriam, xlii. 8, xliv. 1; advice of, to Israelites, xlii. 5
Amtalai, daughter of Barnabo and wife of Nahor, xxvii. 7
Anamim, son of Misraim, xxvii. 4
Anba, built by Turnus, xl. 14
Andaïm, son of Canaan, xxvii. 4
Andrios, a page of Ptolemy, lxxxvii. 1
Angels created on the second day, i. 8; four bands of, i. 9; seven ministering before God, i. 10; destroyed by God, vi. 8; appointed over spirits of men, ix. 2; three ministering, appear to man at his death, x. 5, xii. 3; two bands at gates of Gehinnom, xiv. 1; of death, xvii. 5, lii. 9; of death drives wicked like cattle, xvii. 3; of death flees before Moses, li. 7; of death approaches Moses second time, li. 7; of death approaches Moses third time, li. 7; of destruction, xvii. 1, 5; of destruction punish sinners twelve months in Gehinnom, xvii. 3; of destruction slays Israelites, lv. 12; six thousand, of trembling, xvii. 5; of terror, xvii. 5, lii. 9; of terror try to consume Moses, lii. 9; of anguish, xvii. 5; of peace, xvii. 6; of peace weep at the distress of the law, lxxxii. 3; of mercy, xvii. 6; of mercy dance and sing before the pious, xx. 1, 2; myriads of, guard gates of Paradise, xviii. 1; sixty, at the head of every just man, xviii. 3; seventy thousand, surround God's throne, xxx. 8; dispute who shall rescue Abraham from furnace, xxxiv. 13; appointed over childbirth, xliii. 4; places two stones in child's hand, from one of which it sucks milk

and from the other honey, xlii. 4, xliii. 4; washed children, rubbed them with salt, and bound them in swaddling clothes, xliii. 4; envy Adam, xxii. 1; led astray by woman in the days of Noah, xxv. 1; attacks Moses for his transgression of the covenant, xlvii. 2; Michael, Gabriel, and Uriel save Pharaoh from the sea, xlviii. 12; close all gates of heaven as long as Moses' prayer continued, l. 5; exclamation at death of Moses, l. 15; do not know where God dwells, lii. 6; ministering, xvii. 6; ministering pair went to each of the Israelites, lii. 12; ministering, descend and place two crowns upon every Israelite, lii. 13; ministering, clothe the Israelites, liii. 16; ministering, cry at the weeping of the law, lxxxii. 3

Anias succeeds Latinus, xl. 13

Anias Trognos (Tarquinius) succeeds Latinus II., xl. 14

Animals roared on throne of Solomon, lxxxiv. 8

Annibal arrives in Germania by the sea Oceanus, xcvi. 2; humbles the pride of the Goths, xcvi. 2; King of Africa, reigns over the city called Carthagena, xcvi. 2; crosses the narrow sea between Africa and Sepharad, xcvi. 2; King of Africa, humbled by Rome, xcvi. 2; fights eighteen battles with the Romans in ten years, xcvi. 3; returns to Africa with his army, xcvi. 8; flees to Egypt, xcvi. 9; conquered by Scipio, xcvi. 9; brought to Africa with great honour, but takes poison, xcvi. 9

Anointment of Judah for battle, xci. 3

Anteos, in Lybia, conquered by Erkules in the reign of Tola, lviii. 9

Antiochia, *i.e.*, Hamath, built by Hamathi, xxxi. 18; Romans make war upon, xcvii. 1

Antiochus, the enemy of the Jews, made King of Asia by Alexander, lxxxv. 8; made King of Macedonia, lxxxvii. 6; slays Ptolemy and rules in his stead, lxxxvii. 6; commands his subjects to bow down before the image of the king, lxxxvii. 7; informed by wicked Jews that the Jews rejoice at the report of his death, lxxxvii. 7; prohibits the Jews from observing the Sabbath and from circumcising their children, lxxxvii. 8; smites the Jews in Jerusalem with the edge of the sword, lxxxvii. 8; commands Phillipos to slay every Jew who will not worship images and eat swine's flesh, lxxxvii. 8; leaves his officers in Judea to afflict the people, lxxxvii. 8; seizes seven brothers with their mother for refusing to eat swine's flesh, lxxxix. 1; tears flesh of the Israelites like that of an ox, lxxxix. 1; tries to entice the seven sons, lxxxix. 1 *et seq.*; subdued by the mother of the seven sons, lxxxix. 9; exhorts the mother to induce her last son to escape by obeying him, lxxxix. 10; tortures the seventh son much more cruelly than he did any of the other brothers, lxxxix. 13; leaves Phillip to crush the Jews, xc. 1; musters a mighty army, xcii. 4; goes against the revolted Persians with half of his army, xcii. 4; compelled to flee from Ecbatana by the Persians, xciii. 3; swears he will make Jerusalem a burial-ground, xciii. 8; plagued by God with boils and an internal disease, xciii. 4; takes his enormous army and many elephants in the direction of Jerusalem, xciii. 4; thrown out of his chariot, which is overturned, xciii. 5; stench of the body of, xciii. 5; has his bones broken, in consequence of his being a stout and heavy man, xciii. 5; humbly acknowledges God's righteousness, xciii. 6; prayer of, not hearkened to by God, xciii. 7; succeeded by Eopater, his son, xciii. 7

Antiochus Eupator, son of Antiochus, sends Lysias against Judah, xcv. 2; letter of, to his cousin Lysias, xcv. 6; letter of, to Judah, xcv. 7; King of Greece, defeated and compelled to pay tribute to the Romans, xcvi. 1; breaks the covenant he made with Judah and marches against him, xcviii. 3; lays siege to Bethter, xcviii. 3; nobles fall in battle, xcviii. 5; makes a new covenant with Judah, xcviii. 6; informs Nicanor that unless he will send Judah bound in chains, he will be killed, xcix. 4

Apis, King of Egypt in nineteenth year of Jacob's life, xxxv. 8; deified and called "Sarapis," xxxv. 8; the calf of, xxxv. 8; King of Egypt, built Mof, *i.e.*, Menfis, xlii. 1

Apollonius, sword of, seized by Judah, xcii. 1; captain of the Macedonian host, gathers a large multitude against the Jews, xcii. 1.

Apollopanis, brother of Timotheos, ordered to be beheaded by Judah, xciv. 7

Apostates, punishment of, xvi. 7

Apple-tree wishes to serve as gallows for Haman, lxxxiii. 4

Apumaṣia, concubine of Darius, lxxv. 6

R. Aqiba, concerning infliction of punishments in God's presence, xiii. 6; in first compartment, xviii. 7

Aqôlôn, son of Peleg, xxvii. 5

Aqrabim, sons of Esau surrender to sons of Jacob in, xxxvii. 14

Aqtes, in Greece, built by Ṣiqrops as metropolis, lvi. 1

Aram, in Ham's portion, xxxi. 2; children of, xxxi. 16

Aramaic, language written on the wall, lxviii. 3; language spoken in Syria, xxxi. 1

Aran, son of Shem, xxvii. 5

Ararat captured by Cyrus, lxxviii. 1

Arēlīm cry at the weeping of the law, lxxxii. 3

Argos, extermination of kings of, lviii. 6; kings of, reign 544 years, lviii. 6; passes into the hands of Mesenes, lviii. 6

Argument of the first king's chamberlain, lxxv. 1

Arirah, a kingdom in Kush, lxiii. 8

Aristios, a page of Ptolemy, lxxxvii. 1

Ark in God's mind at creation, i. 4; surrounded by all the banners and pillar of cloud placed by God above it, liii. 6

Armania, tents made of the hair of, lxii. 11

Armenēi, children of Madai, xxxi. 4

Armies represented by the hair of the feet in Isaiah's prophecy, lx. 5

Arpnkhshad, son of Shem, xxvii. 5

Arqa (one of the hells), he who is lowered in, ascends no more, xvii. 3

'Arqi, city of 'Arqes, near Tripolis, xxxi. 18

Arvadi, name of an island, Arvodios, xxxi. 18

Asael, fall caused by power, x. 10

Asaph, governor of the garden of Lebanon, lxxvi. 3

Ashchor did not worship Baal in the days of Yair, lviii. 10

Ashdod, Judah killed at battle outside, c. 5

Asher, constellation of, Scorpio, liii. 13; stone of, the onyx, liii. 13; ensign of, an olive, liii. 14; find seven golden idols and hide them under Mount Shechem, lvii. 13

Ashkenaz, children of Gomer, in land of Greeks, xxxi. 4

Ashqalon, built by Misraim, xxxii. 4

Ashtaroth Karnaim, place where Bakires and Timothios fled to, xciii. 1

Ashur, son of Shem, xxvii. 5; sons of, xxvii. 5; *i.e.*, Bel, son of Nimrod, came from Kalna, xxxi. 18

Asqinus (Ascanias) succeeds Anias, xl. 13

Assimilation of Jews to the people of Antiochus, xc. 1

Assyria, all kings of, called Antiochus, xxxii. 6; camp of, smitten, the only survivors being Sennacherib and Nebuchadnezzar, lx. 5; received by lottery by Cyrus, lxviii. 10

Astiras, the province into which Agnios arrived in ships, xl. 5

Astrubel, son of Agnios and Jania,

King of the Carthaginians, defeated and killed by Latinus, King of the Kittim, xl. 10; brother of Annibal, killed by Scipios in Africa, xcvi. 6; head of, sent by Scipio to Annibal, xcvi. 6
'Athrai, daughter of Pusai, prophecy concerning her, lx. 4
Avisianos succeeds Alba, xl. 14
R. Aybo, concerning the death of Moses, l. 1
Aza, Timotheos flees to, xciv. 5; army of Timotheos utterly defeated by Judah at, xciv. 5; besieged by Judah for five days, xciv. 5; walls of, scaled by Hasmoneans, xciv. 6; gate of, fired by the Hasmoneans, captured, xciv. 6; spoil of, carried by the Hasmoneans to Jerusalem, xciv. 7
Azael, Midrash of, xxv.; advises God not to create man, xxv. 2; assumes human form and sins, xxv. 4; did not repent, xxv. 12; appointed chief over charms and ornaments, xxv. 7
'Azah and 'Azazel, l. 15
Azazel, identified with Azael, who bears Israel's sins, xxv. 18

Baal, i.e., Bel, a Baal Peor and Baal Zebub, xxxii. 5; worshipped by all Israelites in the reign of Yair, except by seven righteous men, lviii. 10
Babel, tower of, destruction, xxx. 5; contained seventy steps, xxx. 7
Babylon, people settle in valley of, xxix. 1; i.e., Ur of the Chaldees, xxxv. 2; war of, with Rome, xl. 20; King of, captures Jerusalem, and thus terrifies Romans, xl. 20; Judah and half Simeon journey the way of, lxiii. 19; two mighty kings raised against, viz., Darius the Mede, and Cyrus the Persian, lxvii. 1; capture of, by Cyrus and Darius, lxviii. 8; terrible vengeance inflicted upon, by Cyrus and Darius, lxviii. 8; most precious things of, burned by Cyrus and Darius, lxviii. 9; rendered a waste land, like Sodom and Gomorrah, lxviii. 9
Bakidos comes upon Judah in Laish, c 1; arranges 15,000 men on the right of Judah and 15 000 men on his left, c. 2; succeeds in escaping to Ashdod, c. 5
Bakires, a Macedonian general, xciii. 1
Balaam lost his soul through wisdom, x. 10; the Enchanter, one of Pharaoh's counsellors, advises king to kill Moses, xliv. 9; counsels people to rebel against Qinqanos, xlv. 2; two sons of (Jannis and Jambris), appointed captains of the host, xlv. 2; the Enchanter, i.e., Laban the Aramean, left behind to guard city of Cush, xlv. 2; stratagem of, xlv. 2; king over the people, xlv. 2; flees to Pharaoh, King of Egypt, and advises king to kill Hebrews, xlv. 8; of Petor, advises that king should destroy Israelites by drowning, xlvi. 4; fearing Moses, flees to Cush, xlvi. 6; ordered by Moses to be summoned before him, xlvii. 6; deep counsel of, to Moabites, whereby the Israelites were punished, lv. 10; tries to escape, flying by means of witchcraft, xlviii. 14; and two sons slain by Moses, xlviii. 14; brought to earth by God's ineffable name, xlviii. 14
Banishment by Nebuchadnezzar on the eve of the 9th of Ab, lxi. 1 (v. Exile)
Banners, four, of tribes correspond to the four elements of which the world is composed, liii. 10
Baqtris belongs to Shem, xxxi. 2
Barak captures Hasor, lviii. 4
Baruch, son of Neriya, carried from Egypt to Babylon by Nebuchadnezzar, lx. 10
Bath-Kol, or heavenly voice, succeeds prophecy in the days of Malachi, lxxxv. 2
Batuah, a kingdom in Kush, lxiii. 8
Bauveri, children of Japheth, xxxi. 4
Beast, huge, from middle downwards like a man, from middle upwards like a goat, xl. 7; of field rear and sustain Israelitish children, xliii. 6
Beath, son of Dodanim, xxvii. 2
Beer Shahat, second compartment of hell, xvii. 2

Behemoth created on sixth day, vi. 1; fed daily from 1,000 hills, vi. 1
"Behold," the Hebrew word = 55,1.1
Beings in the form of men walk about, lvii. 41
Bel succeeds to Babylon in days of Serug, xxxii. 3; god of Babylon, daily order of the offering of, lxxii. 2; said to consume the offering laid upon his table, lxxii. 2; Daniel shows Darius the secret entrances through which priests came in to eat the contents of Bel's table, lxxii. 6
Bela, name of city to which Lot fled, xxxv. 6
Belshazzar, King of the Chaldeans, rebelled against by Cyrus and Darius, lxvii. 1; defiles the holy vessels by drinking wine from them, lxvii. 2; greatly afraid at the words of Daniel, lxviii. 4; princes and dignitaries of, crushed when passing through the gate in their excitement, lxviii. 4; murdered by his doorkeeper, lxviii. 5; head of, taken by the doorkeeper to Cyrus and Darius, lxviii. 5
Ben Azay concerning punishment, xiii. 6
Benjamin, stone of, the amethyst, liii. 13; constellation of, Aquarius, liii. 13; ensign of, a wolf, liii. 14; wished to test whether God's law emanated from God or from Moses, lvii. 15; tribe of, especially hated by Haman, lxxix. 1
Benjaminites smite 18,000 Israelites, lix. 13; 25,000, total number of slain of, lix. 16; 600 flee to the cleft of Rimmon, lix. 16
Ben Nethanel, name given Moses by all Israel, xliv. 7
Berakhel, son of, owner of ship in Naphtali's second vision, xxxviii. 7
Bethel, children of Reuben dwell by, lxiii. 17
Beth Horon, people summoned to by Teron, xcii. 2
Bethter attacked by Lysias with a battering-ram and stones, xcv. 2; inhabitants of, relieved by Judah, xcv. 4

Bidria arose from Elisa and dwell on Rinos, xxxi. 12
Bigthan and Teresh, the relatives of Haman, lxxviii. 2; plot to hand over the king's head to the Macedonians, who were then warring with Persia, lxxix. 2
Birds sang, the, and the trees emitted their perfumes on throne of Solomon, lxxxiv. 6
Birean, brother of Timotheos, ordered to be beheaded by Judah, xciv. 7
Bitanya, city of, built by Taḥpanḥes, lvi. 5
Bitto subdued by Madai, xxvii. 3
Bityah (Pharaoh's daughter), son of, xlvi. 6
Blade, fiery, held by angel of death, xii. 5
Blind among Amorites restored to sight by kissing idols, lvii. 14
Blindness seizes the men who were round about the seven righteous men, lviii. 10
Blood, if decree sealed with, decreed will happen, lxxxii. 5
Blue used in tabernacle reflected in the rivers, liii. 18
Bodea (or Borëa), in Japheth's portion, xxxi. 3
Boël complies with God's wish, vi. 4; name of, changed to Raphael, vi. 4, 5
Bohu created on first day, i. 3; above Tohu, xvii. 4
Books and precious stones to be placed on the top of the mountain by the side of the new altar, lvii. 18; which cannot be burnt by fire or broken by iron to be destroyed by dew, lvii. 18
Borgonia arose from Elisa, and dwell by river Rodano, xxxi. 12 (v. Burgunia)
Boṣrah subdued by Riphath, xxvii. 3
Bricks, twelve princes refuse to make, xxix. 3; made from clay and pitch, xxx. 7
Brittania (= Bytinia?), xxxii. 4
Brook from Garden of Eden habitation of the dead, xix. 1; overflowing world, seen by Mordecai in dream, lxxix. 3
Brothers', seven, martyrdom, lxxxix.

Burgunia, son of Elisa, fought Latinus II., xl. 15

Cadmus Europes Tahpanhes reigns in Greece, lvi. 3; King of Egypt, goes from Thebes and comes to Tyre, lvi. 3; reigns in Tyre and Sidon, lvi. 3; reigns in Thebes in the days of Othniel, lvi. 5
Cæsarea (*i.e.*, Kappadocia), xxxii. 4
Cain, derivation of name, vii. 2; Qalmana, wife of, xxiv. 1; the first to surround city with a wall, xxiv. 1; children of, very numerous, xxiv. 3; descendants of, all evildoers, xxiv. 4; sons of, dwelt in the fields of Damascus, xxiv. 11; seed of, with whom the seed of Seth did not intermarry, xxiv. 11; in land of Nod, xxvi. 11; names of seven cities built by, xxvi. 11; sons of, xxvi. 12; daughters of, xxvi. 12
Caleb in third house in Eden, xx. 6; lots cast in the tribe of, lvii. 2
Calf, golden,' brought by the Reubenites and Gadites from Dan, and a holy temple made for it, lxi. 1; images of, to be prayed to by those desiring sons and daughters, lix. 12; carried away by Sennacherib, lx. 1
Cambisa, son of Cyrus, reigns in his stead, lxxviii. 5; destroys the remnant of the Scythians, together with their queen, Tamirah, lxxviii. 5; son of Cyrus, King of Persia, lvi. 1
Camp, each of the Israelites', like a large city, liii. 15; of twelve tribes in desert described, liii. 15; of the sons of Merari, in the north, opposite Dan's standard, liii. 15; of the sons of Gershon in the west, opposite Ephraim's standard, liii. 15; of Moses, Aaron and his sons to the east of the tabernacle, opposite Judah's standard, liii. 15; of the sons of Qehath, in the south, opposite Reuben's standard, liii. 15; total area of, twelve square miles, liii. 18; between the, an area of 4,000 cubits, liii. 18
Canaan, children of, xxvii. 4; number of children of, xxviii. 4; boundary of, xxxi. 18; a sinner after the flood, lvii. 14
Canaanites in the mountains join Amaleqites, but are defeated, xlviii. 14
Cannibals encountered by Elhanan, lxiii. 20
Canopies, ten, created for Adam, vii. 1; table of precious stones and pearls in, xviii. 2; in Paradise, overgrown by golden vine, from which thirty pearls hang, xviii. 2; two, one of stars, the other of sun and moon, to each scholar, xviii. 6; at erection of, the mountains and hills skipped like rams, lii. 18
Canusi, a large city where the battle between Annibal and the Romans took place, xcvi. 3
Carthagene (Qartaini), built in the time of Yair, lviii. 11; besieged by Scipio, xcvi. 7; men of, inform Annibal that unless he will relieve them they will open the gates to Scipio, xcvi. 7; Annibal in, xcvi. 2
Castor, brother of Theseus, captured in the time of Yair, lviii. 11
Cattle of tribes pasture opposite their encampment, liii. 18
Cedar wishes to serve as gallows for Haman, lxxxiii. 4; replaced in its position by Gabriel after falling upon Haman, lxxxii. 6
Chain, iron, half hot as fire, half cold as ice, to beat man with at death, xiii. 2
Chaldean language spoken in Chaldea, xxxi. 1
Chaldeans dip sons in fire, as other nations dip them in water, xxxv. 6; defeated by Cyrus and Darius, lxvii. 1; kingdom of, divided by lot between Cyrus and Darius, lxviii. 10; furnace of, xxix. 14 (*v.* Chasdim)
Chariot, wheels of, i. 11; God's, noise of, produces earthquakes and lightnings, i. 11; wheels of the, praise God for being no respecter of persons, l. 6
Chasdim, Judah and half Simeon dwell in land of, lxiii. 19 (*v.* Chaldeans)

Cherubim, God speaks between two, i. 11
Child, God decrees future of, ix. 1; formation of, ix. 1-10; birth of, ix. 8
Children in sixth compartment of Paradise, xviii. 7; commanded by God to be swallowed up by the earth, xliii. 5; sustained by beasts of the field, xliii. 6
Chronicles, Book of the, of the Kings of Egypt, xlvii. 8; of the Kings of Media and Persia, lxxviii. 1; of the Kings of Rome, lxxviii. 1
Cinnereth, in Lybia, built in the days of Ehud, lviii. 2 (vide Cyrene)
Circumcision prohibited by Antiochus, lxxxvii. 8; by Jethro, xlvi. 13
Citron wishes to serve as gallows for Haman, lxxxiii. 3
Clay, if decree sealed with, prayers heard, lxxxii. 5
Clouds pass on sounds to the seas, ii. 5; and thick darkness form dishes for moon, iii. 6; of glory surround the Israelites in the wilderness, liii. 1; level high places and raise low places, liii. 1; placed at top of the standards upon which the light of the Divine Presence was refulgent, liii. 1; one arm of seventh, rests on each of the four standards, liii. 2; containing the letter Yod, Hē, went the round of all the camps during the seven days of the week, giving light as the sun by day and as the moon by night, liii. 6; four, upon which Hebrew letters were engraved, followed the Israelites, liii. 7; cleanse the Israelites, liii. 16; divide tribes from their cattle, liii. 18
Commandments, Ten, given by God, xlviii. 15
Corinthus, present name of city of Epira, lvi. 5
Covenant, text of the, between the Romans and the Jews, xcvii. 2
Creatures, holy, quaking, i. 13
Crown, reaches God's throne, when all the wheels of His chariot and throne commence rolling, lii. 6
Cush, children of, xxvii. 4, xxxi. 17; people of, wage war with people of Qedem (East) and Syria, xlv. 1; besieged nine years by Qinqanos, xlv. 8 (vide Kush)
Cushim, son of Canaan, xxvii. 4
Cycrops fled from Egypt, lvi. 1 (vide Siqrops)
Cyprus, i.e., Kittim, xxxii. 4
Cyrene, in Lybia, lviii. 2
Cyrus the Persian raised against Babylon, lxvii. 1; marries the daughter of Darius, lxvii. 1; prevents Chaldeans from pursuing the Median camp, lxvii. 1; receives by lot Assyria and Persia, lxviii. 10; proclaims that whoever desires to go to Jerusalem to help in building the temple shall be paid for his labours, lxxv. 2; reigns over Media and Persia after the death of Darius, lxxvii. 1; reigns over all the kingdoms of the earth, lxxviii. 1; captures mountains of Elef (or Alef), lxxviii. 1; captures all the fords of India and the land of Ethiopia, lxxviii. 1; acts of, written in the Book of Chronicles of the Kings of Media and Persia, lxxviii. 1; acts of, written in the Book of Chronicles of the Kings of Rome, lxxviii. 1; ends his days in battle in the land of Shittim (Scythians), lxxviii. 2; entices the Scythians from their fortresses by a ruse, lxxviii. 3; slays the son of their queen Tamirah, lxxviii. 3; succeeded by his sons Darius, Cyrus, and Artaxerxes, lxxxv. 1
Cyrus and Darius humble themselves and prostrate themselves before God, lxviii. 7; write proclamation to the Arameans, Tyreans, Samaritans, and Asaph, governor of the garden of Lebanon, lxxvi. 8

Da'al did not worship Baal in the days of Yair, lviii. 10
Damascus, xxxvi. 1
Dan, constellation of Cancer, liii. 13; stone of, the beryl, liii. 13; ensign of, a serpent, liii. 14; taught their children what they learned from the Amorites, lvii. 10; determine to leave Canaan and settle in Egypt, lxii. 5; war

waged against tribe of, lix. 13;
Naphtali, Gad and Asher come
to, lxi. 4; tribe of, mighty warriors, lxii. 5, lxiii. 4; refuse to
fight House of David, lxii. 5,
lxiii. 4; determine to fight Jeroboam, lxii. 5; tribe of, arrive at
the other side of the River Pishon,
where they settle, lxii. 6; tribe
of, wish to settle in Edom, Moab,
and among the Ammonites, lxii.
6; birthplace of Elhanan, lxiii. 1;
descendants of met by Elhanan,
lxiii. 4; tribe of, march to the
brook of Pishon, seven years'
journey from Canaan, lxiii. 5;
tribe of, dwell by the sea in Kush,
where are Ethiopians without
number, lxiii. 5; tribe of, arrive
at Kush, *i.e*, Havila, lxiii. 5;
tribe of, resolve to attack Edom,
Ammon, and Moab, lxiii. 5; tribe
of, resolve to attack the Egyptians, lxiii. 5; descendants of, slay
twenty-five Ethiopian kings, lxiii.
6; tribe of, joined by men of the
tribes of Naphtali, Gad, and
Asher, lxiii. 7; tribe of, dwells
with those of Gad, Asher, and
Naphtali, by the rivers of Kush,
lxiii. 8; children of, never close
their houses, as there are no
thieves among them, lxiii. 14;
children of, possess no servants,
lxiii. 14; children of, rebuked by
the children of Levi for swearing
by God's name, lxiii. 14; children
of, smite 22,000 Israelites, lix. 13

Danaus has fifty sons, who marry
the fifty daughters of Egisates,
their brother, lvi. 4; one of fifty
sons of, slays his brothers and
reigns in their stead, lvi. 4

Daniel discovers injustice of Susannah's two judges, lxv. 7; prayed
for Nebuchadnezzar, so that his
seven years became seven months,
lxvi. 1; refuses to be one of
Nebuchadnezzar's heirs, lxvi. 2;
interprets the writing upon the
wall, lxxii. 1; rebukes Belshazzar, lxviii. 2; advice of, to Darius,
lxix. 2; envied by the princes,
who conspire against him, lxx. 1;
prays to God three times each
day, lxx. 3; cast into a den in
which ten lions were enclosed,
lxx. 6; God of, praised by the
bystanders, lxx. 10; brought from
the lions' den sound and perfect,
lxx. 10; points out that the
priests of Bel eat the offerings,
lxxii. 3; discovers by means of
ashes upon the floor of Bel's
temple the stratagem of the
priests, lxxii. 4; leaves for Shushan, in the land of Elam, his
native place, lxxiv. 3; gives all
that the king presented him with
to the suffering exiles of Judah,
lxxiv. 3; prophesied the division
of the kingdom by Alexander,
lxxxv. 8

Danube, *i.e.*, the Dunai, by which
Ugar, Bulgar, and Pasinaq live,
xxxi. 7

Darius the Mede, reign of, xl. 20;
the Mede raised against Babylon,
lxvii. 1; receives by lot Babylon,
its temple, and the land of Media,
lxviii. 10; places Daniel upon a
throne and asks him for counsel,
lxix. 1; issues a decree to his
people to honour and believe in
the God of Daniel, lxix. 3; confirms the decree of the princes by
sealing it with his seal, lxx. 2;
exerts all his strength to rescue
Daniel, lxx. 4; strives with the
princes until sunset, lxx. 5; goes
to the lions' den at daybreak and
hears Daniel singing God's praises,
lxx. 9; orders Daniel's enemies
to be thrown into the lions' den,
lxx. 10; orders the princes to
assist the Jews, lxxi. 2; orders
runners to proclaim the king's
permission to the Jews to rebuild
God's temple, lxxi. 2; appoints
Daniel as his counsellor, lxxii. 1;
sends for Daniel to test his wisdom,
lxxii. 1; prepares an offering to
be brought before Bel, lxxii. 2;
allows Daniel to return to his
native land on condition of appointing a successor, lxxiv. 1;
son of Ahasuerus, reigned thirty-four years after the rebuilding of
the temple, lxxiv. 3; perplexed at
the dicta of his three guardians,
lxxiv. 8; sends a message to Cyrus
to join him in establishing God's

house in Jerusalem, lxxvi. 2; makes Cyrus, his son-in-law, king over Media, lxxvii. 1
Darkness created on first day, i. 3; that existed before creation now in hell, xxi. 11; covering earth, seen by Mordecai in dream, lxxix. 3
Dathan lost his soul through riches, x. 10
David, tradition spoken by, ix. 11; in third house in Eden, xx. 6; speaks in third house of Eden, xx. 7; smites Syria in the days of Romulus II., xl. 15; enticed by a woman, lxxv. 7
Day created on first day, i. 3; twelve hours in, vi. 10; refuses to move that Moses may continue to live, li. 4
Dead, large habitation of, xix. 1; souls of, eat from field and drink from brook on Sabbath eve, xix. 1; robbed by those who drink water between the afternoon and evening services on Sabbath, xix. 2; rest on Sabbath, xix. 3; rise from their graves every Sabbath and new moon, xix. 4
Death, time to quit world, ix. 10; difference in, of man and animals, xi. 5; angel of, appearance of, xii. 5; martyrs inform Antiochus that their souls are given over to, lxxxix. 7; an atonement for their people, lxxxix. 7
Deber, son of Samer, xxvii. 1
Debir built by Misraim, xxvii. 4
Deborah, twin wife of Abel, xxvi. 1
Decrees, the four, concerning the Levites: (1) Sprinkling of water of sin-offering; (2) washing of clothes; (3) heaving; (4) razor, lv. 6
Dedan, son of Japheth, xxvii. 2
Dedazal, son of Reu, xxvii. 6
Degel subdued by Magog, xxvii. 3
Demetrius, with a large army from Rome, attacks Antiochus Eupator, xcviii. 6; slays Antiochus and Lysias, xcix. 1; rules in Antiochia, in Macedon, xcix. 1; sends Nicanor with a strong army against the Jews, xcix. 3
Demons created on second day, i. 3; children of Adam, xxiii. 1

Depaseat, son of Heri, xxvii. 2
Derifa, daughter of Reu, xxvii. 6
Dialus, a wise man who made idols of gold and brass which could speak, lviii. 8
Diensdakh (i.e., Tuesday), iv. 2
Diga, son of Serug, xxvii. 7
Dinim subdues Gudah, xxvii. 3
Dinur, a river in hell, beneath throne of glory (vide Fire; Rigion), xvi. 7
Dionysius builds Niza, in Media, lviii. 2
Diqalbel, son of Yoqtan, xxvii. 5
Diul, a sinner after the Flood, lvii. 14
Divination first practised, xxvii. 9
Do'ath, son of Heri, xxvii. 2
Dodanim, children of, xxvii. 2, xxviii. 3; subdue Qaduba, xxvii. 3; i.e., Rodie, xxxi. 4; i.e., the Daniski, who dwell in Danemarka and Asidania, xxxi. 14; descendants of, xxxi. 15
Doeg the Edomite lost his soul through wisdom, x. 10
Dog kills Piritius and attempts to kill Thisius, who is saved by Heraclones, lviii. 2
Donnersdakh (i.e., Thursday), iv. 2
Dostios (Dositheus), a captain of Judah's army, captures Timotheos, xcvii. 7; a captain of the host slain in a fierce battle between Judah and Gorgias, xcviii. 1
Dove, image of, to be prayed to by those desiring riches, lix. 12; places a scroll of the law upon the knees of Solomon, lxxxiv. 7
Dragon, and Daniel, lxxiii.; fighting seen by Mordecai in dream, lxxix. 3
Dream of Miriam, xlii. 8; of Pharaoh, xliii. 1; interpretation of Pharaoh's, xliii. 2; of Mordecai, lxxix. 3; of Ahasuerus, lxxxii. 7; of Alexander, lxxxv. 4
Drop, bitter, from blade of angel of death, xii. 5
Drought and rain, xxvii. 3
Drowned, in second compartment of Paradise, xviii. 7
Ducsius, elder of the Hassidim, tested in the reign of Antiochus and found perfect, xcix. 6; called father of the Jews, and judge in

Jerusalem, xcix. 6; pierces his bowels, xcix. 7; prays and dies, xcix. 7
Dust, God takes of the, vi. 7

Eagle, image of, to be prayed to by those desiring riches, lix. 12; whose wings are spread over the whole world, so that nothing could withstand it until the great Mede arose and smote it, lxxxi. 1; and peacocks nestled among the branches of the trees on the throne of Solomon, lxxxiv. 3; placed crown upon the head of Solomon, lxxxiv. 6
Earth created on first day, i. 3; over waters as a ship, ii. 2; depth of, ii. 4; destined to become a curse, vi. 6; compact made by God, vi. 14; rebuked, vi. 6, 7; divided into three parts, xxxi. 1; commanded by God to swallow up the children of the Israelites, protect them until they grow up, and then to cast them up, xliii. 5; ploughed by the Egyptians in order to injure children, xliii. 6
Earthquakes in northern corner of the world, i. 7; when Abram in furnace, xxx. 14
Earth-worshippers encountered by Elhanan, lxiii. 20
Ebarim, Mount, under which books concealed, lvii. 10 (vide Abarim)
Eber, son of Shelah, xxvii. 5; sons of, xxvii. 5
Ecbatana, Antiochus compelled by the Persians to flee from, xciii. 3
Eden, Garden of, created before creation, i. 2; gate of, opened by God, ii. 3; Adam and Eve driven from, vi. 10 et seq.; spirit brought from, ix. 2; child carried through, ix. 5; virtuous honoured in, xvii. 6; nine palaces in, xx. 1; length of houses in, xx. 1; every house presided over by angels, xx. 1; sixty myriad species of trees in, xx. 2; every house in, contains canopies of roses and myrtles, xx. 1; fruit of, eaten by pupils of sages, xx. 2; houses in, xx. 3; beams of house in, of white glass and walls of cedar-wood, xx. 4; second house built of silver and walls of cedar, xx. 5; third house built of gold and silver, xx. 6; 310 worlds in, xviii. 6; third house of precious stones, with golden beds, and prepared lights, xx. 7; reason why fourth house of, built of olive-wood, xx. 8; fourth house of, like first man, xx. 8; fifth house built of onyx and precious stones, xx. 9; walls of fifth house of gold and perfumed with balsam, xx. 9 (vide Paradise)
Edessa, i.e., Semari in Syria, xxxi. 18
Edom, land of, where Judah and Gorgias fight a battle, xciv. 2
Edomites, commanded by the two kings to contribute their share in the rebuilding of God's house, lxxvi. 5; ordered to hew the wood from the Lebanon, lxxvi. 5; ordered to pay yearly tribute of five talents of gold, lxxvi. 5
Egisates (or Agestes), the fifty daughters of, married by the fifty sons of Danaus, lvi. 4
Egypt, kings of, called Pharaoh till time of Ptolemy Lagos, from which time called Ptolemy, xxxii. 6; divided into three kingdoms, xlii. 1; gods of, broken up into small pieces and destroyed, liv. 1; every firstborn of, slays his father, liv. 2; Israelites flee to, in twenty-seventh year of Nebuchadnezzar's reign, lx. 10; captured by Nebuchadnezzar, lx. 10; engraved upon a golden table, lxxxvii. 5
Egyptian language spoken in Egypt, xxxi. 1; rabble wish to prevent Israelites from going, xlviii. 12.
Egyptians, two wizards of, liv. 8; more addicted to witchcraft than any other nation, liv. 8; seized with fear on seeing the Israelites, liv. 9; did not wish to enter the sea after the Israelites, liv. 9
Ehud succeeds Othniel, lviii. 2
Eight things created on first day, i. 3
Eight things created on second day, i. 3
Elaf (or Alef), mountains of, i.e., the mountains of darkness, as far as the Snow Mountains, which are impassable, captured by Cyrus, lxxviii. 1

Elah, spokesman of sinners, wants each tribe to be asked separately, lvii. 9; tent of, where the books (?) of the Amorites were hidden, lvii. 12; a sinner after the Flood, lvii. 14
Elam, son of Shem, xxvii. 5
Elash, son of Tiras, xxvii. 2
Elazar, son of Asher the Levite, page, 1, xxxi. 5, 18, xli. 7
R. Elazar of Modin, on Abraham's greatness in magic, xxxv. 4
Elchanan hailed from Dan, and was very wise and pious, lxiii. 1; son of Joseph, a large export merchant, and owner of many ships, lxiii. 1; made a ship containing many chambers, lxiii. 1; a man of valour, lxiii. 2; servants of, partly Jews, partly Ishmaelites, lxiii. 2; ship of, loaded with 10,000 talents' worth of spices, lxiii. 2; ship of, drifts on to the sand in the Sea of Havila, lxiii. 3; majestic in appearance, lxiii. 4; comes upon a people who speak Hebrew, lxiii. 4; passes through lands some of whose inhabitants are fire-worshippers, others earth-worshippers, others worshipped a white horse and were cannibals, lxiii. 20; the Danite came from the land of India, lxiii. 20
Eleazar and Ithamar succeed Aaron, xlviii. 17; the priest exhorts the people, lvii. 38; captain, xlviii. 14; R., question of, to R. Simeon, whether Israelites took weavers with them, liii. 16; the chief of the seventy priests sent to Ptolemy, lxxxvii. 3; brings the various copies to the king, who finds them to be identical, lxxxvii. 4; refuses to eat of the forbidden sacrifice, lxxxviii. 3; refuses to deceive the people by feigning to eat forbidden sacrifice, lxxxviii. 3; captured and brought before Phillip, lxxxviii. 3; aged ninety, martyrdom of, lxxxviii. 4, 5; Judah's brother pierces the elephant with his sword, it falls upon him and crushes him to death, xcviii. 5; blood of, avenged by Judah, xciii. 1
Eliakim, the priest at the head of the Jews returning from Babylon, lxxi. 3
Eliezer, ruler of Damascus, enters Abraham's service, xxxv. 2
R. Eliezer, i. 1, 8, iii. 2, 3; concerning stiffneckedness of wicked, xii. 8; concerning the beating in the graves, xiii. 1; concerning etymology of Gehinnom, xiv. 1
Elifaz, son of Peleg, xxvii. 5
Elijah, four Divine hosts shown him, ix. 11; interview with R. Joshua b. Levi, xv. 1; dwells in the fifth house of Eden, xx. 9; on appearance of, ark will be discovered, lxxvii. 9; beseeches Abraham, Isaac and Jacob, lxxxii. 4; informs Moses of impending doom and of Mordecai, lxxxii. 4; informed by Moses that if the decree has been sealed with blood, then what was decreed will happen, lxxxii. 5; informed by Moses that if the decree is sealed with clay, their prayers may still be heard, lxxxii. 5; goes to Mordecai, lxxxii. 5
Eliochora, Sea of, held by Jonithem, xxxii. 1
Eliodorus, captain of the host of Seleucus, ordered to go to Jerusalem, lxxxvi. 1; places guards round the Temple, lxxxvi. 2 (vide Heliodorus)
Eliosin (Eleusis), name of Akta, xxxv. 9; city of, destroyed by Erkules in the reign of Tola, lviii. 9
Eliphaz, son of Esau, taught by Jacob, does not accompany his brother to war against Jacob, xxxvii. 13
Elisa, children of Yavan, xxxi. 4; i.e., Alamania, inhabit mountains of Iov and Sobtimo, xxxi. 12; sons of, xl. 13
Elishah subdues Tablo, xxvii. 3; number of children, xxviii. 3
Elishah ben Abuyah presides over, not punished, in seventh compartment, xxi. 11
Elohim, children of, of the seed of Seth, xxiv. 10
Emorites (vide Amorites)
Endiana belongs to Shem, xxxi. 2

Enoch, name of a city built by Cain, xxiv. 1; son of Cain and Qalmana, xxiv. 1; the seventh from Adam, purified city of Enoch, xxiv. 3; sons of, xxvi. 8; daughters of, xxvi. 8; desired by God and taken away, xxvi. 8; son of Cain and Temed, xxvi. 11; children of, xxvi. 13; placed in the Garden of Eden, xxvi. 20; author of many writings, xxvi. 20; son of Reuben, fights by the side of Simeon and Benjamin, xxxvii. 6

Enosh, son of Seth, forms a man, xxiii. 6; in the days of, men began to be deified, and had temples built to them, xxiv. 9; sons of, xxvi. 4; daughter of, xxvi. 4; in time of, men made temples to gods, xxvi. 20

Eoropa, in Japheth's portion, xxxi. 3

Ephraim, stone of, the jacinth, liii. 13; constellation of, Gemini, liii. 13; ensign of, an ox, liii. 14; passed their children through the fire, according to the custom of the Amorites, lvii. 15

Ephraim and half Manasseh, tribes of, possess no money, but only spoil from their enemies, lxii. 12; tribes of, are hard-hearted, ride horses, infest the roads, and are pitiless, lxii. 12, lxiii. 18; tribes of, are distant six months' march from Temple, and are innumerable, lxii. 12; exact tribute from twenty-five kingdoms, as well as from a portion of Ishmael, lxii. 12; are good riders, lxiii. 18; a portion of the tribes of, are harsh and hard-hearted, lxiii. 18

Ephron, a large city, besieged by Judah, xcvii. 8

Epira, city of, now called Corinthus, lvi. 5

Epirus, many Romans slain by Annibal at, xcvi. 8

Erekh (*i.e.*, Edessa), xxxi. 18

Eriqtonios, the first to construct a chariot in Greece, lvi. 3; lives in the time of Joshua, lvi. 8

Erkules conquers Anteos, in Lybia, and destroys city of Elios during reign of Tola, lviii. 9; commits suicide by throwing himself into the fire at the time of the death of Jephtha's daughter, lix. 8

Esau separates from Jacob, xxxvii. 1; attacks Jacob and his sons when they are sitting in mourning for Leah, xxxvii. 1; hit on right shoulder by an arrow from Jacob's bow, xxxvii. 4; dies from his wound at Adoram, xxxvii. 4; sons of, xxxvii. 18; children of, made tributary by sons of Jacob, xxxvii. 14; difference in future reward of children of, to that of children of Jacob, xx. 7

Esther, prayer of, lxxx.; in her royal garments appears before the king, accompanied by two handmaidens, lxxx. 4; faint from fasting and trouble, lxxx. 6

Estirah, name of girl seen and desired by Shemhazai, xxv. 5; taught the ineffable Name by Shemhazai, xxv. 5; ascends to heaven, and is placed among the Pleiades, xxv. 6

Esudad, son of Hōri, xxvii. 2

Ethiopia, each of the twenty-five kings of, possesses 1,000 horsemen and 80,000 infantry, lxiii. 6; land of, captured by Cyrus, lxxviii. 1 (*vide* Kush)

Euphrates, in Shem's portion, xxxi. 3; children of Zebulun extend to the, lxii. 11

Eupirus, river where Æmilius and Varros arranged the Roman army in battle array, xcvi. 3

Eve eats the forbidden fruit, xxii. 1 *et seq.*

Evil Merodach succeeds Nebuchadnezzar the Younger, lxvi. 4; rescues Jehoiachin, King of Judah, from prison, lxvi. 5; Nebuchadnezzar's eldest son slandered to his father, who makes Nebuchadnezzar the Younger king, lxvi. 5; three sons of, named Regosar, Lebuzer-Dukh and Nabar (*i.e.*, Belshazzar), lxvi. 6

Excommunication by Upper and Lower Tribunal, lv. 12

Exiles, the eight, lx.; banishment by Titus, on the eve of the ninth of Ab, lxi. 1 (*vide* Dan; Levites; Moses, sons of; Tribes)

Ezra, the priest and scribe, at the head of the four myriads of returning Jews, lxxi. 3

Ezra and Nehemiah pray to God for the holy fire which was hidden by Jeremiah, lxxvii. 3

Faneg, son of Dodanim, first used ships, xxvii. 3; subdued Yedid, xxvii. 3

Fantônya, son of Tubal, xxvii. 2

Fast proclaimed by Judah, xcii. 5

Faunus, successor of Sefo, xl. 10; ruled Italy, lix. 10

Februarius, month of, added by Pompilius, lix. 11

Ficus ruled Italy, lix. 10

Field, in the habitation of the dead, xix. 1 (*vide* Camp)

Fig-tree, wishes to serve as gallows for Haman, lxxxiii. 2

Filop, son of Dedan, xxvii. 2

Fingers, writing on the wall, lxvii. 3

Fire, river of, from the face of holy creatures. i. 18 (*vide* Dinur); Chaldeans drop their children in, xxx. 6; worshippers of neighbours of Issachar, lxii. 10; worshippers of, encountered by Elhanan, lxiii. 20; holy, hidden by Jeremiah, lxxvii. 3; sunk in the earth, under a large stone in the valley of the Mount of Olives, lxxvii. 6; place of, indicated by old priest. lxxvii. 6; in a pit in the valley of the Mount of Olives priests find something like the lees of oil, mud, and honey, lxxvii. 7; suddenly burns the altar, lxxvii. 8; licks the burnt-offering, and cleanses the Temple, diminishes, lxxvii. 8; of Judah's mouth burns sinners, xc. 4; for the altar could not be found by Judah, xciv. 1

Firita, daughter of Reu, xxvii. 6

Firmament created on second day, i. 8; divided into seven degrees, iv. 3

First-born, every Egyptian, slays his father, liv. 2; where no, eldest in the house died, liv. 3; the dead, come to life and die anew, liv. 3; smiting of, liv.

Flame which did not burn, lvii. 40

Flood, the, in God's mind at Creation, i. 4

Foam, hot, vomited by source, lvii. 41

Forma, waters drawn from, brought to Kittim in a vessel for the use of Iania, xl. 11

Fortresses, store-cities of Egypt, so built that no one could enter or leave without king's knowledge, xlii. 3

Foundations, between the, sons of men shall dwell 7,000 years, lvii. 41

Fountain, of hot waters near Gehinnom, ii. 4; yield fishes, birds and fruits and water, lxii. 3; six of which form one pool, lxii. 3

Frankos, children of Gomer, xxxi. 6

Franselin, land of Frankos, xxxi. 6

Fransi, children of Madai, xxxi. 4

Frezes (Phryges), children of Togarmah, xxxi. 4

Gaash, Mount, occupied by Amorites, discomfited by sons of Jacob, xxxvi. 10

Gabriel, head of second band of angels i. 9; driven away by earth, vi. 5; commanded to bring dust, vi. 6; relieves Hananya, Mishael, and Azariah from furnace, xxxv. 3; the angel, assumes the form of one of Pharaoh's counsellors, xliv. 11; advises king to test Moses by bringing onyx stones and live coals before him, xliv. 11; commanded by God to bring the soul of Moses, l. 10; asks God how he can look upon the death of one worth sixty myriads of His angels, l. 10; spreads a garment of fine linen at the head of Moses, l. 14; unable to do anything against Johanai and Mamre, liv. 8; enters the sea in the form of a mare, liv. 9; afflicts the Amorites with blindness, lvii. 34; replaces the cedar in its position after it fell upon Haman, lxxxii. 6; appears in his dream to Ahasuerus in the form of Haman, trying to kill him with a drawn sword, lxxxiii. 7

Gad, constellation of, Capricornus, liii. 13; stone of, the diamond, liii. 13; ensign of. a troop, liii.

14; children of, lie with the wives of their neighbours, lvii. 18; the seer, golden seat put for, lxxxiv. 3

Gad and Gilead, men of, send two letters to Judah imploring his help against Timotheos, xciv. 2

Gadaira, in Ham's portion, xxxi. 2; boundary of Japheth's portion, xxxi. 3

Galathi (or Gavathi), children of Japheth, xxxii. 4

Galilee, Jews of, delivered by Simeon, xciv. 3

Galiṣur the angel prophesies the condition of the crops, lii. 8; so called because he revealed God's secrets, lii. 8; wings of, spread out to receive the breath of the holy creatures, lii. 8; takes a thick covering of iron and spreads it on the river Rigion, lii. 8

Gallows for Haman, trees dispute who shall serve as, lxxxiii. 2

Garden planted upon mountain by Nebuchadnezzar the Younger, to please his Median wife, lxvi. 4; of Eden (*vide* Eden, Paradise)

Gasqonei, children of Japheth, xxxi. 4

Gebi, son of Peleg, xxvii. 5

Gedudim, troops of angels, l. 14

Gehinnom (*vide* Hell), created before Creation of world, i. 2; in God's mind at Creation, i. 4; heat of, created on second day, i. 8; hot fountain near, ii. 4; child carried to, ix. 6; judgment of, ix. 11, xiii. 5; punishment of, x. 4, xi. 4, xiii. 6, 7; fate of one condemned to, xi. 7; description of, xiv. 1 *et seq.*; why so called, xiv. 1; seventh compartment of hell, xvii. 2; fire of = one-sixtieth fire of Shaare Ṣalmavet, xvii. 2; wicked led to, by angels of trembling, xvii. 5; wicked thrown into depth of, by angel of death, xvii. 5; vision of, xxi.

Genealogies, Book of, xli. 2

Generations, Book of the, lxvi. 6

Germania, arrival of Annibal in, xcvi. 2

Gershon not circumcised, by order of Reuel, xlvi. 18; camp of the sons of, liii. 15

Geshem the Arabian slanders the Jews, lxxi. 3

Gezrôn, son of Ashur, xxvii. 5

Gibeah, incident of concubine of, lviii. 1; incident of, in the days of Abdon, lix. 12

Gideon asks for another sign, lviii. 7

Giḥon flows from fifth house of Eden, and illumines the upper world, xx. 9; fragrance of, more exquisite than that of Lebanon, xx. 9; *i.e.*, the Nile in Ham's portion, xxxi. 3

Gilead attacked by Timotheos, xciv. 4

Gilug, son of Cush, xxvii. 4

Giteal, King of the Ammonites, lix. 1

Gizla, daughter of Serug, xxvii. 7

God, Divine presence described, i. 9; throne of, i. 10; footstool of, i. 10; breath creates hosts of heaven, iii. 2; worship of, through fear, x. 4; descends, together with Michael, Gabriel, and Zagzael, l. 14; makes a sign in the heavens, and the day remained at a standstill, li. 5; not able to help Jews, said by Haman, lxxxi. 6; will fight against Antiochus, and uproot him from the earth, lxxxix. 7

Godansdakh (*i.e.*, Wednesday), iv. 2

Godo conquered by Riphath, xxvii. 3

Gog and Magog descended from Sqite (Japhethites), xxxi. 4

Gólaza, son of Magog, xxvii. 2

Gomar, sons of, xxvii. 1; children of, numbered by Pinḥas, xxviii. 3

Gomer, sons of, xxvii. 2; *i.e.*, Gavathi, or Galathi, son of Japheth, xxxi. 4

Gomorrah built by Misraim, xxvii. 4

Gondalus ravages land of the Kittim, xl. 5

Goqar, waters of, equivalent to those of Forma, xl. 11

Gorgias chosen one of the generals of Lysias, xcii. 5; with a huge army, meets Judah in the land of Edom, xciv. 2; defeated and put to flight by Judah, xciv. 2; flies to Arabia to Timotheos, xciv. 2; avoids single combat with Judah, and escapes, xcviii.

1; flies to the desert of Marasha, where he dies, xcviii. 1
Goshen, land of, where certain shepherds reigned, xlii. 1; kingdom of shepherds, granted in honour of Jacob and Joseph, xlii. 1
Goths, pride of, humbled by Annibal, xcvi. 2 (*vide* Guti)
Gozan, the river, lxiii. 18
Grave, beating of, xiii. 1 *et seq.;* judgment of, not on those who die at Sabbath eve, xiii. 5; judgment in, more severe than that in hell, xiii. 5
"Great," the word applied to Moses, l. 5
Greece, assisted by Rome against Babylon, xl. 20
Greek, language spoken in Greece, xxxi. 1; spoken by Judah and half tribe of Simeon, lxiii. 19; persecution by the, *vide* Antiochus, Judah
Gresi, river of, called Yoniu, xxxi. 4
Gudah, subdued by Dinim, xxvii. 8
Guti (Goths), children of Japheth, xxxi. 4
Gutiel did not worship Baal in the days of Yair, lviii. 10

Habakkuk prepares a large dish to feed the reapers, lxx. 8; the prophet returns from harvesting in Judah at the same time as Daniel is cast into the lions' den, lxx. 8; lifted up by a lock of his hair by an angel, and placed with food in the lions' den, lxx. 8
Hadarezer and his sons flee to Kittim, xl. 15
Hadarniel, every word uttered by, accompanied by sparks of fire, lii. 2; stands far above his fellow-angels, lii. 2; rebukes Moses, lii. 2; goes before Moses, lii. 4; acts as messenger for Moses, lii. 4; not able to stand before the fire of Sandalphon, lii. 5
Ham, children of, xxvii. 4, xxviii. 1, 4, xxxi. 17
Haman angered at the execution of his relatives, Bigthan and Teresh, lxxviii. 2; the Amalekites' enmity due to Mordecai being Saul's descendant, lxxix. 1; letter of, lxxxi; counsel of, to blot out all the Jews on one day, lxxxi. 3; cuts down a cedar from his garden to hang Mordecai on, lxxxii. 6; beats the children with iron chains and appoints keepers over them, lxxxii. 7; destroys the wall of his own house to obtain a beam for the gallows, lxxxiii. 5
Hamath in Ham's portion, xxxi. 2; (*i.e.*, Antochia) built by Hamathi, xxxi. 18
Hamatim, son of Canaan, xxvii. 4
Hanokh, son of Heri, xxvii. 2
Haran, dies in the presence of his father Terah in Ur of the Chaldees, xxxv. 1; children of, xxxv. 1
Hararyah, land of, given to Jacob by the Amorites, xxxvi. 12
Harteman, son of Peleg, xxvii. 5
Hasmoneans, graven images found under the clothes of, who were slain in battle, xcviii. 2 (*vide* Judah)
Hasor, battle before, xxxvi. 5; captured by Barak, lviii. 4
Hassidim, assembly of, scattered and exiled, lxxxvii. 8; flee to the forest, lxxxvii. 8; a large number of, mustered by Mattathiah, xc. 2; send the spoil to Jerusalem, xciii. 1
Havilah, son of Yoqtan, xxvii. 5; number of children of, xxviii. 4; *i.e.*, Getili, xxxi. 17; precious stones of, included the bdellium and the onyx, lvii. 14; encampment of Levites, lxii. 8; land of, abounds in gold, sheep, cattle, camels, asses, and horses, lxii. 8; land of, measured, lxiii. 7
Heat of living body, created on second day, i. 8
Heaven, created on first day, i. 3; form of, i. 6; boundaries of, i. 6; north corner not completed, i. 7; created by one word, iii. 2; the seven doors of, lii. 11; seven doors of the seven, opened by God Himself, who reveals Himself to Israel face to face, lii. 11
Heavenly hosts, with their crowns, glorify God, lii. 6; bodies, clothe themselves in sackcloth at the distress of the law, lxxxii. 8
Heber, name given to Moses by his father, xliv. 7

Hebrew, language spoken in Eber, xxxi. 1; the holy language, xxxviii. 11; spoken by tribe of Issachar, lxii. 10; spoken by children of Reuben, lxiii. 17; spoken by Judah and half Simeon, lxiii. 19; children of Hebrews reply to the children of Egyptians, xliv. 3; Hebrews who rebelled slain during the three days of darkness, xlviii. 8

Helena, captured by Theseus in the time of Yair, lviii. 1; captured by Alexander in the time of Elon, lix. 9; comes to Egypt in the time of Abdon, lix. 10

Heliodorus smitten very severely, lxxxvi. 3; sees an awe-inspiring man riding a splendid horse in the Temple, lxxxvi. 3; felled to the ground, lxxxvi. 3; lifted by young priests and placed on his bed, lxxxvi. 4; informs Seleucus that he should only send his enemies to plunder God's house, lxxxvi. 5; ordered to bow down before Honiah, lxxxvi. 5 (vide Eliodorus)

Hell, sea-gate, alluded to in Jonah, xiv. 3; three gates of, xiv. 3; gate of, in wilderness, xiv. 3; world-gate, xiv. 3; five different fires, xiv. 4; gate of, xv. 1; first compartment of, where covetous punished, xvi. 1, xxi. 4; second compartment, slanderers punished, xvi. 2, xxi. 5; third compartment, adulterers punished, xvi. 3, xx. 7; fourth compartment, wantons punished, xvi. 4, xx. 8; fifth compartment, princes punished, xvi. 5, xx. 9; 7,000 windows in each room, xvi. 6; sixth compartment, ten nations, xx. 10; 7,000 vessels filled with venom in each window of, xvi. 6; seven compartments of, xvi. 6; seventh compartment of, six nations, xxi. 11; 7,000 rooms, xvi. 6; 7,000 holes in every compartment of, xvii. 1; names of compartments, xvii. 1; 7,000 scorpions in every hole, xvii. 1; 300 slits in every scorpion, xvii. 1; 7,000 pouches of venom in the slit of every scorpion, xvii. 1; length of, 6,800 years' journey, xvii. 2; no righteous people in, xxi. 1; fire at the gates of, xxi. 3; two brooks in first compartment of, xxi. 4; open pits, fiery lions, xxi. 4; Antiochus will descend to the bottom of hell, that he will be drawn into darkness where there is no life or light, but darkness and shades, where there is no rest or repose, but trouble, sorrow, brimstone, and fire, xxxix. 13 (vide also Gehinnom)

Helpmeet, the word causes the earth to tremble, vi. 14

Heraclones saves Thisius from a dog. lviii. 2 (vide Erkules)

Hōri, son of Ashkenaz, xxvii. 2

Heroës, former name of the city Ramses, xlii. 1

Hetel, river by which families of Togarmah live, xxxi. 6

Heyya, son of Shemḥazai, xxv. 7; invoked by men when they bear heavy loads, xxv. 11 (vide Aheyya)

Hezekiah rules the 13,000 men of Judah and Benjamin who remain in Jerusalem, lx. 5

Ḥiddeqel, i.e., the Tigris, in Japheth's portion, xxxi. 3

High priest sends Ptolemy seventy priests with Eleazar as their chief, lxxxvii. 3 (vide Eleazar, Alkimos)

Ḥol, an immortal bird who rebukes Eve, xxii. 5, 8 (vide Milḥam)

Holy creatures, breath of, unendurable were it not for Galiṣur, lii. 8

Ḥoniah informs Eliodorus that the only gold in the treasury is that presented by Seleucus for the maintenance of orphans, widows and the poor, lxxxvi. 1; the priest fasts, lxxxvi. 2; entreated by the elders of Macedon to pray for Heliodorus, lxxxvi. 4

Horad, son of Melech, xxvii. 2

Horiyah, a kingdom of Kush, lxiii. 8

Horses, fiery, ridden by forty men between heaven and earth, lxxxvii. 7; riders of, fight against one another for forty days, lxxxvii. 7

Hosea, son of Elah, kills Pekah, lx. 1; reigns five years over Israel in Samaria, lx. 1; presents Sennacherib with the golden calf which Jeroboam had placed in Bethel, lx. 2

Hushiel, angel who smites wicked in fifth compartment of hell, xx. 9

I (words with I *vide* also under J and Y)

Iberi, children of Tubal, xxxi. 4

Idols for the first time, xxiv. 9; of gold and brass which could speak, made by Dialus, lviii. 8

Iglesusi, dwell by the river of the great sea, xxxi. 11

Ilag, son of Canaan, xxvii. 4

Inachus, King of Argos at Jacob's birth, xxxv. 7; father of Io, surnamed Izides by Egyptians, xxxv. 7

India, Elhanan came from land of, lxiii. 20; fords of, captured by Cyrus, lxxviii. 1; subdued by Alexander, lxxxv. 8 (*vide* Endiana)

Intriguer descends to hell for ever, xv. 6

Io, daughter of Inachus, by Egyptians given surname of Izides, xxxv. 7

Irad, son of Enoch, xxiv. 4

R. Isaac, proverbial sayings of, xi. 4

R. Isaac b. Parnach, concerning record of man's merits and sins, xii. 1

Isaiah, prophecy of, fulfilled, lx. 5; in Hele, xvi. 1

Ishai, son of Ashur, xxvii. 5

Ishmael, son of Netaniah, slays Gedaliah, lx. 10; R., death of, xxi. 2

Ishmaelites, kings of, pay tribute to Judah and half Simeon, lxiii. 19

Isles of the sea, inhabitants of, descended from Dodanim, xxvii. 2

Ispania, children of Tubal, xxxi. 4

Isqlabi (Slavonians), their boundaries, descendants of Dodanim, xxxi. 15

Israelites, wicked only punished in their lifetime, xx. 7; destroy Hittites, Jebusites, Amorites, Girgashites and Hivites, xxxi. 18; carried manure upon their shoulders, xlii. 3; dug channels in Egypt, xlii. 3; cleansed the channels of Egypt, xlii. 3; refuse to listen to Aaron's admonitions, xliv. 15; destruction of, impossible by fire or sword, but possible by water, xlvi. 4; sent away with many gifts, xlviii. 9; prevail over the Egyptian rabble, who want to prevent Israelites from going, xlviii. 12; dwelling in Egypt flee to Amon, lx. 10; flee to Egypt in the twenty-seventh year of Nebuchadnezzar's reign, lx. 10; refuse to intermarry with the heathen, lxxxi. 6; condemned because they did not ascribe to God the power of delivering them in the days of Nebuchadnezzar, lxxxiii. 1; fast, lxxxvi. 2

Isrub, King of Tapuah, prowess of, xxxvi. 2

Issachar, constellation of, Aries, liii. 12; stone of, the topaz, liii. 13; ensign of, a strong ass, liii. 14; asked the idols what would become of them, lvii. 9; tribe of, fulfil the commandments, lxii. 9; tribe of, are pious men, hating oppression, lxii. 9; tribe of, dwell on the mountains of the great deep in the nethermost parts of Media and Persia, lxi. 4, lxii. 9, lxiii. 15; tribe of, inhabit a large country, lxii. 9; tribe of, dwell in peace, lxii. 9; tribe of, have abundance of cattle, camels and servants, but do not breed horses, lxii. 9; honesty of servants of tribe of, lxii. 9; tribe of, have no warlike weapons, lxii. 9; tribe of, have captains of the army, but never fight, lxii. 9, lxiii. 15; tribe of, speak Hebrew and Persian languages, and that of Kedar, lxii. 10, lxiii. 15; neighbours of, worship fire and marry their mothers and sisters, lxii. 10; children of, dwell on an area of thirteen days' journey in each direction, lxiii. 15; children of, very numerous, lxiii. 15; children of, receive as tribute from the heathen kingdoms a fourth of all yearly produce and a fifth of the flocks and herds, lxiii. 15; children of, fulfil the law, lxiii. 15; children of, possess silver and gold, servants, camels, flocks and herds in plenty, lxiii. 15

Italy, whole of, ruled by Sefo-Janus

Saturnus, xl. 9; ruled by Janus Saturnus, Ficus and Faunus, lix. 10

Itan, land of, where Jonithem was sent by Noah, xxxii. 1

Iteb, son of Dodanim, xxvii. 2

Ithamar succeeds Aaron, xlviii. 17

Izides, surname of Io, daughter of Inachus, xxxv. 7

J (words written with J *vide* also under I and Y)

Jabal, father of those who live in tents, xxiv. 5, xxvi. 14; invented locks against thieves, xxiv. 5, xxvi. 19

Jabin, a prophet called by Kenaz when his days were drawing to a close, lvii. 39

Jabneh, captured by Judah, xcvii. 3; burning of, seen as far as Jerusalem, xcvii. 4

Jacob, sons of, dwell in third house in Eden, xx. 6; speaks in third house in Eden, xx. 7; kills Zehori, King of Shiloh, xxxvi. 4; kills Susi, King of Sartan, Laban, King of Horan (or Heldon), and Shakir (or Shikkor), King of Mahna(im), xxxvi. 6; children of, fight with the Amorites, xxxvii. 1 *et seq.*; grasps two rudders, xxxviii. 7; reproves Joseph, xxxviii. 9; commands his sons not to unite with sons of Joseph, but only with sons of Levi and Judah, xxxviii. 10

Jael, prayer of, lviii. 4; wife of Heber, lviii. 5

Jair commands his servants to burn seven righteous men who spoke against Baal, lviii. 10; and all his house consumed by fire, with Baal and 10,000 of his followers, lviii. 10; servants of, burned instead of the seven righteous men whom they tried to throw in the fire, lviii. 10; buried at Qamon, lviii. 10; the Gileadite makes an altar to Baal, lviii. 10 (*vide* Yair)

Jambris, son of Balaam, appointed captain of the host, xlv. 2; ordered by Moses to be summoned before him, xlvii. 6 (*vide* Mamre)

Jania, only daughter of Usi, married Agnios, King of Africa, xl. 4

Jannes, son of Balaam, appointed captain of the host, xlv. 2; ordered by Moses to be summoned before him, xlvii. 6 (*vide* Johanai)

Januarius added by Huma Pompilius, lix. 11

Janus, festival of, in honour of Ṣefo, xl. 7; smites plundering troops of Gondalus, xl. 8; ruled Italy, lix. 10

Japheth, children of, xxvii. 1, xxxi. 6; numbered by Pinhas, xxviii. 3; number of children of, xxviii. 3

Jaspiṣi, daughter of Astrubel, so beautiful that the men of her generation wove her image upon their clothes, xl. 10; captured and married by Latinus, xl. 12

Javan, sons of, xxvii. 1; subdues Seel, xxvii. 3; are Grēsi, xxxi. 4; children of (the Greeks), xxxi. 8

Jechoniah, second captivity of Nebuchadnezzar caused by, lx. 7

Jedid subdued by Faneg, xxvii. 3

Jehoiachin advises Nebuchadnezzar the Younger to take his father's corpse from the grave, cut it into 300 pieces, and give them to 300 vultures, lxvi. 6; a great and pious Jew in Babylon who married Susanna, lxv. 1; house of, visited by two judges to deliver judgment to the people, lxv. 2

R. Jehudah, ii. 5; concerning punishments for different crimes, xiii. 4; says that the death of Moses is referred to ten times in Holy Writ, l. 2

Jepheth, *vide* Japheth

Jephthah sends messengers to Giteal, King of the Ammonites, lix. 1; prays to God in Mizpah, lix. 1; vow of, lix. 2; daughter of, has four days in the year devoted to her memory by the women of Israel, lix. 8

Jerahmeel, xxxi. 15, xxxii. 1, xxxv. 2

Jered, sons of, xxvi. 7; daughters of, xxvi. 7; name given to Moses by his sister, xliv. 7

Jeremiah carried from Egypt to Babylon by Nebuchadnezzar, lx. 10; prayer of, answered, lx. 11; hides the holy fire, lxxvii. 3; becomes angry with the priests who followed him, and swears they will never discover the ark until he and Elijah appear, lxxvii. 9; carries the ark up to Mount Nebo, and places it in a cave, lxxvii. 9; on the appearance of, the tabernacle, and the tent of the congregation, ark of the testimony, and the two tables of stone will be restored, lxxvii. 9

Jeroboam presides over, but is not smitten, in fourth compartment of hell, xx. 8; orders Israelites to wage war against Rehoboam, lxiii. 4

Jerusalem in God's mind at Creation, i. 4; captured by King of Babylon, xl. 20; the light which illumines man's path, lvii. 41; exiles from, all youths of Judah and Benjamin, l. 9; Judah and half Simeon dwell near, lxiii. 19; walls of, rebuilt by Ezra, Zerubbabel and his company, lxxxv. 1 (*vide* Judah)

Jeshua at the head of the Jews returning from Babylon, lxxi. 3

Jew, Jews, anyone mentioning the name of, to be slain, xc. 1; offers a swine's head upon the altar of Antiochus, xc. 7; terrified at the multitude of Seron's army, pray to God, xcii. 2; make covenant with Romans, xcvii. 2; live in all the cities of the sea coast from Aza to Acco, xcvii. 3; persuaded by the Macedonians to board their ships to have sports on the sea, and are thrown into it, xcvii. 3; mourn for Eleazar, xcviii. 5 (*vide* Israelites, Judah)

Jinôn, son of Ziptḥai, xxvii 2

Jishub, waters of, where sons of Jacob rested, xxxvi. 8

Joab, fall caused by power, x. 10

Job, advice of, that Pharao should do what he pleased, xlvi. 4

Jobah, son of Yoqtan, xxvii. 5

Jochebed, wife of Amram, xlii. 8, xliv. 1; Moses child of, adopted by Pharaoh's daughter, xlii. 9, xliv. 4

Johanai, an Egyptian wizard, liv. 8 (*vide* Jannes)

Johanai and Mamre fly as far as the firmament by means of their wiles, liv. 8; princes of witchcraft, liv. 8

R. Johanan less fair than the angels, xviii. 3; on sinner's confession, xiv. 2; concerning punishment of sinners, xiv. 8; concerning the angels appointed over sinners, xv. 5; b. Nuri, concerning duration of punishment, xiii. 7; b. Zakkai, in third compartment of Paradise, xviii. 7; messenger of Lysias, xcv. 5

Johnios, *i.e.*, Ptolemy, chosen one of the generals of Lysias, xcii. 5

Jonadab did not worship Baal in the days of Yair, lviii. 10

Jonathan buried Judah, c. 5

Jonithem, son of Noah, xxxii. 1; and Nimrod, xxxii. 1; told Nimrod that descendants of Ashur would reign first, xxxii. 1; sent to the land of Itan by Noah, which he held as far as the sea of Eliochora, xxxii. 1

Joppa besieged and captured by Judah, xcvii. 4

R. Jose, legend of Adam told by, xi. 4

Joseph born in Jacob's ninety-second year, xxxv. 9; less fair than the angels, xviii. 3; in Naphtali's vision, xxxviii. 3; children of, will depart from God, xxxviii. 3; mounts a bull, xxxviii. 4; beats his brother Judah, xxxviii. 4; refuses to take his oar, xxxviii. 7; grasps both rudders, xxxviii. 8; quarrels with Judah, and ship founders, xxxviii. 8; beauty of, disturbs Egyptian women, xxx. 2; the Egyptian women peeling apples, xl. 2; coffin of, carried by Moses, xlviii. 10; bones of, searched for by Moses, li. 1; coffin of lead made by magicians of Egypt, weighing 500 talents, and thrown into river, li. 2; coffin of, ascends as a reed, li. 3; coffin of, borne by Moses upon his shoulders, li. 3; R. Joseph, his Midrash of Shemḥazai and Azael, xxv. 1; J. ben Gorion asserts that Joshua decreed that water should be poured upon the ground instead of blood, lvi. 2; ben Gorion, book of, lxvi. 6, xc. 9; ben Gorion, anointed priest of battle, who was exiled from Jeru-

salem in the reign of Vespasianus, Book of, lxxviii. 1
Joshua, Moses prays God to let him rule while he (Moses) may continue to live, li. 6; succeeds Moses, xlviii. 17; decrees that water should be poured upon the ground instead of blood, lvi. 2; J., son of Jehozadak, the high priest, chosen by Ahab and Zedekiah to accompany them in the furnace, lxiv. 4; the high priest not touched by the fire, his garments merely smelling of fire, lxiv. 4; explains his clothes smelling of fire as caused by his being accompanied by two wicked men, lxiv. 5; R., estimates world's depth, ii. 4; R., b. Levi, concerning man's merits and sins, xii. 2; R., b. Levi, concerning man's ordeal at death, xiii. 2; R., b. Levi, interview with Elijah, xv. 1; R., b. Levi, description of Paradise, xviii. 1 et seq.; R., b. Levi, vision of, xx. 3
Josiah, God's beloved, ends his days in battle, lxxviii. 2
Josippon, Book of, xxx. 2; a portion of, added by Eliazer the Levite, xxxi. 4; relates how Abraham sat under an oak, which lasted till reign of Theodosius, in Rome, xxxv. 5; relates buoyancy of Dead Sea, xxxv. 6; according to, incident of Micah and concubine of Gibeah occurred between Joshua and Othniel, lviii. 1 (vide Joseph b. Gorion)
Jotham, King of Judah, during whose rule Remus and Romulus rule over Rome, xli. 1
Jovis, god of Egypt, revealed himself in the form of a ram, and was called Serapis, xlii. 1 (vide Apis)
Jovisdi (i.e., Thursday), iv. 2
Jubal, father of those who play on the harp and reed-pipe, xxiv. 5, xxvi. 14; discoverer of the science of music, xxiv. 6, xxvi. 15; wrote science of music on two pillars, xxiv. 7, xxvi. 16
Judah, prowess of, xxxvi. and xxxvii.; engages Isrub, king of Tapuah, xxxvi. 2; slays Isrub, xxxvi. 2; urges his father to fight with Esau, xxxvii. 4; engages nine comrades of Isrub, xxxvi. 4; first to climb walls of Haṣor, xxxvi. 6; prayer of, accepted by God, xxxvii. 12; takes a staff, jumps upon the sun, and rides upon it, xxxviii. 3; Benjamin and Levi alone remain with, xxxviii. 5; sits upon mast, xxxviii. 7; stone of, the sardius, liii. 13; ensign of, a lion's whelp, liii. 14; the tribe of, selected to lead the people, lvii. 1; confesses the making of a calf, lvii. 9; J. the Maccabean burns the sinners with the fire of his mouth, xc. 4; clothed in a coat of mail, looks like a giant, xc. 4; anointed for battle by his father, Mattathiah, xci. 3; called Maccabee, on account of his power exhorted by Mattathiah to lead his brethren in battle, xci. 3; takes his father's place, xci. 4; fights a fierce battle with Apollonius, xcii. 1; seizes the sword of Apollonius, with which he fights for the rest of his life, xcii. 1; strikes terror into Seron's army and smites them, xcii. 3; proclaims a fast, xcii. 5; marches out to meet Nicanor and prays to God, xcii. 7; commands those who have planted vineyards, or built a house, or have married or are faint-hearted to return home, xcii. 6; smites the camp of Nicanor, xcii. 7; distributes gold taken from the merchants among the poor, xcii. 7; captures Phillipio, xciii. 1; fights Bakires and Timotheos in a severe battle, and puts them to flight, xciii. 1; dedicates the altar of the 25th of Kislev, xciv. 1; with Hassidim goes to Jerusalem, overthrows the heathen altar, and cleanses the Temple, xciv. 1; battle with Gorgias, xciv. 2; smites Gorgias, xciv. 2; judges his people, and weeds out the wicked from their midst, xcvii. 2; with Hassidim passes the Jordan, xciv. 3; puts the Macedonian camp to confusion, xciv. 4; finds Timotheos attacking the city Gilead, xciv. 4;

encouraged by the vision of the five horsemen, smites Timotheos, xciv. 4; and the Hasmoneans in the forests and mountains, xcv. 2; goes out to assist his brethren in Bethter, xcv. 3; and the Hasmoneans enter Jerusalem, xcv. 3; sees a man riding between heaven and earth, xcv. 4; receives a letter from Romans, xcvii. 1; having smitten many Arabs, imposes a tribute upon them, xcvii. 4; after separating the Jews, kills the inhabitants of Joppa and burns the place, xcvii. 4; passes the strongly fortified city of Raspon, xcvii. 5; defeats the army of Timotheos, xcvii. 7; orders the head of Timotheos to be cut off, xcvii. 7; spares the life of Timotheos, xcvii. 7; besieges Ephron, xcvii. 8; marches to Scitopolis, xcvii. 9; returns to Jerusalem three days before the festival of Pentecost, xcvii. 9; marches against Gorgias, xcviii. 1; destroys cities of Edom, xcviii. 2; judges his people, and acts righteously and justly, xcix. 1; meets Nicanor, xcix. 3; summons his Hassidim and Hasmoneans and goes to Samaria, xcix. 4; calls upon Nicanor to meet him in the field, xcix. 8; defeats Nicanor and kills him, xcix. 10, 11; remains at his post with only 800 men and his brothers, c. 1; engages in a battle the army of Bakidos, c. 3; rushes at Bakidos, who attempts to flee, c. 4; is killed in the battle outside Ashdod, c. 5; prospers all the days of his life, c. 5; mourned by Israel for many days, c. 5; buried by Simeon and Jonathan, c. 5; ministered unto the Lord for six years, c. 5

Judah and Benjamin, tribes of, scattered over the whole world, lxii. 12

Judah and half tribe of Simeon journey the way of Mathol and of Babylon, until the city of the madman, lxiii. 19; are very numerous and have lions' faces, lxiii. 19; dwell in a wilderness in tents made of hair, lxiii. 19; speak Hebrew and Greek, and also the language of Togarma, lxiii. 19; are men of faith, versed in the Scriptures, lxiii. 19; wage war with strange kingdoms, lxiii. 19; dwell in the land of the Chasdim near Jerusalem, lxiii. 19; are proficient riders, archers, spearsmen, and swordsmen, lxiii. 19; receive tribute from twenty-five white kings, some of whom are Ishmaelites, and other descendants of Keturah, lxiii. 19

Judgment three days, xiii. 3, 4 (vide Grave, Hell, Paradise)

Julius Cæsar, first king of Rome, after an interval of 464 years, xli. 2

Jupiter, rules on fifth day, iv. 2; appointed over life, iv. 7; appearance of, iv. 7

Kaforisio, mountain, xl. 6

Kaftorim, son of Misraim, xxvii. 4

Kalna, Seleuqos changed name of, to Seleuqia, xxi. 18

Kaphnaya (or Kapanya), plain of, where Kittim dwell, xl. 1; in the land of the Kittim, in which Janus built a temple and reigned, xl. 9

Kaphtor, land of, captured by Cyrus, lxxviii. 1

Kaporisio, mountain climbed by Kittim, xl. 1 (vide Kaforisio)

Karpitos, succeeds Qapis, xlv. 14

Kasluḥim, son of Misraim, xxvii. 4

Kaspon, the inhabitants of, curse Judah, he sets it on fire, xcvii. 5; the pool of blood flowing from this city was two stadia in length and two in breadth, xcvii. 5

Kedar, language of, lxiii. 10; language of, spoken by Issachar, lxii. 10, lxiii. 15; language of, spoken by Reuben, lxii. 11

Kedron, brook of, called Sambatyon, which encompasses the four tribes, lxiii. 11

Kehath, camp of, liii. 15

Kenaz, lot falls upon, as leader, lvii. 2; address of, to the Israelites, lvii. 3; with Eleazar, prays to God to know what to do with sinners, lvii. 7; finds the books of the Amorites under the Mount Abarim, lvii. 10; finds books (?) of the Amorites in the tent of Elah, lvii. 12; finds seven golden idols of the Amorites under Mount Shechem, lvii. 13; enters all the replies of the sinners in a book, and recites them before God, lvii. 15; tests the stones by iron, it slips away from under them, lvii. 20; tests books in fire, it is extinguished, lvii. 20; tests books by water, it becomes dry upon them, lvii. 21; finds twelve precious stones, upon which were engraved the names of the sons of Israel, lvii. 22; puts twelve stones in the Ark of the Testimony with the tables of the Covenant, lvii. 25; people speak against, lvii. 26; thirty-seven men who had spoken against, cast into prison, lvii. 27; calumniators of, burnt with fire, lvii. 37; asks prisoners what complaint they prefer against him, lvii. 37; with a shofar in his hand approaches the Amorites with 300 men, lvii. 30; approaches the camp of the Amorites alone, lvii. 30; prayer of, lvii. 31; lightning sword of, lvii. 32; asks God for a sign of salvation, lvii. 32; smites the Amorites single-handed, lvii. 34; slays 45,000 Amorites, lvii. 34; sword of, cleaves to his hand, lvii. 35; slays an Amorite, and by pouring his warm blood upon his hand separates his sword from it, lvii. 35; finds Israelites in a deep sleep, lvii. 35; prophesies, the Spirit of the Lord coming upon him, lvii. 39; prophecy of, lvii. 40

Kerethi and Pelethi, the students of the Law, thus called in the days of David, lx. 7

Keturah, descendants of, pay tribute to Judah and half Simeon, lxiii. 19

Kings, represented by the head in Isaiah's prophecy, lx. 5; in the riddles, the most powerful persons on earth, lxxiv. 8, lxxv. 1

Kio (or Kiva), river which flows into the Gergan Sea, xxxi. 11

Kittim, number of children of, xxviii. 3; *i.e.*, Qipres, xxxi. 4; *i e.*, the Romans dwell in the valley of Kapania by river Tiberio, xxxi. 14; go to Sabino, take the daughters of Tubal captive, and climb the mountain Kaporisio, xl. 1; encamp in plain of Kaphnaya (Campania), and dwell by the river Tiberio, xl. 1; build three cities by the sea, which they call Porto, Albano, and Arēṣah, xl. 2 (*vide* Ṣefo)

Kiuza, built by Misraim, xxvii. 4

Kor, measure of (or, chorus), discovered in Greece in the time of Abimelech, lviii. 9

Korah, generation of, excepted from dwelling in third house in Eden, xx. 6; presides over, but not smitten, in third compartment of hell, xx. 7; rebellion of, lv.; complained to, by the woman, lv. 2; expostulates with Aaron, lv. 4; weaves 400 garments of blue for 400 men, lv. 5; foolish complaint of wife of, lv. 8; counsel of wife of, lv. 9

Kush, rivers of, where four tribes of Dan, Naphtali, Gad, and Asher dwell, lxii. 4; sons of, pay the Danites tribute, lxii. 6; *i.e.*, Havila, a rich and fertile land, lxiii. 5; sixty-five kings of, dwell on one side of Pishon, lxiii. 6; kings of, engaged in constant battle with the four tribes, lxiii. 7; rivers of, called Zahab Tob, lxiii. 8; names of the kingdoms of, lxiii. 8 (*vide* Cush)

Lailah, angel appointed over conception, ix. 1

Lakhish, built by Misraim, xxvii, 4

Lamp of gold before the throne of Solomon, lxxxiv. 4

Langobardi, children of Japheth, xxxi. 4 (*vide* Lungobardi)

Languages, confusion of, xxx. 5, 8; strange, spoken by the children of Reuben, lxiii. 17

Laqmi, angel who rules over hail, xxxv. 8

Latin, language spoken in Rome, xxxi. 1; alphabet, invented by Nizpa in the time of Jair, lviii. 11

Latini, so called because its inhabitants spoke the Latin language, lix. 10

Latinus, successor of Piqos Faunos, explained language and its letters, xl. 10; succeeds Seliaqos, xl. 13; fought Almania and Burgunia, sons of Elisa, xl. 13

Latusqah, a kingdom in Kush, lxiii. 8

Law, the, created before creation, i. 2; finds all the Israelites dead, lii. 11; meets Satan in widow's garments, weeping, lxxxii. 3

Lebanon in Ham's portion, xxxi. 2

Lebuzer-Dukh, Son of Evil Merodach, lxvi. 6

Led, son of Gomer, xxvii. 2

Lehabim, i.e., the Flaminga, xxxi. 18

Lemech, son of Metushael, xxiv. 4; two wives of, xxiv. 5, xxvi. 14; sons of, xxvi. 9, 14; sons of, purify city Enoch, xxiv. 3

Lesha, i.e., Qaliron, its waters warm, and flow into Salt Sea, xxxi. 18

Letters created on second day, i. 3; by means of the letters Yod Hē, God created the world, liii. 6 (vide Cadmus, Nizpa)

Levi kills king of Ga'ash, xxxvi. 4; takes a staff, jumps upon the sun, and rides upon it, xxxviii. 8; ascends big mast and sits upon it, xxxviii. 7; tested the holiness of the tabernacle, lvii. 9

Leviathan, created on fifth day, v. 1; a huge serpent, v. 1; fed daily by a serpent, v. 1

Levites encamped between the tabernacle and the camps of the other tribes, liii. 15; occupy one-eighth of the whole area of the tribes, liii. 18; occupied in their ministrations at the time of the banishment, lxi. 1; sons of Moses, made ten journeys, lxii. 1; cut off their fingers, so that they cannot play their harps, lxii. 1; together with their wives and children lifted by a cloud, lxii. 2; brought by the Lord to the seashore, lxii. 2; given light by night by a pillar of fire, lxii. 2; surrounded on three sides by the river, and on the fourth by the sea, lxii. 2; journey and encamp at Havila, lxii. 8; journey from one border to another, a distance of four days' travelling, lxii. 8; dwell in tents made of skin, lxii. 8; inflict capital punishment according to Jewish law, lxii. 8 (vide Moses)

Lice, plague of, details of, xlviii. 8

Light created on the first day, i. 3; quarrel between two, iii. 1; enlargement and diminishing of, iii. 1; hidden, shines, lvii. 41; which illumines the path of man is Jerusalem, lvii. 41

Lightning sword of Kenaz, lvii. 32

Lilith, the first Eve, begets demons from Adam, xxiii. 1

Lions at Pharaoh's gate warded off by Moses, xlvii. 5; image of, to be prayed to by those desiring strength, lix. 12; daily fare of, consisted of ten sheep and ten human bodies, lxx. 6; starved so that they should hasten to devour Daniel, lxx. 6; lick Daniel and wag their tails upon seeing him, lxx. 6; destroy his enemies, lxx. 10

Lipukh, son of Cush, xxvii. 4

Lira, river in land of Riphath, xxxi. 6, xl. 14

Lot given by Terah to Abram as his adopted son, xxxv. 1

Lud, son of Gomer, xxvii. 2; son of Shem, xxvii. 5; inhabited by children of Zebulun, lxiii. 16

Ludim, son of Misraim, xxvii. 4

Lunedi (i.e., Monday), iv. 2

Lungobardi arose from Elisa, xxxii. 12; conquered Italia, xxxi. 12

Luon, son of Tisai, xxvii. 2

Lusifer, i.e., Nogah, temple of, built by Latinus II., priests passed through fire on the altar of this temple, xl. 13

Lysias leads an army against Judea, xcii. 4; sends strong armies against Judah, xcii. 5; makes a covenant with Judah, xciv. 4; and his men fly in shame and disorder, xciv. 4; gives battle to Judah at Bethter, xcv. 2; sent by Antiochus Eupator against Judah, xcv. 2; charges the messengers sent to Judah with words of peace, xcv. 5; letter of, to the people of Judah, xcv. 5

Maakh, sons of Tiras, xxvii. 2
Maccabees, Book of the, lxxxv.
Macedon, land of, captured by Cyrus, lxxviii. 1; yoke of, broken asunder from the shoulders of Judah, xc. 3
Macedonia inhabited by Greeks, xxxi. 8
Macedonians take to flight on entering temple, lxxxvi. 3; and the people of Joppa and Jabneh bring about great evil, xcvii. 3
Machik called saffron, lxiii. 2
Madai, number of children, xxviii. 3; subdue Bitto, xxvii. 3; i.e., Edalos, dwell in land of Turkhan, xxxi. 9 (vide Medians)
Madia, kingdom of Mehumat on the borders of, lxiii. 18 (vide Media)
Madman (i.e., Mahomed), city of the, Judah and half Simeon journey as far as, lxiii. 19
Mafshiel, son of Zipthai, xxvii. 2
Magog, sons of, xxvii. 2; subdued Degel, xxvii. 3; number of children, xxviii. 3; i.e., Sqite (Scythians), children of Japheth, xxxi. 4
Mahalalel, sons of, xxvi. 6; daughters of, xxvi. 6
Maipon, son of Cush, xxvii. 4
Maktiel, angel who smites wicked in fourth compartment of hell, xx. 8
Malkah, daughter of Ruth and wife of Reu, xxvii. 6: daughter of Haran given by Terah to Nahor as wife, xxxv. 1
Mamre, an Egyptian wizard, liv. 8 (vide Jambris)
Man short-lived will sin, vi. 8; will repent and be pardoned, vi. 8; height of, vi. 12; creatures afraid of, vi. 12; seven stages, ix. 9; righteous happy, x. 1; wicked unhappy, x. 2; compelled to relate his deeds, x. 6; appearance after death, xi. 6; iniquities engraved upon his bones, xii. 1; merits and sins not testified until his death, xii. 2; "The Old," and his seven counsellors rule Rome and subdue the West, xl. 19; the word applies to Moses, l. 4; images of, to be prayed to by those desirous of sons, lix. 12
Manasseh, stone of, the agate, liii.

13; constellation of Libra, liii. 13; ensign of, buffalo (or reem), liii. 14; did not observe the Sabbath, lvii. 15; presides over penitent in second house in Eden, xx. 5
Manna created on second day, i. 3
Mano in Japheth's portion, xxxi. 3
Maqol, son of Tisai, xxvii. 2
Maresha, desert of, in the wilderness of Edom, where Gorgias dies, xcviii. 1
Markusdi (i.e., Wednesday), iv. 2
Marriage of mothers and sisters, lxii. 10
Mars rules on third day, and his appearance, iv. 2
Marsdi (i.e., Tuesday), iv. 2
Martyrdom of seven sons, lxxxix.; of Eleazar, lxxxviii. 45
Martyrs in first compartment of Paradise, xviii. 7
Mastizrida, son of Elishah, xxvii. 2
Mathol, Judah and half Simeon journey the way of, lxiii. 19
Mattathiah, son of Johanan of Modaith, zealous for his God, xc. 2; sends for his son Judah to assemble those Jews who are willing to rebel against Antiochus, xc. 2; informs Hassidim to pray and to fight, xc. 3; armed for war at the mount of Modaith, xc. 5; is prepared to obey his king, let the Greeks obey their, xc. 6; slays the renegade Jew, xc. 8; gives the signal for war, xc. 8; commands the Jews to fight on the Sabbath, xc. 9; the first to raise his hand against the Macedonian kingdom, xc. 9; and the Hassidim circumcise their sons, xc. 10; on the point of death encourages and exhorts his sons, xci. 1; pours a horn of oil upon the head of Judah, thus anointing him for battle, xci. 3
Matter, four colours of, vi. 7
Mazäger built by Misraim, xxvii. 4
Moah, son of Tiras, xxvii. 2
Mecca, vide Meyuqah
Mecoth, roads leading to, infested by tribe of Reuben, lxii. 11
Medi, children of Madai, xxxi. 4
Media in Japheth's portion, xxxi. 3; nethermost parts of, inhabited by Issachar, lxii. 9 (vide Madai)

Medians descended from Dodanim, xxvii. 2

Medina, four months' journey from kingdom of Mehumat, lxiii. 18

Mehumat, kingdom of, a distance of four months' journey from the city of Medina, lxiii. 18; kingdom of, on the borders of Media, lxiii. 18

Mehuyael, son of Irad, xxiv. 4

Meir, R., concerning punishment, xiii. 5

Meletus, city of, built in the thirty-ninth year of Deborah's reign, lviii. 6

Members, functions of various, of the body, xxxviii. 14

Menelaus comes to Egypt in the time of Abdon, lix. 10; a prince of Rome, xcvii. 1; a godless man, incites Antiochus to injure the Jews, lxxxvii. 7; sent by Antiochus Eupator to speak words of peace to the Jews, xcv. 7; ordered to be taken to a tower fifty cubits high, from which he is thrown and buried in the ashes beneath, xcviii. 7

Menfis, i.e., Mof, built by Apis, King of Egypt, xlii. 1

Merari, camp of the sons of, liii. 15

Mercorius discovers animals called Sirenes in the reign of Gideon, lviii. 8

Mercury rules on fourth day, iv. 2; appointed over, iv. 8; form of, iv. 8

Meriba subdued by Tarshish, xxvii. 3

Merodon (Herodia), citadel of, where Esau's body was found, xxxvii. 14

Mesech, i.e., Saqsoni, xxxi. 10

Mesekhah, city of Qapadoses, xxxi. 4

Mesenes receives the kingdom of Argos, lviii. 6

Meshech, number of children, xxviii. 3

Meshek subdues Nephti, xxvii. 3 (vide Mesech)

Meshullam, son of Zerubbabel, succeeds him, lxxxv. 2; in his days the last prophets Haggai, Zechariah, and Malachi died, lxxxv. 2

Messiah, name of, created before Creation, i. 2; dwells in the fifth house in Eden, xx. 9; beloved by the daughters of Jerusalem, xx. 9; son of David, sits on palanquin in fifth house of Eden, xx. 9; consulted every Thursday by Korah and Absalom, xx. 10; repulses Korah and Absalom, xx. 10; consulted every Monday and Thursday, Sabbath and Holy Day by Moses and Aaron, etc., xx. 10; accompanies Joshua b. Levi in hell, xxi. 2

Metatron, messenger sent by God to Shemhazai, xxv. 8; ordered by God to throw Johanai and Mamre into the sea, liv. 8

Methuselah beseeches God's protection against the demons, xxiii. 2; son of Hanoch, why so called, xxiii. 4; wept for by holy creatures, xxiii. 5; made 230 parables in praise of God, xxiii. 5; mourned by 900 rows of mourners, xxiii. 5; studied 900 sections of the law, xxiii. 5; sons and daughters of, xxvi. 9

Metushael, son of Mehuyael, xxiv. 4

Meyuqa (Mecca?), tribes of Ephraim and half Menasseh dwell opposite city of, lxii. 12

Mezuzah required for a house full of holy books, lv. 5

Micah, presides over, but not smitten, in sixth compartment of hell, xxi. 10; incident of, lviii. 1; zeal of Israelites not shown against, lix. 15; acts as his mother tells him, lix. 12; incident of, in the days of Abdon, lix. 12; makes three images of man, three of calves, and the likeness of an eagle, lion, and serpent, lix. 12

Michael, head of the first band of angels, i. 9; the archangel, vi. 3; first of seventy ministering angels who teach seventy descendants of Noah seventy languages, xxxviii. 11; commands seventy nations to choose their protectors, xxxviii. 12; leads Moses out of Egypt, xlv. 15; assumes likeness of the chief executioner, severs head of the chief butcher, whose face was changed to the exact likeness of Moses, xliv. 15;

weeps at the approaching death of Moses, l. 8; asks how he can witness the death of one of his pupils, l. 10; arranges the bed of Moses, l. 14; upon whose heart God's great name is engraved, to go before Moses, lii. 13; unable to do anything against Joḥanai and Mamre, liv. 8; disturbs the sleep of Ahasuerus, knocking him on the ground 366 times, lxxxiii. 6

Midian, five kings slain by Moses, xlviii. 18

Midwives, Hebrew, Shifrah and Puah, advice of, xliii. 3

Milḥam, an immortal bird which rebukes Eve, xxii. 5, 8 (vide Hol)

Mimoel, son of Yoqtan, xxvii. 5

Minos, son of Eoripi, reigns in Crete, lvi. 5

Miriam, well of, created on second day, i. 3; dream of, xlii. 8; called "the bitter," because lives of Israelites were embittered, xliv. 1; prophesies, xliv. 2; dies, in the fortieth year of their wanderings, on the tenth day of the first month, xlviii. 17; buried in the wilderness of Sin, which is Qadest, xlviii. 17; well of, placed at the entrance of the court near Moses' tent, liii. 17

Misraim, children of, xxvii. 4, xxxi. 18; number of children, xxviii. 4; cities built by the sons of, xxvii. 4

Mizpah, Jephthah prays to God at, lix. 1

Moab, consulted Midian, lv. 10

Mobros, son of Qinqanos, made king by the Cushites, xlvi. 8

Modaith, mount of, where Mattathiah and the Ḥassidim brought their wives and children and armed for war, xc. 5; Mount, burial-place of Judah, c. 5

Mof, i.e., Menfis, built by Apis, King of Egypt, who was made a god, xlii. 1

Mondakh (i.e., Monday), iv. 2

Monkeys, man's form changed to, xxx. 5

Moon, work of, done quickly, iii. 3; habitation of, iii. 6; rules on second day, iv. 2; holds key of heaven and earth, iv. 9; appointed over, iv. 9

Mordecai, at the head of the Jews returning from Babylon, lxxi. 3; discovers the plot of Bigthen and Teresh, lxxix. 2; dream of, lxxix. 3; refusal of, to bow the knee to Haman, lxxix. 4; meets three children coming from school, lxxxi. 7; repeats the lesson each child has learned in school, lxxxi. 7; advice of, disregarded by the Israelites, lxxxii. 1; afflicts the school-children, lxxxii. 6

Moses, birth of, fills Amram's house with great delight, xliv. 2; born circumcised, l. 12; speaks on the day of his birth, l. 12; placed on banks of the Nile, xliv. 4; refuses the breasts of Egyptian women, xliv. 6; prophesies when three months old, l. 12; various names of, with their significations, xliv. 7; takes crown from Pharaoh's head and places it upon his own, xliv. 8, l. 12; seizes the live coal and places it upon his lips, which causes him heaviness of speech, xliv. 11; is reared together with Pharaoh's sons, xliv. 12; reason why he slew the Egyptian, xliv. 12; height, strength, and beauty, xlv. 4; comes to Qinqanos, xlv. 4; king's counsellor, xlv. 4; king over the Cushites, xlv. 5; marries the widow of Qinqanos, xlv. 5; advice to the besiegers, storks trained, xlv. 6; conquers Edom, East of Palestine and Syria, xlvi. 7; does not approach his Cushite wife, xlvi. 7; reigns over Cush forty years, xlvi. 7; accused by his wife, the widow of Qinqanos, xlvi. 8; given valuable gifts and sent away by the Cushites, xlvi. 8; sixty-seven years old when he left Cush, xlvi. 9; assists the daughters of Reuel to water their flock, xlvi. 9; goes to Midian, xlvi. 9; put in prison for ten years by Reuel, xlvi. 9; found alive in prison, xlvi. 11; sees a staff made of sapphires fixed in Reuel's garden, xlvi. 11; uproots staff, which has the ineffable name of God engraved upon it, xlvi. 11;

staff of, history of, xlvi. 12; rod of, created on second day, i. 3; seventy-seven years old when he quits prison and marries Zipporah, xlvi. 13; as wizard, who brought great plagues upon Pharaoh and his household, lxxxi. 3; God appears to, in the burning bush at Horeb, xlvii. 1; appearance of, like that of the children of God, xlvii. 5; wards off young lions at Pharaoh's gate with his rod, xlvii. 5; bids Joseph's coffin ascend, li. 3; takes Joseph's coffin with him, xlviii. 10; searches for Joseph's bones, li. 1; speaks face to face with God, conquers host of heaven, l. 12; does not approach his wife from the day when God revealed Himself to him in the bush, l. 15; rends sea into sixty parts, treads path of heaven, l. 12; performs miracles, l. 12; receives law, is hidden behind a cloud, l. 12; wars with Sihon and Og, l. 12; captures the land of Sihon and Og, xlviii. 13; fights against Midian, xlviii. 13; given the 618 precepts by God, xlviii. 16; informed by God that time for Aaron s death has arrived, xli. 1; accused of killing Aaron by the Iraelites, xlix. 1; proclaims God before sixty myriads of angels, l. 1; exalted by God before fifty-five myriads of angels, l. 1; told by God that the time of his death has approached, l. 1; not to enter the promised land ten times decreed, l. 2; decree that he was not to enter the promised land not sealed until the great tribunal had decided, l. 2; decree of death lightly felt by, since he hoped for pardon, l. 3; prayer moves the earth and very creation, l. 4; fasts and prays, l. 4; prayer of, rent and cut like a sword and was not impeded, l. 5; prayer not to be accepted, l. 5; begs God to annul this decree on account of the anxiety he has suffered on behalf of the Israelites, l. 7; takes a scroll, writes the ineffable name upon it, and recites his last song, l. 10;

the most righteous of all the prophets, l. 8; implores God to let him live as one of the beasts of the field, l. 9; to let him live as a bird that flies in the air, l. 9; hears a voice (Bath-Kol) declare that his last moment has arrived, l. 13; hastens to the house of Joshua, li. 6; separated from Joshua by the pillar of cloud, li. 6; jealousy shown by, to Joshua, li. 6; seizes the Angel of Death and compels him to go before him while he blesses the twelve tribes, li. 7; beats Samael with his staff, l 13; soul of, addressed by God, l. 14; sanctifies himself as one of the seraphim, l. 14; hears a voice say that God Himself will attend his burial, l. 13; death of, xlix. 7, li. ; dies in the same year as Aaron and Miriam, on the seventh day of the twelfth month, i.e., Adar, xlviii. 17; earth weeps at death of, l. 15; Israelites weep at death of, l. 15; soul of, entreats God, l. 15; Heaven weeps at death of, l. 15; God weeps at death of, l. 15; soul of, taken by a kiss of God, l. 15; special merit of which caused God Himself to attend to his burial, li. 1; soul refused to depart from him, li. 8; buried in the valley at the nethermost part of Mount Abarim, xlviii. 17; to be shown the same mercy by God as He showed to Joseph, li. 3; soul of, carried by God to the highest heavens, l. 14; enters the cloud and is carried aloft, lii. 1; walked along the firmament, lii. 1, 2; ascended to receive the law, a cloud appeared before him, lii. 1; meets Hadarniel, lii. 2; God's mercy moved for, lii. 3; protected by God, passes the fire of Sandalphon, lii. 5; comes to Rigion, lii. 7; taken across Rigion by God, lii. 7; meets Galiṣur, lii. 8; every angel handed secret cure to, lii. 9; meets a troop of angels of terror, lii. 9; God opens the firmaments for, shows heavenly temple to, lii. 10; explained the different hues by

God, lii. 10; fire of the lightnings of, stronger than that of the angels, lii. 13; camp of, liii. 15; makes four decrees for Levites, lv. 6; forcibly lifts up the Levites from the ground against their will and heaves them, lv. 7; and Aaron preside over third house in Eden, xx. 6; sons of, lxi.; sons of, bite off their own fingers so as not to be forced to play upon their harps, lxi. 1; sons of, with their sheep and cattle lifted by a cloud and brought to the east of Havila, lxi. 3; land of children of, contains no wild beast, unclean animal, reptile, lxi. 3; sons of, made ten journeys, lxii. 1; no unclean animal or bird or creeping thing seen among children of, lxii. 3; sons of, men of faith, students of the law, lxii. 3; sons of, pious, never swear falsely, lxii. 3; sons of, attain 120 years, and no child dies in the lifetime of its parents, lxii. 3; sons of, sow one seed and reap a hundredfold, lxii. 3; sons of, see three generations, lxii. 4; sons of, do not close their houses in the night-time, lxii. 4; sons of, see only tribes of Dan, Naphtali, Gad and Asher, lxii. 4; sons of, fear no robbers or injury, lxii. 4; sons of, dwell on the other side of the Sabbatyon until the end of the world, lxii. 4; sons of, sow and plough for themselves, having no servants, lxii. 4; sons of, dwell close to the four tribes, lxiii. 11; sons of, received their tradition from Moses and Joshua, but do not know the other sages, lxiii. 13; children of, well versed in the Torah, lxiii. 13; Chronicles of, xli. 2, xliii.

Mother of seven martyrs, seventh son, a mere lad, exhorted by his, lxxxix. 8; of the seven sons, neither feared nor trembled, but standing by the corpses of her sons, exhorts the seventh and last son, lxxxix. 8; falling upon the corpses of her sons, dies with them, lxxxix. 14

Mountains, creation of, ii. 1; of snow, two, where sinners are led on Sabbath eve, xv. 7; above world, xvii. 4; of the deep inhabited by Issachar, lxi. 4, lxii. 9, lxiii. 15; of darkness, children of Reuben possess land in midst of, lxiii. 17

Muzam, son of Yoqtan, xxvii. 5

Naamah, sister of Tubal Cain, xxiv. 8; inventor of instruments for weaving and sowing, xxiv. 8

Nadab, son of Aaron, x. 10

Naftuḥim, son of Misraim, xxvii. 4

Naḥor, son of Serug, xxvii. 7; sons and daughters of, xxvii. 7

Name, ineffable, written upon tables of the law, lv. 12; upon rod of Moses, xlvii. 2; upon the banners, liii. 6

Naphtali comes to Judah's assistance, xxxvi. 6; will of, xxxviii.; implores his children not to join children of Joseph, but the children of Levi and Judah, xxxviii. 2; first vision of, xxxviii. 3; second vision of, xxxviii. 6; constellation of, Pisces, liii. 13; stone of, the jasper, liii. 13; ensign of, a hind, liii. 14; did all that the Amorites did, lvii. 12

Napoli, xl. 16

Nathan the prophet, golden seat put for, lxxxiv. 3

Nation, small, dwelling between two dragons, seen by Mordecai in dream, lxxix. 3

Nebo, Mount, ark placed by Jeremiah in a cave on, lxxvii. 9

Nebuchadnezzar slays Sanhedrin, x. 10; banishes the Israelites four times, lx. 1; banishes Israelites to Babylon, lx. 6; banishes the remnant of Judah and Benjamin, lx. 6; exiles the students of the law, lx. 7; exiles the free and imprisoned, *i.e.*, the kings and queens, lx. 7; captures Jerusalem, lx. 7; makes Zedekiah king of Judah, who reigns eleven years, lx. 8; slays all the Jews found in Ammon and Moab and Egypt, lx. 10; finds Jeremiah and Baruch, son of Neriya, in Egypt, and carries them to Babylon, lx. 10; captures Egypt and reduces it to desolation, lx. 10; besieges Tyre, kills its inhabitants, and exiles its king, lx. 10; King of Babylon, roasts false prophets in the fire, lxiv. 1; told by Ahab and Zedekiah that they were instructed by God, lxiv. 3; tests Ahab and Zedekiah in fiery furnace, lxiv. 4; wandered about in caves for forty days, lxvi. 1; chewed his food like an ox and killed the wicked like a lion, lxvi. 1; appeared like an ox as far as his navel, and from his navel to his feet like a lion, lxvi. 1; wept for his sins during the second forty days, lxvi. 1; changed only in appearance, mind and language, lxvi. 1; roamed among the wild beasts for forty days, lxvi. 1; appoints seven judges, lxvi. 2; wishes to make Daniel one of his heirs, but Daniel refuses, lxvi. 2; lives on herbs and seed whilst repenting for his sins, lxvi. 2; the Younger builds a temple to Bel in Babylon, lxvi. 3; the Younger plants a garden upon a mountain that his wife may gaze upon Media, the land of her birth, lxvi. 4; the Younger, besieges Tyre for three years and ten months, lxvi. 4; God's impotence asserted by Haman, as shown by the Israelites' delivery into the hands of, lxxxi. 6

Nebuzaraddan besieges Jerusalem, lx. 8; besieges sixty cities of the Levites, sons of Moses, lx. 9

Nefesh, son of Reu, xxvii. 6

Nefilim (the fallen) giants, descended from intermarriage of Seth and Cain, xxiv. 12

Nehemiah, son of Hachaliah, details concerning the rebuilding of the temple handed to, lxxxi. 5

Nephti subdued by Meshek, xxvii. 8

Nesa, land of (or, the isles), inhabited by Greeks, xxxi. 8

New Sarento, xl. 16

Niba, wife of Enoch and daughter of Shem, xxvi. 13

Nicanor, made King of Babylon by Alexander, lxxxv. 8; battle with, fought on the sixth day, xcii. 7; brings many merchants with him to buy the captive Jews, xcii. 7; disguises himself as a poor man and escapes to Macedon, where he tells Lysias all that had happened, xciii. 2; sends word to Judah professing his friendship, xcix. 3; sent by Demetrius with a strong army against the Jews, xcix. 3; demands Judah from the priests at the temple and speaks blasphemies, xcix. 5; searches all the houses in Jerusalem for Judah, xcix. 6; sends a messenger to fetch Ducsius, xcix. 7; meets Judah on the Sabbath, xcix. 8; implored by the Jews with him to respect the Sabbath, xcix. 8; gate of, xcix. 11; head and arm of, cut off and hung before the gate of, Jerusalem, xcix. 11; day of, viz., the 13th of Adar, observed by the Jews as a festival, xcix. 12

Nicolaos of Damascus, book of, xxxv. 2

Night created on first day, i. 3

Nimigim, son of Canaan, xxvii. 4

Nimrod, son of Cush, first giant in pride before God, xxvii. 4; prince over children of Ham, xxviii. 1; numbered children of Ham, xxviii. 4; beginning of his kingdom, xxxi. 18; son of Cush, xxxi. 20; allied himself with children of Ham at dispersion, xxxii. 2; the wicked, chooses the angel who taught him language of Kush (so also Put, Mizraim, Tubal, Javan, Meseh, and Tiras), xxxviii. 12; a sinner after the flood, lvii. 14; astrologers of, advise him to kill Abraham, xxxiv. 1; orders Abraham to make an idol, xxxiii. 2; disputes with Abraham, xxxiv. 10; throws Abraham into fiery furnace, xxxiii. 3, 4, xxxiv. 11, 12

Nineveh built by Ninus, son of Bel, xxxi. 18; length of, xxxii. 3

Ninfe, holy ones of, name of seven golden idols of Amorites, lvii. 13; holy gods of the Amorites, who would deliver Israelites into their hands, lvii. 33 (*vide* Nizpa)

Ninus succeeds Bel, and builds Nineveh and Rehoboth, xxxii. 3; makes an image like his father, which he calls Bel, xxxii. 5

Nipim, son of Canaan, xxvii. 4

Nix, name of Sirenes in Ashkenaz, lviii. 8
Niza, in Media, built by Dionysius, lviii. 2
Nizpa (read Ninfa), invents the Latin alphabet in the time of Yair, lviii. 11
Noah, sons of, xxvi. 10, xxxi. 1; God's promise to, xxvi. 21; generations of, xxviii. 1; number of, children of, xxviii. 5
Nōba, twin wife of Seth, xxvi. 1
Nobar, i.e., Belshazzar, son of Evil Merodach, lxvi. 6
Nordmani, children of Japheth, xxxi. 4

Oars, grasped by Jacob's sons, xxxviii. 7
Obadiah, speaks to the proselytes in Eden, xx. 4
Obed, son of Reu, xxvii. 6
Ocean, in the west of Shem's portion, xxxi. 2 (vide Oqeanos)
Octopus, a sea-monster, with arms ten cubits long, xlviii. 3
Ogiges, King of Achayah, xxxv. 9; built Akta, which he called Eliozin (Eleusis), xxxv. 9
Olive-tree, wishes to serve as gallows of Haman, lxxxiii. 3
Olympiad, consisted of four years, lix. 10; established 406 years after fall of Troy, lix. 10
On, ruse of wife, lv. 9
Ophanim, opposite God, i. 11
Oqeanos, waters of, flow round ends of heaven and earth, i. 6 (vide Ocean)
Ordin, son of Canaan, xxvii. 4
Othniel, succeeds Kenaz, lvii. 42
Ox, sang hymns once a year, which day Egyptians kept as a festival, called the day of Serapis, xlii. 2; likeness of an, which arose in the air, and was worshipped by Egyptians, xlii. 2 (vide Apis)

Pahath, subdued by Tubal, xxvii. 3.
Palabus, son of Peleg, xxvii. 5
Palanquin, of Lebanon wood, made by Moses in fifth house of Eden, xx. 9
Palante, giant killed by Titonide, xxxv. 9
Palini, name of a city, xxxv. 9

Pallas, name given to Titonide, after killing the giant Palante, xxxv. 9
Palm-trees on both sides of the throne of Solomon, lxxxiv. 8
Palos, tower between Albano and Rome, xl. 5; nephew of Agnios, head of army, xl. 5
Paltia, son of Peleg, xxvii. 5
Parable of husbandman's death, xi. 1; of rich man's death, xi. 2; of scholar's death, xi. 3; of mule to be killed, xxxiv. 2
Paradise, two carbuncle gates, xvii. 6, xviii. 1; description, xviii. 1 et seq.; four rivers in, xviii. 2; myriads of trees in every corner, xviii. 5; chanting angels in every corner, xviii. 5; tree of life, xviii. 5; clouds of glory, xviii. 6; seven compartments of the just in, xviii. 7 (vide Eden)
Paran, Reuben dwells behind mountains of, lxii. 11, lxiii. 17; mountains of, inhabited by children of Zebulun, lxii. 11, lxiii, 16
Parhiel, angel who smites wicked in sixth compartment of hell, xxi. 10
Paruta, son of Magog, xxvii. 2
Pathrosim, son of Misraim, xxvii. 4
Patriarchs, spirit of, in God's mind at creation, i. 4; dwell in third house of Eden, xx. 6; bow to justice, whereupon God rises from the throne of justice and sits upon the throne of mercy, lxxxiii. 1; seven, sculptured before the throne of Solomon, lxxxiv. 4
Pekah, son of Remalyahu, rules Israel at time of first exile, lx. 1
Peleg, son of Eber, xxvii. 5; in his days earth was divided, xxvii. 5; children of, xxvii. 5
Penitents in fifth compartment of Paradise, xviii. 7; dwell in second house of Eden, xx. 5
Perjurer descends to hell for ever, xv. 6
Persia chosen by Shemites, xxxi. 2; nethermost parts of, inhabited by Issachar, lxii. 9; received by lot by Cyrus, lxviii. 10; kings of, love God's Temple, lxxvii. 10
Persian descended from Dodanim, xxvii. 2; revolt from the Macedonian rule, xcii. 4; put Antio-

chus to flight, xciii. 3; spoken by Issachar, lxii. 10; river, in Shem's portion, xxxi. 2
Pharaoh presides over princes in fifth compartment of hell, xvi. 5; called Tibei, began to rule Egypt on day of Abraham's birth, xxxii. 6; Amenofis, King of Egypt, who knew not Joseph, xlii. 2; dream of, xliii. 1; the three advisers of, xlvi. 1; orders Balaam, Janis, and Jambris to be summoned before him, xlvii. 6; orders Moses to give him a sign, xlvii. 7; magicians of, perform miracles similar to those of Moses, xlvii. 7; desires Moses to tell him of God's power, xlvii. 9; drives Moses and Aaron from his presence, xlvii. 9; pursues the Israelites, xlviii. 12; saved from drowning in the Red Sea, believes in God, remains 500 years in Nineveh, xlviii. 12; resolves to seek Moses himself, liv. 4; voice of, heard in whole land of Egypt, liv. 6; horse of, follows Gabriel, in the form of a mare, into the sea, and is followed by all the Egyptians, liv. 9; entered the sea through the enchantment of the Israelites, lxxxi. 3
Phillip prohibits the Jews the study of the law and performance of God's service, lxxxviii. 1; slays many of the Hassidim, lxxxviii. 1; ordered to blot out the memory of Judah, and to slay anyone mentioning the name 'Jew,' xc. 1; destroys all whom he found observing the law, xc. 2; finds a number of Jews observing the Sabbath in a cave, suffocates them, xc. 4; collects a large army to fight the Judeans, xc. 4; revolts against Antiochus Eupator, xcviii. 6
Phillipio has his house overthrown upon him and is burnt to death, xciii. 1; captured by Judah, xciii. 1
Phillipus, brother of Ptolemy, made King of Macedon by Alexander, lxxxv. 8; the Pelusian, left in Judea by Antiochus to afflict the people, lxxxvii. 8
Philistia, Sea of, in Ham's portion, xxxi. 2

Philistines, land of, army of Seron flees into, xcii. 3
Philo, friend of Joseph, son of Gorion, relates in his book of Kenaz his fights, his prophecy, etc., lvii. et seq.
Phryges, vide Frezes, xxxii. 4
Phrygians left in Jerusalem to afflict the people, lxxxvii. 8
Phut, number of children, xxviii. 4; a sinner after the flood, lvii. 14; conquered by Targômah, xxvii. 3
Pike, sword-like, on Judah's banner, liii. 2; sword-like, on four standards, on each rests one arm of the seventh cloud, liii. 2
Pillars, twelve, by the well, sing the 'Shirah,' liii. 17; on the highest step of the throne of Solomon two huge of ivory, and two golden hollow vines, lxxxiv. 3
Pinehas, son of Magog, xxvii. 2; prince over children of Japheth, xxviii. 1; kills Balaam, xlviii. 14; given maw as reward for his zeal, lv. 12; smites young men of Israel and scourges them through the camp, lv. 12; zeal of, lv. 12; excommunicated Israelites who should drink wine of heathen, lv. 12; pierces Zimri and woman with a spear, lv. 12; son of Eleazar the priest, words of, lvii. 39; called by Kenaz when his days were drawing to a close, lvii. 39; fed by ravens and eagles, lix. 17; closing year of life of, lix. 7; son of Eleazar the priest, prayer of, lix. 14
Pious, place allotted to each, according to his deeds, xx. 1; seven, men sculptured before the throne of Solomon, lxxxiv. 4
Pirati, children of Japheth, xxxi. 4
Piritius killed by a dog, lviii. 2
Pishon, river, to which the sinners are brought down by Kenaz, lvii. 16; tribe of Dan settles on the other side of river, lxii. 6; brook of, lxiii. 5
Pithom, store city built by Israelites at the extremity of Egypt, xlii. 3
Plague of blood, details of, xlviii. 1; of frogs, details of, xlviii. 2; of wild beasts, details of, xlviii. 3;

sent among the Egyptian cattle, xlviii. 4; of fever, which afterwards broke out into boils, xlviii. 5; of hail, details of, xlviii. 6; of locust, details of, xlviii. 7; of darkness, details of, xlviii. 8; of slaying of firstborn, xlviii. 9; destroys 24,000 Israelites, lv. 11

Planets, seven, iv. 1; influence of, iv. 5-10; appearance of, iv. 5-10; the seven, correspond to the four standards, Moses, Aaron and the tabernacle, liii. 15

Plants, production of, ii. 2

Po, river, xxxi. 12, 15

Polios succeeds Numa Popilios, xl. 18

Pollux, brother of Theseus, captured in the time of Yair, lviii. 10

Pomegranate wishes to serve as gallows for Haman, lxxxiii. 3

Pompilios, Numa, succeeds Romulus, xli. 2; succeeds Romulus and reigns forty-one years in the time of Hezekiah, King of Judah, lix. 11; adds two months to the calendar year, viz., Januarius and Februarius, lix. 11

Poor in the seventh compartment of paradise, xviii. 7

Popilios, Numa, succeeds Romulus, xl. 18

Pôra, son of Serug, xxvii. 7

Poṣomanga built by Kittim, xl. 1

Potiphar, wife of, entices Joseph, xxxix. 1

Precepts. 613, given to Moses by God, xlviii. 16

Priamus reigns in Troy during the reign of Tola, lviii. 9

Priest, old, requests his six sons to bear him to the altar that he may inhale the frankincense, lxxvii. 4; tells the chiefs of the fathers where the holy fire lies, lxxvii. 6

Priests interpret the twenty-four books of the law, which the elders translate from Hebrew into Greek, lxxxvii. 4; cry between the porch and the altar, xcix. 5 (*vide* Aaron, Levites)

Princes, flight of, in time of Yoqtan, xxxix. 7; of Persia, agree whoever should pray to any body besides the king to be thrown into the lions' den, lxx. 1; roll a great stone over the mouth of the pit, lxx. 6; are punished, lxx. 10

Procas succeeds Abṭinos, xl. 14

Proselytes in first house of Eden, xx. 4

Ptolemy, son of Lagi, made King of Egypt by Alexander, lxxxv. 8; the Macedonian, King of Egypt, lxxxvii. 1; collects many Median and Persian books, lxxxvii. 1; commands his two pages to collect many books, lxxxvii. 1; informed by his pages that they have collected 950 books, orders them to add 50 more, lxxxvii. 1; advised by his two pages to send to the high priest for wise men to explain their law to him, lxxxvii. 2; puts the seventy priests into seventy chambers, lxxxvii. 4; presents a table of pure gold, weighing 100 talents and having Egypt and the course of the Nile engraved upon it, to the temple, lxxxvii. 5; presents Eleazar and the seventy priests with much money, and sends them back to Jerusalem, lxxxvii. 5; succeeds Ptolemy as King of Egypt, lxxxvii. 6; chosen one of the generals of Lysias, xcii. 5; King of Egypt, delivers Annibal over to Scipio, xcvi. 9

Puah, advice of, xliii. 3

Pul, inhabited by children of Zebulun, lxiii. 16

Punishment, duration of, xiii. 6; of transgressing Israelites, xiii. 7; from Passover to Pentecost, xiii. 7; of consummately wicked, xiii. 7; of law-breakers, burnt to ashes, xiii. 8; of apostates, xiii. 9; of sinners, xiv. 6; of those who let their hair grow for sin, xv.; of slanderers, xv. 1; of those who uncovered their breasts, xv. 1; of those who followed their eyes to sin, xv. 1; of adulterer, xv. 1; of thief, xv. 1; of blasphemers, xv. 2; of those who ate what they stole, xv. 3; of those who abused the poor, xv. 4; on eve of Sabbath, xv. 7; five kinds of, in hell, xvi. 1; three kinds of, decreed by Pharaoh against the Israelites, xlii. 4; some follow at once, x. 3; some come after an interval, x. 3

Purple robes first worn by Tullus, King of Rome, lix. 11
Pusai, father of Athrai, lx. 4; lxiii. 9
Qadesh, burial-place of Miriam, xlviii. 17
Qadima, daughter of Reu, xxvii. 6
Qaduba subdued by Dodanim, xxvii. 8
Qadvah (Qadovah), a kingdom of Kush, lxiii. 8
Qainan, sons of, xxvi. 5; daughters of, xxvi. 5
Qaliron, i.e., Lesha, whose warm waters flow into the Salt Sea, xxxi. 18
Qalmah, a kingdom in Kush, lxiii. 8
Qalmana, twin wife of Cain, xxvi. 1 daughter of Adam, xxiv. 1
Qamo built by Misraim, xxvii. 4
Qamon, burial-place of Yair, lviii. 10
Qapadoses, children of Mesech, xxxi. 4
Qapis succeeds Avisianos, xl. 14
Qappadokia, i.e., Cæsarea, in land of Kaftor, xxxi. 4
Qashē, son of Magog, xxvii. 2
Qedar, vide Kedar
Qedem, people of, at war with people of Kush, xlv. 1 (vide Moses)
Qelalah, a kingdom in Kush, lxiii. 8
Qemuel, angel of destruction, lii. 1 ; guard at the gates of heaven, rebukes Moses, lii. 1
Qenath, son of Elishah, xxvii. 2
Qenaz, vide Kenaz
Qiniza, son of Reu, xxvii. 6
Qinqanos, King of Cush, xlv. 1; army refused entrance into Cush, xlv. 3; widow of, advises people to depose Moses and appoint her son king, xlvi. 8 (vide Moses)
Qinsius Minios, a prince of Rome, xcvii. 1
Qipod, angel who accompanied Joshua ben Levi to the gates of hell, xxi. 2
Qomah, a kingdom in Kush, lxiii. 8
Qorah, vide Korah
Qushiel, angel who smites wicked in second compartment of hell, xx. 6

Ra'amah, number of children, xxviii. 4; children of, xxxi. 17

Rafa, son of Peleg, xxvii. 5
Rain, storehouse of, ii. 5; descends after long drought, xxvii. 3
Rainbow created on second day, i. 3; in clouds, xxvii. 3
Ram, form in which Jovis revealed himself, xlii. 1
Ramses, store city, built by Israelites, at extremity of Egypt, xlii. 1, 3; where the Tibei reigned, xlii. 1
Raphael, head of the fourth band of angels, i. 9; first called Boël, vi. 5
Red Sea in Ham's portion, xxxi. 2; divided into twelve rents for the twelve tribes, xlviii. 12
Regini, children of Japheth, xxxi. 4
Regosar, son of Evil-Merodach, lxvi. 6
Rehoboth, i.e., the wide city built by Ninus, xxxi. 18
Remus rules over Rome during the reign of Jotham, xli. 1; and Romulus suckled by a she-wolf, xli. 1, lix. 10; born during the reign of Ahaz, King of Judah, lix. 10
Renegades, punishment of, xvi. 7
Rents, twelve, into which the Red Sea was divided, xlviii. 12
Repentance created before creation, i. 2
Resigned, who have been in affliction and have not rebelled, dwell in fourth house of Eden, xx. 8
Resin, son of Canaan, xxvii. 4
Resurrection, foretold by fourth son to Antiochus, lxxxix. 5; deniers of, punishment of, xvi. 7
Return home ordered by Judah to those Jews who had vineyards, built houses, married, or were faint-hearted, xcii. 6; to Palestine under Cyrus, lxxvi. 2
Reu, temples erected to men overthrown in time of, xxiv. 9, xxvi. 20; son of Peleg, xxvii. 5; children of, xxvii. 6; daughters of, xxvii. 6
Reuben, constellation of, Taurus, liii. 13; stone of, the emerald, liii. 13; ensign of, mandrakes, liii. 14; sacrificed to the gods of the nations, lvii. 9; love, unity, and peace, between Zebulun and the tribe of, lxii. 11; tribe of,

possess Bible, Mishna, Talmud, and Agadoth, lxii. 11; tribe of, speak language of Kedar, lxii. 11; tribe of, dwell opposite Zebulun, behind the mountains of Paran, lxii. 11; tribe of, divide their spoil with Zebulun, lxii. 11; infests the roads leading to Mecoth and the way to Babylon, lxii. 11; tribe of, have lectures every Sabbath in Hebrew, interpreted in the language of Kedar, lxii. 11; children of, possess a fertile land in the midst of the mountains of darkness, lxiii. 17; children of, dwell between Paran and Bethel, lxiii. 17; children of, watch the roads and capture much spoil, and dwell in tents of hair, lxiii. 17; children of, speak Hebrew and another strange language, lxiii. 17

Reuel advises Pharaoh not to injure the Hebrews, xlvi. 2; takes Jacob's staff with him, xlvi. 4; leaves Egypt and goes to Midian, xlvi. 4; puts Moses in prison for ten years, xlvi. 9; sends to see if Moses still lives in the prison, xlvi. 10

Riadura, son of Yoqtan, xxvii. 5

Rich man dying, parable, xi. 2

Riddles given by Zerubbabel and two captains to each other, lxxiv. 6; of the three guardians of the king placed under the king's pillow, lxxiv. 6

Rifath, i.e., Paflagronas (Paphlagonians), children of Gomer, xxxi. 4; children of, fight against Abtinos, xl. 14 (vide Riphath)

Rifud, son of Peleg, xxvii. 5

Righteous, ways of, in God's mind at creation, i. 4; great banquet of, vi. 1; reward of, x. 12, xi. 4; eight myrtles placed in hands of, xviii. 1; canopy of, xviii. 1; two crowns of, one of precious stones, the other of gold, xviii. 1; clothed with eight cloths, woven from clouds of glory, xviii. 1; led to a well-watered place with flowers, xviii. 1; changed to youth, xviii. 4; changed to a child, xviii. 4; changed to a middle-aged man, xviii. 4; changed to an old man, xviii. 4; the future glory of, not yet fully revealed, xviii. 8; God sits in their midst, xviii. 8; attended and fed by myriads of angels, xx. 2; the seven, who did not worship Baal in the reign of Yair (Da'al, Abi Yezre'el, Gutiel, Shalom, Ashchor, Yonadab, and Shim'i), lviii. 10

Rigion, a river of fire, lii. 7 (vide Dinur)

Rimmon, cleft of, where 600 Benjamites fled for refuge, lix. 16

Rinos, river in Shem's portion, xxxi. 2; boundary of Ham's portion, xxxi. 2

Riphath subdues Boṣrah, xxvii. 3; alone conquers Godo, xxvii. 3; number of children of, xxviii. 3; i.e., Brittanos, xxxi. 6 (vide Rifath)

Riphtah, a kingdom of Kush, lxiii. 8

Riphtania inhabited by children of Riphath, xxxi. 6

Ris, measurement of, xxxvi. 2

Risôn built by Misraim, xxvii. 4

Rivers of oil, balsam, wine, and honey in Paradise, xviii. 2; great, encompassed the whole camp of the Israelites, liii. 17; round the Tabernacle four other rivers issue into the four corners of the court, liii. 17; in desert produce all kinds of dainties, liii. 17; four, encompass camp, and flow between each family, liii. 17; marked the boundary of each camp, liii. 17 (vide Sambatyon)

Rod of Moses, xlvi. 12; created by God after the Creation was completed, xlvi. 12; taken by Adam when he left Eden, xlvi. 12; comes into the possession of Shem, xlvi. 12; taken by Noah, xlvi. 12; planted by Reuel in his garden, nobody able to uproot it except Moses, xlvi. 12

Rodii = Dodanim, xxxii. 4

Roma, city built by Romulus, xl. 17, xli. 1 (vide Rome)

Roman history, abstract, xli.; year originally consisted of ten months, lix. 11

Romania, place of Romulus, xl. 17
Romans ask Judah whether he will be their friend or the friend of the Greeks, xcvii. 1; letter of, to Judah, son of Mattathiah, xcvii. 1; make a covenant with Jews, xcvii. 2
Rome, all kings of, called Cæsar, xxxii. 6; city of, xl. 5; war with Babylon, because Rome assisted Greece against Babylon, xl. 20; the seven kings of, xli. 2; city of (*i.e.*, the Latini) arose during the reign of Aeneas, lix. 10; founded by Romulus and Remus in the reign of Ahaz, King of Judah, lix. 10; first kings of, reign thirty-eight years, lix. 10; the fourth animal which Daniel saw in a vision, xcvi. 1; conquers kingdom of Antiochus, xcvi. 1; the fourth kingdom, which God began to render more powerful than the third, Greece, xcvi. 1
Romidath, land of, flooded, xxvii. 3
Romulus succeeds Agrippa, xl. 14; succeeds Æmilius, xl. 15; wages great wars, and makes a covenant with David, xl. 17; wall of, xl. 17; builds a temple in honour of Jovis, removes that dedicated to Luṣifer, xl. 17; rules over Rome during the reign of Jotham, xli. 1; builds city of Rome, lix. 11; born during the reign of Ahaz, King of Judah, lix. 10
Rôô subdued by Tiras, xxvii. 3
Rossi dwell by the river Kio (or Kiva), xxxi. 11

Sabbatdi (*i.e.*, Saturday), iv. 2
Sabbath in God's mind at Creation, i. 4; observance of, prohibited by Antiochus, lxxxvii. 8; observance of, xc. 4; Mattathias commands Jews to fight on, xc. 9
Sabbatyon, or Sabbatianus, river where children of Moses were brought, lxi. 3; depth of, 200 cubits, lxii. 2; length of, extended to a distance of nine months' journey, lxii. 2; noise of, like an earthquake, sand and stones roll six days, lxii. 2; fire burns all round, and consumes everything, lxii. 3; fire burns from Sabbath eve to conclusion, lxii. 3; width of, in narrowest part less than sixty cubits where the people converse with those on other side, lxi. 3; ceases to flow on the Sabbath, lxi. 3, lxii. 3; flames prevent anyone from approaching within thirty-four miles of, lxii. 3 (*vide* Sambatyon)
Sabino, where Kittim go, xl. 1; built by children of Tubal, xl. 1
Sabta, number of children, xxviii. 4; *i.e.*, Aṣtabari, xxxi. 17
Sabtecha, number of children of, xxviii. 4
Saffron, called Machik, lxiii. 2
Salt Sea, or Leber Meer, site of Sodom, xxxv. 6
Samael, angel of death, induces Eve to sin, xxii. 2; the wicked, chief of the Satans, rejoiced at the coming death of Moses, l. 8; commanded by God to bring him the soul of Moses, l. 11; terrified when he sees Moses, l. 11; clothed with anger, l. 11; returns to God, and is again ordered to bring him the soul of Moses, l. 13; draws his sword and stands over Moses, l. 13
Samanãkh, son of Magog, xxvii. 2
Sambatyon, river from which a flaming fire ascends on the Sabbath eve, so that nobody can approach it, lxiii. 11; noise of, like the billows of the sea, lxiii. 12; river, four cubits wide, as far as a bowshot reaches, lxiii. 12; sand of, if placed in a flask, whirls during the six week-days, but rests on the Sabbath, lxiii. 12; frequented by the four tribes to shear their flocks, lxiii. 13 (*vide* Sabbatyon)
Samson, fall caused by power, x. 10; subdued by a woman, lxxv. 7
Samuel and Saul, xi. 8
Sanballat the Horonite slanders the Jews, lxxi. 3
Sand fence to sea, ii. 1
Sandalphon, fire of, lii. 4; sight of, terrifies Moses, lii. 5; heavenly hosts moved when crown leaves hands of, lii. 6; conjures with the ineffable Name, and the

crown rests on God's head, lii. 6; towers above his fellow-angels, lii. 6; stands in front of the curtain, weaving crowns for his Maker, lii. 6
Sanhedrin, the great, slain by Nebuchadnezzar, x. 10; the ten banishments of the, lxii.; seats on the throne of Solomon, lxxxiv. 4
Saqsonei, children of Japheth, xxxi. 4; dwell by river of the great sea, xxxi. 11
Saqvah, a kingdom of Kush, lxiii. 8
Sarapis, *vide* Serapis
Sardana, son of Ashkenaz, xxvii. 2
Sartan captured by sons of Jacob, xxxvi. 7
Satan enters the image of Enosh and makes it walk, xxiii. 7; accuses Israel before God, lxxxii. 2; ordered by God to bring a scroll for Israel's destruction to be written upon, lxxxii. 3 (*vide* Samael)
Satuldakh (*i.e.*, Saturday), iv. 2
Saturn rules on seventh day, iv. 2; his appointment and form, iv. 5; temple to, erected by Anias Trognos, xl. 14
Saturnus, name given to Sefo in addition to Janus, after the planet Shabtai (*i.e.*, Saturnus), xl. 8; temple of, closed by Latinus II., xl. 13; ruled Italy, lix. 10
Saul, house of, judged, xi. 8; God's anointed, ends his days in battle, lxxviii. 2
Scholar, dying, parable, xi. 3
Sciences spread from Egypt to Greece, xxxv. 4
Scipios dissuades the 320 Roman counsellors from opening the gates of Venusia to Annibal, xcvi. 5; marches to Africa, and kills Astrubal, xcvi. 6; cuts off the head of Astrubal, which he sends to Annibal, xcvi. 6; besieges Carthagene, and destroys it, xcvi. 7; captures the whole of Africa, xcvi. 9; conquers Annibal, xcvi. 9; a prince of Rome, xcvii. 1
Scroll in ark to be referred to, in case the tribes strove to falsify a word, li. 5
Sea above Bohu, xvii. 4
Sebóim built by Misraim, xxvii. 4

Seel subdued by Yavan, xxvii. 3
Seelah, daughter of Jephthah, lix. 4; goes up to Mount Tlag, lix. 5; lamentation of, lix. 6
Sefarad captured by Cyrus, lxxviii. 1
Sefer Hayashar (*i.e.*, Book of the Just) = Pentateuch, xlv. 8; contains remaining history of Moses, xlviii. 17
Sefo, son of Eliphaz, flies to Egypt, xl. 3; appointed captain of host by Agnios, xl. 3; splits open the head of huge strange animal, xl. 7; name changed to Janus, xl. 7; king of the Kittim, xl. 8
Segna, river in country of Frankos, xxxi. 6
Sehabim, son of Misraim, xxvii. 4
Seir, Mount, the sons of Esau flee to, xxxvii. 14
Seleucus made King of Syria by Alexander, lxxxv. 8; King of Macedonia, informed by Simeon of the wealth contained in the Temple, lxxxvi. 1; orders Eliodorus, the captain of the host, to go to Jerusalem, lxxxvi. 1
Seliqos succeeds Asqinus, xl. 18
Semari (*i.e.*, Edessa), in land of Syria, xxxi. 18
Semeramit, wife of Ninus, governs Assyria at his death, xxxii. 7
Sennacherib banishes the Israelites four times, lx. 1; captures golden calf, which Jeroboam had placed in Dan, lx. 1; makes Reubenites, Gadites, and half tribe of Manasseh dwell in Lahlah, Habor, river Gozan, and cities of Media, lx. 1; exiles the tribes of Asher, Zebulun, Naphtali, and Issachar, because they refused to acknowledge Hosea's rule, lx. 2; exiles the tribes of Ephraim and Manasseh in the third year of Hezekiah's reign, lx. 3; takes the tribes of Judah and Simeon captive, lx. 4; conceals the tribes of Judah and Simeon behind the mountains of darkness, beyond the rivers of Ethiopia, lx. 4; pits the tribes of Judah and Simeon against Tirhakah, lx. 4; besieges fortified cities of Judah, lx. 4; besieges Jerusalem, lx. 5; appoints Hosea, son of Elah, king

over Samaria, lx. 2; his two sons slew him, lx. 5; at death of tribes of Gad, Asher, and Naphtali, war with Kushite kings, lxii. 8

Serah, daughter of Asher, points out place of Joseph's coffin to Moses, li. 2

Seraphim, six wings, i. 12; near God, i. 12; of fire, praise God for being no respecter of persons, lx. 6

Serapis, name of Apis, after his deification, xxxv. 8; name of Jovis, in the form of a ram, xlii. 1; day of, xlii. 2 (*vide* Apis)

Seron, captain of the Syrian host, resolves to fight Judah, xcii. 2; corpses of the army of, piled up on the field, xcii. 3; remnant of the army of, flee into the land of the Philistines, xcii. 3

Serpents killed by the young storks, and city taken, xlv. 6; image of, to be prayed to by those desiring long life, lix. 12; of gold encircled Solomon, lxxxiv. 6

Serug, sons and daughters of, xxvii. 7; did not walk in wicked ways, xxvii. 9

Servios succeeds Tarkinos, xl. 18

Seth, sons of, xxvi. 8; daughters of, xxvi. 8; sons of, dwelt in mountains by Garden of Eden, xxiv. 11; children of, xxiv. 10

Seven things created before the world, i. 2; brothers, martyrs, lxxxix.

Shaare Mavet, fourth compartment of hell, xvii. 2

Shaare Salmavet, sixth compartment of hell, xvii. 2

Shabethfin, son of Yoqtan, xxvii. 5

Shabtil, angel who smites wicked in third compartment of hell, xx. 7

Shafat, son of Togarma, xxvii. 2

Shafdifal, son of Peleg, xxvii. 5

Shafra, son of Peleg, xxvii. 5

Shakir destroyed by sons of Jacob, xxxvi. 9

Shalaphtra, son of Yoqtan, xxvii. 5

Shaluia, son of Reu, xxvii. 6

Shalom, son of Dedan, xxvii. 2; did not worship Baal in the days of Yair, lviii. 10

Shampla, son of Tiras, xxvii. 2

Shaphat, of the tribe of Dan, lxiii. 9

Shayish, son of Peleg, xxvii. 5

Shealtiel, father of Susanna, lxv. 10

Sheba, son of Cush, xxvii. 4; number of children, xxviii. 4; comprises the Sabeans, Arabians, and Indians, xxxi. 17

Sheifa, daughter of Reu, xxvii. 6

Shekinah, face of, hidden, i. 12; residence in East, iii. 5 (*vide* God)

Shelah, son of Arpakshad, xxvii. 5; a sinner after the Flood, lvii. 14

Shem, children of, xxvii. 5, xxxi. 16; 406 nations descended from, xxxi. 1; children of, live in Asia, xxxi. 2

'Shem Hammeforash,' the Ineffable Name, li. 7 (*vide* Name)

Shemhazai, Midrash of, xxv.; advises God not to create man, xxv. 2; assumes human form and sins, xxv. 4; children of, eat 1,000 camels, 1,000 horses, and 1,000 oxen daily, xxv. 8; dreams of his sons, xxv. 9; repents and hangs himself between heaven and earth, xxv. 12

Sheol, return of wicked to, xii. 10; described, xvii. 1; consists half of fire and half of ice, xvii. 2 (*vide* Hell)

Shepherds reigned in the land of Goshen, xlii. 1; the abomination of Egypt, xlii. 1

Shiddim, dwelling in the North, i. 7 (*vide* Demons)

Shifrah, advice of, xliii. 3

Shihor, the Nile, xlviii. 10

Shilo, inhabitants of, attack sons of Jacob, xxxvi. 8

Shimi, son of Ninus, succeeds Semeramit and builds Babylon, xxxii. 7; did not worship Baal in the days of Yair, lviii. 10

Shittites (Scythians) shut themselves in their fortresses, lxxviii. 3; with their queen, Tamirah, flee before Cyrus, lxxviii. 3; remainder of, destroyed by Cambises, lxxviii. 5

Shofar (*vide* Trumpet), blowing of, xiii. 5

Shuah, a sinner after the Flood, lvii. 14

Shuri, son of Peleg, xxvii. 5

Shushan, in the land of Elam, the native place of Daniel, lxxiv. 3

Shzŏŭr, son of Peleg, xxvii. 5
Sidon, son of Canaan, xxvii. 4; built by Sidon, son of Canaan, in the land of Phoeniṣe, xxxi. 18
Sidonians ordered to hew the wood from the Lebanon, lxxvi. 5
Ṣihon and Og so tall that the waters of the Flood did not reach their knees, li. 12; war with Moses, xlviii. 18
Silagtaba, son of Tisai, xxvii. 2
Siliŏ, son of Cush, xxvii. 4
Silisia = Tarshish, xxxii. 4
Ṣillah, wife of Lemech, xxiv. 5; children of, xxvi. 18; son of Serug, xxvii. 7
Simeon, stone of, the sapphire, liii. 13; constellation of, Virgo, liii. 13; ensign of, the city of Shechem, liii. 14; of the tribe of Benjamin, informed Seleucus of the wealth in the Temple, lxxxvi. 1; incites Antiochus against the Jews, lxxxvii. 7; exhorted by Mattathiah to advise his brethren, since God gave him might and wisdom, xci. 2; hastens to Galilee, where he slays the enemy and takes their spoil, xciv. 3; buries his brother, Judah the Maccabean, c. 5; R., b. Gamliel, death of, xxi. 2; R., asked by R. Eleazar whether the Israelites took weavers with them, liii. 16
Simim, son of Canaan, xxvii. 4
Sin, no benefit derived from, x. 11; punishment of, x. 7 (vide Hell)
Sinners' punishment, xiv. 6; punishment of, who perfumed themselves, xv. 1; three classes of, who descend to hell for ever, xv. 6; burned to ashes every twelvemonth, xv. 8; redemption through repentance, xvi. 7; punished twelve months in each compartment of hell, xvii. 3; selected from each tribe, lvii. 5; total of selected men 110, lvii. 6; the seven, after the Flood, lvii. 14; to be burnt with fire, lvii. 16; burnt with fire of Judah's mouth, xc. 4
Siqrops, first King of Atinism (Athenians), i.e., the So'anites, lvi. 1; flees from Egypt to Aqtes, in Greece, after commencement of ten plagues, lvi. 1; at death of, seventeen kings and nineteen princes reign in Aqtes, lvi. 1 (vide Cycrops)
Sirenes, like beautiful women, and their lower parts like fishes, lviii. 8; discovered by Mercorius in the reign of Gideon, lviii. 8; called Nikes (Nix) in Ashkenaz, lviii. 8
Sirine, in Lybia, built in the sixty-ninth year of Ehud, lviii. 2 (vide Cyrene)
Sisipo builds city of Epira, now called Corinthus, lvi. 5
Sitopolis (Scytopolis), inhabitants of, beg Judah to spare them, since they had always treated the Jews well, xcvii. 9
Slander, punishment of, xiii. 4
Slanderers, punishment, xvi. 7; descend to hell for ever, xv. 6
Sleep created by God, vi. 14
Snow, earth created from, beneath throne of glory, i. 6; Mountains, which are impassable, captured by Cyrus, lxxviii. 1
So'anites, throne of the kingdom of, built by Siqrops, lvi. 1
Sodom, built by Misraim, xxvii. 4
'Ṣoḥer Tob' mentions story of she-wolf suckling Remus and Romilus, xli. 1
Solomon alludes to 7,000 vessels in hell, xvi. 6; concerning renegades, xvi. 7; in third house in Eden, xx. 6; will place precious stones on cherubim, lvii. 22; King of Israel, throne of, lxxxiv.; on each step two lions, lxxxiv. 2; mounted his throne on six different sides, lxxxiv. 2; on each side of the throne of, golden seats for Gad the seer, the other for Nathan the prophet, lxxxiv. 3; encircled by a serpent of gold, which seated him upon his throne and then crept down at his feet, lxxxiv. 6; had to read some portion of the Law of Judgment upon every step of his throne, lxxxv. 3; heart of, inclined towards woman, lxxv. 7
Sorento, built by Hadarezer, xl. 15; oil-well of, causes city to subside between Napoli and New Sorento, xl. 16

Sosipater, a captain of Judah's army, captures Timotheos, xcvii. 7
Soul of child shown the righteous, ix. 5; carried to Gehinnom, ix. 6; shown every place where it will tread, ix. 7; of the seven brothers will walk to God, to the light that is with the Lord, lxxxix. 3
South, *i.e.*, Arabia, captured by Cyrus, lxxviii. 1
Spark in Kenaz' vision flies out, and remains as a spider's web in a beam, lvii. 41; flies out and remains in the air as a shield, lvii. 41; to be extinguished when sin comes to an end, lvii. 41; source vomits hot foam, lvii. 41
Spirits, evil, dwelling in the north, i. 7; hidden in Garden of Eden, ix. 2; made to enter new being, ix. 4; judgment of, ix. 11
Sqite, *i.e.*, Magog, xxxii. 4.
Staff of Adam, Abraham, Isaac, Jacob, Joseph, Pharao, Reuël, xlvi. 12 (*vide* Rod)
Standard, similar in shape to a lion with golden hooks and sword-like point, liii. 2, 10; of Judah in the East, liii. 2; of Reuben in the South has the appearance of a man similar to mandrakes, liii. 3; of Ephraim in the West, appearance like a fish, liii. 4; of Dan in the North, like a serpent, liii. 5; of tribes corresponds to twelve constellations and twelve stones in ephod, liii. 10, 12; of twelve tribes, liii. 14; the four, with Moses, Aaron, and the tabernacle, correspond to the seven planets, liii. 15; three tribes form under one, liii. 15
Stars created third day, iii. 3; at Abraham's birth, xxxv. 1
Stones, twelve precious, represent the twelve tribes, lii. 13; of the ephod, correspond to the twelve tribes, liii. 10; precious, to be substituted for stones of idolaters and placed in the ephod and breastplate, lvii. 18; light of, shall be seven times more powerful than light of the sun and moon, lvii. 23; will be put in the place whence they were taken by God, and will remain there till the end of the world, lvii. 23; illumine the whole earth just as the sun at noonday, lvii. 25; precious, on throne of Solomon, lxxxiv. 3; upon the altar emit fire, xciv. 1
Strabon of Caphtor states in his book that Nimrod was son of Shem, xxxii. 1
Sun, work done slowly, iii. 3; hours of, iii. 4; Ineffable Name written upon heart of, iii. 4; fiery face of, iii. 4; rising, in a chariot, iii. 4; prostrates before God, iii. 5; in presence of Shekhinah, iii. 5; rules on first day, iv. 2; icy face of, iii. 4; appointed over, iv. 9; and moon created on fourth day, iii. 1
Susanna, history of, lxv.
Swine's flesh abhorred by the Jews, lxxxix. 1
Sword of Kenaz cleaves to his hand, lvii. 35; of Kenaz, separated from his hand, lvii. 35; appearance of, like lightning on a rainy day, lxxxv. 4
Syria, people of, at war with people of Kush, xlv. 1

Tabel, son of Tiras, xxvii. 2
Tables of stone in God's mind at creation, i. 4; of pure gold presented by Ptolemy to Temple, lxxxvii. 5
Tablo subdued by Elishah, xxvii. 3
Tahpanhes, the royal city of Greece, thus called by Cadmus Europes Tahpanhes, lvi. 3; introduces the letters of the Greek writing, lvi. 5 (*vide* Cadmus)
Tamar, concealed the fruit of her conception three months, xlii. 6
Tamirah, Queen of the Scythians, lxxviii. 3; grief of, at the death of her son, lxxviii. 3; smites the camp of Cyrus and Cyrus himself, lxxviii. 4; places head of Cyrus in a bottle, which she filled with blood of the slain, lxxviii. 4; killed by Cambisa, lxxviii. 5
Tanais, river in Japheth's portion, xxxi. 3
Taoro, mountains of, in Japheth's portion, xxxi. 3; mountain in Brittania, xxxi. 4
Tapuah captured by sons of Jacob, xxxvi. 8

Targômah conquers Phut, xxvii. 3 (*vide* Togarmah)
Tarkinos succeeds Polios, xl. 18
Tarkinos II. succeeds Servios, xl. 18; killed by the brothers of a woman whom he took by force, xl. 18
Tarshish subdues Meriba, xxvii. 3; number of children, xxviii. 3; *i.e.*, Traksiani, accepted law of the Macedonians, xxxi. 13; *i.e.*, Silisia, xxxi. 4
Tchilah, daughter of Reu, xxvii. 6
Tehom, above Arqa, xvii. 4
Teled, son of Gomer, xxvii. 2
Temed, wife of Cain, xxvi. 11
Temple, site of, created before creation, i. 2; in God's mind at creation, i. 4; commencement of the rebuilding of, in the first year of the reign of Cyrus over the Chaldeans, lxxi. 2; rebuilding of, discontinued until the second year of the reign of Darius, lxxi. 3; rebuilding of, supervised by the elders of the captivity, lxxvii. 2; service of, stopped until the second year of the reign of Darius, King of Persia, lxxviii. 5; in the vision of Kenaz, lvii. 22; purified by Judah, xciv. 1
Ten things paramount in God's mind at creation, i. 4
Tent of the congregation stood in the centre, surrounded on all sides by the Levites, liii. 15
Tents of hair inhabited by children of Zebulun, lxiii. 16; of hair lived in by children of Reuben, lxiii. 17; of hair lived in by Judah and half Simeon, lxiii. 19
Theseus captures Helena in time of Yair, lviii. 11; brothers of, Castor and Pollux, lviii. 11; mother of, captured in time of Yair, lviii. 11
Thisius saved from a dog by Heraclones, lviii. 2
Thorn wishes to serve as gallows for Haman, because to it the wicked are compared, lxxxiii. 4; beam of, falls upon Haman, thereby taking his measurement, lxxxiii. 5; selected by God to serve as gallows for Haman, lxxxiii. 5
Throne of glory created before creation, i. 2; God's, like sapphire, i. 10; glory of God's, spread about Moses to protect him, lii. 9; of Solomon, lxxxiv.; wheels of Solomon's, rotated when the people approached him for judgment, lxxxiv. 8
Tibei reigned in Ramses, xlii. 1
Tiber caused to flow into other channels, and its bed paved with brass, xl. 20
Tiberio, River, where Kittim dwell, xl. 1; frontier of Tubal, xl. 1
Tiberios succeeds Karpitos, xl. 14
Tilas, son of Canaan, xxvii. 4
Tiller of ground dying, parable of, xi. 1
Tilon built by Sidon, xxvii. 4
Tiluf, son of Kush, xxvii. 4
Timbrel, art of playing upon, discovered in Greece in the time of Abimelech, lviii. 9
Timna given to Jacob by the Amorites, xxxvi. 12
Timothios, a Macedonian general, xciii. 1; goes to Gad and Gilead, and slays many Jews, xciv. 2; and his army flee towards the Jordan, xciv. 4; rallies his men and prepares for battle at Aza, xciv. 5; men of, curse Judah from the walls of Aza, xciv. 6; brothers of, xciv. 7; meets Judah with large army, xcvii. 7; endeavours to escape, but is captured by Dostios and Sosipater, xcvii. 7; flees and hides himself in one of the pits, xciv. 7; entreats Judah for his life, and swears to do good to the Jews all his life, xcvii. 7
Tina, son of Zipthai, xxvii. 2
Tinôs, son of Cush, xxvii. 4
Tipa, son of Magog, xxvii. 2; daughter of Nahor, xxvii. 7
Tiqunah, a kingdom in Kush, lxiii. 8
Tira'h, a kingdom in Kush, lxiii. 8
Tiras, son of Jepheth, xxvii. 2; subdues Rôô, xxvii. 3
Tirhakah, King of Ethiopia, rebels against Sennacherib, lx. 4
Tirus—*i.e.*, the Rossi (or Kurasan)—dwell by the river of the great sea, xxxi. 11
Tisai, children of, xxvii. 2
Tişio, river, xxxi. 12, 15
Tit-Hayaven, third compartment of hell, xvii. 2
Titonide, a virgin versed in the seven

sciences after killing the giant Palante, was called Pallas, xxxv. 9
Tlag, mountain where Seelah laments, lix. 5
Toba, son of Serug, xxvii. 7
Tobiya, the Ammonite, slanders the Jews, lxxi. 3
Toftch (hell), why so called, xiv. 1
Togarmah, children of, xxvii. 2; number of children, xxviii. 3; the ten families of (Cuzar, Paṣinaq, Alan, Bulgar, Kanbina, Turq, Buz, Zakhukh, Ugar and Tulmes), xxxi. 6; language of, spoken by Judah and half Simeon, lxiii. 19 (vide Targoma)
Tohu, created on first day, i. 3; above Tehom, xvii. 4
Torah, intervention of, vi. 8; called the daughter of God, lii. 13 (vide Law)
Toronia, place where the children of Turnus dwell, xl. 14
Toscana, country where the children of Tubal encamp, xl. 1
Traitors, punishment of, xvi. 7
Transformations, according to four watches of the day, xviii. 4; the four, of righteous, xviii. 4
Trases, children of Tiras, xxxi. 4
Trasos, descended from Tarshish, xxxi. 13; the Ishmaelites cause inhabitants of, to flee to Greece, xxxi. 13
Tree of life, seven clouds of glory on, xviii. 6; 500 tastes, xviii. 6; perfume of, xviii. 6; odour of, wafted to the four corners of the earth, xviii. 6; scholars sit beneath the, xviii. 6
Tribes, the twelve, dwell in third house in Eden, xx. 6; twelve, for whom the Red Sea was divided, xlviii. 12; twelve, represented by twelve precious stones, lii. 13; four dwelling together are Dan, Naphtali, Gad and Asher, lxiii. 9; four, armies of, consist of 173 banners and each of 1,500 men, lxiii. 9; four, converse in Hebrew and in the language of Kedar, lxiii. 10; four, each of the, sews three months, lxiii. 10; four, consists of pious men, lxiii. 10; four, possess many wells, which irrigate the land, lxiii. 11; four, dwell in houses built like towers, lxiii. 11; four, the only people who have seen the flames of the Sambatyon, lxiii. 11; four, reap a hundred-fold, lxiii. 11; four, no unclean bird or animal among them, lxiii. 11; four, encamp by the brook of Kedron, lxiii. 11; four, possess the worms that make the crimson colour, lxiii. 12
Tritolymus builds ships to carry wheat and merchandise, lviii. 2
Troy, in Dardanim, built in the time of Ehud, lviii. 2; 406 years after the capture of, Olympiad begins, lix. 10; city of, captured in the time of Abdon, lix. 10
Trumpets blown by priests when they notice four clouds moving, liii. 7; used for assembling the people, liii. 8; hollow and emitted a loud sound, liii. 8; one cubit in length, and a thin reed placed at the mouth, liii. 8; used as a signal for war, liii. 8; one long drawn sound to assemble the people and bring the princes together, liii. 8; a long, even sound upon two, to assemble the whole congregation, liii. 8; used for the Sabbaths and festivals, liii. 8; at the sounds of the, the camps under the banner of Judah moved first, liii. 9; a 'Teru'ah' to continue the journey, liii. 9; a 'Teqi'ah' and a 'Teru'ah,' signal for war or a festival, liii. 9
Truth reigns supreme over kings, wine and woman, lxxv. 8
Tubal subdues Pahath, xxvii. 3; number of children, xxviii. 3; i.e., Tuscans, dwell by River Pisa, in Tuscania, xxxi. 10; children of, encamp in Toscana, having River Tiberio as their frontier, xl. 1; daughters of, taken captive by Kittim, xl. 1; children of, overbearing to Kittim, xl. 1; children of, subdued by Janus, King of the Kittim, xl. 8
Tubal Cain, son of Ṣillah, xxiv. 8, xxvi. 17; first forger of iron war-implements, xxiv. 8; inventor of axe, pincers and hammer, xxiv. 8; discoverer of art of joining iron and lead, xxiv. 8, xxvi. 17

Tudan, son of Kush, xxvii. 4
Tuflita, son of Dedan, xxvii. 2
Tullus Ostilius succeeds Numa Pompilios, xli. 2; succeeds Numa, and reigns thirty-two years in the reign of Manasseh, King of Judah, lix. 11; King, who first clothed himself in purple robes, lix. 11
Turnus, King of Benevento, who sought Jania for wife, xl. 4; children of, fight against Abtinos, xl. 14; tower in, between Albano and Rome, xl. 5; built by Turnus, xl. 14; sons of, fled from Agnios, King of Afriqi, built Purnus and Anba, xl. 14
Tyre, city of, built 240 years before the temple at Jerusalem, lviii. 8; besieged by Nebuchadnezzar the Younger for three years and ten months, lxvi. 4
Tyrians ordered to hew the wood from the Lebanon, lxxvi. 5

Uriel, head of third band of angels, i. 9
'Usi, a man who lived in the land of the Kittim, in the city of Posomanga, xl. 4
'Unim, son of Yoqtan, xxvii. 5

Vabni (?), son of Kush, xxvii. 4
Varrus at the head of the Roman army, xcvi. 3; escapes to Venusia, xcvi. 4
Vckhal, son of Ashkenaz, xxvii. 2
Venitiqia Sea, into which the rivers Tisio and Po flow, xxxi. 12, 15
Venus rules on the sixth day, iv. 2; form of, iv. 8; appointed over kindness, etc., iv. 8
Venusia, a city situated between the mountains and the plains, where Varrus escapes to, xcvi. 4; besieged by Annibal for eight days, xcvi. 5
Vespasianus, reign of, lxxviii. 1
Vindredi (*i.e.*, Friday), iv. 2
Vine wishes to serve as gallows for Haman, lxxxiii. 2
Virtuous saved from hell, xiv. 7
Vredakh (*i.e.*, Friday), iv. 2

Walnut-tree wishes to serve as gallows for Haman, lxxxiii. 3
Water created on first day, i. 8; tumultuous rising of, ii. 1; above bottom of sea, xvii. 4; children dipped in, xxxvi. 6; fountain of, brought by Agnios to Carthage captured by Latinus, xl. 10; which had no source, lvii. 40; turned partly into blood and partly into fire, lviii. 7
Well, waters of, swell into rivers, surround the camp of the Israelites, liii. 17; in the desert causes various kinds of spices and sweet-smelling herbs to grow, liii. 17 (*vide* Miriam)
Wicked, judgment of, between Passover and Pentecost, xi. 5; punishment of those, who ate on fast days, xv. 2 (*vide* Sin, Punishment, Hell)
Wilderness, the generation of, dwell in third house in Eden, xx. 6
Willows of the brook wish to serve as gallows for Haman, lxxxiii. 3
Winds, four, created, i. 7; four, from the desert blow myrrh and frankincense, liii. 7
Wine the most powerful thing on earth, lxxiv. 8, lxxv. 2; of heathen not a prohibited thing in the days of Balaam, lv. 10
Wizards come with Amaleq, xlviii. 13 (*vide* Balaam, Jannes)
Woman of Moab enticing Israelites to sin, lv. 10; the most powerful being on earth, lxxiv. 8; two, who circumcise their children are hanged by their breasts and hurled with their children from the top of a tower, lxxxviii. 2
World, light of future, in God's mind at creation, i. 4; seven now, await child, ix. 9; above waters, xvii. 4 (*vide* Paradise)
Worshippers of white horse encountered by Elhanan, lxiii. 20; of fire, lxii. 10, lxiii. 20
Writing created on second day, i. 8; on wall in Hebrew characters, but language Aramaic, lxviii. 3

Y (words written with Y *vide* also under I and J)
Yaftir, son of Togarma, xxvii. 2
Yair, *vide* Jair
Yedid subdued by Dodanim, xxvii. 3
Yequtiel, name given to Moses by his mother, xliv. 7

Yiskah, *i.e.*, Sarai, given by Terah to Abram as wife, xxxv. 1
Yoniu, river of Grecia, xxxii. 4
Yoqtan, son of Eber, xxvii. 5; daughters of, taken to wife by sons of Peleg, xxvii. 5; children of, xxvii. 5; chief over children of Shem, xxviii. 1; tries to save rebellious princes, xxix. 6; tries to save Abraham, xxix. 11

Zaaq, son of Elishah, xxvii. 2
Zabel built by Judah, xxxvi. 12
Zagzagel spreads a rug at the feet of Moses, l. 14; teacher of Moses and scribe of all the heavenly host, l. 5
Zahab Tob, by the rivers of Kush, on the border of the land of Havila, lxiii. 8
Zakar, son of Peleg, xxvii. 5
Zaqlah, a kingdom of Kush, lxiii. 8
Zaryonah, a kingdom in Kush, lxiii. 8
Zebulun, constellation of, Sagittarius, liii. 13; stone of, the carbuncle, liii. 13; ensign of, a ship, liii. 14; eat the flesh of their children to know whether God would be pleased with them, lvii. 10; tribe of, encamp on the mountains of Paran and extend to the Euphrates, lxii. 11; tents made of the hair of Armenia, lxii. 11; children of, possess the Torah, Talmud, and the Mishna, lxiii. 16; tribe of, dwell on the mountains of Paran, in tents of hair, in the land of Pul and Lud, lxiii. 16; children of, men of valour, fight four months in the year, lxiii. 16; children of, good riders, and possess servants, horses, sheep, oxen, camels and asses, lxiii. 16; children of, tilling the ground, lxiii. 16
Zechariah, blood of, avenged by Nebuzaraddan, lx. 8
Zedekiah, Sanhedrin of, slain by Nebuchadnezzar, x. 10; captured by Nebuzaraddan, brought to Riblah, lx. 8; ben Ma'aseyah, false prophet of Midrash, lxiv.; goes to daughter of Nebuchadnezzar, inducing her to sin, lxiv. 2
Zepho, *vide* Sefo
Zera, father of Methushael, xxvi. 13
Zeridah, a kingdom in Kush, lxiii. 8
Zerubbabel, son of Shealtiel, son of Jechoniah, King of Judah, appointed by Daniel as his successor, lxxiv. 2; appointed overseer of the two captains of the host and guardians of the king, lxxiv. 4; finds favour in the king's eyes, lxxiv. 4; and the two captains decide to test each other's wisdom by means of riddles, lxxiv. 6; argument of, lxxv. 4; embraced by the king in the presence of his people, lxxv. 9, lxxvi. 1; reminds Darius of his vow to rebuild the temple, lxxvi. 1; son of Shealtiel, details concerning the rebuilding of the temple handed to, lxxvi. 5; returns to Babylon, where he dies after the rebuilding of the temple, lxxxv. 2
Zifd, son of Peleg, xxvii. 5
Zipporah, daughter of Reuel, feeds Moses whilst in prison, xlvi. 9; wedded by Moses, because he plucked the staff from ground, xlvi. 12; bears Eleazar, xlvi. 13; bears Gershon, xlvi. 13; goes the ways of the women of Israel, xlvi. 13; circumcises her son, xlvii. 2
Zipthai, children of, xxvii. 2
Zondakh (*i.e.*, Sunday), iv. 2
Zoroaster the Wise, discoverer of Nigromancia, vanquished by Ninus, xxxii. 4; reigns in Bractia (Bactria) and writes down seven sciences on fourteen pillars, seven of brass and seven of brick, xxxii. 4; taught magic science by Abraham, xxxv. 4

THE END.

BILLING AND SONS, PRINTERS, GUILDFORD.

Fol. 22ᵃ

אדם הוליד שלשה בנים והוא לש מבנות קין והוומת לעבוד
אשתן והבל ותאומתו דבורה ואשת ושת אתיוולטן
גופלו יושתו: ויהי אדם את חוה אחר אשר שת שנת שבע ומאה
יולד בנים ויולד עשר. וכאשר שלונה גולה שמות בנו על
שאול צרי עלומיו ברוב בנו ות זרמולה אשא מחטי וענת.
ושם הבנות חוה מעושה אחי פולאם חסד היטיוה שבא עטן
ויחי שת ומאת וחמש שנה ויולד את אנוש: ותחי שת אחרי
הולידו את אנוש שמנה מאות שנה. ויולד בנים שלשה
ושתי מנות ושם הבנים קינא קנען וידעה. ושם הבנות
נועא ונחלא. ויחי אנוש תשעים שנה ושמונים שנה תעל מתקין
ויחי אנוש אחרי הולידו את קינן שני בנים יוהר ושמעו ובת
אחת קינמת. ותיץ הוליד ומהר גהוליולי ג שנה ותרך ומסו
ולושא: וב מנת חנה לויסא. ונהלאל הוליד ותרי ידד
ג בנים עירין וניסא ויצר מלי מישש ווידמיאל לד אזוני.
וב בנות עדה נועה ויעל ויעדה עלה: ירד הוליה אחרי חנן
ל טדם ועשר ענן סכפי יתר: וב בנות הזכו לחך: חנך
הוליד אחרי ויתשילח ה בנים עבע לישון עשמון קלדי חיני
וב בנות תימוד ליפתר לעי עד וחסוץ כתער ויתחתו:
אד מתושלה אחרי לקח ממס ב ובנות ב עינב רמטי עלויתה
עדונה. ולמך הוליד את נח לאור זה יחרימנו וינח לארץ ולא
יעשר עליה כי יסתך יי דעה על היורץ לינחם החרם ואשר מ
מעשיך. ונח הוליד ג בנים שם נחם ויפתץ וישב קין אשתחן
כמיד גורד עד יודעת קין את אשתו תעוד בן עו שנה ותילד
את חנוך ויבן שבעה עירות ויחרו המשובה כשם בנו חנוך
עיפוך לעד גוזה לשנה חלך יבבל. ויולד קין ואחרי חנוך ג
בנים חוופ לרגן קיזל וב בנות עישא ומת. ויקח חנוך יות
עדא כת שם לאשה ותולד לו את עירד ויית קאעת ויות נעדא

האדמה וישיב השאול אות חוט. ומעבדון ישיב חלון יושיב דורשע
כפרי מעולו. וישמעו כן בשר ונפשו. ויגוח נהשקע העולם. ועל
הרעות ועצת ושאול הסכר אותפה. ולא יהיה שר הארץ על צמח
ולא יעקדו יושסה. ולא ישתאווה המשפטים כי הארץ חדשה ושמים
חדשים יהיו לישיבת עולם: בני יפת גומר והגוג ומדי ויון ותובל
ומשך ותירס: ובני גומר אושכנז וריפת ותוגרמה: ובני יון אולישה
ותרשיש כתים ודודנים: בני גומר פולוד להד דרגילד: בני ותוגר
קשא עיפת פורשעי שמיאל פנחם. גולוחמ פנעך: כני דדן שלום
פילון עומלוים: בני תובל פיטושואע יועיפן: בני תירס וירך
טבאל בועבה שמפלא מיבה מיולש: בני מוך – ־ יודורדד הוד
בצלה בועדה: בני אושכנז ועל סרדגע יוענן: בני עלי הרי יעצבר
רועת ד'פסיות וחצך: בני תוגרמיה אוביתיגר שפט ויפטיר:
בני אלישה דעה הנת הסס ידילא: בני יוסת והמשיאל טינם אוויג
אוויגין: בני עיסי מהיל היון עלצויאב: בני דודעם ויועב
הסאת ופעג: תאוה גברון יושכי ארץ פרם. ומדי. ואוי היס: ויעל
פעג בך הודעם ויחל להיות ספך כיעבות הים איז נפעת שליש אורך
רומית: ויעשו פש את ידיך: ובני הוג גבשו להם אות דיגל: ובי
עדי כבשו אות בעוע וכפיין כבשו אות שרין וכני תוכל כבשו אות
סחת: ובני ותשך כבשו אות נפני: ובני תירס כבשו אות רויו ובי
יונים כבשו את אולדר. וריפת בלו בני כבשו את גודי וכי ריסת
כבשו אות כועדה ובני תוגרמה כבשו את פוט: בני אולישה כבשו
אות טבלו ובני תרשיש אות הידינן ובני כתים: ובי דודנים אות
הרצא: ויון החלו לעבוד אות הגוריה ושמשר צבאה לגוים ויקאו
אלו. ויהויה משך: ויה טרדת הגשם ועויר הקשת כעץ ויראו יושב
יושבי הארץ אות אות הברית ויברכו אותו: ובי חם בנש ומצרים
ופטו וכנען: ואלה בני בוש שבא ועודן ובני מיסטו סיעש ע
עלצוועויטמ אלוות לסוך: ובני כנען עידן והנדרווים דרצין ט
שינדים חודואין עמינעם חוויתים גיפים עושם אולע עישים:
ועט ילד אות נמרוד הועו חחל להיות נפול גבור לפעלך: וועציס
ילד את לודים נות ענעים נות להטב נות נפטוחים וסלד

ופתרוסים וכסלוחים וכפתורים: והם החלו לנטת עירות ולהד
עידן ובעתיה ריסון מיוודא מזאגר ישתלון דנד הוו טולון לכובש
סדום ועדומה ואדמה וצביים: ובני שם עילם. ואשור וארפכשד
ולוד וארן: ובני אושור גמרן יש'י: וארפכשד ילד אית שלח ושלח
ילד אית עבר: ולעבר יולד שני בנים שם היוחד פלג כי ממיו נפל
נפלגה הארץ ושם אותיו יקטן. ויקטן ולד אית ילמודד ואת שלף
שומערא ואת מודאם ודויד ודרא ועוזיב דיקלב ויאווזאל ג
שביט הפן חזילה יובב: ובני מלג יעג רימוד שטרג אתילון זר
שך גבי שורי שדייור סלאטוט תחי פלעוג שתריאל שייש ש
ונרעואל אולף... אלה בני פלג. ואלה שמותם ויחיו לחס
נשים הנטת יקטן וילדו בנים: ובנת ותולו הארץ מהס. ויחל
לו רעל אית מלג בת רות לאשה ויולד את שרוג וימלאו ימיה
ללדת ויאומר רע וידק יצעו עד דוד רמע יושר יום כסיו עלה
ויהנדו חמיס צדיק ודוג העוון ביים לו יעשק עדיות וימלאון ה'
ירע אית השולם: ויולד רעל יוחרי שרון ל בנים וביאול שבד ש
שולמון דידל קעדא עדור נפש והב בנות הדיולי דרפא שיופף
פריעג תהילה: ויולד שמר אחרי נחור ל בנים עלה דישון סוטא
ושורא ובר כטת גדלת תצלה שליפא: ויולד נחור יוחרי תרה ובני
רבב דדיובי בייבב. ושמאביעל שף מדב המוון ונ בנות יסכה
טיפא ברוא קעטא: ויקח אית יודתלאו בת ברנב: ויחי תרח על
שנה ויולד את אברם ואית נחור ואת הרן והרן אוליד יות לוט
וית החל ישבי הארץ לגויות במצלות ולחיות חויב גובעי
לההסוס כהמים והי מתענס בעהס ובעתיה ב גיוש ושתת
ונעש להיהלט בדרביכב: ואלה תלדות עם טוצעותה למשכחות
לשותות ונפעו נעייהם נארץ נאור אותר המבול. ויניאו בני חם
וישיות עליהם יות עדור לשר ולעבר וגם בני יפת נתנו עליה
יות פעמס לשר ולעבר וגם בני שם נתנו עליהם יותיגעו לשר
ולעבר: ויבאון שלושת העעדים האלה ויועצו יחדו להרב יחד
אית עמש אליהם עעור עם אויבהס חי ויקרע על העמ יולדהם ול
ויהיו לעם אחר וחר ד שי השלום בארץ: ויהי נשנת שש מיאות

היושבים בארץ תשתחוו על עפר פסאי · ומשך הם סרסר · תירס הם הוקי טוקי
טפטע וחולקלב ישובים · על עפר יב גדול רול · הונם · על עפר מוד · ושוסך בים
אלישה הם אלעניה היושבים בן הרי איטליאו וישבו בה על הים הדר
ברזנת · תרשיש · והרי יוב · ושבתמו ויפטור · את איילאן · ואדם בדריאן היל
אושר בוא סרן · וכרמיון · ומהם ברטנא היושבים · על עפר הרדן · ואדם בדריאן היל
היושבים · על עפר ריוש · היושב בים הגדול · ורכמתו · ופיתן טושבים בים בטרי
בטויקיא תרשיש הם תוקוסיאני באו על סא מקורבא ברת · ודהם תרשים
עפי סופי · ולמהשטעוסנאס · את אורך תבסרן · ברמן אובין בעול בני יון · והב
כיתם הם רומני · החומש בסקעת
מחרים · עם היושבים אשר בתרסוס
מצוא על עפר חברון · דודנים הם דענשקי היושבים במך הים הגדול · אשר אזן
אוקריענב טורץ · העוררו וכמירגישו במך הים הגדול אשר עטובע לסרוי
יושבן ודומרים · ויתחמדו במך על · יב אוקיענוס · לא יכול כי הגענה מרשולת
מואה · עב אחרית · אחרי הם אוקיענוס · ונם מורדית · וכרטואי · וסרדון · ולריגן
ולינוק · וכרוכר · וכפרדין · מבני דדעים · יופטת · והם חתום בחוף הים מעבוך מלוב
על בלעטריקיו על הים · ומשם מושכים · יצב גבול טוקטוע · על הים הגדול הסר
הקראים איסקליבי · ואוקרים · אחדים · כי הם מבני כנעל · אך הם מתיחסים לבני
יון כן עבדי היסיפון · וכתיב סלעתורץ הגדולים לרה בספינו בני
אושוב · ארל · וסגרא עשו אהלב · אדם · חור אלולי ירדעהל
טו · ערצים עולריאנס · אטור · אשורייץ · ארפכשר קלדעא · לוד לידיאה · ארם
שויי · ובני אדם עוץ · אשר איוב על שם · נעע קרטנאע · מעש · ואלה חתו מעבוד
אדם · עד · אוקיענוס · ובני חם כוס ומצרים · ופוט · וכנען · כוש נגריאות
אקטיפסיגה · מצרים מצריאים · פוט לוביאה · כנען אדם · וכם פלו
סבא · וחוילא · וסבתא · ורעמה · וסבתבא · ובני רעמה שבא ודדן · סבא סמרי · ם
עביאי · ואיעריאלי · חוילי · גימלי · סבתה · בביא אטסטברי · סבתכא ורעמה · לוי · סירואתי
וכם רעמה סבוא מלכת · ודדן אוריה · היא אשור · למדרת אוריל כוש
וכוש ילד את נמרוד · והי ראשית ממלכתו בבל · וארך ואריסיאן · אכד עבד · פאלילו
כלנה כלונקום בינל · מן השם יצא · אשור בן שם כלעוכריאל · מן הארץ ההיא יצא · אשור
היא בן מרוד · והעיד כל אזת נעם · אשר בנה את נעוה העיר הגדולה · ואת
רחובות · את רחב העיר · ומועדים · ילד · את הלודים · ואת ענמים · ואת להבים · ואת
אן נעתוני · כי אלההות · חן כן פני כוש · וכל עבדים · ותענסו יחד · ולא ניסתוו
וטוחיעכי · אוני המוד ליטפר · הבים הם · ולתיעעו · וחמורה · בלהב אסי · ושל
תנע הבים סיעהם · ובעיעל · ילד את מצרון בכור · ועל שמו סדראת · ידדון
ער מולוך בספינתו חת · ויכוס אימורי · ועתסו · וחוי · בני ישיה הלסועיאן
עריה צור · סרקטי · איעל נטריפוליטי · אורדני · שמעוני · ארוודיאטי · מצרי הוח
ארישיטוה · סורידין · רריני · חמות · בינה חמה · הוא אנטוכיאי · ויהי גבול הכנעני
מעיד בוא בגיבה · עב סרוה · ועל · על · ישבע הוא קליון · ועיוע · חזיים · וטובים בים
המלח · חולה · כני חם הם הלסועיאתיה · לשתנותם · בארעתם · בגויהם · וכטל
בן חם הולדו · את · עלוד · הוא האל אלוהיה · עבור יעד בארץ · על פני א שמיה
יצא רוח רע אדם · בגבורתו · והוא דוחסם · להשתהות · ולעשות · את · ועוסה · על עפר · הכ
ולעברו · וכל · כן יוסף · לברות · ולעשות · עוד ועצבי · בבל · אשר שם · הלוכל · בראן
המדיד עז הקבה · וכל כן יאמר במשל · הקדמונים · כעדרוד · גבור · יציר · לפני א · ולכן
שהיה מורד עז הקבה

www.ingramcontent.com/pod-product-compliance
Lightning Source LLC
Chambersburg PA
CBHW031956300426
44117CB00008B/778